D1602696

EAST CENTRAL EUROPE
IN THE MODERN WORLD

Andrew C. Janos

East Central Europe in the Modern World

THE POLITICS OF THE BORDERLANDS FROM
PRE- TO POSTCOMMUNISM

STANFORD UNIVERSITY PRESS

STANFORD, CALIFORNIA

JN
96
.A58
J36
2000
west

Stanford University Press
Stanford, California
© 2000 by the Board of Trustees of the
Leland Stanford Junior University

Printed in the United States of America

Library of Congress Cataloging-in-Publication Data

Janos, Andrew C.
    East Central Europe in the modern world : the politics of the borderlands from
pre- to postcommunism / Andrew C. Janos.
        p.   cm.
    Includes bibliographical references and index.
    ISBN 0-8047-3743-6 (alk. paper)
        1. Europe, Central—Politics and government.   2. Europe, Central—Politics and
government—1989–   3. Europe—Politics and government—20th century.
4. Regionalism—Europe.   5. Social stratification—Europe.   6. Europe—Foreign
relations.
    I. Title.
    JN96.A58 J36   2000
    947'.0009'04—dc21   00-036557

♾ This book is printed on acid-free paper.

Original printing 2000
Last figure below indicates year of this printing:
09   08   07   06   05   04   03   02   01   00

Designed by Eleanor Mennick
Typeset by G&S Typesetters in Sabon, with Sanvito

To her without whom . . .

Contents

Illustrations

Acknowledgments

Research projects have a life of their own. This one was conceived in 1987 and was originally planned to be a historical comparison of the politics of the early nation-states of East Central Europe with those of the Soviet Bloc, in order to contrast patterns of integration into the world market with integration into a full-blown imperial system. But just as research, some of it in the "field," got under way, the Soviet Bloc dissolved and was replaced by a new international order, in which Western liberalism and the market once again played important roles, offering opportunities for further comparisons. There was also the reasonable expectation that the fall of communist governments would produce a literature of revelations that would invite us to revise some of our earlier conclusions about our subject.

To be sure, the first few years of transition were turbulent and the results of new research into the past took some years to emerge. Certainly, the time was not propitious for producing synthetic work on the region's past, present, or future prospects. By 1995, however, distinct trends began to emerge, and, at the same time, new and often rich evidence became available about the ever-so-secretive socialist states. This encouraged resumption of the project after a hiatus of five years. The actual work of writing began in mid 1995, and, after considerable diversions by competing professional obligations, it continued until the spring of 1998, when the finished manuscript was submitted to Stanford University Press. As history, the study ends on May 1, 1998, with no subsequent attempt made to update the text. Accordingly, the many momentous events that have shaken the region since that date—such as the Kosovo war, the accession of three states of the region to NATO, and the fall of the Mečiar government in Slovakia—are not part of this narrative. However, I believe these recent events are in line with the interpretation I have presented here. In this sense, these subsequent events provide a test of sorts for the utility and validity of the intellectual framework which serves as the backbone of the volume.

xiv   *Acknowledgments*

During these years of intermittent research, writing, and gestation, I have been the beneficiary of considerable help from both institutions and individuals. As to the first, I wish to express my gratitude to the International Research and Exchange Board (IREX) and the National Fulbright Committee, whose joint grant permitted me to spend the year 1991 in East Central Europe, both catching up on research and observing firsthand the emergence of postcommunist states. I am equally grateful to a number of intramural funding sources at the University of California, Berkeley. They include the university's Committee on Research, the Center for Slavic and East European Studies, and the Center for German European Studies, whose fiscal generosity provided resources for travel, research assistance, and for the preparation of the manuscript for publication. I am further grateful to the staff members of Radio Free Europe / Radio Liberty, then in Munich, and of the Institut für Sozialwissenschaften (Section VI, DDR), in Berlin, for the generous access they granted to their archives, and for helping to structure my project of interviewing refugees in 1986–87, which, at that time, seemed to be a major source of information on the inner workings of communist states. In this respect, I am especially indebted to Vladimir Kusin, then research director of RFE, to the late Vlad Georgescu, to Anneli Meier, Alfred Reich, Michael Shafir, and Vladimir Socor, who were tireless in directing me either to human subjects or to the materials of their departments. Several years later, I received equally friendly receptions from the staffs of the archives of the Hungarian Socialist Workers' Party (MSzMP) and of the Institute of Political Science of the Hungarian National Academy of Science, in possession of the manuscript collection of the former Institute of Social Research of the Central Committee of the MSzMP. During a year of research and meditation in Hungary, I became especially indebted to Sándor Balogh, the then director of the party archives, László Bruszt, Elemér Hankiss, István Stumpf, János Simon, and László Szoboszlai (the latter five persons being political sociologists affiliated with various institutes of sociology and political science in Hungary).

Closer to home, I wish to acknowledge the intellectual companionship of colleagues, among them especially of Victoria Bonnell, George Breslauer, Beverly Crawford, Kenneth Jowitt, Jeffrey Kopstein, and Barbara Voytek. I am also pleased to express my thanks to long-time research associates George J. Svoboda and Stanyan Vukovich, who rendered invaluable help by providing translations of texts from the Czech, Slovak, and South Slav languages. Thomas Grabowski, likewise, helped me with the summary and translation of some Polish materials. Among my able research assistants, I am especially indebted to Carol Timko, Jeffrey Sluyter-Beltrao, Laura Henry, and Mieczyslaw Boduszynski, who provided precious research and editorial assistance at various phases of the project. In addition to them, I had the benefit of the assistance of a number of enthusiastic yet unwitting helpers: graduate students, many of them by now distinguished professionals, who over the years wrote research papers for my seminars that either directed me to sources or provided ideas useful in writing this book, especially Chapter 6 on the post-Stalin years of European communism. In this respect, I feel duty-bound to cite the names of Peter Blitstein, Karen Breslau, Christine Chinni, Susan Erickson, Russel Faeges, James Goldgeyer, Peter Lavalle, Jason McDonald, and Susan Overdorf. Other names to mention are those of Gordon Adams, who spared neither time nor effort to share his valuable knowledge of computer languages, of Norris Pope and Grant Barnes of Stanford University Press for their encouragement and interest, of Mary Severance at the Press for shepherding this project from manuscript to final product, and of Doug Easton for preparing the index.

While the composition of this study required concentration of effort and a carefully constructed research design, some of the themes in this book—above all the politics of backwardness and the nature of the Soviet system—have long engaged my attention and been the subjects of some of my earlier writings. Part of this scholarly output appeared in monographic studies on Romania and Hungary (Janos 1977 and 1982). References to these studies are to be found in the notes at appropriate places in the text. In addition, I have engaged in a number of preliminary attempts to formulate generalizations about the dynamics of communist regimes and the various causes of backwardness. Three of these articles have been published in *World Politics* (Janos 1989, 1991, and 1997) and one in *Studies of Communism and Post-Communism* (Janos 1996a). Permission to use parts of these articles is gratefully acknowledged here to the Johns Hopkins University Press and to the editors of *Studies* and the Department of Political Science at the University of California, Los Angeles.

Needless to say, projects and books, and more generally ideas, are not formed in a vacuum, but are inspired by the collective effort of a larger community of scholars. My gratitude to this community, and to its individual members, will be acknowledged in the footnotes accompanying the text. Still, a few names should be mentioned here, because footnotes alone do not express the extent of the debt. Among those who qualify as classics I wish to mention the names of the Romanians Stefan Zeletin and Constantin Dobrogeanu-Gherea and the Hungarian Julius (Gyula) Szekfű, all three of them authors of path-breaking studies on various problems of East European liberalism in its milieu of economic backwardness. Among contemporaries, some of them now late, I wish to acknowledge, in alphabetic order, my debt to the contributions of Attila Ágh, Ivan Berend, Paul Bairoch, Mihály Bihari, James F. Brown, Karen Dawisha, Csaba Gombár, Raul Hilberg, János Kornai, Marvin Jackson, John Lampe, Aylmer Macartney, Bruce Parrott, György Ránki, Henry Roberts, Joseph Rothschild, Peter Sugar, and Eugen Weber. Clearly, without the contributions of these scholars, the work could not have been written, or at least not written in its present form.

Last but not least, thanks are due to my wife, who has, over the years, put up patiently, and sometimes heroically, with the trials and tribulations of partnership with an academic. More than that, throughout all this time, she provided an infrastructure for the effective pursuit of my interests, combining traditional and modern spousal virtues in an admirable synthesis, while pursuing a career of her own. Words alone are insufficient to express my gratitude. Without her solicitude, this volume would likely not have seen the light of the day.

A.C.J.

EAST CENTRAL EUROPE
IN THE MODERN WORLD

Introduction

This book is political history written by a social scientist. As such, it addresses two audiences: (1) historians and area scholars of East Central Europe, and (2) students of political sociology, economy, and culture interested in such subjects as modernization, development, and decay. To historians, the message of the book is best summarized by a paradox conveyed by the familiar French aphorism: The more things change, the more they stay the same. For while, on the one hand, the modern political experience of the region may be best described in terms of endemic political change, on the other hand, none of the ever-changing political regimes could avoid facing the challenge of the same stubborn facts of East Central European life: the region's ever-increasing economic inferiority vis-à-vis the West, the debilities of small nationhood, and the cultural divide between the lands of Eastern and Western Christianity.

To political scientists, the book offers another set of messages. It tells them that theories of macropolitics and macropolitical change abound in the existing body of literature on the subject. Some of these theories are structural, others are institutional; some are economic, others political; and some are based on "societal" factors, while others emphasize confining conditions that arise out of the larger global environment. What comparative politics needs is not brand-new theory, but one that can strike a reasonable balance among these competing explanations. This book is an attempt to take a step toward such a synthesis and should be judged by that standard.

METHOD AND SCOPE OF INQUIRY

This dual—historical and analytic—focus of inquiry has imposed upon the writer a twofold task. The first was to survey the existing body of literature on political change in order to establish an intellectual baseline for research and to position the work in relation to competing interpretations.

This survey was undertaken as part of a broader intellectual endeavor, and its results appear in Chapter 1. The second task was to test the analytic framework against the political history of East Central Europe by sifting through the existing literature on the countries of the region in the major Western languages, as well as in Hungarian, Romanian, and, with the help of able assistants, in the Czech, Slovak, and South Slav languages. Needless to say, the volume of this literature is vast and has been plowed through as part of a longer professional commitment to the politics of the region.

Although that search was in and of itself daunting, a study of this chronological scope and analytic ambition could not have been written without at least some forays into primary sources of information: statistical works, including compilations and raw data on individual countries, the daily press both in the original and in translation, archival materials (largely provided by Radio Free Europe and by various German centers of research and learning), and, finally, personal contact with participants and observers of the contemporary political process.

Of these endeavors, two stand out in importance and should be noted in this Introduction. The first involved years of patient work on the social composition of Hungarian and Romanian elites, based on standard sources on the composition of parliaments and cabinets, mostly the registers of members of parliament in selected years between 1887 and 1939.[1] This bibliographical information was checked and tabulated with respect to education, occupation, and family origin, with particular reference to familial connections to the traditional elites of the two countries. This was achieved by matching the information against various tables and almanacs of the Hungarian and Romanian nobility.[2] This research was complemented by a much more modest inquiry into the family backgrounds of leaders in other countries in the precommunist period, and while never published the results were presented at the Third International Congress of Southeast European Studies (Bucharest, 1974) and subsequently used in my monographic studies of Romania and Hungary.[3] For the sake of simplicity, some of these data are cited as "Elite Project" (1974–82).

Another study, only partly completed, was originally designed to fill gaps in firsthand information about daily life and grassroots politics in communist societies. Some such information was collected in the summer of 1987 by way of questionnaires and in-depth interviews with Hungarian, Roman-

1. For Hungary, Sturm 1887, 1892, 1897; Végváry and Zimmer 1910; Kun, Lengyel, and Vidor 1920, 1922, 1927, 1931; Haeffler 1935, 1940; also Hungary, *Tiszti cim- és névtár* 1878, 1927, 1938. For Romania, Nicolescu and Hermely 1899, Nicolescu 1903, Petrescu 1910, 1912; *Anuarul Parlamentar* 1931; also *Politics and Political Parties in Romania* 1936, and Predescu 1939–40.

2. Kempelen 1911–31, 1–11; Lecca 1937; Filitti 1915.

3. Janos 1977 and 1982.

ian, and East German defectors in West Germany, followed up by interviews with members of the staff of Radio Free Europe (in Munich) and conversations with personal acquaintances in East Central Europe proper. After 1990, much of this information, so laboriously garnered, entered the domain of public knowledge; thus, no systematic attempt was made to tabulate the data, and only a handful of the interviews in depth were deemed relevant for quotation under the original numbers and dates assigned to these cases.

Although I have sought to make the study comparative, it was not always possible to achieve a perfect balance in covering individual countries. This is partly because of the multitude of languages involved, which no single individual, or even cohort of assistants, could ever fully master, and partly because of the great discrepancies in the quality of available sources, both primary and secondary, about individual countries. Statistics vary greatly in their reliability. To mention only the most glaring example, statistical information about Albania is virtually absent before 1945 and notoriously unreliable thereafter. Finally, there were the vagaries of the histories of nation-states. Some of our countries, notably Poland, Czechoslovakia, and Yugoslavia, did not exist as organized entities before 1918, hence their history is restricted to information about precursors like Serbia or about particular regions in a larger imperial context.

THE REGION AND ITS POPULATION

The Region Defined

The purposes and methods of this study having been discussed, there remains the task of identifying East Central Europe, the region that will serve as our subject and empirical referent. On the surface, this designation is one of geography, a "first cut" serving to indicate as accurately as possible the territorial boundaries set for the study. This is to say that if we divide the European continent into three more or less equal parts—one western, one central, and one eastern—from the Iberian Land's End to the Ural Mountains, the countries to be discussed here will be found in the eastern half of the central sector. However, the term "East Central Europe" is not purely geographic, but historical and political as well. Historically, it refers to the borderlands of two early medieval empires—the Byzantine and the Carolingian—that is, east of the rivers Elbe and Leitha and north of what are now known as Greece and European Turkey. In modern times, the region has been most frequently defined so as to coincide with the combined territories of a number of smaller and weaker nation-states that emerged, or re-emerged, gradually after the middle of the nineteenth century, first to serve as buffers between Russia and German-speaking Europe, and then, between 1945 and 1989, as the client state of the Soviet Union and as part of the Soviet "outer empire." Because the boundaries of Russia, Germany, and the borderlands themselves have changed a number of times during this same period, we have to recognize that in speaking about East Central Europe we are dealing with a geographical entity without precise physical or political boundaries, Indeed, the very number of states in our region has changed several times over the past two centuries. In the late nineteenth century, East Central Europe included only five states: Serbia, Montenegro, Bulgaria, Romania, and semi-sovereign Hungary (within the larger Austro-Hungarian Monarchy). In the wake of the Balkan wars (1912–13) and World War I (1914–18), these boundaries were redrawn, creating seven states by 1920 (Albania, Bulgaria, Czechoslovakia, Hungary, Poland, Romania, and Yugoslavia), covering 509,000 square miles and inhabited by 91.3 million people. Further changes were to follow during and after World War II, and when the dust settled and the Soviet Bloc emerged in 1949, the region consisted of eight states, with a part of the former Reich (roughly speaking, the part between the Elbe and the Oder) being added under the label of the German Democratic Republic (GDR, or East Germany). This new East Central Europe extended over a territory of 492,600 square miles with a combined population of 133.9 million (1980). As is well known, this map, created by the victors of World War II, was redrawn again in 1989–92. East Germany now became part of a reunited Germany, while Czechoslovakia split into two and Yugoslavia into five parts (Bosnia, Croatia, Macedonia, Slovenia, and rump Yugoslavia, consisting of Serbia and Montenegro). According to the latest estimates, the territory of the "borderlands" has receded to about 450,000 square miles, and its twelve constituent states had a population of 123.6 million.

Alas, to make matters more complex, the same territory and combination of states is also known by another name, Eastern Europe—a designation largely reflecting the spirit of the Cold War years, during which time the lesser nations of the Eastern Bloc were regarded as "captives" of an imperial power, while that power itself, the Soviet Union, was treated as a non-European entity. Inaccurate as this usage was in geographical terms, it was widely, perhaps universally, accepted in Western Europe and the United States for more than fifty years. This will be evident to the reader attentive to relevant bibliography, footnotes, and direct quotations from participants in the political game. In the text itself, however, the two terms have distinct meanings. "Eastern Europe" is used to designate the broader geographical entity that includes Russia or the Soviet Union, while "East Central Europe" refers to the geohistorical and geopolitical entity delineated above.

Under whatever label, this geographical-political entity has been, in both

TABLE 1

Territories and Populations of East Central European Countries,
1930 and 1980

	1930		1980	
	Territory[a]	Population[b]	Territory[a]	Population[b]
Albania	11.1	1.0	11.1	2.6
Bulgaria	39.8	5.5	42.8	8.7
Czechoslovakia	54.2	14.7	49.4	15.3
Hungary	35.9	8.7	35.9	10.7
Poland	150.0	30.7	120.7	35.1
Romania	122.3	17.4	91.6	22.4
Yugoslavia	96.1	13.3	98.6	22.4
East Germany	—	—	42.5	16.7
Total for Region	509.4	91.3	492.6	133.9

SOURCES: *Statesman's Yearbook* (1931); *Worldmark Encyclopedia* (1984), vol. 5.
[a]In thousands of square miles.
[b]In millions.

TABLE 2

Territories and Populations of East Central Europe,
1992–93

Country	Territory[a]	Population[b]
Albania	11.1	3.2
Bulgaria	42.8	9.0
Czech Republic	30.5	10.2
Slovakia	18.9	5.4
Hungary	35.9	10.5
Poland	120.7	38.2
Romania	91.6	23.3
Serbia-Montenegro	39.4	10.5
Slovenia	7.8	2.0
Croatia	21.8	4.7
Bosnia-Herzegovina	19.7	4.6
Macedonia	9.9	2.0
Total for Region	450.1	123.6

SOURCE: *Statesman's Yearbook* (1994).
[a]In thousands of square miles.
[b]In millions.

scholarly discourse and the vernacular, divided into several subregions. The most commonly known of these entities is the Balkans, the region traditionally defined to be south of the rivers Danube and Sava, or, with some modification after 1918, as the area covered by the territory of Bulgaria, Yugoslavia, Albania, and Greece (although the latter is historically excluded from both Eastern and East Central Europe). The Balkans, a living term in the vernacular, have often been juxtaposed with the "northern tier" of the region in scholarly discourse, including the rest of the countries of what are here designated as the borderlands. Another line may be drawn across the

region by a line drawn from the Baltic to the Adriatic, giving us the culturally, and economically meaningful subdivision between the northwestern
and southeastern tiers (the former not to be confused with another key region, the northwestern "triangle" of Atlantic Europe, the economic core of
innovations on the larger continent).

Language, Religion, and Peoples

Whatever the exact boundaries of the region we shall be dealing
with, counting only groups exceeding 100,000, it has at any time during
this century had a population divided into no fewer than nineteen peoples,
so defined, or self-defined, either because they speak a common language or
because they possess a common religious heritage, or a combination of these
two factors. The list of these peoples appears in Table 3. From a purely linguistic point of view, these nineteen peoples may be divided between Slavs
and non-Slavs, by religion between (Roman) Catholics and (Greek) Orthodox, with Protestant and Greek Catholic minorities in their midst together
with Jews in the Northwest and Moslems in the Southeast.

TABLE 3

*The Ethnic Composition of East Central
Europe, 1930 and 1980*

(in millions)

Ethnic Group	1930	1980
Albanians	1.5	4.7
Bulgarians	5.6	7.4
Belorussians	1.0	—[a]
Croats	3.2	4.4
Czechs	6.1	9.8
Germans	6.0	0.4
Gypsies	0.3	2.5
Jews	4.7	—[a]
Macedonians	—[b]	1.6
Magyars	10.4	13.4
Moslems	1.2	2.0
Poles	18.8	35.3
Romanians	13.0	20.0
Russians	0.4	—[a]
Serbs	6.0	8.1
Slovaks	2.7	4.7
Slovenes	1.1	1.8
Turks	0.8	0.9
Ukrainians	4.4	—[a]

SOURCES: *Statesman's Yearbook* (1931, 1944); Seton-Watson 1967, 416; *Worldmark Encyclopedia* (1984), vol. 5.
    [a]Total not available; no single country census indicates more
than 100,000.
    [b]Counted as Serbs.

It is not the purpose of this book to belabor the complexities of these ethno-religious divisions beyond a few remarks to avoid confusion among readers less familiar with the region. To begin with, Slavic speakers are usually broken down into three major subgroups by geographical location: western, eastern, and southern. The first group includes the Poles, Czechs, Slovaks, and a minuscule Wend (or Sorb) minority within the territory of East Germany. The second, and numerically largest, group includes Russians, Ukrainians, and Belorussians, three peoples that, while not East Central European by our definition, have had frequent political contact with East Central Europe and have at times formed ethnic minorities in the region's national states. In the Balkans, where the majority of the population are southern Slavs, ethnolinguistic identities become especially tangled, with most Yugoslavs speaking four mutually intelligible but somewhat distinct dialects, while the Slovenes speak a language of their own. Other Slavic languages are spoken by the Bulgarians and Macedonians, with dialects sufficiently similar to prompt futile efforts at creating a common vernacular and anchor it to a common identity. When it comes to nationality, however, religion enters the picture, separating Orthodox Bulgarians from Moslem Pomaks, and Catholic Croats from Moslem Bosniaks, Orthodox Serbs, and Montenegrins.

The non-Slav peoples of East Central Europe are, somewhat arbitrarily, divided into "natives" and "immigrants," in terms of whether they settled in the area before or after the turn of the first millennium. The natives include Hungarians, Romanians, and Albanians. The Hungarians are a Ural-Altaic people who preserved the main elements of their Ugric language. They came to the region relatively late, in the last decade of the ninth century, to settle in the Pannonian Basin and the adjacent highlands. The Romanians speak a romance language embellished with Slavic elements. Their origins have been the subject of recurrent and politically charged debates between those who place their origins with the linguistically closely related Vlach (Arumanian) tribes of Macedonia, and those who place their homeland within their present borders and regard them as Dacians conquered and Latinized under Roman rule in the imperial provinces north and south of the Carpathians. Just as moot, although less vigorously debated, is the origin of the Albanians, whose language appears to be the sole survivor of the extinct Illyrian family, enriched with romance elements that show Vlach and, indirectly, Latin influence. It should be noted here that modern Albanian language is divided into two regional dialects: Tosk, spoken south of the river Scumbini, and Gheg, spoken north of that line, including much of the Kosovo region outside Albania proper. Minor though the differences between the two dialects appear to be, they have at times acquired political significance, having been tied to different patterns of social and economic organization: Tosk with a feudal agricultural society in the planes, and Gheg with the pastoral society of the mountains.

The rest of the non-Slav peoples include a number of minorities that at various times have played crucial roles in the social and economic lives of given countries. Historically, perhaps the most important representatives of these ethnolinguistic groups are the Germans who settled east of the Elbe and Leitha rivers in several great waves between the twelfth and eighteenth centuries. In 1930, more than two million Germans lived in the successor states of "old" Hungary: in Hungary proper, in Slovakia, Transylvania, and the Banat (known today as the Voyvodina). In addition, there was a German minority more than two million strong in the Czech lands, and one of several hundred thousand in Poland. Since that time their numbers have dwindled to minuscule proportions as a result of expulsions, deportations, and voluntary migration, although some organized settlements still remain in Hungary, Romania, and Poland. Another ethnolinguistic minority, the Balkan Turks, entered the region as the harbingers of imperial rule in the sixteenth and seventeenth centuries. Turkish settlers from Asia Minor included soldiers, administrators, traders, artisans, and the holders of imperial land grants. At one time their numbers were substantial, but as the countries gained independence from Ottoman rule, most of these populations could not weather post-imperial purges and expropriation that, incidentally, continued even under communist rule in the second half of the twentieth century. Today, only one country, Bulgaria, has a substantial Turkish minority, representing close to 10 percent of the country's population. Their presence in the country continues to be one of the pivotal issues of Bulgarian politics.

In addition to Germans and Turks, a number of diaspora peoples identify themselves along ethnolinguistic lines. They include relatively small groups of Armenians, Greeks, and Balkan Vlachs (Koutsovlachs, also known as Arumanians), who under imperial rule performed both mercantile and administrative functions, but who now largely assimilated into the surrounding communities. Perhaps the largest of these diaspora groups are the Roma, or Gypsies, who have a distinct language of their own but mix it freely with a variety of local tongues. Consistently undercounted in the census of national states, they have come to new prominence in the postcommunist period, and the new statistics in the near future will most likely show their numbers in excess of two million, most of them living in Romania, Hungary, Slovakia, and the Czech lands. The Jews, already mentioned, are best described as a cultural minority because the bonds that give them a common identity are neither strictly religious nor linguistic, but derive from a shared historical heritage. Prior to World War II, their numbers were substantial: a population of some 5 million was reduced to perhaps less than 100,000 by genocide during the war and immigration thereafter.

TABLE 4

Number of National Minorities by Country, 1992

(in millions)

Country	National minority	Population
Albania	Greeks	0.6
Bosnia-Herzegovina	Moslems	2.2
	Serbs	1.5
	Croats	0.8
	Other	0.1
Bulgaria	Turks	0.8
	Pomaks	0.4
Czech Republic	Roma-Gypsies	0.2
Slovakia	Hungarians	0.5
	Roma-Gypsies	0.3
Hungary	Germans	0.3
	Roma-Gypsies	0.3
Poland	Ukrainians	0.3
	Belorussians	0.3
	Germans	0.3
Romania	Hungarians	1.8
	Germans	0.3
	Gypsies	1.0
Yugoslavia	Albanians	2.2
(Serbia-Montenegro)	Hungarians	0.5
	Moslems	0.3
Slovenia	—[a]	—
Croatia	Serbs	0.7
	Moslems	0.1
	Other	0.3
Macedonia	Albanians	0.5

SOURCE: *Statesman's Yearbook* (1994).
[a]No national minority with more than 100,000 members.

Given this large number of peoples and a turbulent history of intra-regional migrations, the typical East Central European state in history has been a multi-ethnic state. A prototype of such a state was Hungary prior to 1918, with only about 50 percent of the country's inhabitants being ethnic Hungarians (Magyars), the rest being Romanians, Slovaks, Serbs, Croats, Germans, and Ruthenes (Carpatho-Ukrainians). After 1918, multi-ethnic Hungary was carved up and shared among its neighbors. But this did not change the fundamentally multi-ethnic character of East Central European states. For, much like Hungary before 1918, the new Yugoslavia, Romania, and Czechoslovakia—as well as the reborn Poland—all had substantial ethnic minorities. Indeed, according to the compilations of Hugh Seton-Watson, in 1930 more than one-third of East Central Europeans could be classified as people living in an "alien" state.[4] Table 4 shows the dimensions of the problem.

4. H. Seton-Watson 1958, 413–15.

After 1945 attempts were made to reduce this complexity, by massive population transfers of Germans, Hungarians, and Turks, and by redrawing the boundaries of Poland, Czechoslovakia, and Romania to transfer regions with Slavic minorities to the Soviet Union. But even after these transfers and expulsions, Romania, Bulgaria, and Slovakia still have restless ethnic minorities, and the ethnic map of the South Slav countries shows a veritable mosaic of Moslems, Serbs, Croats, Albanians, and Macedonians living within each other's sovereign territories, with little inclination to accept one another. Multinationality is clearly a factor that aggravated the social and economic tensions plaguing each and every one of these separate ethnic communities.

1 | Social Science, History, and Political Change

From Change to Progress

The study of political change is as old as the discipline itself, but political thinking acquired a new cast in the eighteenth century and thereafter, mainly under the influence of revolutionary changes in the human condition itself. First, from the Italian Renaissance onward, social thinking emancipated itself from the idea of a divine plan and compelling laws of nature and discovered the concept of interest as the motive force of social change. Second, under the obvious influence of the Copernican-Newtonian revolutions in kinetics, the old Aristotelian polis became transformed into an interdependent, self-sustaining social system, in which the change of one component was seen to bring about changes in all others, thereby moving from a state of equilibrium to disequilibrium, and then back to equilibrium. Finally, the economic revolutions of the eighteenth century focused attention on the means of production and, in a broader sense, on the relationship between man and nature. It was from these epistemological innovations that the new "productionist" or "modernization" paradigm of politics emerged, based on the fundamental premise that there was an important nexus between man-to-object and man-to-man (intersubjective) relations: whenever the relationship between humans and the physical environment changes, so this paradigm held, one can also anticipate changes in the division of labor and the structure of authority, one preceding the other. This being the case, one of the major tasks of the political scientist would be to identify critical thresholds in technological innovation with particular reference to "dexterity," Adam Smith's translation of the Greek word *techne*.[1]

More specifically, the Newtonian and industrial revolutions gave social science a three-tiered paradigm in which economy, social structure, and cul-

1. Smith [1776] 1980, 46, 109–15.

ture mediated between technological sophistication and political change. The major force of change, and hence the key independent variable of the paradigm, is the degree of human mastery over the physical environment. When this mastery increases, it produces greater wealth for the nation, differentiation in the social structure, and rationalization in human behavior by increasing the awareness of choice over fate, by devaluing the sacred, and by upgrading the value of utilitarian expediency. Separately or together, these processes of change are seen to have an impact on the political system and to manifest themselves in (1) ever-increasing degrees of political participation and empowerment, (2) the functional specialization and professionalization of governments, and (3) the secularization of the principles that uphold the legitimacy of governments. Since the key variable of the scheme is human mastery, and since the growth of such mastery is seen as inexorable and unidirectional, the paradigm is one, not just of change, but of human progress as well.

The chief protagonists of this "productionism" were the Scottish moral philosophers of the eighteenth century and the Marxian economic theorists of the nineteenth. Both of these schools of thought subscribed to the view that political change originates in technology, while technology is linked to the division of labor or the social structure. But some of the differences between the two schools are just as important as these similarities. Whereas Marxists, inspired by Jeremy Bentham's philosophical radicalism, taught that human behavior and cultural systems may be reduced to the rational calculation of material interests, Smith and his Scottish compatriots recognized the existence of such virtues as "fellow feeling" and "self-command," which originated from the "author of nature," and, in any case, from outside the division of labor or material needs. From these variations there developed two different sets of theories of social and political change: one foreseeing universal and unconditional progress, the other envisaging variable historical outcomes, tying economic and political progress to variations in factors other than the division of labor or economic interest.

Paradigm Shift: From the Social to the Global System

Whether in its Smithian liberal or Marxist radical form, this paradigm of politics had an enormous impact on social thought and for a good while remained dominant in studies of political change. This should not be surprising. The theories that this paradigm has spawned were parsimonious and had seemingly powerful logical underpinnings. They located the ultimate source of institutional change in the mode of production and pointed to the division of labor and the division of social goods as intervening variables between the means of production and political change. In this manner, they reduced the complex and multifaceted experience of the Occident to a few manageable general categories that, if nothing else, provided a number of convenient shorthands that no student of Western history could henceforth ignore.

These seemingly universal laws, however, ran into masses of contradiction once social scientists began to apply them to explain society and politics outside the narrower confines of the Western world. This first happened when Russian and Eastern European socialists began to look at their own societies around the turn of the nineteenth century, and then again when American comparativists and political economists carried their European baggage to study the societies of the "Third World" in the 1950s and 1960s. In both these instances, political change seemed to be omnipresent, or at least much in the air. But in neither case were political tensions the results of advances in the system of production. To the contrary, they were the result of the absence of technological advancement and economic change.

The response of intellectual communities to this seeming anomaly conforms closely to T. S. Kuhn's characterization of a "paradigm crisis."[2] In both Russia in the 1900s and the United States in the 1950s and 1960s, the first instinct of the discipline was to respond by stretching facts to meet the expectations of the paradigm, specifically the premise that agricultural and industrial revolutions were in fact taking place.[3] For a while, practitioners of productionism and modernization went around in circles. But in the end, in both Russia and the United States, groups of practitioners and scholars emerged who became dissatisfied with the search for multiple roads and variations in sequences and chose to define the experiences of non-Western societies, not as variants of an old theme, but as a fundamentally new historical phenomenon requiring the discovery of new categories and causal relationships. The thinking of these innovators still accepted the relevance of technological breakthroughs as major forces of political change and as the centerpieces of a larger package of social changes under the label of modernization. But it rejected the old notion that societies were relatively closed "natural systems,"[4] and replaced the narrower concept of the social division of labor with a broader concept of a modern world system divided into central (or core), peripheral, and semiperipheral areas (the last two occasionally lumped together as the "peripheries").[5] In this new scheme, the "industrialization and democratization of Europe" came to be regarded as "a

2. Kuhn 1962, 77.
3. The classical example of such stretching is V. I. Lenin's first work (Lenin [1898] 1964). In the United States, we can point to some 70 library entries between 1958 and 1970 all addressing problems of societies in "transition." Perhaps the best known of these is Lerner 1958.
4. Bendix 1967.
5. Wallerstein 1974b. The Russian antecedents of this thinking can be found in Trotsky [1908] 1969. See also Lenin [1916] 1970b, 667–768. Both of these works were heavily influenced by the work of Alexander I. Helphand (Parvus). See Scharlau 1964 and Scharlau and Zeman 1970.

singular historical breakthrough . . . culminating in a century-long and specifically European development," [6] the success of which, while inspiring imitation on the peripheries, would also become the source of endemic stress,
social disequilibria, and discontinuities, which the elites of peripheral societies have been trying to escape. If valid, this new perspective reorients our
theorizing. Instead of searching for variations in the politics of modernization, we shall have to realize that we are dealing with two distinct, although
empirically related, patterns of political change: one in the core societies,
driven by the need to adapt to ongoing, successful technological innovation,
the other on the peripheries, driven by the need to overcome the debilitating consequences of economic inferiority, produced and reproduced by the
economic progress of the core.

THE POLITICS OF BACKWARDNESS

The Politics of Development: Institutions contra Structures

What, then, is the proper and likely response of economically inferior societies desirous of breaking out of the grips of backwardness? What
can and should their elites do to "reduce their a-timic [outdated] status,"
and to "catch up with the well-placed nations of the world?" [7] This question
was raised by two British political scientists in the 1960s, and the answer
to their question, in perfect harmony with the disciplinary mainstream in
political science, was that such societies should "develop" by modernizing
their infrastructures and modes of production so as to increase the international competitiveness of their economies and to raise the per capita wealth
of their populations. While the qualitative institutional changes in their economic systems would presumably increase their adaptability to their natural and international environments, the rising welfare of their populations
would make them happier and politically more stable. The ends, in essence,
were economic, but the means of achieving them was political. Adjusting
means to ends would create a new political phenomenon: the developmental state.

Although this mode of thinking has a pedigree that goes back to eighteenth-century French mercantilism and nineteenth-century German political economy, it took root in the United States only after World War II, when
the country was entering the arena of world affairs with a new geopolitical
agenda of its own. Once established, this new branch of political theorizing
went through two stages of development. In stage 1, under the unmistak-

6. Bendix 1972, 410.
7. Nettl and Robertson 1968, 56–57.

able, but rarely admitted, influence of Marxism, the economic emphasis of the theory was on the accumulation of capital, its political emphasis on the coercive capacities of the state capable of mobilizing nonvoluntary savings from reluctant populations. This was well reflected in what Albert Hirschman calls a "competition of metaphors"[8] such as "takeoff" (Rostow), "big push" (Rosenstein-Rodan), "great spurt" (Gerschenkron), "critical effort" (Leibenstein), and "hump" (de Schweinitz), all in reference to capital shortage as a singular historical condition that must and can be overcome before a society can reach a plateau of "self-sustained growth" and "normal" economics. In stage 2, inspired largely by the experience of the newly industrialized countries of the Pacific Rim, the focus of inquiry shifted from coercion to coordination, and from the harshness of the "mobilization system," to the "soft authoritarianism" of the "capitalist developmental state," the chief functions of which were to relay market signals from the world economy to local enterprise and to absorb some of the risks of foreign export ventures.[9]

On the whole, these theories may be described as optimistic, for sometimes implicitly, sometimes explicitly, they suggest that the choice of appropriate institutional forms alone could produce positive developmental outcomes. This optimism, however, ran up against both logic and statistics. As to the first, common sense alone suggests that, just as the finest seed sown into barren soil cannot guarantee an ample harvest, so the best institutional forms alone will not be able to produce a high rate of growth amid external conditions of adversity. As to the second point, both the long- and the short-term statistical evidence on developmental outcomes is dismal. It shows that a gini index of income distribution among nation states, the gap between rich and poor nations, continued to grow throughout the modern period. We can cite here Paul Bairoch's samples drawn from what he calls the the First and the Third Worlds. They show that, even if adjusted to purchasing power parities, the ratio between the respective per capita incomes of these large world regions have moved from 100:77 in 1830 to 100:32 in 1910, and to 100:19 in 1950.[10] Other, more complete and recent samples show still greater disparities. Comparisons of the average income of the top and bottom 25 countries of the world (from a list of 125) meanwhile show that in the quarter of a century between 1978 and 1993, these disparities have increased from 1:50 to 1:88, or from 1:15 to 1:23 if adjusted to purchasing power parities.[11]

Inspired by the above reasoning and the burgeoning statistical evidence

---

8. Hirschman 1981, 10.

9. For the original formula of the capitalist developmental state, see C. A. Johnson 1982; id. 1987; Haggard 1990.

10. Bairoch 1981, 7.

11. Based on World Bank 1978, 76–77; id. 1993, 238–39.

on growing income inequalities in the world, another paradigm emerged in the 1960s, competing with these "classical" development theories. These new theories shifted the weight of explanation from internal institutions to confining conditions in the external economic, cultural, and political environment of the national state, focusing on those elements of the environment that seemed not only to frustrate developmental designs but to reproduce and augment the initial condition of backwardness. In short, the new constructs spawned by the structural mode of thinking are not theories of development but theories of decay.

The economic explanations for the perpetuation of backwardness are twofold. One, associated with Marxism, locates the problem of peripheral economies in processes of exchange and is based on three interrelated and controversial assumptions: (1) that trade is the key factor in the accumulation of capital and national wealth; (2) that the typical export profile of a peripheral economy consists of "lower-ranking" goods, including large amounts of human (as opposed to machine) labor; and (3) that when these lower-ranking goods are exchanged for "higher-ranking" goods, surplus is transferred from the labor intensive to the capital-intensive economy.[12] The other school shares the Marxist view of the competitive disadvantage of economically backward countries, although it takes a broader view of market forces beyond the mechanics of trade. Unlike the Marxists, this school rejects the theories of surplus value and unequal exchange in favor of more standard categories of economic analysis.[13] These include differences in income elasticities of demand for the products of the core and the peripheries, and unequal rates of return and remuneration in different sectors of the world economy that result in a steady flow of capital and highly skilled labor from the high-risk low-wage economies of the peripheries toward the more secure and remunerative economic environment of the core societies. Of these forces, the last one is particularly pernicious, for it presents the economic planners of the periphery with another Hobson's choice. They can either regulate the flow of talent at the expense of bureaucratic regimentation or they may permit free labor migration, which will drive up the costs of highly skilled labor to world market levels and thereby result in increasing income inequalities and the potential for destructive social and political conflict.

The second set of arguments is psychocultural and is best subsumed under the label of the "international demonstration effect" (IDE). This effect is generated by the material progress of the "pioneering" societies in the historical centers of innovation: while the standards of consumption, comfort, health, and life expectancy of these societies are the products of ongoing

12. See, e.g., Frank 1972, 3–46.
13. See Hirschman 1962, esp. 183–98; Myrdal 1958, 23–38.

technological innovations within their own national boundaries, the images of these standards cross boundaries and travel fast, creating new expectations that the mode of production in economically backward societies cannot fulfill. In the short term, the net effect of these expectations is an increase in the propensity to consume and a decrease in the propensity to save. Faced with declining investment rates, the peripheral state may step in with its coercive instruments to accumulate capital, as the various theories of development suggest. But such accumulation of capital may create discontent, frequently aggravated by the "paradox of the peripheral state": whereas the mobilization of scarce resources requires strong states, such states on the periphery readily turn into rent-seeking instruments in the hands of a political class that uses them to raise its own material standards to those set by the middle and upper classes of the core states.[14]

Terms like "international demonstration effect" and "relative deprivation" are of recent vintage, but the ideas underlying them go back a long way in intellectual history. Thus in the eighteenth century David Hume and Adam Smith spoke of the relativity of scarcity and needs generated by "commerce with strangers,"[15] but generally assumed that the demonstration effect of new commodities would be beneficial to society, because new "desires" would stimulate enterprise and economic productivity.[16] Similarly, Marx in the nineteenth century recognized the relativity of "immiseration" and the flexibility of human needs, but, unlike Hume and Smith, he saw this relativity of deprivation as a source of strain (at least for the capitalist system). In his own words: "Our desires and pleasures spring from society, we measure them, therefore, by society and not by the objects which serve their satisfaction. Because these [desires and pleasures] are of a social nature, they are of a relative nature."[17] And, still more forcefully: "A house may be large or small, as long as the surrounding houses are equally small, it satisfies all social demands for a dwelling. But let a palace arise next to a hut, . . . the occupant of the small house will feel more and more uncomfortable, dissatisfied and cramped within its four walls."[18]

Marx's insights into the relativity of "immiseration" were further developed by Thorstein Veblen in the first decades of the twentieth century. According to Veblen, the economic expectations of the individual are shaped by the consumption patterns of "others with whom he is accustomed to class himself,"[19] while the consumer behavior of classes is shaped by that of

14. Platteau 1984, 63–88.
15. Hume 1970, 14.
16. For an excellent summary of early British thinking about scarcity, see Xenos 1987, 12–21.
17. Marx [1849] 1972, 180.
18. Ibid.
19. Veblen quoted in Xenos 1987, 20, 32n.

other classes, and especially by the behavior of those who hold higher status in society. In the modern age, when technological revolutions almost daily create new amenities, these amenities will first be available to the upper echelons of society, and it is from these echelons that consumer tastes will spread downward "with great facility" driven by the "force of emulative imitation." [20] Thus modernization and its core process, technological innovation, will create, not just new amenities, but also "standards of reputable expenditure also known as 'decent living,'" [21] which over time become so deeply ingrained that falling short of them will be an experience of a "spiritual nature." [22]

In recent years, Veblen's theory of consumption has inspired further investigations by a number of economists. Apart from giving us the term "demonstration effect," [23] or, alternatively, "Veblen effect," [24] these economists have provided us with a cogent critique of classical theories of marginal utility by demonstrating empirically that both consumption and saving are shaped, not just by income levels, but by the behavior of others and by the subject's own personal experience. From here on, adding "international" to demonstration effect is but a small step, easily made once we expand our concept of the "social" to include reciprocal expectations within a larger supranational context, in which individuals may seek out reference groups beyond national boundaries and in which societies may restructure their expectations by following the example of the more advanced and the more powerful. [25]

These empirical hypotheses, however carefully constructed, still leave us with the significant question of why the demonstrated welfare of others, whether national or international, should turn into a "desire" or expectation with measurable consequences for economics and politics. This question becomes especially salient in view of the fact that prior to the eighteenth century, while noticed by astute observers, international inequalities did not have the same unsettling consequences that they have had in the modern age. One possible explanation is provided by the special, indeed historically unique, qualities of the products of the industrial age. Unlike innovations of previous centuries, those of the industrial revolution brought about not just marginal increases in human comfort, but far-reaching changes in the quality and even the quantity of life, including new levels of control over nature, health, space, and time. In the last analysis, this explanation derives from the pleasure principle of utilitarianism. Alternatively,

20. Veblen [1915] 1954, 147.
21. Ibid., 208
22. Ibid.
23. See Duesenberry 1967, 27.
24. Ibid; see also Leibenstein 1950, 183–207.
25. See esp. Nurkse 1962, 57–81.

however, one might argue, as does Ted Gurr, that the demonstration effect of material progress is rooted in the cognitive realm[26] as part of what Karl Mannheim designated as the process of "fundamental democratization."[27] In one way or another this process encourages the belief that people are "in the same boat"[28] with respect to their entitlement to life's amenities. It is in thus in the broader context of universalism and egalitarianism that material inequalities are defined as a form of injustice. Jose Ortega, a skeptical observer and acerbic critic of modernity, combines these two explanations by linking the endemic instability of modern societies to the dual ills of "technicism and egalitarianism."[29] On the one hand, technicism was the creator of new forms of bounty. On the other hand, the ideas of universalism and egalitarianism transform the bounty of the few into an entitlement for the many, engendering an endless quest for more that cannot be fully satisfied by technical innovations alone.

There still remains a third theory of external constraints on development, and one that puts the weight of explanation in the domain of external politics. The brutal logic of its underlying argument goes back to Thucydides, who spoke of the proclivity of the strong to take what they can and the fate of the weak to surrender what they must. As throughout history, in the modern period, this principle has been practiced with vigor, perhaps nowhere more obviously than in the case of classical colonialism. More recently, the theory gained new currency in the writings of radical critics of capitalism like Paul Baran, who sees powerful nation-states bending the rules of the market;[30] like Albert Hirschman, who writes about the economic sources of political power, which, once politicized, can be used to extort further economic gain;[31] and like Susanne Bodenheimer, who writes about the nexus between the local client classes and the centers of power in the larger world scene.[32]

If institutionalism ignores external constraints and the sheer weight of statistical evidence that dims the prospects of development, structuralists fail to account for obvious exceptions from the law of averages, ignoring the countries that, external constraints notwithstanding, have been successful in moving from poverty to prosperity. What we have thus are two rather rigid intellectual constructs. What we need is a synthesis between these two approaches that will enable us not only to account for exceptions to the statistical average but also to explain the success and failure in particular cases.

26. Gurr 1970, 101.
27. Mannheim 1940, 43–44.
28. Runciman 1969, 9.
29. Ortega y Gasset [1930] 1957, esp. 54–67.
30. Baran and Sweezy 1971, 69–84.
31. Hirschman 1945.
32. Bodenheimer 1971, 155–82.

Such a synthesis can be accomplished in two steps. First, we have to ac-knowledge that institutions, however cleverly crafted, are fulfilling only the necessary, and not the sufficient, conditions of development. Second, we shall have to "soften" the hard structure of external constraints by recog-nizing flexibilities and variations in them. The appropriate analogy to the nature of these structures is the electromagnetic field of the Earth: while its relevance is universal, the intensity of the field varies over space. In a like manner, the force field of the confining conditions of development should not be treated as uniform in intensity, but as variable over both geographi-cal space and historical time. Specifically, three caveats are in order to up-grade the predictable effects of external forces on the politics and econom-ics of national states:

1. The practitioners of political economy should bear in mind that markets are not reified objects (to which one can "adapt" once and for all). Rather, markets are the domain of the relationship between supply and de-mand, one that can abruptly change with respect to particular commodities, rewarding or punishing particular producers irrespective of collective virtue or institutional configurations. In part, at least, this fluidity is the result of the unpredictability of streams of technological innovations that can turn some producers into paupers, while lifting others from poverty to prosper-ity. A good example to illustrate such a change is the discovery and wide-spread use of the internal combustion engine, which turned previously use-less crude oil into a valuable commodity and lifted half a dozen or so exporters into the ranks of the ten or fifteen richest nations of the world. There are some other examples, such as Scandinavian ore, wood pulp, and dairy products, all of them "rewarded" by the markets mainly for being at the right place at the right time, profiting from proximity to England and, later, to Germany during the Industrial Revolution. Conversely, the inven-tion of artificial fibers turned the producers of silk and other natural fibers, if not into paupers, then into less advantaged exporters and entrepreneurs. Such fluctuations in demand are especially important in the early phases of development, when they can make or break as yet undifferentiated econo-mies. But even in the later phases of development, economies are not invul-nerable to changing market forces affecting production lines or ingrained management styles. Indeed, the road to the core of the world economy is not a one-way street, as the example of the post-1945 history of Britain so ad-equately demonstrates.

2. It is equally important to remember that the international demon-stration effect, although universal in relevance, will vary over time and space, and especially with the geographical and cultural distance of a country from the high consumption regions of the global core. Unfortunately, only few

studies of these variations have been undertaken by contemporary scholarship. One of them, by Daniel Lerner, suggests the growing relevance of the IDE in the modern period because of dramatic changes in communication technologies.[33] Another set of studies have arisen from comparisons between consumption patterns in Russia and Japan, one being part of the *Kulturkreis* of Europe, in close proximity to the great centers of innovation, the other possessing an insular culture at a great geographical distance from the Industrial Revolution in England and northwestern Europe. In this respect, the words of Henry Rosovsky, a student of both countries, are highly illuminating. Whereas in Russia, the gentry quickly adopted foreign styles of consumption and the masses measured their condition against Western lower-class standards,

> Tokugawa seclusion allowed Japan, slowly and peacefully, to reach a base point from which it could leap into industrialization. . . . Two hundred years of isolation solidified a style of life that could not be demolished even by the powerful impact of the industrial revolution. . . . To put the matter in more economic terms, Tokugawa isolation created an effective defense against the erosions of the consumer demonstration effect. In a large line of commodities, mostly those of everyday life, consumer aspirations continued to be directed toward the outputs of the traditional sectors.[34]

Rosovsky's conclusions seem to be corroborated by the quantitative study of the Japanese economist Ryoshin Minami, who draws a sharp distinction between consumption patterns before and after World War II. Whereas, before the war, Japanese consumption patterns were were set "by previous habits," after the war, they were influenced by increases in per capita income, "although the influence of past behavior is still there."[35]

3. Finally, there remains ample room for revising the conventional structuralist view of the nature of world politics and of the relationships between strong and weak states. For many years, the bulk of the relevant literature, and, above all, the literature of political economy, has emphasized the extractive and exploitative nature of this relationship. It has done so with considerable justification, for instances of the rich and powerful exploiting the poor and powerless abound in modern history. But this emphasis ignores the fact that while most powerful states will be inclined to use their political assets to improve or maintain their economic positions, they are also concerned about their security and at times will be willing to pay an economic price for physical and cultural survival. Consequently, when dealing with the problem of international mobility, we should pay heed not

---

33. Lerner 1958, 55–58 and passim.
34. Rosovsky 1961, 86.
35. Minami 1994, 163. Minami's work and the Russia-Japan comparisons were brought to the author's attention by Tadashi Anno.

only to international competition, but also to various forms of international cooperation, including the transfer of resources from richer to poorer countries, or to co-optation by opening up marketing opportunities to politically preferred junior partners. Such co-optation, although not entirely unknown in earlier periods, became the main weapon of the United States and other Western countries in their fifty-year confrontation with Soviet communism. The major examples of these co-optive ventures are well known: they include the Marshall Plan and its Far Eastern counterparts, the international trading regime based on the Bretton Woods agreements, the co-optation of semiperipheral Italy into the Common Market, and, later, the expansion of the European Community to include Spain, Portugal, and Greece.

These and other experiences provide us with some of the elements necessary for constructing a much-needed theory of co-optation in juxtaposition with the familiar theories of exploitation. As in the case of Adam Smith's butcher and baker, the major factor motivating international co-optation will be self-interest, although "benevolence"—or, in the language of political psychology, self-validation—may also play a role. Obviously, the terms of economic co-optation will vary with the hegemon's material resources, on the one hand, and the dimensions of the threat to its security, on the other. The richer the country, the more imminent the threat, the more generous the terms of admission to the circle of privilege. Just as with the adverse uses of hegemonic power, these benign uses may be direct or indirect. They may be restricted to aiding the economic development of the client country or may involve attempts at restructuring its political culture and institutions as well.

Beyond Development: The Uses of the Politico-Military State

During the half century in which the developmental state has been an academic subject in the United States, the concept has stimulated a great deal of useful research about Latin America, Africa, the Pacific Rim, and, more recently, about the emerging postcommunist states. However, like many other useful categories, this one has been overused, stretched first, then turned into a virtual master concept of comparative politics as the discipline was seeking ways to explain the politics of international inequality. For many years, the widely held assumption among political economists was that "non-Western" countries were actually developing, or that whatever the elites of these countries were doing was oriented in one way or another toward economic development.

This approach to the problem of international economic inequality tends to overlook the all too obvious fact that throughout the history of human-ity, tribes, peoples, and nations have been improving, or trying to improve, their international competitive positions, not only by seeking to change their modes of production and gain new market shares, but by conquering or plundering their neighbors, or by some other means of "reconstructing" their external environments. The term "reconstruction" has been borrowed from Karl Mannheim[36] in recognition of the fact that such "external al-ternatives" not only refer to the crudest forms of external appropriation but may involve grand designs for changing existing international norms of resource allocation and interstate behavior in reference to the tenets of ideology.

The overuse of the concept of development has nowhere been more ob-vious than in the study of revolutionary regimes, including those of com-munism, fascism, and national socialism, which many practitioners of com-parative politics were willing to see as nothing but radical developmental states. This tendency was particularly strong in the case of communist stud-ies, where the students of the Soviet Union and its satellites were inclined to see Stalinism as the epitome of a "mobilization system," an efficient, if overly rough, shortcut to the building of a modern industrial society.[37] There have been similar attempts to turn varieties of fascism into developmental states,[38] to present them as a particular road to modern industrialism,[39] or to present them in the developmental frame of reference as the embodiments of anti-developmental and anti-industrialist regimes that somehow lost their way on the road to modern industrialism.[40] For those uncomfortable with the de-velopmental frame of reference, the escape route was through paradigms of stress, social marginality, and cultural despair, categories that reduced these movements to the status of social pathology and their goals to utopias.[41]

This relative neglect of the war-making state by comparative politics, and its abandonment of the subject to the subdiscipline of international politics, is all the more surprising because long before the twentieth century, there existed and flourished a school of political science in which war was well rec-ognized as an alternative to development, or more generally the "continua-tion of politics by different means."[42] Some of these writers, like Treitschke,

36. Mannheim 1940.
37. Deutscher 1953; Laue 1971; Kautsky 1972; Nove 1961, 29–38; Black et al. 1975; Hoettding 1959.
38. Gregor 1979.
39. B. Moore 1966.
40. See, e.g., Masse [1964] 1981; Moehler 1970; Kautsky 1962, 97–106.
41. Arendt 1951; Cohn 1961, 307–20; Talmon 1960; Walzer 1967, 109–34; Stern 1961.
42. Clausewitz [1832] 1943, 169. For others who developed this idea into a historical, em-pirical construct, see Ranke [1836] 1962, esp. 60–61; Delbrück 1886, 1–2; Hintze 1975, 4; Treitschke 1886.

were unabashed advocates of German expansionism; others, like Clause-witz, Ranke, or Hintze, were empiricists more interested in social than in normative theory. In either case, though, they pass as political economists, for their emphasis is on economic scarcity and on the means of subsistence, which, together with status and wealth, can be appropriated either inter-nally, by economic development, or externally, by means of war.

The relative neglect of the war-making state by American political soci-ology is still more puzzling because, although most of its students were Ger-mans, the most succinct juxtaposition of war and development comes from an Englishman, Herbert Spencer, who made it one of the cornerstones of his evolutionary scheme.[43] Like most of the great "productionists" of his cen-tury, Spencer believed that societies move from higher to lower stages by in-novations in technology, but unlike other productionists, he drew distinc-tions between "industrial societies" that meet the evolutionary challenge by such "internal activities" as the "growth of agriculture, manufacture and commerce,"[44] and "military societies" that rise in the world by external ag-gression and expansionism. It is important to note that Spencer's "military society" is not just one that is run by soldiers, but a society that is organized like an army and legitimated by its "external purposes." To be sure, Spencer was well aware that, especially in modern times, the success of military ac-tivities required manufacturing industries and a sophisticated economy. But he also tells us that in the case of a military society, this "industrial part" continues to be essentially a "permanent commissariat existing solely to sup-ply the needs of governmental military structures, having left over for itself enough merely for bare maintenance."[45] Hence, Spencer added perceptively, and with some foresight, its activities would be closely supervised and co-ordinated by political authorities. Thus more clearly than Smith and Marx before him, he recognized the distinction between the technologies of pro-duction and destruction, and, further, between producing for the market and producing for war. Unlike many recent students of industrial society, Spencer clearly understood that the term "industrialization" can actually be applied to two very different processes. In one, it refers to the rise of a military-industrial complex based on the technologies of destruction, a pro-cess led by the state and for the state; in the other, it refers to a process that leads to increasing popular welfare and international competitiveness.

Albeit more than a hundred years old, Spencer's conceptualization may provide a useful tool of social science and a corrective for the heavy devel-opmental bias of the discipline of comparative politics in recent years. Some amplifications may be in order, however. For one, we must reiterate the dis-

43. Spencer [1876] 1972, 149–66.
44. Ibid., 152.
45. Ibid., 154.

tinction already drawn, between states that set out to increase their power incrementally by territorial conquest and plunder, and states that conquer territory as part of a larger scheme of "reconstructing" the international environment. The prime examples of such reconstructionist states in the modern world have been communism and National Socialism, with their designs respectively for worlds of perfect equality and inequality. In contrast, Wilhelmine imperialism and Italian Fascism serve as examples of ideologies aiming at improving their relative positions of power without illusions, in Mussolini's own words, about the ability of the "human family" to secure "final settlement of all its difficulties." [46]

The project of "bringing war back" into comparative politics and historical sociology also invites theories of the dynamics of militarism, especially when used as an instrument of international upward mobility. Here again, German theorizing from Clausewitz to Hintze, and the history of Prussia, may provide us with a helping hand. Indeed, since Prussia was an economically marginal state on the periphery of the European continent in the eighteenth century, its experience may be a good model for how an economically disadvantaged state can fight its way "up" from the periphery to the center of the modern world economy and polity. The model that emerges from this experience is both linear and cyclical. Its linearity derives from Clausewitzian military doctrine, which teaches that one should chose one's final target carefully, avoid nibbling around the periphery, and always strike at the main force of the enemy. But each step upward contains a cycle that begins with the mobilization of resources of a relatively poor society and ends in war at the point when a favorable military balance obtains, or, when there are no more resources to be mobilized. If successful, war leads to the acquisition of new resources or the conquest of territory with new, and preferably more advanced, productive capacity. This permits the replenishment of resources and offers a breathing space for the population before embarking on a new cycle of mobilization and austerity. Of course, these cycles may be broken by defeat, as was the case with the Axis powers, or by exhaustion and deterrence, as was the case with the Soviet Union.

Finally, to make Spencer's scheme more workable, we may have to strip it of its rigid functionalism. True, in one sense, societies do interact with each other through their states, so they may serve as units of analysis. But societies are composed of classes with divergent interests, and these class interests may take precedence over the interests of the whole. In this respect, it is especially important to remember that societies are not only divided into economic classes, but also between economic and political classes, the former being the producers of material goods (and the managers of man-to-nature relationships) and the latter the producers and reproducers of soci-

46. Mussolini 1935, 10.

ety, with a vested interest in the institutions of the state. If we remember this, we shall be able to solve a number of puzzles that holistic, "societal" models of functionalism cannot. Above all, we can explain why nations strive to be independent, even though the economic consequences of independence may turn out to be detrimental to society as a whole and beneficial only to those who control the state machines.

CULTURE AND CONTINUITY

Whatever its scope, a process of change will always, by its very nature, raise the issue of continuity. Change, whether it occurs in societies, classes, or individuals, is never total and should not be confused with the metamorphosis of one object into another. By the time Bob turns from a teenager into an adult, he will have undergone a number of major changes. But he will still be Bob, and as such will carry a heavy baggage of psychological and physical characteristics that have been with him since early childhood.

And so it is with societies, the structure and cultural characteristics of which, or at least some aspects thereof, are in Joseph Schumpeter's words, "like coins that do not readily melt. Once they are formed they [will] persist, possibly for centuries." [47] But, as Schumpeter continues, the fact is that different structures display different degrees of resilience in the face of external challenges, such as the challenge of technological change. Informed by the newer modes of thinking in sociology, we may extend Schumpeter's wisdom to other forms of change, such as those generated by external economic and political forces, the forces of the world market and world politics that were examined on the previous pages. When society is exposed to these, there will be both change and continuity. Insofar as societies showed variations in their "traditional" stage, some of these will carry over into the modern world, providing us with another source of potential distinctions among societies over space.

To give a few examples, late entry into the world market will heavily burden a country's agricultural enterprise. But the nature of emerging capitalist agriculture and the distribution of the burdens of responding to market signals will be different in countries where, at the point of entry, the agricultural economy was based on individual, as opposed to communal, ownership, or was owned by peasant smallholders as opposed to feudal aristocrats. As an obvious corollary, political development in "plebeian" societies will differ from that in those subject to a traditional ruling elite with conspicuous solidarities and privilege. Both tribal and feudal societies will bend

47. Schumpeter 1947, 12–13.

to technology and to market forces, but they will bend in different ways, while ethnically homogeneous and heterogeneous societies will respond differently to demands for establishing a national state.

The same Schumpeterian wisdom applies to culture, a catch-all term often used to designate widely divergent sources and manifestations of social consciousness. Thus, in current academic discourse, "culture" may refer to the symbolic representations, or to norms reflecting the logic of social organization, as in the culture of a corporation, academic institution, or militarized state. Most frequently, though, culture is used to refer to a kind of cognitive processor rooted in collective experience, the memories of which will help to interpret the surrounding world and provide routinized responses to challenges, whether emanating from the object world or from the human environment. These experiential roots may be in series of loosely related events located in the the past. Or, as Max Weber tells us, they may originate in the pronouncements of a charismatic-prophetic figures, whose message reaches society in a moment of unusual vulnerability.[48]

It is in this last manner that religion enters society and becomes part of its collective consciousness. Its original purpose is to structure the individual's relationship to the transcendental realm, although, inevitably, this endeavor will spill over into the secular domain to offer injunctions concerning appropriate forms of social behavior. Functioning in this manner, religion will preempt neither the pursuit of status or material gain nor the exercise of authority. But it will circumscribe the ways in which people order their priorities, and hence will impinge on the character and viability of political arrangements.

The economic implications of this were elaborated by Max Weber; its political implications were explored by Ernst Troeltsch, among others.[49] Both of these writers see religious norms as shaping social outcomes. But their most significant insight, made more explicit by Talcott Parsons, was not just that religious beliefs impinge on social behavior, but that these norms will, as a result of habituation, continue to exert their influence even in an age of modern secularism.[50] When they do so, these "habits of the heart" compete with the rational calculation of material, social, and political interests. The task of the student of society is to discern typical ways in which habit, a value in itself, interacts with conscious choice, and, further, to strike a reasonable balance between the respective weights of the division of labor and culture in predicting political outcomes.

This discussion of culture must be concluded by a caveat with epistemological implications. While culture—whether rooted in religion or histori-

48. Weber [1925] 1947, 358–63.
49. Weber [1904–5] 1958; Troeltsch 1958.
50. Parsons 1966, 9.

cal accident—may be assumed to be a force of continuity, its presence cannot be always easily discerned by decoding political discourse and behavior. For one thing, it takes some time for culture to seep into the fabric of institutional life and make itself manifest in political practices. For another thing, repression, trauma, and collective ecstasy may make it invisible in the short run. To give an example, Mussolini and his Fascists believed, and made the outside world believe, that they had freed themselves from elements of Italian culture that ran counter to the purposes of their regime, only to find that in the long run these patterns reasserted themselves. Or, to take the case of Stalin, his system of mass repression succeeded in blurring cultural distinctions among the institutions of the countries of East Central Europe, yet these distinctions resurfaced quickly under his successors to shape and color political reality.

2 | East Central Europe

A HISTORICAL OVERVIEW

The Origin of Medieval States

When tracing the origins of the modern European state, political historians usually go back to the middle of the first millennium. It was then that the great migration of Eurasian peoples destroyed the Roman Empire of the West and reduced the Greco-Byzantine Empire of the East to the status of a regional power on the edges of the Continent. Thereafter, for several centuries, much of Europe was thrown into a state of turmoil as successive waves of migrating warrior peoples—Gepids, Vandals, Goths, Huns, Avars, and many others—made their way from the Eurasian steppe to the Mediterranean and the Atlantic, some of them marching even further across the Iberian peninsula to North Africa. Time and again, the chieftains of these nomadic peoples attempted to form territorially bounded empires or states. But these attempts proved futile, for the political organization of these nomads disappeared as fast as they had emerged on the European political scene.

By the beginning of the eighth century, however, some of the Germanic tribes and their Latinized cousins in Italy and Gaul began to consolidate their societies by converting to Christianity and abandoning their tribal organization in favor of a new social division of labor between warriors and agricultural producers, the former protecting the latter from the depredations of nomadic marauders. It was from this rudimentary system of reciprocities, in which producers surrendered part of their surplus in exchange for the security of life and limb, that there developed a new type of political order, designated by posterity as feudalism. In the meantime, inspired by their common religious allegiance to the Christian faith and by their common need to defend themselves from new waves of "barbarian" migrants, a

MAP 1.   Europe in the Ninth Century.

number of the warrior chieftains developed a system of alliances that, by the
last year of the eighth century, was consolidated into a new "Holy" Roman
empire under the scepter of Charlemagne (800–814). This new empire en-
compassed much of today's France, Italy, Austria, the Low Countries, and
western Germany, and extended from the Pyrenees in the southwest to the
river Elbe in the north and the river Leitha in the southeast. As some historians pointedly remind us, these were the very same boundaries chosen by
the victorious Allies after World War II as they divided Europe between East
and West.[1] We should note here that, whether by accident or design, these

1. Berend 1986, 2; Szűcs 1986, 616–68.

MAP 2. Europe in the Middle Ages.

"Cold War" boundaries also followed those of the medieval Byzantine empire by assigning Greece and Turkey to the "West."

Whatever meaning we assign to these historical continuities, there can be little doubt that the initial division of Europe along the Elbe and Leitha had far-reaching consequences for societies on both sides of the divide throughout the entire second millennium. For the West, the boundary became a strong and reliable line of defense that, while occasionally pierced by roving bands of nomads, put an effective end to the stream of migrants and conquerors from the steppes of the East. Charlemagne defeated the Avars in 796, just as his successors would defeat the Hungarians in 933 and 955, and

MAP 3. Europe at the Time of the Congress of Vienna (1815).

although the Mongols were able to devastate Europe east of the Elbe and the Leitha in the thirteenth century, their depredations stopped at the imperial boundaries. Likewise, although in the sixteenth century the Ottoman Turks conquered southeast Europe, their seemingly inexorable march came to a halt before the walls of Vienna, at the gateway to the Cisleithanian regions of the Continent. From the point of view of the West, the imperial boundaries thus became a protective wall behind which civil society and civilization could develop in relative safety from external enemies.

From the perspective of the East, however, these ramparts of the empire

MAP 4. Europe in 1945.

acted more like a powerful breakwater, from which successive waves of nomadic invasions rolled back into the adjacent region, turning it into a "shatter zone" where the turbulence of the "people's migration era" [*Völkerwan-
derung*] continued for some time after it had come to an end in Western
Europe. Most immediately, this "shattering" of successive waves of migrations resulted in populations that were ethnically far more fragmented than
their counterparts in the West. In addition, the shatter effect delayed the rise

of organized societies, and when states finally made their appearance, they were much more fragile than their western neighbors, for they continued to face threats to their existence not only from the steppe nomads but from the territorial ambitions of their better-organized imperial neighbors as well.

The first identifiable precursors of contemporary states appeared in the region toward the end of the first millennium. In the Balkans, south of the Danube-Sava line, there was a Bulgarian state as early as the eighth century, followed in the ninth and tenth centuries by the principalities of Raška, Zahumlye, Zeta, Dyrrachium (also known as the tributary despotate of Epirus), and Primorje—the forerunners of today's Serbia, Bosnia, Montenegro, Albania, and Dalmatia—together with the duchy of Croatia occupying the lands between the rivers Drava and Sava. Croatia and Raška-Serbia eventually became kingdoms, Croatia in association with the kingdom of Hungary, a neighbor state it joined in 1102 without surrendering its institutions and internal autonomy. In the Danubian and northern tiers of the area, there existed a Czech state in some shape or form from the end of the ninth century onward. Its neighbors to the north and the south were Poland and Hungary, the latter including Hungary proper within the arc of the Carpathians, the duchy, later principality, and still later grand duchy of Transylvania, and the already-mentioned associate kingdom of Croatia (officially, Croatia-Slavonia). Poland and Hungary both became kingdoms in the year 1000, when they were so recognized by Pope Sylvester II, who sent royal crowns to their respective tribal princes. The two Romanian principalities of Wallachia and Moldavia came into existence some time later, in the fourteenth century, on the eastern slope of the Carpathians north of the Danube.

From Kingdoms to Empires

As would be the case in later centuries, the political fate and fortunes of these dynastic states of East Central Europe, and the greatness of some, were all related to changes in the larger configurations of power on the Eurasian supercontinent. Between the ninth and the thirteenth centuries, the fledgling states of East Central Europe faced powerful empires in the south and the west, as well as waves of warrior nomads in the east. During these centuries, their existence was precarious. After the middle of the thirteenth century, however, the danger of nomadic incursions abated as another ring of states was to form around Muscovy and Kiev, while the Western Empire was weakened by internecine conflict as well as by disputes between popes and emperors. It was during these centuries that some of the states of East Central Europe experienced their "golden age." Most remarkable was the ascent of the Commonwealth of Poland, itself a multinational empire, created by dynastic union between Poland and Lithuania

(1386) and enlarged by extending its boundaries deep into the territories of today's Belarus and Ukraine. The kings of Hungary likewise used the favorable balance of forces to consolidate a multinational realm inside the arc of the Carpathian mountains, then added new feudal dependencies to their domain in the Balkans and in the Transcarpathian provinces. The power of this imperial state apexed under Mathias Corvinus, king of Hungary, who won the crown of Bohemia and ruled his realm from Vienna after temporarily subduing the neighboring duchy of Austria. On a lesser scale, Serbia flourished as a regional state, reaching the apex of its power under Tsar Dušan of the House of Nemanja in the middle of the fourteenth century. Indeed, indicative of their political fortunes, many of the kings of the region in the fourteenth century were adorned by posterity with the adjective "great," including Louis of Hungary, Charles of Bohemia, Stefan of Moldavia, and Kazimir of Poland, while Dušan of Serbia and the tsars of Bulgaria could hold on to the fiction that they were ruling imperial states.

These moments of glory, however, were to pass soon as the configurations of power changed in the larger Eurasian space. In the west, the apparently moribund German-Roman empire was resuscitated under the hereditary rule of the house of Habsburg, the archdukes of Austria with numerous family possessions, whose power in the sixteenth century reached as far as Spain and, through Spain, the New World. Simultaneously, in the east there appeared a new band of conquering people, the Ottoman Turks, who, after a quick march through Asia Minor, were ready to project their power onto the European continent. In 1389, they were already battling, and significantly weakening, the Serbian state in the epic confrontation of the Blackbird Field. In 1393, they occupied Bulgaria, and in 1453 they dealt a coup de grâce to the Greek empire of Byzantium by occupying Constantinople. The Ottomans extinguished the independence of Serbia in 1459 and of Bosnia in 1463. In 1482, the same fate befell the principality of Herzegovina. The princes of Wallachia and Moldavia submitted to Ottoman overlordship in 1462 and 1512 respectively. By now the entire Balkan peninsula was in Ottoman hands, and except on some of the high mountains of the west, Ottoman power was effective. Then in 1526, Ottoman armies crossed the rivers Sava and Drava, and defeated the army of the king of Hungary in the battle of Mohács, with the king himself left dead on the battlefield. Within the next fifteen years, the Ottomans established themselves on the Pannonian plain and turned Transylvania into a tributary state of the empire. From here on, however, Ottoman advances were stymied, for on the Pannonian plain, Turkish armies met the Habsburgs, one of them, Prince Ferdinand, having been elevated to the Hungarian throne by the country's desperate estates. The new king and his successors used rump Hungary as a glacis, or buffer, to protect their western holdings and their imperial capital, Vienna.

From this defensive position, they repelled three major Ottoman onslaughts in 1529, 1552, and 1683, turning the last one into a prolonged and devastating war for the possession of the lands of the Hungarian crown. Successful in this last enterprise, the Habsburgs, soon to be hereditary monarchs, extended the boundaries of their realm to the line of the Sava and the Carpathians. Although de facto part of a larger imperial system, de jure both Hungary and Transylvania remained separate entities, where the Habsburgs ruled by virtue of the consent of the local estates.

In the northern tier of the region, the political landscape was reshaped by the confrontations of three powers. One was Poland, a country that had remained a first-rate European power well into the eighteenth century. However, in the interim, the rulers of Muscovy finally defeated the Mongols and consolidated their domain in a new Russian empire, while in the West, German immigrants colonized the area between the Elbe and the Memel to become the subjects of the duchy of Brandenburg and of the Order of the Teutonic Knights. In 1701, these territories came to form the core of the new Protestant kingdom of Prussia. These three states—Prussia, Poland, and Russia—waged a number of wars against each other, as well as against the aggressive and ambitious kingdom of Sweden, for primacy in northeastern Europe. For a long while, Poland appeared to be the likely candidate for the position of the regional hegemon. But the country was eventually subdued by an alliance of Prussia and Russia, joined for the spoils by the house of Habsburg. After three successive partitions, Poland disappeared from the map of Europe in 1795.

Although imperial domination of the region was complete by the end of the eighteenth century, the nature of foreign rule varied considerably from country to country, mainly with respect to the degree of social and political autonomy enjoyed by the local populations. In the case of Ottoman Turkey, the countries and provinces of the Balkan peninsula were divided into administrative districts (larger *vilayets* and smaller *sanjaks*) directly governed from Istanbul by Moslem administrators. An exception to this rule was mountainous Montenegro, whose inhabitants were supposed to pay a tribute to the Porte, but where the collection of taxes was poorly enforced, mainly because of the region's physical inaccessibility. Under direct Ottoman rule, the native administrative and landed classes were either exterminated or expelled, which turned Serbia and Bulgaria into "peasant societies" in the post-imperial period of independence. The same pattern was followed in the Turkish-occupied parts of the Hungarian plain, except that these regions were subsequently resettled by both nobles and peasants in the eighteenth century. In a few places, most notably in Bosnia-Herzegovina, some of the local landowners, including members of the free peasantry, converted to Islam to escape expropriation or expulsion. In contrast, the regions north of the Danube—Wallachia, Moldavia, and Transylvania—were under indirect Ottoman rule. In these provinces, the imperial government was content to exercise a power of veto over the person of the prince, to collect an annual tribute, and to keep Ottoman garrisons in key fortresses. In the eighteenth century, this form of rule deteriorated, in that the princes of Wallachia and Moldavia were appointed by the Porte, or sold outright to the highest bidder, who promised to collect maximum revenue for the imperial treasury in exchange for the opportunity to enrich himself.

In the larger domain of the house of Habsburg, initially at least both Bohemia and Hungary were independent entities, where the emperors ruled in their capacity of kings elected by the local estates. In 1618, however, the estates of Bohemia launched a revolt against the overbearance of imperial officials. The result was a bloody civil war in which the Czech estates were defeated, and the nobility was expelled from the country or exterminated with the same thoroughness as was the Christian nobility of the Balkan countries. Henceforth Bohemia would be ruled directly from the imperial capital of Vienna. In Hungary, there were similar rebellions in the seventeenth and eighteenth centuries, but the imperial forces could never fully prevail, so the constitutional arrangements of the Middle Ages survived, and the emperors continued to rule Hungary as a kingdom affiliated with the empire but not an integral part of it. This further meant that the power of the nobility remained unimpaired and survived well into the modern period. Likewise, the Polish provinces of the Habsburg empire were given a measure of administrative autonomy. While Galicia became an integral part of the Austrian imperial domain, the local nobility were given a measure of autonomy and an active role in the administration of their country. Compared to this model, Prussian and Russian rule over Poland was harsher and more direct. Under Prussian rule, the annexed Polish provinces were governed with an iron fist and in complete disregard of local interests. In Russia, the initial autonomy of the Polish provinces was gradually whittled down, and after 1863, it was abolished altogether, reducing the local ruling class to the status of a marginal intelligentsia with radical sentiments.

From Empires to Nations

The expansion of imperial rule over East Central Europe culminated in 1795 with the third partition of Poland. In that year, no piece of soil in the region could fly its own flag or claim other symbols of dynastic or national independence. Ironically, though, hardly had the colonization of the region been completed in the north, when signs of restlessness began to multiply in the south, stimulated as much by the internal decay of Ottoman administration as by the example of rising nation-states in the western half of the Continent. The Serbian uprising of 1804 was still little more than a peasant jacquerie triggered by corruption, maladministration, and the depredations of Turkish soldiers. But between 1815 and 1830, popular dissatisfaction acquired a new political and ideological cast, in that the populations now aspired and fought for national autonomy and independence. There will be no attempt here to chronicle these movements in any detail. Suffice it to say that between 1830 and 1878, Serbia, Montenegro, and Bulgaria became independent in all but name, and so did Wallachia and Moldavia, now united as the principality, later kingdom, of Romania. In the interim, Hungary fought a bitter civil war against the Habsburgs, lost its constitutional autonomy within the empire (1849), and then regained it in the compromise of 1867 that expanded the country's autonomy and liberties. It was within this particular historical context that the first states emerged and that the modern age, the subject of the rest of this volume, unfolded.

CULTURE AND TRADITIONAL INSTITUTIONS

Christianity: East and West

As elsewhere in Europe, on the eastern perimeters of the Continent, the rise of the medieval state was closely intertwined with the spread of Christianity. When a pagan prince or chieftain converted to the new faith, and subsequently coaxed his people into following suit, he received not only the blessings of other Christian rulers—the medieval equivalent of admission to the United Nations—but a religious doctrine as well, which was to provide much-needed ideological cement for the building of an orderly political community. In the first place, Christian religious tenets tended to discourage wanton murder and plunder as a way of life. They further provided a concept of solidarity that went beyond the narrow confines of the kinship group and tribe and, at the same time, encouraged obedience to secular authority on the grounds that rebellion against it might jeopardize the immortal soul of the subject.

However, as already noted, from its very beginnings as an organized religion, Christianity was divided between its Eastern and Western branches, and over the centuries the chasm between the two steadily increased until 1054, when the two branches formally broke with each other. By then, the Western branch was closely associated with the papacy and the "Holy Roman" Empire, and as such its doctrines and organization were heavily influenced by the individualist, legalistic, and rationalistic legacies of Roman antiquity. Within this tradition, God's image as a loving and forgiving father was overshadowed by the Roman image of justice in which a judge applies rewards and punishments dispassionately according to a preestablished scale. As a corollary, sin becomes analogous to a breach of contract or violation of the law. Avoiding it becomes a matter of individual responsibility, albeit in Catholicism, this responsibility is supposed to be discharged under ecclesiastic guidance. In life, humans are given the chance to absolve themselves by doing penance in a carefully specified manner. But should they die in a state of mortal sin, the consequence is eternal damnation, the spiritual equivalent of life imprisonment without parole. If the idea of God's love still looms large in holy texts, it refers to a quantity given in exchange for compliance with the explicit terms of ever-renewed covenants. In the words of the German theologian Ernst Benz: "From the beginning, the West has understood the fundamental relationship between God and man primarily as a legal relationship. God has established certain laws for man. By sinful conduct man violates these laws. Justice requires him to make amends to God. The church supervises this relationship."[2]

In contrast, the theology of the Eastern Orthodox Church was shaped by Hellenic traditions and under the philosophical influence of the Orient. Unlike the traditions of Roman antiquity, those of Hellenic Byzantium tended to emphasize introspection over worldly deeds, relationships dominated by affect, and what the Russians would later call *sabornost'*, meaning communal sentiment and collective responsibility for salvation.[3] Thus, if in Catholicism—and still more so in Calvinism and Lutheranism after the sixteenth century—the ideas of divine justice tend to overshadow the idea of God's love, in Orthodoxy the very opposite is the case. Whereas in Western theology, sinning is regarded as a breach of contract, in Orthodoxy, it is seen as a diminution of essence, an act that increases our distance from God, although without rupturing the relationship. For centuries, writes Benz, the Eastern Church was flirting with the idea of universal salvation, in which the day of the Last Judgment was to be a day of ultimate redemption. Rather than separating those who have been saved from those who have been doomed, God, in a truly paternal fashion, might give everybody the fresh chance of a new beginning. "At the end of all eons everything evil will have been winnowed out; the fallen angels, and even Satan himself, will turn back to the divine Logos."[4] Instead of a theology of reciprocal legal obligations, we encounter here one that emphasizes the reciprocal obligation of love and devotion. On the surface at least, this theology provides an attractive model for statecraft, more appealing than the cold impersonality of law and contract. The problem though is that when hierarchy is based on such reciprocal obligations, the parties to the relationship may be faulted not only for breach of fixed norms but also for not being sufficiently loving and de-

2. Benz 1963, 43–44.
3. See Benz 1963, 41–42; Hussey 1961, 126; Walters 1988, 64.
4. Benz 1963, 52.

voted. Love is a subjective category, and making its practice mandatory may pave the way to arbitrary and despotic government.

These differences in theology were further accentuated by the respective positions of the two churches in society and in their relations to secular authority. Both of these churches were elevated from the catacombs by imperial states in compromises that made them instruments of secular authority. But shortly after this occurred, the Western Empire collapsed, and the Church of Rome acquired an institutional independence that, by a series of historical accidents, it was able to preserve and strengthen throughout the centuries. Thus, when the Western Empire was reestablished under Charlemagne, it encountered a powerful supranational institution of equal standing in the world, and it was on this platform of equality that Church and state were to build their future relationship. While the new empire and its many princes legitimated their power by claims of divine stewardship, this claim could be substantiated only by the Church through the sacred rituals of coronation and anointment. In exchange for the sacralization of their authority, emperor and kings had to respect the laws of the Church and its institutional integrity. True, over the centuries, kings, emperors, and their servants were often tempted to change the balance of power in this relationship. But the pope, as the head of the Catholic Church, could deny these malefactors the benefits of his blessing or excommunicate them from the Church, thus delegitimizing their rule and implicitly inviting their subjects to resist their acts of government. On the whole, this element of reciprocity permitted the Western Church to maintain its institutional integrity, which in time would serve as a model for others in their struggle for privileges and immunities.

Not so in the East, where the empire had survived the vagaries of the migration period, and where the subordinate position of the Church found justification in theories of kingship imported to Byzantium from the Orient. In these theories, the sacrality of rulers did not derive from ascription, ritual, and the charisma of office, but from hereditary charisma, vested in a biological person; that is to say, rulers were not made but born sacred or "saintly."[5] As a result, the Eastern ruler "had a sacrosanct status without parallel in [Western] Europe . . . and extraordinary liturgical privileges in keeping with their divine election and charismatic position in society."[6] The Byzantine emperor could "like the clergy, enter the sanctuary and partake of the sacrament."[7] The ruler of the East was therefore "not only God's servant, but his representative watching over the purity of the faith,"[8] in charge

5. Dvornik 1962, 142.
6. Papadakis 1988, 38.
7. Ibid.
8. Josif Sanin, abbot of Volokolomsk in the fifteenth century. Quoted in Dvornik 1962, 372.

of the salvation of his people, whom God entrusted to his care.[9] He was "shepherd, benefactor and savior to whom divine honors were to be paid, surrounded with ceremonial that was religious in character and closely connected with ecclesiastic liturgy."[10]

In conformity with this Hellenistic-Oriental concept of rulership, as early as the fourth century, the rulers of Byzantium "began to take the lead in ecclesiastic matters, to interfere personally in theological controversy, to convoke councils, and even to legislate on heresy and schism."[11] Their successors attempted to tilt the balance of power still further toward themselves. In the last five hundred years of the empire, nearly one-third of all the patriarchs of Constantinople were forced out of their office by imperial mandates.[12] Surely, there were "limits beyond which the emperor could go only at his peril."[13] But throughout the centuries, imperium and sacerdotium remained closely intertwined, with superior power on the side of the secular rulers, who would deprive the Church of its independence and merge the spiritual and temporal realms into a single, all-encompassing politico-religious sphere. While the medieval state was never powerful enough to penetrate every "nook and cranny" of social life, this blurring of boundaries between state and society anticipated some of the features of modern totalitarianism and made some of its practices easier to accept when and where they would occur.

The Evolution of Juridical Feudalism

In the countries of Western Christianity, the history of the Middle Ages is one of the gradual development of juridical feudalism and of the legal state, culminating in the development of parliamentary institutions and government. Throughout the Continent, this development can be traced through three separate stages. In the first one, the newly converted monarchs began to supplement the ranks of their kinsmen and household retainers with retinues of hired vassals, often foreigners, who were to perform administrative and military services in exchange for specific rewards and benefits guaranteed by contract and confirmed by reciprocal oaths of fealty. On the one hand, the vassal promised to render specific military or administrative services; on the other, the kings promised their vassals the usufruct of land, together with protection of their persons and property. In the second stage, the vassals' privileges became hereditary and gradually extended to other

9. Ibid., 377.
10. Papadakis 1988, 39.
11. Ibid., 38.
12. Ibid., 41.
13. Hussey 1961, 89.

categories of royal subjects, among them the household servitors of the kings, common knights, members of the clergy, craftsmen, and traders. The individual privileges of vassals thus became converted hereditary and collective rights, and new social entities, the estates, arose, the first among them being the estate of the nobility. From here on, the third stage of development was logical, if not inevitable: since the royal charters invariably promised not to use coercion against the privileged estates (except in case of high treason or felonious conduct), and since they usually granted subjects the moral right to resist royal breaches of contract, the kings were forced to engage in "parleys" whenever they needed the cooperation of the estates or their financial contributions to the commonweal. It was out of these parleys that the medieval institutions of parliament emerged, convoked to raise royal revenues and conscripts and, conversely, to enable the nobles to petition the king for the redress of their grievances against him or his servants.

This three-stage model of institutional and social development is familiar from the histories of England, France, Italy, and the western provinces of Germany.[14] But the model was also quite closely followed in the borderlands of western Christianity: in Poland, Lithuania, Bohemia, and Hungary, as well as in Croatia-Slavonia and Transylvania, associated with the Hungarian crown. In all of these countries, contractual vassalage played an important part in consolidating the early monarchies. Foreign knights were invited by the monarchs not only because of their administrative and military expertise, but also because of their willingness to protect the kings from their own contentious kinsmen (a fact that István, the first king of Hungary, bluntly admitted in the "Admonitions" that he drafted for the benefit of his son and successors). Contractual vassalage turned into a society of estates in the thirteenth and fourteenth centuries, when these individually granted privileges were extended to whole categories of subjects by royal charters. The first in a series of these charters was the Hungarian Aurea Bulla of 1222, in which King Andrew II of Hungary made all the privileges of his chief vassals hereditary and at the same time conferred those same privileges upon his household servitors, thus transforming them into a noble estate. Significantly, the document also recognized the collective right of this knighthood to take up arms against the king should he be found in violation of his letter of patent. Two years later, the same king issued his Diploma Andreanum delineating the rights and immunities of German settlers in seven boroughs of Transylvania.[15] Thereafter, similar documents, or "statutes" were issued by other Catholic monarchs. The Statute of Little Poland was issued in 1347, and that of Greater Poland in 1348, followed by the Charters of Mo-

14. For this process of development, see esp. Bloch 1965, esp. 1: 145–63, 190–210, 219–30; 2: 283–92.
15. Molnár 1971, 1: 76–78.

ravia (1377) and Transylvania (1437), and in the wake of the statutes there emerged new civil societies of privileged estates. In the Czech lands, the medieval constitution recognized four of these: barons, knights, clergy, and burghers.[16] In Poland, medieval law recognized the estate of warrior freemen (*szlachta*), divided into magnates and lesser knights, as well as the estates of the clergy and burghers, the latter divided again into Jews and gentiles. In Hungary and Croatia, the estates consisted of nobility, clergy, and burghers, the former two being divided after 1608 into higher and lower ranks, following the Polish pattern. Transylvania recognized the privileges of three "nations": Hungarians, Szeklers, and Saxons. In reality, however, these three nations were estates in disguise, for "Hungarians" referred to the nobility, "Szeklers" to the free peasants of the Eastern Carpathians, and "Saxons" to the German burghers of privileged cities.

The development of institutions of self-government followed the rise of the estates. At the local level, the most important of these institutions were the counties of the nobility (in Hungary and Poland) and the cities governed by the councils of burghers. At the national level, we find the already-mentioned diets, or parliaments. In Hungary and Poland, these national assemblies were bicameral. In Poland, the Sejm consisted of a senate and a chamber, one composed of the great lords temporal and spiritual, the other of delegates elected by the county assemblies, or *sejmiks*. In Hungary, a similar division had existed for centuries but was not formalized by legislation until 1608, when the Diet was divided into a "table" of magnates (temporal and spiritual) and a table of the lesser "corporations and estates," including the elected representatives of the common nobility, lower clergy, and the free cities. In the Czech lands, the Diet consisted of three chambers: the magnates and knights each had their own, while the third chamber included representatives of the burghers and the clergy. In Croatia-Slavonia and Transylvania, the Sabor and Diet, respectively, were unicameral, but based on the same principles of representation as the Hungarian Diet. Thus, the Croatian Sabor included magnates and prelates, as well as the representatives of the "lower" estates, while the Transylvanian Diet consisted of the representatives of the three "nations." The constitutional powers of these diets increased with the political power of the estates and reached its apex in the sixteenth century, when the parliaments codified all earlier privileges and enacted constitutional legislation that put the estates on equal footing with the kings. The Czech and Moravian estates accomplished this during their long session between 1499 and 1508, after which they published the *Legislation, Justice and Tables of the Land of Bohemia;*[17] the rights and privileges of the Hungarian and Croatian nobility were codified by the Diet

16. Dvornik 1962, 70–72.
17. Dvornik 1962, 335.

of 1514–17 and published as the *Corpus Iuris Tripartitum*, and a similar code of noble privileges was compiled upon the instructions of the Polish Diet of Toruń in 1520. Thereafter, the pendulum of power began to swing back to the monarchies under the impact of imperial encroachments and within the broader sweep of developments in the continental economy. The Diet of the Czech lands was dissolved in 1627 after the country's failed attempt to gain religious and political independence from the house of Habsburg. But the Sejm of Poland, often to the detriment of the commonweal, retained most of its powers until the partition of the country in 1795. Finally, the institutional identity of the Hungarian (Transylvanian, Croatian) diets was preserved until 1848, when they dissolved themselves in order to give way to more modern forms of representative government.

In all of the countries discussed above, the monarchy was elective at one time or another during the Middle Ages. In Poland, this arrangement commenced upon the extinction of the first, and native, dynasty of the Piasts, and led to the rise of the Rzeczpospolita, or noble commonwealth, which was to last until the end of the eighteenth century. Similarly, in Hungary, the monarchy became elective in 1301 upon the extinction of the founding dynasty of the Árpáds and remained elective de facto until 1540 and de jure until 1687, when the principle of hereditary succession was recognized by the Diet under considerable pressure from the house of Habsburg. In Transylvania, the princes of the Ottoman period were elected by the Diet between 1552 and 1692. In the Czech lands, kings were elected after the extinction of the medieval dynasty of the Przemyslides, and the monarchy remained elective de jure until 1627, when the Habsburgs turned the country into one of their hereditary domains. While in force, the elective principle changed the very institution of the monarchy. Although the principles of rule by divine right were never formally abandoned, in reality, the legitimacy of the monarchy derived from the various pacts and *constitutiones* that a prospective ruler had to sign with the estates as a condition of being elected.

While the culture of legalism was most evident in shaping the relationship between kings and estates, it also had a discernible impact on relations between lords and peasants. There should, of course, be no mistake: the large majority of the populations, the peasants who tilled the land, were, to use the contemporary phrase, "outside the protective bastions of constitutional liberties." They were not, as they have subsequently been referred to at times, a fourth or fifth estate, but rather a group of people recognized as a non-estate. They were also a downtrodden class. They were, in the blunt terminology of the Hungarian *Tripartitum*, the *misera plebs contribuens*, the wretched common folk who carried the tax burdens. Their own institutions of village government were poorly developed, withering and waning as the powers of the nobility grew. They were thus weakest at the time when the powers of the nobility reached their apex in the fifteenth and sixteenth centuries. But even in better times, these institutions served the interests of the landowning class, for the principal functions of village judges and aldermen were to enforce the order of production and to apportion and collect the obligations of the village toward the local landowner. The office of the village judge, therefore, carried little status, and in hard times it was even imposed upon a reluctant candidate under the pain of severe physical punishment.[18]

Still, over the centuries, there remained three important principles at work that set certain limits to exploitation by the crown and the landed nobility. The first of these principles was that serfdom and land tenure represented economic rather than personal relationships, hence peasants were not in personal bondage, but were free to move from one manor to another after discharging their obligations. The second principle was that, even though all land was owned by the nobility, serfs enjoyed hereditary rights to the tenure of their parcel. Although the peasant was free to leave, his lord could not forcibly evict him and his family. The third principle was that his rights and obligations and, above all, the terms of his tenancy were to be incorporated into written copyhold agreements, with disputes between him and his landowner to be adjudicated by juries from which the serf's own lord was excluded. Critics, to be sure, will be quick to point out that at times these principles were observed only in their breach. Such was the case in the early sixteenth century, when there was a strong movement in most countries of Central and Eastern Europe to restrict peasants' mobility from one estate to another and to increase servile obligations in labor and in kind. But these and other times of feudal reaction would pass, and the right of free migration was restored again and again. The royal courts of appeal were also effective enough to review the system of servile obligations and, overall, to prevent the institutionalization of the worst kinds of abuse by the noble owners of the land.

Autocracy and Paternalism

The historical experience of the Orthodox countries was different from the above patterns. Indeed, it is questionable whether we can speak at all of a "path of development," for over the centuries, public authority followed cycles of weakness and strength without noticeable departures from the principles of autocracy and paternalism. In a milieu in which the tsar was an "autocrat" who "wielded power over all things"[19] or, still more tell-

18. Szabó 1948, 12–16.
19. Dvornik 1962, 377.

ingly, was the "supreme owner of every person and all property," [20] social relationships based on the reciprocity of rights and obligations could not flourish. True, there existed in these societies, too, a class of boyars, a term that sometimes refers to princely administrators, sometimes to landowners. In the words of a distinguished historian of boyardom, they were a "privileged class," but "few ever knew who qualified for membership and what the privileges were." [21] There was undoubtedly an enduring desire on the part of royal retainers to establish themselves as a ruling class through the acquisition of property. But it was the very ability to check this tendency toward aristocratization and entrenchment that separated strong rulers from the weak in the eyes of both their contemporaries and subsequent historians. Thus, in Russia, Ivan II is remembered as "the Meek one," mainly because he was unable to rein in his boyars, while Ivan III and IV are remembered as great, even though "terrible," rulers, because they successfully curbed the influence of both landowners and officials. The Ivans had their counterparts in Balkan rulers such as Vlad Ţepeş, "the Impaler," who virtually exterminated the boyardom of Wallachia, or Vlad Vîntila, who had the endearing habit of "arresting his boyars, cutting off their noses, mutilating their mouths, and throwing them in the dungeons of Poinari castle." [22]

In the same way, the absence of strong cultural models for contractualized authority thwarted the rise of feudal diets and other institutions of civil society and self-government. We do, of course, find frequent references to national assemblies, such as the *zbor*, the *skupstina*, and the *stanak* of Balkan countries, and the *sfăt*, the *divan*, or the *adunarea* among Romanians, and there are historians who credit these institutions with the drafting of important constitutional documents. A case in point is the attribution of Tsar Dušan's Code of 1349 to the Serbian Diet at Skopje. The functions of these assemblies are best seen as advisory, since they did not possess the power of the purse or the right to refuse the collection of taxes in the manner of the Polish, Hungarian, or Bohemian diets. In this respect, it is instructive to compare the functioning of the Serbian *skupštine* and the Bosnian *stanaks* with the Croatian Sabor,[23] or the divans of Moldavia and Wallachia with the diets of neighboring Transylvania. As to the latter, a highly respected Romanian source records 306 of its meetings between 1529 and 1691.[24] The laws that the diets passed during this period appear in two major works, the *Approbatae Constitutiones* and the *Compilatae Constitutiones Regni Transylvaniae et partium Hungariae*. The diets legislated in such

20. Xenopol, quoted in Giurescu Jr. 1940, 2: 360.
21. C. Giurescu, Sr. [1918] 1943, 227.
22. Ciurca 1970, 87–88.
23. Dvornik 1962, 136–43.
24. D. Giurescu 1981, 248.

weighty matters as the freedom of religious practices (1564), the status of serfs and free peasants, and the use of land held in common. In contrast, the princes of Wallachia "ruled with the help of a hierarchy of high officials . . . [and] with a well organized state apparatus the multifold activities of which were dependent on centralized authority."[25] The *sfâts*, or later divans, are described as "akin to a [modern] council of ministers" that the princes consulted regularly on judicial, administrative, and military matters.[26] Time and again, to be sure, the divans of the principalities were called upon to choose the new ruler upon the extinction of a princely line (until such powers were effectively seized by the Ottoman government in Istanbul). But the act of election was not accompanied by the signing of constitutional contracts, and the powers of the "all powerful princes" were limited only by the vaguely articulated customs of the land (*obicei pămîntului*), which rarely prevented the ruler from undoing the privileges of the same boyardom and clergy that had elected him.

These characteristics of paternalistic rule were also manifest in the relationship between lords and peasants. Much like the relationship between ruler and retainers, that of masters and servants was ill defined and purposely diffuse. Thus, as the former prince of Moldavia, Dimitrie Cantemir, wrote in 1716, landowners were entrusted with the general welfare of their serfs, who were regarded as part of the lord's household, and custom required that lords provide livelihood for young families, sometimes by granting them arable land for cultivation from the acreage of their estate. In exchange, the peasant owed the landowner the *clacă* (*corvée*), and was to be in personal bondage under his jurisdiction.[27] In practice, though, the paternalistic formula seemed to permit, or even encourage, arbitrary behavior on the part of the landowners, checked only by cyclical shortages of labor, the flight of serf peasants to neighboring Transylvania, or rebellions that punctuated long periods of peasant apathy. When writing about the subject, many economic historians say that in the Orthodox East, serfdom and feudalism did not exist in the European sense.[28] The crucial difference was that the status of the rural poor, much like the status of the landowners themselves, remained ill defined or not regulated at all. Time and again, princely edicts, like Dušan's Code in Serbia, the *Prăvila* of Vasile Lupu in Wallachia, or Mavracordat's edicts for the Romanian principalities[29] were issued to improve the condition of the peasantry. But these were of little avail, and the

25. Ibid.
26. C. Giurescu [1918] 1940, 2:386; Xenopol 1940, 25, 30–31.
27. According to (1700), the "boyar may sell a Moldavian subject, but not outside his native village. However, if he sells a whole estate with its peasants, that sale is valid" (Cantemir, *Descriptio Moldaviae* (1716), quoted in Warriner 1965, 126–27).
28. Dragaşanu 1942, 67.
29. "Decrees of Constantin Mavracordat," in Warriner 1965, 130–131.

true condition of the peasantry—at least in the Romanian principalities—is perhaps best summarized in Cantemir's *Descriptio* at the dawn of the eighteenth century. "Of whatever race they may be," he writes of the peasants, "they are bound to apply themselves continually to their lord's work. There are no limits set to their toils; their master's will alone decides how many days they must work." [30] Somewhat incongruously, then, Cantemir goes on to describe the many rights of the peasants: "no part of the peasant's personal property belongs to the lord; if he extorts any[thing] judicial remedies are available to restore it"; and, most significantly, "to kill him [the peasant] is forbidden by the law." [31] But thereafter Cantemir admits, with engaging bluntness, that neither law nor custom is very effective in defending the serfs, for "if the lord wants to act unjustly, he beats the peasant until he voluntarily [sic] surrenders what is desired." [32] At any rate, whatever his obligations to the lord, "he pays as much tribute as the prince decrees, and there is no limit laid down for that." [33] The reality was one of personal bondage and license for exploitation, mitigated only by temporary shortages of labor, or by periodic rebellions that followed long periods of rural apathy.

Just as in the lands of Western Christianity, so too in those of Orthodoxy we encounter various forms of village government, which populists and other romantics have often described as a potential, or even real, cradle of peasant democracy. Such arguments though are not easy to defend. For while we do indeed find an officialdom in the villages, often chosen by the peasants themselves in some procedure resembling modern elections, and find that these officials had jurisdiction over local affairs, in the final analysis, local functionaries served at the pleasure of local landlords or of the authorities of the imperial states. In the Balkans, the *seoski knez*, or village headman, and his council of aldermen were empowered by the Ottomans to perform judicial and police functions within village boundaries, yet their main function was to apportion among individual families the tax levied collectively on villagers by the *ispahi* landowner or the Ottoman authorities. Thus, just as in Hungary and Poland, elders under Ottoman rule were compelled to serve, and could pay with their lives for lack of cooperation with officials of the state.[34] Rather than being democratically elected officials of self-government, these local officeholders confirmed and conformed to a cultural image of being "sacrificial beasts of burden for the cares of the whole community." [35]

30. Warriner 1965, 127.
31. Ibid.
32. Ibid.
33. Ibid., 127–128.
34. Stavrianos 1958, 120; Halpern 1967, 17.
35. Walters in Ramet 1988, 64. See also Utechin 1963, 78–127, 64.

BEFORE THE MODERN AGE: MATERIAL CONDITIONS

Like its political fate and fortunes, the economic landscape of medieval Europe was tangibly affected by the geopolitical division of the Continent in the year 800. The empire of Charlemagne and of his successors
created at least a modicum of security for life and limb, and hence for the
production and exchange of commodities. Consequently, under imperial authority, exercised through a complex set of relationships among territorial
vassals, large stretches of land that had been laid waste by the depredations
of robber knights and foreign intruders were once again brought regularly
under the plow. Producers were willing to invest time and effort once again
in the immovable stock of vineyards and orchards, and in the production of
"culture crops" that require permanent fixtures or changes in the lay of the
land. At the same time, there was a revival of ancient handicrafts, while new
technologies such as the waterwheel were developed for use in milling and
mining, innovations that would gradually be diffused by immigrants from
the west to the east of the continent. Finally, as part of the general economic
upswing at the turn of the millennium, a number of large population centers
emerged, among them London, Paris, Venice, and Bologna. By the twelfth
century, these cities had not only acquired large populations but were also
notable for their magnificent architecture and universities. In this sense at
least, the borderlands of East Central Europe were less developed than the
imperial West, a fact that some historians have interpreted to mean that between the ninth and the eleventh centuries, the economies of northwestern
Europe pulled ahead of the rest of the Continent, indeed the rest of the
world.[36]

This relative advance, however, was temporary, and limited overall by a
number of factors—above all, by the inefficiency of agricultural technologies for producing staples, which in the case of Europe were cereals like
wheat, rye, barley, and oats. According to commonly accepted calculations
quoted by Fernand Braudel, throughout the Middle Ages, European farmers produced what by modern standards would be considered extremely
low yields. The yield of wheat hovered between 5 and 7 hectoliters (15 to
21 bushels) per hectare (2.41 acres), representing an average yield ratio of
1:4, or about one-twenty-fifth of yields in the advanced societies of our
day.[37] The yields for oats and barley, at about 1:3.7, were apparently still
lower, both in relative and in absolute terms.[38] And if, during the turbulent
centuries of continued migrations, the East may have lagged behind the West,

36. L. White 1963, 277–82.
37. Braudel 1974, esp. 79–81.
38. Ibid.

by the late Middle Ages (1250–1500), yield ratios of cereals across the continent varied but little, the figures being 4.7 for England, 4.3 for France, 4.2 for Germany, and 4.1 for Eastern Europe.[39] From the point of view of the East, these small differences in productivity were amply offset by a much lower population density,[40] the legacy of prolonged migrations and recurrent invasions by nomadic neighbors; unlike the Rhineland, Flanders, Burgundy, Lorraine, and Lower Saxony, much of East Central Europe was, moreover, forest available for clearing by settlers and rich natural grazing lands that permitted the raising of cattle both for export and for local consumption. Throughout much of the pre-industrial period, only three-quarters of arable land was under the plow in Hungary, and only one-sixth in the Romanian principalities.[41] Thus, while the West could dazzle with its urban civilization and with the refinement of its arts and crafts, East Central Europe was compensated for the absence of this sophistication by an abundance of land available for settlement and substantial deposits of copper, iron ore, and precious metals,[42] which made the region a magnet for immigrants from the West from the thirteenth century right up to the beginning of the industrial age in the last decade of the eighteenth century.

Still, in both East and West, the low productivity of agricultural labor inhibited economic expansion in a variety of ways. Primitive technologies meant that the overwhelming majority of the labor force had to be engaged in the production of comestibles and to live in rural areas. Even in the western half of the Continent, only about 15 percent of the population lived in towns, the rest in the countryside,[43] and a substantial number of town-dwellers were engaged at least part-time in tilling adjacent tracts of land.[44] Indeed, in some regions, like the Hungarian Plain, the majority of town dwellers were agriculturists.[45] In Bohemia-Moravia, Arnost Klima notes, the agricultural sector substantially exceeded 80 percent of the population, leaving only a minority to engage in crafts, mining, trading, navigation, administration, and military service. The low level of productivity ipso facto limited the capacity to generate surplus, and much of this surplus was directly expropriated from the producer in the form of tithes and taxes. This left very little to trade. There is to be sure some evidence for the rise of grain exports from Bohemia and Poland,[46] from which overly bold conclusions

39. Ibid., 80.
40. See, for instance, Kochanowicz 1989, 92–93.
41. Warriner 1965, 2.
42. Gunst 1989, 62–63.
43. Bairoch 1977, 452–67.
44. Klima 1979, 51.
45. For Hungary's urban population, Marczali 1910, 29. Hóman and Szekfű 1935, 5: 242–44. Also Danyl and David 1960, 50–51.
46. Kochanowicz 1989, 96–97.

have been drawn concerning the origin and persistence of regional eco-nomic inequalities on the Continent and the rise of labor repressive econo-mies in the sixteenth and seventeenth centuries.[47] But as Arnost Klima ob-serves, as late as the seventeenth and eighteenth centuries, "only a very small fraction of the total production"[48] was traded across political boundaries, only a "tiny section" of the population was involved in such trade, and "only a similarly small section of the population [of the Continent] was in any way involved in the importing of produce."[49] One gains the same im-pression from the Hungarian Henrik Marczali's studies of the production of surplus grain on the Hungarian plain.[50] As late as the eighteenth century, the most advanced manufacturing regions of the Continent, England and the Low Countries, exported only 3 and 13 percent respectively of their to-tal consumption across political boundaries,[51] while overall only 1 percent of the grain produced on the continent circulated via what might qualify as channels of international trade.[52]

Not only were levels of productivity generally low, but harvests were at the mercy of the elements. Poor harvests were frequent, and two poor har-vests in a row meant devastating famine. The record is spotty but telling. It shows that France had 20 poor harvests during the thirteenth century, and 14 in the fourteenth. In the case of Tuscany, 111 harvests over a 316-year period are designated as "poor," meaning a yield ratio of 1:2, instead of the customary 1:4. In Poland, scholars have discerned 26 bad harvests over a 200-year period.[53] Periodic famine weakened human immunity to disease and accounts in part for periodic plagues. In general, life expectancy at birth is estimated to have been 36 years throughout the Middle Ages—to which, by virtue of better nutrition, the rich could add another decade.[54] At the same time, infant mortality rates varied between a low of 183 and a high of 515 per thousand, or a secular average of 350 per thousand.[55] In general, whether in the East or the West, the amenities of medieval life were few and far between. While the poor were constantly hovering on the verge of star-vation, the rich themselves "lacked real luxury or sophistication of eating habits."[56] The middle class, judged by the family budget of urban crafts-men, spent almost three-quarters of their wages on comestibles, 44 percent

47. Above all, in Wallerstein 1974a.
48. Klima 1979, 60.
49. Ibid.
50. Marczali 1910, 54.
51. Klima 1970, 60.
52. Bairoch 1977a, 477.
53. Braudel 1974, 38, 80.
54. Cipolla 1976, 150.
55. Ibid., 284–85.
56. Braudel 1975, 124.

on bread alone, leaving a mere 15 percent for animal proteins, even though Europeans were deemed to be carnivorous in comparison to the peoples of other cultures and continents.[57] The same artisan spent a mere 14.5 percent of his family income on housing, and 6.1 percent on clothing.[58] Given these percentages, it should not be surprising that housing was modest, household furniture sparse, "so if moderns were to enter into the interior of the past, they would soon feel uncomfortable."[59] Eating utensils were, with the exception of knives, generally unknown. Braudel locates the first fork in European cultural history in a painting by Jacopo Bassano dating from 1599.[60] The notion of fashion, the idea of items of clothing changing their style from year to year or season to season, was nonexistent. Only the more prosperous wore shirts and body linen. As to the poor, a category that included the majority, perhaps two-thirds, of the population, "clothing" really meant "rags to cover [their] nudity," while their dwellings were "shelters rather than houses intended to meet the most rudimentary needs of men and domestic animals,"[61] often huddling together on straw separated only by a screen. The shelters themselves were often mere hovels built around an open fireplace—rural dwellings acquired chimneys only after the fourteenth century—or holes dug in the ground and thatched over to provide some protection from the elements.

Apart from the mode of production, the conduct of life was circumscribed by the technologies of transport and warfare. Overland transport depended on the muscular energy of people, horses, and draft animals, while watergoing vessels were propelled by oarsmen and by primitive, fixed sails that did not permit navigation beyond coastal waters. As to the art of war, personal valor and physical endurance were decisive factors. Battles were fought at close range, involving hand-to-hand combat or the use of manually propelled projectiles. Fortified castles were well-nigh impenetrable. Laying siege to them meant, not an attempt to breach their walls, but seeking to compel surrender by exhausting the supplies of the defenders. This represented as much a challenge to the central authority of governments as to the mobility of foreign intruders. The art of such fortification was first practiced in the West and, except for the imperial city of Constantinople, did not exist in East Central Europe until the major Mongol incursions in the middle of the thirteenth century. When they did arise, the authority of princes and kings declined, and a period of "feudal anarchy" set in. Given this level of military technology, the mainstay of armies across the Continent was the ar-

57. Ibid., 90.
58. Ibid.
59. Ibid., 266.
60. Ibid., 141.
61. Ibid., 197.

mored cavalry, which, together with the proliferation of fortified castles, encouraged the rise of warrior aristocracies to a position of influence.

Overall, these material conditions, and the low capacity to control the physical environment, was reflected in political institutions and consciousness. Unable to grasp and control the forces of nature and leading a life that was "nasty, brutish, and short," always on the edge of famine and disease, society was "saturated in every part with conceptions of Christian faith." [62] Institutions were seen as God-given, handed down by immortal precepts of tradition, and hence immutable—which is one reason why it is more profitable to start with religion, rather than economics, in trying to explain differences among and between medieval states. This, one should hasten to add, did not mean that either state or society was static in reality. But change was the result of piecemeal and often unconscious adaptations to man-made, natural, or demographic disasters and not of deliberate institutional experimentation that would overstep the boundaries of culture, defined largely by religious doctrine. As Eric Hobsbawm points out, primitive rebellions were movements aimed at restoring a real or imaginary order created by precedent, rather than attempts to introduce new social and political principles. [63] When noblemen rose against a king, they did so because they believed that the ruler had deviated from traditional norms. The object was the "redress of grievances" and not to reform or abolish the monarchy. Tyrannicide was practiced, but always directed at the person of the king rather than against the institution itself. By the same token, peasants burned down manor houses and killed the collectors of taxes and dues, but they did not contemplate abolishing the system of land tenure; their objective was only to force their superiors to adhere to the norms and obligations that had evolved throughout centuries. The phenomenon of social banditry, so well captured by Hobsbawm, likewise did not aim at abolishing or reversing social hierarchies, but at the expropriation of wealth that had been accumulated by improper means. [64] To put it differently, medieval Europeans both East and West, like their counterparts in other premodern societies, were quite ready and able to perceive deviations from divinely sanctioned norms. But institutional and social engineering as a remedy for injustice was beyond their imaginative reach.

62. Huizinga 1954, 67.
63. Hobsbawm 1963, 57–92.
64. Ibid., 13–29.

3 | Liberalism and the Nation-State

The Great Transformation

By the near-general agreement of historians and social scientists, the conditions described above began to change under the impact of a triplet of technological revolutions—in transport, in the art of war, and in the mode of production—that transformed the traditional relationship between humanity and its natural environment. The appropriate chronological boundaries of this "great transformation," to borrow Karl Polanyi's term,[1] though, is a matter for scholarly debate.[2] But we may not be wide of the mark if we take Fernand Braudel's four centuries of the rise of "capitalism and material life," from 1400 to 1800,[3] for it was between these dates that the great technological breakthroughs of European civilization worked their way through the structure of the "pioneering" societies of northwest Europe and that the profound changes in the relationship between man and nature began to manifest themselves in both national and international politics.

As Carlo Cipolla tells us, revolutions in transportation began with the invention of the compass and the rigging of sails that permitted vessels to leave the coastal waters and to head toward the open sea.[4] These changes in the art of navigation ushered in the age of geographical discoveries, and, concomitant to them, an age of routinized access to distant parts of the world.

1. Karl Polanyi 1957, 5.
2. Immanuel Wallerstein chooses the dates 1460–1640 and refers to the intervening period as the "long sixteenth century"; for John U. Nef, the critical period of transition lies between 1540 and 1640; Carlo Cipolla points to the centuries between and describes the three hundred years after 1400 as critical to the formation of a modern world economy. See Wallerstein 1974a; Nef 1957; Cipolla 1957 and 1965.
3. Braudel 1967.
4. Cipolla 1965, 166–67.

In Wallerstein's words, the old "two-hundred-day world" gave way to a new "sixty-day world,"[5] a far cry from today's "global village," yet an accomplishment through which the peoples of the world became mutually aware of each other and available for commerce, conquest, and colonial domination. The term "world system" is of recent vintage, but the validity of the concept goes back to the age of discoveries and of the navigational revolution. The words of Sir Dudley North, a seventeenth-century Englishman, are worth remembering here: as a result of the advances in shipping, the "whole world became like one nation in trade," and within this larger "nation," countries became like individuals in society competing with each other for advantage.[6]

Revolutions in the art of war meanwhile were stimulated by the invention, or reinvention, of gunpowder, with concurrent advances in metallurgy that permitted the use of this new source of energy to increase the range and destructive force of projectiles. The lines of causality are intricate, but the subsequent introduction of gunnery into the military arsenals of Europe had major effects on both domestic and interstate affairs. On the domestic scene, the use of artillery increased the vulnerability of the two political mainstays of the feudal nobility: the fortified castle and the armored cavalry. The fact that the walls of noble fortifications could be breached by cannons permitted the gradual subjugation of feudal lords and invited the eventual extension of centralized governmental authority, the hallmark of the modern national state. At the same time, gunnery diminished the military significance of armored cavalry, thus undermining the power of warrior aristocracies and the legitimacy of their claims for special privilege. As for interstate relations, military might became less dependent on the physical prowess and fortitude of fighting men than on economic infrastructure capable of producing and supplying firearms. The decline of warrior nobilities in Western Europe was thus accompanied by the decline of the great nomadic empires, and by the rise of Europe to an undisputed hegemony over the other parts of the world.

The revolutions in the mode of production likewise implied a twofold process of change. First, there came the fruits of successful gadgeteering and the invention of new mechanical implements: the iron plow and harrow in agriculture or the famous spinning jenny with its manipulable multiple rows of spindles in manufacturing. These combined with imaginative ways of utilizing inanimate sources of energy, beginning with the uses of the waterwheel and culminating in James Watt's invention of the steam engine. Most immediately, these inventions multiplied the volume of the social product: consumption was increasing and so was surplus, increasing the frequency of ex-

---

5. Wallerstein 1974, 17.
6. Quoted in Rich and Wilson 1977, 5: 214.

change and the importance of markets as distributive mechanisms. As part of the process, producers were transformed from being providers of scarce commodities into risk-taking entrepreneurs, soon to replace the warrior aristocracies as the main pillar of society, given their ability to accumulate new forms of wealth. While these developments were strictly regional, confined to England and the northwestern "triangle" of the Continent, their images traveled far and wide with continental, and later worldwide, consequences that will be discussed somewhat later.

One by one, and altogether, these technological breakthroughs had a profound effect on human thinking, and, ultimately, on political consciousness. In the Middle Ages and before, humanity was overwhelmed by the forces of nature, by exposure to disease, by physical phenomena it did not comprehend, and by the sheer effort of traveling from one geographical location to another. In more than one sense, nature made human existence precarious. But now the tables were turned. The technological revolutions, so it seemed to contemporaries, released people from their medieval state of helplessness. Rather than being slaves of the forces of nature, they suddenly seemed to have become their masters. Nowhere is this attitude more thoroughly personified than in Daniel Defoe's Robinson Crusoe, who, stranded on a desert island, created a flourishing agricultural economy with a kit of tools, sheltered himself from the elements, and asserted his superiority over intruding savages by the judicious use of his firearms. What we see here is a new relationship between man and nature, as, indeed, between man and man, and a new sense of personal efficacy on the part of those in possession of what passed in this age as modern technology. But this was only a first step in the evolution of modern consciousness for, slowly but inexorably, the sense of efficacy spilled over into social relations. If humanity could change its material environment, why not take charge of its political destiny? This question seemed justified to many, and in answer to it there emerged a new political consciousness, rooted in the belief that society itself was a human construct and that political authority must find justification in finite and discernible human purposes.

Latched onto the economic interests of the new entrepreneurial classes, this new consciousness became the cornerstone of the ideology of liberalism. This ideology embraced the ideas of the freedom of markets from political intervention, the freedom of the subject from arbitrary rule, and finally the freedom to participate in the affairs of government. The practical application of these ideas, to be sure, was a long and tortuous affair: in France, it involved the outright rejection, in England, the ritualization of the divine right of monarchical institutions. Even where they struck root, liberal political institutions passed through two distinct stages. In the first, the rights of representation were won, whether by reform or revolution, by the successful class of capitalist entrepreneurs and professional classes; in the second, equally grudgingly, these rights were universalized and extended to all classes of the adult male populations.

The Development of Underdevelopment

In the first instance, the economic revolutions of Europe played themselves out with respect to the mode of agricultural production, or, in the more colorful idiom of two English historians, in "man's ways of wresting a living from the gifts of nature."[7] The use of new implements to pulverize the soil more effectively, the more systematic use of fertilizers and irrigation dikes, and the concomitant abandonment of the old two-field system in favor of the more efficient three- or four-course rotation of the crops, did raise productivity, although the use of the term "revolution" to describe these improvements is somewhat hyperbolic. The innovations themselves were slow to take root and to produce measurable results. Thus it took the farmers of Flanders, England, and the Rhine region more than a century and a half to raise seed-harvest ratios from the traditional 1:4 to 1:6, and then yet another century, the eighteenth, to raise their yields to the critical 1:10 ratio, about one-seventh of today's average wheat yields.[8] This would release one-quarter to one-third of the labor force to be available for nonagricultural pursuits, such as manufacturing, commerce, public administration, and military service in the new mass armies of modern states.

As part of a larger process, these improved methods of cultivation spread at a painfully slow rate of three to four miles per annum, moving from the northwest toward the south and east of the Continent. At this rate, the technologies invented in the Low Countries, England, and to some extent in the Rhineland during the "long sixteenth century" (1450–1640) reached Bavaria, Saxony, Bohemia, and the French Midi around 1750, Hungary, Poland, and the Balkans between 1825 and 1850, and Russia still later. Because innovation in the core region was not a one-time affair but an ongoing process, regions located six to eight hundred miles from the epicenter of economic change remained some two hundred years behind the core regions in terms of yield per acre.[9] Overall, the distribution of agricultural productivity and income distribution across the Continent acquired a neatly regressive geographical pattern that transcended both climatic and cultural bound-

7. Cole and Postgate 1957, 101.
8. Braudel 1967, 80–82; Habakkuk and Postan 1965, 85. Also Milward and Saul 1977, 344.
9. For cereal yields and for the development of geographically regressive patterns of income distribution on the Continent, see Braudel 1967, 52, 81, 230, 393; Habakkuk and Postan 1965, 6: 3–4, 12, 544; Rich and Wilson 1977; Milward and Saul 1977, 234, 349, 379; Cole and Postgate 1957, 69; Cipolla 1976, 29; also Berend and Ránki 1982, 15–16.

aries. It is this pattern that enables us, by 1800, to distinguish clearly among three economic regions of Europe: the center of innovation in the northwest, characterized by high yield ratios and commercialized agriculture; the adjacent regions of continental Europe bounded in the west, south, and east by the rivers Loire, Elbe, and Po, where agricultural innovations made some headway, but where farming retained a distinctive mode with limited reliance on wage labor; and finally the regions further to the southeast and the south, where the innovations of the northwest had yet to make a dent in the traditional mode of agricultural production. Because this geographically regressive pattern of productivity and relative income distribution would persist until 1945,[10] and, with some minor modifications, even later, and because these economic patterns closely correlated with patterns of authority and behavior, we are justified in designating these three regions as the core, semiperiphery, and periphery of the modern European economy.

The second revolution, with its origins in the industrial breakthroughs of eighteenth-century England, is more appropriately designated as such, for the introduction of labor-saving devices and their successful harnessing to steam-powered engines created spectacular advances in the volume of manufactured goods. The amount of raw cotton imported to Britain and processed by the new factories increased from a mere 2.5 million pounds in 1760 to 22 million pounds in 1787, and then to 366 million pounds in 1837, the latter a sixteenfold increase within a period of fifty years.[11] The total amount of iron processed into steel in English factories was 68,000 tons in 1788. This figure rose to 250,000 tons by 1806, and 678,000 by 1830.[12] In the wake of these changes, domestic consumption grew rapidly, giving rise to what has been described as the "first of the world's consumer societies."[13] The availability of cheap cotton "made it possible for millions to wear drawers and chemises where before there had been nothing but coarse and dirty undergarments,"[14] while the more prosperous began to succumb to "the sovereign authority of fashions,"[15] and, "impressed by the color and elegance of cotton prints learned to distinguish more and more between seasons and [to] dress for the summer in muslins and calicoes."[16] Or, as another work notes, "where once the ability to wear such fashions was limited to the very few, now rising family incomes brought them increasingly

10. See League of Nations 1943, esp. 86–91.
11. Braudel 1967, 282–83; Habakkuk and Postan 1965, 274–75. Another set of statistics speaks of 5 million pounds imported in 1781, 124 million in 1810, and 164 million pounds in 1816, a 33-fold increase within a third of a century (Mitchell 1980, 427–29).
12. Habakkuk and Postan 1965, 274–75.
13. McKendrick et al. 1982, 13.
14. Habakkuk and Postan 1965, 313.
15. Braudel 1967, 231.
16. Habakkuk and Postan 1965, 313.

within the reach of the many."[17] The consumption boom, of course, extended beyond textiles to "tobacco, soap, candles, spirits, beer, kitchen utensils, glassware, soap, matches, household furniture."[18] The consumption of these commodities increased more than twice as fast as the population.[19] Increases in the consumption of some commodities were truly stupendous. While between 1785 and 1800 the population of Britain increased by 14 percent, the consumption of tea increased by 97.7 percent, and the domestic sale of printed fabrics by 141.9 percent.[20] There were further changes in the pattern of housing, nutrition, and hygiene, and in the process, notions of luxury and staple were rapidly reevaluated. "Luxuries came to be seen as 'decencies' and decencies turned into necessities."[21] To be sure, the distribution of consumer gains remained highly uneven, their principal beneficiaries having been the "middling" element in society that had risen from manual labor to professional status and entrepreneurship. Still, "more men and women than ever before in human history enjoyed the experience of acquiring material possessions"[22] and became the beneficiaries of better housing, nutrition, sanitation, and of the rises of life expectancy that were closely related to them.

These revolutionary changes in consumer styles provide a convenient starting point for explaining the intricate relationship between development and underdevelopment in Europe. True, the earlier agricultural-commercial revolutions, too, had generated income inequalities: there were a great number of seventeenth- and eighteenth-century observers who noted how bread got darker and how the poor got poorer as one traveled from the northwest to the southeast of the Continent.[23] But the effect was far less dramatic than the "emulative imitation" of the consumption culture generated by the Industrial Revolution of England between 1780 and 1830. This is amply evident from both trade statistics and the observations of contemporaries. Within just two decades, between 1760 and 1780, British exports rose from an estimated 5 percent to 35 percent of the country's national income. By 1810 they had reached 50 percent,[24] a figure that implied "commerce so active and universal that traveling from Prussia to St. Petersburg, from Amsterdam to the farthest point of Sweden, from Dunkirk to the southern extremes of France [the traveler] was served at every turn from English earthenware. The same fine articles adorn[ed] the tables of Spain, Portugal, and

17. McKendrick et al. 1982, 1.
18. Ibid., 29.
19. Ibid.
20. Ibid.
21. Ibid.
22. Ibid., 1.
23. Habakkuk and Postan 1965, 280–81, 544.
24. Ibid., 51.

Italy, and provide[d] the cargoes of ships to the East Indies, the West Indies and America." [25]

Consequently, in Eastern Europe, as one observer of the Romanian scene notes, "after 1829 a drastic change took place in the [earlier] patriarchal way of living. From the style of dress to the use of kitchen utensils and hand tools, one can quickly discern the West European influence." [26] Or, to quote the testimony of others, in the Romanian principalities the use of "perfumes, champagne, glass, silverware, mirrors, matches and furniture spread quickly among the members of the upper and the middle classes." [27] The same classes could barely restrain their urge to consume goods "so much refined, so beautiful in appearance . . . having also the charm of novelty." [28] Or, to quote a Hungarian author writing in the year of 1828: "people are developing new tastes every day. Silverware, until now seen only in the houses of the rich, now appears in many households. The watch, once as rare as a white crow, has now turned into an article of necessity." [29] Consumption in the Balkan countries did not lag far behind the northern tier of the region. In Bulgaria, "people who had before been content to wear native homespun now [in the 1870s] elected to dress *a la franca*," [30] and all classes of consumers "threw themselves at European manufacturers." [31] In Serbia, meanwhile, "the intellectual, professional and bourgeois classes imitated the ways of living which were common among the middle and professional classes of the Austrians and Germans. They took from them their fashions in clothes (always an important matter where classes are differentiated out of a classless society), in furniture and household utensils. . . . Tea, coffee, sugar were passing out of the class of luxury goods into more common use. Town-made lamps were replacing home-made candles. [Even] in peasant homes a few books were to be found. . . . Although the number of purchased articles in [these] homes were small by urban standards, nevertheless they represented considerable change." [32]

The imitation of Western lifestyles was not restricted to the eastern half of the Continent, nor was it a uniquely European phenomenon. Half a world away, the same patterns of consumption came to Latin America, where in the words of one observer, there was likewise "a breathless desire to be like the French and the British, . . . to dress like fashionable Europeans," to pay hom-

25. Faujas de St. Fond, *Voyage en Angleterre* [Travels in England] (1818), quoted in McKendrick et al. 1982, 137.
26. Quoted in Schuster 1939, 20–21.
27. Colson 1841, 210.
28. Dobrogeanu-Gherea 1910, 33–34.
29. von Csaplovits 1828, 254.
30. Palairet 1997, 189.
31. Ibid., 190.
32. Trouton 1952, 71–72.

age to the "intrinsic worth of the way in which Europeans went about build-ing their houses, educating their young or spending their leisure time."[33] In Valparaiso, the shops sold "German glass and toys, American furniture, En-glish hardware, textiles, carpets, household furniture, chinaware."[34] Or in the words of another historian: "The houses of the better classes were as re-plete with objects of American and European manufactures as would be true for the citizen of London or Boston."[35]

Whether defined as luxuries or necessities, these patterns of consumption were incongruous with existing modes of production, and the further away we move from the great centers of industrial innovation, the greater was the degree of incongruity. While such imitation clearly influenced the pattern of accumulation and development in the center of the Continent, it appears to have stunted these processes altogether farther to the south and east. There, too, landowners wished to imitate the normal "decencies" available for their western counterparts, but the methods of cultivation were as primitive as those "used in Western Europe during the twelfth or thirteenth centuries."[36] All relevant written accounts about Hungary or Poland, as well as lands fur-ther away from the core regions of the continental economy, reveal condi-tions familiar from medieval economies: the system of crop rotation was ru-dimentary, plows were made of wood, and there was a shortage of beasts of burden.[37] Changing consumer aspirations thus created considerable strain for these economies. While in the innovative core of the world economy consumer tastes had developed as part of an organic process, and were re-lated to an "agriculturally induced increase in home demand,"[38] on the pe-ripheries, especially after the beginnings of the Industrial Revolution, ex-pectations ran ahead of real income, and thus were apt to create both micro- and macroeconomic adversity. The "breathless desire" to acquire Western products boosted effective demand for manufactures, and hence the rela-tive movement of prices to the disadvantage of primary producers. More significantly, this "taste-induced" consumer revolution was bound to lower marginal rates of saving and private investment. This tendency toward dis-investment then became the starting point for the "downward drift" of the peripheries, and the first hint that effective accumulation would have to be accomplished outside the private sector. Again, the more backward the econ-omy, the greater would be these ill effects.

This is not to suggest that all peripheral societies, and within them all

33. Veliz 1980, 168, 172.
34. Glade 1969, 205.
35. Anderson 1967, 22.
36. Jackson and Lampe 1982, 115.
37. Marczali 1910, 55–56. Jackson and Lampe 1982, 115. Klima 1979; see Chapter 2, n.44.
38. McKendrick et al. 1982, 24.

individuals, turned overnight into profligate spenders. Some societies, like Hungary, did; others, like Romania, did not—at least according to the testimony of trade statistics throughout the first half of the nineteenth century. According to contemporary figures Hungary went on a genuine consumer binge between 1825 and 1848, financed largely by the export of coin and precious metals.[39] In the absence of such accumulated wealth, the same spending spree could not take place in the Romanian principalities, so in spite of anecdotal accounts to the contrary, the country maintained a positive balance of trade throughout most of the nineteenth century.[40] In Serbia, exports generally exceeded imports in the first half of the century, but the trend was reversed in 1856, and a negative balance characterized the country's foreign trade until 1896, when it saw another decade of favorable balances.[41] But those who did apply consumer restraint did so at considerable social and psychological cost to themselves and, even with stationary or slowly rising incomes, felt that they were becoming poorer with every passing year.

True, most peripheral economies responded at first to the progressive redefinition of wants and needs by increasing the exports of their own primary products. To the extent that individual countries found a niche in the world economy, they experienced export booms that in turn created euphoric expectations about the opportunities inherent to trade. There was thus a "golden age" of Hungarian wool (1806–18), of Hungarian and Romanian wheat (1829–38, and then again, 1855–73), Serbian plums and pigs (1843–64),[42] of Bulgarian cereals and rose oil (1842–46, 1850–66),[43] just as there was a golden age of Spanish wool and Portuguese wine toward the end of the eighteenth century, or of Brazilian coffee, Cuban sugar, Chilean copper, and Argentinian beef toward the end of the nineteenth and the beginning of the twentieth century.[44] But closer study of these cases will quickly reveal that these export booms were based on the utilization of surplus land or the exploitation of existing natural resources rather than on the intensification of production and capital investment. Consequently, these "golden ages" tended to be brief, and the "false euphoria"[45] of the early years quite rapidly gave way to a sense of malaise, gloom, and self-pity that permeates both the public and the literary life of these countries in the second half of the nineteenth century.

39. Fényes 1842–43, 1: 248–49, 270.
40. Chirot 1976, 122.
41. Sündhausen 1989, 341–42. Also Palairet 1997, 106.
42. Palairet 1997, 106.
43. Jackson and Lampe 1982, 113–65, 138–39; also Tomasevich 1955, 63; R. Seton-Watson 1934, 211; Zeletin 1925, 47.
44. Herr 1958, 120, 146–47; Veliz 1980, 168–72.
45. Furtado 1963, 97–98.

International Politics and the Concert of Europe

The gunpowder revolution and the advances in navigation ensured the preeminence of Europe over the rest of the world. But this global hegemony was not exercised by a single, vertically organized political entity, but by a number of states with traditions of mutual enmity and a record of fighting each other for continental hegemony. Indeed, at times these rivalries grew so bitter that they took precedence over fighting powerful invaders from outside the Continent, the Arabs in the southwest and the Ottoman Turks in the southeast. These wars involving France, Spain, Britain, and Austria throughout the seventeenth and eighteenth centuries need not be recounted here in detail. Suffice it to say that the struggle for hegemony reached epic proportions during the Napoleonic wars, at which time France attempted to bring the entire Continent under its hegemonic rule under the guise of an ideology that ingeniously combined elements of both aggressive nationalism and humanistic universalism.

The defeat of France by the European coalition was a historic milestone, marking the beginnings of a hundred years of European peace, under an international regime constructed at the Congress of Vienna in 1814–15. By Karl Polanyi's count, in the seventeenth and eighteenth centuries each there were 60–70 years of major wars fought among the great powers. In the nineteenth century, including the Crimean and Franco-Prussian wars, they fought each other for a total of 36 months.[46] Carefully institutionalized as a "Concert" of great powers that would hold periodic "congresses" to adjudicate disputes, the regime was maintained by common interest in peace, dictated by preoccupations with new economic opportunities, but, above all, by the opportunity for European expansion into the non-European world.

The mainstay of the international regime was a system of enforcement in which successful coalitions could be built against any one of the players tempted to seek hegemony. In this system of enforcement England, being the predominant naval power and trading state of the world, played a critical role, always ready to check the power of an aspiring hegemon by supporting its adversaries. The proverbial pragmatism of British foreign policy was most forcefully expressed in Palmerston's well-known dictum that his country had neither eternal allies, nor permanent enemies, only eternal interests.[47] The two major conflicts of the century do well reflect both the pivotal role of Britain and the nature of the international regime. In 1854–55, England and France took to arms to curb Russian designs to gain advantage against the decaying Ottoman empire in the east; in 1870, the powers accepted German unification, not least because of Britain's determination to

46. Polanyi 1957, 5.
47. Quoted in Kissinger 1994, 96.

check the renascent ambitions of France under Napoleon III. In each of these instances, though, the aims of the wars were limited and, responding both to British nudgings and to their own interest in the regime, the victors refrained from crushing the defeated adversary. In the spirit of this pragmatism, Britain and France may at first have conceived of World War I as such a limited war, a means of enforcing the old rules of the game against Austria and Germany. By then, however, the common interest in moderation had substantially waned, and the conflict assumed unanticipated proportions that embittered the losers and exhausted the winners to the point where the regime could no longer be sustained.

In the first place, the Concert was a construct to regulate international politics, but from its inception, it was to have implications for the domestic affairs of nations across the Continent, indeed, across the world. In the first half of the century, the common interest of the great powers was masked by an ideology that, as a throwback to the discourse of an earlier age, justified the maintenance of existing institutions across the Continent by invoking religious principles. But in the second half of the century, the ideology of the Concert became secularized, the "holiness" of the alliance having been replaced by an unabashed pragmatic utilitarianism. But whether expressed in religious or in secular terms, some rules adopted by the Concert remained universally binding and unchanging. One of these was the principle, first formulated in Westphalia in the seventeenth century, that maintaining internal order was both the prime purpose of statecraft and the prime criterion of statehood itself. A government and state that could not maintain internal order were not worthy of recognition as a sovereign entity, and hence fair game for great power occupation, colonization, or discipline. But this was not all, for mainly in deference to the British tradition and trading interests, power, if arbitrary, would not qualify as meeting the requisites of international civility. In order to meet these, a state also had to have legal foundations and institutions, so as to operate under self-imposed restraint and have institutions capable of enforcing contracts and offer other protections for international trade. This legalism was more in harmony with the traditions of the western than with the eastern half of the Continent, yet by the 1860s, it was universally adopted as the sine qua non of international comity. By this time, even Russia, although autocratic by tradition, accepted the principle and created a "Western-style" set of legal institutions that, acting as impediments on autocratic impulse, enabled the country to become part of the world system of trade.

There was more ambiguity about parliamentarism and the institutions of representative government. While Britain regarded her institutions as unique and did not make concerted efforts (in the manner of Americans in the twentieth century) to impose them on others, the very success of Britain in both economics and empire building, together with the value of gaining the sympathies of the public of the island nation, made parliamentarism a desirable institutional form that many countries of the world adopted as a matter of status and prestige, or as a proof of their standards of civility in an attempt to preempt colonial subjugation. The weaker the country was, the greater was the urge to adopt a form of representative government. Russia, a great power with a strong autocratic tradition, resisted these subtle pressures throughout the nineteenth century, but finally adopted a limited form of parliamentarism in 1905–6, soon to be followed by such non-European powers as Persia, Japan, and Ottoman Turkey, all struggling to maintain their international position in the face of the global hegemony of the West.

STATE AND SOCIETY ON THE PERIPHERY

Class Formation and Social Mobility

While the problem of relative pauperization was common to all strata of peripheral societies, those most directly affected were the proprietors of medium-sized estates and others located close to the middle of the social pyramid. The reasons for this appear to be twofold. On the one hand, these classes were those most likely to identify with the bourgeois and professional classes of the Occident, whose rise was the very hallmark of the consumer revolution of the turn of the eighteenth century. On the other, the lesser nobility (wherever such a class existed) had no vast reserves of fallow land that could be brought under the plow, and no large reserve army of serfs whose labor productivity could be increased by more efficient, or more coercive, forms of organization. In the absence of such reserves of land and men, new patterns of consumption could only be indulged in by selling off old assets of coin and precious metal hoarded over generations, or by mortgaging and eventually selling land to creditors. Again, it should be emphasized that not all landowners were profligate spenders who would actually adopt Western standards of living. But those who were not began to view themselves as *déclassés* as a result of ever more common comparisons of their own living conditions with those of the business classes, country gentry, or even the prosperous yeomanry of the advanced countries. Certainly, this is the story that Max Weber tells us about the *Junkers* of East Elbian Prussia,[48] and the same story has been told again and again about the Polish *szlachta*, the Hungarian "common nobility," later dubbed the gentry (*dzsentri*), and the lesser boyars (*mică boierime*) of the Romanian principalities. Indeed, it is a story common as well to the *dvoryanstvo* of Russia, the petty nobles of Portugal

48. Weber 1924, 472. Bendix 1977, 33.

and Spain, and to the *patriciates minores* of South American countries. Quite frequently, the demise of these classes has been attributed to their heroic-military traditions, which supposedly prevented their successful adaptation to the impersonal rationality of the capitalist market mechanism. This hypothesis, however, is contradicted by the fact that not only the majority of the nobles, but also a substantial part of the non-noble middle class—the artisans and craftsmen of the precapitalist period—perished together with them. Thus, the urban classes of the Polish kingdom, the Hungarian crown, and the Balkans likewise reached a low point during the first decades of the nineteenth century. Indeed, while the older generation of these merchants and craftsmen tried to withdraw behind the walls of established, often imperial, privilege, members of the younger generation were leaving their fathers' small enterprises in droves to invest their meager family resources in education rather than business. It is thus that they became, together with the offspring of the bankrupt country gentry, members of a "free floating intelligentsia,"[49] or, in the contemptuous words of a contemporary, a "proletariat of the pen."[50]

Under whatever name, these were the "marginal men" of peripheral society, whose "condition could not possibly worsen by a change in the organization of society. [Rather] the prospect of change opened up new horizons for them,"[51] particularly to the extent that their education provided them with the qualifications necessary for service in the apparatus of the modern state. Much as in the countries of the non-European world, "for these groups without space or status . . . a government job was not only an alternative, it was a virtual imperative."[52] Thus while the history of the modern Western state may well be described as one of the rising middle classes in quest of larger national markets, the history of the peripheral states is one of declining middle classes trying to escape the vagaries of the market and hoping to find safe haven in political, rather than economic, entrepreneurship.

However, as a political class in the making, the marginal intelligentsia of Eastern and East Central Europe was not only motivated by narrow material considerations, but also by the desire to find status, honor, and acceptance in the larger international community. For any prospective political class, such acceptance was closely related to the extent that their societies and economies approximated the models set by the leading societies of the Occident. By now, the east–west economic gradient had become a gradient of culture—witness the German word *Kulturgefälle*—and civilization. Thus

49. In German, "freischwebende Intelligenz" (Mannheim 1936, 153–64).

50. More accurately, as a "proletariat of the penholder" (*ai condeiului*) (the words of the Romanian poet Mihai Eminescu, as quoted in Zeletin 1925, 142). For the formation of this intelligentsia, see also Chalasiński and Ulatowski 1947, quoted in Wynot 1974, 8–9.

51. Filitti 1915, 408.

52. Anderson 1967, 224.

while finding employment in the state was an economic necessity, catching up with the West economically, politically, and culturally also became part of the public agenda of the educated classes as a matter both of self-respect and of self-interest. Thus, while their concern for personal income and status drove them in the direction of etatism, their preoccupation with international status and power drew them toward the ideas of Western liberalism. While in opposition, this preoccupation with their international image took extreme and theatrical forms. There is a well-known story of young Hungarian liberals in the 1840s being chastized by their elders for trying to act out the roles of the heroes of Lamartine's *L'Histoire des Girondins* (1847). "This is a dangerous book. It is not history, not a novel, but least of all a bible that you are trying to make it," the older Francis Deák grumbled about this role-playing.[53] Strikingly, one can read the very same story about the young liberals of Chile[54] and of Romania of the same period.[55] What this indicates is a genuine, even exaggerated desire to imitate the Western political model, one that would eventually founder on the shoals of non-Western realities once the marginal intelligentsia had turned into a political class in power.

On the lower end of the social spectrum the peasantry was less affected by the material progress of the northwest, but also lacked the resources which enabled the middle classes to adapt to potential economic adversity. During brief periods of opportunity in the nineteenth century, peasant farmers participated in production for the domestic and export markets. But once the boom years were over, the majority of them retreated into subsistence farming. This tendency was characteristic for the area as a whole, but was most pronounced in the lands of the Hungarian crown and in the Romanian principalities (later united Romania), where as late as the end of the nineteenth century, only 11 and 14 percent of peasant proprietors, respectively, were producing commodities for cash.[56] The rest, while diversifying production, did so for their own consumption trying to satisfy their needs for cash, and hence for nonfarm commodities, by hiring themselves out as seasonal labor, or by engaging part-time in nonagricultural pursuits. Such pursuits provided only for a bleak existence, and for living standards that at times fell below historical levels. Yet, precisely because of their poverty, few peasant families could accumulate the savings necessary to invest in new technology or in education, as did the urban classes and the declining gentry. To put it differently, the emerging boundary line between "middle" and "lower" class in these societies lay between those who did, and those who did not, have the amount of savings required for access to the educational system. With

53. Hóman and Szekfű 1936, 5: 310.
54. Veliz 1980, 164–65.
55. Xenopol 1911, 1: 176.
56. For Hungary, see Janos 1982, 121; for Romania, Roberts 1952, 61.

opportunities limited in both markets and the state, many members of the rural lower classes sought opportunity for improvement neither in enterprise nor in schools, regressing instead into various forms of primitive rebellion, such as periodic riots and widespread social banditry, which made the countryside unsafe. In most of the countries of the European periphery, the period between 1825 and 1860 was one of the *haiduki* and the *betyár*; that is, of Slavic, Romanian, and Hungarian highwaymen who, romanticized by popular poetry, terrorized the prosperous and made travel on rural roads a hazardous undertaking. As the economic pendulum was swinging from bad to worse, this low-level but endemic violence became punctuated by periodic outbursts of peasant fury, directed less against the social order itself than against its visible representatives: tax collectors, landowners, farm managers, moneylenders, and local bureaucrats in charge of land deeds and tax records. The most memorable of these were the "cholera revolt" of 1830 in northeastern Hungary, the Galician jacquerie of 1846, the Serbian "Timok rebellion" of 1883 (exacerbated by the costs of public policy), and finally, the "great peasant uprising" (*rascoală mare*) of Romania in 1907. More will be said about these later.

At the apex of the social pyramid, the large landed proprietors of the Polish provinces, the Romanian principalities, and of the lands of the Hungarian crown (then including Hungary proper, Transylvania, and latter-day Slovakia), much as their counterparts in Iberia, Russia, or the East Elbian provinces of Prussia, could keep up with the changing lifestyles of the modern world, and with their chief international reference group, the aristocracy of Britain. They could do so simply because of the vastness of their estates. They could not, however, consume and save at the same time. Throughout the nineteenth century (and in some instances until 1945), their principal problem was thus how to accumulate capital for the modernization of their estates without jeopardizing their international status by diminished spending. Some members of the aristocracy, like the Romanian boyars Constantin Golescu[57] and Heliade-Radulescu[58] or the Hungarian Count József Dessewffy[59] pleaded with members of their own class to spend less and to return to the more frugal ways of an earlier age. Others, like the Hungarian Count Széchenyi, one of the most notable figures of early economic reform in Eastern Europe, fixed their eyes on foreign capital, hoping that the investment crunch of the great estates could be solved by developing a modern credit system. Thus in his first, and major, programmatic work, characteristically titled *Hitel* [Credit], published in 1830, he advocated the abolition of the system of entailment, which was impeding the free circulation of money and

57. Golescu 1915, 89.
58. Xenopol 1882, 95.
59. Dessewffy 1831.

the commodification of land. While the more puritanical exhortations fell on deaf ears, hopes for generating Western bank capital for Eastern agriculture were dashed by the disinterest of foreign lenders both before and after the abolition of feudalism. Increases in agricultural output therefore could only be attained by bringing surplus land under the plow, and, when such surplus acreage was no longer available, by tightening the working conditions of the labor force.

The politics of the aristocratic classes reflected these dilemmas as well as the exigencies and opportunities of international trade. Thus, although the magnates always fearful of rebellions from below, in the economically promising 1820s and 1830s, the idea of liberal reforms, including the abolition of the system of feudal land tenure, had numerous supporters. In those years, Polish aristocrats made common cause with the gentry against the foreign monarchies. The Hungarian reform movement included the bearers of some of the most illustrious names in the country: Counts István Széchenyi, Lajos Batthyány, Gyula Andrássy, and Baron József Eötvös. The Romanian "opposition" to reactionary princes meanwhile could boast the names of the powerful Filipescu, Băleanu, Suțu, and Ruset-Rosetti families, and in the Divan of 1841, only 22 of the grand boyars supported the princely government, while 37 were its opponents.[60] In the economically tighter 1840s, however, many of these aristocrats drifted away from reform movements, opting instead to support the integrity of imperial markets and traditional economic and political institutions. At the time of the revolutions of 1848, most aristocrats sought accommodation with existing princely and larger imperial structures. In the more prosperous 1850s and 1860s, a number of magnates returned to the reformist fold, although skeptics have dismissed them as a mere "bunch of feudals who [had] discovered the advantages of free trade."[61] Such skepticism was not without justification, for as the price of agricultural commodities plummeted in the 1870s, most aristocrats abandoned the cause of liberalism once again, henceforth to form the nucleus of a conservative pressure group that persistently lobbied for the restoration of traditional labor controls, as well as greater "social discipline" vis-à-vis their tenants and agricultural laborers. In the end, attempts to distinguish between "good and bad landowners were an irrelevance, for losses made them all into exploiters,"[62] competing with the political classes for ways to squeeze the agricultural labor force more intensely.

As the "indigenous" classes of peripheral society were retreating from markets either to "retraditionalize" or to become political entrepreneurs, the more risky and demanding economic functions were gradually taken

60. Xenopol 1911, 1: 10.
61. Constantin Garoflid, quoted in Mitrany 1930, 64.
62. Milward and Saul 1977, 343–44.

over by immigrant members of low-status ethnic communities. In this process, we see the reverse side of Veblen's hypothesis, for if high-status expectations undermine the propensity for saving, low-status expectations encourage it. Free from the burdens of convention, and from the concomitant pressures of status, the outsider will take risks shunned by natives, and is more likely to restrain consumption to increase marginal rates of saving. The capacity to do so is especially high if the process involves "homeless" peoples; that is, those who do not have reference societies of their own. Such homeless peoples therefore become prime candidates for what one student of developing economies has described as "pariah entrepreneurship."[63] The extent and character of this type of entrepreneurship varied with the geographical distance of the country from the core of the modern world economy. Thus in Germany and in Bohemia-Moravia, countries to be discussed later in this chapter, the percentage of ethnic entrepreneurship was relatively small and restricted to a few branches of the economy, such as money management, retail trade, or the manufacturing of textiles. However, further to the south, and especially toward the east, the percentage share of ethnic entrepreneurs was relatively large and their activities covered the whole spectrum of modern economic pursuits.

In East Central Europe, to be sure, even traditional, precapitalist entrepreneurship had been foreign. It consisted of Germans in the northern tier, of Greeks, and of Armenians in Romania and the Balkans. Over the centuries, though, these foreigners became integrated into their social environment and responded to the rise of modern capitalism much like their indigenous counterparts, that is, by attempting to abandon economics for the sake of politics. This in turn opened up entrepreneurial roles to a new wave of immigrants. Often blamed for ruining the precapitalist bourgeoisie, these immigrants arrived when that bourgeoisie was already well on its way to economic bankruptcy and political entrepreneurship. This was certainly the case in Romania, and especially in Hungary, where, as recent research has shown, the entry of the non-noble classes and the largely German and Greek bourgeoisie into political life and the state bureaucracy took place almost simultaneously with the flight of the gentry from the land between 1825 and 1875.[64]

In the northern tier of the periphery, the new class of immigrant entrepreneurs was largely recruited from members of the Jewish communities of southern Poland who, under the population pressures of their own environment, moved into the neighboring countries to take advantage of op-

---

63. For this term, see Riggs 1966, 188–93.
64. For Romania, even the highly tendentious Schuster 1943, 27—but also the far more objective Zeletin 1925, 63–7—notes the demise of native traders and their proletarianization before Jewish migration to Wallachia in the second half of the nineteenth century. For Hungary, see Pukánszky 1931, 46–48.

portunities provided by the rise of the new continental economy. Part of this emigration flowed toward the east, to Russia, and part toward the west, to Germany. But most of the migrants of the early nineteenth century headed toward the adjacent Romanian principalities and the countries of the Habsburg realm, including Austria, Bohemia, and the various provinces of the kingdom of Hungary, including Transylvania and the future Slovakia. As a result of these migrations, the percentage of Jews in the populations of these countries increased substantially. In Hungary and the associated principality of Transylvania, the census of 1787 had found a Jewish population of 75,089, representing less than 1 percent of all inhabitants. By 1841, this number had grown to 241,632, or 2.5 percent of the population.[65] But the bulk of Jewish immigration took place after the Diet lifted certain occupational and residential restrictions in 1841, peaking at 938,458, or 5.1 percent of the population of the country, in 1910.[66] In Romania, the trend was similar: the number of Jewish inhabitants increased from approximately 12,000 in 1803 to 118,992 by 1860, and almost three times as many in 1910.[67] After these migrations there still remained a Jewish population of approximately 3 million (2.8 million by nationality, and 3.1 million by religion) in the provinces that would become Poland.[68]

These figures changed for the individual countries as a result of the boundary changes of 1918–20. While the peace treaties following World War I reduced the territory of Hungary, they increased the size of Romania by adding Bukovina, Bessarabia, and Transylvania to that country. Consequently, Hungary was left with a postwar Jewish population of 473,355,[69] while Romania would, by 1930, have a Jewish population of 756,930, most of them concentrated in the provinces of Bukovina, Bessarabia, and Moldavia.[70] The same boundary changes that reapportioned the Jewish populations under Romanian and Hungarian sovereignty were also responsible for creating "new" Slovak and Subcarpathian Jewish communities under Czechoslovak authority with subsequent histories of their own, numbering 136,737 and 102,542 members respectively in 1930.[71] Overall, these numbers represented substantial percentages of the respective populations— 9.8 percent in Poland, 5.1 percent in Hungary, 4.2 percent in Romania, 4.1 percent in Slovakia, and 14.1 percent in the province of Subcarpathian Rus[72]—figures far in excess of those in the more developed countries of the European core and semiperiphery.

65. Fényes 1842–43, 1: 82.
66. Újváry 1929, 553; also Hungary *Annuaire statistique hongrois* 1911, 17–18.
67. Verax 1904, 13.
68. Mendelsohn 1983, 23.
69. Ibid., 99.
70. Romania 1931, 441.
71. Mendelsohn 1983, 142.
72. Ibid., 23, 99, 159–60, 179.

Following patterns common to all immigrants, and confined, at least initially, by legal restrictions on residence and occupation, Jewish tradesmen and artisans sought out branches of the economy that "were relatively new, which enabled a rapid turnover of working capital, and required ingenuity rather than savings, sharp instincts rather than social connections."[73] In time, though, with the development of an adequate infrastructure, Jewish economic activities were extended into other branches of commerce, banking, industrial enterprise, and, to a limited extent, even to agriculture, so that by the end of the nineteenth century, all modern branches of the national economies became closely associated with the Jewish minorities. The statistics pertaining to this association were too often compiled by less than impartial observers, but whatever their shortcomings, throughout the region they show occupational structures that set these minorities apart from majorities. Thus we will find that from country to country about one-half of the gainfully occupied Jewish populations were active in commerce and finance, about one-third in the crafts and in the modern industrial sector,[74] the rest in transport, services, and other sectors of the economy, including agriculture, where they played a significant role as agronomists, managers, and tenants of large estates. As Yehuda Don points out, "rationally managed agro-business was profitable and Jewish entrepreneurs played an active role in [it]."[75] Indeed, in this last respect, the numbers are quite stunning. In Hungary (1910) not less than 73.2 percent of the tenants of parcels over 1,000 Hungarian acres (hold) were Jewish.[76] In Romania, Jews were tenants of 36.6 percent of all land leased by owners, and 72.38 percent of all land leased by the owners of large estates.[77] There is some question, and debate, as to how this "participation" translates into shares of national wealth and income, especially in view of large Jewish proletariats in Romania and Poland. But even here, it seems, the Jewish populations tended to cluster around the middle of the income structure, while on the top there were sufficient numbers of prosperous traders and industrialists to sustain popular images of Jewish wealth in contrast to the poverty of the "native" lower classes.[78]

73. Simon Kuznets, quoted in Don 1990, 137 and 149 n. 15.

74. In Hungary, Jews made up 37.7 percent of the owners of mines, 12.3 percent of all "independent owners" of industries, 53 percent of the owners of commercial establishments, 80 percent of the owners and employees of financial institutions. In Romania (1930) they provided 31.3 percent of the total manpower in trade, 32.1 percent of the owners of industry, and 81.3 percent of the independent artisans. In Poland, the proportion of Jews in commerce was 62.6 percent; in industry, around 20.0 percent. See, among others, Kovács 1923; Spulber 1966, 105; Mendelsohn 1983, 25–27.

75. Don 1990, 129.

76. Alajos Kovács 1923, 44, 72.

77. Creanga 1907, 144.

78. Janusz Zarnowski, a leading social historian of Poland in the interwar period, believes that of the roughly 3.1 million Jews of the country, 100,000 belonged to the class of bourgeois

From the early nineteenth century onward, the presence and success of these large immigrant communities in the economic lives of the countries created multiple sources of tension. In retrospect, of course, it is not possible to gauge these tensions accurately, except to say that adverse sentiments varied over time and from region to region. On the one hand, the recurrent, almost routinized and ritualized pogroms of tsarist Russia were absent in the countries west of that empire. On the other, it is safe to say that such sentiments were constantly simmering, a fact reflected in popular stereotypes as well as in the low level of social contact between the Jewish and non-Jewish segments of the population. Indeed, latent hostilities did occasionally burst into the open. The "cholera rebellion" of northern Hungary (1830), the Galician jacqueries of 1846, and the great peasant uprising of Romania (1907), while not principally directed against Jews, all acquired a tinge of anti-Semitism once passions had begun to flare.

Throughout all of this, the attitudes of the "native" upper and middle classes toward Jews ranged from the ambivalent to the benign. Consider first the great landowners. As we noted above, their basic attitude toward the world was one of conservative anti-capitalism, which one might expect to have put them squarely into the camp of anti-Semitism. Surely, evidence for such anti-Semitism is not hard to find, most frequently manifested in the form of outbursts against speculators and the evils of the commodities and stock exchanges. But this form of anti-Semitism, so prevalent among the non-Jewish artisan and smallholder classes of Central and Eastern Europe, did not become a predominant aspect of the ideology of landowners, for general grievances against the capitalist economy were accompanied by highly profitable personal relationships among aristocrats and Jewish businessmen, accountants, moneylenders, and, above all, the aforementioned tenants and estate managers. It was largely as a result of these relationships that the anti-Semitic sentiments of landowners acquired a somewhat abstract quality, their rhetoric being combined with a great deal of protectiveness to-

---

entrepreneurs, 2,000,000 to the middle and lower middle economic strata, and 700,000 (or 23 percent) to the proletariat. He estimates that 300,000 were members of professional and white collar classes not counted in any of the above categories. See Mendelsohn 1983, 27. In Hungary, a contemporary (and hostile) student of Jewish social stratification reports that in 1935 9.9 percent of the community was "upper and upper middle" class, 28.3 "middle class," 37.6 percent "lower middle class," and 24.2 percent "lower class" (Bosnyák 1937, 70–75). An earlier study of the "virilists" of the counties (paying 1,000 forint or more in direct taxes) shows that 20.05 percent of those in this category were Jewish, including 62.2 percent of those who listed their occupation as businessmen, 64.6 percent of tenants of estates, and 12.5 percent of landowners. See Janos 1982, 114. For Romania, the information is more anecdotal. Summarizing it, Mendelsohn 1983, 179–80, concludes that the Jewish populations of Bukovina, Bessarabia, and Northern Transylvania were relatively poor, while the Jewish role played in the old provinces of Moldavia and Wallachia was more substantial, with a "few famous Jewish banking families of great wealth and a solid and influential Jewish bourgeoisie concentrated in Bucharest."

ward individuals. It was an attitude later much bemoaned by the radical anti-Semites of the fascist movements, who cited the phenomenon as one of the major obstacles to the solution of the "Jewish problem." In the end, the relationship between the aristocracy and the Jewish community found a modus vivendi. The great landowners of these countries accepted Jews much as if they were another medieval estate, with particular rights and obligations, so long as they did not attempt to encroach upon the property rights of the "historical classes." That this would not happen was eventually guaranteed by appropriate legislation. In Hungary, legislation passed in 1868 provided for the effective re-entailment of at least part of aristocratic estates,[79] while in Romania, Articles 1430 and 1431 of the Civil Code of 1865 (in force until 1923) denied citizens' rights to Jews and Armenians, thereby preventing them from acquiring landed property.[80]

The attitudes and behavior of the rising political classes were guided by similarly conflicting considerations. On the one hand, as nationalists, the liberals could not but lament the rise of an alien entrepreneurial class in their midst. On the other hand, as economic rationalists, they could not overlook the fact that Jews were an "industrious and constructive segment of the population,"[81] a group of entrepreneurs who paid their taxes to sustain the national state and were the prime agents of an economic process that was expected to propel these backward countries into the modern age. In Hungary, there was yet another factor that made the political classes protective toward the Jewish population: listed by language rather than religion in the official census, the 5 percent strong Jewish minority provided the critical numerical margin that made Magyar speakers a majority, rather than a mere plurality, in their own country. Out of these interests, there emerged a tacit compact that would regulate the relationship between Jews and the political classes. While the latter were to protect Jewish property as well as lives and limbs, Jews were to refrain from seeking employment in the apparatus of the state, or from challenging the primacy of the political establishment. Written into the constitution in Romania (where Jews were denied citizens' rights), while remaining informal in the rest of the region for almost a century, this compact was rather meticulously adhered to and remained one of the main pillars of the liberal state in the countries of the European periphery. The political machinery of the state protected entrepreneurs from both expropriation and personal injury, while the entrepreneurs paid their taxes (together with an occasional bribe to members of the liberal establishment), founded factories and banks "for the fatherland," and, in Hun-

79. Janos 1982, 131–32.
80. Schuster 1939, 75.
81. The words of Hungarian Premier Kálmán Tisza in 1882. See Hungary Napló 1882, 5: 64.

gary, showed considerable zeal for spreading the national culture and language among often recalcitrant ethnic minorities.

So far, we have discussed only the bourgeoisie of the northern tier of the European periphery. In contrast to this region, the Jewish populations of the Balkan countries were relatively small. To be sure, the minute Sephardic Jewish communities of Turkish times were augmented by immigration from Poland around 1870. But even after the influx of new immigrants, their communities represented less than 1 percent of the populations of the South Slav countries. But the concept of ethnic, or "pariah," entrepreneurship was far from being unknown to the region. We will recall that in traditional Balkan society entrepreneurial functions were performed by Armenians, by Greeks (especially from the Phanar quarter of Constantinople), and, to a lesser extent, by Turks who moved to the peninsula in the wake of the Ottoman conquest. In the early nineteenth century, the Greek and Armenian merchant classes rapidly melted into the surrounding populations and, much like the German artisans and traders of Hungary or Poland, joined the local notables in their quest for political, rather than economic, functions. The urbanized Turks meanwhile were expelled during and after the various skirmishes for national independence, and their place was subsequently taken by a new generation of Greeks (now from the Girokaster [*Argyrokastro*] and Korçë regions), and by the Tsintsars (Koutsovlachs, or Arumanians) of the borderlands between Macedonia and today's Albania.

The last of these groups, the Tsintsars, whose history closely resembles the Jewish socioeconomic experience, contributed the most conspicuous ethnic entrepreneurs of the Balkans. Like the Jews, the Tsintsars were a "homeless" people, without a state and society of their own; indeed, they were a people "without history"[82] who first came to be known as sheepherders tending their flocks in the center of the peninsula, speaking a tongue nearly identical with Romanian (a fact that gave rise to the endless debates on the origins of the Romanian people itself). In more recent centuries, some of these sheepherders moved to cities like Moskopolje, and embarked upon careers as stock traders and itinerant merchants. Like the Jews of Galicia, they began moving out of this region around 1760, the date that signals the beginnings of great economic changes in Europe stimulated by the Industrial Revolution of England. Their influx into neighboring countries was accelerated by disaster, more specifically by the pillage and destruction of Moskopolje by one of the Ottoman pashas in 1769. At first this migration followed international trade routes. But by the time of the uprisings of 1804 and 1815, the Tsintsars were evident all over Serbia, as well as the Croatian provinces of the Habsburg realm. They carefully avoided the parts still

82. Popović 1937, 9. Much of the rest of the discussion of the Tsintsars is based on this authoritative work that summarizes the extant literature on that group.

under direct Turkish rule: Bosnia, the Sandjak of Novibazar, and much of the territory of latter-day Bulgaria. By mid-century, there were substantial Tsintsar populations in many Serbian cities: Kragujevac, Šabac, Požarevac, and Belgrade itself—where in 1865 they constituted the majority of city councilors.[83] More significantly, they were the dominant element in the Belgrade *čaršija*, the infamous "marketplace," where deals were made not only among merchants, but also between them and the political class that administered the young Serbian state. Some of the most famous clans (Papakosta, Kapra, Papamosca) were Hellenized. Others (Kika, Fica, Ţipa) retained their Arumanian names and identity.[84]

Much like the position of the Jews in the Danubian and Polish societies, that of the Tsintsars in Balkan society was both tenuous and anomalous. Popular prejudice against them was rampant, instances of which have been meticulously recorded by Popović. For one, there were the usual stereotypes based on physiognomy: the Tsintsars were supposedly recognizable by the shape of their nose, by their bushy hair and eyebrows, and by their dark complexion. They were said to be cunning, bent on cheating, bribery, tax evasion, and avoiding military service.[85] In a hierarchy presided over by the devil, they preceded the Armenians, but "were just as bad as the Greeks."[86] The group's very name is evidence of popular prejudice, for in the Arumanian dialect, as indeed in Romanian, *tsintsar* means "gnat" and refers to the blood-sucking qualities of that insect.[87] Yet Popović also discerns and conveys more dispassionate and positive popular images. Many apparently recognized that the Tsintsars were clever traders who knew when to buy and when to sell: they were seen to be industrious, and as bearers of a great propensity for saving. There were also those who took note of the moderation with which they ate and drank, as well as the sexual puritanism of both males and females.[88] Overall, the family structure of the Tsintsars revealed obvious differences from that of the Balkan Slavs: wives are said to have had business accounts and property separate from their husbands, which they were free to dispose of or invest in whatever ways that pleased them.[89] Here we thus discern, once again, a considerable degree of ambivalence, which was further reflected in the attitude of the Serbian political classes, who shared the disdain felt by the average Serb, but who saw in the Tsintsars a vehicle of economic progress. Indeed, not only did Tsintsar merchants provide a re-

83. Ibid., 180.
84. Ibid.
85. Ibid., 57–59, 104, 107.
86. Ibid., 107.
87. An alternative etymology ties the name to the word "cinci," the word for the numeral five in both Romanian and Arumanian. See Sündhausen 1989, 69.
88. Popović 1937, 65.
89. Ibid.

liable revenue base (both legal and illegal) to the officialdom of the country, but they taught Serbs many of the sophisticated arts and crafts, as well as an urban lifestyle and bourgeois tastes.[90] Out of these mixed experiences there emerged arrangements similar to the ones we encountered in the Danubian countries. Under the terms of these arrangements the Serbian state undertook to protect the lives and capital of ethnic entrepreneurs, but prevented their acquisition of rural property, their penetration of rural markets, and their participation in national (as opposed to local) legislative bodies and affairs.

Following the familiar patterns of pariah entrepreneurship, Serbo-Tsintsar relations began to change in the fourth quarter of the nineteenth century, as younger members of established mercantile families acquired higher education and sought new avenues of social mobility. It was then by no means coincidental that, in 1876, the sons of a number of prosperous merchants in the Smederevo district refused to serve in the Serbian army on the grounds that they were not full-fledged citizens of the state. Their refusal provoked violent incidents, which the authorities attempted to control only in a half-hearted way. In time, emotions did simmer down, and the riots may now be seen as a kind of watershed in Serbian social history. Although no enabling legislation was passed, from then on Tsintsar families found it easier to acquire citizenship and to join the mainstream of Serbian society on equal terms. By 1930, there remained not more than 12,000–15,000 identifiable Tsintsars in Yugoslavia, and 41 percent of the 1,716 prominent Tsintsar families listed by Dušan Popović[91] had Serbian names. As with all processes of assimilation, this one may have taken its toll on some individuals. But the common religion of Greek Orthodoxy facilitated passage from one group to the other—above all, by the expedient of intermarriage. If on the one hand, this expedient contributed significantly to the dissipation of mercantile fortunes, it also permitted many Tsintsars to enter political life, or to act as brokers between the *čaršija* and the political elite. Thus, unlike the Danubian Jews, there is no evidence for the massive concentration of Tsintsars among the ranks of rising revolutionary counter-elites.

State Building and Modernization: The Impulse to Reform

In most of East Europe, the liberal intelligentsia played a significant and direct role in extricating their countries from foreign tutelage. Thus, in Hungary, the Romanian principalities, the Bulgarian provinces of the Ottoman empire, and (unsuccessfully) in partitioned Poland, the educated classes not only agitated for national independence, but also took part in the armed

90. Ibid., 161–63, 303.
91. Ibid., 313–480.

struggles of 1830, 1848–49, 1863, and 1877–78. That participation earned them considerable prestige, thereby accelerating their political ascendancy in society. The role of the intelligentsia was slightly different in Serbia and Montenegro. In the former, the uprising of 1804–14 was led by illiterate peasants and livestock traders who subsequently elected one of their own, Karadjordje, to be their prince. In Montenegro, independence was not a major issue, for the small Christian enclave had for centuries effectively defied Ottoman overlordship. In these two countries, no intelligentsia existed to speak of in the first half of the nineteenth century. But once their international status became clear an educated stratum emerged rapidly from among the urban classes as well as from the ranks of the *prechani*. The latter were Serbians living "across the river" in Hungary, where a South Slav intelligentsia already existed and, having no immediate access there to the state machine, was understandably eager to fulfill its national political mission by migrating to the two mother countries. In Poland, struggle against Russia failed, and was hopeless against the military might of Prussia. Except for their participation in local government in Austrian-ruled southern Poland, the largely noble Polish intelligentsia was excluded from public employment and affairs; as a result, many members of this marginal nobility were reduced to menial occupations. During this same period, the *déclassé* gentry grew in terms of both bitterness and numbers, while its liberalism, untested by harsh realities, retained an air of innocence and romantic idealism until the end of World War I.

In their ascent, the rising political classes remained true to their liberal principles as the chief driving force of political and economic reform. The centerpiece of these reform projects was the establishment of constitutional government. In united Romania, the Constitution of 1866 completed a gradual process of evolution that began with the externally imposed Organic Statutes of 1830, followed by the appropriately named Statute of Evolution (*Statutul Dezvoltător*) of 1864. In Serbia, the point of departure for a similar evolutionary process was the Hatisarif of 1838, granted by the Ottomans to the rebellious Serbs, developed further in the Constitution of 1858, in which the princes still retained the power of appointing part of the legislature, culminating in the outspokenly liberal constitutional document of 1889. In Hungary, the "April Laws" (following the March Revolution of 1848) were likewise the products of a long period of constitutional gestation during the preceding Age of Reform. In 1849, this constitutional legislation was suspended after the country's defeat in the war of independence against the imperial government, but later restored by the Compromise Act of 1867. In Bulgaria, a constituent assembly was called immediately upon the declaration of independence and that body voted a democratic constitution in 1878. In Montenegro, constitutionalism evolved slowly between

1860 and 1905, from an appointed senate of advisors to an elected parliament. In Albania, representative institutions were established only after World War I, but, dissolved in 1923, were not to be reestablished until the end of the Communist period.

The franchise, introduced or extended as part of the liberal project of constitution making, was broadest in the Balkan states, where the principle of representation was not an organic part of the political tradition. In Serbia, under the Constitution of 1889, 23 percent of the population, all of them males, were entitled to vote.[92] In Bulgaria, suffrage was still broader, although only about a fifth of the eligible voters are said to have exercised their rights.[93] Montenegro, late though she was in joining nations with popularly elected parliaments, had liberal provisions concerning suffrage.[94] Hungary and Romania, on the other hand, were more cautious in shaping their electoral institutions, reflecting the remaining influence of landowning classes, who now were giving up their earlier constitutional prerogatives. In Hungary, the Electoral Law of 1848 extended the right to vote from about 1.5 percent to 6.5 percent of the general population. This figure, on a par with that of contemporary Britain, included property owners and taxpayers of certain categories, the educated classes, and finally voters by "ancient right" (i.e., members of the nobility whose names, or those of direct ancestors, had appeared in one of the pre-1848 voting registers). Unlike in Britain, however, this percentage figure was not to increase further until 1920. Indeed, subsequent legislation in 1874 actually reduced it to 5.9 percent of the population.[95] In Romania, meanwhile, the electoral system followed the curial principle, which is to say that a relatively large proportion of the population was enfranchised, although voting was by colleges, or *curiae*, strongly favoring the landed and the educated urban classes due to the disproportionate weight of their votes. Initially (1864), the Romanian electorate was divided into four of these colleges. The first consisted of a few hundred large proprietors, the second of the owners of medium-sized estates. The third college included urban proprietors and the professional classes, while the fourth was to provide indirect representation for rural small proprietors and taxpayers. In 1884, the first and second colleges were merged. But the other features of the system, including the heavily weighted suffrage and the indirect representation of the voters of the fourth college, now third, remained in force. In 1905, 15,973 voters of the first college elected 72 members of the lower chamber (*camera*), 34,742 urban voters of the second college 71, while the 42,907 "electors" of the third college, themselves desig-

92. Dedijer, Božić, and Ćirković 1974, 379.
93. See Stoianovich 1963, 322.
94. Miller 1908, 466.
95. Hungary, *Annuaire statistique hongrois*, vol. 19 (1910), 438.

nated by about a million peasant voters in a two-stage process, was granted a representation of 40 members.[96]

One of the gentle ironies of the nineteenth century was the survival—and in some cases, revival—of the monarchy, a quintessentially medieval institution, in the modern age. To be sure, most monarchies of Europe, whether in the east or the west, were subject to constitutional limitations, having to exercise their prerogatives through cabinets responsible at least in some degree to elected parliaments. Nonetheless, even in the context of constitutionalism, the monarchs of the age had their own unique position, which gave them a degree of autonomy from other state institutions and made them political actors in their own right. While the educated and the urban classes were on the whole beholden to the principle of popular sovereignty, a significant portion of the rural populations was still susceptible to the mystique of divine right, especially in countries where that institution had a long and unbroken history. One of the significant functions—and hence, sources of power—of the monarchy was to serve as a buckle between these two segments of the body politic. Just as significantly, European monarchs, including such "most constitutional" rulers as Queen Victoria and King Edward of Britain, served as important intermediaries between their own national state and the international community. Once so recognized, kings and queens became members of the most exclusive peer group and social club in the world, that of European royalty, whose members married among each other, attended royal baptisms, funerals, and other ceremonial functions, bestowed upon each other splendid decorations, and, in the process, also struck deals on behalf of their governments. By performing these functions they were important players in the Concert of Europe, but the failure of the concert to prevent the cataclysm of 1914–18 was widely seen also as a failure of this informal system of royal connections. Once the system failed, monarchical rulers either disappeared—as was the case in Germany, Russia, and Austria-Hungary—became mere symbols without policy making functions, or, alternatively, were compelled to seek new legitimacy by transforming themselves into popular tribunes.

In the nineteenth century, though, monarchs still had both charisma and utility. So the new parliaments of eastern European countries either confirmed existing institutions or quickly restored old ones, hastening to invite occupants with appropriate credentials. Thus when the Hungarian parliament dethroned the house of Habsburg in April 1849, it was careful not to abolish the institution itself. Subsequently, in 1867, parliament "compromised" with the emperor of Austria, and arranged for his coronation as Hungarian king with unusual pomp and circumstance. Similarly, in tiny

96. R. Seton-Watson 1934, 357; Romania 1919, 10–11.

Montenegro, the rulers of the house of Petrović were confirmed in their office in 1863, although they themselves decided to modernize the institution by abandoning the religious function of the *vladika* (prince bishop) in favor of the secular title of prince. United Romania at first retained the elective form of the monarchy. But the first elected national prince, Alexander Cuza, soon had to vacate his throne to make way for a hereditary line of rulers from the Siegmaringen branch of the powerful Hohenzollern dynasty. In Bulgaria, the monarchy declared by the National Assembly was first occupied by Prince Alexander of the Battenberg family. Then, after a coup d'état expelled him, the title went to Prince Ferdinand of the house of Sachse-Coburg-Gotha. The Serbians alone elected princes from their own plebeian ranks, thumbing their noses at the luster that accompanied an established royal family, but paid a certain price for their national pride in terms of international influence and domestic political stability. In due course, these princely titles were upgraded. The rulers of Romania (1881), Serbia (1882), Bulgaria (1908), Montenegro (1910), and, belatedly, Albania (1927) promoted themselves to the rank of kings, as a symbol of the progress of their own societies. The more prestigious monarchs of the Continent tended to receive them with the same bemused benevolence that the Soviet leaders would show half a century later as their junior partners were advancing from people's democracies to socialist republics.

In tandem with constitutional reform, the liberal intelligentsia and its political parties were also engaged in changing economic institutions, so as to integrate their countries into the rising world economy. In this respect, the first step was the abolition of feudal institutions, whether of the eastern or the western variety. Like political reform, economic reform was first pursued during the period of liberal gestation prior to the countries' independence, and while some of the motivations behind it were political—diminishing, or, in the Balkans, expropriating the landed aristocracies—others were purely pragmatic and economic, designed to lay down the foundations of a modern, capitalist, export-oriented agricultural economy. This last objective was to be accomplished by establishing a modern system of property rights and by marketizing, or commodifying, land and labor, the principal factors of production in these relatively underdeveloped economies. One of the most articulate proponents of this pragmatic anti-feudalism was the already-mentioned Hungarian Széchenyi, who argued that abolishing the antiquated laws of entail would allow landowners to raise capital, while the replacement of the *corvée* and other servile obligations with wage labor would enhance overall productivity. More or less the same argument was made in the essays of the Serbian reformer Vladimir Jovanović published in *Srpska Novine* in 1857. According to these, agriculture was the base of progress, for it was there that surplus was produced. To produce surplus, an economy needed efficient labor rather than the labor of indentured serfs, while land itself had to be commodified by abolishing both land tenure and the kinship-oriented *zadrugas* prevalent in the South Slav lands.[97] Others, like Jevrem Grujić and Milovan Janković (educated in Germany and France), concurred in "strongly worded articles suffused with the spirit of *laissez faire*." [98]

These ideas bore fruit, for when the time came, the governments of the newly emerging states abolished the traditional institutions of land tenure. Portions of the land cultivated by peasants in exchange for labor services became their property, while simultaneously the new parliaments put an end to the legal fiction that all land was owned by the crown and that the lords of the manor were but hereditary tenants of the prince. In the Balkans, where this legislation followed wars of liberation, and where the landowners were members of a foreign military class, land was taken and distributed without exacting compensation. In Hungary, Romania, and in divided Poland, where the progressive intelligentsia had close ties to the landowning classes, cash compensation was exacted from the new peasant farmers, and substantial portions of all arable land remained in the hands of the former seigneurs, with only the smaller part of the former feudal holdings—33 percent in Romania, 27 percent in Poland, 25 percent in Hungary, and 15 percent in Transylavania[99]—turned into peasant freeholds.

An integral part of the program of modernizing the economy was the reform of the legal systems. In part, these reforms were a response to the logic of the market and to the needs of a new society of private proprietors engaging in business transactions with each other and with the outside world. In part, though, as Gale Stokes tells us, the reform of the legal system was part of a "civilizing process," [100] or adaptation to the prevailing political culture of the Western countries. Indeed, to quote the preamble of the new Serbian Legal Code of 1873, the reforms were introduced "in order to erase the memory of the time when Serbia was below the European peoples," and in order to secure the country a place "within the ranks of the rest of the cultivated European states." [101] As in Serbia, so in the other countries of the region, the 1860s and 1870s produced a flood of new legislation establishing commercial codes to regulate business transactions, including the newly founded stock and commodities exchanges, new penal codes and bodies of administrative law, the latter as much to protect the administrative classes from political interference as to protect the public from arbitrary administrative behavior. All this went hand in hand with the establishment of a ju-

97. For Jovanović, see Stokes 1975, xiv, 15.
98. Ibid., 17.
99. Janos 1982, 29, 85, 88–89; Dobrogeanu-Gherea 1910, 52; Wandycz 1974, 197.
100. Stokes 1990, 166.
101. Ibid., 26.

dicial system in which judges were generally appointed by political authorities, but were also granted sufficient immunities and security of employment.

If the establishment of modern commercial law and courts to enforce it were designed to encourage the flow of foreign capital into the countries, another set of policies was to serve the purpose of facilitating the outflow of local commodities toward the West European markets. In general, the economic strategy of all countries was first export-oriented, and above all oriented toward the export of grain, the commodity that seemed to have the greatest comparative advantage on the global market. As an integral part of the strategy, all countries of the region engaged in ambitious projects to improve infrastructure, and, more specifically, the system of transportation. Indeed, by the late 1860s and early 1870s, railroad building turned into a virtual rage across the region. "Civilized man," the Romanian Ion Brătianu exulted in 1876, "is the product of trade," and the best marks of civilization were "highways, railroads and waterways."[102] Were they not the first conveniences built whenever a civilized country set about to colonize a primitive one?[103]

For a while this economic strategy appeared to be successful. In the 1860s and 1870s, East European grain found markets in the industrializing West, competing effectively with other farm economies of the Continent. Indeed, a number of European economists, among them the French Eugene Bontoux (teaching at the University of Vienna), and the Germans Max Wirth and Heinrich Ditz, wrote alarmist scholarly tracts envisioning large quantities of cheap eastern grain crushing German and French agriculture.[104] But the competitive advantage of East European agriculture was short-lived. It was terminated abruptly in 1877–78 upon the appearance of cheap overseas grain on the European markets, reaching its new destination via newly built railroads and the sudden appearance of steam-powered cargo ships capable of transporting bulk. Literally from one season to another, grain prices fell. At the Danube port of Pest, or the Black Sea port of Brăila, American (and later Canadian and Argentinian) grain produced on cheap land with capital-intensive methods was suddenly less expensive than Hungarian or Romanian grain produced by cheap labor. This change in prices precipitated what has been since known as the great commodities crisis of 1878–96. But, in fact, with the exception of a few short intervals, the relative price of grain never recovered to its earlier level, and the East Europeans had only rare moments of trade advantage between 1878 and World War II.

This rather traumatic experience forced the governing elites of the region

102. Quoted in Zeletin 1925, 47, 121.
103. Ibid.
104. See Bontoux 1861, 2d ed. 1868, esp. 3; Wirth 1868, 31; Ditz 1866.

to reevaluate their economic strategy and priorities. Infrastructure still remained an important calculus in the overall design, although few would voice the opinion that its development could in and by itself serve as the vehicle of accumulation and industrial development. Indeed, the priorities of governments were now reversed. Their immediate target became industrial growth, in order to reduce reliance on imports, with the state being assigned a role in creating a system of tariff protection. One after the other, the smaller Balkan states thus imposed duties on the import of industrial products ranging from 8 to 14 percent *ad valorem* in the Balkans to 20 percent in Romania (rates that were subsequently raised to 25 and 33 percents respectively).[105] Not all countries of the area, however, were in control of their own foreign trade. Hungary, for instance, was part of a larger imperial tariff system, while Bulgaria was for a while subject to the "capitulations" of the Treaty of Berlin that prohibited the country from imposing duties on certain products. These countries used the alternative method of indirect subsidies first created by Sándor Wekerle, Hungary's minister of finance (and later prime minister) by providing tax exemptions, cash payments, preferential freight rates, government contracts, and a variety of profit-guaranteeing schemes. These became an integral part of the Hungarian Industrial Act of 1881 and the Bulgarian Industrial Act of 1882. In time, the system was copied by Romania and Serbia as well in their own industrial acts of 1886, 1893, 1898, and 1910.[106] Insofar as these measures did not have immediate and dramatic effect, the governments of both Hungary and Bulgaria attempted to further supplement them by patriotic efforts to mobilize public sentiment in favor of buying the products of local industry. The Hungarian Protective Association (*Védegylet*) founded in 1842 and the Tulip Movement initiated in 1906 served these purposes, as did various campaigns of the Bulgarian government to encourage—indeed oblige—public servants to wear locally manufactured clothes, including the traditional leather sandals (*opănca*) of Balkan peasants. Amid this general pattern for East Central Europe as a whole, the eastern provinces of Poland represented a somewhat special case, for while the country remained the dependency of a foreign power, on balance, the policies of the tsarist governments favored local industries by giving them preferential access to the internal markets of a vast country.[107] The position of the Hungarian economy was somewhat more ambiguous, since the country was part of a customs union with a number of industrially more advanced regions of the Continent. But while this circumstance put the new Hungarian industries at a competitive disadvantage, the economy

105. Jackson and Lampe 1982, 266.

106. For these policies see Gratz 1934, 2: 224; Berend and Ránki 1982, 86–88; Pasvolsky 1930, 27; Spulber 1966, 22; Jackson and Lampe 1982, 256–66.

107. Wandycz 1974, 201–2.

of the country was compensated by the Austrian tariff imposed on comestibles, which had a beneficial effect on agricultural producers in the eastern half of the Austro-Hungarian realm.

From Parliaments to Political Machines: The Corruption of Liberalism

In the long run, however, no aspect of the politics of the liberal intelligentsia was more consequential than the building of the bureaucratic and military organizations of the modern state. Much like the building of the parliamentary institutions, this process was spurred by the desire of national elites to conform with the "civilized" international standards set by the pioneering states of modern industrialism. Thus from the early nineteenth century onward, in most of these countries, the idea was prevalent that one needed a cadre of professionals and a centrally controlled administrative system in order to bring modernity, under whatever name, to these countries, and especially to their backward countryside. Almost all liberals of the period feared local particularism and rued the traditionalism of their peasantries. Some, like the Hungarian Baron Eötvös, one of the looming figures of East Central European liberalism, dreaded the autonomy of the counties, and made the issue of administrative centralization the centerpiece of his own political program.[108] Others, like the Serbian Vladimir Jovanović, were more cautious. They feared centralized bureaucracies but accepted them as a necessary evil as long as the large masses of people remained ignorant and devoid of national consciousness.[109]

Whatever doubts lingered, it was in the name of progress and enlightenment that the central, ministerial bureaucracies of these countries began to expropriate powers hitherto reserved to municipalities and village government. While the appearances of autonomy and self-government were often preserved, in reality local administrations were drawn ever closer to the center and subjected to the ministries, with the ministries of interior taking direct charge of the police forces. Thus, in Serbia, "local government which had flourished for centuries under the Turks now began to wither with the appearance of elected officials."[110] The father and creator of this system was Iliya Garašanin, a *prečanin* Serb, who recruited most of his country's first generation of genuine civil servants among fellow Serbians "from across the river" in Hungary. The administrative developments in Bulgaria, some twenty years later, were not much different. While under Ottoman rule, lo-

108. The best summary of his ideas in his own *Die Reform in Ungarn* [Reform in Hungary] (1847). See also Body 1972.
109. Stokes 1974, 224.
110. Stavrianos 1961, 254.

cal self-government was firmly in the hands of local notables (the *chorba-djiya*), from 1882 onward the autonomies of village and district government were whittled away, so that by 1895, Premier Stambulov could boast that "not even a bee could hum" in the provinces without the knowledge of the central government.[111] In Romania, the reform of 1864 abolished most of the traditional functions of village government, and the 1866 constitution divided the now united principalities into administrative districts (*judeţe*), with prefects who were to act as "petty satraps" on behalf of the ministry in Bucharest.[112] In tiny Montenegro, the late-nineteenth-century rulers of the country secularized and rationalized the administration of the country by establishing clear divisions between religious and temporal authority, by creating ministries with specialized functions, and by recruiting a group of educated young men from Belgrade to serve as their first functionaries. But in so doing, they also managed to "check the independent spirit of the chieftains and to curtail the autonomy [they] had exercised over their districts."[113] In Hungary, a country extremely proud of the ancient prerogatives of its counties that for centuries had served as a bulwark against dynastic attempts at centralization, the post-1867 governments quickly extinguished local autonomies by a series of legislative acts ostensibly passed to "modernize" the country's administration. Thus Public Law IV separated the administrative and judicial functions of the counties, placing the new court system under the authority of the minister of justice. Public Laws XX–XXII of 1878 effectively reduced county and municipal assemblies to the performance of ceremonial functions and subordinated local organs to the authority of lord lieutenants (*főispán*) appointed by the government. Finally, Public Laws XX–XXIII of 1886 provided for a ministerial review of all elections to local administrative offices.[114]

If in the long term the rise of this centralized bureaucratic apparatus was justified by the lofty objectives of civilization and economic progress, more immediately the process was pushed forward by the interests of the declining middle classes in finding dignified salaried employment and avoiding the rough-and-tumble of modern economic life. Under these pressures, from country to country, public administration changed not only in form but in size as well. Once the nations gained independence from their imperial masters, their administrative services were inundated with applicants, and started to grow at a rate that far exceeded any objective need (measured by the rate of economic progress or social differentiation), or, for that matter,

111. Hulme 1895, 63.
112. R. Seton-Watson 1934, 354.
113. Miller 1908, 432.
114. For a summary of this legislation, See R. Seton-Watson 1908, 240–42.

the relative size of the bureaucracies of their models in the advanced countries of the Occident.

The definition of bureaucrat, of course, varied from country to country, as does the reliability of figures on public employment. Even so, the available figures are illuminating. In Hungary (with a population of about 14 million), there were in 1867 around 16,000 public employees of the white-collar class. The number doubled by 1875,[115] and it doubled again by 1890 (while the population increased a mere 20 percent). Thereafter the ranks of public administration increased still more rapidly. There were 97,835 public servants in 1900 and 119,937 in 1910.[116] These figures include only the employees of the central (ministerial) state apparatus. The total number of public employees (including those of local governments) was 265,447 in 1904, and 387,922 in 1914.[117] These figures may be compared to those from Germany, a country with a population more than three times that of the Hungarian kingdom (on its pre-1918 territory), where the number of public employees in the administrative sector was 635,000 in 1913.[118] In Great Britain, the most advanced country in Europe at that time, the number was 309,432.[119] In Bulgaria, a country of 5 million, the state employed 35,920 officials in 1908, but the number was to rise to 88,000 (or 144,000, if municipal officials are counted) in the next twenty years, even though the country suffered crushing financial and economic losses in World War I.[120] In Serbia, the proportions were somewhat lower. Here, with fewer than 2.5 million inhabitants, we find some 25,000 civil servants at the turn of the century.[121] In Romania, the government paid 87,000 employees, excluding technical personnel and the employees of municipal governments.[122] In each and every one of the above cases, public employment is said to have exceeded 5 percent of the total labor force,[123] compared to 1.5 percent for Germany and 0.9 percent for England and Wales.[124]

Numbers, however, represented only one dimension of the problem. The truly troublesome aspect of administrative development was not just that

115. Keleti 1889, 5.
116. Hungary, *Annuaire statistique hongrois*, 1900, 80, and 1910, 93.
117. Buday 1921, 44.
118. Germany, Statistisches Reichsamt 1929, 41, 224.
119. Great Britain, Census Office 1934, 679.
120. Roucek 1948, 54.
121. Jackson and Lampe 1982, 235. Another source speaks of 4.97 percent of the population being in "public service and the free professions" (1890); see Ekonomski Institut N.R. Serbije 1953, 70. Yet another identifies 18,137 persons on the payroll of the central state apparatus (1900); see Sündhausen 1989, 461.
122. Jackson and Lampe 1982, 235.
123. Ibid.
124. See above, Statistisches Reichsamt 1929, 41, 224; Great Britain, Census Office 1934, 679.

there were more bureaucrats than justified by the existing levels of social complexity and economic development, but that the expectations of the bureaucratic personnel, shaped by foreign examples, were thoroughly incongruous with the economic underpinnings that these societies could provide for the modern state. Nonetheless, the intelligentsia continued to constitute a powerful interest group in its own right, and was determined to obtain a share of national income that would allow it to exist at levels established by the middle classes of Western societies. This objective required 25 to 40 percent of state revenues, and 15 to 20 percent of national income during the first decades of nationhood.[125] One should hasten to add here that such officially appropriated revenue was only part of the real income of the political classes, for the revenues of the "state bourgeoisie" and their hangers-on were further augmented by private income collected from either the entrepreneurial classes or from individual members of the general public. While in Hungary (and later, Poland) a good part of this revenue was "legal," in that it consisted of the fees of various "political brokers"—attorneys close to the seats of power, ex-ministers serving on the board of businesses and acting as "fixers"—in Romania and the Balkans, this form of skimming profits was accompanied by the petty corruption of officials who used their position to extort bribes. In either case, these revenues represented a substantial overhead for conducting routine business, as well as another flow of funds from the economic to the political classes. In one way or another, these peripheral states were becoming grand instruments of income equalization—not, to be sure, among the different strata of the local populations, but between elites of the backward and advanced societies of the European continent.

This burden on national income was made heavier by the obligations undertaken by the governments to build infrastructure, and compounded by defense expenditures, which in the last quarter of the nineteenth century made up at least a quarter of the national budgets.[126] Here again, the logic of underdevelopment was at work. A modern state requires a modern army, but the cost of maintaining such an army was usually incommensurate with the ability of the economies to sustain the expenditure. The cost of an artillery piece, or machine gun, especially if imported, was not significantly less in Bulgaria than in Germany or France. Germany, for example, spent 16 gold francs per capita on national defense in 1890.[127] With only about 40 percent of German national income per capita, Romania, Serbia, and Bulgaria spent 13, 12, and 9 francs per capita, respectively.[128] The case of

125. Jackson and Lampe 1982, 235.
126. Banks 1971, 99–126.
127. Jackson and Lampe 1982, 234.
128. Ibid.

Hungary was somewhat different. Only a small portion of the defense out-lays show up in the annual budget, yet, under the terms of the Compromise of 1867, Hungarian taxpayers had to bear 33 (later 37) percent of the costs of the monarchy's military outlays, one of the highest in per capita terms in Europe.[129]

Under these pressures on scarce resources, budget expenditures were in-creasing by leaps and bounds, and certainly in excess of the rate of economic development that the countries could take credit for. In Hungary, expendi-tures in the national budget increased by 58 percent during the seven years following the restoration of the autonomous Hungarian state in 1867 (and this figure did not include expenditures for the common Austro-Hungarian army), then increased by almost 250 percent in the next quarter century.[130] In Serbia, budget expenditures tripled every twenty years between 1839 and 1889, doubled between 1889 and 1910, and increased overall by a factor of 33 during the seventy-five years between 1835 and 1910.[131] In Romania, the size of the budget increased fourfold between 1859 and 1889.[132] After the turn of the century, the growth of state expenditures continued unabated. During the fourteen years between 1898 and 1910, public spending in Ro-mania increased by 232 percent, in Bulgaria by 200 percent,[133] and in Hun-gary by 287 percent.[134] To put the social burden of these expenditures in perspective, we must note here that while this rapid expansion of the bud-gets occurred, per capita national income increased by not more than 50 to 75 percent.[135] Consequently, as Jackson and Lampe observe, the relative eco-nomic burden of this spending was far heavier in the east than comparable increases in the central (semiperipheral) or western (core) regions of the continent.[136] This observation is borne out by more systematic comparisons of per capita income and public spending. As Table 5 A–B and Table 6 show, in 1880 average per capita state expenditure of East Central European states was exceedingly high in relation to per capita income and product when compared to figures for Western Europe. In 1880 eastern countries spent on average 81.2 percent of the amount spent by the United Kingdom, and 87.1 percent of the average expenditure of six highly developed countries of the Continent, with only 38.0 percent of the British per capita income and 51.4 percent of the West European per capita income. Our tables also show that these ratios further deteriorated between 1880 and 1910. The phe-nomenon was areawide, most pronounced in the southeast (Table 7).Yet the

129. Banks 1971, 101.
130. Matlekovits 1900, 2: 867–69.
131. Sündhausen 1989, 463–64; Karić 1887, 575.
132. Dobrogeanu-Gherea 1910, 480.
133. Jackson and Lampe 1982, 234.
134. Calculated from figures for Austria-Hungary in Banks 1971, 101.
135. Berend and Ránki 1982, 15–16.
136. Jackson and Lampe 1982, 233.

TABLE 5A

Western State Expenditures per Capita, 1880–1910

(current US $ with adjustment to purchasing power parities)

Country	1880 US $	1880 PPP	1890 US $	1890 PPP	1900 US $	1900 PPP	1910 US $	1910 PPP
United Kingdom	11.85	12.79	11.18	12.07	15.82	17.08	17.12	18.48
Germany	16.24	18.83	22.25	25.81	28.07	32.56	33.90	39.32
France	17.46	24.79	16.58	23.54	18.41	26.14	21.12	29.99
Netherlands	11.29	14.22	14.82	18.67	11.71	14.75	14.12	17.79
Belgium	10.30	7.21	13.3	9.6	16.7	11.6	21.70	15.22
Sweden	4.44	4.08	6.22	4.80	6.90	6.34	11.31	10.40
Switzerland	2.83	3.05	4.25	4.59	5.88	6.35	8.39	9.06
Average	9.86	11.93		14.13		15.62		19.94

SOURCES: Banks 1974, 99–137; Clark 1940, 51, 132–45. German figures adjusted to reflect budgets of Länder from Germany, *Vierteljahrhefte zur Statistik des deutschen Reiches* (1902), No. 2, 257, and (1914), No. 2, 1.

TABLE 5B

Eastern State Expenditures per Capita, 1880–1910

(current US $ with adjustment to purchasing power parities)

Country	1880 US $	1880 PPP	1890 US $	1890 PPP	1900 US $	1900 PPP	1910 US $	1910 PPP
Czech Lands Bohemia- Moravia	11.79	15.71	16.24	21.64	22.87	30.48	29.72	39.61
Hungary[a]	8.84	10.25	11.75	13.63	16.77	19.45	21.05	24.41
Romania	5.25	7.98	6.14	9.33	6.42	9.75	12.89	19.59
Bulgaria	9.17	13.84	5.25	7.92	4.60	6.94	7.72	11.65
Serbia	2.50	3.70	4.12	6.09	5.94	8.79	7.65	11.32
Average of Above	7.51	10.39	8.50	11.72	12.89	15.08	15.80	21.31
Average Minus Czech Lands	6.44	8.94		9.24		11.23		16.74

SOURCES: Banks 1974, 99–137; Clark 1940, 51, 132–45; Bohemia-Moravia and Hungary based on Austria-Hungary, adjusted following Matlekovits 1900, and Berend and Ránki 1982, 30–31.
[a] Hungarian expenditures from 85%–90% of Austro-Hungarian average; Czech = 120%.

problem was not unique to East Europe but was apparently common among peripheral societies and represents one of the political consequences of economic backwardness. Indeed, using the same databases we will find that Portugal and Greece fall in the same category, while six Latin American countries for which data are available have been even more profligate spenders with slightly weaker economic bases than the East Central European states.[137]

137. Banks 1971, 99–36; Bairoch 1976, 286; summarized in Janos 1989, 339–41.

TABLE 6

Relative State Expenditures per Capita, East and West, 1880–1910

(adjusted to purchasing power parities)

	1880	1890	1900	1910
	STATE EXPENDITURES			
East as % of UK	81.2	97.1	88.3	115.3
East (minus Bohemia) as % of UK	69.9	76.6	65.7	90.6
East as % of West	87.1	82.9	96.5	107.9
East (minus Czech Lands) as % of West Europe	74.9	65.4	71.4	84.0
	PER CAPITA INCOME			
East as % of UK	38.0	35.2	35.7	38.9
East as % of West	51.4	50.0	49.5	47.6
East (minus Czech lands) as % of West Europe	46.9	44.6	43.2	41.3
East (minus Czech lands) as % of UK	34.7	31.4	31.2	33.7

SOURCES: See Table 5A–B. Expenditures from Banks 1971, adjusted according to Clark 1940, 51; per capita income from Bairoch 1976, 289. See also Table 7 below.

TABLE 7

State Expenditures per Capita, Southeastern Europe, 1910

Country	Gold francs	Adjust to PPP	Percent of UK	GNP/cap. % of UK
Serbia	43	63.6	47.5	31.2
Bulgaria	42	63.0	47.0	29.8
Romania	75	113.2	84.8	33.9
Austria-Hungary	67	84.4	62.9	39.8
United Kingdom	126	134.0		100.0

SOURCE: Jackson and Lampe 1982, 234. For adjustment to PPP, Clark 1940, 51; for GNP per capita, Bairoch 1976, 286.

Faced with an obvious and increasing gap between state budgetary needs and the capacity of their underlying economies, the political classes of Eastern Europe first attempted to deal with the problem by resorting to the expedient of foreign borrowing. Thus the foreign liabilities of the states— virtually nonexistent in the 1860s—began to accumulate in the 1870s, reaching extraordinary proportions by the first decade of the twentieth century. In Romania, the leading debtor nation in the region, public debt amounted to 299.6 French francs per capita, representing 116 percent of the total national product. In Serbia, the figure was 238.8 francs, which represented an estimated 120 percent of the national product. Bulgaria, one of the least profligate of the peripheral states, was indebted to the tune of 149.2 francs per head, or some 50 percent of the national product. While these figures declined from the high points in the early 1880s, by the early twentieth century interest payments still made up between one-fifth and one-third of the state budgets and, together with defense, developmental expenditures, and administration, took the lion's share of public revenue.[138]

However, the expedient of borrowing could only postpone the need to raise revenues from local sources, and when the governments finally faced up to that task, they went about it by extremely harsh means. Given the reluctance of parliaments to raise tax rates, fiscal authorities sought to raise revenue by arbitrarily increasing the assessed value of taxable items. And when local governments did not collaborate, the "central government got its money by sending its own assessors around the country. These central servants spared no one, and often the new assessment was as much as ten times higher than the first." [139] Once taxes were assessed, collection drives took the form of military campaigns, in the course of which army and gendarmerie would descend upon villages, seizing anything of cash value. This is what happened during the Hungarian tax collection campaign of 1869, which the authorities themselves described in military terms.[140] But even short of such methods, raising revenue remained a brutal business, which relied heavily on excise taxes levied on such staples as salt, kerosene, liquor, and tobacco, as well as on fees levied on licenses and transactions, a system that was developed by such renowned ministers of finance as the Russians Ivan Vyshnegradsky and Sergei Witte and the Hungarian Sándor Wekerle. Where the system of collection remained ineffective, funds were extracted from the public nonetheless by individual bureaucrats, who used the powers of their office to extort bribes, which served to maintain lifestyles regarded as commensurate with their social position. But even in "high-tax" countries with relatively effective systems of collection, political figures would take advantage of their position by collecting retainers, *honoraria*, and legal fees—in effect, protection money—from the hapless and vulnerable ethnic entrepreneurs.

Not surprisingly, these methods of revenue raising, and the transfer of income from the economic to the political classes, engendered widespread opposition on the part of the tax-paying public. To forestall it, the governments of the day began to convert their administrative leverage—their powers of assessment, collection, licensing, and regulation of public health and safety—into political power by cajoling and persuading the weak and semiliterate rural electorates into sending deputies to the national assemblies who then would do the bidding of the bureaucracies and the central governments. This was an effective means given some significant differences

138. See Milward and Saul 1977, 444; Jackson and Lampe 1982, 232; Stavrianos 1961, 419; for Serbia, see also Sündhausen 1989, 499.

139. Petrovich 1976, 2: 403.

140. The term used, *adószedési hadjárat*, literally means a "military campaign for collection." Molnár 1971, 2: 79.

between societies in the east and the west of the continent. Whereas in the pioneering countries of northwestern Europe, state administrative bodies had been called into being by classes of vigorous and self-confident agrarian and mercantile entrepreneurs, in the backward societies of the European periphery, the public consisted of an illiterate peasantry, a declining (or alien) middle class, and, where it existed at all, an agrarian upper class highly ambivalent about its future place in the rising market economy. There were, in other words, no social forces potent enough to act as an effective counterweight to the influence of the administrative services. The abolition of serfdom enhanced rather than retarded administrative influence, for the rural smallholder and laborer effectively became wards of the administration, and just as strictly accountable to it as they had been to local landowners. Bureaucrats—particularly in those ministries at the apex of the bureaucracy—could now subject them to various forms of economic harassment, fines, and incarceration. Consequently, much as happened elsewhere under similar historical circumstances, the bureaucracies became "formidable enough to recast the system of government in [their] own image,"[141] by converting their administrative power into political power via the control of the electoral process.

In most countries of East Central Europe, electoral fraud was as old as bureaucracies and parliaments. But in the third quarter of the nineteenth century, bureaucratic meddling in the electoral process became routinized under the growing fiscal pressures generated by the rise of the modern state. From the mid 1870s onward, we can no longer speak of a parliamentary system merely riddled with abuses, for "abuse became the system itself."[142] These are the words of a historian of Spain, but they are eminently applicable to the countries of the eastern periphery as well. In this new system, to produce predictable majorities, bureaucracies expropriated the normal function of the voting publics through a variety of fraudulent practices: the withholding of tax assessments until after elections, the denial of licenses, the imposition of fines on obstreperous individuals, the doctoring of voters' lists and electoral results, and even the blocking of highways and thoroughfares to prevent unfriendly voters from reaching polling places, usually located in only one or two townships in a given constituency. While it functioned, the system was not entirely devoid of reciprocity. This reciprocity obtained, however, not between the public and the parliament, but between the bureaucracy and a parliamentary majority specifically crafted to serve and articulate the bureaucracy's political perspective.

A sterling example of such debased parliamentarism is provided by the

141. Rosenberg 1966, 1.
142. Carr 1966, 256.

political machine of the Hungarian Kálmán Tisza, premier of Hungary between 1875 and 1890. Originally the leader of the "Left-Center" opposition to the Compromise between Austria and Hungary, Tisza himself was victim of electoral irregularities in 1869 and 1872. In 1875, however, Tisza made his peace with the constitutional compact, and was called upon by the emperor-king to form a government. In the years that followed, it was Tisza who firmly centralized the administration of the country, then established a solid electoral base for his Liberal Party by creating about 160 "rotten boroughs" inhabited largely by the Slovak and Romanian minorities of the country. In these districts, non-Magyar voters were either struck from the voting lists or rendered so thoroughly helpless in the face of administrative harassment that they would obediently elect deputies to serve as the hard core, or "mameluke guard," of the prime minister's supporters. Some fifty constituencies, furthermore, became "pocket boroughs" effectively relinquished to the control of aristocratic landowners who, while independent from the government, could be induced to support it by a variety of concessions. Elsewhere, approximately 200 constituencies remained "open boroughs" in the sense that there the government refrained from using some of the more obvious forms of administrative pressure. So structured, the Liberal Party had a clear upper hand, coming to be known simply as the "Government Party" in Hungarian political parlance. Only once, in 1905, did this system fail to produce the predictable majority, and after a short interval, machine politics was restored, surviving—with minor adjustments—until 1944.[143]

Neighboring Romania closely, and one may assume consciously, followed the Hungarian model. In that country, too, electoral fraud had been widespread since the Organic Statutes of 1830 had given the principalities a form of feudal parliamentarism. But much as in Hungary, in 1876, Ion Brătianu's Liberal Party seized the reins of power, and Brătianu proceeded to consolidate his gain by setting up a symbiotic arrangement between administration and parliament. To strengthen his hand, Brătianu abolished the old first college of the electoral system, dominated by powerful boyar families, and merged it with the second college of lesser landowners, whose ranks were more sympathetic to Brătianu's etatist brand of liberalism. They were also more susceptible to administrative pressure. Indeed, as Seton-Watson notes, the new regime "made it exceedingly difficult to agitate against the government . . . even for members of the boyar class."[144] In Stefan Zeletin's words, "as the power of the salaried bureaucracy increased, the power of the old

143. This system is described in detail in Janos 1982, 96–109. See also R. Seton-Watson 1908, 249–74; 1911; May 1951, 252–69; and finally a series of electoral maps in Fodor 1922, vol. 3B, Annex vii.
144. R. Seton-Watson 1934, 354.

landed classes proportionately declined." [145] And if the great landowners lost much of their power, the peasant smallholders and their chosen "electors" became virtually defenseless against the political machine, which henceforth dutifully turned out sweeping majorities.

In Bulgaria, the establishment of constitutional government at first led to political *immobilisme* verging on anarchy. The democratic Tirnovo constitution of 1879 produced a liberal government, but the liberals were soon overthrown by a conservative coup orchestrated by Russian administrators and backed by the Orthodox Church. For a while, the constitution itself was suspended, but once new elections were held, the liberals found themselves back at the helm of government. Although elected with an overwhelming majority, their leader, Stefan Stambulov, left little to chance, proceeding to consolidate his party's rule by measures still harsher than those employed in the neighboring countries. Not content to establish a network of prefects with docile municipal councils under them, Stambulov set up a "political machine of hired thugs and rumor mongers to create an atmosphere of fear." [146] Under this regime, suffrage was nominally universal, but in reality only some 5 percent of the electorate went to the polls (although official documents reported the participation of as many as two-thirds of the electorate).[147] Worse still,

> the election machine was almost completely under government domination with local officials filling in spurious pro-government ballot slips, destroying opposition votes or physically excluding known opposition supporters. To do this the government secured control of the electoral bureau which was responsible for conducting the poll and which was to consist of the first voters to arrive at the polling point. If the government failed to do this then there were other more desperate measures; in Pleven in 1887 when anti-government activists established control over the electoral bureau the police promptly arrested them *en bloc*, whilst in other constituencies the authorities declared they could not guarantee order if the elections took place, in which case voting would be postponed giving the government faction time to ensure its victory.[148]

As elsewhere in East Central Europe, in Serbia, electoral fraud had been resorted to sporadically ever since the Hatisarif of 1838 introduced the concept of a legislative assembly.[149] But the first political machine was established by the "Defenders of the Constitution" (*ustavobranitelji*), led by Iliya Garašanin and Tomas Vučić, two Serbs from Hungary who served as ministers to the weak princes Milan I and Michael Obrenović. Garašanin was

145. Zeletin 1925, 77.
146. Stoianovich 1963, 322.
147. Ibid., 216.
148. Crampton 1983, 140–41. For Bulgarian elections, see also Stavrianos 1961, 437; Black 1945, 203; Jackson and Lampe 1982, 199.
149. See Stokes 1975, 158.

apparently deeply concerned with the material welfare of the people, but that concern was overshadowed by his obsession with the powers of the state, the foundations of which he was inclined to derive from higher principles rather than from the idea of popular sovereignty.[150] Both Vučić and Garašanin were consummate administrators who idolized the autocratic Francis I, ruler of Austria and Hungary in their youth. It was in his spirit that "they laid down the foundations of bureaucratic politics. They were the kinds of politicians and bureaucrats who did not believe in the political consciousness of the people and its ability to govern themselves. Rather, they themselves felt called upon to tutor the people without their approval and against their will."[151] The Defenders wanted law and order in administrative practices, as well as an "advanced and responsible state apparatus."[152] They wanted liberal economic policies and attention paid to education. They passed laws to accomplish these objectives, then set about to Serbianize the towns and the larger cities. It was also in order to accomplish these goals that they began to manage elections. Thus, as Vasa Čubrilović notes, while their social and economic thinking was progressive, their politics was bureaucratic and conservative.[153]

The methods of the Defenders were perfected by Jovan Ristić's liberal government (1876–80). Installed as prime minister by free elections, Ristić "gathered around himself those liberals who were willing to accept his bureaucratic way of operating,"[154] and, "confident that they understood the needs of the nation itself, they used the state bureaucracy to impose their policies, and to ensure that the Ristić government would remain in power."[155] Like the Defenders, Ristić was not a reactionary. As one of the foremost historians of the period states, "he understood that after the French revolution the people had to be represented in a legislature, and that in a modern state the legislature should confirm the actions of the government."[156] He also agreed with the general line of argument that "Serbia could be made politically modern,"[157] although his model for a modern state was neither England nor France, but Prussia. Consequently, his liberalism meant "control of the state on behalf of the people, not direct democracy."[158] In practice, this meant that instead of facing the electorate squarely, his machine resorted to the customary methods of intimidation and the falsifying of vot-

150. See Jovanović 1933, 329–31.
151. Čubrilović 1958, 145.
152. Ibid.
153. Ibid., 148.
154. Stokes 1975, 221.
155. Stokes 1990, 178.
156. Ibid., 115.
157. Ibid., 11.
158. Ibid., 90.

ing registers and results as well as, in one critical election, an order to soldiers on active duty to vote for the government's candidates.[159]

Corrupted Parliamentarism and the Legal State

By so manipulating the voting process and electoral results, the political machines of these countries eventually emerged as powerful, even pivotal, political actors in these regimes. But while clearly dominant at most times, they were far from being the omnipotent Leviathans that the communist states would become in the second half of the twentieth century, for they had to act within a complex web of restraints. On the surface, these restraints appeared to be "self-imposed." In reality, their roots were in the structure of external hegemony, that is, in a set of reciprocal expectations with which the rulers of these countries had to comply in order to maintain their international respectability and viability. It is this circumstance that explains why those in power had to put up with a pesky and intrusive press, and why, in worst-case scenarios, had secretly to hire thugs, rather than sending their policemen after their opponents. Again, these external restraints account for the fact that even after the most carefully managed elections, there remained a handful of opposition deputies who could scrutinize budgets, filibuster legislation, denounce the corruption of ministers, and agitate against the incumbent government both on or off the floor of parliament, and who could move around the cloak of parliamentary immunity, a mystical veil with which the authorities were loath to tamper.

The formal instrument through which these restraints operated was the judicial system. It would, of course, be vain to argue that these systems were perfect, or even equal in their judiciousness across the region. Nor could one make the case that poor illiterate peasants enjoyed the same protection from their institutions as members of the educated and propertied classes did. It is also hard to ignore the fact that at times of widespread rioting and civil disorder, the army and the rural gendarmerie often proceeded with brutal dispatch to restore what they saw as law and order. The volleys the Hungarian gendarmerie fired at striking agricultural workers and restless Slovak nationalists, King Milan's court-martials after the repression of the Timok uprising of 1883, and General Averescu's punitive expedition after the Romanian jacquerie of 1907 are to be remembered as part of the overall record of class relations in these societies. And yet the judicial system, with its trials by jury in the glare of publicity, provided protections that extended far beyond the domains of wealth and social privilege.

The evidence to this effect is overwhelming. In Romania, for instance,

159. Ibid., 120.

only about half of all criminal prosecutions ended in convictions during the first decade of the twentieth century. The figures were 44.9 percent for 1905, 51.9 percent for 1906, and 51.0 percent for 1907, the year of the great and bloody peasant uprising.[160] In Serbia, from 1881 to 1908, on average 41 percent of defendants were sentenced by the courts and 59 percent acquitted.[161] Roughly the same proportions apply to the experience of Hungary.[162] Perhaps still more revealing is the fact that the same, or an even higher, percentage of acquittals occurred in "political" cases—that is, in cases where defendants were charged with subversion, treason, and violence against authorities. In Serbia, the number of these cases is exceedingly small: of 10,000 cases tried in 1906, only 372 were committed "against the state."[163] In the other countries, if only for definitional and methodological reasons, the number is greater. But the percentages of acquittal were as high as—or higher than—those for common criminal cases, with punishments often being little more than symbolic. In Hungary, between 1898 and 1908, 719 persons were hauled into court on charges of national agitation. The average sentence meted out to those found guilty was two months.[164] During more or less the same period, 916 people were indicted for activities relating to strikes and "socialist agitation." On the average, these defendants drew sentences of 12 days.[165] Although far from complete, these statistics tend to corroborate impressions of judicial independence that one gains from other items of historical evidence. "In political cases," writes one observer of the turn of the century in Hungary, "conviction was difficult and rare."[166] Indeed, in two spectacular cases, those accused of attempting to assassinate the Romanian king (in 1871) and the Hungarian premier (in 1912) were acquitted by juries on the grounds that their motives had been patriotic and that they had committed their desperate acts in defense of a constitutional system.[167] While the charges were less grave, no less conspicuous was the trial of the Serbian Pera Todorović and his associates, hauled into court upon direct princely orders on charges of sedition in 1876. The defendants "used the occasion to denounce the bureaucracy and to put up a generally stirring defense against the prince in the name of the naked, hungry and oppressed people."[168] Other defendants refused to answer the questions of the investigating magistrate. Still, the trial vindicated the accused. "All thirty indictments for 'preparing a traitorous undertaking' were dis-

160. Romania, Direcţiune generală a stătisticei 1919, 322.
161. Sündhausen 1989, 572.
162. Hungary, *Annuaire statistique hongrois* 1910, 524.
163. Sündhausen 1989, 572.
164. Based on R. Seton-Watson 1908, 448–66.
165. Böhm 1923, 19.
166. Horváth 1961, 337.
167. R. Seton-Watson 1934, 328; Janos 1982, 104.
168. Stokes 1990, 102.

missed for lack of evidence, a good indication—the historian notes—of the relative fairness and independence of Serbian courts, even when the prince was vitally interested in convictions." [169]

Perhaps just as significantly, these webs of direct and indirect restraints on political authority operated effectively to maintain a wall of separation between the private and public spheres, another major contrast between this corrupted parliamentarianism and the communism of future years. This left a whole host of private organizations to act as *pouvoirs intermédiaires*, buffers between the individual and the state. The family and the churches thus remained on the whole free from bureaucratic intervention, as did numerous voluntary associations, ranging from agrarian cooperatives to trade unions and chambers of commerce, each protecting different economic interests. Still more conspicuous were the autonomies of the universities, which, following closely the tradition established in Western Europe, were not only free to shape curricula but enjoyed immunity from the investigative and police powers of the government. Under the protective cloak of this immunity, the universities became hotbeds of anti-government agitation by radicals of both Right and Left, whose members not only organized behind the walls of these institutions but also retreated there after physical confrontations with the government. Time and again, rebellious students would taunt the police, whose club-wielding members would then chase them to the gates—only to stop, as if by magic, at the physical boundaries of the premises. When, in the 1930s, the magic finally wore off, and police detectives crossed the invisible line of autonomy to apprehend communist or fascist students, their steps signaled the end of one era and the beginning of another, in which politics was no longer subject to institutional restraints.

Simulating Democratization

The organic process of political development, or decay, in East Central Europe was interrupted by World War I, and by the victory of the Allied powers, who then dictated the terms of the peace. As a result of the territorial provisions of the peace treaties, the Austro-Hungarian monarchy and the Ottoman Empire were to disappear from the map of Europe. In their places, there emerged a number of successor states. Yugoslavia and Czechoslovakia were carved out of the territories of Austria and Hungary respectively. Poland was restored to the status of an independent state, with boundaries that, although they did not extend to the historical boundaries of the Commonwealth, were generous enough to include large Ukrainian, Belorussian, and German minorities. Romania more than doubled its territory and nearly trebled its population by the annexation of Transylvania (and

169. Ibid., 102.

adjacent territories on the Hungarian plain) together with Bukovina from Austria and Bessarabia from Russia, all inhabited by a variety of ethnic groups. Bulgaria had to retreat behind boundaries established after the Second Balkan war and surrender southern Dobrudja (Dobrogea) to the Romanian state. Hungary, the principal loser in these new arrangements, lost two-thirds of its prewar territory and half of its prewar population, including Hungarians living on the territory of the new Yugoslav, Romanian, and Czechoslovak states.

The war buried the old Concert of the Powers under its debris. In its place came a new international regime shaped and institutionalized at Versailles by the victors, among them a non-European great power, the United States. While America was soon to distance itself from these arrangements, the operational principles and institutions were shaped by the political views of its president, Woodrow Wilson. Instead of congresses attended by great powers, the new security arrangements were to be collective and to include powers both great and small. This pluralism found institutional expression in the structure of the League of Nations, although the system of enforcing the regime would still fall to the victorious great powers, and, after the retreat of the United States (and in the absence of the Soviet Union), would remain notoriously weak. With Germany defeated, and with Italy sulking over the meager spoils of victory, much of the burden for upholding the security system was carried by Britain and France, bolstered by alliances with a number of the countries of East Central Europe who were believed to have profited sufficiently from the war.

Incongruous with these weaknesses, and still bearing the stamp of Wilsonian principles, the new international regime was far more activist than its predecessor had ever been. In contrast to the minimalist approach of the Concert and the informality of conditionality under its regime, through the formal provisions of the several peace treaties, the new hegemons set explicit standards for the domestic behavior of governments. For the first time in modern history, a number of European states were requested explicitly to recognize the existence and rights of ethnic and religious communities. Romania for one was obligated to grant citizenship to her Jewish inhabitants. All other of the small countries—but remarkably not Germany—were to grant civil and cultural rights to their national minorities. Less formally, but no less strongly (and still under Wilsonian influence), the victorious powers expressed their preference for popular governments and advised both former enemies and allies to extend the suffrage and to democratize their parliaments. One after the other, the countries of East Central Europe complied, and elections under a broader franchise were first held in the years 1919–21.

The clear expectation, shared widely among local democrats and the hegemonic powers, was that these reforms would spell the end of bureaucratic etatism. Such expectations were soon to be disappointed. For, while the governments of East Central Europe quickly adopted the new political principles of secrecy and universality, with the exception of Czechoslovakia they returned just as quickly to their previous practices of electoral rigging. Albania's first elections ever were held in 1923, but the results created a sharp Left-Right split, eventual civil war, the expulsion of liberal-minded Bishop Fan Noli, and the presidency of the Gheg chieftain Ahmed Zogu, who in 1928 proclaimed himself king and proceeded to rule with a mere rubber-stamp parliament.[170] In Hungary, a national assembly elected under universal suffrage and the secret ballot in January–March 1920 was dominated by a coalition of two new parties: the Smallholders and Christian Nationals. The effect of electoral reforms was nullified in 1922, however, when, after some parliamentary maneuvering, Premier István Bethlen introduced a more restrictive suffrage (with some 29 percent of the population eligible) together with a variable system of balloting: secret in 49 urban constituencies, but open in 199 rural ones.[171] These procedural reversals led the way to the full restoration of machine politics. In C. A. Macartney's words:

> For complete efficiency of working, the system was dependent on the close and frictionless cooperation between the [government] Party and the administration, which was not technically under direct Party control. It was controlled by the Minister President, who appointed the Főispáns [lord lieutenants] and certain other functionaries, and under him by the Minister of the Interior, who was the direct head of the administration, and in particular of the gendarmerie and the police. But it was the keystone of Bethlen's system that the Party Leader should also be the Minister President; and in any case there could be under normal conditions little danger of friction, for under Bethlen's system the word "party" should not be held to imply a rigid distinction between politics and administration: the Party was simply the legislative or parliamentary aspect of a machine whose other often more important functions were carried out elsewhere: in the Ministry or county office, on the magistrate's bench . . . and at the village notary's desk.[172]

In Romania, the secret ballot and universal suffrage were introduced in 1919, and the system of curial voting was replaced by a bicameral parliamentary system. These institutional arrangements remained untouched until 1938. But the electoral process was instantly compromised by administrative terror against candidates campaigning in opposition to the government party of the day, by the notorious 40–60 rule (which, after 1926, gave a 20 percent bonus to the largest party, and thus released the bureaucracy from the need to garner a majority of the votes for the governing party), and, finally—as a last recourse—by the routine stuffing of ballot boxes by

170. Rothschild 1974, 361–62.
171. For this electoral law, see Molnár 1971, 2: 381.
172. Macartney 1961, 1: 48.

TABLE 8

Composition of the Lower Chamber Romanian National Assembly, 1920–30

Party	1920	1922	1926	1927	1928	1930
Liberal	17	260	16	318	13	12
People's League	209	11	292	—	5	10
National Peasants	44	28	32	49	333	30
National Union (Iorga)	—	—	—	—	—	287
Others	99	70	37	20	37	50

SOURCE: Roberts 1952, 28, 95, 97, 103, 105, 131, 172; Rothschild 1974, 299, 305.

the local prefectorate and its employees. The effect of these methods is all too obvious from the composition of the lower chambers elected in quick succession after the war. Just as before, the opposition was invariably reduced to a few deputies, while electoral majorities shifted violently from one party to another as the political machine picked its winners and losers (see Table 8).

In Bulgaria, universal manhood suffrage had been the rule even before World War I. Although elections were now by secret ballot, they remained as corrupt as before. Both Left (1920–23) and Right (1923–34) employed methods of electoral intimidation by requiring that candidates collect large numbers of signatures nominating them. These "nominators" would then become obvious targets of economic and physical intimidation. When this failed to achieve the desired result, as in the notorious elections of 1927 and 1931, still cruder methods of intimidation and ballot box stuffing were resorted to. In Yugoslavia, likewise, suffrage had already been broad prior to the war, and now these standards were extended to former Austro-Hungarian territories. The result was parliamentary chaos, leading to the royal coup of 1929, followed by a reduction in the number of voters and by the restoration of the open ballot, much as had been the case in neighboring Hungary. But even beforehand, in the "democratic" 1920s, the administrative machine had performed its traditional tasks. Charles Beard and George Rodin describe these elections thus:

> The heads of the administrative machine in the several localities are appointees of the Minister of the Interior. They stand directly under his authority in many relations. They represent all the political functions of the government in their respective regions. They report to the Ministry on local events. Through them, the use of the police is directed from the center. Political meetings can be hampered and, if utterances too radical are made, they may be dissolved under the law against communists. If that is not sufficient, a more general statute for the defense of the state may be brought into play. In addition to interfering with meetings, the police can take a hand in inducing voters of the proper political color to come to the polling places and take part in the balloting. Ordinarily, from twenty to thirty percent of the electorate fails to exercise the right of franchise in elections,

and by a little judicious pressure, perhaps not going beyond friendly suggestion, the police can increase the number of active voters.[173]

Poland, restored to independent statehood after 123 years of imperial rule, had, like Hungary, a respectable tradition of feudal parliamentarism, together with an extensive record of progressive movements throughout the nineteenth century. This progressivism remained uncorrupted because, under foreign domination, its principles were never tried out in political practice. The reunited country elected a constituent assembly in 1919 under universal suffrage and the secret ballot, which was followed by several more elections and six years of chaotic politics, in which 36 parties vied with one another. It was this parliamentary system that Marshal Pilsudski's coup d'état overthrew in 1926. The marshal, a hero of Poland's reunification, could easily have dissolved this unwieldy legislature. But like many leaders of the immediate postwar years, he preferred to govern behind a façade of simulated parliamentarism, largely in order to curry favor with his major allies in the West. For this reason, he was content first to reduce the powers of parliament by constitutional amendment and then to take steps to establish control over the legislature by organizing a government party, officially called the Nonpartisan Bloc for Cooperation with the Government (BBWR). Once the BBWR was in place, Pilsudski proceeded, with the help of the administrative bureaucracy, by the familiar methods of pressure and fraud. He succeeded in gaining a plurality for his party in the elections of 1928 and then, by using uncommonly harsh measures of intimidation, in gaining control over the majority in parliament.[174] "At the apex of the regime," writes Joseph Rothschild, "a statist-managerial theory held sway. . . . Poland was to be purged, cleansed, modernized through state direction, not political competition. She was to be administered, rather than governed. Interest of the state, not of class or party, would alone determine the government's social and economic policies."[175] As elsewhere on the European periphery, this was not effective democracy, but democracy simulated.

BETWEEN CORE AND PERIPHERY

Cleavage and Conflict on the Semiperiphery

So far, we have focused on the countries of the eastern periphery, contrasting them mainly with the experiences of the European core. Between these two sectors, however, we have also recognized the existence of a third

173. Beard and Rodin 1929, 88–89.
174. Rothschild 1966, 217–78, 353–54. See also Rothschild 1974, 56–65.
175. Rothschild 1974, 60.

one, the semiperiphery, encompassing much of France and Germany, northern Italy, Switzerland, Austria, and Bohemia. As already noted, this sector
had profited from the diffusion of the agricultural innovations of the core
region prior to the critical half century of the British industrial revolution between 1780 and 1830—that is, before modern mass consumer tastes began
to form across the Continent. Consequently, the agrarian economy could
best be described as semideveloped. This term implies a higher degree of labor productivity than in the peripheral regions further to the south and the
east, but also lower productivity and capital intensity than in the core countries. At the same time, this "semidevelopment" also involved the prevalence of semicapitalist enterprise in agriculture—above all, the mixing of
wage labor with more traditional forms of labor exploitation (such as sharecropping). Given these mixed forms, most agrarian proprietors of the semiperiphery differed from traditional seigneurs or peasant cultivators. Yet they
were not an agrarian bourgeoisie either, retaining instead a separate socio-
economic identity perhaps best reflected by the rise and sustained existence
of self-labeled agrarian parties in the twentieth century.

This experience of the agricultural economy set the stage for a distinct
pattern of industrial development within which the role of the state was far
from negligible. But state intervention left sufficient room for private initiative, which, as Alexander Gerschenkron informs us,[176] had a strong finance
capitalist component. That is, much of the investment capital for infrastructure and heavy industry came from private savings channeled into the economy by a highly developed banking system. This institutional device was a
logical response to the needs of the semiperipheral economies, as well as to
the unique opportunities they afforded. On the one hand, these areas were
less developed than the core; this created pressures to "catch up," and hence
the need for larger concentrations of capital than the individual entrepreneur could provide. On the other hand, the semiperiphery possessed a more
developed agricultural sector than the peripheral regions, which made it
possible to rely on voluntary savings. The brothers Pèreire, who invented
the *crédit mobilier,* had to do so in an economic setting such as this one.
Their invention would have been superfluous in England, and meaningless
in, say, Bulgaria or Russia, where rates of personal savings were low and
where, as Gerschenkron tells us, business ethics were too weak to inspire
confidence on the part of institutional lenders.[177]

This pattern of development created its own peculiar contradictions,
class configurations, and cleavages. The autonomous development of the
agrarian sector, and the participation of private capital in the rise of the industrial economy, created a bourgeoisie and civil society much stronger and

176. Gerschenkron [1959] 1962, 12–13.
177. Ibid., 17–18.

more differentiated than those on the periphery of the Continent. Nowhere does this difference become more obvious than in some of the great social novels of the semiperiphery and the periphery, which reveal telling differences between the characters in Mann's *Buddenbrooks,* Balzac's *Lost Illusions,* or Stendhal's *The Red and the Black,* on the one hand, and the heroes of Chekhov's *Cherry Orchard,* Tolstoy's *Anna Karenina,* or Goncharov's *Oblomov,* on the other. If the first set of novels describes an ascendant bourgeois society, the second portrays bureaucrats, landowners, military officers, impoverished peasants, and scoundrel entrepreneurs. At the same time, the bourgeoisie and the civil societies of the semiperiphery were more ambivalent and weaker than their counterparts in Britain. In part, this was simply due to the competitive disadvantage these semideveloped economies faced in trying to carve out for themselves a slice of the global market dominated by Britain. But this weakness was further compounded by the fact that, unlike those of Britain, the propertied classes of the Continent were split—between agriculture and industry, between finance capital and family enterprise, as well as between the "ethnic" and the "native" entrepreneur —into groups that viewed each other with "mutual incomprehension" [178] that left public opinion and parliaments "too divided to parcel out the contested social product." [179] Consequently, while bureaucratic-military machines would never gain the same ascendancy as that attained in southern and eastern Europe, they were strong enough to insulate large areas of public affairs from the jurisdiction of parliaments.

This rough equilibrium between state and society, between political and economic classes, was institutionalized in different ways, reflecting the particular traditions and histories of individual countries. In republican France and under the constitutional monarchy of Italy, bureaucracies exercised their powers de facto, by moving into the political vacuum created by parliamentary *immobilisme.* Public finance, defense, and the administration of colonies were largely left to professional officers and civil servants, although no laws existed to that effect. In countries with strong monarchic traditions, the division between publics (represented in parliaments) and the bureaucratic-military structure of dynastic states was a matter of constitutional law. While the monarchies recognized parliaments with liberal suffrage and clean elections, they also reserved for themselves prerogatives with respect to defense and foreign affairs, including powers over the appointment of ministers and over the conduct of war.

By its very nature, however, this equilibrium between political and economic classes, between bureaucracies and publics, was tenuous, and it began to tilt in one direction or other in the second half of the nineteenth century,

178. Stearns 1978, 54.
179. Maier 1975, 353.

producing two different political outcomes. In their attempts to explain differing historical outcomes, historians as well as social scientists have usually turned to variations in the social structure or to the cultural makeup of individual countries. The presence and survival of traditional economic and social sectors appears to be a particularly appealing hypothesis.[180] Nonetheless, we may do better overall by approaching the problem within the context of state interaction with the international political environment, for much as in the case of the peripheral countries, variations in elite choices and political outcomes are closely linked to the power potential of a given society in the international system. On one end of the political spectrum, the elites of smaller semiperipheral countries were constrained in their choices by the rational assessment of their inability to change the international system to their own advantage. These experiences may well have persuaded the respective political classes that they should improve conditions in their countries, not by waging war, but by helping the rising bourgeoisie to adjust to the vagaries of global markets. Thus, over the years, public policy moved through successive stages of economic liberalism, neomercantilism, and finally welfare etatism.

This was not the case, however, in the major countries of the semiperiphery. In the larger and potentially more powerful entities, the political classes could reasonably entertain the strategic alternative of improving their position, not by adjusting to the rules of the market, but by adjusting those very rules by military and political means. However, the political classes of these societies could not have carried out this strategy on their own. In order to pursue it effectively, they needed allies, and in search of them, they turned to the struggling entrepreneurs of their countries, offering them both protection from socialist harassment and a heroic vision of a new continental order in which they, the bourgeoisie, would be able to compete successfully with rivals from the core countries. In times when the economy was good, the bourgeoisie tended to resist these blandishments, but in times of hardship, entrepreneurial support for parliamentarism eroded quickly, producing periodic "migrations of bourgeois republicans to the Right over economic and social issues."[181] As crises deepened, this "free-floating Right" tended to join hands with the political classes of the state to form a Bona-

180. It should be noted that the semiperiphery is primarily an economic concept, and that only a few of the continental governments presided over "pure" semiperipheral economies. The main culprit here was ethnic nationalism, the rise of which lumped together regions with different economic characters solely because their inhabitants spoke the same language. Thus the heartlands of both the German and the French economies were semiperipheral, but they coexisted uneasily with core-type economies in the northwest, and peripheral-type economies in the south and east of the two countries respectively. In Italy, a semiperipheral north faced an undeveloped peripheral south. In Czechoslovakia (after 1918), the more advanced, semiperipheral provinces were dominant but had to coexist with the backward economy of Slovakia.

181. Maier 1975, 353.

partist dictatorship under the leadership of a heroic figure who promised to raise, or to restore, the nation to its rightful place in the international system. Over time, the idiom would change, but the constituent elements of the coalition would remain the same. Bonaparte and Hitler, Boulanger and Mussolini (or Pétain), appealed to the same social instincts, although their rhetoric and ideological formulae reflected some fundamental differences between the milieux of the nineteenth and twentieth centuries.

In retrospect, these Bonapartist experiments seem to have been costly exercises in futility. Above all, the maintenance of large civilian and military bureaucracies required the diversion of resources from productive investment into partly unproductive state consumption. Meanwhile, the smaller countries not only prospered, but also developed democratic institutions cast in the British mold. In the long run, to be sure, even the larger countries attained political democracy and economic prosperity, but only after external forces had reduced them to the status of small powers in the international system. This was the experience of Germany, Italy, and Japan after World War II, and of France after the wars in Indochina and Algeria. Ironically, the path of these countries from the semiperiphery to the core was paved, not by military victory, but by defeat and the overall reconstitution of the international political system.

Democracy and Bureaucracy:
The Politics of Czechoslovakia

Within the geopolitical and geohistorical area designated here as East Central Europe, only Czechoslovakia, or, more accurately, Bohemia-Moravia (the "Czech lands"), qualifies as semiperipheral in contrast to the peripherality of the rest of the eastern half of the continent, largely owing to the proximity of the Czech lands to the innovative societies of the core. As a result, their agricultural economies developed early, having profited from the spontaneous and market-driven diffusion of new technologies from the northwest to the southeast long before the British industrial revolution generated its backwash effect on the continental economies. Consequently, the Czech economy was producing a surplus as early as the eighteenth century, and by the end of the nineteenth century—at 17–23 metric quintals (30–40 ctws) of grain per hectare—reached a level of productivity far above the levels attained by Poland, Hungary, and countries further to the south and east, although below those attained in the northwest.[182] In both productivity and structure, Czech agriculture closely mirrored Brandenburg Prussia, where sharecropping arrangements were dominant throughout the nineteenth century and where more than one quarter of the land was owned by

182. League of Nations 1945, 86.

larger estates (over 200 hectares in size).[183] In both countries significant productivity gains were attained by economies almost evenly divided between small farms and larger estates. In East Elbian Germany (1910), 40.5 percent of land was held in parcels in excess of 100 hectares; in Czechoslovakia (1918), 28.5 percent of arable land was the property of estates over 200 hectares, or 500 acres.[184] And while, as in East Elbia, larger estates took the lead in technological innovation in the eighteenth century, by the mid nineteenth century, there was little difference between the productivity of bigger and smaller farms. Accordingly, the Czechoslovakian land reform law of 1923, largely motivated by the desire to break the power of former imperial landowners (Austrians and Hungarians), created little disruption, and did not bring about a fall in volume or productivity as occurred in Romania. At any rate, levels of agricultural productivity were robust enough both before and after World War I to permit respectable rates of domestic saving that, together with foreign (largely Viennese and German) capital, could be mobilized by the banking system for purposes of infrastructural and industrial development. While the development of machine and heavy metal industries benefited greatly from the policies of the Habsburg imperial state, other branches of industry, among them textiles, chemicals, and food-processing, arose by private initiative, with banks such as the Viennese Creditanstalt and the Czech Zemská or Živnostenská playing a significant role in their development.[185] Whatever the precise ratio between bank and nonbank capital, the system was sufficiently successful by 1910 to reduce the share of the population dependent on agriculture to 32.1 percent in the Bohemian provinces of the Austro-Hungarian Monarchy.[186] As we shall see below (in Chapter 4), in the interwar years, these figures were to decline yet further, to 26.6 percent for Bohemia-Moravia and 36.6 percent for Czechoslovakia as a whole.[187] Although World War I affected the economy of the country adversely, the low proportion of the economically active population employed in agriculture, combined with the relatively high efficiency of labor in both industrial and agricultural sectors, produced relatively high incomes per capita, at least by the standards of the times. According to Colin Clark, Czech per capita income in the years 1925–34, adjusted to purchasing power parities, was $545 in U.S. prices, or 84.5 percent of the figure for Germany.[188] Still other sources put the Czech (as opposed to Czechoslovak)

183. Milward and Saul 1977, 57.
184. Ibid., 57; Garver 1978, 19.
185. Milward and Saul 1977, 17, 25, 31; Hermann 1975, 90–91; Monroe 1910, 364.
186. Milward and Saul 1977, 20.
187. Mitrany 1945, 26; the figure for Bohemia-Moravia has been extrapolated from the Czechoslovak aggregate on the basis of Mamatey 1973, 210.
188. Clark 1940, 86. The Czech figure has been extrapolated from the data given for Czechoslovakia by Clark (ibid.). Another source, using the same method and expressing pro-

standard of living just 20 percent below Germany's, or at a level some 40–50 percent above the figures for neighboring Hungary, 138 percent above the figure for Romania, and 181 percent above the figures for the Balkan countries.[189]

These developmental experiences went hand in hand with a pattern of social mobility that can perhaps best be described as a two-track system. Much as in the rest of Eastern Europe, one of these tracks led upward via education and entry into the large and powerful imperial army and bureaucracy, which were receptive to candidates from the Czech lands. But a second track led through participation and investment in the economy, which, in the nineteenth century, was responsible for the rise of a class of native entrepreneurs that rapidly replaced the traditional German bourgeoisie and preempted the rise of immigrant entrepreneurship. Thus, notwithstanding Jewish immigration from the Austro-Polish provinces from 1780 onward, the percentage of Jews in the overall population was less than 1 percent in Germany and 1.07 percent in Bohemia.[190] Moreover, in about 1890, even this small percentage began to decline, and while the immigrants' second and third generations made their own thrusts into the *Bildungsbürgertum* of both Bohemia and Germany in the national economies proper, they occupied a far narrower niche than in neighboring Romania, Hungary, or Poland. That niche was marked by a heavier concentration in trade, relative insignificance in industry, and virtual absence from the management of the agrarian economy.[191]

Much as elsewhere in semiperipheral Europe, in the Czech lands, the economic classes were divided not merely between agriculture and industry, but also between the larger "native" and the smaller "foreign" element, between white-collar employees and the ever-increasing number of professionals, and between small, family-operated and large, bank-financed enterprises in the manufacturing sector. As in Germany and France, and perhaps to a much larger extent than in Britain, these middle classes faced a strong socialist movement that split after 1920 between moderate and radical factions, with the latter eventually joining the Third International. All this was well reflected in the "hexagonal" pattern of the party system, in which

---

ductivity in 1960 dollar prices, puts the ratio between German and Czechoslovak per capita income at 100:76.1 ($770 vs. $586), from which we can extrapolate the figure of $663.74 for the Czech lands, representing 86.2 percent of German per capita income. See Paul Bairoch 1976, 297.

189. Mitrany 1945, 100.

190. This small percentage, however, applies only to the Czech provinces. The figures were much higher in peripheral Slovakia (4.1 percent), and higher still in the underdeveloped backwater of the Ruthenian counties (14.1 percent), annexed from Hungary in 1918–20. Mendelsohn 1983, 142.

191. See Don 1990, 121–54.

the Agrarians and National Democrats represented agriculture and big industry respectively, a People's Party and a democratic-progressive party, National Socialist in name only, represented the divided middle classes, and the Social Democratic and Communist parties—organizational expressions of the divided socialist movement—represented the industrial workers and various discontented groups among the lower classes. As in Germany and in France, this "hexagonal" pattern of party politics was further complicated by a "free-floating right," hidden throughout the 1920s among the voters of conservative and centrist persuasion, but which surfaced in the turbulent 1930s in the form of two small fascist-type parties. These parties garnered 7.6 percent of the vote in 1935, but did not have a major impact on politics.[192] The political spectrum was in any case further complicated by the prevalence of Slovak and Ruthene autonomists, as well as of German and Hungarian separatist parties (in the Sudetenland and the eastern provinces respectively).

These political cleavages largely circumscribed the relationship between the public and the powerful apparatus of the state, built by the Habsburgs and passed on to the new Czechoslovakia. Historically, under the Habsburgs, this state apparatus, consisting of a civilian bureaucracy and the army, had enjoyed a privileged position, which continued even after the introduction of suffrage and the institutions of modern parliamentarianism. In the Austrian half of the dual monarchy, parliamentarism was not subject to the same debasement by electoral manipulation as in the societies further to the south and the east, but the position and privileges of the bureaucracy and the army, and their potential freedom from parliamentary review, were written into imperial constitutional documents that explicitly exempted defense, foreign, and certain common affairs from effective control by elected bodies. To be sure, the Czechoslovakian democratic constitution of the post–World War I era did away with these prerogatives and subordinated the executive branch to the authority of parliament. But such subordination was imperfect at best, and the bureaucracy and army gradually reasserted their autonomy. The army was elevated above public debate by tradition and consensus, and the creeping emancipation of the bureaucracy from parliamentary review was fostered by recurrent parliamentary deadlock among the five major coalition partners—the *petka*—that time and again resulted in the formation of caretaker governments by "politically neutral" technocrats and financial experts.

This process of creeping emancipation was accelerated and formalized by a number of legislative acts during the lifetime of the republic. The Czech political elite, once fierce defenders of local autonomies under the Habsburgs, quickly changed their minds once in command of their own country. The

192. Rothschild 1974, 126.

Administrative Law of 1920 divided the republic into 21 districts, interposed between the center and the local organs of administration, with district chiefs and their staffs directly responsible to the Ministry of the Interior in Prague.[193] This was only a prelude to another Administrative Law, that of 1927, which was passed over the objections of progressives and socialists in parliament. The latter law vastly enhanced the de facto power of the bureaucracy by abolishing the old county system and replacing it with a small number of provinces, to be presided over by appointed career prefects, with their self-government diluted by the appointment of one-third of their members.[194] On the political side, the powers of the state apparatus were enhanced by a number of laws that increased the powers of administrative organs and diminished the legal rights of the citizenry. The first of these was the Law on the Protection of the Republic. Passed in 1923, and modeled after a German law of the same year,[195] the law banned a whole series of acts "committed or intended" against the state, and gave administrative authorities broad powers to investigate and bring charges against communists, fascists, national minorities, and autonomist Slovaks and Ruthenians. These protections of the state were further augmented by the Law on the Security of the Republic, passed in the summer of 1933, authorizing police and administrative officials to suspend newspapers and to initiate the suppression of subversive political parties.[196] While the objectives and results of these laws were obvious to the casual observer, they were made explicit in the 1930s during the tenure of the blunt-speaking premier Jan Malypetr, who prided himself on presiding over a "government of the strong hand." Malypetr believed that the executive and the bureaucracy were the best guarantors of democracy and wanted to "insulate the executive from any influence coming from the political Right or Left."[197] With some justification, his critics described the regime as an "authoritarian democracy."[198]

Taking advantage of coalition deadlocks, parliamentary inertia, and the stipulations of these laws, the Czech-dominated state apparatus carved out large domains of policy functions for itself. As under the Third and Fourth French Republics, the army was elevated above politics, or, more specifically, above public criticism and debate.[199] Something similar happened to the Ministry of Finance. Creating a new tax system and balancing the budget had been painful tasks in all of the new states of East Central Europe. Czechoslovakia was no exception, and the leaders of the parliamentary par-

193. Slapnicka 1975, 134.
194. Mamatey 1973, 134.
195. Ibid., 113.
196. Slapnicka 1975, 141; Mamatey 1973, 148.
197. Slapnicka 1975, 141.
198. Ibid., 139.
199. Kostrba-Skalicky 1979, 518.

ties of the immediate postindependence period were all too happy to leave these unpopular tasks to a group of technocrats. One of them, the energetic and brilliant Alois Rašin, quickly made his department the locus of budgeting, of managing the currency, and of planning for economic development. As to taxation, the relatively efficient Austrian and Hungarian systems were streamlined by Rašin's subordinates. Beyond fiscal management, Rašin's technocrats had ambitious plans to turn Czechoslovakia into an export economy, following a policy of laissez faire modified by some regulatory features of the wartime German economy, sardonically nicknamed *Kriegssozialismus*.[200] As to fiscal policy, Rašin "abhorred inflation"[201] and was determined to maintain the value of the koruna by austerity measures that the parliament was loath to take. In the process, he became a lightning rod for adverse popular sentiment and was assassinated by an irate citizen, dying "for the strength of the koruna and its exchange rate on the international market."[202] In accepting the blame for hardships, he may have saved both the koruna and Czech democracy, while his sacrifice made him a hero figure for the Czech bureaucracy. While apparently contrary to the logic of an export-oriented economic policy, the stabilization of the currency turned out to be a spectacular success, for it prompted a flow of funds into Czechoslovak banks from the inflationary economies of neighboring countries. That flow in turn provided capital resources for recovery and for the rise of the country to the positions of both leading exporter and most rapidly growing industrial sector on the continent in the 1920s.[203] In the face of this success, few parliamentarians had the desire or courage to make economic decisions. Much like the Japanese MITI a generation later, the Czechoslovak Ministry of Finance acquired a great deal of autonomy, which it retained in the less auspicious 1930s while supervising a contracting and floundering economy.

Perhaps still more significant, and politically more fateful, was the role played by the Czech bureaucracy in "civilizing" Slovakia and in integrating it into the highly centralized Czechoslovak state. After being annexed from Hungary, the province and its Slovak population were in a parlous condition. It had been a long-standing aim of Hungarian policy to extinguish Slovak national consciousness by capturing and assimilating the upwardly mobile strata of the population. Under Hungarian governments, the Slovak educational system was allowed to atrophy and young Slovaks were encouraged to attend Hungarian gymnasia and universities. Having done so, they were offered the opportunities that the Hungarian economy and state could afford. Many of them became members of the Hungarian intellectual

---

200. Mamatey 1973, 110. See also Pryor 1973, 188–210.
201. Mamatey 1973, 110.
202. Ibid.
203. In 1929, 33 percent of Czechoslovak industrial products were exported (Mamatey 1973, 142).

elite and political class after changing their names and eradicating all traces of their ethnic origins and markings. Thus, when the Czech occupying army entered the formerly Hungarian territories, they found only 1,946 Slovak nationals with high school (gymnasium) diplomas or university degrees, out of a total population of some 2.9 million.[204] Among these were 150 lawyers, one judge, and 164 officials with administrative experience.[205] Hungarians, representing less than one-third of the active labor force in the region, occupied two-thirds of positions in transportation and three-quarters of professional, managerial, and public service jobs.[206] Except for agricultural smallholdings, the economy was largely in Hungarian and German hands, and Slovakia (then including the Ruthenian region of the Carpatho-Ukraine, or Subcarpathian Rus) was substantially less developed than the Czech lands. While these eastern regions had 28 percent of the population of the Czechoslovak state, they had only an 18 percent share of the gross national product of the new economy,[207] with per capita income varyingly estimated between 42 and 66 percent of the figure for the Czech lands.[208] Moreover, having supplied only 17 percent of prewar Hungary's industrial production, Slovak industry was weak and represented only 10 percent of the industrial production of the new Czechoslovak state.[209] Created largely for political reasons with subsidies from the prewar Hungarian state, this small industrial sector was in a poor position to compete with either Czech industry or with other European economies.

The Czechoslovak bureaucracy moved to rectify these conditions with commendable, if overly paternalistic, zeal. Once again, the bureaucracy entered a domain that parliament was too skittish to handle. Consequently, the newly formed Ministry for Slovak Affairs was closely integrated with the other branches of the centralized system of administration, run almost exclusively by Czechs. The portfolio was treated as a purely bureaucratic, nonpolitical post.[210] As one of its first acts, this agency took upon itself the task of banning the sale of alcoholic beverages in Slovakia, a blow to Slovak spirits, especially in view of the fact that no similar measure was in effect in the Czech lands.[211] On the more practical side, the ministry, together with the Ministry of Education, moved rapidly and efficiently to create a system of Slovak gymnasia and institutes of higher learning. The results were impressive. A mere three years after the creation of the new Czechoslovak

204. O. Johnson 1985, 31.
205. Lipscher 1975, 151–52.
206. Leff 1988, 14.
207. Pryor 1973, 210.
208. For the low estimate, Capek and Sazama 1993, 212. For the high estimate, Pryor 1973, 210.
209. Pryor 1973, 210.
210. Mamatey 1973, 134.
211. George J. Svoboda, personal information to author, October 1995.

state, there were already 13,157 students enrolled in Slovak gymnasia, and the number would increase to 18,051 in 1929 and 27,692 in 1938.[212] During the same period, the Slovak universities produced over 10,000 graduates, and approximately the same number completed their studies in the more advanced Czech lands.[213] There were 1,379 lawyers and 554 candidates in training for the bar in Slovakia in 1935.[214] Unquestionably, then, an educated class of Slovaks had emerged by the end of the interwar period.

The problem that this intelligentsia faced, however, was the familiar one encountered all over the peripheral regions of East Central Europe: economic development did not keep pace with the development of the system of education. There was, as noted, a careful design for development, and one that was highly successful at least during the first decade of the republic. But this design reflected technocratic-managerial principles of rationality, aimed at maximizing the national product with little regard to political exigencies. And whether so intended or not, these policies favored the Czech lands over the eastern provinces. Hard budgeting and deflationary policies were hardest on Slovakia, where cash savings were small and where the credit crunch hurt the chances of recovery in the immediate postwar years. The industrial tariff, designed to enhance the competitiveness of Czech industries abroad, turned out to be disastrous for the weak, previously subsidized industries of Slovakia. Indeed, during the decade of greatest economic expansion, the 1920s, Slovakia underwent a process of "deindustrialization."[215] To be sure, Slovak peasants profited from the Land Reform Law of 1919, which distributed the large estates, previously held almost exclusively by members of the Hungarian nobility. Also, in 1925, at the behest of the Agrarian Party in parliament, a move was made to protect the interest of producers in the eastern provinces by the introduction of an agrarian tariff, which was eventually raised to new levels in 1929.[216] However, ironically, the principal beneficiaries of these tariff policies were not ethnic Slovaks but Hungarians. For even after the reforms, the latter owned most of the land producing cereals, sugar beets, and tobacco, and subsequently showed their gratitude by voting in disproportionate numbers for the Czech Agrarians. Altogether, while the Slovak economy experienced some structural changes—in the 1920s, the number of those employed in agriculture declined from 60.9 to 57.6 percent, and those employed in industry increased from 13.9 to 18.9 percent[217]—the ratio between Czech and Slovak incomes remained stagnant. And this occurred despite the flow of some

212. O. Johnson 1985, 128.
213. Ibid.
214. Czechoslovakia, *Manuel statistique* 1938, 270.
215. Mamatey 1973, 114–15.
216. Kosta 1975, 20.
217. O. Johnson 1985, 77.

1.6 billion koruny from the Czech lands to the eastern provinces over a period of fifteen years. "Slovakia was a losing proposition [*na Slovensko se dopláci*]," Malypetr said laconically in 1934.[218]

As had so often happened before in the less-developed countries of East Central Europe, adverse economic conditions encouraged the rising intelligentsia to seek refuge in the apparatus of the state. This was the case in Slovakia as well. Those graduating from the institutions of higher education expected to find employment in the administration of the state—above all, in the administration of their own provinces. Their problem was that the doors of the bureaucracy and the army remained largely closed to their numbers. The causes of this remain murky. While many Czech observers point to the rigorous meritocratic standards maintained by the Czech bureaucracy and to the competitive disadvantages of Slovak candidates—43 percent of educated Slovaks came from peasant stock, as opposed to the largely professional, middle-class pool of Czech applicants[219]—others, more sympathetic to the Slovak cause, point to conscious or subconscious discrimination against Slovaks, who were generally deemed childlike and reckless by their Czech brethren.[220]

In any case, the Czech-dominated apparatus of the state showed little willingness to open itself, or to bend its own rules, for the sake of political expediency. And if ever there was such a willingness, it rapidly declined after 1930 when, during the Great Depression, the state apparatus rationalized itself by transferring superfluous bureaucratic personnel from the western to the eastern parts of the country.[221] The figures speak for themselves. In the central ministries, in 1938, only 1.6 percent of the personnel of the executive class was Slovak; in the Ministry for Slovakia (later Ministry for Unification), the Slovak proportion was 11.8 percent.[222] As to the army, after 20 years of the republic, in 1938, only 422 of 11,820 career officers (3.6 percent) were Slovak, with only one Slovak among the 139 general officers.[223] The ratio was just as unfavorable among career noncommissioned officers, with only 421 (5.0 percent) out of 8,333 hailing from the eastern regions. In the reserve, we find 830 Slovak subaltern officers among a total of 20,800 (4 percent).[224] In politics, Slovaks were recipients of only 17 out of 322 ministerial appointments over the history of the republic, and behind this façade of ministerial turnover among "perpetual ministers," there was a still starker reality, for 94 percent of the "Slovak posts" were held by a mere three people,

218. Mamatey 1973, 151.
219. O. Johnson 1985, 192.
220. Přihoda 1995, 128–38, esp. 132–33.
221. Suda 1995, 106–27, esp. 114.
222. Leff 1988, 193.
223. Kostrba-Skalicky 1975, 520.
224. Wolchik 1991, 189.

Milan Hodža, Ivan Dérer, and Vavro Šrobár.[225] These numbers, and the protectiveness of the Czech political class, produced social conflict. Rejected by the Czechoslovak bureaucracy and army, the educated Slovaks became a free-floating intelligentsia that, together with a number of uneducated hangers-on, became a radical political counterclass in pursuit of their own state. While the idea of Slovak autonomy had long been harbored by the Slovak Catholic People's (later National Union) Party, from 1930 onward the young members of the Forward Group (Nastupišti) turned to more grandiose schemes. Their leaders—Karol Sidor, Ferdinand Ďurčanský, and Jozef Tiso—would eventually be the leaders of the Slovak fascist state. In time they, too, would be overtaken by still more radical politicians who were ready to break with the idea of the nation-state and to seek their own, and their nation's, fortunes within a German-led "new order" on the European continent.

CULTURE AND THE POLITICS OF DIVERSITY

A good way to take stock of political developments in the age of liberalism is to contrast the politics of the period with the politics of traditionalism in the Middle Ages. The political institutions and practices of that earlier period were, to invoke Johan Huizinga again, deeply permeated with religious thinking, which was omnipresent and stimulated by the precariousness of the human condition. The proximity of the living to the dead made the afterlife a public as well as a private concern, a focus of both institutionalizing political authority and the state-society relationship.

In contrast, people of the modern period—that is, after the sixteenth and seventeenth centuries—turned increasingly to the material world in search of an anchor for their social existence. The causes of this shift have been discussed extensively in the literature on the rationalization and secularization of authority. While they are complex, they had something to do with man's growing ability to know and conquer the forces of nature, which originated in the few innovative societies at the center of the world economy and was diffused from there to the rest of the world. That politics thereafter followed economics, rather than religion, can be demonstrated clearly by examining the structure of authority across the European continent. There, in the second half of the nineteenth century, the already-existing economic gradient turned into a political gradient as well. Moving from west to east, civil societies got weaker and states stronger. In Marx's pungent formulation, the further east one goes on the Continent, the more cowardly the bourgeoisie and the more savage and arbitrary the apparatus of the state.

225. Leff 1988, 192–93.

As in economics, the top end of the gradient began in England (along with Holland and Belgium), where the public exercised effective control over political elites, and where civil societies were dominant over state machines through parliamentary institutions. From there on, the gradient gently descends through France, Germany, Italy, Austria, and the Czech lands (of Bohemia-Moravia), where parliaments coexisted with bureaucracies, and where states and civil societies existed as co-equal and autonomous entities. At this point, the gradient becomes steeper, with the balance of power tilting more and more obviously away from the public to the elite, and from civil society to the state. These variations in the balance of power can be demonstrated historically by examining the ratio between opposition and government on the benches of parliament—that is, between freely elected representatives of the public and deputies elected under the auspices of the state machine. Such an examination reveals some variation over time, and significant variation over space as we move from Hungary to Romania and Bulgaria. In Hungary, the ratio between opposition and government deputies (1875–1939) in the House of Representatives was 39:61; in the Romanian Lower House (1895–1937), it was 17:83; in the Bulgarian Assembly (1882–1910), it was 11:89.[226] Finally, at the bottom of the slope, there was Russia, where no parliament existed before 1905. Indeed, when the Duma was finally called into being by the Constitution of 1905, its powers were so severely circumscribed that it could do little more than express adverse opinions about policies initiated by the executive.

Although economics now emerged as the controlling variable of politics, religious doctrine did not disappear, but continued to exert influence on political institutions and behavior, now functioning as a building block of political culture. Tradition, as Joseph Schumpeter and Reinhard Bendix have both observed,[227] remained a significant force. It not only provided values and meanings to political institutions imported from the West but also, to use the metaphor of Marianne Weber, acted as a "railroad switchman," designating the tracks upon which the train of politics would move forward behind the locomotive of material interest.[228] Depending on its contents, culture either reinforced the prevailing liberal trend or helped to derail it by pitting the material interests of the ruling classes in liberal arrangements against the "habits of the heart" that had developed throughout the centuries. To put it differently, while the degree of authoritarianism across the Continent was a function of the level of economic development, the quality of this authoritarianism—its scope, style, and effectiveness—continued to reflect qualities of culture that had their roots in religion and history.

226. Elite Project (see Introduction, nn. 1, 2); Crampton 1983.
227. Schumpeter 1942, 9; Bendix 1967, 292–346.
228. Marianne Weber 1950, 379–80.

In the countries of Western Christianity—Czechoslovakia, Hungary, Poland, and the South Slav provinces of Catholic heritage—the transformation
from the feudal to the modern state took place in the cultural matrix of legal-
rationality. Diets there had existed in one form or another since the thirteenth century: bargaining and "horse-trading" in politics were regarded as
acceptable behavior in conflicts between kings and nobility, the latter often
masquerading as the *populus*. Here, suffrage did not have to be introduced.
It had existed in some limited form since the Middle Ages and hence only
had to be extended. Still more significantly, the idea of the legal state, with its
spirit of impersonal rationality, was well established. In Bohemia-Moravia,
Hungary, Poland, and Croatia, procedure was respected, if not sacrosanct.
Litigation and "lawyering" (in Hungarian, *jogászkodás*) were virtual pas-
times for the Polish and Hungarian gentry. In Hungary, the feudal lords'
benches (*úriszék*) were in fact juries drawn from the county nobility. "Modernizing" the legal system represented quantitative rather than qualitative
change. It simply meant that, after 1848, jurors were also to be empaneled
from the non-noble, although propertied, classes of the population.

These cultural continuities were, in the first place, reflected in the nature
of political discourse in the northeastern sector of East Central Europe. In
all these countries, the political spectrum was divided among liberals, radicals, and conservatives. The structure of authority was shaped by economic
conditions: in the Czech lands, it was democracy; in Poland and Hungary,
bureaucracy. Whether in the arts or in politics, radicals were critics of the
existing order who demanded not less but more modernity and a closer imitation of Western models. In the arts, there was a division between romanti-
cism and realism. The dilemma of the romantics, however, was not whether,
but how, national identity could be integrated with the larger civilization of
the West. In politics, nineteenth-century radicalism in the northwest meant
radicalism of the Left, demanding not less but more liberalism, democracy,
and liberty. At the same time, the conservatism of big agrarians, while nos-
talgic about the past, and while harping a great deal on the principles of hierarchy and social discipline—code words for a labor-repressive extractive
economy—also found good words for the whiggish concepts of liberty, legalism, and parliamentarianism. This is true not only of the Czech Agrarians, who, in time, evolved into a highly pragmatic, market-oriented party,
but also for Polish and Hungarian conservatives. Thus the Polish aristocracy, while "fearful of the Left's espousal of land reform, [was] also alienated by the Right's raucous chauvinism" and cultivated "an ideology that
was conservative but not Rightist in the integral nationalist sense."[229] The
Hungarian aristocracy, while opposed to the nationalism of the gentry and
its espousal of the modern state, was first to protest the suspension of the

229. Rothschild 1974, 33.

Hungarian constitution and, after its restoration in 1867, its perversion by the bureaucratic political machine. Reactionary to the core in economic matters, Hungarian aristocrats founded the Puros movement to protest the corruption of the electoral process in 1895,[230] and in the interwar period, they turned out to be the last defenders of the constitution against the anti-parliamentary onslaught of the Right.

This convergence between self-interest and the norms of culture may well explain the self-assurance of the political classes, which in turn goes a long way toward explaining both the success of the Czech democratic experiment and the relatively smooth functioning of the liberal political machine in Hungary, where the Government Party set up by Kálmán Tisza survived under a succession of premiers, shaken only briefly by political crisis in 1905–6. In 1918, to be sure, the Hungarian regime collapsed along with the larger monarchy. But by 1922, the old machine was back in place, and although the country experienced a changing of the guard in 1931, the structure of the old order remained intact until the Arrow Cross coup of October 1944. In Poland, another country in the Western cultural sphere, the neoliberal experiment was short-lived and therefore does not lend itself too well to comparison. But overall, in the judgment of history, the Pilsudski regime was efficient and effective, capable of exercising its authority without becoming mired in petty graft or public disorder.

These models of politics stand in stark contrast to the experiences of the countries of the southeast, where political culture had been shaped by the religious tenets of Orthodoxy. Here the historical change from imperial traditionalism to modern liberalism and parliamentarianism was abrupt. The idiom of liberalism was not a bridge that connected tradition and modernity but a wall of separation that needed to be scaled. The political class, to be sure, embraced the liberal agenda because it served its economic interest. But this agenda clashed with deeply rooted "habits of the heart," creating cognitive dissonance and ambivalence. As the Romanian statesman Petre P. Carp noted, when his countrymen embraced the liberal state with its spirit of legalistic impersonality, they "had to break with their own past,"[231] becoming men who, in the sardonic words of Constantin Dobrogeanu-Gherea, wore top hats and frock coats while sporting the traditional sandals of the peasant on their feet.[232] In the Balkans, raised in the spirit of familialism (*kumstvo*) and kinship (*probratinstvo*), the "liberal intelligentsia [had to] wrestle with the dilemma of ideology vs. culture."[233] It was in this spirit that the young Serbian philosopher Svetozar Marković could both extol democracy and equality and, in much the same breath, like the Russian Slavo-

230. Gratz 1934, 1: 211.
231. Quoted in Zeletin 1925, 222–23.
232. Dobrogeanu-Gherea 1910, 373.
233. Čubrilović 1958, 200.

philes, also celebrate his country's backwardness and urge his countrymen to build socialism on the existing communal institutions of the village (*op-ština*) and the extended family.[234] Under these cultural pressures, "Serbian liberals distorted the constitution not just to accommodate the state but the patriarchalism of the Serbian tradition as well."[235] In Bulgaria, likewise, it was through the institutions of the village community and the Church that the intelligentsia had "developed the political habits which in a large degree characterized the public administration of their country after liberation."[236] The Bulgarian poet-patriot Kristo Botev professed to be genuinely committed to the ideas of democracy and liberalism, but he also looked back in time to the "golden age" of village communes and feared "uninvited guests" from the materialist West.[237] Much in the same vein, the intelligentsia of Romania was tormented by fears that by embracing liberalism, Romanians might commit a "sinful deviation from higher norms,"[238] and "betray their own national self."[239] Indeed, as Zeletin notes in his social history of the liberal period, even more so than in the Balkans, the creative intelligentsia of Romania was, almost to a man, opposed to the principles of liberalism and dedicated to articulating the values of a tradition of communalism and patriarchalism.[240] As early as 1864, Romania's cultural elite gathered in the Junimea of Iaşi, a literary circle that eventually became a magnet for conservatives of all stripes, including a number of big landowners. They shared a desire for material progress, tempered by concerns about retaining the paternalistic value system and structure of traditional society. It was from this alliance between the cultural and the landed elite that Romania's Conservative Party emerged, "traditionalist" like Hungary's and Poland's, but representing a tradition of a different kind.

As one would expect, the ambivalence and cognitive dissonance of the political classes of the southeast diminished their ability to act as a cohesive force vis-à-vis other classes and institutions, including the monarchy. At first, to be sure, the political machines seemed to have the upper hand over both society and king. In Romania, Bulgaria, and Serbia, the political machines under the command of prime ministers removed weak princes and replaced them with others. In Romania, a native prince was thrown out in favor of a foreigner; in Bulgaria, one foreign prince was exchanged for another; in Serbia, a native prince was expelled and another put on the throne in his stead. But as weak monarchies met weak political classes, the

234. Tomasevich 1975, 251. For a more extensive treatment, see McClellan 1965.
235. Stokes 1990, 181.
236. Black 1943, 48.
237. Crampton 1987, 329.
238. Zeletin 1927, 132.
239. Zeletin 1925, 222.
240. Zeletin 1927, 132.

political systems quickly deteriorated into what S. P. Huntington has labeled "praetorianism":[241] a political condition in which the stability of expectations is low, conflict among elite groups rampant, and resolution of conflicts is likely to come through violence. Indeed, as we examine the modern political history of Serbia and Bulgaria, and Romania after 1918, we are hard pressed to identify a clear-cut and predictable pattern of politics. The best we can do is to identify a cyclical pattern of change from royal to ministerial (machine) supremacy, and from there on to anarchic parliamentarianism before returning to royal supremacy once again. In the course of each cycle, kings sought to weaken the prerogatives of bureaucracy and to purge personal opponents from the machine. In Serbia and Romania, for example, the rights of civil servants were vaguely formulated to permit dismissal in the interest of the state.[242] But abused subordinates, in turn, did not shrink from attempts to expel, or even assassinate, the king. The body politic, as a result, lurched from one crisis to another.

In Bulgaria, these cycles were relatively long. The first years of the national state (1878–86) present us with one cycle, which began with a weak parliamentarism that eventually succumbed to a princely coup (1881) and ended with the coup (1886) that expelled Prince Alexander Battenberg, while bringing Prince Ferdinand to the country and electoral victory to Stambulov. The second cycle then consisted of the rise, ascendancy, and fall of the Stambulov machine (1887–94). That cycle came to a conclusion with the assassination of Stambulov, an event that simultaneously marked the beginning of princely rule. The latter phase lasted for 23 years, ending with the country's military defeat and the exile of (the now king) Ferdinand in 1918. This was followed by five years of turmoil, figurehead monarchy (King Boris), and dictatorial rule by Premier Stambulisky's Orange Guard and Agrarian Party machine. In 1923, Stambulisky was assassinated in a coup, with King Boris's apparent connivance, an event that ushered in phase four: eleven years of political anarchy and futile attempts by the Tsankov and Liapchev governments to establish machine control over the turbulence of parliamentarism. Anarchy thus reigned until 1934, when King Boris's coup established a royal dictatorship with mock parliamentarism, a state of affairs that was to last until 1943, when Boris died, a possible victim of poisoning. For another year, regents governed on behalf of his infant son, whose reign was cut short by Soviet occupation and exile. Altogether three rulers of modern Bulgaria were thus forced into exile, and there is good reason to believe that the fourth was assassinated.

In Serbia (later Yugoslavia), the prevalence of praetorianism is still more obvious, and the cycles between anarchy and royal dictatorship were even

241. Huntington 1968, 52, 192–96.
242. See Höpken 1989, 7–8. Also Janković and Guzina 1962, 243.

shorter. Over the 130 years that preceded the rise of communism in the country, we can identify ten of these cycles, in the course of which there were at least a score of unconstitutional royal attempts to curtail the powers of bureaucracy, ministries, and parliament, half a dozen coups directed against the monarchy, and a number of popular uprisings against identifiable power holders. Between 1804 and 1941, Serbia had a total of ten rulers (two of them reigning twice). Of these ten, one resigned voluntarily, one died in office of natural causes, four were forced to resign and to go into exile, and another four were assassinated. So prevalent were these coups and other violent events that throughout most of its modern history Serbia-Yugoslavia had not one but two dynasties, the houses of Karadjordjević and Obrenović, each of which maintained its own entourage of family retainers and its own brand of foreign policy. When one house was overthrown, it sometimes opened the way for the pretender from the other house, waiting in exile for his turn to seize the throne. A sketch of the ten cycles of change, scanning the events of these turbulent years, may best be achieved through brief summary:

1804–39. Wars of independence. Princely autocracy punctuated by palace coups. The first elected chief of all Serbians, "Black George" Karadjordje, assassinated in 1813. His successor, Miloš Obrenović, rules like a patrimonial despot. Coup forces him to abdicate in 1839.

1839–58. Miloš followed by Milan and Michael Obrenović (the former died in office). Weak princes and rapid rise of the Defenders' political machine under Garašanin and Vučić, accompanied by a series of peasant risings in the 1840s.

1858–68. Power struggles between political machine and prince. Princely ascent of Michael Obrenović cut short by assassination (1868).

1868–80. Liberal Constitution of 1869. Representative government preempted by the rise of the Ristić-Blaznevać political machine. Power struggle between Prince Milan II and Ristić ends with the latter's resignation.

1880–93. Parliamentary supremacy and political turmoil. As a protégé of Franz Joseph of Austria, Prince Milan proclaimed king of Serbia (1882). Peasant uprising of Timok (1883). Radical opposition wins elections (1883), followed by a royal coup and the dissolution of parliament. Attempt to co-opt Radicals in a royal-liberal political machine (1887). Abdication of King Milan under pressure (1889). Regency and democratic constitution: extended suffrage, irremovability of judges, guarantees for the freedom of the press. Regency and parliamentary regime.

1893–1903. Royal dictatorship. King Alexander I arrests regents, suspends constitution, and proclaims royal dictatorship. Alexander thoroughly purges bureaucracy of personal and political opponents, creates new political machine by coopting the "court factions" of the Liberal and the Radical parties.

1903–18. Parliamentary supremacy with factional struggles. Alexander I and his wife assassinated by military conspirators (1903). Peter Karadjordjević called to the throne. Democratic constitution of 1903 expands the scope of representative government. Elections bring Radical majority, split between the "old radical" faction of Pašić (favoring etatist-progressive economic policies) and "independent radicals" (promoting anti-bureaucratic, peasant populist interests). After 1908, a triangular power struggle among the king (Peter I; after 1910, Alexander II), the Radical Party machine under Pašić, and nationalist radical officers of the army led by Colonel Dragutin (Apis) Dimitrijević. Apis executed by royal court-martial in Salonika (1917).

1918–29. Unstable parliamentarism in the new Yugoslavia. The "old radicals" of Pašić attempt to create radical political machine to control parliament. When these attempts fail to stabilize the politics of the new country, a royal coup suspends the constitution.

1929–41. Parliamentarism returns under the open ballot and limited suffrage. Political machines able to control elections. King Alexander II assassinated (1934), succeeded by Peter II under regency of Prince Paul.

1941. Regency overthrown by military coup, an event that triggers declaration of war by Germany. Peter II in London exile.[243]

In the history of Romania, we must distinguish two periods: one before, the other after World War I. In the first period, there developed a rough equilibrium between the monarchy and the political machine, leading to an arrangement in which kings and political machines collaborated in sizing up the public mood and in bringing about appropriate changes in the government by engineering the required parliamentary majorities. Thus unlike the other countries of East Central Europe, Romania had something in the nature of a "working" two-party system, as liberal and conservative governments alternated with each other to serve as fronts for an essentially authoritarian bureaucratic system. While the bureaucracy had to provide spoils for malcontents among the public, the king's role was to adjudicate among competing factions in the bureaucracy itself. In the language of one observer, the system worked by making sure that "the juiciest morsel [al-

243. See Čubrilović 1958, 140–44, 200–222; Dedijer et al. 1974, 367–96. Janković and Guzina 1962, 240–44; Stokes 1990, passim; Vucinich 1954, 63–68.

ways went] to the most vicious dog."[244] The social mainstay of the system was a network recruited from the traditional classes of boyars, usually from the lesser boyardom, whose members were abandoning landownership in the second half of the nineteenth century. Their class solidarity transcended political differences, and their presence gave political structures considerable stability. Thus the system survived the Great Peasant Rising of 1907, in the wake of which it was capable of designing new social policies. But after 1918 the country's territory and population more than doubled, and aspiring politicians from the new provinces, including Romanian nationalists from Transylvania, had to be co-opted. In the process, the proportion of public officials from the boyardom of the old provinces declined precipitously: from 34 to 11 percent among the deputies of parliament, from 55 to 14 percent among cabinet ministers.[245] At this point Romanian politics began to follow the Balkan pattern of a perennial tug-of-war between kings and ministries, punctuated by assassinations and the periodic breakdown of public order. These in turn led to the bloody repression of political malcontents and the forced departure of Carol II from the throne of his father and grandfather.

244. German Foreign Minister Bülow to Chancellor Caprivi (Stavrianos 1961, 438).
245. Lecca 1937; Filitti 1929. Elite Project (see Introduction, above, n. 2).

4 | The Crisis of Liberalism

ECONOMIC PROGRESS AND POLITICAL DECAY

East Central Europe in the World Economy

During the eighty years between the first stirrings of liberalism in East Central Europe and World War I, and still more conspicuously in the half century between 1860 and 1910, the economies of the region underwent significant changes, propelled in part by the forces of the market and the private sector, in part by the intervention of governments eager to reduce the material gap between their own lands and the countries of the rapidly advancing Occident. However, the mix of the role of the market and politics varied. The closer a country was to the core regions of innovation, the stronger the role of entrepreneurship and private capital. Conversely, the farther away a country was toward the east, the weaker the entrepreneurial impulse and the larger the role played by the state. It is in terms of these differences that we may distinguish among three economic sectors of East Central Europe: (1) the Czech lands of Bohemia-Moravia; (2) Hungary, Poland, and Romania; and (3) the Balkan countries of Bulgaria and Serbia (with Montenegro). For the sake of completeness, we may add a fourth sector, represented by Albania, liberated from Ottoman rule in the course of the Balkan wars of 1912–13. But one is inclined to describe this sector as one that had not yet been, and would not be for some time, integrated into either the economy or the material culture of the Occident.

As already noted in Chapter 3, in the Czech lands, economic development took off early—that is, before the rise of the consumer cultures of the core countries, with their debilitating effect on savings and investment. As a result, making money by entrepreneurship was attractive and provided an impulse for both agricultural and industrial development. This is not to say that state intervention was absent. Indeed, both the Austrian imperial and the Czech republican states played a considerable role in the process, the one by generating demand for the products of Czech heavy and armament industries, the other by designing policies favorable to an export-oriented economy. It was as a result of this twofold stimulus that the Czech lands, with a mere 9 million inhabitants, produced more than half of the industrial goods of the dual monarchy, with its 56 million inhabitants.

The pattern of economic development was substantially different in the peripheral countries of East Central Europe—that is, in the countries trying to "take off" economically *after* the consumer revolutions of Britain and after the early industrial revolutions of the West. Here, the state was to play a more prominent role in the development of both agriculture and industry. But the further east we go on the map, the more we find that this role was undertaken by weaker and weaker states. It is in terms of the degree of this weakness that we may further distinguish between sectors 2 and 3.

Sector 2 on this continuum includes Hungary, Romania, and the Russian provinces of Poland, where effective (and repressive) states were trying to cope with economic challenges of far greater magnitude than those faced by the Czech lands (or Czechoslovakia after 1918). In all three countries, agriculture was dominated by larger estates (of over 100 hectares), which together comprised about two-fifths of all arable land.[1] In each of these countries, this sector of the economy experienced brief spurts of innovation between the Napoleonic wars and the second half of the nineteenth century. Yet overall, agricultural development, especially after the 1870s, was labor- rather than capital-intensive, a polite phrase for increasingly stringent labor repression, culminating in the labor codes of 1882 in Romania and 1898 in Hungary, each of which declared agricultural strikes illegal and ordered the forcible return of fugitive laborers in "breach of contract" during the planting and harvesting seasons. In Russia, and hence in the Russian-governed part of Poland, labor discipline was enforced under a broader government mandate that made the state's policing powers available for the repression of the labor force.[2] For some time at least, these measures had their effect. They permitted all three countries to make impressive gains in the production and export of cereals, doubling, and, in the case of Romania, trebling, the total amount of grain harvested over a thirty-year period. Those gains came despite highly adverse marketing conditions due to the influx of overseas grain to the continent during the last quarter of the century.[3] But throughout these years, agricultural production remained relatively undiversified, concentrating on the production of cereals for export. By 1910, it had become abundantly clear that levels of production could no longer increase within the existing institutional framework of the rural economies.

1. Berend and Ránki 1974, 37.
2. Janos 1982, 130; Mitrany 1930, 73; Blum 1961, 606.
3. Berend and Ránki 1974, 55.

In all three countries of sector 2, states played a significant role in stimulating the development of industry, partly by creating demand, partly by encouraging investment—although they did so with different degrees of success. An examination of the development of Polish industries in the Russian Empire reveals some similarities with the Czech experience within the Austro-Hungarian customs union. While Russian distrust in Poland was considerable, and was exacerbated by the failed Polish uprising of 1863, the geographical location of the kingdom, its endowment with cheap coal, and its proximity to major European markets made it a logical location for the development of industries. Thus Polish industries benefited both from direct state intervention and from their place in a larger imperial customs area within which the Polish provinces could play the role of an industrially more advanced trading partner of the underdeveloped Russian hinterland. Nevertheless, since compared to the Czech industrial takeoff, the Polish one was delayed by at least seventy years, and since the takeoff was made from a much lower level of economic development, neither the advantages of a moderately protected market nor favorable public policies were sufficient to close the gap between the two countries. While in 1910 per capita industrial production in the Czech lands was estimated at 66 percent of that of the British index figure, Poland's was approximately 22 percent,[4] and the agricultural population of the country remained at 60 percent, compared to the 34 percent figure for the Czech lands.[5]

In Hungary, the effects of the imperial nexus were more ambiguous. Whereas Polish factories represented a significant industrial concentration within an economically backward imperial economy, those of Hungary had to compete against the more advanced industries of the Czech and German Alpine provinces. On the other hand, Hungary unquestionably benefited not only from a guaranteed export market for its grain but also from the economic clauses of the Compromise Act of 1867, according to which a quota of 33 percent of all military orders was set aside for Hungarian industries. In addition, as we have seen, governments in Budapest tried to foster industrialization by increasingly generous subsidies from 1882 to 1914. Put together, these policies and legislation reaped measurable rewards. Hungary's own industrial revolution took off in the 1880s, and in the two decades before World War I, Hungary registered annual growth rates comparable to those of the Czech lands. Once again, however, these rates are calculated from a much lower initial base than in Bohemia-Moravia. Also, the industrial development of the country was more lopsided. A textile industry had barely developed before the 1920s, prior to the time when the country gained

4. Bairoch 1982, 330–31.
5. Berend and Ránki 1982, 157–59; Hertz 1970, 93. Polish figures extrapolated from postwar and Russian figures.

control over its customs territory. Altogether, by 1910, the contribution of industry to gross national product was 26 percent, and per capita industrial production reached 23 percent of the British index figure used above, or roughly equivalent to the level of Polish development.[6] As in Poland, the percentage of the labor force in agriculture dropped from 75 to 64 percent during the two decades prior to World War I. After 1920, however, when the boundaries of these countries were redrawn, Hungary emerged as the more industrialized of the two, as Poland gained and Hungary lost economically underdeveloped regions. The value of Hungary's per capita industrial income consequently rose to 30 percent of the British figure, while the percentage of people employed in the agricultural sector dropped to 51 percent.[7]

A somewhat different story line emerges from the Romanian experience. Romanian governments made considerable efforts to develop industries by radical protectionist measures unavailable to Hungarian and Polish nationalists. But despite these efforts—or perhaps because of them—growth in the manufacturing sector was negligible until the turn of the century, and in 1910, 78 percent of the labor force was still employed in agriculture, with a mere 45,000 workers employed in modern factories. These were only scarcely above the levels achieved by the Balkan countries in sector 3 and, at 13 percent of the British index figure, only half of the per capita value produced by the Hungarian and one-fifth that by the Czech industries.[8]

In the third sector, comprising Serbia and Bulgaria, we encounter yet another pattern of economic development. Here, liberation from Ottoman domination went hand in hand with the distribution of the *spahiluk*, the lands held in Ottoman military fiefs. The agrarian economy thereby became essentially an economy of small, undercapitalized peasant farms, and subsequent increases in agricultural production were not the result of capital improvements but of a gradual extension of cultivable land by the clearing of forests. Throughout the Balkans methods of cultivation remained primitive: the quality of seed was poor, beasts of burden were scarce, and even after the introduction of the iron plow around 1900, the number of wooden plows was dominant and increasing.[9] The result was a level of productivity that Marvin Jackson and John Lampe compare with Western Europe in the sixteenth and seventeenth centuries.[10] By the turn of the century, land for clearing and settlement ran out. At this point, there were some desperate attempts to maintain the existing balance between output and population growth by increasing labor inputs, notably in Bulgaria, where the work week

6. Berend and Ránki 1982, 157–59.
7. Ibid.
8. Jackson and Lampe 1982, 184.
9. Berend and Ránki 1977, 94–95; Palairet 1997, 318.
10. Jackson and Lampe 1982, 184.

reached 68 hours, the longest on the European continent.[11] But such efforts notwithstanding, the balance between population growth and farming output could not be maintained at their pre-independence levels. While Jackson and Lampe register increases in total output throughout the peninsula,[12] the more recent calculations of Michael Palairet show a precipitous decline in per capita farming productivity: 27.5 percent in Serbia, and 14.3 percent in Bulgaria, between 1870 and 1912.[13]

These patterns of agricultural development produced low rates of domestic savings, inadequate in and by themselves to support effective policies of industrial growth. In neither country did industrialization begin in earnest before 1900, and although in Bulgaria both Palairet and Leo Pasvolsky note a spurt of industrial growth in the years 1906–13,[14] it would be difficult to speak of a genuine "takeoff" of industrialization in this sector of the continental economy before World War I. Indeed, Lampe thinks it appropriate to describe both the Serbian and the Bulgarian ventures into import substitution growth as "varieties of unsuccessful industrialization."[15] This judgment seems to be borne out by relevant statistics. In 1910, for example, the overwhelming majority of the population, 79 percent for Bulgaria and 81 percent for Serbia,[16] was still employed in agriculture, and the number of factory workers—as opposed to traditional craftsmen—was only about 16,000 in each country.[17] According to Alan Milward and S. B. Saul, the combined horsepower of the machinery used in the Balkans in 1914 was less than that used in Prussia in 1860.[18] The per capita values of the industrial product of Serbia and Bulgaria were only 10 and 12 percent, respectively, of the British index figure for 1900.[19]

What is remarkable about this developmental record is the iron consistency with which East Central Europe and its individual countries remained locked into the structural positions created when the agricultural and industrial revolutions of the West intersected in time—that is, during the decades between 1780 and 1830. Thus, if we take the arithmetical averages of per capita income figures (adjusted to purchasing power parities, as in

11. Clark 1940, 140. Palairet is skeptical of these efforts, and points to their absence in Serbia and Montenegro, citing indolence and/or the heroic qualities of culture in these societies. Palairet 1997, 111–12.

12. Jackson and Lampe 1982, 164–65.

13. Palairet 1997, 340–41, 362–63.

14. Ibid., 325; Pasvolsky 1930, 27–29.

15. Lampe 1975, 83.

16. Berend and Ránki 1982, 159. This figure refers to those gainfully engaged in economic activity. The percentage of population dependent on agriculture is a few percentage points higher. See Pasvolsky 1930, 23.

17. Milward and Saul 1977, 431.

18. Ibid.

19. Bairoch 1982, 330–31.

TABLE 9

Evolution of per Capita GNP in Western and East Central Europe

(in 1960 dollars, adjusted to purchasing power parities)

	1860	1870	1880	1890	1900	1910
			WESTERN EUROPE			
United Kingdom	558	628	680	785	881	904
Belgium	490	571	589	630	721	854
France	365	437	464	515	604	680
Germany	354	426	443	537	639	705
Holland	452	506	542	586	614	705
Sweden	225	246	303	356	454	593
Switzerland	480	549	676	705	785	895
Average without UK	394	456	503	554	636	739
			EAST CENTRAL EUROPE			
Czech lands[a]	345	366	378	433	517	586
Bulgaria	210	220	210	250	260	270
Hungary[b]	230	244	252	288	310	351
Poland (Russian-ruled)	196	266	246	200	272	315
Romania	200	210	230	246	275	307
Serbia	220	230	240	250	260	282
Average	234	256	259	277	315	352
Average without Czech lands	211	234	236	247	275	305

SOURCE: Bairoch 1976, 286.
[a] Czech lands calculated as 120% of Austria-Hungary level, 1860–90; 125% 1900–1910.
[b] Hungary calculated as 80% of Austria-Hungary level, 1860–1910; 75% 1900–1910.

TABLE 10

Eastern GNP/Capita as Percentage of Western, 1860–1910

	1860	1870	1880	1890	1900	1910
East[a] as % of UK	41.9	40.7	38.0	35.2	35.7	38.9
East as % of West Europe	59.4	56.1	51.4	50.0	49.5	47.6
East minus Czech lands as % of UK	37.8	37.2	34.7	31.4	31.2	33.7
East minus Czech lands as % of Western Europe	53.5	51.3	46.9	44.6	43.2	41.3

SOURCE: Bairoch 1976, 286.
[a] "East" as East Central as in Table 9.

Tables 9, 10, and 11), we will find that East Central Europe as a region not only failed to narrow the gap between itself and six advanced countries of the West, but that this gap was increasing with merciless consistency from decade to decade. This is also true in the case of the Czech lands, the most successful economic entity of the region, where per capita income figures declined from 86 to 79 percent of the per capita income figures in the Western sample between 1860 and 1910 (see Table 9). As a whole, during the half century after 1860 the arithmetical averages of East Central European in-

TABLE 11

*Eastern Income per Capita of Labor Force
Compared to Western, 1910–13[a]*

United Kingdom	1072
Belgium	589
France	786
Germany	829
Netherlands	975
Sweden	567
Switzerland	764
Average without UK	752
Bulgaria	317
Czech lands	411
Hungary	298
Poland (Russian territories)	306
Romania	274
Serbia	271
Average	313
East Percentage of Western Six	41.6
East Percentage of UK	29.2

SOURCE: Clark 1940, 78–175, esp. 151.
[a] Adjusted to purchasing power parities in 1925–34 dollars.

TABLE 12

Population in Agriculture

(%)

	1860	1910
Bohemia-Moravia	55	34
Hungary	75	64
Poland	—	—
Romania	81	75
Bulgaria	82	75
Serbia	89	82

SOURCE: Hertz 1970, 93.

come figures fell from 59.4 to 47.6 percent of the aggregates of the Western sample (see Table 10). Or, if we take the five peripheral societies of the region (excluding the Czech lands of Bohemia-Moravia), the decline is from 53.5 to 41.3 percent. Other calculations, based on the average wage of working populations (also adjusted to purchasing parities, as in Table 11), corroborate the size of the income gap between East Central Europe and the West, in that for 1910 they show an average income in East Central Europe at 41.6 percent of that in the Western "six," and at 29.2 percent of the average income in the United Kingdom. These figures, together with other customary yardsticks—such as percentages of the labor force in agriculture, horsepower used, railway density (see Tables 12 and 13)—also show that

TABLE 13

Indicators of Economic Development in East Central Europe,
1910–13

Country	% Population in agric. 1910	Wheat yields[a] 1913	Industrial hrspwr[b] 1913	Railway density[c] 1900
Czech lands	34	17.9	—	5.8
Bulgaria	75	6.8	24.0	1.0
Hungary	64	15.7	570.4	4.8
Poland	—	—		2.9
Romania	75	10.5	115.8	2.2
Serbia	82	9.9	24.0	1.2

SOURCES: Hertz 1970, 93; League of Nations 1943; Berend and Ránki 1974, 78, 115–46; Matlekovits 1900, 663–65.
[a] Measured in ctw per hectare.
[b] Total horsepower used by national industries, measured in thousands of kilowatts.
[c] Kilometers of railway line per 100 square km.

while economic differentials between East and West were increasing, economic differentials within the Eastern region also persisted or increased.

This pattern of persistence, reproduction, and increase in national and regional income inequalities invites us to contemplate the dynamics of economic marginalization on the European continent. Certainly, based on elementary logic and common sense, the neatly regressive geographical and chronological pattern permits us to eliminate a series of possible, and fashionable, explanations. Thus, we may reject explanations based on culture, "national character," and leadership on the grounds that virtue is not likely to be distributed geographically. Nor can one put all the weight on the role of exploitative imperial policies, a favorite of nationalist historians, for in a number of the instances cited—Poland, Hungary, Bohemia—and in different ways, such policies helped rather than hindered economic development, although not to the point where any one of these countries would have been able to "break out" of its position on the great European gradient. We may also reject explanations based on climatic factors that may have an influence over agricultural production (and hence on a significant initial component of the gross national product). Indeed, conditions favorable to the growing of crops are almost inversely related to yield-per-acre ratios on the Continent: for the production of almost any of the crops produced for cash—but above all for grain—the Hungarian, Romanian, and Polish plains, or the valleys of Bulgaria, are better suited than the arable lands of Holland, England, or western Germany.

In contrast, the consistency and reproduction of a neatly regressive geographical pattern of income inequalities tends to support hypotheses concerning the international demonstration effect of the rising material culture of the Occident. While the effect may be taken as more or less constant over space, or expressed by a slightly sloping curve, the initial economic inequalities also represented a constant reproduced in two ways. In the decades from 1800 to 1860, the effect operated to boost levels of consumption among the middle and upper classes imitating higher Western material standards and thus diminishing the rate of saving and investment: what should have gone into technological innovation in agriculture, went instead into spending for the new "decencies" of Western middle-class life. Phase 1 then led to phase 2. After independence, the low rates of private savings spurred the involvement of the states in the economy and served to justify greater bureaucratic autonomy from the weak institutions of representative government. This in turn enabled classes of political entrepreneurs to use the institutions of states to accomplish what they had not been able to accomplish as economic entrepreneurs: to raise their standard of living to the level enjoyed by the middle classes of the advanced societies of the Occident. It was in this manner that the East Central European states became to varying degrees "rent-seeking" states. The costs of this rent-seeking, combined with the other costs of maintaining the apparatus and accoutrements of modern states, was demonstrated by Tables 5, 6, and 7 in the previous chapter. Once again, in a new vicious cycle, this put new pressures on investment in an environment of increasing public spending. As Ivan Berend and György Ránki observe, throughout the region and the period, "state intervention led to no rise of real incomes, the funds for state intervention coming from what [would have been] consumer demand."[20] Or, as Lampe notes about the Balkans, "the state drew more fiscal resources away from productive investment than it had contributed itself."[21]

Weighty as the influence of the international demonstration effect was, the troubles of Eastern and East Central European economies were aggravated by adverse market conditions. To return to a point made earlier, economically backward nations may profit a great deal by heavy demand for primary products that they inherit from premodern society by accidents of history. In much of Eastern and East Central Europe, this commodity was grain. It was with respect to cereals that most of these countries seemed to have a natural comparative advantage given the favorable ratio between their populations and large stretches of flat, arable acreage. Whatever economic development they experienced between the Napoleonic wars and the middle of the century was largely owing to periodic spurts of demand as a result of Western shortages. As the states began to develop modern infrastructures of transportation, the prospects of grain looked particularly auspicious, only to be undercut by the development of new means of transport that brought cheap overseas grain to Europe. From 1878 to 1899, the price

20. Berend and Ránki 1982, 71.
21. Lampe 1975, 83.

of grain fell by 40 percent, and the general agricultural price index declined by 32 percent,[22] and did not recover until World War II, except for brief periods of time as a result of overseas crop failures.

It is, of course, impossible to say with any certainty what might have happened had the price of grain remained high for another half century after 1860. Could these societies have overcome the "hump" of initial development and have generated enough momentum for the takeoff toward more diversified economies? There are no direct answers to prove counterfactual hypotheses, but analogy, above all the contrary case of the Scandinavian countries, may be somewhat illuminating. Only slightly more advanced than some of the Eastern European nations in the 1860s, the Scandinavian economies flourished, and continued to flourish even after 1878, presumably aided by proximity and available sea routes to the great heartlands of the Industrial Revolution, and, above all, by an export profile that largely excluded grain, but included iron ore, timber, and wood pulp to feed the demand created by the new steel industries of the last quarter of the century, and the equally important demand for paper generated by the educational revolution in Europe. It was from this base that, one after the other, they progressed toward diversifying their economies, eventually entering the ranks of the very high-income nations at the core of the modern world economy.[23]

World War I and the ensuing territorial dispensations outlined above unquestionably caused economic disruptions for the region. The former destroyed physical plant and economic capacity, especially in Serbia and Poland, and the latter disrupted established trading units and encouraged a protectionist trend that had begun earlier but culminated in the 1920s. But the effects of these disruptions should not be exaggerated. The fact is that within five years after the end of the war, the economies recovered sufficiently to share in the worldwide boom of 1924–29, with most of the countries of the region experiencing remarkable bursts of industrial development, the dimensions of which are presented in Table 14. It was in this time period that Czechoslovakia emerged as one of the great export economies of the Continent, with 25 percent of its national income derived from foreign trade.[24] As before, the agricultural economy remained a problem. Indeed, compared to 1913 (see Table 15), cereal yields per acre were declining in most countries as part of a continentwide trend caused by a chronic shortage of capital in that sector. In some countries, especially Romania, the trend was aggravated by land redistribution schemes that cut deep into the

22. Prices at the commodities market of London. For grain prices, Kühne 1910, 63–64; for the price index of agricultural products, Milward and Saul 1977, 485–87.
23. For the Scandinavian experience, see Senghaas 1985, 71–94; Jörberg 1975, 92–135, esp. 124–25.
24. Pryor 1973, 193.

TABLE 14

Levels of Industrial Development in East Central Europe, 1910–38

(UK 1900 = 100)

Country	1913		1928		1938	
	Total	Per capita	Total	Per capita	Total	Per capita
Czechoslovakia	—	—	22	66	23	60
Hungary	—	—	6	30	9	34
Poland	—	—	16	22	19	23
Romania	2	13	4	11	5	11
Bulgaria	1	10	2	11	3	19
Yugoslavia	1	12	5	15	7	18

SOURCE: Bairoch 1982.

TABLE 15

Cereal Yield by Region, 1913–36

(metric ctw per hectare)

Country	1913	1928	1936
Holland	26.7	25.1	25.5
Belgium	24.3	26.5	26.2
Germany (western)	22.5	22.9	22.7
Denmark	21.0	22.8	22.4
France (northeastern)	19.9	26.3	18.9
Italy (northern)	19.4	16.8	—
Germany (eastern)	18.5	17.0	16.5
Czech lands	17.9	16.1	15.6
Hungary	15.7	15.3	13.6
Romania	11.7	10.0	11.1
Italy (southern)	10.5	9.0	—
Poland	10.5	10.1	9.6
Yugoslavia (Serbia)	9.9	13.2	12.2
Bulgaria	6.8	11.7	13.3

SOURCE: League of Nations 1943, 86–91.

volume of agricultural exports.[25] The major exception was Bulgaria, where both agricultural income and productivity increased as a result of intensified labor inputs.[26] Overall, the rate of economic growth of these countries hovered around 5 percent per annum in per capita terms.[27] With these rates, per capita GNP reached prewar levels by 1926–27, and by 1928—

25. Roberts 1951, 56–57.
26. Clark 1940, 140. By Clark's calculations, about 18.5 percent of Bulgarian per capita income was derived from labor input in excess of 48 hours per week, the European standard. The higher Yugoslav figures derive from the incorporation of more productive agricultural land into the territory of the new country. The higher Hungarian figures, in contrast, reflect the loss of unproductive lands located on the country's mountainous periphery.
27. Bairoch 1976, 295.

TABLE 16

*Per Capita GNP Levels in East Central Europe
and Western Europe, 1913–38*

(in 1960 US dollars, adjusted to purchasing power parities)[a]

Country	1913	1928	1933	1938
	EAST CENTRAL EUROPE			
Czechoslovakia	524	586	501	548
Hungary	372	424	396	451
Poland	320	350	332	372
Romania	307	316	296	343
Yugoslavia	284	341	292	339
Bulgaria	263	306	270	420
Average of Above	345	387	348	412
	WESTERN EUROPE			
Belgium	894	1,098	952	1,015
France	695	982	846	936
Germany	757	770	716	1,126
Holland	754	1,008	753	920
Sweden	680	897	816	1,097
Switzerland	963	1,265	1,233	1,204
Average of Above	791	1,003	886	1,049

SOURCE: Bairoch 1976, 297.
[a] Calculated for postwar territories, adjusted to changes in boundaries.

the last pre-Depression year—exceeded prewar levels across the region (see Table 16).

Whatever these trends may have promised for the future, they came to an abrupt halt in 1930, when the first waves of the Great Depression reached the countries of East Central Europe. The crisis, generated by overproduction in the industrial sectors, affected both agriculture and industry. In agriculture, there was a fall in prices without precedent in modern economic history: between 1929 and 1933, the price of wheat fell by an average of 49 percent, the price of rye by 59 percent, and the price of corn by 72 percent.[28] Losses in industrial exports were commensurate. They amounted to 45.5 percent in Hungary, 46.6 percent in Romania, 51.6 percent in Yugoslavia, 63.2 percent in Poland, and a staggering 70.9 percent in Czechoslovakia.[29] These in turn were reflected by the decline of the gross value of national product, ranging from 36.6 percent for Bulgaria to 55.2 percent for Hungary (see Table 17).

This extraordinary degree of output collapse, accompanied by massive unemployment and underemployment, was a wrenching experience, which triggered some of the political events to be discussed in the rest of this chap-

28. Average prices in Hungary, Romania, Bulgaria, and Yugoslavia based on Berend and Ránki 1974, 244.
29. Hertz 1970, 80–81.

TABLE 17

Loss of Value of Gross National Product

(base year 1929)

Country	Year	% Loss
Czechoslovakia	1934	38.7
Hungary	1932	55.2
Poland	1933	48.8
Romania	1932	51.6
Bulgaria	1933	36.3
Yugoslavia	1932	44.2

SOURCE: Clark 1940, 133, 137, 173–75.

TABLE 18

Central Government Expenditures

(averages in 1935–37 as percentages of total budgetary expenditure)

	Economic expenditure	Education	Public welfare	Defense	Administration	Debt service	Unclassified
Bulgaria	14.1	16.2	3.3	24.7	15.1	22.9	3.7
Czechoslovakia	17.9	7.5	9.1	32.2	15.8	10.2	7.3
Hungary	15.7	15.5	4.8	21.3	31.4	7.4	3.9
Poland	17.7	12.3	1.9	34.7	17.8	5.2	10.4
Romania	9.6	16.6	3.9	33.2	16.5	12.9	7.3
Yugoslavia	17.1	11.1	2.5	25.9	16.9	10.7	15.8

SOURCE: Based on Mitrany 1945, 119.

ter. But although the trauma of the Depression shook most states to their foundations, the economic effects were temporary; for, driven by a number of external and internal factors—including government austerity programs, preparations for a new war, and German trade policies—most of the economies of the region repeated some of the experiences of the first postwar decade. By all indications, the years 1933–34 to 1937–38 were productive for most industrial economies of the region, as they were for the rest of Europe: by 1938, Czechoslovakia had reached 1929 levels of industrial output, while all of the other countries' industrial sectors, with the exception of Poland's, had exceeded pre-Depression levels by 25 to 40 percent.[30]

Although the states of the region unquestionably contributed to this spurt of economic development, one cannot overlook the fact that, much as they had at the turn of the century, they continued to exact a heavy toll from their societies by using revenue for nonproductive expenditures. Table 18 shows that, even in Czechoslovakia, noneconomic (i.e., defense, administration, and debt service) expenditures—not including "unclassified" (and largely nonproductive) items—continued to outweigh infrastructural (economic

30. Clark 1940, 66; Lampe and Jackson 1982, 300–301.

TABLE 19

Eastern per Capita GNP as a Percentage of Western, 1913–38

(in 1960 dollars, adjusted to purchasing power parities)

	1913	1928	1933	1937–38
West Europe[a]	791	1003	886	1049
East Europe[b]	345	387	348	412
East as % of West	43.6	38.6	39.3	39.3
East without Czechoslovakia	309	347	317	384
East without Czechoslovakia as % West	39.1	34.5	35.8	36.6

SOURCE: Bairoch 1976.

[a] West = average of 6 countries: Belgium, France, Germany, Holland, Sweden, and Switzerland.

[b] East = average of 6 countries: Czechoslovakia in 1928, 1933, and 1937–38; Bohemia-Moravia in 1913 (see Table 16).

and educational) and welfare expenditures in national budgets. The ratio of items in the infrastructural and noneconomic categories is approximately 1:2; moreover, as David Mitrany notes, even though some infrastructural expenditures may have come from local budgets, the high proportions of expenditures for defense, public administration, and debt servicing are the most salient facts to emerge from an analysis of East Central European budgeting of the interwar period.[31]

While clear-cut causal connections are hard to establish between this pattern of state spending and the overall historical record of development, it is noteworthy that neither the region as a whole nor its individual countries — with the possible exception of Bulgaria, which forged ahead of Yugoslavia — were able to break out of their earlier positions in the continental or regional economy. Indeed, as Table 19 indicates, the gap between the average per capita income figures of the Eastern and Western "sixes," used throughout this study as a basis of comparison, continued to increase, following the historical trend. Whereas in 1913 the average GNP figures for the East were 43.6 percent of those for the West, by 1938 this figure had declined to 39.3 percent. Excluding Czechoslovakia, the calculations reveal a decline from 39.1 to 36.6 percent. At the same time, the historical pattern of disparities in income persisted along the northwest-southeast geographical axis that had been established at the time of the agricultural revolutions of northwestern Europe. The persistence of the pattern is confirmed by a plethora of economic indicators: the percentage of populations dependent on agriculture, the length of railroad lines per square km of national territory, the consumption of certain staples, industrial production as a percentage of industrial production in the United Kingdom, and national income per capita unadjusted to purchasing power parities (see Tables 20 and 21).

31. Mitrany 1945, 118.

TABLE 20

Indicators of Economic Development I, 1937–38

	% of population in agriculture	Wheat yields[a]	Sugar consumption[b]	Meat consumption[b]
Czechoslovakia	28	17.8	23	31
Hungary	51	13.9	11	26
Poland	65	11.5	12	22
Romania	78	10.6	5	17
Bulgaria	79	11.7	3	21
Yugoslavia	80	12.7	5	16

SOURCES: Berend and Ránki 1974, 306; Mitrany 1945, 19–21.
[a] In metric ctw per hectare.
[b] In kg per year.

TABLE 21

Indicators of Economic Development II, 1937–38

	Railway density[a]	Industrial production[b]	National income[c]
Czechoslovakia	9.7	60	170
Hungary	9.3	34	120
Poland	5.3	23	100
Romania	3.6	11	81
Bulgaria	3.3	19	75
Yugoslavia	4.2	18	80

SOURCES: Berend and Ránki 1974, 306, 309; Bairoch 1982, 330–31, Mitchell 1980, 613.
[a] Km of railway line per 100 square km.
[b] Per capita, percentage of United Kingdom.
[c] Per capita, in current dollars and unadjusted to purchasing power parities.

Enter the Masses: The Crisis of Mobilization

The problem of the continued marginalization of the economies acquires full meaning when examined through the prism of the concurrent entry of the masses into politics. The reality behind this metaphor has two dimensions, each related, among a number of other factors—increase in commerce, travel, universal conscription—to the revolutions in primary education and to the concurrent spread of literacy, both of which had made impressive strides between 1860 and 1910 (Table 22). One dimension of these changes was the exposure of large masses of people outside the educated elite, not just to Western standards of material life, but also to Western political experiments with universal suffrage, trade unionism, more equitable distribution of social income, and, last but not least, with the sense of personal efficacy, which, according to Alex Inkeles, is the major defining characteristic of modern man.[32]

32. Inkeles 1974, 50–60.

TABLE 22

Literacy Rates in East Central Europe, 1880–1910

(%)

	1880	1890	1900	1910
Bohemia-Moravia	79.0	82.0	88.0	99.6
Hungary	53.5	61.4	68.7	84.8
Poland	—	54.2	61.4	68.7
Romania	—	18.0	22.0	40.0
Bulgaria	14.5	—	29.6	42.2
Serbia	10.0	14.0	40.3	49.5

SOURCES: UNESCO, *Progress of Literacy in Various Countries* 1953, 45, 105, 162; and *The States-man's Yearbook* 1880, 1890, and 1900.

The second dimension of this process of modernization is behavioral. As so many social scientists have pointed out, by acquiring some of the rudimentary skills of social communication, people become "mobilized,"[33] that is, available for sustained, systematic, and organized political action, in sharp contrast to the primitive rebellions of the traditional universe.[34] Thus, greater consciousness of the world and material aspirations go hand in hand with new forms of political participation, most obviously manifest in the rise of political parties articulating the interests of the lower classes. In this respect, parties of urban industrial workers led the way. Workers' organizations, mutual aid societies, and the like made their appearance in the 1870s and 1880s, while social democratic parties, stimulated by the organization of the Second International, began forming in the 1890s. By the turn of the century, all the countries of the region had had at least one of these parties, although the socialists of Russian Poland had to stay underground and many others were harassed regularly by the authorities.[35] The parties of the peasantry came a decade after the urban social democrats. First among them was the Bulgarian Peasant Union (1899), followed by the Polish Piast in Austrian-ruled Galicia, the Hungarian Peasant Smallholders and Agrarian Socialists, and the Croat Peasant Party, all of them formed in the politically turbulent years 1905–6. The more radical Polish Wyzwolenie, or Peasant Liberation Party, and the Romanian Peasant Party of Ion Mihalache were formed in 1915 and 1918 respectively.[36] In the egalitarian spirit of the European Left, all of these parties appealed to class sentiment, and all of

33. See Deutsch 1961, 493–502; Huntington 1968, 55.
34. Hobsbawm 1963, 1–13.
35. For the early history of these parties, see Dziewanowski 1959, 1–54; Tökés 1967, esp. 1–82; Roberts 1951, 5–6, 104, 131, 144, 244; Ghita Ionescu 1964, 1–35; Rothschild 1959, 11–57; Zinner 1963, 25–36; Banac 1984, 196–97, 109–10, 154–55, 295–97.
36. For the rise of the peasant parties, see Mitrany 1951, 138–41, 135, 144–45, 138, 146–48, 200, 272–73; also Jackson 1966, 3–25; Banac 1984, 226–31; Rothschild 1959, 85–113; Bell 1977, esp. 22–55.

them had both maximal and minimal programs. Minimally, they injected into public consciousness demands for shorter working days, for the right to form trade unions, plans for redistributive measures, and for universal manhood suffrage, based on the British Reform Acts of 1867 and 1881. At their most ambitious, they wanted to effect major changes in the ways in which their societies were organized and income was redistributed, issues that further stimulated the spread of mass political parties by rallying the middle classes in the defense of the status quo.

The entry of the lower classes into politics had been rather troublesome even in the core countries of the advanced industrial world, for the ruling classes could not be certain about the final outcome of expanding franchise and participation in politics. In this respect, Disraeli's admission of industrial workers into the English electorate was anything but casual or routine, and the process was still more agonizing in France, where universal manhood suffrage was introduced and repealed a number of times between 1789 and 1871. But on the eastern half of the Continent, the issue created still more stress. For while the lower classes in the West were enfranchised in an environment in which the economies were constantly growing, and in which the fruits of development could be redistributed, the lower classes in the East were demanding political rights at a time of ever-growing relative scarcities. Satisfying their demands would have required the redistribution of assets, not of gains. This was also an environment in which the rate of economic development lagged far behind the rate of political mobilization and the injection of effective demands into the political process. This gap between economic development, measured by the growth of per capita product, and political participation, measured crudely by the literacy of the population, can be expressed in numerical terms in comparisons between the countries of Eastern and Western Europe. According to the calculations of Colin Clark, in 1910, average per capita product on the eastern peripheries was 317 IU,[37] corresponding to the British figure for 1688 and the French figure for 1789. Yet the degree of literacy corresponds more closely to the British and French figures for 1860.[38] This gap between political participation and economic development, a recurrent concern of political scientists of the past decades,[39] becomes still more evident if we construct an index by dividing per capita product by the percentage figure for literates in given societies at ten-year intervals over the fifty-year period (1880–1930) when the masses were entering the political arena of East Central Europe. A chart plotting the results of this exercise would yield a steeply regressive curve, indicating

37. Per capita income adjusted to U.S. prices expressed in 1925–34 dollars. See Clark 1940, 83, 132–40; see also Table 11 (above).
38. See *The Statesman's Yearbook*, 1870, 142; ibid., 1900, 517.
39. Deutsch 1961; Huntington 1968, 54–55.

ever-smaller amounts of social product available per head of the "mobilized" population. In contrast, the figures for England and France from the middle to the end of the nineteenth century would show a steeply rising curve indicative of increases not only in national income per capita but also in the income per capita of the politically activated populations.

What this seems to suggest is that the societies of the East faced a genuine "redistribution crisis."[40] It indicates not only that the existing distribution of social resources was highly inequitable, but that even a most equitable pattern of distribution could only have been attained by increasing the rate of economic development and overtaking the rate of participation.[41] This circumstance did not augur well for political democracy. Indeed, for a whole century after 1890, the politics of East Central Europe would move in a direction that was diametrically opposite to the northwestern European experience of expanding political rights and civil liberties. Rather than expanding, after 1900 these rights and liberties continuously shrank, while political power passed into the hands of ever smaller and more resolute minorities. It is, of course, easy to blame culture, national character, or the moral failings of leadership for this rather consistent trend. Yet, as Henry Roberts observed nearly half a century ago, what we are really dealing with is a vicious circle of inadequate economics and exploitative politics, one feeding off the other to produce a downward drift. This, Roberts concludes, "can only be understood in the light of the all pervasive influence of the West,"[42] exercised not by conquest or exploitation, but by the skewing of expectations via the international demonstration effect.

Indeed, in the inhospitable environment then prevalent in East Central Europe, it is not hard to find a great number of "Westernized" leaders who were genuine democrats eager to govern their countries in the manner of Britain and France; but without exception, when at the helm of governments these leaders were frustrated by conditions that were very far from those of the West. Take, for example, Nikola Pašić of Serbia-Yugoslavia; Stefan Stambulisky of Bulgaria; Iuliu Maniu of Romania; and Mihály Károlyi, Oszkár Jászi, and István Nagyatádi of Hungary. Much like Aleksandr Kerensky in Russia, Károlyi and Jászi were motivated by the purest of principles, but in refusing to ally themselves with the Right, fell prey to the autocrats of the communist Left.[43] Pašić and Nagyatádi were peasant tribunes, pure at heart, who in power became persuaded piecemeal that a little corruption was preferable to much anarchy and reverted slowly to the bureaucratic methods of

40. See Pye 1966, 66.

41. Huntington 1968, 55.

42. Roberts 1951, vi.

43. For the two Hungarian revolutions, the democratic and the Bolshevik, see Böhm 1922, 19–21.

the prevailing regimes.[44] Another peasant tribune, Stambulisky, went the other way. Although a professed democrat, as premier of Bulgaria, he quickly concluded that democracy would have to wait, perhaps for as long as forty more years.[45] But the most poignant of these biographies is the Romanian Maniu's. With a lifelong record of political probity and civility, he became premier in 1928, just before the Great Depression set in, with a program of liquidating corruption in politics. By 1930, however, he had clearly failed to overcome the weight of the traditional culture and structure of Romanian politics. He resigned and retired from politics, saving his good name, although his resignation only hastened Romania's drift into still more perilous and murderous waters.[46] Many more names familiar to students of East Central European history could be cited, those of József Eötvös, Virgil Madgearu, and Wincenty Witosz among them. The more we study their biographies, the more we are bound to see the history of East Central Europe as a stellar case of the victory of structure over design and personality.

Unlike these dedicated democrats, the great realists of the liberal machines concluded early on that democracy was dangerous and resisted its advances either by raw power or trickery. Yet at the same time the "old guard," or at least some of its more astute members, grasped quickly that the rise of mass politics was not merely a matter for the police. Like the Hungarian Ágost Pulszky, they regarded socialism as a "malady," but one that was not contracted accidentally; rather, it was an integral part of industrialization "and a price that all civilized nations must pay for economic progress."[47] Hungary's liberal premier István Tisza was of a similar opinion. In his words, "the problem of workers was not created here in parliament. It was created by the growth of the manufacturing industries of the country. The rise of a working class is an unavoidable concomitant of industrialization, and is a problem common to all modern societies."[48]

It was in this spirit that, in the first decade of the century, the governments of the region began to craft social policies aimed at ameliorating the condition of the lower classes while trying to avoid their effective incorporation into the prevailing political order. These policies follow a discernible pattern, in that they were initially designed to accommodate industrial workers at the expense of the peasantry. Beginning in the 1890s, motivated partly by liberal commitments to industrialization and partly by the belief that industrial workers were politically more dangerous than the rural population,

44. For Pašić, see Dragnich 1974; on specifics, Ćubrilović 1958, 449, or Tomasevich 1955, 253; for Nagyatádi, see Macartney 1961, 1: 12, 24, 26.

45. Rothschild 1959, 86.

46. For Maniu, see H. Seton-Watson 1962, 201–2. Also Roberts 1951, 135–36.

47. Z. Horváth 1961, 97.

48. Lower House of the Hungarian Parliament, *Napló* (1891), vol. 22, p. 45; quoted in Janos 1982, 164.

TABLE 23

Relative and Absolute Industrial Wages, 1925–34

	Wage per week in US $	Industrial wage as % of per capita income	Industrial wage as % of British average
United Kingdom	17.3	94	100.0
Switzerland	15.0	79	86.7
Germany	13.8	129	79.8
Holland	13.9	106	80.3
Uruguay	12.0	127	69.4
Czechoslovakia	11.0	125	63.6
Spain	9.4	120	54.3
Poland	8.0	148	46.2
Italy	7.1	120	41.0
Yugoslavia	7.1	111	41.0
Mexico	6.0	130	34.7
Estonia	5.2	106	30.1
Bulgaria	3.7	111	21.4

SOURCE: Clark 1940, 40–41, 47.

most governments of the area permitted industrial workers to organize and to strike for wages, while also designing for them the first rudiments of a system of health insurance and social security. At the same time, wage demands by the agricultural labor force were stymied, invoking earlier bans on labor mobility and strikes, in order to keep the price of food low and urban wages competitive, in what amounted to a subtle policy of horizontal income redistribution from rural to urban wage earners. Alternatively, governments tried to redistribute the costs of social overhead among the peasantry itself, by diminishing direct taxes on property owners while increasing indirect taxation.[49] Meanwhile, they attempted to insulate the rural population from the demonstration effects of the outside world. This last policy was most conspicuous in Serbia, where its main legislative instruments were the Commercial Act of 1860 and the Village Commercial Stores Acts of 1871 and 1891, all of which remained in force until 1929. The Commercial Act "protected" the smallholdings of peasant farmers by prohibiting their mortgage, thus effectively removing them from the credit system and the capitalist market. The other acts regulated the opening of shops in rural areas and banned the sale of a wide range of "luxury" articles, including textiles, coffee, sugar, tea, woolens, and finer types of cooking utensils.[50]

Aided, too, by market forces, these pro-industrial labor policies of the governments bore some fruit. As Table 23 shows, throughout the region, in-

49. For the diminishing tax burdens and tax legislation, see Palairet 1979, 719–46, esp. 732–33.
50. Tomasevich 1955, 45–46.

dustrial wages rose, pushing the class of skilled laborers toward the middle of the income distribution scale.[51] But from the point of view of the liberal reformers, the political gains were marginal at best, counterproductive at worst, for the gains were made at the expense of the peasantry, which already viewed urban life with jaundiced eyes. While industrial workers continued to look West and aspire to the wages, working hours, and living conditions of their counterparts in Britain and in Germany, the peasants developed a sense of relative deprivation when they compared their own lives with those of their cousins in the cities. It was more this sense of relative deprivation than an actual decline of rural living standards that from the 1890s onward accounted for the growing unrest of the countryside, not only in East Central Europe, but all over the European periphery.[52] The endemic agrarian troubles of the Hungarian plain, the periodic outbursts of peasant fury in Serbia, the twelve "minor insurrections" in Bulgaria between 1835 and 1876,[53] "[t]he horrors wreaked by the Romanian peasantry [in 1907], the bloodthirsty land struggles of Ireland, Galicia and Andalusia, the turmoil of Russia [in 1905–6],"[54] were all products of the same peripheral desperation in an age of growing self-awareness and stagnating material standards.

A World in Crisis: Economic and Political

From the turn of the century onward, the societies of the periphery labored under increasing stress generated by growing demands for social redistribution and by the rise of new political classes competing for the loyalty of politicized masses in an economic arena of relative scarcities. These factors explain the increasing intensity of social conflict. But they do not tell us how these conflicts were woven into new ideological cloth, giving rise to political movements that rejected not only the incumbent elites but also a number of the most fundamental tenets of nineteenth-century politics. In order to understand this new dimension of conflict, we shall have to go beyond national boundaries and examine a larger crisis, a crisis of the principles of liberal capitalism that had provided the "old order" with its cohesion and legitimacy.

This larger crisis was triggered by a number of unanticipated changes in the structure and dynamics of the world economy that cast increasing doubts on the validity and wisdom of the larger liberal project's fundamental as-

51. As Colin Clark points out, this result is consistent with the "Fisher principle," so named after the British economist A. G. Fisher, who explained the phenomenon by pointing out that the more underdeveloped the economy, the more technical training and skills are at a premium (Clark 1940, 225).

52. Milward and Saul 1977, 227–29.

53. Palairet 1997, 158.

54. Habakkuk and Postan 1965, 461.

sumptions. One of the first to go was the theory of comparative advantage that had made liberalism compatible with theories of development. The idea underlying the Ricardian theory was that a complex division of labor, whether at the level of national or global economies, allowed participants to prosper by providing each with a proper niche within which virtue was to find its proper reward in economic mobility. This theory seemed to have been corroborated by the experience of core societies, in which the new division of labor had brought about increasing popular welfare and new forms of social mobility. In the international arena, however, the experience was different, for what the global division of labor brought about was not universal prosperity but progressive immiseration. Although this immiseration was only relative, it led many observers to see development as an elusive objective and to conclude that the problem lay not merely with the corruption and inefficiency of local elites but within the structure of the world economy and with the dominant principles of liberal capitalism.

As a corollary to these disappointed expectations of material progress, liberal capitalism experienced another crisis, brought on by increasing tensions between its legitimating and operational principles. As a historical phenomenon, modern capitalism had been the product of surplus production. It was precisely the existence of surplus that had turned markets into arenas of uncertainty and made risk-taking the defining character of entrepreneurship. And yet, from the inception of capitalism, unequal outcomes had been justified in terms not of the rewards of risk but of the rewards of labor and "self-command," or commitment to sustained and systematic endeavor. *Pace* Max Weber, this mode of justification had always been subversive of the entrepreneurial essence of capitalism; witness Ben Jonson's contempt for Volpone profiting from betting on the loss or return of seafaring vessels from long and perilous journeys.[55] In the second half of the nineteenth century, however, industrial economies became more and more monetized, and the management of large volumes of capital acquired increasing centrality in the processes of production and investment. The role of banks became highly visible, while stock and commodities exchanges became conspicuous venues of personal enrichment. In this new economy, farmers, craftsmen, and other small producers, even when applying themselves to their economic tasks with equal vigor from year to year, garnered profits that bore little correlation to their investments of labor and personal endeavor. At the same time, the forces of the market appeared to reward—the prevalence of losses was generally disregarded—many who were not industrious in the traditional sense of the word, but rather reaped rewards for "merely" buying and sell-

55. Jonson, *Volpone* [1606] 1898. For a modernized version, see Stefan Zweig's *Ben Jonson's Volpone: A Loveless Comedy of Three Acts* (1928).

ing paper at the right moment. While the trend was systemwide, it was, as Gerschenkron has noted, most salient in Central Europe.[56] Thus it was here that "finance capitalism" was denounced most loudly and that capitalism itself was rejected by both Left and Right as an essentially parasitic system divorced from personal savings or endeavor. In both cases, the critique pivoted on a rather traditional concept of work and its just rewards. While the Left pointed to the expropriation of those rewards by force, or by the logic of the system, the Right decried capitalism as a system that rewarded "speculation" and not the "hard work" of the struggling "little man." In this manner, Marx's labor theory of value and Christian discourse on the nonproductivity of capital became two sides of the same coin of anti-liberal and anti-systemic politics.

This crisis of confidence in capitalism was further deepened by the increasingly aggressive pursuit of markets by some of the great trading states of the world. That aggressiveness tended to undermine another great shibboleth of classical liberalism: that economic exchange produced not only material wealth but also peace on earth. It shall be remembered here how Sir Dudley North spoke of the world as "one nation in trade,"[57] an idea further elaborated by Scottish economists who hypothesized that the logic of an interdependent world of commerce was antithetical to war. This theory, long popular with British economists, was reiterated in the second half of the nineteenth century in Herbert Spencer's hope and belief that over time the "industrialism" of the trading nations might supersede the militaristic tendencies of the modern state.[58] Alas, only a decade after the formulation of his ideas, the great industrial nations began their "mad scramble" for new markets on other continents, raising the specter of war among themselves and increasingly associating trade, not with peaceful capitalism, but with old-fashioned imperialism. When the war actually came, it destroyed the moral dimension of capitalism, the claim that it was one of the progenitors of universal peace. Indeed, now the tables had been turned, for capitalism's critics, from Hobson to Lenin, pilloried it as the main cause of the unfolding human tragedy. The trauma caused by the Great War was universal and deep. The experience not only gave aid and comfort to the skeptics of the periphery but destroyed the moral fabric of the liberal capitalist heartlands, dividing their publics and demoralizing their elites. Liberal morale would be eventually restored in the wake of capitalist triumphs in Western Europe, Japan, and the United States after World War II, but the interwar period was one of liberal self-doubt, which itself served as encourage-

56. Gerschenkron [1959] 1962, 11–16.
57. See Chapter 3, 55n. 6.
58. Spencer [1876] 1972, 149–66.

ment to the forces of anti-liberalism. While the new challengers were self-righteous in the opposition, England and France were hesitant and erratic in defending liberal democracy and their interests on the Continent.

In damaging the moral fabric of liberal capitalism, the war also created a new international system. The term "order" may be a misnomer here, for when the old Concert of Europe broke down, three powerful blocs of states emerged in its place, legitimating themselves by three competing and mutually exclusive ideologies, less interested in restoring a balance of power than in recasting the world in their own images. The first of these blocs more or less coincided with the core region of liberal capitalism, whose leading nations, as if to compensate for their weaknesses and doubts, were now more inclined to moralize than ever before. The second center of power was the Soviet Union, a large political entity that inherited the imperial possessions of Russia, and, in the egalitarian traditions of the European Left, turned itself into the center of a new global counterculture and a base of operations on behalf of the dispossessed of the world. The third center of power emerged from the geographical middle of the European continent, with Italy and Germany challenging the "plutocracies" dominating the world economy. But the political agenda of Middle Europe, inspired by the authoritarian-hierarchical traditions of the Right, was more than just another rebellion against existing patterns of international inequality. For while the ideology of fascism was revolutionary in its enmity to global privilege, it was counter-revolutionary in its desire to repress the egalitarian onslaught launched by the great proletarian power of the East. Over time, the initial balance among these powers would change, and it was in this larger international political context of change that the domestic and foreign politics of the smaller nations of the borderlands would unfold for the better part of the twentieth century.

MARXIST DESIGNS

Radical Intelligentsia or Political Class?

At the turn of the century, the crisis of liberal regimes in East Central Europe was catalyzed by the rise of a new political class, often referred to as the radical intelligentsia that would undertake to challenge the liberal regimes. Its rise was the result of the interplay of three factors. First, given the progressive marginalization of the economies and the unfavorable ratio between risk and return (as well as the continued preeminence of the state in both economic and public affairs), politics as a vocation continued to be attractive to talented young men (and, increasingly, women). Second, upward mobility increased as a result of the expansion of the educational systems.

For although the number of university graduates was still pitifully small by today's standards (and would remain so until the 1920s),[59] there was a sufficiently large pool of people produced by the gymnasia and lycées with politically usable skills. Third, and most significant among these points, was the rise of the masses itself, for the process provided the exhilarating and adventurous alternative of revolutionary action to advancement through the many ranks of increasingly stodgy and inert bureaucratic machines. Thus, in time we will encounter cleavages not just between liberals and radicals but also between the radical of the left and those of the right.

Social differences between the liberals and leftists was in large part due to the policies of inclusion and exclusion practiced by the liberal establishments. In Hungary and in Romania, this practice implied a bias in favor of employing the traditional gentry in the state machine. In the Balkans, it meant a discernible preference in favor of kith and kin, operating through traditional clientele arrangements both among the urban mercantile and rural communal notables. Accordingly, and not surprisingly, the new political class in ascent through the peasant and workers' parties was more "plebeian" than the liberal elites. Just as in Russia, the new political class was a *raznochinstvo*—a mixed group consisting largely of people devoid of the social markers of traditional rank and privilege. In most countries, the peasant movements and populist parties of the pre–World War period were led either by peasants, like the Hungarians András Achim and István Szabó, or the Croat Stepan Radić, or by village schoolteachers of peasant origin, like the Romanian Ion Mihalache and the Bulgarian Stefan Stambolisky. In this respect, Constantin Stere, the great ideologue of Romanian peasantism and leader of the populists of Bessarabia, was an exception as a landowner with ancestors who were members of the table of both Russian and Romanian boyars.[60] The rule also holds for the composition of the rising socialist parties. In Hungary, among 457 functionaries of various socialist movements (1900–1919), genealogical research reveals that only four (possibly nine) persons had family connections to traditional privilege.[61] For Romania, we

59. In 1900, the number of students enrolled in Bulgarian universities was 2,455. The figure was 5,925 for Romania, 13,737 for Russian and Austrian Poland, and 11,893 for Hungary. These totals represented .049, .069, .057, and .053 percent of the respective populations. The figures for Germany and France were .110 and .059 percent. In the same year, in Hungary, 1.2 percent of the total population had high school diplomas. See Laky 1932, 12–14. For high school graduates, see Hungary Ministry of Foreign Affairs 1922, 3: 217. Today, on average, about 2.5 percent of the populations of advanced industrial countries is enrolled in institutions of higher learning, and between 12 and 25 percent of the populations have higher degrees.

60. Roberts 1951, 144.

61. This list included delegates to Social Democratic congresses, identifiable members of the radical Galileo Circle, the Revolutionary National Council of October 1918, and of the central committees of the Communist Party (November 1918) and the united Socialist-Communist parties. For a breakdown, see Janos 1982, 177. Names on the list were checked against Kempelen 1911–31.

have a much smaller sample of 39 names, culled from a history of the early socialist and communist movements.[62] It is virtually certain that none of the names of these prominent early socialists and communists, including members of the parties' central committees (1900–1923), were connected with families that appear on compiled lists of boyar families.[63] The profile of the Polish party, however, is more ambiguous. As M. K. Dziewanowski tells us, in the absence of a functioning Polish state, and under imperial tutelage, not just plebeians but the *szlachta* as well were "barred from public office," so the early socialist movements were led by a "mixture of Jewish intelligentsia and descendants of the ruined nobility,"[64] although in time even here the majority of the radicals came from outside the ranks of the gentry class.[65] Dziewanowski himself identifies only five persons—among them the later famous, or infamous, Feliks Dzierżyński—as being of such family origin.[66] Their names, and some biographical particulars, are part of a narrative on the foundation of the Polish People's, Polish Lithuanian Social Democratic, and Communist parties.[67]

Even more conspicuous than its "plebeian" character is the connection of the new political class, and especially of the socialist elites, with the phenomenon of ethnic marginality. One writer on the subject of radical socialism treats this as an area-wide phenomenon, and identifies a variety of marginal groups—*prečanin* Serbs from "across the rivers," outside Serbia proper, Greeks resettled from Asia Minor, and Macedo-Bulgarians—as being prominent in the early socialist and communist movements, and explains their disproportionate presence by the attraction of socialist internationalism, with its declared objective to assign social status irrespective of ethnic origin.[68] Still, the major example of the connection between an ethnically marginal group and radical socialism is provided by the Jews of Eastern Europe. Often interpreted with a conspiratorial twist, Jewish participation in opposition politics follows the logic of the social position of a group that, being heavily urbanized and associated with the bourgeoisie, showed higher than average mobility, yet was barred from political office by the unwritten ethnic "contracts" imposed and enforced by the ethnic majority. The phenomenon is too well known to need belaboring here beyond a few statistics

62. G. Ionescu 1964, 1–70.
63. Elite Project (see Introduction, n. 2); checked against Lecca 1937; Filitti 1929.
64. Dziewanowski 1959, 8, 32.
65. Chalasiński 1947, 37–38.
66. The others that are, or can be, so identified by reasonable inference are Ludwik Warinski, one of the founders of the socialist movement, Stanislaw Budzyński, Ignacy Daszyński, and Julian Leszczyński. See Dziewanowski 1959, 16, 65, 90.
67. Dziewanowski's narrative and description of the social composition of the formative years of the Social Democratic Party of Poland and Lithuania appear to be corroborated by a more recent study on the subject. See Blobaum 1984, esp. 55–71.
68. Burks 1960, esp. 57–59, 93–94, 101–2, 115, 126.

that emerge from a variety of samples. One of these shows that in Hungary, 43.5 percent of 457 officers of the early socialist and communist parties were Jewish—or, more accurately, of likely Jewish parentage on the paternal side—with another 17.9 percent being "possibly Jewish."[69] Likewise, 48.6 percent of the much smaller Polish contingent and 30.7 percent of the names in the Romanian sample were Jewish.[70] In the case of Romania, ethnic marginality played a significant role beyond Jewish participation, for another 11 of the 39 names are those of Hungarians, Bulgarians, Germans, and Ukrainians.[71] Analyses of vote and party membership show further correlations between Jews and radical socialism.[72] Thus while the majority of the Jewish communities may have been apathetic or even hostile toward Left radical movements, the high visibility of Jews in leadership created an irresistible temptation for rivals and opponents to ethnicize future political confrontations between the parties of the Left and Right.

Whatever its social and ethnic origins, the attitudes and behavior of the radical political classes were defined by the context of the new phenomenon of mass politics and the looming crisis of liberal capitalism. As to the first, the radicals were not pencil-pushing bureaucrats, or parliamentarians representing constituencies of notables, but agitators and propagandists, the street-hawkers of ideas, who were "going to the people" in order to raise its political consciousness. This required special, new skills in the arts of political drama, and in translating complex issues into the language of the masses. As to their goals, they were inspired by grand chiliastic dreams of replacing the status quo and making a leap into the unknown. To some of their critics, such a leap is proof of nothing but personal and social pathology. Yet their behavior was consistent with the principles of economic rationality: while they were assuming higher risks, they were also expecting higher rewards, and were thus political entrepreneurs in the true sense of the word. That many of them failed to reap these rewards, or even lost their lives in pursuing them, does not by any means invalidate the proposition.

Marxism: The Ideology

In the last quarter of the nineteenth century, and for some time thereafter, the most powerful ideological expression of this radical anti-liberalism was provided by the doctrine of Marxism. The tenets of this doctrine are too well known to require elaboration in detail. It will be enough to remind ourselves that they include a comprehensive critique of capitalism, a vision

69. Janos 1982, 177. An illuminating addition to these numerical data is McCagg 1972b, 78–105.
70. Based on Dziewanowski 1959, 3–22; 365–69; G. Ionescu 1964, 1–35.
71. Ionescu 1964, 1–35.
72. Ibid., 158–63.

of the ideal human condition, and a methodology borrowed from science, in which inductive analysis is combined with the logic of dialectic in ways capable of justifying practical political action at critical junctures of history.

The critique arises from the simple premise that labor, and labor alone, is capable of producing value. It is, in other words, the only valid factor of production, and the "ultimate commodity." Translated into simple terms, this theory provides the eye-catching argument of a surplus value that does not reach the laborer but is expropriated in exchange; hence, markets are not morally neutral (or beneficial) but arenas of concealed expropriation. As to the underlying vision, it is one of progress in the best tradition of the eighteenth century, in which humanity rises from lower to higher stages by means of increasing control over its material environment. Industrialism is one of the major dynamos of this historical progress, for it creates both the foundations for material abundance and a working class of the machine age with special qualifications to liberate productive energies from exploitative selfishness.

Formalized in the voluminous writings of Karl Marx and Friedrich Engels, these theories won considerable popularity among both the workers and the educated classes of the Continent, and more than anywhere else, in the German-speaking countries. If workers were easily persuaded that the rate of return over capital was a form of theft, the intellectual counterculture of the age was attracted to the doctrine's skillful use of scientific idiom in building political arguments. By the end of the century, the prospect of socialism was no longer distant: the major issues that separated the faithful were on matters of tactics concerning the ways of overthrowing capitalist regimes. While the "orthodox" followers of the now deceased Marx were convinced that the "bourgeois" state could be dislodged only by cathartic violence, the "revisionists" gathering around Edouard Bernstein and Otto Bauer put their faith in the power of universal suffrage and in the institutions of parliamentarism. As industrialism progresses, so the revisionist argument went, the number of class-conscious workers will constitute an electoral majority capable of outvoting and expropriating the capitalist minority.

Paradigm Shift: From Marx to Lenin

Although a number of workingmen's associations and socialist clubs had existed in East Central Europe as early as the 1870s, it was in the last decade of the century, following the establishment of the Second International, that socialist parties made their appearance in the countries of the region. By the end of that decade, socialist parties were functioning everywhere, even in Russia and its possessions, including Poland. But as Marxism migrated across the region en route to Russia, some of the squabbles of Austrian and

German socialists were traveling along with the creed. Indeed, the squabbles often became exacerbated, for in the political milieu of East Central Europe, the relative virtues of uprising versus universal suffrage acquired renewed salience. To be sure, in 1907, Bohemia, as part of the Austrian empire, became the beneficiary of universal manhood suffrage. But in all other countries, including the Hungarian parts of the dual monarchy, the socialist parties were hamstrung either by limited suffrage or by bureaucratic harassment. This in itself made revolution-making more attractive than the long road through parliamentarism, the attractiveness of the strategy being further enhanced by the weakness of some of the local structures of authority. Revolution, in other words, was far more likely to succeed in Bulgaria, Russia, or Romania than in England, Germany, or the United States. In recognition of this fact, most parties would be soon divided between those eager to promote a general uprising against their weak government and those who put their energies into broadening the suffrage and into supporting the emancipation of the weak bourgeoisie from the tutelage of open or disguised autocracy. In 1903, the Russian Social Democratic Party split along these lines, and this split between Mensheviks and Bolsheviks was replicated in Bulgaria between the Broad and the Narrow constructionists of Marxism,[73] and, less formally, by the split of the Hungarian party between the "German" and the "Russian" factions.[74] Clearly, in that year, the patience of young political entrepreneurs was wearing thin, while their revolutionary enthusiasm was further stimulated by increasing signs of agrarian and industrial unrest.

This impatience is easy to detect in Lenin's early work. His first book, *The Development of Capitalism in Russia* (1898),[75] conceals a not-so-subtle attempt to show to both populists and diffident Social Democrats that Russian agriculture and industry were developing at very high rates, and that the takeoff of these revolutions, as we would say today, had already been accomplished, so that the day of revolution was in the not-too-distant future. Seven years later, he made a stronger and more convincing argument based on comparisons between Western and Eastern history.[76] In the West, as Marx had pointed out in volume 1 of *Capital*,[77] the commercial and agricultural revolutions preceded the revolutions in industrial technology, and while the first two of these revolutions had been the creators of bourgeois hegemony, the Industrial Revolution signaled the beginnings of bourgeois demise. Not so in the East, where, Lenin argued, the economic revolutions were sequenced differently, owing mainly to the intervention of the states.

73. Rothschild 1959, 38–40.
74. Süle 1967, 196.
75. Lenin [1898] 1964.
76. Lenin [1905] 1970d, 1: 462–541.
77. Marx 1967, chs. 26–33.

Here, industrialization preceded the rise of agrarian and commercial capitalism, and the proletariat was arising before, or together with, the bourgeoisie. The bourgeois and proletarian revolutions could therefore be "telescoped" into a single event—to start under liberal auspices but to then be taken over by the industrial proletariat or, more accurately, by its political representatives. By the logic of this argument, the socialist parties of Russia and the peripheries were justified in preparing for political revolution by tightening the discipline of their ranks.

This analysis seemed to suggest that the proletarian revolution was possible, and that the impatient political entrepreneurs of the Marxist movement would not have to wait another century to get a taste of power. But it left open the larger question of whether the overthrow of the old order would indeed produce socialism—or, more specifically, whether a revolution by socialists could in the long run sustain a democratic form of government. In this respect, Lenin stood on weak ground. The counterargument was most forcefully expressed by Gheorghii Plekhanov, the "father of Russian Marxism," who made his case in terms of economic dynamics and exigencies. Plekhanov's premise was based on the purest of Marxist principles: socialism without industrialism was folly, for a society without industry would lack both the wherewithal to satisfy material needs and the social consciousness that was to provide socialism with inner restraint and fellow feeling. Should socialists seize the helm of government in a backward corner of the periphery, they would be saddled with the dirty work of primary accumulation, of investment by forcible savings, which would alienate their very own constituents. Under such circumstances, revolution in a backward society would not yield democracy but a "political monstrosity exemplified by the ancient Chinese and Peruvian empires,"[78] or, translated into the language of contemporary politics, in a totalitarian developmental state.

This round of the debate was won by Plekhanov, Martov, the Mensheviks of Russia, and the democratic socialists of East Central Europe. It established a platform that, in 1905–6, no socialist was willing to contest, at least not in open debate. But some time between the defeat of the first Russian revolution and the outbreak of World War I, the radicals, now speaking with the voices of Alexander Helphand-Parvus and Leon Trotsky, affected a genuine intellectual breakthrough that was to change the course of history.[79] Their stroke of genius was not to deny the validity of Plekhanov's argument but to redefine the entire world historical context: while they readily conceded that constructing socialism in a backward society was an

78. This quotation from Plekhanov in Medvedev 1972, 359. For more on Plekhanov's views, see Wittfogel 1957, 391–95.

79. For the elements of this breakthrough, see Trotsky [1908] 1969. For the influence of Parvus, see his "Samoderzhanie i reformi" [Self-government and reform], cited in detail in Scharlau 1964. Also Trotsky, *Mein Leben*, quoted in Scharlau and Zeman 1970, 74–75.

inappropriate undertaking, they now explained that the Russian revolution would not merely be a matter of revolution in Russia but of carrying the "revolutionary conflagration to Europe" and the "establishment of socialist organizations in all countries of the world."[80] This idea, first floated by Parvus and Trotsky, was picked up by Lenin in 1914 and further refined in the latter's *Imperialism, the Highest Stage of Capitalism*.[81] Underlying the argument was the premise of an interdependent global economic system, conceived metaphorically as a chain, the durability of which would depend on the strength of its weakest link. Russia—with its overcommitted and underlegitimized autocratic state, discontented peasants, and rebellious workers—appeared to be the epitome of this very link, which made it a logical venue for beginning the grand historical project of revolutionizing the world.

It is, of course, tempting to dismiss this "paradigm shift" in Marxism as empty bravado and sheer opportunistic sloganeering, except for the fact that once the Bolsheviks seized the helm of government, they proceeded almost immediately to institutionalize and set into motion their revolutionary internationalism. The institution involved was none other than the Communist International (Comintern), set up in Moscow but staffed by radical socialist collaborators and émigrés from all over the world. The strategy of the Comintern was simple and direct: to foment insurrections against the governments of capitalist countries, mainly on the European continent. The logic of this strategy was impeccable: if it could overthrow capitalism in the advanced countries, socialism would be victorious in their dependencies across the world shortly thereafter. Moreover, establishing socialism in the advanced countries first would save poor countries like Russia from the agonies of primitive accumulation in the process of industrial development— for it was an article of faith among the Bolsheviks that the new socialist governments in the core region of the world economy would readily offer their surpluses to aid economic development elsewhere. This strategy owed a great deal to the thinking of the Prussian general Carl von Clausewitz, whose study *On War* was avidly read by Lenin and his associates.[82] In it, Clausewitz urged prospective disciples always to prepare for a *coup de main*, a strike at the main force and heartland of an adversary, and to avoid any wasteful nibbling around the peripheries. His maxim would inform Soviet strategic thinking even after the demise of the Comintern.

In the spirit of Clausewitz, between 1919 and 1923, the Comintern fomented uprisings in Finland, Estonia, Austria, and, several times, in Germany. It also aided short-lived Soviet republics in Hungary and Bavaria and encouraged mutinies in the French navy and a wave of strikes in England,

80. Lenin [1915] 1970b, 663.
81. Lenin [1916] 1970b, 667–763.
82. Clausewitz [1832] 1943. For his influence, see Lenin [1930] 1957.

the United States, and Italy. While these projects came to naught, the exhilarating experience of fomenting them created its own political culture that helped to sustain the "utopian" and "Leftist" impulses in many spheres of Soviet intellectual and social life. The chief elements of this culture were an exuberant anarchism and iconoclastic anti-traditionalism,[83] manifest in a thriving feminist movement, in Aleksandra Kollontai's panegyrics in favor of "free love" and against the "bourgeois" family, and in a radical egalitarianism that spouted contempt for all differences, material or symbolic, in status and rank.[84] In the arts, this culture produced the great decade of Soviet modernism, which, like its counterparts elsewhere on the Continent, celebrated revolt by rejecting structure and form, whether in poetry, prose, painting, or music. In philosophy, the same rebellion manifested itself in "Bogdanovism," associated with Aleksandr Bogdanov, alias Malinovsky, who, like the postmodernists five decades later, asserted the primacy of culture over structure, and even questioned the existence of an objective reality existing independently from the human mind.[85]

Authoritarianism and the Logic of Salvationism

In the interim, though, the institutionalization of socialist power had to be resolved in Russia proper. Here, in the throes of protracted and bloody civil war, the democratic traditions of the Enlightenment soon clashed with the hard realities of the minoritarian position of the Bolsheviks amid their numerous adversaries. Unquestionably, in order to survive the turmoil, they had to shelve their earlier rhetorical commitments to democracy. Lenin at first tried to maintain the democratic fiction by resorting to verbal acrobatics: the Bolsheviks, he maintained, while a minority of the population as a whole, represented the majority of the country's most progressive class, the industrial workers. "Should sixty peasants have the right to decide and ten workers be obliged to obey?"[86] he queried petulantly. But when confronted with a loss of his majority even among those workers, he finally gave up any pretense. "Majority vote! This is what they tell us, and we tell them that they are clowns."[87] What the revolution needed was not the counting of heads, not even a dictatorship of the proletariat, but "dictatorship by a small, conscious contingent of the proletariat."[88]

Such arrogance required justification, and the Bolsheviks found it in the

83. See McClelland 1980, 403–6.

84. For Kollontai, see McClelland 1980, 419–20. For an English-language biography, see Clements 1979; for Kollontai's autobiography, see Kollontai 1970.

85. Utechin 1958, 113–38; see also McClelland 1980, 408.

86. Lenin, quoted in Harding 1977, 1: 202.

87. Ibid., 215.

88. Ibid., 226.

scientific pretensions of Marxism. Unlike the French Jacobins or their hapless populist-peasantist adversaries, they were not reduced to weak arguments about momentary exigencies and their own revolutionary instincts. They instead drew on an elaborate epistemology from which a political formula appropriate for the moment might be extracted. More specifically, the scientific pretensions of Marxism permitted them to pose as a priesthood in possession of sacred knowledge, and thereby to replicate the traditional logic of divine right legitimacy in a modern, secular context. As in that traditional logic, if subjects asked why they should obey, rulers could answer that their commands were the correct ones at this particular juncture of history. If their subjects challenged them by asking how such things could be known, the rulers could now answer by invoking their special training in scientific method, which, in the context of the twentieth century, served as the functional equivalent of God. It is true, of course, that most of the Bolsheviks' adversaries were unmoved by these arguments. But the premise and the syllogisms were accepted by the faithful select, and this acceptance permitted them to overcome any doubt or hesitation in the exercise of authority, which would soon become absolute. This, we should repeat, was a luxury unavailable to radicals since the age of the Enlightenment, and one that may well explain why the Bolsheviks succeeded in consolidating their power where others, like the populists, had so abysmally failed.

One should hasten to add that this was not conventional authoritarianism, familiar from the annals of history. This authoritarianism was that of a revolutionary state, because its political formula was cast in chiliastic-salvationist terms that endowed it with "transcendental significance" and infused it "with all the mystery and majesty of a final eschatological drama."[89] The essence of such salvationism is the idea of creating a society of terrestrial harmony. In the case of Marxism, it refers to a condition in which humanity was to be free, not only from material privation, but also from boredom and frustrations generated by the division of labor and the production process. So described, socialism would not only be better than any other known form of society, but perfect in design and actuality, and as such it would represent the stage of ultimate fulfillment in human history.

The credibility and appeal of communist salvationism have been the subject of frequent debates among historians and social scientists. To some, this salvationism was a mere cloak and mask, a clever invention of leaders determined to mobilize the less sophisticated masses by dazzling them with promises of paradise. To others, it was nothing but a paranoid "fantasy,"[90] the product of desperation born out of catastrophe or rapid sociocultural change. Still others argued that there are such things as "true believers,"

89. Cohn 1961, 308.
90. Ibid., 310.

who arise at particular points in human history when rare conjunctures of favorable elements create a mood of excessive optimism—as was the case in the nineteenth century, when rapid technological advances increased human control over nature and, by extension, over society as well. It is not within the scope of this work to attempt to adjudicate this debate. Suffice it to say that salvationism was an integral part of original Marxism and the same tenets were fully embraced, even developed further, by the Russian Bolsheviks. This proposition may strain the credulity of a skeptical posterity. But only a true believer in the faith could have spent, as did Lenin, the precious and precarious prerevolutionary months in drafting a huge essay on the withering away of the state,[91] or, like Trotsky, make "red paradise" a standard phrase of his vocabulary,[92] and, together with Bukharin and Preobrazhensky, embellish Marx by proclaiming that under socialism, "human culture will climb to heights never attained before" and the intelligence of the average person would soar to that of a Michelangelo, a Marx, or an Aristotle.[93]

Far from being empty political rhetoric, this salvationism came very much alive in operational principles and logic that shaped the structure of the Leninist state. In general, this logic calls for charismatic leadership: where the task is extraordinary—like the salvation of all humanity from misery and conflict for all times—leaders and their followers are likely to attribute to themselves supernatural qualities. It was by such logic that the Bolshevik party identified itself as a "special breed of men . . . cut out of particular stuff" (as Stalin did in a famous funeral oration over Lenin's grave).[94] The logic of charismatic salvationism, in turn, is the logic of total devotion, rather than of mechanical obedience. In the name of that devotion a leader can demand inordinate sacrifice and impose it on others with total disregard to cost: where paradise is the reward, the price of human life and suffering are all too easily paid. By the same token, the vision of a magnificent future can emancipate political activists from the narrow and awkward restraints of law and traditional morality, an attitude that paved the way toward subjectivism and arbitrariness in the exercise of authority. Finally, the logic of charisma is the logic of perfectionism. By self-definition, the charismatic cadres have superhuman qualities and do not make mistakes. Hence, when mistakes do occur, they will not be treated as statistically probable or inevitable events, like accidents on crowded highways, but will be attributed instead to the withdrawal of goodwill, to sabotage, or to the deeds of infiltrators. It is in this context of charismatic salvationism that the Marxian

91. Lenin 1970c, 2: 276–376.
92. Trotsky in Cohn 1961, 312; also in Kernig 1969, 746.
93. Bukharin and Preobrazhensky [1921] 1966, 71–72.
94. From Stalin's "Oath to Lenin," quoted in Deutscher 1960, 270.

tenet of "no accidents in history" acquires operational meaning, and explains the communist routines of the purge, replete with extracted confessions, which otherwise strike the outsider as irrational, if not downright insane.

These operational principles had been evident from the very inception of the Bolshevik regime, perhaps nowhere more conspicuously than in the operation of the Leninist judicial system. Revolutionary tribunals were constantly exhorted against being guided by the dead letter of the law rather than by revolutionary conscience and instincts. "Don't tell me," Lenin's chief prosecutor is quoted as saying, "that our criminal courts ought to act exclusively on the basis of written norm. We live in the process of revolution. A tribunal is not the kind of court in which fine points of jurisprudence and clever strategems by lawyers are to be restored." [95] Most tellingly, this was a system of "revolutionary justice" in which the "the proof of guilt [was] relative and approximate." [96] An interrogator was to base his conclusions, not on illusory objectivity, but on "intellect, party sensitivity and moral character," [97] weighing, among other things, the social status and the political proclivities of defendants.

The same principles are also evident in the operational code of the rising party apparatus and administrative system. As in any large-scale organization geared toward the performance of a multiplicity of complex tasks, administrative and political functions had to be routinized by subjecting them to certain impersonal rules. But these rules served as guidelines of only limited relevance, for, unlike the ideal-typical bureaucrat, the communist functionary was called upon to make critical judgments, above all the judgment as to whether any particular case should be handled "by the book" or in terms of the political expediency expressed in an ever-changing party line. The cadre who was seen to "cling slavishly" to the rules, who refused to make critical judgments at critical moments, was liable to be removed from positions of responsibility. Thus, although the "quantity" of coercion varied over time, in spirit, political culture, and quality, the Leninist system was already as arbitrary, and had as little respect for the boundaries between state and society, as its Stalinist successor.

Although subject to recurrent debates, these continuities between Leninism and Stalinism have been recognized by historians and political scientists. What has been far less generally, if at all, recognized is the duality of the early Bolshevik political culture, and the tensions between the political culture of charismatic salvationism and that of revolutionary insurrectionism. While the logic of the former dictated single-minded, total devotion and dis-

95. Public prosecutor Krylenko, quoted in Solzhenitsyn 1974, 308.
96. Ibid., 101.
97. Ibid.

cipline, that of the latter bred rebellion against philistinism and hierarchy. Lenin, deadly serious and obsessed with discipline, clearly stood on one side of the cultural divide. Ever suspicious of the "aristocratic anarchism" of those who spoke of the party organization "as a monstrous factory," who "confused discipline with serfdom," and responded to the necessity of a "division of labor and directions from the center . . . with a tragicomic outcry against cogs and wheels,"[98] he was the one who led the attack against the "left-wing infantilism" of the Workers' Opposition at the Tenth Party Congress of 1920. But, weakened by illness after 1922, he did little more than grumble about Kollontai's antics or Bogdanov's thinly veiled radical subjectivism. However, the coexistence of these two cultures was precarious, and their contradictions defied attempts at synthesis. In time, one or the other would have to perish.

Nationalism and Communism in East Central Europe

Perhaps the greatest triumph of the Comintern era was the proclamation of the short-lived Hungarian Soviet Republic by a coalition of Left socialists and ex–prisoners of war returning from Russia imbued with communist ideas. They seized power without shedding blood or firing a single shot, since they moved into a political vacuum left by the resignation of Count Mihály Károlyi's democratic government, dismayed by the peace terms handed down by the French military commission in March 1919.[99]

The Hungarian Soviet Republic was based on the principles of Marxism and the logic of Leninism. Its powers were vested in a Revolutionary Governing Council of People's Commissars, in principle responsible to periodically convened congresses of delegates elected by local councils;[100] these delegates were elected from a single list of candidates, the councils themselves were run by *direktoria*, or executive committees, and the Congress of Councils was convened only once, to be disbanded after four days when deep divisions became manifest among the delegates.[101] Overall, there was little attempt to hide the fact that this was a "dictatorship of an active minority on behalf of the by and large passive proletariat . . . at least until such time that the revolution spreads elsewhere in Europe"[102] As in Russia, martial law was declared and administered by revolutionary tribunals whose di-

98. Quoted in Daniels 1960, 24.
99. For an excellent description of the ascent of the Hungarian communist movement in 1918–19, see Tőkés 1967, 83–99.
100. "A Tanácsköztársaság ideiglenes alkotmánya," April 3, 1919, in Hungary Magyar Munkásmozgalmi Intézet 1955–59, 6: 100–103.
101. Böhm 1922, 300; Janos 1970a.
102. Commissar László Rudas, quoted in Tőkés 1967, 180.

rectives ruled out "formal investigative procedure, written charges, appeals or recourse to clemency." [103] To enforce the decree, a Hungarian version of the Russian Cheka was set up, and its flying squads were let loose against open counterrevolutionaries and sympathizers with and officials of the old regime, as well as against farmers and railroad men who showed lack of enthusiasm in performing their obligations to the Republic. Although these flying squads claimed only a few hundred victims—a paltry number by the standards of the twentieth century—they effectively flaunted their arbitrariness, and made public executions part of the political theater of the new regime.

Other than seizing power in embattled Hungary for a period of 133 days, communism made little headway in East Central Europe, notwithstanding the social tensions experienced by most of these societies in the first two decades of the twentieth century. In explaining this lack of success, we must examine the larger context of external relations: in 1918–20, France and Britain together were powerful enough to contain the Soviet Union and excise the "cancerous growth" of communism from these small, weak countries. The most obvious case in point is that of the Hungarian Soviet Republic. Although it was not hugely popular among its own citizens (there were several counterrevolutionary risings during its brief rule), the Republic was not overthrown by internal forces but by the joint military venture on the part of Romania, Czechoslovakia, and Yugoslavia, sponsored by the French Balkan command and its forces stationed in southern Hungary. In fact, French commanders in the city of Szeged were harboring Admiral Horthy and were responsible for equipping his National Army. A year later, France was instrumental in organizing Polish resistance against the invading Soviet armies. Although French forces were absent from the battlefields, the French government urged Poland's neighbors to provide logistical support, armaments, and ammunition to forestall a Soviet victory. Still more indirectly, France supported the region's governments morally in the repression of communist parties by often harsh police measures.

Military power could, of course, be instrumental in preventing the rise of communist governments, but it could not stem the popular appeal of communism. Such appeal, even if not overwhelming, did exist, although it varied a great deal from country to country and sometimes from year to year. These variations suggest that, by and large, the populations of these countries did understand quite well that communism had a larger geopolitical design, and that by embracing communism, a country, region, or individual also embraced the idea of partnership with Russia in a larger political game. This observation seems to be supported by the pattern of variations in which

103. Hungary Magyar Munkásmozgalmi Intézet 1955–59, 6: 32, 167.

TABLE 24

East Central European Marxist Parties,
Electoral Results, 1918–30, Peak Years for CPs

Country	Year	Party[a]	% Vote
Czechoslovakia	1925	Communist	13.2
		Social Democratic	8.9
Hungary	1927	Communist	1.7
		Social Democratic	11.8
Poland	1928	Communist	7.9
		Social Democratic	13.1
Romania	1922	Communist	0.6
		Social Democratic	1.0
Bulgaria	1920	Communist	20.2
		Social Democratic	6.1
Yugoslavia	1920	Communist	12.4
		Social Democratic	2.9

SOURCES: Burks 1960, 78–83; Dziewanoski 1959, 127; Rothschild 1974, 65, 110, 215, 335; Zinner 1963, 64–65.

[a] Front organizations: Hungary, Socialist Labor; Romania, Independent Socialists; Poland, Union of Workers and Peasants, Hramada, Ukrainian Socialists.

the popularity of communism correlated closely with the images of Russia in particular societies and ethnic communities. Overall, by the measure of electoral results, communism was most popular in Bulgaria, Czechoslovakia, and Yugoslavia, countries with substantially different social structures and political cultures, but uniform in regarding Russia as an "older brother" and protector, whether from Germany, Austria, or the Ottoman Turks.[104] As Table 24 shows, in all three countries, communist parties, while legal, gained over 12 percent of the popular vote, no mean accomplishment in Czechoslovakia, and especially impressive under the electoral regimes of the Balkan states. The same table shows that in all three of these countries, communists outpolled democratic socialists, at least in the few elections in which both parties were allowed to run for parliament. These figures are corroborated by less quantifiable historical evidence. In the case of Bulgaria, the Comintern felt confident enough of popular support to encourage an armed uprising in September 1923. The uprising failed. But even underground, as we shall see later in this chapter, the party remained a significant political factor and continued to be represented under a variety of aliases in the mock parliaments that continued to function under the years of a royal dictatorship. In Czechoslovakia, as in Bulgaria, a large majority of prewar Social Democrats opted for membership in the new Communist Party; they continued to outvote the socialists and survived all the vicissitudes of World War II to emerge as the single most powerful party of the short-lived demo-

104. Burks 1960, 76–78.

cratic republic, with 38 percent of the vote.[105] In Yugoslavia, Serb enthusiasm for Russia was mixed with regional protest movements to give the Communist Party respectable electoral strength in the nationwide elections of 1920. The party's share of the Serbian vote, at 15.4 percent, exceeded the national average of 12.4 percent.[106] Here, too, the party was suppressed early, but as an underground organization, it continued to enjoy the support of the young intelligentsia and could maintain a strong enough cadre to mount a nationwide partisan war against German occupation in 1941–44.

The cases of the remaining countries show a different pattern, but the image of Russia once again appears to be the crucial explanatory variable. In Hungary, a negative image was rooted in the tsarist suppression of the War of Independence of 1849, in the war of 1914–17, in which Hungarians and Russians fought on different sides, and, after the short-lived Soviet Republic of 1919, in the widespread and unjustified blame put on communism for the country's staggering loss of territory and population to its neighbors. In Poland, still more than in Hungary, the imperial domination of the country by Russia, and the history of numerous unsuccessful risings against imperial rule, was responsible for a great deal of negative sentiment. But the image of Russia was further darkened by the march of the Red Army to the Vistula in 1920. As in Hungary, the cause of local communism suffered, and the 7.9 percent communist vote shown on Table 24 included few cast by ethnic Poles.[107] Like Poland, Romania had her grievances against imperial Russia, stemming from the tsarist expropriation of Moldavian territory between the rivers Pruth and Dniester in 1812, and by a subsequent, and unusually haughty, tutelage exercised by Russia over the principalities for the first half of the nineteenth century. As in Poland, ill feelings were rekindled by Soviet resistance to Romania's recovery of the lost provinces in 1919–20. As a result, the underground party in Romania remained heavily identified with ethnic minorities, with all but one of the general secretaries of the party recruited from their ranks. Time and again, the party resurfaced in parliamentary elections under different names. But the best these bogus parties could do was to capture a minuscule fraction of the total vote, and by 1944 the underground party had virtually no identifiable membership.[108]

Finally, there is the case of Albania, a small and undeveloped country under Ottoman rule until 1912, where there was no tradition or party representing socialism. A handful of Albanians, including the later infamous

105. Rothschild 1959, 102, 114.
106. Banac 1984, 389.
107. Burks 1960, 78.
108. G. Ionescu 1964, 1–35; for a brief history of the party underground, see Roberts 1951, 241–55.

Enver Hoxha, were exposed to communist ideas during their studies in western Europe, but the Comintern never deigned to invite them to form a party under its auspices. Further discounting the country's importance, and showing continued contempt for its potential as a communist base, Stalin was even ready to donate Albania to the Yugoslavs and leave the fate of Albanian communism in their hands.[109] Needless to say, communism had few supporters in the country during the interwar period.

Outside national mainstreams, communist parties received consistent support from ethnic minorities, not on grounds of ideological appeal or historical sympathies, but because in their early years the parties were opposed to ethnic discrimination and to the very idea of ethnic states. In time this opposition was modified by a touch of opportunism, in that the Comintern began to distinguish between good and bad nation-states, the latter including mainly those that were allied to France and constituted the notorious *cordon sanitaire* between Europe and Bolshevism. Thus, the fact that the Comintern and the Soviet Union harbored hostile designs on Romania and Czechoslovakia made minorities in those countries more eager to vote and support communism in ethnic self-defense and protest. While Hungarians in their own land turned their back to communism after the fiasco of 1919, their conationals were prominent in the Romanian underground, and in Czechoslovakia gave 22–24 percent of their vote to communist candidates.[110] But if minority status correlated with voting for communist parties, this correlation was especially notable among ethnic minorities whose status was coupled with positive historical or cultural memories of the homeland of communism. Thus the communist party garnered 42.0 percent of the vote in the formerly Hungarian, now Czechoslovak, province of Ruthenia (Sub-Carpathian Rus), 33.5 percent among the Belorussian minority in Poland, 33.0 percent in Yugoslav Macedonia, and 38.0 percent in Montenegro, the latter being as resentful of annexation into Yugoslavia as it was warmly sympathetic to things Russian.[111] Jews, as Richard Burks notes, represent a somewhat special case, for their above-average participation in communist organizations and share of the communist vote was not just a protest against discrimination by ethnic majorities but also a sign of the appeal of socialist internationalism and of the prospect of a political order in which social and political status would be divorced from ethnicity.[112]

One way or another these correlations show that particularism—ethnic, regional, religious—did continue to play a significant role in the politics of East Central Europe, and that some of these particularist attachments tran-

109. Gibianski 1997, 293–94.
110. Burks 1960, 151–54; Zinner 1963, 61–63.
111. Zinner 1963, 78; Banac 1984, 389.
112. Burks 1960, 163–64.

scended the boundaries of class. For the communists, this was a dramatic discovery, for the leaders of both the Comintern in Moscow and of local communist parties were strongly wedded to their universalistic purpose and identity. At first this universalism was unbending and their contempt for particularism was complete. Nowhere was this rigid internationalism more obvious than in the Hungarian Soviet regime, whose leaders denounced all "petty bourgeois overtures . . . to social patriotism and bourgeois nationalism" [113] and never tired in repeating the internationalist mantra that they felt "no more akin to the Hungarian proletariat than, let us say, to the American, Czech, or Russian." [114] Indeed, throughout the 133-day existence of the Republic, its leaders banned the national anthem, ended the use of national insignia, and saw to it that the statues of national heroes were removed from public places. Remarkably, one of the last messages sent by the commissars to the troops fighting at the river Tisza warned commanders not to hoist the national colors next to the red flag of the revolution.[115] This resolutely antinational, internationalist stance not only accelerated the demise of the red regime but also substantially aided the counterrevolutionary governments of the interwar period in painting the communist party with the brush of treason and reducing its mass appeal. Indeed, the charge of treason rubbed off on the Social Democratic Party as well, with the result that, by the 1930s, Hungary was a country in which radicalism was almost entirely monopolized by the Right.

The Hungarian fiasco and the lessons of subsequent elections were not entirely lost on the communist leadership, and they started a long and agonizing reappraisal of the proper relationship between communism and nationalism. The fact that the Bolsheviks were trying to recover territories lost by Russia during the Civil War and to expand their domain over the Caucasus and Central Asia made the problem still more acute. It was in this context that minorities were discovered to be a "surrogate proletariat," [116] and that the notion of distinctions between "good" and "bad" nations were rediscovered among some of Marx's more casual and careless remarks. Russian nationalism was thus for some time branded as chauvinistic and reactionary, while the nationalisms of the Khazaks and Tadjiks (as indeed of Macedonians and Montenegrins) were described as progressive. But both theory and practice exuded opportunism, and it would be one of Stalin's tasks to establish new principles more suitable to the needs of a modern empire that the Soviet Union was rapidly becoming.

113. Kun 1919, 66–67.
114. Tőkés 1967, 130.
115. Böhm 1922, 414.
116. For this term, with slightly different meaning, see Massell 1974.

FASCIST EXPERIMENTS

The Dynamics of Fascism

The rise of the radical Right—or, to use the more common if historically imprecise synonym, fascism[117]—was driven by some of the same forces as the radicalism of the Left: the continued marginalization of the economies of East Central Europe, the increasing mobilization of the masses as a result of the further growth in literacy rates from 1910 to 1940 (shown in Table 25), and the rise of another class of political entrepreneurs searching for their "place in the sun." To be sure, it would be a mistake to try to pluck fascism out of its historical context. For one thing, there was the prior rise of the radical Left, which acted in and by itself as a causal factor by mobilizing and radicalizing the political Right. For another thing, there were the experience and memories of World War I, which reshaped both the political playing field and the consciousness of both elites and masses across the Continent.

The most immediate and obvious consequences of the war were major changes in the map of Europe, especially in the east. The exact dimensions of these changes have already been described above. Here it will suffice to outline them only briefly. Most dramatically, the Treaty of Versailles, and the subsidiary treaties identified with St. Germain, Sèvres, and Trianon-Neuilly, created a number of independent states from the domains of defeated empires: Poland, from territories long held by the German, Austrian, and Russian imperial states, reaching in the east well beyond obvious ethnic boundaries; Czechoslovakia, from the formerly Austrian provinces of Bohemia, Moravia, and Silesia as well as from the Hungarian "Highlands" (Felvidék), now to be designated as Slovakia and Ruthenia (also Sub-Carpathian Rus, or Carpatho-Ukraine); and Yugoslavia, cobbled together from the old kingdoms of Serbia and Montenegro (including Macedonia and the Kosovo, won by Serbia in 1913), along with the formerly Austro-Hungarian provinces of Carniola-Carinthia (now Slovenia), the Bácska-Bánát (now Voyvodina), and the province of Bosnia-Herzegovina, which had been under Austro-Hungarian administration since 1878. There was now also an independent Hungary, although one shorn of most of the territory and population it had enjoyed as a component of the Austro-Hungarian monarchy, while neighboring Romania more than doubled its size through the transfer of the provinces of Transylvania, Bucovina, and Bessarabia from Hun-

117. The designation originates from the name of the Italian movement, which, while copied by many parties of the Right, was rejected by others, including the National Socialist German Workers Party.

TABLE 25

Growth of Literacy Rates, 1910–40

(percentages)

Country	1910	1920	1930	1940
Czechoslovakia[a]	99.6	92.6	95.3	—
Hungary	84.8	—	90.4	92.4
Poland	68.7	84.8	90.4	—
Romania	40.0	—	57.0	76.9
Bulgaria	42.2	53.3	68.5	77.0
Yugoslavia[b]	49.5	—	55.0	74.6

SOURCE: UNESCO 1953, 45, 105, 162.
[a]Bohemia-Moravia before 1918.
[b]Serbia before 1918.

gary, Austria, and Russia respectively. For Bulgaria and Albania, the treaties confirmed boundaries established after the Second Balkan War of 1913, thus in each case adjudicating territorial disputes in favor of neighboring Romania, Yugoslavia, and Greece. As a result, the majority of Slavo-Macedonians and about half of the Albanian population of the Balkans became subjects of the newly formed South Slav entity in 1918.

Another consequence of the war was to accelerate the secular trend toward the political awareness of the masses. If, in 1910, substantial parts of the rural population were still unaware of the outside world, by 1930 its images had been brought to the villages. As before, this was the result of increasing the rate of literacy, but more directly the war was instrumental in exposing members of large conscript armies to foreign lands, "from the Urals to the Pyrenees."[118] Or, as Jozo Tomasevich observes,

> World War I [was] a great school for the southeast European peasantry as a result of which the peasant had grown politically. . . . As a fighting soldier or as a prisoner of war, the peasant from all South Slav provinces became during World War I a great "traveler." He was able to observe not only the difference between life in his village and in the cities, but also the difference in the ways of working and living of peasants in countries and areas on much higher levels of cultural and economic development than the way of life to which he and his neighbors were accustomed. . . . No doubt these experiences during the war served as an impetus in the attempts of many peasants during the interwar period to improve their economic lot and conditions of life in the village generally.[119]

But apart from "mobilizing" the peasantry, the war contributed to social tensions in yet another and more subtle way, which is generally ignored by many of its historians. While this war had been fought in the name of na-

118. Z. Szabó 1936, esp. 200. In a similar vein, see Gusti 1968, 486–91.
119. Tomasevich 1955, 230.

tional power and prestige, beneath the surface it was, as the radical Left kept reiterating, about the "uneven development" of capitalism and about a widespread sense of the futility of trying to improve one's lot by conventional strategies of economic development. The ennui of the prewar years, so much touted by historians, and so well captured by the literature and visual art of "modernism," was the boredom of people who, like Sisyphus, were tired of rolling rocks up hills without tangible, not to say dramatic, improvements in their daily lives. The joyous crowds of August 1914 expressed this feeling, together with an undercurrent of hope that war would both liberate them from futility and accomplish what the daily routines of buying and selling could not. Needless to say, these expectations were left unfulfilled. The peace treaties changed national boundaries and redistributed territories, but did not create new economies. The Polish peasant now had a country of his own, and the Italian or Romanian peasant a larger country than before, but their economic lot had either deteriorated or remained the same. The result was a massive disillusionment in all the countries of the periphery, not just among the defeated but among the victorious nations as well. While the defeated nations felt ravaged by ruthless victors, the victors themselves felt cheated out of a "just reward" for their sacrifices: Italians complained about being excluded from the redivision of colonies, Yugoslavia about Italian high-handedness, Romania about the major allies' orders to relinquish Hungarian territories it had held beyond the armistice lines, the Poles about not being able to recover their old empire in its entirety. If the 1920s were a decade of sulking and blaming the political dispensations of the major powers, the 1930s encounter with the Depression filled these national grievances with new economic content and linked anger about international politics with anger about international capitalism.

These compounded frustrations provided a natural backdrop to the rise of a new political class, the third major dynamic in the rise of the radical Right in the politics of East Central Europe. As in the nineteenth century, secular trends in modernizing educational systems played a role. Indeed, after 1920, most countries expanded their systems of higher education, creating an ever-widening gap between educational accomplishment and social mobility. The cases of Poland, Hungary, and Romania are the most conspicuous. In Poland, the number of university students increased almost threefold between 1910 and 1930 (from 13,737 to 36,364) at institutions located in the territory of postwar Poland, mostly as part of an official design to create a culturally homogeneous intellectual elite. In Hungary, during the same period—and while the population of the country decreased by 60 percent—the number of university students increased by 8 percent (from 11,893 to 12,788), reflecting the government's desire to accommodate middle-class refugees from the lost territories. In Romania, the number of university students increased fivefold (from 5,925 to 29,930), in gross disproportion to the doubling of the general population.[120] Herein were the makings of a "free-floating intelligentsia," as one distinguished contemporary, Karl Mannheim, designated the phenomenon.[121]

But once again, the war entered as an independent factor of social change, giving the secular trend a sharp twist by raising the aspirations of significant segments of the younger generation. It did so by requiring the induction of tens, indeed hundreds, of thousands of young men with certificates of "maturation"—or high school diplomas—who, almost uniformly in all belligerent countries, were trained to be junior officers of reserve status to command the millions of peasant and worker recruits, the bulk of all armies in the field. Consequently, a very large number of young men—and particularly those struggling with their education or careers while lacking the proper social and ethnic credentials—suddenly attained exalted rank, together with all its perquisites. They may not have been, as one observer suggests, weaned "to a carefree life" or "financial liberties,"[122] but they certainly were shielded from the vagaries of the marketplace and enjoyed a good measure of economic security: food at the officers' mess, appropriate attire, and manservants to look after them. But above all, they had the experience of hierarchy and command—indeed, that of power over the life and death of subordinates—an experience that would define the outlook of a whole generation of educated people aspiring for status and privilege. When the war ended, these privileges ended overnight, and the loss was hard to absorb. It was, of course, most bitter among the returning members of the defeated armies, where career officers, soon to become the hard core of the various officers' detachments, joined reservists (and some noncommissioned officers) at emergency food lines. The more famed examples of Germany's "free corps" thus found their counterparts in the alliance of the Twelve Captains (*tizenkét kapitányok*) of Hungary,[123] each of whom would play a prominent role in one movement of the Right or another, becoming members of the university brigades (*egyetemi zászlóaljak*) of demobilized reservists, or of the Hungarian National Defense League. In Bulgaria, the Military League (later Reservists' Association) was formed under Damian Velchev, which the public dubbed the Captain's League.[124] But even in the victorious countries—Poland, Romania, and the new states of Yugoslavia and Czechoslovakia—demobilized soldiers faced problems. There, too, returning officers encountered unemployment, the resumption of their interrupted stud-

120. See Laky 1932, 18–22.
121. Mannheim 1936, esp. 154, 161-62, 181–83.
122. Ránki 1971, 66.
123. J. Erős 1981, 124.
124. Rothschild 1974, 341.

ies while facing an uncertain future, or the boredom of relatively low-level jobs, like teaching in a village school, which, after commanding a company or even a squad, was a devastating experience. Thus a substantial portion of the returnees, especially men without social connections, sought support among old comrades. Poland, like Hungary and Bulgaria, had its own captains of Pilsudski's Legion (to reappear as the "colonels" of the fascist regime of 1937). These were sometimes followers of Dmowski's Greater Poland Camp, while others formed into nameless groups, like the one that plotted and carried out the assassination of President Narutowicz in 1921.[125] In the new Yugoslavia—the "Kingdom of Serbs, Croats, and Slovenes" until 1929—demobilized officers tried to find social support and a venue to relive their wartime experiences in numerous para- and ex-military organizations: the Union of Chetniks, the Society of Reserve Officers, the Federation of Volunteers, the Union of Slovene Soldiers (BOJ), the Croatian Ustasha, and the revitalized Internal Macedonian Revolutionary Organization (IMRO).[126] In Romania, soldiers returning to the student bodies of the universities were among the first to join Codreanu's Legion of the Archangel Michael, the forerunner of the better-known Iron Guard, and the Fascia Româna.[127] Even in relatively placid and content Czechoslovakia, some of the members of the wartime Czech Legion entered the Czech National Fascist Community (Narodni obec fašistická).[128]

In 1929–30, the governments of East Central Europe were still busy, and largely successful, in their attempts to accommodate this new "generation of the fronts" (Frontgeneration) when they were shaken by the turmoil of the Great Depression. Once the Depression struck, labor markets collapsed. Governments, in desperate budgetary straits, not only could not hire long-waiting candidates but were forced to cut the existing body of public employees. "Intellectual unemployment," or "underemployment," was now on every front page and on every lip. Demoralized university students quickly understood that they were being "overproduced" and that there might now be more profit in brawling than in attending lectures, passing exams, and writing doctoral theses. Organizations of radical students and unemployed graduates mushroomed everywhere and were especially evident in Hungary, Poland, and Romania, where they were now joining such organizations as the MOVE, the NARA, and the Iron Guard respectively.[129]

Not surprisingly, Right radical elites resembled their rivals on the Left in their social composition. Given the persistence of discrimination, they were

125. Wereszycki 1971, 87–88.
126. A. Djordević 1971, 130.
127. E. Weber 1966, 501–741.
128. J. Zacek 1971, 59.
129. A remarkable 114 of the 252 legionary "martyrs" of the royal dictatorship were students. See Almanahul Cuvântul, 1941 (1940), 315–17.

more plebeian and *raznochyntsi* (born without the traditional social markers of privilege), or at any rate more plebeian than their liberal-conservative counterparts: this emerges from comparisons of their social profile with those of earlier governments in Romania and Hungary.[130] There are also at least some parallels between Left and Right elites with respect to ethnic marginality: both attracted individuals teetering uneasily on the borderline between two identities and often crossing that line in search of social mobility. The most striking examples of this are provided by the history of interwar Hungary, a multinational country before 1918 in which public-sector employment (1) excluded Jews, but (2) was also used to encourage the ethnic assimilation of upwardly mobile Germans, Slovaks, and South Slavs. After 1918, however, with the sudden shrinking of employment opportunities in the rump country, not just Jews, but other people of "suspicious" and "ambiguous" origin became targets of discrimination by "true-born" Hungarians flouting their ethnic credentials in search of preferential treatment. This discrimination was informal rather than formal and institutional, yet it produced a statistically identifiable association between the new Right and the psychologically wounded, assimilated elements. Thus between 1932 and 1944, 12 out of 19 identifiable Right radical cabinet ministers were of non-Hungarian ethnic origin, as were 14 of the 17 members of the Arrow Cross National Council.[131] But the Hungarian Right was not alone in attracting ethnic marginals. Herzegovinans of the "borderlands" played (and still play) a significant role in Croat radical nationalism, as did resettled Macedo-Romanians (Arumanians, or Vlachs) in the elite groups and councils of the Iron Guard,[132] and the role played by recent assimilees was conspicuous in the top echelons of nearly all fascist movements. Prominent examples include the Hungarian prime ministers Gömbös (Knöpfle), Imrédy (Heinrich), Sztójai (Stojaković), and Szálasi (Saloşean), the Romanian Guardist leader Codreanu (Zelenski), and the "three musketeers" of Czech national radicalism, Rudolf Gajda (Geidl), Karel Perger, and Jiři (earlier Ferdinand) Strýbni. One might also add to the list some of the leaders of the new Slovak Right: Jozef Tiso, who before 1918 was editor of the Hungarian *Nyit-*

130. In Romania, boyar descendants represented 30.5 percent of the delegates in the "liberal" parliaments of the 1920s as opposed to only 15.2 percent in the rightist National Union government of 1930–31, 7.9 percent of the deputies of the fascist Romanian Front, and boyar descendants made up 8 percent of Iron Guard deputies, but only 2–3 percent of the names on the list of 388 Iron Guard candidates, and they were absent from the list of Iron Guard "martyrs." In Hungary, 55.9 percent of the deputies of the ministers of the liberal-conservative Bethlen government were members of the titled aristocracy or the gentry, as opposed to 25 percent of national radical ministers (1934–44), and 17.7 percent of the Arrow Cross National Council. For Romania, see sources of the Elite Project, Introduction, n. 2. For the list of Iron Guard candidates, see *Buna Vestirea* (Bucharest), December 2, 1937. For the list of martyrs, see *Almanahul Cuvântul*, 1941, 315–17. For Hungary, see tables in Janos 1982, 282–84.
    131. Janos 1982, 282–84.
    132. E. Weber 1966c, 544.

rai Szemle, and Vojtech (earlier Béla) Tuka, a professor of law at the Hungarian University of Pozsony who rediscovered his Slovak roots after 1918 and, as his detractors charged, learned to speak his native Slovak only at the age of forty.[133]

The rise of this new political class changed the political spectrum and the very nature of conflict in most of the societies of East Central Europe. If in the first two decades of the century, politics was neatly dichotomized between old and new, between peripheral liberalism and socialism, in the 1920s the politics of most of the societies of the region acquired a tripartite character, with radicals of the Left and Right fighting both each other and the liberal establishment. This competition is well reflected in the political ideology of the new Right, most prominently in its militant reassertion of the politics of particularism, juxtaposed with the economic universalism of the market and the political universalism of socialism. While anti-Semitism was not an integral part of the doctrine, given the ethnic background of some of the left-wing elites, it was never far from the surface.

The word "particularism," however, has different meanings and has applications in different contexts. It may refer to the particularism of the ethnic nation. But it can also be used in reference to communities of culture and race. All of these communities, in the last analysis, are "imagined," social constructs. But each definition has a logic of its own, and it is in terms of this logic that we may identify varieties of fascism, most significantly the fascism of national communities, as opposed to supra- or international communities of religion and race.

Varieties of Fascism

The first of these two varieties, national radicalism, has its roots in some of the frustrated ambitions of Europe's major nation-states. In Germany, for example, there existed a long-standing tradition, cultivated even during the years of "saturation" under Bismarck's chancellorship, that glorified national greatness and accepted war as a normal instrument of pursuing national contentment. Cultivated by a series of military thinkers and historians from von Clausewitz to Leopold von Ranke and Friedrich Treitschke, the tradition resurfaced in the 1890s to provide rhetorical underpinnings for the more aggressive foreign policies of Wilhelm II and for the ensuing German quest for hegemony. In France, the wounds inflicted by defeat at the hands of Prussia in 1870 never quite healed. There were large numbers of Frenchmen who, throughout the half century after the Franco-Prussian war, nurtured resentments about the loss of their country's continental he-

---

133. For the Czechs, Havránek 1971, 50; Zacek 1971, 59–61. For the Slovaks, see Baerlein 1940b, 309–10.

gemony and grieved over the loss of Alsace and Lorraine. Elements of the French Right appealed to this large constituency, suggesting that the cause of *revanche* might best be served by restructuring French society and by toughening French political culture and institutions. Some of the names associated with this advocacy were those of Edouard Drumont, author of an anti-Semitic tract, *La France juive*, the publication of which is said to have denoted "in a verifiable sense . . . the beginnings of the Dreyfus affair";[134] Maurice Pujo, the founder of the street-brawling Camelots du Roi;[135] and, last but not least, of Charles Maurras, who made the first successful attempt to pull together the loose strands of radical conservatism into a coherent doctrine of "integral nationalism."[136] In essence, this doctrine stated that the rights of the nation take precedence over the rights of the individual, that military organization and means were superior to "government by lawyers and professors,"[137] and that authoritarian government was neither a natural condition nor something ordained by divine law, but an instrument crafted to mobilize society for national survival and greatness.[138] By the same logic, integral nationalism provided a bridge between Maurras's political philosophy and the raw sentiments expressed by Pujo and the French anti-Semites of the turn of the century. For if one applied its logic, one could argue that effective mobilization for national purposes required not only political but national homogeneity as well. If the liberal state had been ambivalent about the rights of cultural minorities in the national state, the doctrine of integral nationalism made minorities unambiguously and altogether unwelcome.

As it happened, though, both before and after World War I, Italy provided a more fertile soil than did France for the principles of radical nationalism. Like France, although for quite different reasons, from the 1880s onward, Italy harbored national grievances. The Risorgimento had failed to pull all Italians together into a single state, and a large number of compatriots remained Austrian subjects. Furthermore, as a latecomer among the great national states, Italy had been unable to compete effectively in the race for the distribution of colonies in the non-European world. Accordingly she remained, in the picturesque phrase of the times, a "beggar at the banquet" of the great colonial powers, England and France. Unlike France, moreover, Italy had failed to achieve effective national integration of the poverty-stricken South with the relatively prosperous North, a circumstance that no doubt contributed to the slow growth—indeed, progressive marginaliza-

134. Nolte 1966, 48; E. Weber 1962, 45, 71, 198.

135. For Pujo's recollections of the early years of the movement, see his *Les Camelots du Roi* (1933); for description of the Camelots, see Nolte 1966, 69–70, 89–92, and E. Weber 1966a, 71–127.

136. E. Weber 1962, 53–54.

137. Maurras, *Le mauvais traité*, vol. 2, quoted in Nolte 1966, 111.

138. Nolte 1966, 110–13.

tion—of her economy in comparison to other semiperipheral countries of the continent. For the first time in history, national radicalism thus turned into an ideology of economic backwardness.

The Italian who perhaps more than anybody else articulated these concerns in the radical nationalist frame of reference was Enrico Corradini. A socialist in his youth at the turn of the century, and a contemporary of Lenin and Trotsky, Corradini borrowed freely from Marxist teaching, although he added a number of interesting twists to the doctrine after his conversion to nationalism. Most significantly, Corradini treated nations as analogous to Marx's classes, and international relations primarily as conflict between rich and poor, or between plutocratic and proletarian nations struggling for scarce resources from a position of economic inferiority.[139] Although he recognized that the postmedieval concept of sovereignty gives states the status of independence, in Corradini's view such independence remains purely formal so long as it is not accompanied by economic and cultural equality. By his analysis, Italy of the turn of the century was the paradigmatic case for such a proletarian nation: although nominally independent, her reality was one of dependency (*dipendenza*)[140] on the more powerful and economically more successful capitalist nations. The task confronting Italy and other economically dependent, nominally sovereign states, then, was to break out of the confining conditions of foreign tutelage. Such liberation could be accomplished only by collective action, and preferably by such action involving violence, for it was through the experience of combat that nations would be built and transformed from mere communities of interest into "spiritual communities." A devoted student of Sorel, Corradini on this point broke with Marx and Bentham, becoming master and forerunner of Antonio Gramsci and Frantz Fanon by emphasizing that solidarity is the function of collective experiences of peril, violence, and risk-taking, and that politics, in the final analysis, is a test of competing wills.

The most important representative of Italian fascism, Benito Mussolini, was a disciple of Corradini,[141] although his doctrinal writings were also influenced by other thinkers of his age, one of them German, the others mostly Italians. The German was Friedrich Nietzsche, from whom Mussolini borrowed three major themes. One was the already-familiar idea that war is not only an instrument of politics but one of the main instruments of building the moral character of individuals and nations. Much like Nietzsche, Mussolini was full of contempt for the humdrum economic pursuits of the bourgeoisie; he turned Nietzsche's celebration of adventure into a celebration of the political entrepreneurs he would eventually lead to victory.

139. See Corradini 1923a, 103–19.
140. Ibid., 109.
141. For Mussolini and Corradini, see Gregor 1969, esp. 72–82.

The second borrowed element was Nietzsche's secularism and contempt for traditional morality, best expressed by his familiar aphorism "God is dead," interpreted by Mussolini as an injunction against sentimentality and restraint in politics. Morality was, at best, the error of honest men; at worst it was an instrument of deception wielded by defenders of the status quo in order to cloak the universal struggle for domination among states. Third, Mussolini embraced Nietzsche's profound pessimism about the human condition and his perception of life as a perennial struggle for survival in a "dog-eat-dog" world. It was in this spirit that Mussolini rejected "the possibility of 'happiness' on earth as conceived by the economistic literature of the eighteenth century," and the "teleological notion that at some future time the human family [would] secure final settlement of all its difficulties."[142] Man's reward was to be not in paradise but in domination over other men, although in the long run, this reward could prove elusive. In the grand scheme of history, hegemony and domination were temporary, so peoples and elites should seek fulfillment in the existential experiences of adventure and violence.

These Nietzschean ideas were further complemented by what Mussolini learned from the sociology of two contemporaries, Vilfredo Pareto and Gaetano Mosca.[143] Pareto's view that history is not linear and evolutionary, but rather composed of recurrent cycles of fortune and misfortune, further corroborated Mussolini's Nietzschean pessimism. In addition, Mussolini was impressed by Mosca's view that societies are divided not only among upper and lower economic classes but also between economic and political classes, the latter exercising power by the sheer force of character and initiative. But what may have touched Mussolini most of all was Pareto's theory of the circulation of elites. According to this theory, societies operate most effectively when ruled by elites of natural talent rather than by elites of hereditary right. That principle was to exercise a powerful influence over the new class of political entrepreneurs, recruited, as Mussolini was, from the lower strata of society, and impeded in their upward mobility by effete conservative and liberal establishments.

Much as in France and Italy, national radicalism first manifested itself in East Central Europe before World War I as an angry nationalism impatient with institutional and moral restraints that seemed to stand in the way of national unification or independence. The best-known and best-remembered organizations of this kind were in the South Slav lands, where the memories of fighting bands (the Bulgarian *cheta* and the Serbian derivative *chetnik*)

142. Mussolini 1935, 10.
143. For a critical summary and review of the vast oeuvres of these two men—including Pareto's *Cours de economie politique* (1896) and *Trattato di sociologia generale* [Mind and society] (1916), and Mosca's *Elementi di scienza politica* [The ruling class] (1896)—see Meisel 1965.

lingered long after 1878. Their tradition was revived by the the Internal Macedonian Revolutionary Organization (IMRO). Founded in 1904, IMRO for the next thirty-five years played much the same role as the PLO, Hezbollah, and Hamas are playing in our own days. In the Serb lands, the chetnik tradition sustained the organization of the Narodna Obrana (National Defense), the Mlada Bosna (Young Bosnia), and the Ujedinjenje ili Smert (Unification or Death). The latter was founded in 1911 by Ljuba Jovanović and the Colonel Dimitrijević-Apis, who eventually became its best-known member. If the name of the organization summarized its purposes, the title of their journal, *Pijemont* [Piedmont], reflected its leaders' conception of strategy: the use of Serbia as a base from which actions could be started to unify all Serbs in a single country.[144] The Ujedinjenje, popularly known as the Black Hand, encouraged the group of young Bosnian Serbs who carried out the assassination of Archduke Francis Ferdinand in Sarajevo, an act that eventually served the purposes of the organization by triggering World War I. But while plotting such momentous events, the members of the organization also harbored plans for the reorganization of the Serbian state along lines more in harmony with an externally aggressive and expansive foreign policy. Once the world war began, however, these designs brought them into sharp conflict with the more senior members of the Serbian establishment, including a once sympathetic crown prince, later King Alexander II of Yugoslavia. Fearful of a military coup, the crown prince and his entourage effected the arrest of these dangerous men in 1917. The leaders of the organization were then tried by a special tribunal and sentenced to die by firing squad.

Right radicalism became a political force in East Central European politics after World War I, which had left in its wake both a class of new political entrepreneurs and an air of near-universal disappointment. Part of the ideology of the new political entrepreneurs was borrowed and part was original or, at least, represented a genuine reinvention of doctrinal wheels that the actors themselves were not directly familiar with. But the radical designation was in any case justified. For unlike their predecessors, who had been willing to play by the rules of the international game, the newly emerging political class put its faith in war and external conquest as a means of righting national wrongs, and most of their operational principles followed the logic of those "higher" political purposes. If war, rather than development, was the way to lift the nation out of its doldrums, the nation would have to be mobilized for effective combat, while its "bad elements" were to be neutralized or weeded out. Consequently, the radicals quickly rejected both the "farce" of parliamentarism and the judicial protection of political and national minorities.

144. See McKenzie 1982, 323–44.

As a corollary, the mobilization of national energies required new institutional forms and the abandonment of parties for "movements," or the monopolization of their political power—innovations that, incongruously, entered the program of the radical Right from the vocabulary and experience of the Soviet Communist Party model. Finally, the logic of mobilization for combat required the liquidation of traditional privilege and rule by elites of virtue and talent, qualities that the new political classes now attributed to themselves. Suddenly, the old ruling classes were denounced and their property was declared to be subject to expropriation, as the radicals of the Right joined those of the Left in forging programs of social redistribution. This was especially true in Poland, Hungary, and Romania, societies with great and highly visible social and economic inequalities. The two most obvious objects were large landholdings in the countryside owned by aristocratic proprietors and the capital and means of production associated with the rising urban economy. Fortuitously for the radicals, in a number of these countries, redistributive demands could easily be harmonized with ethnic themes, for much of the landed aristocracy was of foreign—Austrian, Hungarian, or Greek—origin, while commerce and industry were disproportionately the domains of Jewish and other ethnic entrepreneurs. Ideally, then, the land of these foreign and idle magnates would be distributed among the "native" peasantry, while the property of the Jewish entrepreneur would be transferred in one way or another to the members of a "native" middle class, who, together with the peasants, would serve as the backbone of a revitalized national community.

This nativist impulse took two distinct forms, sometimes merging awkwardly into a single symbolic system. One version conjured up the images of primitive tribal society yet uncorrupted—vide Nietzsche—by the civilizing influences of Rome or Christianity. It was in this spirit that the Romanian Right found solace in juxtaposing the Dacian origins of Romanians to their more refined Latin-Roman heritage, and that Hungarian radicals performed pagan rituals in the hills of Buda, while naming one of their most influential associations after the Etelköz, the region east of the river Pruth, whence the Hungarian tribes launched their conquest of the Pannonian plain in the last decade of the ninth century. Alternatively, radical nationalists expropriated the idiom and symbolism of the populists by celebrating the hearty primitiveness of the peasantry, its propensity for suffering and austerity. Some of the great peasant novels of East Central Europe—the Polish Reymont's *Chlopy* (Peasants), the Hungarians Zsigmond Moricz's *Sárarany* (Gold in the Rough) and Dezsö Szabó's *Elsodort falu* (Village Adrift), and the Croat Mile Budak's *Ognjište* (The Hearth)—either presaged or expressed this radical fascination with peasant life. In magnificently efficient political theater, Codreanu's fascists rode to the villages to be one with their inhabitants, scenes reminiscent of the radical Left's old "going to the people" strategy.[145] The Hungarian Gömbös could weep at the mere sight of a "peasant in costume" or of a "primitive tableau of cattle drinking from a *gémkut* (a shallow well to draw water for cattle),"[146] and when the Romanian king wanted to flaunt his radical credentials, he named himself "the first peasant" of the land.[147] Slovak fascists in fact expropriated the populist label by referring to themselves as Ludaks (men of the people). Never were peasant costumes more popular with a political elite than in East Central Europe during the interwar period. The image was most convenient. It symbolized not only the primordial resolve of a new elite, but also the raw strength that their nations would need in order to conquer or reconquer territories denied to them by the trickery of diplomacy and by the treachery of stronger competitors in the jungle of world affairs.

Given this public celebration of the peasant and of the virtues of primitivism, it was only natural that the new nativists were initially strong and relentless critics of the economic policies of the old liberal-conservative regimes. Indeed, the political rhetoric of the new Right in the 1920s is filled with stark denunciations of the peasants' exploitation and with dark forebodings about the rise of an industrial working class, which most radicals of the time regarded as the harbinger of Marxist internationalism. Within a few years, however, this anti-industrial, anti-urban rhetoric began to crumble under the weight of the inexorable logic of power in the modern world. The main promoters and articulators of policies that adapted to that logic were a number of engineers, economists, and former staff officers (who during the war had been confronted with some of the complexities involved in managing war economies). These men shared a number of traits with their nativist colleagues: they too were members of the front generation, exposed to the experience of war; they too favored strengthening both the hand of the elite at the expense of the mass public and the state at the expense of society; and they, too, were preoccupied with national greatness and the restoration of historical frontiers. But they would also be inclined to remind their comrades-in-arms that a policy of external conquest required a modern army, which in turn required a modern industrial base. They also seem to have learned the true lesson of the World War: that territorial conquest alone would not change the fundamental dynamics of economic backwardness on the periphery of the modern world economy.

These technocrats, who surfaced in public life at the time of the Depression, never challenged the long-term goals of other radicals outright, and they ritualistically repeated the primitivist and peasantist rhetoric of their

145. E. Weber 1966c, 532–41.
146. Macartney 1961, 1: 35.
147. Roberts 1951, 211.

fellow intellectuals and officers. But for the short term, they introduced a new set of priorities by insisting on meticulous planning and economic analysis, and by juxtaposing the virtues of social redistribution with both the benefits of economies of scale and the necessity of capital accumulation for large-scale investment projects. As to minorities, and particularly Jews, the technocrats may have shared the nativists' distaste, but that distaste was tempered by the fear that the harassment and expropriation of Jewish business might hurt the national economy.

While we will meet a number of these technocrats on the following pages, none of them summarized their particular brand of national radicalism better than the Romanian Mihai Manoilescu.[148] An engineer by training and an economist by profession, Manoilescu had won early recognition in Europe as an advocate of import-substitution industrialization in the context of an interdependent modern world system.[149] Much like Corradini and the *dependencistas* of our own day, Manoilescu emphasized the structurally inferior position of peripheral nations, "the differential evolution of terms of trade between exporters of primary goods and producers of manufactures." He further denounced the "growing wealth and productivity gap between the central-developed and peripheral-underdeveloped countries and the role of international politics in enforcing regional disparities."[150] Again like the *dependencistas*, Manoilescu believed in the Marxist theory of unequal exchange and at least implicitly distinguished between "higher" and "lower" ranking goods, depending on the amount of labor required in producing particular commodities. Accordingly, the fundamental problem facing Romania was one common to underdeveloped countries: by trading agricultural products and raw materials for industrial commodities, it was being shortchanged in the process of exchange.[151] For this reason, Manoilescu progressively disengaged himself from the Peasant Party's program of land redistribution in the belief that such a program merely reduced the efficiency of the economy as a whole. The only way out was to industrialize the country by imposing a strict etatist regime of accumulation. "An agricultural country," he stated in his main work, "cannot raise slowly and uniformly the income of all producers. . . . The real work of progress begins at the centers, or nuclei . . . and such nuclei can only be provided by industries, which require superior productivity."[152] The main project and immediate priority of a backward society is therefore the rapid development of the industrial

148. A most recent, and most astute, summary of Manoilescu's life work, including a careful analysis of his lesser writings, is to be found in Love 1996, 71–100. See also Roberts 1951, 193–98; Schmitter 1978, 117–39; Janos 1970, esp. 213–14.

149. Manoilescu [1930] 1986, 21.

150. Schmitter 1978, 120–21.

151. Manoilescu [1930] 1986, 21, 178–85.

152. Ibid., 63.

sector. The realization of such a project required in the first place the rationalization of production, allocation, and investment. As Henry Roberts observes, Manoilescu saw the ideal society "as a planned work of engineering."[153] "One day," Manoilescu predicted confidently, "the principles of scientific organization will dominate all of society and will be applied to the entire system of national production as to a single enterprise."[154] But—and this is Manoilescu's significant departure from liberal principles—the project of development cannot be restricted to economics; it must embrace the entire social and political life of the nation. "In order to exist as a civilized state, Romania must have a political and social form that will realize her energies to a maximum."[155] The specific forms that Manoilescu envisaged were the corporatist society and the one-party state.

Manoilescu's ideas on the single party reflected the same managerial-bureaucratic concerns with capacity and efficiency that inform his economic writings. That is, he saw the monopolistic party not merely as an instrument of popular mobilization but also as one of political rationalization. The peoples of the world, Manoilescu stated, were generally tired of the inefficiency and waste of energy that resulted from inept state administration and the futile bickering of competing political factions.[156] "For this reason," the idea of rationalization would make "more and more headway in the soul of the people, and even become a kind of myth. The fact that the term 'rationalization' does not enjoy universal popularity does not change the validity of this proposition."[157] Indeed, given its ability to guarantee public order, stability, and continuity, the advantages of the one-party state were so overwhelming that it would be able to attract the best and most idealistic elements of the nation, which in turn would guarantee the political purity of the regime.[158] Political-structural and economic change therefore had to go hand in hand. The only question was whether changes in the domestic political structure alone could do the job. Manoilescu did not explicitly answer that question, but his structural analysis of the global capitalist economy strongly suggested that mobilization of one country's resources alone would not suffice, and that the weak countries of the periphery needed either to unite, as some of the populists had suggested, or to partake in a larger rebellion of continental powers, thereby creating the political underpinnings of a new global economy. His own personal political history—involving pilgrimage from peasantism to the royal dictatorship, his flirtation with the

153. Roberts 1951, 194.
154. Manoilescu 1922, 50.
155. Quoted in Roberts 1951, 194.
156. Manoilescu 1941, 42.
157. Ibid.
158. Ibid., 52–85.

Iron Guard, and accommodation with the idea of bringing Romania into the orbit of National Socialist Germany—seems to suggest that he was in search of solutions beyond the nation-state. If so, his dreams were crushed on the day when Italian and German arbiters of the Romanian-Hungarian territorial dispute held against his country, revealing their willingness to admit only a truncated Romania into the emerging New Order of the Continent. Manoilescu, then the country's foreign minister, fainted on the scene, and subsequently faded away as a figure in Romanian politics. He eventually perished in communist captivity.

If national radicalism aimed at raising the status of one nation over all others, rightist internationalism had a far more grandiose scheme to create a new order of continental, and ultimately global, scale. The nation as a category was not necessarily absent from this grand design. But the nation and its welfare were no longer ultimate ends. Instead, the nation came to be seen as a means destined to accomplish a historically ordained higher purpose, to which its happiness, and even its survival, could be subordinated. The history of fascism provides a striking number of examples of this kind of thinking. Hitler, for one, believed that the German nation was chosen by fate to create a new order of perfect harmony in the world. He was willing to gamble with the very existence of the nation, and when he was about to lose his gamble, he was inclined to leave the country in smoldering ruins for having been unworthy of the mission assigned to it. Some of his minions, too, were complicit in the destruction of their own countries, often to prolong their own lives, although they justified their behavior by invoking imperatives over and above the existence of the national state. It was in this vein that the Hungarian Ferenc Szálasi declared the Magyar nation to have been destined by fate to create a new order in southeastern Europe, adding in 1936 that if it proved to be "incapable of doing so, it should be cleared out of the Danube Basin and another nation be put in its geographical position." [159] What sounded like gibberish in 1936 became a terrifying reality in 1945, when the Hungarian Arrow Cross joined the German army in destroying the country's capital in a last-ditch attempt to hold up the advance of the Soviet army. Years later, surviving subordinates of Szálasi's still took pride in the fact that Hungary was sacrificed in order to save Europe from Bolshevism. [160]

In this sense, fascist internationalism shares some of the characteristics of Marxist internationalism. However, the differences between the two are at least as important as the similarities. For while Marxism as an idea rose out of the Enlightenment's paradigm of progress, international fascism harkened

159. Quoted in Macartney 1961, 1: 163.
160. See Sulyok 1954, 542.

back to the conservative idea of a golden age, which, although lost on account of misfortune or malevolence, was recoverable by sustained, virtuous endeavor. The images of the golden age varied, and so did the ideologies of international fascism. While one was drawn from the pre-Christian age and the migration of Teutonic peoples to the European continent, with their raw and unbridled power, the other found inspiration in the Christian Middle Ages, with its purported harmony based on the idea of divine right. Both of these images transcended the idea of the nation-state—one in the name of a racial, the other in the name of a religious community.

As Hannah Arendt so powerfully reminds us, race thinking in politics originated not on the peripheries but in some of the most advanced core countries of the early modern world. Thus it was in France that the Comte de Boulainvilliers coined the phrase "race of aristocrats"[161] in an attempt to give new legitimacy to the declining upper class of feudalism in genetic terms, and in England that Houston Stewart Chamberlain, John Davidson, and Charles Dilke further developed the race idea in search of an ideological justification for the "mad scramble" for colonies.[162] In both cases, race served not as an idiom of rebellion but as one of defending established configurations of power. If in France the implications of racism remained local, in England they became global and closely intertwined with the victorious march of *techne* during the early industrial age. In more than one way, economic superiority and successful innovation became the evidence of racial superiority, while racial superiority became justification for the rapidly evolving hierarchical relationships among nations and continents.

The ideology and politics of race, however, underwent further metamorphosis as it migrated from England and France to Germany. While British purveyors of the racial idiom used it to justify hierarchical relationships between European and non-European peoples, in the hands of German scholarship and statesmanship, it was applied to European peoples, and most of all to peoples in the eastern backyard of imperial Germany. The racial inferiors were no longer the savages of "dark continents," but the "whole repulsive mixture of Czechs, Poles, Ruthenians, Hungarians, Serbs and Croats," whom the young Hitler met in the streets of Vienna, and deemed to be the very "embodiments of the desecration" of a superior race.[163] Like the earlier notion of the *Kulturgefälle*, the racial notion followed closely the economic gradient of the European continent as another justification for German hegemony. But cast in racial terms, the theory now made hierarchy more "natural," and hence immutable and absolute.

161. Arendt 1951, 163–64.
162. Ibid., 180–84.
163. Hitler [1926] 1971, 123.

Another aspect of this metamorphosis turned out to be still more momentous, and ultimately more fateful. Migrating from England to Germany, these ideas were traveling not so much from one culture to another as from one sector of the global economy to another, and this made a great deal of difference. England (and her overseas offshoots) were hegemonic powers of the global core. But semiperipheral Germany, while regarded by her own racial thinkers as the aristocrat of nations, was also a loser in the competition for new territories, outdistanced by the Anglo-Saxons and French, with their colonial empires and higher per capita incomes. From the point of view of the true believer in racial theory, these disparities represented a monumental incongruity: how could a superior race occupy an inferior position in the distribution of spoils in world politics? Racial theory, it was argued, was about natural hierarchy: a grizzly bear everywhere and inevitably is as superior to the gray wolf, as the gray wolf is, in turn, to the caribou. A condition of relative political and economic inferiority endured by a superior race goes against the laws of nature, especially if, as in the case of Germany, that condition was reaffirmed by defeat in war. By this logic, such incongruity becomes an intellectual puzzle that can only be solved by invoking external agency—in this instance, conspiracy and trickery.

The key to the puzzle was again provided by Friedrich Nietzsche. Although not a racial theorist, Nietzsche was preoccupied with power, will, and hierarchy. His philosophy offers a conception of human consciousness that emphasizes the power of persuasion over and above the power of the impersonal forces of history. Nature's way is thus to establish a hierarchy between masters and slaves on the basis of military virtue and physical strength, but the relationship is complicated by the existence of a "priesthood," whose power derives from its ability to determine what is good and what is bad.[164] By its very nature, priesthood—an allegory for intellectualism—attracts cerebral but impotent men, jealous of aristocratic beauty, strength, and proclivity for risk-taking. That jealousy finds expression in the creation of morality and in the justification of the slave's rebellion.

This is powerful stuff, and it was picked up by a variety of political figures, including Mussolini, who used it to explain the nobility yet feebleness of Italians in international affairs. But Nietzsche took his theorizing a step further by identifying the Jews as a "priestly people" capable of inverting the values of the warrior by teaching that inequality and hierarchy are "bad," and that "only the poor, the powerless are good, only the suffering, the sick and ugly are truly blessed."[165] The strong enforce submission by

164. For this analysis, see, especially, Nietzsche 1951, 86–90, 126–27, 156–57, and Nietzsche [1872, 1887] 1952, esp. 158–89.
165. Nietzsche [1872, 1887] 1952, 167–68.

combat and physical violence, the weak pursue the same objective by psychological aggression—by filling the strong, happy, cruel aristocrat with a sense of profound guilt.

For Nietzsche, then, what in essence had taken place was the triumph of intellect over brute force. For the coffeehouse circle of right radicals in German-speaking countries, however, it became the perfect explanation as to how a superior race could turn out to be an underdog in the global competition of power and privilege. By all indications, Hitler never read Nietzsche. Neither *Mein Kampf* nor Hitler's *Table Talk* (*Tischgespräche*) mentions his name. Nietzschean ideas reached him through the filter of Alfred Rosenberg's *Myth of the Twentieth Century*,[166] and, more simply, through what was coffeehouse *Quatsch* in Vienna and Munich. This at least is the impression he gives in his published conversations with Dietrich Eckart.[167]

Whatever its origins, this theory of conspiratorial voluntarism, coupled with the view of a natural order in a state of disequilibrium, became the cornerstone of all racial theories of fascism, as well as one of the key differences between the national and international brands of Right radicalism. The anti-Semitism of national radicals was opportunistic, and even at its extreme was limited to the objectives of establishing their political and cultural hegemony in the nation-state. These objectives could be pursued with brutality or subtlety, but they could be attained by expulsions or by the encouragement of migration to some other land. In contrast, the anti-Semitism of racial thinkers was informed by a truly chiliastic vision of restoring a natural equilibrium in the affairs of humanity upset by that priestly people of devilish influence, and the logic of such reasoning left no room for solutions other than the finality of eradication by genocide. This logic lends credibility to the argument that Hitler's final solution was an objective of war, which was given top priority precisely at the time when the prospect of military victory was beginning to slip away. By promoting a policy of genocide, the war could not be won, but humanity might presumably be saved. The same logic explains the behavior of members of the Romanian Iron Guard in 1941 and of the Hungarian Arrow Cross in 1944–45, when, encircled in their capital cities and doomed to certain defeat, its members went on a last, murderous rampage against the Jewish inhabitants of Bucharest and Budapest.

In view of the above, it is easy to agree with Arendt that it was this apocalyptic vision of deliverance that made Hitler into an international figure whose charisma, like that of Lenin or Stalin, transcended political boundaries.[168] But the appeals of Lenin and Stalin, unlike Hitler's, were never burdened by a laundry list of inferior nations, many of which, whether by dint

166. Hitler [1926] 1971; id. [1951] 1953; A. Rosenberg 1930.
167. Eckart 1925.
168. Arendt 1951, 357–58.

of fate or the logic of geopolitics, turned up eventually as Germany's wartime allies and ideological camp followers. Some of these potential disciples swallowed their pride and were willing to take this racism for what it was, a codeword for their own economic backwardness. It was in this spirit that some, like the Hungarian Béla Imrédy (first premier, then leader of the Party of Hungarian Renovation) and András Mecsér (a maverick right-winger and personal friend of Hitler), or the Romanian Horia Sima, accepted the notion of eventual subordination in the hope that German hegemony would bring to their countries German order, efficiency, and cleanliness, or, in the language of today's sociology, modernization.[169] Sima, a survivor among the fascist leaders, in fact describes Hitlerism as a forerunner of today's united Europe, insofar as it allowed the more developed countries to exercise benevolent tutelage over the small nations of the periphery that were struggling to break out of the confining condition of their underdevelopment.[170] Others, like the leaders of the Slovak Ludaks, Vojtech (Béla) Tuka and Alexander (Sanyo) Mach, were ready to downplay the Slavic origins of their own people, arguing that its heroism and anthropological characteristics had earned it a place among the Nordic races,[171] or to go as far as Ante Pavelić's Croatian Ustashas (Ustaše), who as early as 1936 sent several memoranda to high German circles from his Italian exile pleading that Croats were not of Slavic stock, but rather descendants of a Gothic tribe Slavicized in the course of the Continent's great migration of peoples.[172]

Others, though, proved troublesome; unable to swallow their pride, they created their own imaginary communities of race that would put them on equal footing with the Nordic Teutons. The majority of Romanian fascists could fall back on their Dacian or Roman ancestry, or on a mixture of the two, which made them descendants of glorious imperial peoples, while some Polish fascists were ready to argue the pre-Slavic, Sarmatian origin of their nation to demonstrate their racial equality with northern Europeans.[173] In Hungary, select groups of fascists (and some nonfascists) tried to revive their Turco-Turanian ancestry, thereby linking them to the great Timur, the Ottomans, and even Japan, which some Hungarians of the 1930s described as the "other sword of Turan" (the number one place being reserved for themselves).[174] While some Hungarian Turanists went as far as to argue that they were racially healthier than and superior to other Europeans (including Ger-

---

169. For Imrédy, see Macartney 1961, 1: 394, 401; 2: 154–56, 195–96; for Mecsér, his correspondence with Szálasi, in Karsai 1978, 55.

170. Sima 1959, esp. 48–49.

171. Jelinek 1976, 88.

172. Hory and Broszat 1964, 29.

173. Chalasiński 1947, 43–44.

174. The major work on Hungarian Turanism is by Kessler 1967; for the Japanese reference, Barátossy-Balog 1930, esp. 9–12.

mans, who were already corrupted by Judaism),[175] others felt more modestly that, as Turanians living in Europe, they might provide an important bridge between East and West and thus play a role in world politics out of proportion of their numbers or of the size of their country. This geopolitical argument was carried to absurd extremes by the Hungarian Ferenc Szálasi, head of the Arrow Cross–Hungarist movement, who believed that, owing to their unique historical and geographical position, Hungarians might play a role equal to, or even more important than, Germany in building the new European order, while Szálasi's own charisma might eventually help him supersede Hitler as the leader of the international movement. In his words:

> It is my conviction that the whole ordering of Europe can be effected only by this little people despised by the Germans, the Magyar people following the basic principles evolved through me. He who does not identify himself with my doctrine, who does not recognize me as a leader without reservations, and does not agree that I have been selected by higher divine authority to redeem Magyardom, he who does not understand me, or loses faith in me, let him go. . . . [T]he fall of Hungarism would mean the end of national socialism.[176]

Such extreme constructs of the mind, together with some of the more conventional expressions of national pride and local patriotism, were obvious obstacles to German foreign policy toward the region and required creative statesmanship that went beyond erasing offending passages from translations of *Mein Kampf*. This became especially urgent because there were also a great number of good German citizens who were in fact Slavic and Dinarian assimilees, likely to fail the more stringent test of Nordic physiognomy. This was a classic dilemma of ideology and power, one that, for the time being at least, was resolved by creating a second, less stringent, criterion of racial purity. Coexisting uneasily with Hitler's list of the racially inferior, this criterion was based on the notion of a new super race of heroic Aryans that would embrace all who by today's equally loose American standard were Caucasian, or white—all, that is, with the exception of the Jews, who were held up as the great identity-building Other. This definition still left out such important allies as the Japanese, the mufti of Jerusalem, and Hindu sympathizers of National Socialism. But the category was codified in the Nuremberg race laws, opening the door to minor European allies, and, during the last, desperate and manpower-strapped years of the war, permitting the SS (that paragon of racial purity) to set up Ukrainian, Bosnian, Hungarian, and Croat divisions in its own uniform and under its own insignia.

Radicalized racism was one form of fascist internationalism. Radicalized and politicized Christianity was another. While the roots of the former go

175. *Turan*, vol. 8 (1921), 74, quoted in Janos 1982, 274n.
176. Quoted in Macartney 1961, 1: 163.

back to the premedieval right of conquest, those of the latter may be traced to the divine right heritage of European traditionalism.

The route from the medieval principle of divine right to Christian fascism was a circuitous one. One of its principal way stations was the active counterrevolutionism of the French thinkers Joseph de Maistre and Ernest Renan, who not only distanced themselves from the liberal spirit of the Enlightenment but demonized and denounced it as "Satanic and evil . . . [a force] aspiring to overthrow the very foundations of an eternal order."[177] This militant spirit of the religious Counter-Enlightenment then became intertwined with the rising anti-capitalist sentiment of the post-1873 period in the German-speaking countries, reflecting and shaping writers such as Adolf Stöcker, a German clergyman; Karl von Vogelsang, a Lutheran "refugee" to Catholic Austria; and the Austrian Georg von Schönerer, a source of inspiration for Adolf Hitler. There was also the Austrian Karl Lueger, who, under the label of Christian socialism, made such ideas an active force in Austrian politics.[178]

Although French and German in origin, these ideas found adherents in all the societies of Christian Europe, from Protestant Germany to Orthodox Romania and Russia. But they flourished most in the Catholic middle, where the teachings of the Church had provided the foundations for the doctrine of a "just wage and return" and had historically been hostile to speculative risk-taking, the charging of interest, and the "ruthless search for profits" under capitalism.[179] At the same time, the Catholic view of society as an organic entity fostered some of the activist aspects of the Christian social agenda, including its advocacy of the corporatist principle of functional representation and a more expansive view of the state than held by nineteenth-century liberalism.[180] A justification for the structure of authority could likewise easily be found in the rich texture of the Roman Church's past. Although the medieval Church never opposed the contractualization of relations between king and subject, under its doctrine of divine right the king's powers, while limited by contract, were free from direct accountability and hence contrary to the liberal principles of popular sovereignty.

In the 1890s, to be sure, the Church attempted to find a modus vivendi with the modern state. Christian politicians and ideologues who accepted the principles of representation thereby came to the fore, which led to the formation of a number of political parties of the Catholic democratic type in Germany, Austria, the Low Countries, the Czech lands, Hungary, and Slovakia. For some time, these parties served as effective instruments for mobiliz-

177. The quotation is from Joseph de Maistre, *Considérations sur la France*, quoted in Nolte 1966, 35. For Renan, see Nolte 1966, 124.
178. See Diamant 1960, esp. 5–50. Also Pulzer 1964, 99–100, 133, 144–53.
179. Baxa 1926, 52–53.
180. Diamant 1960, 30.

ing a segment of the faithful against the secularism of socialist and radical, anticlerical parties. But tensions between the Christian agenda and democracy remained pronounced and, after 1918, the majority of them drifted into the authoritarian camp. The German Zentrum, the Christian Democratic parties of the Low Countries and of Italy, and the Czech Catholic People's Party remained voices of conservative democratism. But the Austrian Christian Socials, the Slovak Catholic People's Party, the Hungarian Christian Nationals, the Polish Christian National Workers' Party, and Christian Alliance for National Unity all either faded electorally, split, or drifted further to the Right by adopting a platform of unabashed authoritarianism.

Catholicism added to the Christian social movement an internationalist cast that had largely been absent from political Christianity in Protestant and Orthodox societies. At the one end of the spectrum—and even in rebellion—German Lutheran political thought amounted to little more than another attempt to reaffirm the primacy of the national state, to protect society from the excesses of capitalist enterprise and the perils of fraud in the modern business world.[181] At the other end of the spectrum, the "love, tradition and the popular, organic nature of Christian Orthodoxy"[182] was less conducive to internationalism than to a parochial, communal view of the nation as the extended family of the village community.

Not so in the case of Catholicism, which by name and institutional structure was both a supranational creed and a natural base for a political movement that aimed at rising above the national state. Moreover, by historical accident, the cultural space of Catholicism was located between the rich countries of Protestantism and the poor countries of the Orthodox East, which gave its political practitioners a semiperipheral mindset. This mindset could blame the "fathers of the revolution in Wittenberg and Geneva"[183] for the aberrations of semiperipheral capitalism, while in the same breath preaching a crusade against the threat to Western civilization represented by the heretics of the Balkans and the Russian steppe. The aggressive antiOrthodoxy of Polish and Croat political Catholicism were products of this crusading spirit of the Janus-faced semiperiphery, rather than merely manifestations of national sentiment fortified by a common religion. In the Balkans, its fruits included ethnic purification and forced conversions during World War II, as well as the more recent excesses marking the dissolution of Yugoslavia.

Although the ideal world of Catholicism was built on virtue rather than raw biological strength, the disjuncture between moral qualities and economic rewards raised basically the same question as that which preoccupied

181. See, for instance, Pulzer on Stöcker's "sozial-ethisch" principles. Pulzer 1964, 99–101.
182. From the Romanian guardist intellectual Nae Ionescu's *Conversations*, quoted by E. Weber 1966c, 535.
183. Renan, quoted in Nolte 1966, 124.

the racial supremacists: why do the virtuous not occupy a more favored position in God's universe? Some, like Renan, blamed this condition of relative inferiority on the "revolt" of Protestantism against the authority of the eternal Church. Others gave their answers a conspiratorial twist by pointing to the secretive manipulations of Freemasonry, designed to undermine the pillars of a divinely ordered international community. These explanations were quite popular in France and Spain, where Freemasons were numerous. But the hypothesis carried little weight in Poland, Hungary, or Slovakia, where Masons were few, while Jews—associated with both capitalism and socialism—were more conspicuous. Thus, perhaps inexorably, much like the racial thinkers of the radical Right, the practitioners of political Catholicism in these countries fell back on the idea of a Jewish conspiracy in order to explain perceived global disequilibria. With different nuances and degrees of intensity, therefore, many of the founders of Central European political Catholicism—von Vogelsang, Lueger, and Spann—may also be counted among the creators of modern political anti-Semitism.

What, then, were the differences between the ideologies of racial and religious fascist parties? In principle, these differences were substantial, for unlike their racial and national counterparts who believed that "God is dead," the Christian political movements subscribed to God's commandments and, accordingly, declared themselves subject to moral restraint in politics. As a corollary, influenced by medieval doctrine, they accepted a pluralist-corporate notion of society that implied a strict division between civil society and the state. In the language of contemporary political discourse, this amounted to the difference between authoritarianism and totalitarianism. As for their brand of anti-Semitism, it was based on religion rather than race, and therefore on the ultimate redemptive power of conversion and integration, rather than on expulsion and extermination. Adolf Stöcker, a self-described anti-Semite, preached, for example, that "the Christian spirit penetrate[d] the barriers of race . . . when Israelites are baptized, they become . . . brothers." [184]

In practice, however, the distinctions between the two movements frequently became blurred. True, in their early years, when they were still competing for power, Christian radicals crossed swords with the secularized Right and its Nietzschean nihilism. It is also true that in a few instances—in Austria and Portugal, to take the best examples—Christian fascism made efforts to set up corporatist institutions and refrained from the systematic persecution of phantom enemies once it was in power. But in most countries of East Central Europe, corporatism remained an empty shell, with the divisions between state and society frequently breached and the restraining force of the Ten Commandments often superseded by the more militant

184. Quoted in Pulzer 1964, 100.

legacies of the Crusades, the Inquisition, and the Counter-Reformation. As to their "Jewish laws," Christian fascist regimes did pay heed to religious criteria of exclusion and inclusion, but more often than not, they compromised that distinction by introducing cutoff dates—usually the year 1918— as a proof of bona fide conversion and genuine intent. And if, at first, like most other fascist factions, Christian radicals advocated "humane solutions" (meaning emigration or "mere" legal discrimination in the medieval mold), at critical junctures of history they, too, succumbed to pressures and became complicit in the more radical policies of concentration and deportation promoted by racial ultras both within and beyond their countries' boundaries.

Semi-Fascism: The Conservative-Radical Alliance, 1930–1938

National radicalism made its debut immediately after World War I. Thereafter it was forced into hibernation throughout most of the 1920s, after an initial spurt of conspicuous advances. In Hungary, Bulgaria, and Poland, the forces of the radical Right were compelled to retreat, while neo-liberal regimes and their bureaucratic machines were gradually restored following the initial years of chaos, revolutions, and democratic experiments. Having used the zeal of radical organizations and officers' detachments to beat back the left, most of the governments of the region made strenuous and largely successful efforts to neutralize the new Right. Their favored technique was to bribe leaders of the radical Right with jobs and, after giving them modest access to the trough, to shunt them off from the mainstream of political life to provincial garrisons and administrative posts. Those who failed to take the bait were politically marginalized by rigged elections, which, except in Czechoslovakia and Albania, resumed after brief experiments with freely elected democratic government. In Hungary, the diehards of the "white terror" and the "Christian Course" (of 1919–21) were eliminated from parliament one by one. Their leaders—Gömbös, Tibor Eckhardt, and Bajcsy-Zsilinszky—became dispirited men. Gömbös eventually accepted a junior position in István Bethlen's cabinet; Eckhardt and, later, Bajcsy-Zsilinszky left their Party of Racial Defense and eventually gravitated to the political center. In Poland, Pilsudski's coup d'état, undertaken in 1926 in the name of a somewhat dubious "supra-partisan tradition of public service," [185] set up a state that was *dirigiste* but "conservative rather than rightist in the integral nationalist sense," while the National Democrats (Endeks)—the "locus of raucous, chauvinistic nationalism of the Right"—were

185. Rothschild 1974, 33.

reduced from their earlier two-fifths to a mere 8.2 percent share of the Sejm.[186] In Czechoslovakia and Yugoslavia, the new Right was a waning force in domestic politics in the 1920s. In the Czech lands, openly fascist groups could never break the 5 percent mark in national elections; in Slovakia, the integral nationalists of the Nastup [Forward] group remained a small minority in Andrej Hlinka's more traditionalist autonomist People's Party. In Croatia, the regional political scene was dominated by the Peasant Party of the Radić brothers; the right-wing Ustasha emerged only in 1929. In Romania, too, the electoral machine of the old political class was successful in preventing the election of radical Right candidates. Alexandru Cuza's anti-Semitic Christian National Defense League was allowed to garner some half dozen seats in a few of the electoral districts of Bucovina and Moldavia with large Jewish minorities,[187] but the Fascia Naţională never made it to the polls, and Corneliu Codreanu's budding cohorts proved unable to win a single seat in parliament throughout the decade.[188] On the other hand, Codreanu's student radicals remained active throughout the 1920s, engaging in acts of petty terror against Jewish shopkeepers and liberal opponents in the vicinity of the universities of Iaşi and, later, Cluj.[189]

Whether they were dubbed liberal, neoliberal, liberal-conservative, or, with increasing justification, just conservative on account of their desire to maintain the status quo, in 1929 the old political machines and their social allies were in control of the governments of East Central Europe, except for Czechoslovakia, where democracy functioned throughout the interwar period. But the control was not firm, for beneath a superficial calm social discontent was simmering, and when the economic crisis suddenly enveloped the region, the discontent of the lower classes burst into the open, sometimes in violent ways. The various national radical factions were gaining strength and followings by using populist rhetoric mixed generously with nativist sloganeering against Jews and other ethnic minorities. The conservative establishment was gripped by a justified sense of political crisis, and, in country after country, leaders were seeking ways to co-opt radical groups while surrendering as little as possible of their political power.

What followed was a marriage of necessity between two camps that shared a common commitment to the national idea but were divided sharply on at least three major issues of practical politics. For the next seven to eight years, the art of government in East Central Europe was the art of mediating between these two camps and their numerous factions so as to give a semblance of coherence to public policy. The degree to which such coher-

186. Ibid., 47, 49, 63.
187. E. Weber 1966a, 114.
188. Ibid., 110–13.
189. E. Weber 1966c, 523–28.

ence was attained depended in part on the balance of forces in any given society and, not least, on the availability of a leading personality capable of commanding some respect on both sides of the political spectrum. The archetype of such a leader was Admiral Miklós Horthy, who, as a one-time aide-de-camp to Emperor Francis Joseph, enjoyed the support of the conservatives, but as a person closely associated with the "White" counterrevolution of 1919, also commanded the loyalty of the young radicals of the Right. Much the same can be said of King Boris of Bulgaria and King Carol II of Romania, who brought the aura of the monarchy to the task. On the other hand, Paul of Yugoslavia, as prince regent during his nephew's minority, was in a weaker position, reduced to political intrigues that ultimately led to his expulsion by the military coup of March 27, 1941. In Poland, the death of Marshal Jozef Pilsudski left a political vacuum that no single person could adequately fill. Under these conditions, politics was marred by the bickering of factions, above all the factions within the national radical camp. Such disunity may well have contributed to Poland's quick collapse under the blows of the German army in September 1939.

The first major issue on which conservatives and radicals were divided concerned the form of government itself. In this respect, the radicals favored a one-party state based on the Italian model, and, after 1933, on the model of National Socialist Germany. The conservatives meanwhile were committed to the old parliamentarism with its democratic façade and corrupt electoral system. There was considerable seesawing on this matter, but within a few years a synthesis of sorts emerged between the two conflicting principles. On the one hand, the old governing parties were transformed into political parties in the new style—the Camp of National Unity in Poland, the Party of National Unity in Hungary, the National Union, and later the Front of National Rebirth in Romania, and the Radical Community in Yugoslavia, each with local organizations, central committees, propaganda departments, green or blue shirts, and sections for youth, women, industrial labor, and peasantry—but the conservatives held on to the parliamentary institutions and an electoral system over which conservative interior ministers still held considerable sway. There were some exceptions to this rule: in Romania, the royal coup of 1938 abolished the old parliament altogether, and the king became the official leader of his single-party state, while in Bulgaria, a parliament of sort was allowed to function until another royal coup abolished all political parties while resisting the temptation to follow the Romanian model.[190]

190. The literature on this subject is immense and includes H. Seton-Watson 1962; Rothschild 1974; Macartney 1960, esp. vol. 1; Roucek 1948; Roberts 1951, esp. 170–241; Wynot 1974; F. Zweig 1944; Dragnich 1983; Crampton 1987.

A second area of contention was the "Jewish problem"—at least in Poland, Hungary, and Romania, the countries where Jews were a substantial minority. Here the conservatives' strategy was to maintain the parameters of ethnic politics set in the nineteenth century—that is, to contain the political influence and participation of the Jewish communities in national life while continuing to protect Jewish entrepreneurship for national benefit. The radicals, in contrast, wanted to eliminate Jewish influence and participation from the economy as well, ultimately by expropriating the Jewish business class, either to redistribute its property among worthy gentiles, or to etatize it so that the young "native" intelligentsia could find lucrative employment as managers of the economy. But while right-wing agitation on this issue was noisy and persistent, its results, at least in the 1931–38 period, were limited in scope and effects. True, in the second half of the decade, "Jewish laws" were passed in Poland (1936), Romania (1938), and Hungary (1938). But by the standards of things to come, these laws were rather lenient and passed by the parliaments amid what may be construed as virtual conservative apologies. Thus the Romanian Premier Armand Călinescu felt constrained to explain that the law had been passed merely *"pour calmer l'opinion publique,"* [191] while his Hungarian counterpart, Kálmán Darányi, expressed himself to the same effect and promised that the law would be the last one of its kind. [192] Most remarkable of all, the Polish legislators described the passage of the bill "as an act of necessary cruelty," [193] and expressed the hope that its provisions would be carried out without "brutality," lest they "harm the dignity and prestige of the country." [194] The effects of the laws were mitigated by revisions (in Poland), by bureaucratic inertia (in Hungary), and by corruption (in Romania). But the damage had been done. Notwithstanding all the expressions of regret, precedents had now been created, and while the conservatives still had control over legislative agendas, the tone of public discourse was set by the radicals and was such that it would desensitize large segments of the public to further infringements of property rights, and, ultimately, to harm to life and limb.

There remained finally the issues of social and economic reform. With respect to these, apart from the expropriation of Jews, the radicals pursued various land redistribution schemes and the opening up of avenues of mobility to talent from the lower and lower middle classes. The conservatives were opposed to redistribution of any kind. But the liberal wing of the conservative camp was in favor of economic development and welcomed the

191. Mendelsohn 1983, 73.
192. Macartney 1961, 1: 218–19.
193. Wynot 1971, 1035–38.
194. Ibid. For the measures, see Mendelsohn 1983, 71–72.

opportunity to steal some radical thunder to increase the effectiveness of its social policies. The buckle that connected the two camps was the technocratic wing of the Right, which was quite comfortable with populist rhetoric, but then set to work to rehabilitate and aggressively develop the countries' industrial economies.

The technocratic paradigm of politics was first clearly established by Premier Gömbös of Hungary. Fascist in style—he addressed managed crowds from a balcony in the manner of Mussolini—and nativist in his theatrical outbursts, he set to work by recruiting a number of technical experts to serve in the Ministry of Industry and Commerce, including his "Sofort Boys," all "humble, and incidentally of non-Magyar origin, able and pushing," chosen to execute "economic measures of a severely technical kind." [195] In order to reassure conservative forces, these technocrats quietly laid to rest the idea of land reform, much debated in radical "reform circles" in 1930–31. On the "Jewish question," Gömbös reversed himself outright by declaring all Jewish war veterans to be his brothers-in-arms and pledging that no discriminatory legislation would ever be submitted by his government.[196]

The Romanian experience bears close similarities to that of Hungary, except that the first attempts at austerity and remedial economics under Nicolae Iorga's National Union government were drowned in a sea of corruption and inefficiency.[197] These policies were suspended between 1932 and 1938, then resuscitated by the National Rebirth regime under the leadership of the king. While the propaganda ministry of the new regime turned out paeans of praise for "patriotism, family, sacrifice, nationhood and dignity," [198] and the king declared himself the country's "first farmer," the populist rhetoric mainly served as a disguise for revitalizing the old drive for industrialization. A key figure of this drive was Manoilescu, who served first as the king's minister of industry and commerce, and later as minister of foreign affairs. All talk about redistribution was suspended, in accordance with the overall design—indeed, public discussion of the distribution of land was prohibited by law. Rather than favoring land distribution schemes, the royal dictatorship sought to consolidate large agricultural units capable of producing a surplus. Its plans for building a modern industry relied upon enforced savings, which were likely to be extracted from the agricultural labor force. With these objectives in mind, the Bank for Industrialization and the Valorization of Agricultural Products (BINAG) was set up in December 1938, and the following year, the regime crafted an ambitious economic plan to en-

195. Macartney 1961, 1: 117, 120.
196. Kónya 1968, 40.
197. Roberts 1951, 173.
198. E. Weber 1966c, 555.

courage the cultivation of oil seeds, textile, industrial, and medicinal plants, with an eye to building new agricultural industries.[199]

In Poland, likewise, the "Colonels' Regime" of the Camp of National Unity bristled with the rhetoric and symbols of nativism. The official ideology of the Camp was "Polonism"—an appropriate comparison can be made here with the ideology of Hungarism—the purpose of which was to "make Poles masters in their own house" and the "true ruling nation of the country," while externally, it was to "give new content to the idea of Polish independence."[200] The official pamphlets of the Camp contained terms like "discipline, organized will" and "unified leadership" and describe the regime as one of a "totalitarian character."[201] Meanwhile, however, a number of Polish technocrats, led by Finance Minister Eugeniusz Kwiatkowski, pursued an ambitious design for national industrial development, "using the outer trappings of fascism while rejecting its real essence and the extreme methods that gave this movement its dynamic character."[202] This design included a four-year plan for developing the Sandomierz region in the middle of the country, together with a broader fifteen-year plan for industrial development.[203] The argument of national defense was both a valid purpose and as selling point. But the development of defense industries was part of a larger design "to step up the tempo of Polish development, to make up for industrial arrears, and to equalize Poland with other countries in national culture as a prerequisite of effectiveness in the rivalry of the international arena."[204]

This technocratic design for development eventually had the effect of blunting the anti-Semitic impulses of the Camp. Kwiatkowski, above all, was fearful of the flight of talent and capital, as well as of adverse reactions of international financial markets, and to preempt these from happening, he followed Gömbös's policy of protecting the Jewish business community from excesses. To this effect, he lobbied hard, and not without success, to revise the insulting 1936 law that had restricted ritual slaughter, and then conspired with Colonel Adam Koc, a member of the Camp's triumvirate, to engineer a declaration that Jews were welcome in the Camp "provided that they had proven themselves good nationalist Poles by their past behavior."[205] Colonel Slawek, another member of the triumvirate, closer to the nativists, remonstrated. Koc fell in the struggle among factions. But in 1939

199. Roberts 1951, 213.
200. *New York Times*, February 12, 1937, 1.
201. *New York Times*, June 6, 1937, 8; Wynot 1974, ix.
202. Wynot 1974, ix.
203. F. Zweig 1944, 121.
204. Ibid., 92–99; see also Wynot 1974, 76.
205. *New York Times*, April 22, 1937, 12.

the technocrats succeeded once again, if only more discreetly, in welcoming into the Camp "all patriots irrespective of national origin." [206] This was not exactly philo-Semitism. But it was a gesture toward businessmen and investors, as well as an intimation that socialist agitators and commissars need not apply.

In the Balkans, the most outstanding technocratic politician was Milan Stojadinović, who presided over the Yugoslav government from 1935 to 1939. An economist by profession, Stojadinović studied budgetary theory under Professor Walter Lotz at the University of Munich,[207] then served as an intern in the French Ministry of Finance and Office of Public Accounts. His experiences made him a lifelong admirer of bureaucracy as a general model of political organization, and of German efficiency and French bureaucracy in particular. What impressed him most was the way France had been able to exist as a stable and powerful state despite the deep internal cleavages in the French political system, an outcome that Stojadinović attributed to the de facto autonomy of the bureaucracy from cumbersome parliamentary tutelage. Indeed, from the beginning of his political career in his own country, Stojadinović viewed parliamentarianism as little more than a necessary evil, an instrument to legitimate the more serious work of governments, to be performed by technical experts. Certainly, as an instrument of national welfare, parliamentarianism was inferior to rationalized and disciplined hierarchies. "It seemed to me then," he mused about his youth, decades later in exile, "that the state is more likely to prosper under an authoritarian chief than under an ineffectual president of a republic subject to the daily attacks of the newspaper cartoonists and the comedians of the evening." [208] These principles and experiences, combined with his considerable talents, served him well, for after his return to Yugoslavia, Stojadinović rose rapidly within the public service to become the director of budget and minister of finance in Alexander's Yugoslavia. Along the way, he earned recognition for "saving the dinar" through his drastic reorganization of the country's finances.[209]

He was called to the premiership with a mandate for economic and national consolidation and maintenance of the political status quo. In this respect, his position is particularly reminiscent of Gömbös's in Hungary. Like his Hungarian and Polish counterparts, Stojadinović was convinced that economic reform was impossible without political reform, that in order to generate economic development, he would have to effect major institu-

206. Buell 1939, 240.
207. Stojadinović 1963, 30–40.
208. Ibid., 41.
209. Ibid., 155–56, 273.

tional changes in the political system. Thus shortly after being named premier, Stojadinović set out to create a new political base for himself, copying Mussolini's rhetoric and organizational principles. Whether his final goal was to create a one-party state or, as he claims in his memoirs, a manipulable two-party regime with a strong, autonomous bureaucratic core,[210] he quickly renamed the old governing party the Yugoslav Radical Community (Jugoslovenska Radikalna Zajednica) and proceeded with plans to turn it into a nationwide political organization capable of accomplishing the tasks of economic mobilization and national unification. This, of course, required local organizations, a reliable cadre, and a card-carrying membership. It also produced a green-shirted vanguard group, who received the prime minister on the occasion of his numerous local visits "with a fascist-type salute and rhythmic shouts of 'vodja, vodja.'"[211]

Stojadinović's first priority was to mobilize the country for economic development, which, he believed, would facilitate the rise of a common Yugoslav national identity. Like all Yugoslav politicians from the 1870s onward, Stojadinović had to deal with the agrarian question, and this was particularly important in light of his hopes of drawing the peasantry into his political movement. Debt restructuring and relief to small farmers were thus brought in to buy their support for the government. But the premier's real love was for industry, for he was convinced that only by developing a manufacturing base could his country's dependence on the great powers be reduced, and only by means of such a base could long-range solutions to the country's problems of "overpopulation" (the contemporary term for economic underdevelopment) be found. In his own words: "We are constructing factories in order to raise the standard of living and to employ hardworking people. We are creating our own industry to fulfill the needs of national defense and to secure the boundaries of our own state. We have raised chimneys to honor those who have fallen for that state."[212]

The same lyrical qualities, the lyrics of a true technocrat, are evident in most of the speeches of his premiership. A representative example is one he delivered to celebrate the opening of a new chemical plant in Šabac:

Today, this new factory of the Yugoslav Association of Chemical Industries is opening its gates. It will produce for the benefit of other industries, for the benefit of agriculture, and also for the benefit of national defense. The same firm hands that until yesterday carried weapons in the defense of the country today will op-

210. Ibid., 350.
211. Ibid., 590. He maintains that he discouraged the practice, not on principle, but because the rhythmic repetition of the word made it sound like *djavo*, the Serbian word for devil.
212. Stojadinović 1939, 30.

erate machines to expand the economic foundations of our great fatherland, the one and indivisible Yugoslavia.[213]

Carried away by the momentum of an election campaign, Stojadinović proclaimed:

> Bosanska Krajna, like all of Bosnia, is a land of unexploited natural wealth. [But] our country saw little benefit from this natural wealth. . . . Our miners toiled to enrich foreign capital, to give foreign workers jobs, and to enhance the security of foreign powers. I have put an end to this suicidal course. My government rescued your lumber business by creating new markets, and from your mines my government is creating a Yugoslav Ruhr.[214]

The task of the historian, of course, goes beyond the unearthing of legislative record and repeating rhetoric. The historian's most important task is to assess the economic effectiveness and the accomplishments of these semi-fascist regimes. In this area, the regimes must be deemed successful, albeit in varying degrees. Within only four years the countries partaking of the fascist experiment and of campaigns of rearmament made impressive strides toward recovery and, as Table 26 shows, toward industrial development, although (as was shown above in Tables 15, 16, and 18) not to the degree where they would have narrowed the gap between East and West, or brought about changes in the economic ranking of individual countries. Economic historians may rightfully quibble as to whether this spurt of development was because or in spite of the switch to more authoritarian politics. The fact that democratic Czechoslovakia was slower to recover lends some credence to the hypothesis that the higher rate of development was owing to some balance between local economic *dirigisme* and the special barter trade agreements that were part of Germany's new economic design for its southeastern European "space."

The political accomplishments of this coalition of radicals and conservatives, however, were far less impressive. From the conservative point of view, the main reason for co-opting the radicals was to gain popular legitimacy, and enough spontaneous support on the part of the populations to permit the coherent conduct of public policy. However, once the radicals had been coopted, they were tarred with the conservative brush, and the politics of often austere technocratic *dirigisme* was unable to capture the affections of the large masses of the dispossessed. Indeed, one of the common features of this technocratic experience is the absence of the masses from the political structures built with the sole intention to tie them to the regimes. Ironically, all the studies of the subject seem to indicate that the membership of

213. Ibid., 31.
214. Ibid., 42.

TABLE 26

Indexes of Industrial Output

(1913 = 100)

	1932	1938
Hungary	84	128
Poland	52	105
Romania	113	180
Yugoslavia	116	190
Bulgaria	195	245

SOURCE: Berend and Ránki 1974, 299–300.

these fascist-type, technocratic parties consisted mainly of public employees: village clerks, policemen, mailmen, and even members of fire brigades pressed into service by eager governments.[215] The masses of peasants and industrial workers remained aloof from this "official" fascism, and eventually threw their support to political parties that, whether on the left or right, had found ways to establish their radical credentials by word as well as deed, above all, through leadership without ties to the old regimes. In the Balkan countries, where things Russian had a measurable prestige, this free-floating popular radicalism was largely captured by the parties of the left—more specifically, by radical Marxism and populism—although the parties themselves were frequently forced underground by brutally efficient police authorities.

The case of the Bulgarian Communist Party has already been noted. Banned in 1924, the party soon returned in the guise of a Labor Party that, by 1930, counted 30,000 card-carrying members, while its trade union ranks drew 10,000 from among the minuscule industrial labor force. In the general elections of 1931, this crypto-communist party won 12.7 percent of the vote and 31 seats to the Sobranie.[216] In 1934, the party was repressed for a second time and its members expelled from the Sobranie; some of them died under torture in police custody.[217] But the party had not lost its appeal to the lower classes and to certain segments of the intelligentsia. In 1938, its poorly disguised members won 11 seats in the ostensibly nonparty elections held under the new constitution. A similar feat was accomplished in 1940, when nine communist deputies were elected to serve under an ostensibly fascist government. During the war, they abandoned the political stage, but after the armistice had been signed in September 1944, they reappeared without disguise to preside over the execution of their opponents. Their regime

215. For Poland, see O. D. Tolischus, *New York Times*, October 4, 1937; for Hungary, Macartney 1961, 1: 119; for Romania, Roberts 1951, 208.

216. Rothschild 1974, 346–47; also id. 1959, 259–87.

217. Rothschild 1974, 348.

would indeed be far less lackadaisical in these matters than their predecessors. The Yugoslav case was much the same. Although there were no crypto-communists in the controlled parliaments of the 1930s, as noted above, the party was capable of maintaining a strong enough underground organization to reemerge as a political force to counter the country's occupation by Germany and Italy.

A diametrically opposite picture, however, emerges from the experience of Romania and Hungary. Given the general and strong anti-Russian sentiment of these populations, radical energies were channelled into support for hard Right opposition parties, the Iron Guard under the leadership of Corneliu Codreanu, and the Arrow Cross under Ferenc Szálasi. The character of the underlying culture did rub off on these movements and their leadership: Codreanu's Iron Guard is often described as the product of the communalism and mysticism of Orthodoxy,[218] and of the populism of the peasant village, while Szálasi and his Hungarists chose for themselves the model of medieval feudal hierarchy, whose symbols they were wearing,[219] and whose institutions they were imitating by setting up a corporatist state during their brief reign under German auspices.[220] Although this may well have been a matter of personality rather than of national culture, it is worth contrasting Codreanu's contempt for and cynical utilization of the legal process with Szálasi's pathetic insistence on correct legal form in his ascent, when he sought and seized power through Horthy's blessing; in defeat, when he assumed that the Allies would recognize him as the head of a legitimate government; and, finally, before the "people's court" that would sentence him to death as a war criminal, where in his defense he invoked legal technicalities.[221] But beyond these differences, the two movements had something in common: their leaders went in and out of jail and were brutalized by the police of conservative and semi-fascist governments, which gave them an aura of martyrdom that was sufficient to establish their radical authenticity with the masses. This authenticity paid off in elections: in 1937, the Guard won 16 percent of the vote in the Romanian general elections, and the Arrow Cross garnered 25 percent of Hungarian votes in 1939, including 30.7 percent of the vote in Budapest and 41.7 percent in the formerly "red belt" of industrial outskirts surrounding the capital city.[222]

As we have seen, Poland was something of an intermediate case between the Balkan and Danubian cases. Communism aroused suspicions on ac-

---

218. E. Weber 1966c, 520–21, 527–29.

219. These were the white and red stripes of the coats of arms of the medieval dynasty of the Árpáds.

220. Teleki 1974, 251–52.

221. Karsai 1978, 488. And see E. Karsai and L. Karsai 1988, esp. 44–46, where the defendants argue that they are still the country's legitimate government.

222. *Uj Magyarság*, May 30–June 2, 1939. See also Lackó 1966, 169–70.

count of its association with Russia, but an equally strong hostility toward Germany somewhat diminished potential ardor for fascist internationalism. Much as in the other countries of East Central Europe, the technoconservative coalition had some difficulty in capturing popular enthusiasm, however, and alienated national radicals therefore began to congregate under the banners of the NARA (an acronym for national radicalism). The regime's control over the electoral process makes it hard to assess the extent of the NARA's electoral strength. In the general elections of November 6–13, 1938, the official list of the Camp of National Unity won 78 percent of the seats in the still-functioning Sejm, against a bare 7 percent for the Right radical opposition. But, as Joseph Rothschild notes, a more genuine picture of public opinion may be gained from the municipal elections of December 18 of the same year. Apparently exhausted from "managing" the earlier campaign, the pro-Camp official electoral machine failed effectively to control the outcome of thousands of local races. Of 3,944 contested seats, the official Right won only 1,332, or 33.8 percent, with the rest divided almost evenly between the Socialists and candidates of the anti-government Right.[223]

In the Shadow of Empire, 1939–1945

Academic convention divides the history of East European fascism into two periods with the Great Depression serving as a watershed. But the years 1939–41 provide another chronological divide, created largely by events external to the region itself. Specifically, these years mark the final decline of the continental order established by Britain and France after World War I. They also mark the transformation of Germany from a challenger of the international status quo into temporary European hegemon, as well as into a regional imperial power in ascent over East Central Europe.

Weak to begin with, the British-French continental order began to unravel with the Great Depression, a process hastened by the fact that the security system established at Versailles had no economic underpinnings. Although willing to act as sponsors and spokesmen of their lesser European allies, neither England nor France was in a position to be a viable trading partner for the region, and especially not to act as the buyers of agricultural produce so vital for most of the local economies. After 1918, intra-regional trade fell to one-sixth of its pre–World War I volume.[224] Except for Czechoslovakia, the countries of the region could not find new markets in the advanced societies of northwestern Europe. Indeed, trade between these countries and most eastern countries fell significantly: from 46.6 to 18.8 percent

223. Rothschild 1974, 72; also Wynot 1974, 234.
224. Hertz 1970, 83.

of the total value of exports in the case of Hungary,[225] from 61.1 to 17.8 percent in the case of Romania; from 36.6 to 17.9 percent for Bulgaria. Yugoslav trade with the advanced capitalist nations of the Continent stagnated at around 10 percent of the nation's exports.[226] After 1933, the slack was taken up by Germany, following an economic design based on bilateral trade agreements. As a result of these agreements, Germany's share of Yugoslav exports increased from 13.9 in 1933 to 35.9 percent in 1938, while France's share of Yugoslav trade continued to hover around 2 percent.[227] Exports from Bulgaria to Germany tripled in value between 1934 and 1938. Hungary, always dependent on trade with Austria and Germany, also increased its share of exports. Following the Anschluss of Austria to Germany in March 1938, 59.9 percent of all Hungarian export income derived from trade with the German Reich.[228] These figures gave Germany virtually complete control over the local economies.

This economic penetration proved to be an effective prelude to political penetration after 1938. In that year, by virtue of the Anschluss, Germany became a next-door neighbor not only of Poland and Czechoslovakia, but of Hungary and Yugoslavia as well. In October 1938, Germany secured the Munich agreement from the Western powers; the resulting dismemberment of Czechoslovakia transformed the Czech lands into a Reich protectorate in 1939 and made Slovakia into an independent state, albeit under the "protective friendship" (*Schutzfreundschaft*) of National Socialist Germany. In September 1939, Germany attacked and quickly defeated Poland: parts of the country were incorporated into the Reich, parts of it were to be administered under a so-called *Generalgouvernement* in the manner of a colony, while territories east of the Polish ethnic boundary became incorporated into the Soviet Union. The following year France was defeated by Germany and Romania's boundaries were adjusted under duress in favor of the Soviet Union, Hungary, and Bulgaria. In 1941 Yugoslavia, together with Hungary, Romania, and Bulgaria, joined the Tripartite Pact of the Axis. But the officer corps of the Yugoslav army balked and overthrew the country's pro-German government, an act that invited the German invasion of the country and the proclamation of a Croatian state under German-Italian tutelage, followed by boundary changes in favor of Germany, Italy, Bulgaria, and Hungary. By mid-summer 1941, German influence over the region was preponderant, and the territory of East Central Europe was divided between three occupied states—Serbia, Poland and the Czech lands—and five client states of National Socialist Germany—Bulgaria, Croatia, Hungary, Romania, and

225. Ibid.
226. Jackson and Lampe 1982, 366.
227. Zagoroff, Végh, and Bilinovich 1955, 320.
228. Ibid., 210, 373.

Slovakia. The latter countries were for the time being allowed to retain the most important trappings of sovereignty, though further curtailment of their independence was planned and well within the realm of possibility.[229] Momentarily, though, the German government preferred the status quo while it pressed for compliance with demands for (1) military contributions by clients to the German war effort; (2) an increasing volume of exports of food, raw materials, and processed goods; (3) special privileges for German ethnic minorities; and (4) local cooperation in the solution of the "Jewish problem," at first in the restriction of Jewish participation in national life, and later in the deliverance of Jewish populations for extermination.

Germany's leverage in pressing these demands was formidable (albeit variable over time and space). Unlike in the earlier period, this leverage was no longer economic—indeed, wartime scarcities gave eastern exporters the economic upper hand—but rather political and military. Some of the leverage was derived from positive inducements and some of it from negative inducements. The most important of the former was Germany's ability to resolve territorial disputes and to satisfy long-standing territorial aspirations. Thus, Hungary was tied closely to the German imperial system and its network of alliances by a succession of territorial gains resulting from German-Italian arbitration or German fiat. By these means, Hungary regained part of the "Hungarian Highlands" (southern Slovakia) in 1938, Ruthenia in 1939, northern Transylvania in 1940, and part of the Voyvodina in 1941. Likewise, Bulgaria became a German ally as a result of the transfer of territories from Romania to Bulgaria in 1940, from Yugoslavia and Greece to Bulgaria in 1941. Croatia's ties to Germany were strengthened and emotionalized by the German-Italian joint decision to make Bosnia-Herzegovina part of the country. Finally, Germany gained considerable support from Albania, when, in 1943, albeit under German military occupation, the country was united with western Macedonia and the Kosovo province, which were linked to the mother country by ethnic ties. However, gaining supporters by territorial awards could be tricky, for some of these territorial adjustments had to be made at the expense of other prospective clients, as in the case of the territorial awards made to Hungary at the expense of Slovakia and Romania. Slovakia presumably was compensated by the grant of independence; Romania was subsequently (and temporarily) compensated by the reconquest of territories lost to the Soviet Union in 1940 and by the annexation of new territories east of the river Dniester.

Leverage by way of negative inducement was exercised both directly and indirectly. The former implied the threat of force in case of noncompliance—a threat made credible by several precedents for German military in-

229. See Pritz 1997, 159–234.

tervention in the countries' internal affairs. In January 1941, German tank divisions helped General Antonescu to seize the helm of the Romanian government and to put an end to the anarchistic rule of the Iron Guard. In March 1944, German troops occupied Hungary while Regent Horthy was visiting Hitler in Germany and installed a new government more friendly to Germany. This was repeated in October 1944, when German SS troops swooped down on Budapest to remove Horthy himself and to install the Arrow Cross at the helm of the country for the last months of World War II. At about the same time, and in the wake of a "national uprising" in eastern Slovakia, a Reich plenipotentiary took charge of the country, and subsequently German personnel were used to accomplish the last phase of the deportation of the Jewish population. However, such interventions had high political costs and tended to cause severe disruptions in the local economies. So, for most of the war, Germany tried to accomplish its short-term goals by supporting, overtly or covertly, local forces known to be enthusiastic and unqualified supporters of the larger imperial design. This strategy both reflected and hastened major realignments in the politics of the non-occupied countries of East Central Europe. If in the past politics had pivoted around the issue of political and economic reform, now the main cleavages formed principally along divisions concerning foreign policy, and specifically concerning the issue of relationship toward hegemonic Germany. In other words, foreign affairs now trumped domestic social and economic concerns. In the common parlance of the times, the term "Right" now came to be used to designate the unqualified supporters of Germany, and the supporters of the European New Order over and above the interests of the nation-state. The term "Left," meanwhile came to refer to resolute opponents of the German imperial design—ironically enough, since this motley group included not only socialists and liberal democrats but also many arch-conservatives fearful of their future under the international order associated with National Socialism. In between these two camps we find what could then be seen as the political center: a coalition of radical and conservative forces, both opportunistic and reluctant, who followed Germany out of pragmatic considerations and expectations but were trying to maintain as much independence for their countries as was possible under the circumstances.

With all its ambiguities and fluidity, this framework of domestic politics, together with the geo-strategic position of a given country, will give us an important key to client behavior and the degree of autonomy individual clients could win for their states. In this respect, the strength or weakness of the domestic Right was of particular importance, for the presence of a strong and agile right wing provided Germany with a point of leverage, whereas its absence left Germany no choice but to work with the reluctant collaborators of the political center.

Hence, the two countries of the region most immune to German meddling were Romania and Bulgaria. In Romania, ironically, this constellation was brought about as a result of Germany's desire to see the Iron Guard smashed to ensure the continued flow of Romanian oil to the Reich, and, more generally, to re-establish the stability of the country's economy. By helping General (later Marshal) Antonescu to become the undisputed head of government, German policy did achieve its economic purposes, but, at the same time it created a leader who was a francophile at heart, had a nationalist agenda of his own, and harbored considerable suspicion concerning Germany's ultimate war aims.[230] Antonescu seized power in 1941 when the likelihood of German military victory and continued hegemony over southeastern Europe was high, but he was aware throughout that he was engaged in a political gamble. Throughout the war he remained in close contact with members of an officially suppressed leftist opposition, including Iuliu Maniu, whom he regarded as a logical successor should the Allies win the war.[231] One thing this calculation did not take into account was the possibility that the Soviet Union, and not the Western Allies, would exercise influence over the east of Europe. But of course this is what eventually happened and with fateful results, for not just Antonescu but Maniu, too, eventually perished at the hands of the new Soviet hegemon.[232]

Clearly motivated by common interest rather than infatuation with the National Socialist vision for the continent, Antonescu joined the war against the Soviet Union. His armies recovered territories seized by the Soviet Union in 1940, as well as new territories east of the Dniester. But then his troops fought all the way to Stalingrad, second in numerical strength and fighting qualities only to the German army. An unusual war effort was made, partly in pursuit of victory over Soviet communism and partly as a political strategy, for it enabled Antonescu to resist other demands habitually made by Germany. This was most obvious with respect to economics.

To be sure, for four years during the war Romania was Germany's single most important supplier of grain, minerals, and oil. But whereas others were forced to accept promissory notes, the Marshal insisted on cold, hard cash, or commodities of equal worth. As a result, Romania at the end of the war was left with virtually no outstanding German payments, and the Roma-

230. These views were shared by a number of German diplomatic observers including Paul Schmidt, Hitler's personal interpreter, and Hans Joachim Kausch, the chief of German intelligence in Romania. See P. Schmidt 1949, 548–49. Also Hilberg 1961, 490n.

231. A volume of almost weekly correspondence of Antonescu with Maniu, Ion C. Brătianu, and Gheorghe Tătărescu, September 21, 1940–April 6, 1944, was recently published and testifies to the point. See Pelin 1993.

232. The literature on Antonescu is large, still burgeoning, and more controversial than ever. For a sympathetic view, see Watts 1993 and Rotariu 1994. For an account of Antonescu's trial, see Pantazi 1990, 343–63. See also Hitchins 1994, esp. 529, and the still more recent evaluation of Antonescu's role in Romanian history in Temple 1996, 457–503.

nian treasury had doubled its gold reserves.[233] Even so, Antonescu steadily
rose in Hitler's esteem.[234] Soon he was regarded as the third, later second,
most powerful man of the Axis, the one who managed to elicit Hitler's promise of benevolent neutrality should Romania want to recover northern Transylvania from Hungary after the end of the present war.[235]

Even Antonescu, however, was not completely immune to German pressure. On the matter of the German minorities in southern Transylvania he
had to give way and accept quasi-autonomy and the right of these minorities to opt for service in the German, rather than Romanian, army. This was
a price originally set for German territorial guarantees of the fall of 1940,
and perhaps not deeply injurious to the sentiments of the ethnic nationalist.
As for Jews, Antonescu was inclined, like most Romanian officers, to believe
that they were a "problem," and he was prepared to believe reports of Jewish collaboration with the Soviets in Bessarabia. He articulated this view in
a remarkable exchange of letters with the president of the Jewish community of Bucharest, in which he tried to justify atrocities committed by his
troops in the first weeks of the war by citing examples of this collaboration
and armed resistance.[236] Whatever the truth of his allegations, not all of
these atrocities were committed upon his direct orders. The massacre at Iaşi
at the beginning of the war was a spontaneous event probably triggered by
mass hysteria.[237] In any case, his government bears responsibility for the fate
of the Jews of northern Bucovina and Bessarabia, 110,000 of whom (out of
a total of 185,000) perished in the fall of 1941 as a result of forced marches,
exposure to hunger and cold, and wholesale shootings.[238] But Antonescu,
as an officer of the old school, also tended to differentiate between "unas-
similated" and "assimilated" Jews, and the treatment of the latter was to be
more lenient. While the Romanian government decreed the establishment of
concentration camps and the wearing of discriminatory insignia, enforcement of the decrees was lax and mitigated by large numbers of exemptions
granted on grounds of indispensability to the war effort. If there was a Jewish "problem," Antonescu wanted to solve it in the Romanian and not the
German way. Thus, when confronted with explicit demands for the deliv-
ery of Romanian Jews to concentration camps in August 1942, Antonescu
flatly refused on grounds of national principle that may well have been further strengthened by his creeping doubts about the prospects of a German
victory.[239]

233. Berend and Ránki 1974, 332–34. For the gold reserves, Temple 1996, 468.
234. Arimia, Ardeleanu, and Lache 1991; also Hitchins 1994, 458–60, 467.
235. *Mémorial Antonesco: Le IIIe homme de l'Axe* (1950); Buzatu 1990, 370–72.
236. Hilberg 1961, 495.
237. Ibid., 491. Temple 1996, 480.
238. Hilberg 1961, 495.
239. Ibid., 502.

Compared to Romania or the other satellites, pro-Russian sentiments were strong in Bulgaria, and there were few genuine enthusiasts of the German New Order. The political game was to check the Left by holding out the prospect of German intervention, while using the strength of the Left and the prevalence of pro-Russian sympathies as arguments to minimize contributions to the German war effort and reap maximum advantage for the Bulgarian side. In this respect, Bulgaria was more successful than any other German client state, although the ultimate objective of neutrality proved to be just as elusive for Bulgaria as it was for Romania and Hungary. Many commentators attribute this success to King Boris's personal qualities. A leading historian of the Bulgarian war effort describes him as a Machiavellian fox, a "great feigner and dissembler," [240] while Joseph Goebbels referred to him as a "sly and crafty fellow," an apparent master at "playing a double faced game." [241] Apart from these qualities, however, he was also aided by his country's geographical location—its relative remoteness from the crossroads of the great land armies—and by political circumstances, particularly the weakness of the Ratnici and other right-wing organizations that might otherwise have served as instruments of greater German leverage.

Whatever the reason, the rewards for Boris's policies consistently exceeded the price he actually paid. His political game started in September 1940, when, in exchange for the king's vague promises, the German government pressured Romania to cede the southern part of Dobrudja to the Bulgarians. Then, in the course of the Balkan war of 1941, Bulgaria was permitted to annex both Slavic Macedonia from Yugoslavia and Aegean Macedonia from Greece, together with large portions of Eastern Thrace (Belomorie). In both instances, Bulgaria refrained from providing front-line troops, although it had to endure bombing by the British and the Americans, having declared war on both powers in 1941.[242] Two months later, when Germany and her minor allies unleashed their war against the Soviet Union, Bulgaria refused to join on "historical" grounds, her king pleading, with some truthfulness, that such a step might provoke popular resistance in the country.[243] Thereafter, Bulgaria's military contributions to the war effort were virtually nil, and although the German debt to Bulgaria at RM 680 million by far exceeded the amount owed to Romania, it was far less than what had been exacted from Slovakia and Hungary.[244]

The ups and downs of the country's Jewish population must also be examined in the context of the regime's opportunism. The Jewish population of Bulgaria was small, a mere 48,565 in 1934, to which another 15,000

240. Miller 1975, 1.
241. Goebbels 1948, 61–62.
242. Miller 1975, 24–31, 45–51.
243. Ibid., 60–61.
244. Berend and Ránki 1974, 332–34.

were added through the acquisition of territories in 1940–41.[245] Unlike the Jewish populations of the Danubian and northern tier countries, that of Bulgaria carried little economic or political weight; thus it was neither the target of economic envy nor a significant competitor to the native intelligentsia. Historically, the presence of the Jews aroused no popular passions. They were, in Hilberg's words, a "mere surplus commodity,"[246] traded dispassionately for political benefit or in order to satisfy the ideological whims of the regional patron power—in this case, National Socialist Germany.

The first anti-Jewish measure was passed in November 1940, as an obvious payoff for the acquisition of southern Dobrudja. It was enacted, in the words of a socialist deputy on the floor of the Sobranie, "so as not to stay behind Romania in the expression of loyalty to Hitler."[247] Although the letter of the law was severe—it barred Jews from public service and set strict quotas for both the professions and the educational system—its enforcement was lax and, as in Romania, alleviated by numerous exceptions in order to minimize economic disruptions. This, however, was only the beginning. The next step taken was again a payoff to the Reich, this time for taking the side of Bulgaria in a little-remembered confrontation with Italy in Macedonia, which involved the region's Albanian minority.[248] The Bulgarians responded by passing new anti-Jewish measures in August 1942; these narrowed the definition of Jewishness, created a Commissariat of Jewish Affairs, confiscated Jewish bank accounts, introduced living space restrictions, and made the wearing of the Jewish star compulsory for the entire target population. But this was also the summer of the failed German offensive on the Russian plain that, to the perceptive observer, signaled adversities to come even before the Stalingrad disaster. Thus, the passage of the bill notwithstanding, German emissaries reported "disturbing incidents" in their client country, such as an exchange of friendly telegrams between the king and leaders of the Jewish community.[249] Two weeks later, Interior Minister Gabrowski personally accepted the petition of a Jewish delegation and addressed them with friendly words, "to the amazement of all ministry officials."[250]

However, in January 1943, just as the drama of Stalingrad was unfolding, the German government raised stern demands for Bulgarian participation in the occupation of Serbia, as well as in the fight against Yugoslav and Greek partisans. This was a step that Boris was loathe to take. There followed a process of prolonged haggling, at the end of which the Bulgarian government had its way but, as yet another payoff to the Reich, consented

245. Hilberg 1961, 475.
246. Ibid.
247. Dimo Kazasov, quoted in Miller 1975, 27.
248. Ibid., 30.
249. Hilberg 1961, 481.
250. Ibid.

to the deportation of 11,434 Jews from the newly occupied territories, while taking no such steps against Jews on the territory of prewar Bulgaria.[251] For the moment, this human sacrifice relieved the pressure on the government. It was one of King Boris's last acts before his death in August 1943. The gambit only further tarnished Bulgaria's wartime image, but within a year the game was over. Even though the Bulgarian government had refused to join Germany in the eastern campaign, the Soviet Union declared war on Bulgaria on September 5, 1944, making sure that its troops arrived in the country before those of the Western allies.

If Romania and Bulgaria represent one class of countries, Hungary and Slovakia may be seen as another in the larger scheme of wartime politics. The centrist leaders of these countries may have been just as eager to extricate themselves from German embrace while pursuing their own national interests, but their actions were hemmed in by different circumstances: by a closer geographical proximity to Germany, which made them more susceptible to occupation, and by a history of friendship—or minimal animosity, in the case of Slovakia—toward Germany, which also accounts indirectly for the prevalence and for the greater strength of a pro-systemic or pro-hegemonic opposition to their governments. As a result, their freedom of maneuver was more constrained than that of the two southeastern countries, and both countries eventually became victims of German occupation during the last years of World War II.

The mainstay of the political center in Hungary was Admiral-Regent Miklós Horthy, whose support was drawn from both conservative and radical elements now worried about Germany's increasingly overbearing power in the East Central European space. Like Antonescu, Horthy was a military man who fought World War I on the opposite side, as the aide-de-camp of the Austrian emperor and as the commander of the Austro-Hungarian fleet. As such, he clearly felt more comfortable with Germany, though this attitude did not fully extend to the National Socialist regime, which he felt was distasteful in its many breaches of traditional political norms.

He also had a healthy, perhaps exaggerated, respect for sea power, and was inclined to believe that even if Germany could establish itself as a Continental hegemon, it would never be able to defeat Britain, not to mention the United States. On the issue of Hungary's borders he shared the revisionist passions of Hungarian nationalists, although when the hour struck he generally acted as a moderating force more willing to abide by the ethnic principle than by the objective of restoring the integrity of old Hungary. On the Jewish question he was far more tolerant than Antonescu. Like many Hungarian liberals and conservatives, he believed that the main body of Jewry performed useful functions for the nation as a whole, though he per-

251. Ibid.

haps had little patience for Jews who turned communist or socialist, and there is at least some reason to believe that, like many others both among the Magyar and the Jewish communities, and indeed like Antonescu, he was ready to draw a sharp distinction between long-term inhabitants of the country and more recent "Galician" immigrants.[252]

These proclivities, with the sole exception of joining the eastern war, demonstrated Horthy's considerable aversion to committing Hungary's weak army to military engagements. In 1938, when Hitler in fact offered up to the Hungarians the whole territory of Slovakia—with the proviso of regional autonomy—in exchange for an armed attack against Czechoslovakia (in which Germany would come to the aid of embattled Hungary), Horthy refused, provoking Hitler's sardonic remark about those who "want to banquet without wanting to participate in preparing the meal."[253] In a like manner, the Hungarians refused to join the Polish campaign, pleading the case of historical ties. In 1940 the joint Italian-German arbitration commission decided in favor of Hungary, restoring to the country a substantial part of Transylvania; it did so in exchange for legislation to ensure the by now usual privileges to the German minority, and for promises of closer collaboration. Nevertheless, a few months later the Hungarians agonized and temporized in the face of what was in effect a German ultimatum that they join the war against Yugoslavia.[254] (The Hungarians eventually complied but only after prime minister Pál Teleki committed suicide as an act of remorse and protest, and their troops refused to cross historical boundaries, an act of foot-dragging for which they were punished by being kept out of parts of the Voyvodina east of the river Tisza that had been originally promised to them.) In June 1941, however, Horthy and his government joined in the eastern campaign with apparent enthusiasm, expecting an early victory. Their miscalculation became evident soon, above all to Horthy himself, who by the winter of 1941 apparently had a change of heart. Within only three months he appointed a new premier, Miklós Kállay, with a mandate to minimize Hungary's war effort, and, after the early months of 1943, to seek accommodation with the Western Allies in the vain hope that the Soviets might be kept from occupying Hungary. As this policy matured, Germany became increasingly apprehensive, and in March 1944, at a time when Horthy was visiting his headquarters, his armies would occupy the country of his unreliable ally. For the next few months Hungary was reduced to the status of an occupied country, with a government virtually appointed by a resident high commissioner of Germany. By mid-summer, however, the military situation deteriorated sufficiently to undermine the effectiveness of German

252. Reported conversation with Lászlo Baky in June 1944. Macartney 1961, 2: 283n.
253. "Wer mittafeln will, muss auch mitkochen!" For the visit to Kiel, see Ibid., 1: 238–48.
254. Ibid., 474–77.

control over the day-to-day conduct of Hungarian affairs. Thus, Horthy would reassert his powers one more time and used them to sue for armistice on October 15. A second German invasion followed on the same day. Horthy was arrested and taken to Germany, and the Arrow Cross party was installed in the government to hold out fighting until the bitter end.

In minimizing Hungary's contribution to the war, the governments of Hungary followed a different strategy than that of Romania. They got away with this policy (until March 1944), but they had to redeem themselves by paying tribute to Germany in commodities. Beginning in 1939 successive Hungarian governments delivered to Germany large quantities of food, the major part of Hungary's modest oil reserves, and the productive capacity of Hungarian industries, including the capacity of the country's substantial armament industries. Significantly, and in stark contrast to Romania and Bulgaria, after a while these deliveries were in exchange for promissory notes, rather than gold, money, or manufactured goods. As a result, and again in contrast to Romania, by war's end Hungary accumulated a German debt of RM 1.5 billion, the largest amount held by any Axis country at the end of World War II.[255]

Horthy's clever, but ultimately futile, maneuvers were also applied in trying to deal with German demands concerning the country's large Jewish population—by now three-quarters of a million strong. German influence over the region increased so that in 1939 the provisions of the earlier, more moderate legislation of 1938 were overridden by a Second Jewish Law that set more stringent occupational quotas. Further and still more stringent legislative acts were passed in 1941 and 1942, but according to reliable sources these laws represented a mere payoff to Germany and to the local Right and their provisions were not designed to be fulfilled.[256] In any case, there was little attempt to interfere with the conduct of Jewish business, especially in the manufacturing sector. Throughout the years 1939–44, the Jewish-owned machine and defense industries, including the huge Csepel concern of the Weiss family, continued to produce airplane parts, ammunition, tanks, and other military equipment for the Axis war effort, and its contributions and efficiency were standard excuses trotted out by Hungarians each time they were confronted by another demand for more drastic anti-Jewish measures. True, during the same period Hungary's Jewish population suffered many rhetorical indignities and its younger male members were called up for compulsory labor service on the eastern front, where they were often

255. Berend and Ránki 1974, 332–34.
256. Based on personal interviews, Macartney concludes that premier Kállay gave secret assurances to this effect to prominent members of the Jewish community (Macartney 1961, 2: 99). His findings have been corroborated by the more recently published correspondence between Kállay and Ferenc Chorin, the dean of Hungary's Jewish business community (Vida 1977, 362–89).

212 EAST CENTRAL EUROPE

victims of harsh treatment by unsympathetic officers, both commissioned
and noncommissioned. But in the country proper Jewish personal property
was safe; Jews were not required to wear discriminatory insignia, and there
were no attempts to remove them from their regular places of residence. All
this, however, came to an abrupt end in March 1944 when, upon the explicit instructions of the Reich high commissioner, the government by decree introduced a series of harsh measures, including the expropriation of
assets, concentration in ghettoes and in special housing units, and the wearing of the yellow star. These measures were preliminary to deportations to
German concentration camps that took place essentially during a single
month, in June 1944. In the presence of German police organs in the country, the Hungarian bureaucracy executed the project, and, paralyzed by its
own fear of the advancing Soviet army, the general public stood by more or
less idly while two-thirds of the Jewish population, mostly from the countryside, was removed from Hungary. Foreign protests had some effect, and
as Horthy was regaining some freedom to maneuver in mid-summer, he
intervened to stop the deportations. Those left behind, however, were decimated during the months of Arrow Cross rule, especially in embattled
Budapest.

Although Slovakia was a small and newly created country organized as
a one-party state, its wartime politics show some resemblance to those in
Hungary. Here, the political center consisted of a number of clerical and
Christian fascist politicians under the presidency of Jozef Tiso, himself a
former parish priest. He enjoyed the support of a wider circle of nationalist
Slovaks, who were more inclined to think of themselves as part of a larger,
Continent-wide Christian and conservative coalition than as protagonists of
a National Socialist New Order under the overlordship of Germany. As in
Hungary, the Left was relatively weak and heterogeneous, and some of its
elements were willing to accept Tiso as the lesser of two evils—the other
evil being rule by a group of secular racists and populists associated with
the already mentioned names of Tuka and Mach, who celebrated the New
Order as an ethical construct and Hitler as the "joint Fuhrer" of both Germans and Slovaks.[257] Both of these fascist factions were ensconced in the
institutions of the one-party state. While the center could count on the
support of the state bureaucracy, of the army, of the police, of the office
of the president, and of a network of parish priests ministering to the religious rural population, the pro-systemic, or pro-hegemonic, Right drew its
strength from its control of the party machinery and from the Hlinka Guard,
a paramilitary organization emulating the German SA and the Romanian
Iron Guard.

Whether consciously or instinctively and under the pressure of analogous

257. *New York Times*, June 29, 1939, 10; November 30, 1940, 6.

circumstances, Tiso tried to emulate Horthy's policies. With little choice in this matter, which was one of the conditions of Slovak independence under a formal treaty of "protective friendship" (*Schutzfreundschaft*), his regime gave special privileges to the country's German minority, but showed little enthusiasm for military ventures. Slovakia, like Hungary, participated in the eastern campaign, where Slovak troops fought poorly and were plagued by desertions. As compensation for this poor performance, the government put the Slovak economy at Germany's disposal and provided goods to Germany largely on credit. By war's end, Germany's debt to Slovakia stood at RM 1 billion, technically less than its debt to Hungary but twice as high in per capita terms.[258]

As elsewhere in Axis Europe, one of the major issues defining relations between the center and the Right, between client state and hegemonic power, was the "Jewish question." Under dual pressure from Germany and local racial radicals a Jewish Law was passed in 1939 to deal with the status of the country's 137,000 Jewish inhabitants.[259] While passed under external and internal pressure, the law still reveals strong centrist—that is, Christian fascist—influence,[260] particularly with respect to the religious definition of Jewishness and the granting of a large number of exemptions. There is no question that at that point, as well as later on, the clericals tried to delay the passage and the execution of further anti-Jewish measures by methods of feigned compliance.[261] The effectiveness of the first measure was sabotaged by dividing authority over Jewish matters between Mach's Interior Ministry and a Central Economic Office under the control of the presidency. Under external and internal pressure, however, these "deficiencies" were corrected by the Second Jewish Law of September 1941, with its more stringent definitions of Jewishness, prohibitions of intermarriage, and confiscatory provisions. Religious affiliation was overridden by genealogical criteria, although some exemptions remained in place, based primarily upon the economic needs of the state. On March 26, 1942, deportations from the country began under the authority of the Ministry of the Interior. About 60,000 Slovak Jews were thereby transferred to the Reich. But on May 12, in what amounted to a coup d'état, the Council of State amended the 1941 law to bring forward the date of valid baptisms from 1918 to March 14, 1939, a measure that affected about 30,000 persons.[262] In addition, and under pressures from the Vatican, as well as from the Slovak Council of Bishops, de-

258. Berend and Ránki 1974, 332–334.
259. Mendelsohn, 1983, 142. Of the rest of the Jews of the now dissolved Czechoslovakia, the Czech lands were left with 117,700, Ruthenia (or Carpatho-Ukraine), now administered by Hungary, had 102,500.
260. For the law itself, see *The New York Times*, April 19, 1939, 2; for the element of pressure and "payoffs" to the Germans and local radicals, Hilberg 1961, 458.
261. Instructive on these tactics is Grébert 1975, 5–18.
262. Hilberg 1961, 466–67.

portations were suspended altogether.[263] The clericals seemed to have won a partial victory. In December 1943, however, Hitler issued a personal ultimatum and threat to President Tiso. The president now submitted, holding out in vain for the enactment of special exemptions for some 10,000 persons, in the hope of eventually sabotaging the deportations. Indeed, on May 15, Tiso stopped deportations once again, but in the last desperate months of the war, the final roundup of Slovak Jews was carried out by German personnel, who did so without consulting local authorities.[264] In history, Tiso's role remains controversial. A great number of historians, and still more Slovaks, believe him to have been a reluctant collaborator succumbing to superior forces. Others see him either as too weak in resistance or as eager to collaborate. Certainly the Czechoslovak tribunal trying him in 1946 shared the latter opinion. Unlike Horthy, who finished his life in relatively comfortable exile, Tiso was found guilty and executed in 1946.[265]

The political spectrum of the Croat state associated with the Ustasha movement was similar to that of the Slovak Republic. As in Slovakia, political authority was exercised by a one-party state, but the party itself was divided between secular racists and assorted Christian groups, some of them conservative, others fascist. The German emissaries who set up the state hesitated for some time as to which faction to support. Pavelić, a secular racist, was barely known in Zagreb and virtually unknown in the villages.[266] General Gleise von Horstenau, the commander of the German army of occupation, apparently favored a conservative or military government, fearful that the Ustasha would plunge the country into a reign of terror and chaos in the manner of the Romanian Iron Guard. Subsequent events proved him correct. But the German ambassador and Reich plenipotentiary, Siegfried von Kasche, an SS officer, did not trust any of the established parties, and his word prevailed in Berlin.[267] While the Vatican remained ambivalent toward the new state, Pavelić eventually found supporters among the local hierar-

263. Mikus 1972, 124; Hilberg 1961, 469.

264. Hilberg 1961, 471; Hoensch 1973, 291.

265. For Horthy's no less controversial role, interrogations by Allied authorities, and exile to Portugal, see "Interrogation of Horthy," *World War II War Crime Records,* National Archives, Record Group 238. Horthy makes his own case in his *Memoirs* (1957), and receives sympathetic treatment from a former U.S. ambassador to Hungary (Montgomery 1947). Less sympathetic observers are Fenyo 1972, 238–39, and Pintér 1968, 335–41. For more recent research and correspondence of the British Foreign Office, see Haraszti 1993, 48–63; Sakmyster 1994, 382. For the trial of Tiso and associates, see *Dr. Jozef Tiso, Dr. Ferdinand Durčanský a Alexander Mach pred sudom naroda* [Tiso, Durčanský, and Mach before the People's Court](1946). For an enthusiastic defense, see Vnuk 1967. For a more balanced account, Abrams 1996, 255–92.

266. Hory and Broszat 1964, 65.

267. For an account of this debate, including attempts to recruit the account's author as a collaborator, see Maček 1957, 240.

chy and parish priests. But the German Foreign Office and the foreign division of the National Socialist Party were apparently not interested in having another "parish republic" in their domain. So Pavelić became Supreme Leader (*Poglavnik*); his power was based partly on his armed militia, and partly on the goodwill of the occupying powers—which, after 1943, became a single occupying power, Germany. This certainly made it hard, if not impossible, to develop a base for centrist politics, nor did Pavelić demonstrate the will to develop an independent policy defying Germany. Croat participation in the Russian campaign was purely symbolic, much of the fighting forces of the Ustasha, the militia, the regular army, and later a number of SS divisions having been tied down in fighting Tito's partisans in Bosnia and in committing atrocities on their own among the Serbian population of the new state. The deportation of the country's 30,000 Jews, although initially sabotaged in the Italian zone of occupation, was executed in a smooth, almost indifferent manner, as a gesture of goodwill to the patron power.[268] Ustasha energies were largely spent on repressing the new country's Serbians, in a three-pronged policy of expulsions, conversions, and executions. These policies affected an estimated 500,000 persons.[269] While the figure is hard to verify, the number of deportees to Serbia was 118,000 in 1941 alone, and those forcibly converted to Catholicism approximated a quarter million.[270]

War and Fascism: The Balance Sheet

The wartime political experience of the countries of East Central Europe can hardly be separated from the larger geopolitical venture of National Socialist Germany to create an imperial system, that, by its own formula, was to last 1,000 years. As it happened, German power peaked toward the end of 1941 and thereafter gradually declined, following the changing fortunes of war. If we carefully examine the wartime history of Germany's minor allies, it will be quite obvious that the shrewdest of the region's political leaders took Germany's failure to break Soviet resistance in 1941 as a serious warning signal. Hence, even before the Stalingrad disaster, the year 1942 was already a time of maneuverings to diminish the impact of military defeat.

During the first years of the war, the local economies profited from the German war effort and the seemingly insatiable appetite of the war machine for food, raw materials, and industrial products. This demand stimulated

268. Hilberg 1961, 456–57.
269. Avakumović 1971, 135–45.
270. Tomasevich 1975, 106.

industrial production[271] and resulted in a measure of prosperity. The trend began to level off after 1941, mainly because, as they had during earlier periods of high demand, the agricultural economies had soon reached the outer limits of their expandibility, limits imposed by available infrastructure and technology. Also, as noted before, by the end of 1941, Germany's ability to pay or barter had become severely limited, and most of the exports of the client states were paid for by promissory notes. Still, quite remarkably, these letters of credit kept the local economies afloat even when the defeat of the Axis began to loom large in 1944. Inflation rates remained within manageable bounds, and none of the Axis countries experienced the disastrous shortages that had broken the morale of their working classes during World War I.

To some observers, the short-term success of these economies might suggest that this German design for regional cooperation could have provided a long-term solution to the problem of relative backwardness and broken the historical cycle of spurts of growth followed by troughs of decline. This belief was especially strongly held in the region proper during the years of extreme and artificially created scarcities in the postwar decade. However, given the ideological underpinnings of the so-called New Order, there is little reason to believe that, under the imperial rule of a victorious Germany, the minor countries of East Central Europe would have become anything but a permanent agricultural hinterland and raw materials base, exporting primary goods in exchange for the less competitive product lines of the weaker sectors of German industry. Indeed, these countries might quite possibly have been reduced to mere colonies, their subordinate status justified in terms of the inherently hierarchical design of National Socialism. In any case, the Axis lost the war, and in this process most of the modest gains of the previous ten years were wiped out. Some of the economies sank to new depths, from which they had to work their way out while paying tribute to new imperial masters. Accordingly to Jean Marczewski, war damage amounted to 374 percent of prewar (1938) GNP in Yugoslavia, 350 percent in Poland, 194 percent in Hungary, 115 percent in Czechoslovakia (incurred primarily by Slovakia), 29 percent in Romania, and 33 percent in Bulgaria.[272]

Needless to say, not only economic infrastructure was involved. Over and above the loss of material assets, the countries of the region incurred enormous losses in human life and suffering. Apart from the casualties of war,

---

271. Berend and Ránki 1974, 329–34. See also the more recent, and more striking, study of the wartime economic boom in the various countries of East Central Europe in Gross 1997, 19–20.

272. Marczewski 1956, 121.

military and civilian, there were the victims of terror and genocide. There are no accurate tallies of these losses. But if we add the civilian casualties of Poland and Yugoslavia and the losses of the client armies (including prisoners of war and deportees who died in captivity) to those who were the victims of planned genocide, the number of ten to twelve million does not appear exaggerated. These extensive losses in human life, aggravated by the ways in which they were incurred, left not merely demographic but deep psychological scars as well. These scars have not yet completely healed, even after the passage of more than fifty years. In the immediate postwar period, this legacy of violence seemed to justify, and hence facilitated, the rise of a new imperial order under Soviet auspices, and after the fall of the Soviet empire, memories of the war reentered public discourse in arguments for both international cooperation and the dissolution of long-established national states.

5 | Communism

BUILDING THE IMPERIAL CORE: THE STALINIST MODEL

Setting the Agenda

The point of departure of the preceding chapters was the rise of the West—specifically, the agricultural and industrial revolutions of northwestern Europe in the seventeenth and eighteenth centuries, which created the nucleus of the modern world economy and of a global material culture. Both of these then played significant parts in shaping the domestic social, economic, and political structures of the peripheral regions of the world economy, including those of East Central Europe.

The appropriate starting point for the second half of this narrative, however, lies neither in the West nor in the dynamics of the world economy. Instead, this part of the study must begin in the East, with an examination of Russia's revolutions, in particular the "second revolution" of 1929–39, which is associated with the name of Stalin. For while the first revolution thrust the Soviet Communist (Bolshevik) Party into the role of a revolutionary government, it was the second revolution that turned the Soviet Union into an imperial state able to challenge the global status quo.

This new Soviet imperial state provided a focus for discontent with the status quo throughout East Central Europe in the interwar period, and after 1939, the USSR began its westward expansion, culminating in the creation of the Soviet "Bloc" in 1945–48. If, before, the key to understanding the politics of East Central European countries had been their peripheral status in the capitalist world economy, now the key became their peripheral status in a larger political system imperatively coordinated from its Moscow "Centre." [1] To be sure, even thereafter, these societies were not totally im-

---

1. Deutscher 1984b, 104; Jowitt 1987, 296–348.

mune to the influence of the larger world economy and the material culture emanating from the capitalist West, but these external forces were filtered and mediated by the mechanisms of the Bloc. So, for the half century commencing with World War II, political change in the region would be closely related to the Soviet Union's pursuit of its larger imperial interests.

Stalin and the Etatization of Revolution

From 1919 to 1923, there was an effective division of labor between the two main institutions of world communism. While the Soviet government fought hard to establish effective control over its territory and to reunite the former tsarist empire under the red flag, the Comintern took up the project of revolutionizing the external world, from Estonia to Germany, and from Mongolia to the United States. The effort was genuine and considerable, and in making it, the Comintern worked like a capable general staff, dutifully analyzing opportunities as they arose and providing advice to its local operatives as to how to switch from politics as usual to armed uprising.

Nevertheless, the results were disappointing, for capitalism and parliamentary democracy were more resilient than had been originally contemplated by Lenin and Trotsky. By 1923, the revolutionary impulse of the European masses appeared to have spent itself. So, twenty years after the Bolshevik-Menshevik split, Lenin's companions had to raise the old Russian dilemma of "What is to be done?" again. Since Lenin soon succumbed to his long and debilitating illness, the search for an answer entailed years of acrimonious debate, in which the competition of alternative visions became closely intertwined with the competition for Lenin's mantle of leadership.

The first of these visions was that of Trotsky's permanent revolution, although it seems that his personal commitment to this idea faltered rapidly after 1924.[2] The second formula, associated with Nikolai Bukharin, emerged from the chaotic experiments of the New Economic Policy (NEP) period and amounted to nothing less than the abandonment of the externally oriented, forward-looking geopolitical design of revolutionary Bolshevism in favor of "socialist development." The gist of this design was a project of capital accumulation via the still-existing private sector of small agricultural enterprises and a developmental state that would extract surplus by means of taxation. Taxes in turn would be invested in consumer industries, to raise the standard of living of the Soviet working class progressively above the levels prevailing in the advanced capitalist countries. In the long run, Bukharin argued, the economic success of the policy would create its own international demonstration effect that, by the force of example, would persuade

2. Deutscher 1960, 294–312; Carr 1970, 185–89.

the working classes of the world of the superiority of socialism and lead to the gradual liquidation of capitalism in the advanced countries.[3] Had Bukharin's vision gained the upper hand, and had his strategy been successful, one would presumably have seen a flow of migrants from West to East, and eventual sweeping majorities for the communist parties of France, England, and the United States.

For the majority of Bolsheviks, however, the plan held too little promise. On purely doctrinal grounds, there were legitimate objections to a policy design that raised the specter of the "restoration of capitalism" in the agrarian sector and would have altered the internal terms of trade—if only temporarily—in favor of the peasantry, at the expense of the urban working classes. But objections could also be raised on grounds of historical experience. After all, Russian politicians and economists were fully cognizant of the difficulties involved in pursuing developmental strategies and of the discouraging record of the previous century, during which few of the peripheral economies had managed to improve their relative economic positions in the world economy. Bukharinism received its coup de grâce in the realm of politics rather than economics. The not unreasonable concern was that while Soviet society might thereby enrich itself peacefully, it would also leave itself vulnerable to aggression in the ruthless game of great power politics. It was from this position that Stalin proceeded, after 1926, to formulate the political design that eventually emerged as victor in the debate.

For mostly opportunistic reasons, Stalin expropriated Bukharin's slogan of "building socialism in one country," for which he was promptly denounced by Trotsky, now an émigré, for betraying the idea of the world revolution.[4] This view of "the revolution betrayed" later became widespread among students of Soviet communism. In reality, though, Stalin did not abandon the global project, but simply changed its strategy and instruments: rather than relying on untidy and uncontrollable insurrections led by undisciplined foreigners, he decided to accomplish the grand design by using the military power of the Soviet state.[5] Thus, as Stalin was gaining personal power over the Soviet state, the strategy of armed insurrections became transmuted into a strategy of armed interventions. As the editors of a recent volume of his correspondence conclude, Stalin had become the architect of an "imperial bolshevism" in which "the further progress of the international communist revolution and the territorial expansion of Soviet Russia . . . became one and the same process."[6] The methods of this interventionism,

3. S. Cohen 1975, 161–201.
4. Trotsky 1937.
5. For this shift in grand strategy, and the rise of a "militarized society," "barracks economy," and a "garrison state" in the Soviet Union, see Janos 1991, 81–112. For a more recent, powerful articulation of the idea, see von Hagen 1996, 51–76.
6. Lih, Naumov, and Khlevnik 1995, ix.

outlined well in one of Stalin's early letters to Molotov,[7] were first tried out in Manchuria and the Soviet Far East, and then further refined in the two major Soviet thrusts westward into Europe in 1939–40 and 1944–48. As the shift in strategy was being accomplished, the Comintern was progressively marginalized, and, as its main function was being transferred to the Soviet state, its leaders were arrested and physically liquidated. The institution itself was allowed to linger on until 1943, when, as a gesture to anxious Western allies, it was dissolved, and its surviving veterans were absorbed by the Soviet diplomatic and intelligence services. Some of them would return to their homelands after 1945 in the footsteps of the Soviet army.

While Stalin's many detractors, both inside and outside the Bolshevik movement, have long held that by turning to the Soviet state, Stalin also betrayed the classical ideals of socialism, a strong argument may also be made to the effect that he merely creatively adapted them to the logic of his design and to the necessities of the historical moment. To put it differently, one may argue that rather than abandoning them, he put socialist ideals and principles through the filter of a revolutionary *raison d'état* then at the center of his system of thinking. Pushing this argument further, we can then say that those elements of classical Marxism that passed etatist muster were retained as part of the new state doctrine, while elements deemed incongruous with the functional requisites of a strong state were filtered out as useless. Stalin thus unhesitatingly carried out the Marxist vision of eliminating private property, because this "socialization" of the means of production in effect meant etatization, leading to a form of ownership that accorded the state direct access to society's manpower and resources. Similarly—and much like Bismarck or Hitler, who had little love for Marxism—Stalin embraced some of the welfare aspects of classical socialism, including improvements in public health and education, because these old socialist objectives neatly converged with the interest of the state in recruiting literate and physically fit cohorts for the army and economy. The same holds true of the Stalinist celebration of certain aspects of high culture—the cultivation of classical novels, opera, and the ballet—which were to serve as the means of identifying Soviet society as a superior form of civilization. At the same time, and again much like its Prussian counterparts, Stalin's *raison d'état* had no use for feminism, sexual license, or challenges to the traditional family, so these elements of the Enlightenment tradition were dropped from the new socialist agenda together with the "leftist" idea of strict egalitarianism in both army and industry. Indeed, any mention of the latter was now contemptuously dismissed as "egalitarian gamesmanship" (*uravnilovka*), and the earlier com-

---

7. Stalin proposes to turn loose the Soviet army, then "establish a revolutionary government, massacre the landowners, bring in the peasants, create Soviets in the cities and towns and so on." October 7, 1929 (ibid., 182).

mitments to equality of rank and appearance were superseded by the symbols and realities of hierarchy and discipline.[8]

Out of this Stalinist filter, then, there emerged a new political culture, that of etatism, which was much more in harmony with the charismatic salvationism inherited from Lenin than with the libertinism and anarchism of the 1920s. Indeed, the culture of rebellion, irreverence, and anarchism vanished—many of its advocates and practitioners were killed, and an almost equal number were driven into exile or suicide—to be replaced by a strange mixture of socialist philistinism (*meshchanstvo*) and Prussian-style military discipline. Military officers were given back their insignia (including golden braids for generals), together with all the privileges that officers of the tsarist army had once enjoyed. In civilian life, managers were allowed to acquire cars and chauffeurs, and, over the years, state functionaries would gradually shed their workers' and soldiers' tunics for dark suits and neckties. In social relations, emphasis now shifted to the respectability of rank, and gender relations were expected to conform more closely to traditional social patterns. In artistic renderings, "the stiff leather jackets, black tobacco, straight bobbed hair and bi-sexual boots" of the 1920s fell out of favor, while "coiffeurs, cosmetics, clothes, the [traditional] trappings of femininity gained social significance and made the classical theme of the Bolshevik amazon singularly obsolete."[9] Public pageantry became increasingly masculinized and militarized. Adding a particularly striking insult to these injuries of classical socialist ideals, hunting—the ultimate symbol of hierarchy and anathema to all good Marxist humanists—became one of the most universal signifiers of rank and power throughout the communist world, more de rigueur for the communist high functionary than for the English or Prussian aristocrat.

Needless to say, in order to accomplish its external purposes, the Stalinist state required an industrial economy. To a great number of historians and historical sociologists, this imperative meant that Stalinism should be seen as a kind of developmental dictatorship seeking to replicate what England had accomplished in the nineteenth century, if by somewhat unconventional and radical means. But such a depiction of the Stalinist economic design is highly misleading. The Stalinist economic model pursued industrialization not only through but also almost exclusively for the state. It resulted in an economy that, in Herbert Spencer's classical formulation, was the "mere commissariat" of a militarized society, serving the primary purpose of external expansion.[10] The true aims of this policy were not carefully hidden. In the words of a contemporary party resolution, they were "the develop-

8. For the above passages, see Janos 1991, 97–98.
9. Dunham 1990, 41, 43.
10. Spencer [1876] 1972, 154.

ment of those branches of the economy, and of industry in particular, that [play] the main role in matters of ensuring defense and war-time economic stability." [11] But available statistics are equally telling. Even according to the grossly understated official figures of the period, between 1933 and 1938, the output of the Soviet defense industry increased by 286 percent, while the share of military expenditures as a percentage of the Soviet budget rose from 3.6 to 18.7 percent in 1933, jumping to 25.6 percent in 1939, and to 32.6 percent in 1940.[12] These figures suggest a military buildup on the scale of Hitler's Germany, although undertaken by a far less advanced economy.

Characteristically, the model and organizational principles for this great effort were borrowed not from Marxist economists but from the military planners of Wilhelmine Germany, who, in desperate straits after 1916, created the first modern system of what they variously called a "war economy" (*Kriegswirtschaft*) or "administered economy" (*Verwaltungswirtschaft*). At least in part designed by the brilliant economist-politician Walther Rathenau, put into practice by General Erich Ludendorff, and named the *Hindenburgprogramm* after Field Marshal Paul von Hindenburg,[13] this model contained the main elements of the Bolshevik "war economy" of 1919–21 and subsequently of the Stalinist economy of the post-1929 period: the preeminence of a Supreme War Office (*Oberster Kriegsamt*), anticipating the Soviet Central Planning Office; wage and price controls; a system of forced deliveries in agriculture; various designs for the total mobilization of the labor force (including a plan for drafting into the army all German males between the ages of sixteen and sixty to ensure maximum labor discipline); reliance on forced labor (from Belgium); the appointment of military officers to supervise the transportation system; and the appointment of military officers to serve as commissars in factories, anticipating the future role of party secretaries.[14] In some respects, though, the differences between the German model and its Stalinist application were quite significant. Whereas Rathenau and the German generals regarded the system as a temporary expedient designed to win a war, in Stalin's hands, the model became an instrument of mobilization for creating a war economy that, with minor modifications, would be sustained for the next six decades. Just as significantly, whereas in Germany the model served to mobilize the resources of the then second-largest industrial economy in the world, in Soviet Russia it was used to extract surplus from a backward economy ravaged by civil war and social experimentation over the pre-Stalin decade.

11. *KPSS v rezolyutsiakh* (1970), cited in Gaddy 1996, 32.
12. Nove 1992, 230.
13. Kitchen 1976; Hecker 1983.
14. See Raupach 1966, 86–101. Also Neurath 1919; Hecker 1983; Buckelow 1974, esp. 20–85.

Given this last circumstance, the Soviet system of mobilization had to resort to extreme measures that neither the German generals nor other pre-communist protagonists of a modern *Kriegswirtschaft* had ever practiced or contemplated. For one thing, the system of forced deliveries used by Germany during World War I was apparently not radical enough to be able to feed the rapidly increasing number of Soviet industrial workers while simultaneously meeting the levels of wheat exports needed to pay for imported industrial technologies. Soviet agriculture, unlike that of Germany, was noted for the low productivity of its labor force. During the process of Stalinist industrialization, that productivity continued to diminish: an increasingly smaller and more demoralized cohort of peasants was expected to feed an ever-larger number of urban laborers. To compensate for the loss, Soviet agriculture was not only taxed, or subjected to a system of forced deliveries, but also "collectivized." The resulting larger units, while not inherently more productive, were expected to facilitate the capture of the yield for the purposes of the state. This method of capturing "surplus" exacted immense current and future costs. The immediate price was paid by the millions who starved during the "great famine" of 1930–32. The long-term price, meanwhile, was paid via the chronic undercapitalization of Soviet agriculture, which transformed Russia from the world's largest exporter of grain in 1910 into its single largest importer in 1970.

More so than ever in history, the Russian peasantry thus had to bear the burden of building an industrial economy. But the peasantry was not alone in bearing the burden. With about a quarter of the country's gross domestic product representing "producers' goods" (including military equipment) and another quarter reinvested to sustain high rates of growth, real wages declined across the board. According to Janet Chapman's estimates, the downward trend in real wages leveled off in 1935–36. Even so, in 1937 real wages were only 58 percent of their 1928 level.[15] Depressed social consumption, in any event, was only one side of the coin. The other side involved the introducing of draconian measures to strengthen "labor discipline" that put feudal labor exploitation to shame: beginning in 1930, absenteeism became punishable by the loss of six months' wages; in 1932, chronic absentees from the workplace were further punished by the loss of living quarters and ration cards; also in 1932, the internal passport system was introduced, under which changes of domicile and employment required official authorization; Article 58 of the new Labor Code, promulgated that same year, made petty pilfering punishable by ten years' imprisonment, grand theft punishable by the death penalty.[16] In 1938, as the war industry

15. Chapman 1963, 153.
16. Nove 1992, 230.

switched into high gear, managers who failed to enforce these penalties themselves became subject to them. In June 1940, those more than twenty minutes late to work without medical excuse became subject to compulsory labor at their own workplace; unauthorized changes in one's employment became punishable by imprisonment—in the case of defense and defense-related industries, by five to eight years in a labor camp.[17] With the enforcement of these stringent regulations, the number of detainees in labor camps increased rapidly, by various estimates, to six million in the 1930s and perhaps as many as fourteen million in the immediate postwar years (although the latter number also includes prisoners of war).[18]

These methods of resource extraction, unprecedented in the history of modern militarized economies, explain why terror is commonly described as the main feature of the Stalinist regime. The term itself refers not only to the degree of coercion, but to its randomness and its detachment from preestablished legal norms and procedures. To be sure, such arbitrary violence was not absent from the practices of Bolshevism prior to Stalin's ascent to personal leadership: what happened after 1929 was not so much a change in the modus operandi as a large quantum jump in the number of people affected by it. The record on this point is too extensive to need repeating here in detail. What should be remembered though is that this massive and arbitrary violence was only one part of a larger design to keep the Soviet population both subservient and mobilized at the same time. The other part was the nearly total isolation of the Soviet population from the rest of the world. To accomplish the objectives of this policy, travel was curtailed: after 1930, only the highest and most trusted officials were allowed to leave the country, and even they were usually required to leave members of their families behind to serve as hostages in case of defection. As for illegal departures, they were made exceedingly difficult by restraints on internal travel, by the transformation of regions adjacent to borders into special security zones, and by the establishment of a variety of physical barriers. However, isolation was not only important to prevent the outflow of people—and with them the loss of both manpower and credibility as a superior society—but also to prevent the inflow of ideas, and especially to insulate the Soviet population from the demonstration effect of the higher living standards in the West. This policy was startlingly effective in the 1930s. Its success became evident in 1944–45, when large numbers of Soviet soldiers entered East Central Europe and were stunned by the material standards they found, not only in highly developed Germany but in the more underdeveloped Balkan countries as well.[19]

17. Ibid.; Fainsod 1965, 107.
18. Dallin and Nikolaevsky 1947, 86; Weissberg 1951, 318–19.
19. Naimark 1995, 69.

The Purges

The "revolution consuming its own children" is a familiar phenomenon in modern history. The phrase itself was coined in the context of the French Revolution, but the English Revolution, too, had culminated in "[Colonel] Pride's purge" of recalcitrant Puritans from the victorious Parliament. Under whatever label, the phenomenon fits the logic of charismatic salvationism. On the one hand, the latter is inimical to human folly and imperfection; on the other hand, the grandiose nature of revolutionary eschatology is immune to legal and moral restraint. Accordingly, it should not be surprising that the Soviet elite subjected itself, or was subjected by its leaders, to campaigns of ecstatic purification. The first *chistka* was initiated by Lenin in 1921–22, when he called upon the party to rid itself of "rascals, bureaucrats, dishonest or wavering communists, and Mensheviks who repainted their facade, but who remained Mensheviks at heart."[20]

What we need to bear in mind, however, is that behind the term "purge," whether used by its perpetrators or observers, lie a multiplicity of phenomena and objectives. In this respect, Lenin's statement of 1921 is itself instructive. It includes those who may have harbored alternative political designs ("Mensheviks"), those not sufficiently zealous and principled in applying political criteria ("bureaucrats") and those who may have succumbed to the temptation of using their official positions for personal gain ("rascals"). Stalin, one might argue, was dealing with the same categories, although on a much larger scale: his purges were directed against identifiable political enemies, such as the "Bogdanovites," "Bukharinites," and "Trotskyites"; against corrupt officialdom threatening to transform the revolutionary state into a rent-seeking one; and against those who failed to apply administrative regulations, "too slavishly" ignoring the "party line" of the moment. Of course, one might argue that Stalin could have simply pensioned off or dismissed from service all of those with insufficient ability or zeal. But dismissing them with pensions would have strained the meager resources of the Soviet economy, while dismissing them without some emolument in a society where politics was the chief source of status could have created a large group of potential opponents of the dictator and his regime. By this logic, people who did not do a good job, or who had outlived their usefulness, "had to" be imprisoned or executed.

Although the major differences between the purges of the 1920s and those of the 1930s were mainly quantitative, Stalin must still be credited with introducing novel elements into the process. The most conspicuous of these was the show trial, which turned purges of the elite into grand political theater for the masses. The list of these trials is known to all students of Soviet

20. Quoted in Fainsod 1965, 146.

history: they began with the "Shakhty trial" of engineers in 1927–28 and culminated in the great purge trials of 1934–38. Each of these trials was preceded by the elaborate use of physical torture, whereafter the accused were to memorize carefully crafted scripts, in which they would confess to charges of espionage, sabotage, or plotting assassinations in the service of foreign governments.[21]

Once again, the questions of motivation and rationality must be raised. While on one level these may indeed be related to personal pathology, on another level it appears that in designing them, Stalin tried to accomplish at least three distinct political objectives, and that he was staging the trials for three different audiences. The first of these objectives was to create a "siege mentality" within the party by persuading its "true believers"—some of whom, incidentally, included the victims themselves—that the enemy was in their midst, and that they should conduct their affairs with utmost and unceasing vigilance. A second objective was to terrify incorrigible opponents by demonstrating the regime's boundless severity. This stratum of the populace knew all too well that confessions had been fabricated, but the show trials were also persuasive indications that resistance was folly, and that even the strongest could be broken by the security police. Last but not least, Stalin targeted the gray mass of the common people, neither believers nor active opponents of the regime. For this audience, the trials were to demonstrate the prevalence of a kind of rough-and-ready egalitarianism in a system of immense political inequalities. As under the old tsarist regime, so under the new, the political class wielded considerable power over the population without formal rules of accountability. But in contrast to the old, in which privilege had been entrenched and even hereditary most of the time, in the new regime the high and mighty, too, were insecure, and could fall from one day to another into the hands of the executioner or the bottomless pit of the concentration camps, to the obvious delight of the hopelessly dispossessed. In a perverted way, the purge was a substitute for egalitarianism and a proof of equal opportunity.

The Pillars of Personal Power

The purges raise yet another question, however, perhaps even more critical than the question of their purpose and utility: how could the regime and the dictator's personal power be maintained while Stalin was killing off his own auxiliaries? At one level, the answer is simple and easy: he could terrorize the party because, as General Secretary, he had established personal control over the security police, which he used to exact the party's blind obedience. But this answer raises Juvenal's classical dilemma of *quis cus-*

21. Beck and Goodman 1951, 106; Fainsod 1965, 691.

todiet ipsos custodes, a pivotal problem of tyrannical politics. For while the tyrant can rule his people by deploying a praetorian guard, that guard can in turn assassinate or overthrow him, as was the case with countless Roman emperors.

Stalin's political genius is manifest, not only in his understanding of the dilemma, but in his design of an elaborate system of controls to protect himself from such a turn of events. The essence of this design was a strict division of labor, functions, and images between the two key branches of the regime, the party and the security organs. While the party's membership was decimated, the party itself, as an institution, continued to be surrounded by an aura of sanctity and legitimacy. Contrary to the oft-repeated cliché that the purges "destroyed" it, the party was instead glorified and remained the fountainhead of all political wisdom and munificence. At the same time, the security police became an instrument of naked force, celebrated as the "cutting edge" of the regime, but on the whole deprived of any aura of benevolence and legitimacy. In sharp contrast to the party, the dictator allowed that police force to lose its earlier image of benevolence. Indeed, by permitting the circulation of rumors about its brutality and ruthlessness, and by encouraging its members to flaunt their material privileges, the police force was at once desacralized and made into an object of popular suspicion, even hatred. Nowhere was this more evident than in the course of subsequent rebellions against the satellite regimes in Poland and Hungary, when spontaneous expressions of popular wrath invariably turned against security policemen, but rarely against rank-and-file members of the party itself.

This division of labor and imagery certainly diminished the likelihood that the security police would turn into an institutional base for rebellion. But the effectiveness of the system, and Stalin's ability to manage it, depended on yet another element: the successful cult of his personality, and his own skill in insinuating it into popular consciousness. This imagery was contrived and subtle, in that it was once again designed to target multiple audiences. One of these clearly were the cadres of the party, to whom Stalin became the "leader of oppressed humanity" and a great modern hero-scientist, with contributions not only to economics and social science but also to linguistics, genetics, and theoretical physics. The other constituency was popular, and for their sake Stalin projected the image of a "wise father" radiating a "primitive magic,"[22] based on a quaint mixture of personal warmth and spatial distance more reminiscent of the imagery of Byzantine emperors and Oriental god-kings than of modern revolutionaries. After World War II, this imagery was further embellished with themes of military virtue, as Stalin bestowed titles upon himself—first that of Marshal, and later that of Generalissimo.

22. Deutscher 1984a, 106–18.

THE RISE OF THE BLOC

Communism Comes to East Central Europe

The political design of Stalinism, refined and routinized before the war, was eventually imposed upon the countries of East Central Europe in the years 1945–48. There is relatively little that conventional political economy and sociology can add to our understanding of the event. Local economies, social configurations, and historical memories obviously affected the process, but they did so at a relatively low, tactical level. The key to explaining the Stalinist outcomes rests squarely in the domain of the great power politics of World War II and in the events surrounding the defeat of Germany by the Allies in 1944–45.

In the larger continental political arena, this defeat opened a vacuum of power, which the old hegemons of the post-Versailles order, France and Britain, were unable to fill. France lay prostrate in the wake of its earlier defeat, and its efforts were concentrated on attempts to regain a status of nominal equality among the major belligerents. Britain, too, was exhausted by the war effort, increasingly reduced to the status of a lesser player, dependent on the goodwill of the United States. Significantly, Britain's two major wartime projects had come to naught. One of these was to save Poland from Soviet domination by restoring the country's government-in-exile under British auspices. The other, still earlier project, had envisaged the launching of military operations on the Balkan Peninsula, the final target being the Pannonian Plain. The first of these projects was frustrated by the early arrival and physical presence of the Soviet army in Poland. The second plan, never seriously contemplated by American military decision makers, made too little sense. Conducting operations in the Croatian Karst would have been immensely wasteful, while targeting the Pannonian plain ran counter to the central objective of the war: the quick military defeat of Germany. All too obviously, Anglo-American forces would thereby have been marching against the Soviet armies rather than against the common enemy.

The position of the United States was more complex. To begin with, the United States had no traditional interests in the region and scant familiarity with its component nations. While some of its citizens were of Eastern European origin, their influence upon national politics was minimal, leaving U.S. presidents and their advisors considerable room for maneuver. During the years 1942–44, President Roosevelt and his advisors used this freedom in an attempt to construct a new worldwide system of collective security in which the Soviet Union was to play a major role, if not invited outright to become a partner in a Soviet-American superpower condominium over the world. This plan was colored by the president's dislike of European colonial empires, by the view that Japan and Germany were outside the pale of the larger human community,[23] and finally by the view, made fashionable by Reinhold Niebuhr, the theologian-ideologist of the American establishment, that while the fascists were "children of the darkness," the communists were only "misguided children of the light," redeemable, with some patience and effort, for the grand projects of liberalism.[24] There is certainly evidence that Roosevelt could see the rough edges of Soviet communism. Indeed, if we can believe Cardinal Spellman, the president spoke to him about the "barbarism" of Russia.[25] But he felt nonetheless that the Soviet Union could be tamed and retained as a reliable ally against the potential resurgence of German and Japanese fascism. True, as time passed, such cooperation seemed less and less likely, and Roosevelt's continued courting and humoring of Stalin was more and more dictated by realpolitik and the lack of viable alternatives.

A fundamental shift in American thinking thus came only after Roosevelt's death. His successor, Harry S Truman, was, no doubt, more willing to see communists as the other children of darkness, and his inclinations were strengthened by Soviet behavior in Poland and Romania, where communist-dominated governments were installed under Soviet auspices. For a few years, American thinking about the Soviet Union wavered between the extremes of preventive war and abject surrender. But eventually the "wise men"[26] of the foreign policy establishment had their way. Unlike the public at large, they understood the fundamental premises on which U.S. policy had to rest. On the one hand, they knew that a partnership between the world's richest and one of its poorest countries would be inherently unstable. On the other, they were also keenly aware that the Soviet Union (and later, China) were simply too big either to occupy with Western troops or to co-opt into the world economy with preferential treatment and foreign aid. Out of this realization emerged the middle course of containment and, later, of carefully managed conflict. The fundamental premises of the policy remained as valid today as they had been fifty years ago.

In any case, the result of this attitude was a temporary vacuum in the eastern half of Europe, and the Soviet Union took advantage of it, moving to complete a regional project that had been rather clearly outlined as early as 1939–40. During the two major encounters between Molotov and Ribbentrop, the former laid claim not only to Romania, Bulgaria, and Hungary but also to the Dardanelles and Sweden as well.[27] Conventional interpreta-

23. Rose 1973, 9.

24. Niebuhr 1944.

25. Gannon 1962, 222–24.

26. For their story, see Isaacson and Thomas 1986.

27. For the second of these meetings, during which Molotov indicated Soviet interest in Romania, Hungary, Bulgaria, and the Dardanelles, see Shirer 1941, 565–66; 1967, 1053–61. And see also Mastny 1979, 31.

tions of Soviet motivations emphasize military considerations—more specifically, perceived Soviet needs for a widened defense perimeter around the country. Such considerations, to be sure, went back to tsarist days. But in mid-century, they acquired new meaning in the context of Stalin's etatist revolution. That revolution had imposed immense sacrifices on the Soviet population and political class alike, and in the long term, evidence was required that they had not been in vain. Assurances were also needed that the Soviet geopolitical project was making progress. In search of such evidence and assurances, then, the Soviet Union did not merely seek to establish "friendly" or neutral governments, but communist regimes. The effective takeover of the region was accomplished neither by the entry of Soviet troops nor by the signing of bilateral agreements guaranteeing the preponderance of Soviet interests, but rather by the establishment of the political monopoly of communist party states.

Under these circumstances, the real question is not *why* Stalin moved into East Central Europe, but rather why he did not respond to the prospect of an American-Soviet condominium dangled before him by Roosevelt. The answer may be cast in terms of "traditional" Russian mistrust and xenophobia, which had sufficient basis not so much in American intentions as in the realities of global economics and politics. A masterful and intuitive analyst, Stalin likely realized, perhaps well before the Americans, the inherent instabilities of partnerships between rich and poor nations, and the limits of what the USSR could expect, even under the best-case scenario, in terms of postwar American economic aid. Not least of all, however, he could not have been blind to the implications of a foreign-financed strategy of economic development, with its inevitable concomitants of opening Soviet society to foreign personnel, methods of organization, and collection of statistics. Equally, there were well-founded fears of images of a better life penetrating Soviet consciousness and of the general peril inherent in a policy of decompression in the highly charged environment of domestic Stalinism. (The fact that forty years later one of his successors, operating in a much calmer environment, failed in the pursuit of such a policy seems to justify Stalin's apprehensions.) True, when economic aid was formally offered in the framework of the Marshall Plan, the makers of American foreign policy were no longer interested in a condominium design or Soviet participation.[28] But the wartime and postwar attitudes cited above and Soviet suspicions of the West make it reasonable to conclude that Stalin and his comrades-in-arms could have accepted unconditionally granted gifts, but were averse to the idea of economic cooperation and foreign penetration.

There remains the question of whether the conquest of East Central Europe marked the beginning of a phase of Soviet saturation and imperial con-

28. Gaddis 1996, 114–15. Parrish 1997, 273–74; Mastny 1996, 27.

solidation, or whether it was just another stage in the larger geopolitical design of Soviet expansion toward the heartlands of European capitalism. The balance of the evidence, much of it recently garnered, favors the second interpretation. To be sure, just as in the previous decades, Stalin's geopolitical ambitions were accompanied by considerable operational caution and an understanding that, after the exertions of the war, the Soviet Union required a "breathing spell." This was consistent with Bolshevik strategic thinking, and in his historic memorandum to Stalin, Ivan Maisky, deputy minister for foreign affairs, spoke of the need for "about ten years [to heal] the wounds inflicted by the war."[29] During this period, Stalin was to display considerable operational flexibility, mixing offensive and defensive moves, and was careful not to push aggression beyond certain prudent limits. Also, after 1947, he gave apparent priority to reducing American influence on the Continent rather than to establishing communist governments in West European states. It was in this vein that leaders of the Italian and French Communist parties were instructed to prepare for armed insurrections, even if these insurrections produced chaos rather than communist victory.[30] As to actual takeovers, Stalin most likely shared Maisky's opinion that drawing Western Europe into the socialist camp might take as much as thirty years.[31] It is debatable whether Soviet moves such as the Berlin blockade and the Korean War were offensive or defensive in intent. What matters is that Stalin felt reinvigorated by the simultaneous communist victories in China and in East Central Europe, and it was under the impact of these events that he decided not to abandon the "revolutionary-imperial paradigm"[32] of Soviet politics.

The Imperial System

The political vacuum that had opened up in the wake of the defeat of Germany virtually invited the Soviet Union to perform the functions of traditional *Ordnungsmacht* in East Central Europe even before its hegemony in the area was formally established. Most immediately, the performance of these functions implied the need to make the territorial dispensations codified by armistice agreements and peace treaties. Wartime agreements gave broad "police powers" to the Soviet Union in the liquidation of fascist governments in the region, and the Western powers raised few objections even to extremely broad and self-serving interpretations of them.

The redrawing of territorial boundaries followed three general principles.

29. Zubok and Pleshakov 1996, 28–29.
30. Mastny 1996, 33.
31. Zubov and Pleshakov 1996, 28–29.
32. Ibid., 111.

First, the Soviet Union was to retain all the territory it had seized in 1939–40 under the provisions of the Hitler-Stalin pact. To have done otherwise would have been an open admission of error, or even guilt. Moreover, such a course of events would have run counter to what we must assume was Stalin's sentimental objective, to see the boundaries of the tsarist empire restored under the red flag. It was apparently based on such reasoning that the Soviet Union reoccupied not just the strategically significant Baltic countries and the eastern provinces of Poland, with their Belorussian and Ukrainian inhabitants, but also the strategically meaningless and economically worthless Bessarabia, with its largely Romanian population. As a corollary, the boundary changes made over the years of German hegemony were to be nullified. Hungary had to return the territories "recovered" in 1938–41 from three of its neighbors; Macedonia and the Kosovo reverted to Yugoslavia, and, of course, Slovakia was reunited with the Czech lands. The only exception to this rule was the southern part of Dobrudja, a strip of land ceded by Romania to Bulgaria, where in the interim a population exchange agreement had been effected; perhaps in recognition of the outstanding record of its Communist Party, Bulgaria was thus permitted to retain sovereignty over territory it had gained as a result of German patronage. Finally, the former Axis countries were further punished by additional changes in their territorial boundaries. The greatest loser in this respect was Germany, in that she had to cede all the Reich's territories east of the Oder and Neisse rivers and put up with the resettlement of millions of Germans from these lands. Italy, too, was forced to cede part of the Istrian peninsula, Fiume (Rijeka), and a few islands to Yugoslavia, while Hungary lost five more villages to Czechoslovakia, so as to provide suitable conditions for widening the Danube port of the Slovak capital, Bratislava. Finally, reflecting none of the above principles, Ruthenia, a region that had changed hands between Hungary and Czechoslovakia three times, was now deeded by the Czechoslovak government to the Soviet Union so that its inhabitants could join the Ukrainians on the other side of the Carpathians.

These early steps taken under the cover of wartime agreements were followed by more resolute measures aimed at the integration of the seven countries of the region and the Soviet zone of occupation of Germany into the larger imperial system. To the surprise and disappointment of some of the local communist leaders—including the ambitious Tito, who had already cast himself in the role of Stalin's heir as leader of the international communist movement[33]—the countries of East Central Europe were not transformed into Soviet republics, but were allowed to maintain, indeed flaunt,

33. For Tito's ambition, see Khrushchev in Zubok and Pleshakov 1996, 187. According to more recent research, these ambitions received some encouragement from Stalin. See *Cold War History Project* (1998), 122.

some of the attributes of national sovereignty. However, as even the most
cursory observation of Soviet–East Central European relations will quickly
reveal, their sovereignty was largely symbolic, and they in fact were part of
a hierarchically organized supranational political system ruled from a single
center of power, located in the capital of the Soviet Union. Ironically, the
eventual exception would be Tito's Yugoslavia, which, in a monumental miscalculation, was "expelled" from the rising empire in 1948 and thereafter
maintained its precarious independence as a communist state wedged between the more clearly marked political boundaries between East and West
on the European continent.[34] For all the other nations, policy priorities were
set in Moscow by Stalin, Andrei Zhdanov, and a few associates who were
formally in charge of the affairs of "fraternal countries," while the execution of policy was supervised by Soviet ambassadors (who now were to be
treated with special dignity), by a large number of Soviet "advisors," and by
special liaison officers mediating between identical branches of the Soviet
Union and the client states. Perhaps still more important, and descriptive of
the imperial system, was the fact that personnel decisions likewise were
made in the Soviet capital. First secretaries were appointed and dismissed
direct from Moscow, and all appointments at the Politburo level had to be
cleared with the Soviets. This was a major difference between the nature of
Soviet and of earlier hegemonies, including the more inchoate imperial hegemony of Germany before and during World War II.

Like all imperial systems, the Bloc of "fraternal states," possessed not
only a single line of authority but also a single, tightly integrated economic
system. True, in the first decade of Soviet rule, no systematic attempt was
made to create a central coordinating mechanism. The Council of Mutual
Economic Assistance (CEMA), or Comecon, remained largely an empty shell
until the early 1960s. But the formerly diverse and uncoordinated foreign
trade was quickly turned into a single, integrated trading system by rerout-
ing trade flows to the Soviet Union and other Bloc countries. As Table 27
indicates, by 1952, this process of reorientation had made significant headway. Indeed, in an essay of the following year, Stalin could boast that the era
of a single world market dominated by capitalism had ended.[35] To be sure,
this common economy lacked most features of a genuine market, for over
the years, and in particular during the first decade of the Bloc, the imperial
power freely used its political supremacy to set prices and to establish terms
of trade. In these years, an attempt to bargain over these terms became one
of the most heinous crimes that an East European official could commit
against the spirit of imperial comity. Indeed, many of these underlings would

34. For some recent contributions to the vast literature on this expulsion, see Banac 1988
and Gibianski 1997, 291–312.
35. Stalin 1972a, 467–69.

TABLE 27

Trade Patterns of Five East Central European Countries, 1937–52

(percentage of foreign trade)

	With USSR		With CEMA (Bloc)	
	1937	1952	1937[a]	1952
Czechoslovakia	1	35	11	71
Poland	1	32	7	67
Hungary	—	29	13	71
Romania	1	58	18	85
Bulgaria	—	57	12	89

SOURCE: Spulber 1957, 410.
[a] With USSR and the five countries listed.

land in concentration camps as a result of such actions, even when the "bargain" had been sought in good faith, in an attempt to persuade Soviet superiors of their long-term benefits.[36]

Apart from politics and economics, the imperial character of the system was most obvious from the coordination of military affairs. It was not until 1955 that this coordination was formalized by the signing of a multilateral treaty of cooperation in the form of the Warsaw Pact. The integration of East Central European armies into a single military establishment was achieved through the loyalty of their governments and ministers of defense—a Soviet marshal in the case of Poland, in others a handpicked old functionary, often a returning "Muscovite"—and was made effective by a network of Soviet military advisors, who in case of war were ready to assume the command of divisions and regiments.[37] The soldiers of the client states were provided with Soviet arms and equipment, and, again with the exception of Poland, where some concession was made to national tradition, with Soviet-style uniforms.[38] After 1948, often in violation of the explicit provisions of prior peace treaties, troops were raised by the reintroduction of universal conscription. But for a good many years thereafter, they remained an ill-equipped, ragged lot, no doubt because they were regarded as unreliable, or at least as less reliable than their Soviet counterparts. Although this changed in later years, the brunt of the burden of common defense continued to rest with the armies of the imperial power, which provided its material exactions with a veneer of legitimacy.

36. See Loebl 1969, 27–30. For an admission to this effect by the former Polish first secretary, Edward Ochab, see Toranska 1983, 46–47.
37. Brzezinski 1961, 122.
38. See Z. Barany 1991, 148–64. Literature on the early phase of the development of Soviet-style armies in East Central Europe is scarce, but a number of books devoted to the later period provide appropriate background. See Z. Barany 1993, 24–51; Simon 1985, 1–10; Rice 1984, 7–58.

Legitimating Hierarchy: Theory and Reality

Like all hierarchies, the vertical relationships between the imperial core and its peripheries in the Bloc required legitimation, so as to facilitate the accommodation of the subordinates and to raise the self-confidence and cohesion of the superiors. The fact that these relationships violated conventional popular expectations concerning the sovereignty of the nation-state, and, at the same time, contradicted socialist principles of equality, made the need for such justifications only more urgent. Unlike Hitler's empire, which was built on the crude and offensive principle of natural hierarchies, the Soviet Union could fall back upon Marxist theories of history, which, much like American theories of modernization, posit the existence of different stages of historical development. While societies at a higher stage of progress can serve as examples and tutors of the less advanced, those at the earlier stages of the evolutionary timeline are not regarded as ipso facto inferior, but can look forward to their own progress, provided they follow in the footsteps of those who have traveled the road ahead of them. In this manner, theories of progress may serve to justify temporary inequalities of power without being downright offensive to those of inferior rank.

In the Soviet–East European context, this concept of uneven development found expression in the theory of "people's democracy." Formulated between 1945 and 1948 in the Soviet Union, this theory distinguished among three types of modern political systems in the order of their place on the scale of historical development.[39] At the lowest level, there were the "bourgeois democracies" of Western Europe and the United States, in which parliamentary institutions were said to be but a façade for the rule of the propertied classes and capital. The highest stage, meanwhile, was occupied by socialist societies, then exemplified by the Soviet Union. In between the two were people's democracies, now represented by the countries of East Central Europe, which were no longer bourgeois, but not quite socialist yet either. The more precise definition of the concept changed over time as the people's democracies were drawn ever more tightly into the Soviet orbit. At first, people's democracy was defined as the "highest stage of bourgeois democracy in which progressive forces, led by the Communist party, had seized power without liquidating either the private ownership of the means of production or a multi-party system."[40] Then, in 1947, the term was redefined by Zhdanov, the Pole Hilary Minc, and the Hungarian József Révai, to refer to the lowest stage of socialist democracy or to societies whose institutions were consistent with those of the dictatorship of the proletariat,

39. For the evolution of this theory, see Brzezinski 1961, 22–40.
40. Ibid., 76.

made "meaningful by the struggle against world imperialism," yet "historically incomplete" because the class structure had not yet been fully homogenized, because institutions of social welfare had not yet been fully developed, and because the consciousness of the masses had not yet fully matured.[41] To give this theory substance, and contrary to the Soviet model, except for refractory Yugoslavia, countries of East Central Europe retained a structure of bogus political parties, with representation in parliament elected by single list. What both theory and practice were to convey was the idea that there was a single path of historical development, upon which the Soviet Union was far ahead of its East Central European allies, which ipso facto entitled it to provide them with tutelage. Although on the whole a primitive construct, this "theory" provided a proper idiom in which uncomfortable commands could be comfortably verbalized and conveyed in meetings with the leaders of the subordinate parties.

However, theory is one thing, and reality is another. The fact of the matter was that, like all Europeans, and perhaps like most modern people, Eastern Europeans had the tendency to associate technological sophistication with economic development, and by these standards the Soviet Union, and within it Russia, failed the tests of a superior civilization on its Central and East European periphery. While in her "inner empire" of Central Asia and the Soviet Far East Russia could credibly present itself as an advanced society with a corpus of literature, arts, and an Academy of Science, in the regions acquired after 1939, the Russians were seen as charming primitives at best, and at worst as a nation of savages imposing their "Asiatic barbarism" on "European nations." The fact that the imperial propaganda machine continued to proclaim the glories of Russia's cultural and technological superiority, claiming for Russians most of the great discoveries of modern technology and science, only made matters worse. In the 1950s, the Russian plant biologists I. V. Michurin and T. D. Lysenko became the butt of irreverent and politically seditious joking, as did Popov, the presumed inventor of radio, and the unnamed Russian inventors of the X-ray.[42] Meanwhile, lecture tours of "leading Soviet scientists," surgeons, shock workers, and engineers created quiet consternation among local specialists, with their earnest attempts to purvey long familiar or outdated forms of knowledge and know-how.[43] These incongruities between social modernity and power could not be effectively papered over by Zhdanovite theories of socialist progress. No matter what, the empire was seen by most of its newly acquired subjects

41. Ibid.

42. Gati 1990, 21–22.

43. For an extensive discussion of this problem, see Naimark 1995, 398–471, esp. 410, 418, 451. For the reaction of the locals to the Soviet army, see the recollections of a Polish woman in Hungary: Orme 1950.

as a political entity in which the culturally inferior were ruling peoples of greater sophistication and civility. This perception changed little over the years, and throughout the existence of the empire continued to be one of its most serious liabilities, and one with which few of the great imperial powers of the modern world had had to contend. When the Germans, French, British, and Americans played their own roles of regional hegemons and colonial powers, they were often seen by their subjects and clients as cold, calculating, heartless, and ugly, but these perceptions would be compensated for by creeping admiration for their material prosperity, technological sophistication, and efficiency.

Perhaps nowhere were these incongruities more debilitating than in the attempts of the imperial center to communicate its political message to the countries of East Central Europe. For two decades prior to its westward expansion, the Soviet Union was consolidating its own eastern imperial holdings, developing its routines and symbols of communication for an illiterate and semi-literate rural, or only recently urbanized, population. These routines—involving news broadcasts, works of art, movies, and newspapers— may have scored successes in their own milieu, but they failed miserably when, essentially without adjustment, they were introduced into a far more urbanized and educated environment. This was obvious to casual observers of the empty movie houses and art galleries of Warsaw, Prague, and Budapest in this period. By 1945, however, the Soviet propaganda machine, like other Stalinist organizations, had become too rigid to adjust, and lacked personnel with either the necessary initiative or international experience. Although founded by astute Westernized intellectuals, in the end the Bolshevik movement became too parochial and was ineffective in projecting its message westward—certainly less effective in East Central Europe than its great competitor, the National Socialist propaganda machine.[44]

Horizontal Integration: Stalinism and Ethnic Nationalism

By definition, empires are vertically coordinated political systems that recognize the separate identities and characteristics of their constituent elements. This means that empires, whether Roman, German, British, or Soviet, must not just be able to command, but to maintain peace amid diversity. As a rule, for protracted periods of time, such a *pax imperii* cannot be maintained by brute force alone: in order to be truly effective, its subordinate entities, or at least their local leaders, must be persuaded to put their conflicts aside and to live with each other in peace. It was in this respect that

44. Many of these themes are developed in Kenez 1985; on movies, see Kenez 1992, esp. 157–253.

the Nazi imperial system was especially weak, for its particularistic idiom did not blunt but further incited regional hostilities. Hitler's satellites lived with daggers drawn at each other. The best Hitler could do to hold them together was to threaten the use of superior force or urge them to suspend their mutual hostilities until the end of the World War.

Marxism, with its universalistic foundations, was more suitable as an ideology of imperial peace, although it was not entirely free of problems. As the example of East Central Europe in the interwar period has shown, radical universalism can offend national sensitivities and alienate potential supporters. As already noted, the Comintern and early Leninism tried to overcome the problem by distinguishing between progressive and regressive nationalisms and justified the distinction by invoking the principles of dialectics. Suspicious of Great Russian ethnic and imperial sentiment, the Bolsheviks at first branded Russian nationalism reactionary, while desirous of taking credit for the liberation of hitherto subject peoples.[45] Still more transparently, in East Central Europe, the friends of the status quo were branded reactionaries, while its enemies, and their national grievances, were described as progressive.

All this was to change in the early 1930s under the auspices of Stalin. While many standard sources on the subject are all too eager to see this change as part of the "great retreat," and a crude reassertion of Russian nationalism,[46] the new policy, and the subtly articulated doctrine behind it, were infinitely more complex. Rather then merely appealing to Russian nationalism, Stalinist rule "actually contributed to the making of nations by constructing ethnic political units, educational and cultural institutions in their own language" and by promoting "native cadres into positions of power."[47] More fundamentally, Stalinism retreated from the earlier distinction between oppressor and oppressed peoples, and allowed all nationalities to construct positive self-images, as long as this was not accomplished at the expense of a Hegelian-Heideggerian "other." Rather than invoking negative images of the outsider, henceforth every group—big or small, majority or minority—would be encouraged to take pride in its own folk tradition, literature, and, more generally, of its own contributions to the saga of universal human progress. In applying these principles to East Central Europe, history books could dwell at great length on wars of national independence (described as "bourgeois revolutions") and heroize their struggles against feudal and imperial oppressors, but would be expected to downplay past conflicts with other imperial peoples. To be sure, among the peoples of the

45. See Slezkine 1994, 414–53, esp. 418–20.
46. See ibid., 425.
47. Suny 1993, 101.

Soviet empire, Russians were accorded special attention, with significant efforts being made, not only to neutralize hostility to them, but also to make them seem worthy of special admiration. In this spirit, the Soviet Friendship societies of East Central Europe sought to promote the Russian language and love of Russian literature, music, and culture. To use Yuri Slezkine's metaphor, the Russians would occupy the great hall and the kitchen of the "communal apartment," but all the others were given their room and living space.[48]

Like any other high-minded agenda constructed with a long-term perspective in mind, this one had its own contradictions, and at times it would be in conflict with short-term but acute priorities. Such a conflict was most evident during World War II, when Stalin, desperately trying to rally a still largely peasant population, found it expedient to junk the more benevolent view of the ethnic "other." Thus if, for the early Bolsheviks during World War I, a German soldier had been a "fellow proletarian" and victim, stuck into the trenches by greedy German capitalists, in World War II, the same soldier became the member of a subhuman tribe, deserving no sympathy or restraint. Writing in *Pravda*, for example, the novelist Ilya Ehrenburg exhorted Soviet troops "to kill one German and then another"[49] on the day when Soviet troops finally entered the territory of the enemy. The same principle of tribal vengeance was conveniently applied across the countries of East Central Europe, whence ethnic Germans were expelled en masse, murdered, or deported to the Soviet Union.

And yet, once the passions were spent and the short-term objectives of the war accomplished, Stalin's earlier formula of "Hitlers come and go, but the German people remains,"[50] was resurrected in the interests of the long-term stability of the Bloc, and by the end of 1945, it would become the "slogan of slogans in Soviet-occupied Germany."[51] German history would be treated rather cagily for years to come by both Russian and East German communists, but the Stalinist view of ethnicity, welded to Marxist theories of history, allowed the future GDR to forge a new collective identity out of "progressive working-class traditions" and based on technological progress of German industries in the nineteenth and early twentieth centuries. Furthermore, making good use of Marxist theories of class and history, the National Socialist past could be conveniently laid to rest. Unlike in the West, where culture was invoked to establish collective responsibility, in the East, German wartime guilt was explained in class terms, blame being laid on a relatively small clique of officials, Prussian Junkers, and monopoly capital-

---

48. Slezkine 1994, 453.
49. Ehrenburg 1967, 26–27.
50. The statement was first made on February 23, 1942. See Naimark 1995, 76.
51. Ibid.

ists, whose members were treated with great severity in what were in effect extermination camps.[52] Once these people were buried, socially and physically, the task of building a socialist community could begin and the GDR could take its place as a trusted ally and favorite client of the Soviet Union, indeed as a model held up to others in the region to imitate. Thus, in the long run, theory triumphed over momentary expediency.

A different, and perhaps more serious, challenge to these principles of internationalism was presented by the Jewish populations of Eastern Europe. To be sure, the challenge was not new to Marxism. For early Marxists and for Marx himself, Jews represented a "problem" partly because of the religious roots of their identity (which was supposed to wither away under socialism), partly because of their lack of a common language and territorial dispersion. The problem also preoccupied the moderate Austrian socialist Otto Bauer, who, while capable of understanding the existence of a common Jewish identity based on a common destiny, thought that in the long historical run this identity might be unsustainable in the absence of a common territory.[53] As for Stalin, his preoccupations started early and had their roots in his encounters with the Jewish socialist Bund of Russian Poland and its skirmishes with the Bolsheviks. In any case, he felt strongly about the subject. In his relatively short essay on the national question, he makes no fewer than nineteen references to Jews and their relationship to the socialist movement.[54]

To resolve the "problem" within its own imperial context, the young Soviet state first attempted to turn Jews into a nationality by cultivating Yiddish, then by giving them a common territory in inhospitable Birobidjan. Characteristically, the shift from one identity to the other was accompanied by a wholesale purge of the Yiddish cultural establishment and of the executors of the policy. But the real challenge came after 1948. When a Jewish territorial state was established in Israel, Stalin at first supported it, partly in order to diminish British influence in the Middle East and by the hope of gaining the friendship of the new state, and partly in an attempt to appeal to the remnants of the Jewish educated classes in Eastern Europe, especially in Poland, Hungary, and Romania, where the native intelligentsia had been badly compromised by its past support of anti-Soviet causes. He

52. According to Soviet documents, 122,671 Germans apparently fitting this description were arrested in the four years of the occupation period, 42,889 of whom died in captivity. Of 8,827 members of Germany's nobility, about half of whom lived in the German East, 660 "died in flight," 249 were murdered by Russians or Poles, and 453 died in concentration camps. These figures do not include captives held subsequently in camps run by local authorities. Ibid., 143–46, 376–77.

53. Bauer 1907, 324–25.

54. Stalin [1913] 1972b, 54–84. The edition used to make this count excluded sections IV, V, and VI of the work, discussing different nationalist manifestations in Russia and Central Europe.

was to be gravely disappointed. For while part of the Jewish intelligentsia did indeed take refuge in the communist parties of East Central Europe, the new Jewish state gravitated not toward the Soviet Union but toward its Cold War rival, the United States. This, and the massive emigration of Jews from Romania and Poland, compromised those who were left behind, and left them open to charges of treason and double-dealing.

While a great deal has been written about this subject, the motivation for and scope of Stalin's planned retribution still remain shrouded in mystery (or in the memories of a handful of highly placed survivors). It is quite possible that, by the end of 1952, Stalin had decided that all Jews in his empire were unreliable, and that his desire to liquidate them was tempered only by practical political considerations (above all by the attitudes of communist and left-wing parties in the West). But it is at least equally plausible that in ordering the arrest and show trial of a few scores of "Zionist conspirators," Stalin was merely following his old recipe of picking a designation that—like "wrecker," "saboteur," and "bureaucrat"—would fit a great number of individuals, who would be intimidated into still more zealous collaboration by the public humiliation of a few selected and falsely accused victims.

Whatever the case may be, the public record is full of contrived ambiguities and attempts to demonstrate that the trials were motivated not by particularism and prejudice but by the application of universalistic criteria of justice. In the Slánský case, the most famous of the "anti-Zionist" trials, Jewish defendants were tried together with Slovak "bourgeois nationalists," each group being equally vilified for having betrayed the cause of proletarian internationalism.[55] Still earlier, during the Rajk trial in Hungary, pains were taken in the obviously scripted exchanges between judge and defendants to indicate that, while some of the defendants were Jewish, loyalty and not race was at issue. This effect was accomplished by making Rajk point out that, while his father's name was Reich, he was of "pure Aryan stock," a remark that invited an equally contrived angry rejoinder by the presiding judge to the effect that Rajk's remark was both irrelevant and inappropriate.[56] Less subtly, and almost without fail, throughout the entire campaign, official Soviet and client media continued to denounce Zionism and anti-Semitism in the same breath. Indeed, the announcement of the infamous "Jewish doctor's plot" and orchestrated commentaries took pains to denounce the racism and anti-Semitism of Britain and the United States and anti-Semitic manifestations like the "trial of the Rosenbergs."[57]

55. Suda 1980, 247–49.
56. For the transcript, see Kende 1989, 120.
57. Report by Tass, January 13, 1953; the lead article of the Hungarian *Szabad Nép*, January 14, 1953; Rothstein 1953; writings by Besse (*Cahiers de communisme*), and an essay by Pierre Hentges in *Democratie nouvelle* (1953); all are quoted in Kende 1989, 134–38.

The death of Stalin terminated the anti-Zionist campaign but not the Jewish "problem," which, with American demands for free emigration (enshrined in the Jackson-Vanik amendment of 1974), became increasingly intertwined with Cold War issues. In this environment, the official policies toward the ever-shrinking Jewish communities can be best described as one of "don't ask, don't tell." Some, like the Romanian party, welcomed Jewish emigration as a step in the direction of creating a homogeneous national community. But with a few conspicuous exceptions—like Moczar's purge of the Polish intellectual community in 1968—most parties in East Central Europe refrained from anti-Semitic agitation, and even actively discouraged it. At the same time, the parties were equally averse to open displays of Jewish identity, especially in their own ranks.[58] While ideology obviously failed to resolve the "Jewish problem" for the Soviet empire, its universalistic core idiom managed to restrain the worst impulses of both the apparatus and top leaders.

There were, of course, a number of other minorities in East Central Europe, and during the Stalin period most of them fared no worse than the majorities in whose midst they lived. Some of them, like the Hungarian minority of Romania or the Sorb (Wend) minority in East Germany, were singled out for special treatment, the Hungarians being granted, at Moscow's insistence, an autonomous territory on the Soviet model. The Hungarians of Czechoslovakia, subject to expulsions and deportation to the Sudetenland between 1945 and 1948, had their lot alleviated once the country had a full-fledged communist government. In time, at least in Romania and Hungary (although not in Czechoslovakia and Poland), even German minorities were recognized as having cultural rights and given nominal representation in the institutions of the states.[59] To be sure, after Stalin's death, like most other aspects of politics, the treatment of minorities, too, became more diverse. But with a few notable exceptions, assimilationist or discriminatory policies continued to be veiled in a cloak of cultural solicitousness. Till the end of communism, an ethnic slur, if uttered in a public place, would draw some form of official retribution or admonition, even in countries like Romania, which could in the later Ceauşescu years rightly be dubbed national communist. The universalist rhetoric of the communist movement may not have provided protection against inequities, but it did provide a thin veneer of civility in public discourse. It is this thin veneer that, ironically, has quickly vanished as communism turned into postcommunism.

58. For the many ambiguities of these policies, and Jewish reactions to them, one can consult a large body of literature emanating from Hungary, the locus of the largest Jewish minority outside the Soviet Union. In addition to Kende 1989, see Gati 1986, esp. 100–107; Szabó 1995; "A zsidókérdés itt és most" (1989), 438; Kovács 1988, 605–12; Erős, Kovács, and Lévai 1985, 132.
59. For an overview, see King 1973a.

THE POLITICS OF CONFORMITY

Institutions and Policies

As is often the case with revolutionary powers and rapidly changing societies, Soviet foreign policy contained a strong element of self-validation. So motivated, the political formula designed for the countries of East Central Europe by Stalin and Zhdanov allowed for little deviation from the Soviet model. In some sense this was anomalous because, even in communist theory, Soviet and East Central European societies represented different stages of development, one having achieved "socialism," the other still lingering at the stage of "people's democracy." Still, except in the most shallow sense (by permitting the existence of bogus political parties in most countries of the outer empire), these differences in theory were overlooked in practice. Nor did the planners of the new institutions acknowledge the existence of differences in culture and levels of economic development in East Central Europe itself. Ideally, under the Soviet imperial system, Czechoslovaks and Albanians were to live under the same institutional arrangements, and any deviation from the macropolitical model was quickly dubbed an attempt to seek a "separate road to socialism," a cardinal sin for which many a suspect was put to death, and for which Yugoslavia was drummed out of the Bloc in 1948. Perhaps the most visible exception to the rule was East Germany, showcased for a while as a "less advanced" and "more capitalistic" society, most likely because Stalin was weighing the possibility of a deal among the great powers that would establish a united, neutral Germany, detached from the West. The fact that the ruling Socialist Party of Unity (SED) contented itself with a "mere" 66.1 percent of the vote in May 1949,[60] at a time when all other satellites boasted figures in the 99 percent range, was intended to serve as evidence of this "lower" level of socialist development.

Given this Zhdanovite modus operandi, much like the Soviet institutions themselves, those of East Central Europe must be approached at two separate levels. At one level, the purely formal, these institutions were reflective of the "Enlightenment paradigm" of popular sovereignty enshrined in copious constitutional documents.[61] The obvious model for these constitutions was the Stalinist document of 1936, with its 146 articles. Among its East Central European counterparts, the shortest document was the constitution of Hungary, with a mere 70 articles; the longest was the Basic Law of Czechoslovakia, with 178.[62] All of these constitutions provided for legislative institutions and a cabinet type of government (in the form of a Council of Ministers), while also containing excruciatingly detailed provisions for

60. Childs 1983, 23.
61. See Triska 1968.
62. Ibid., 181–96, 395–452.

the structure of administration and local government. All of them guaranteed a broad range of civil, political, and economic rights, including freedom
of speech and assembly and the right to work. Most likely for reasons mentioned above, the East German (GDR) constitution also included freedom
of enterprise, and even the right to strike,[63] but, in a display of exceptional
frankness, banned all political expression aimed either at "boycotting" the
state or inciting people against it.[64]

The fact of the matter was that many of the provisions for a democratic
form of government were vitiated by the very procedures ostensibly created
in order to translate them into political reality. Elections, for example, presented voters with a single list of handpicked candidates, which could only
be rejected in toto at polling places that provided no pencils and often no
privacy. National Assemblies, once elected, would be convened only once or
twice a year, for a period of one to three days, to rubber-stamp a large number of decrees passed by various executive organs. Indeed, until the January 1957 reform of the Polish Sejm, no divisions in these parliaments ever
occurred; the votes, in other words, were always unanimous.

The real world of politics operated behind this institutional façade, and
its practices were justified, not by the principles of popular sovereignty, but
by the "higher" historical requirements of building socialism both at home
and abroad (the latter purpose being carefully described as "international
class struggle" or as a "relentless struggle against imperialism"). The institutional embodiment of this higher purpose, and hence the real legitimating
principle of the regimes, was not the parliamentary institutions but the party,
acting as the guardian and representative of a collective wisdom about the
means of achieving these higher purposes. But, ironically, like the politics of
the masses, the politics of the elite was bifurcated, split between the for-
malities of democracy and the realities of hierarchy. Formally, the party was
a vanguard, whose members enjoyed equal political rights and privileges,
among others, the privilege of gathering in congresses to elect the members of the Central Committee, a quasi-parliamentary body to formulate
the party line between congresses, a secretariat to deal with the day-to-day
management of the affairs of the membership, and, indirectly, via the institution of the Central Committee, a series of "buros," first of all, the " Politburo," or central executive organ of the party itself.

In reality, once communist parties had seized power, these institutions
became a mere façade for a rigidly hierarchical organization in which power
relations were the exact reverse of what the statutes stipulated. First (or general) secretaries emerged by virtue of their control over the party bureaucracy, or *apparat* (or were simply appointed by Moscow), but their subor-

63. Ibid., 218–19.
64. Ibid., 219.

TABLE 28

Communist Party Membership, 1950s

Country	Party members	Total population	% of Total population
Albania (1952)	44,418	1,246,000	3.6
Bulgaria (1954)	455,251	7,467,000	6.1
Czechoslovakia (1954)	1,489,234	13,089,000	11.6
East Germany (1957)	1,472,932	16,100,000	8.5
Hungary (1959)	810,227	9,808,000	8.4
Poland (1954)	1,290,000	27,400,000	4.7
Romania (1955)	583,815	17,489,784	3.4
Yugoslavia (1954)	654,669	17,799,000	3.8

SOURCES: Shoup 1981, 71–83; Dellin 1957, 130; Busek and Spulber 1957, 20, 69; Helmreich 1957, 46, 125; Byrnes 1957, 71; Halecki 1957, 124.

dinates and the members of the various party institutions, including the Central Committee, were co-opted from above, and the representatives who voted at party congresses were carefully selected by the party officialdom. And while the Politburo remained a significant fulcrum of power and decision-making, the first secretary of each party was given wide discretionary powers of selecting its members. By the time the parties became institutionalized, their millions of members (see Table 28) were sharply divided between the party elite and a mass membership devoid of either power or privilege, constituting a prime manpower pool available for the performance of menial political tasks—organizing rallies, snitching, and agitation in the workplace—and a reservoir of political talent for potential recruitment into the elite. In general, the tasks to be performed by the membership—quite often after normal working hours at the plant or collective farm—were onerous, time-consuming, and often distasteful. For these reasons a good part of the membership joined under subtle institutional pressure, in the hope of a future career, or, more frequently, in exchange for some immediate reward such as preferential treatment in the allocation of living space, providing some justification for the parties' constant concern about "opportunism" in the ranks.

It should be pointed out here that the party elite itself was divided both along functional lines and in terms of position in the political hierarchy. Functionally, this elite was divided between the "cadres," or full-time professional political workers under the jurisdiction of the secretariats, and those communists occupying important nomenklatura positions—that is, executive positions in the administration, education, economy, and justice that were normally reserved for party members (or, alternatively, required clearance from party organizations). These two groups, the cadres and the officials of the nomenklatura may be regarded as the members of the communist political class, the functional equivalent of the old politico-bureaucratic officialdom of the precommunist period. The cream of the cadre crop was the apparatus (in Russian, *apparat*) of the central party organs.[65] The ratio of cadres to the general membership ranged from 1:8 to 1:4, depending on the country, period, and special circumstances.[66] For simple definitional reasons, the size of the apparat is hard to establish, but the term designated only a few thousand people in most of the countries of East Central Europe and a few tens of thousands in the Soviet Union.[67]

The Politics of Revolution

The "higher" revolutionary purpose did not exist in a vacuum but was to be attained by meeting three shorter-term objectives, the pursuit of which provided the logic for the operational framework of public policy and the political system. Specifically, in order to create better, or perhaps perfect, societies at home, while pushing further forward the geopolitical design of the movement, material resources had to be mobilized, the structure of societies had to be changed, and a cultural revolution had to be effected to change the existing state of social consciousness.

The policies of mobilization of the client regimes were two-pronged. First, resources had to be extracted from war-torn economies for the quick restoration of the Soviet infrastructure and defense establishment. This purpose was accomplished by extracting reparations from former enemies, by establishing joint ventures with Soviet participation, by giving Moscow the power to set prices and terms of exchange devoid of any objective or market-oriented yardstick, and, in the extreme East German case, by dismantling a quarter or more of the industrial plant in the Soviet zone of occupation and transferring it to the Soviet Union. The amount of this tribute, exacted over a period of ten years, has been varyingly estimated between 14 and 20 billion "gold" dollars, calculated at 1938 prices.[68] This amount, which may appear trivial to those accustomed to reading today's U.S. budget figures, was truly exorbitant in its own time. It represented 18–25 percent of the GNP of the United States in 1938, and, adjusted to 1947 prices, exceeded the $16 billion (at 1947–52 prices) provided by the United States to Western Europe under the Marshall Plan.[69] While an estimated two-thirds of this

65. See Kaplan 1987, esp. 113–21; Avtorkhanov 1968, 58–74; Neugebauer 1978, 28–46, 124–27, 154–56.
66. Avtorkhanov 1968, 88; Kaplan 1987, 180.
67. Avtorkhanov 1968, 153; Kaplan 1987, 115.
68. Marer 1976, 61; Wszelaki 1959, 68–77.
69. The total GNP of the United States in 1938, in current prices, was $84.6 billion. The $16 billion figure for the Marshall Plan reflects the already inflated price levels of 1947, and represents about 5–6 percent of the U.S. GNP of $231.3 billion of the year 1947. For these figures, see U.S. Department of Commerce. United States, Bureau of the Census 1975, 224.

TABLE 29

Proportions of Producer to Consumer Goods

(gross value, producer goods/consumer goods)

Country[a]	Prewar	Postwar
Czechoslovakia	44/56	62/38
Poland	47/53	63/37
Yugoslavia	43/57	57/43
Bulgaria	24/76	45/55

SOURCE: Spulber 1958, 303.
[a] No data for Hungary and Romania.

amount was extracted from a single country, East Germany—by dismantling part of its industrial plant and putting the rest to work for the Soviet
economy—the remaining $5–7 billion still amounted to a full year of the
gross national product of the five other affected countries, Hungary, Poland,
Czechoslovakia, Romania, and Bulgaria. But this was only one part of the
overall economic effort, for the manpower and resources of the countries
were also mobilized to create new heavy industries to enhance the Bloc's
military preparedness. In all countries of the Bloc, investment in the first five-
year development plans was set at between 20 and 27 percent of the national
income. Highly developed Czechoslovakia was an exception with its investment rate of 13 percent. These figures should be compared to the 9–10 percent rates during the immediate postwar years and to 4–6 percent during
the interwar period.[70] If we add the sums obtained from these countries in
the form of reparations or via manipulated terms of exchange, the total
amount extracted from them grows by another 5–10 percent (in East Germany by 25 percent). When we add up all the figures, we may find that the
rates of enforced savings exceeded the Soviet effort of the 1930s, although
this amount was extracted from societies with somewhat higher incomes
per capita.

As in the Soviet Union of the 1930s, these extractive policies could only
be sustained by depressing real wages and by a radical shift of investment
priorities between consumer and producer goods, as is shown in Table 29.
The burdens of high investment rates were spread across the board, although as in the earlier Stalinist experience, the brunt of the burden was carried by the agricultural sector, which had to produce both for export and
to feed the rapidly increasing urban labor force. As Table 30 shows, the
progress of collectivization was slower than in the Soviet Union and varied
from country to country, reflecting in many cases the relative strength of the
party, and, except for Poland and Yugoslavia (where the project was eventually abandoned), it was finished only in the 1960s. But the same effect of

70. Spulber 1957, 297

TABLE 30

Collectivization in East Central Europe

(% of arable land)

Country	Year	Collective	State	Private
Albania	1953	7.1	—	—
	1960	69.5	9.0	21.5
	1970	85.2	14.1	0.7
Bulgaria	1953	51.7	—	—
	1960	79.9	10.9	9.2
	1970	68.0	21.3	10.7
Czechoslovakia	1953	40.0	—	—
	1960	62.1	20.4	17.5
	1970	55.7	29.4	14.9
GDR	1953	—	—	—
	1960	72.8	8.1	19.1
	1970	78.2	8.1	13.7
Hungary	1953	20.0	13.0	—
	1960	48.6	19.3	32.1
	1970	67.6	15.3	17.1
Poland	1953	7.2	—	—
	1960	1.1	11.6	87.3
	1970	1.2	14.4	84.4
Romania	1953	10.0	7.7	—
	1960	50.2	29.3	20.5
	1970	54.1	30.1	15.8
Yugoslavia	1957	3.5	5.9	—
	1960	5.7	5.4	88.9
	1970	5.0	12.4	82.6

SOURCES: Wädekin 1982, 85–86; Sanders 1958, 72, 81, 99, 105, 145, 147; Hoffman and Neal 1962, 273.

rapid extraction was increased by a system of forced deliveries and by keeping rates on investment low in the farming sector, strategies that become amply evident from the balance between industrial and agricultural output targets reported on Table 31, and from comparisons between pre- and postwar growth rates in the industrial and agricultural sectors (see Table 32).

Economics, however, is only part of the story. The second objective of the imperial regime was to bring about the restratification of societies, and, above all, to lay down the political "foundations for restructuring the elites." [71] To this end, the members of the old political classes were dismissed from public service, the professional classes were purged, and the propertied classes were expropriated. Then, after 1948, special efforts were made to draw large numbers of students with peasant and working-class backgrounds into the system of higher education by offering them special one-year preparatory courses, along with other incentives, to "lift them out" of their workplaces into nomenklatura positions. This went hand in hand with

71. Connely 1996, 367–92.

TABLE 31

Industrial versus Agricultural Output Targets,
First Five-Year Plans

(prewar = 100)

Country	Industry	Agriculture	Ratio, I/A
Czechoslovakia	213	138	1.5
Poland	417	115	3.6
Hungary	438	140	3.1
Romania	306	160	1.9
Bulgaria	403	135	3.0
Yugoslavia	494	151	3.3

SOURCE: Spulber 1958, 287.

TABLE 32

Proportions of Industrial to Agricultural Output

(gross value, industrial/agricultural)

Country[a]	Prewar	Postwar
Czechoslavakia	72/28	81/19
Poland	52/48	75/25
Yugoslavia	45/55	64/36
Bulgaria	27/73	47/53

SOURCE: Spulber 1958, 303.
[a] No data for Romania and Hungary

policies of discrimination against the offspring of the former political and "exploiting" classes.[72] These discriminatory measures, pursued with considerable vigor, were reflective of the traditional cultural milieu of Russian communism. Unlike Chinese communists, who believed in salvaging "class enemies" through reeducation, Soviet and Eastern European communists considered family to be destiny, and that idea guided their social policies, at least in the 1950s. True, the system was not absolutely airtight, and within a few years the rigor of discrimination was relaxed in favor of more meritocratic principles.[73]

The third objective of the imperial regime was to revolutionize culture. This objective had several components, reflecting the broad range of meanings attached to the term. At one level, this cultural revolution merely implied the continuation of educational policies of the prewar regimes. The results of these policies were respectable, although by no means striking. Except in Yugoslavia, where educational progress was slower, illiteracy in

72. M. Kovács and Örkény 1991, 13–17.
73. According to the only study of this kind, some two-fifths of the children of the educated upper middle class of the prewar period found their way into high-status occupations under communism, representing about 16 percent of the new, and enlarged, upper stratum of communist society. See more detailed discussion in Chapter 7, pp. 358–59.

TABLE 33

Reduction of Illiteracy in East Central Europe

(percentage of illiterates)

Country	1930s	1940s/50s		1950s/60s	
Albania	—	74.5	(1945)	28.3	(1955)
Bulgaria	31.5 (1934)	23.0	(1946)	14.7	(1956)
Hungary	9.0 (1930)	4.9	(1949)	3.8	(1960)
Poland	23.1 (1930)	5.8	(1950)	2.7	(1960)
Romania	38.9 (1930)	23.1	(1948)	10.1	(1956)
Yugoslavia	44.6 (1931)	25.4	(1948)	21.0	(1961)

SOURCE: Shoup 1981, 169–78.

the Balkans was dwindling at about the same rate as during the prewar period (see Table 33), while enrollment in academic institutions rose from about 1.2 percent of the age cohorts in the prewar period to about 3.6– 4.0 percent during the first two decades of communism.[74] (Later the numbers would increase further, yet competition for the positions remained cutthroat, reflective of the significant correlation between education and social mobility.) But, as in the Soviet Union, the "cultural revolution" also referred to projects designed to spread the appreciation of the arts among wider popular strata. These projects were relatively successful, for the urban working classes in particular began to read books and attend theater performances of classics. At its most ambitious, of course, the cultural revolution aimed at creating a new, socially conscious "socialist man," devoid of selfishness and "false" material needs. This project was promoted partly by compulsory sessions of indoctrination, partly by filtering out "destructive" cultural influences such as Western jazz or movies depicting the material standards of Western countries. By all evidence, this aspect of the cultural revolution was an abject failure, for it did not eradicate either selfishness or materialism. All indoctrination and the collective experience created was a more exaggerated set of expectations concerning the proper role of the state in satisfying material needs.

The sum total of these social and cultural policies had the potential for attracting popular support for communism, but their political effectiveness was undermined by the regimes' policies of economic mobilization and their impact on the general standard of living, and by the perception that material deprivation was the result of systematic surplus transfer to the imperial center. In any case, the sense of deprivation was so widespread that the policies could only be sustained by police terror: harsh punishments for grumblers and rumormongers, random arrests, and forced labor camps, together with a widely and subtly created awareness of the physical torture and gross

74. Shoup 1981, 176–80.

abuse of political detainees. The exact number of victims of this terror is still being compiled and will probably never be reliably assembled. But recent research has estimated the number of Stalin-era detainees at 80,000 in Czechoslovakia, 200,000 in Poland,[75] and, adding the inmates of camps run by Germans to those run by the Soviet Union, 240,000 in East Germany (with a grand total of 95,000 fatalities).[76] In Hungary, a document released recently by the office of the prime minister reports a staggering 511,270 arrests in 1950–53 alone, resulting in 387,177 prison sentences, with 33 to 50 percent of these for infractions that may qualify as political.[77] Taken together these figures amount to 1–2 percent of the total population and, since the great majority of the victims were men, to 6–8 percent of adult males.

The Political Machines: Beyond Bureaucracy

The ambitious, externally imposed, political objectives of the regimes, required—in addition to terror—a complex network of organizations that turned Lenin's early prediction about communist society being administered by political amateurs into a pathetic historical relic of Marxist optimism. As in the Soviet Union, this network consisted of six identifiable hierarchically organized branches: (1) a civil administration (including the routinized administration of justice); (2) the central and local management of the socialized, or, more correctly, etatized, economy; (3) a plethora of mass organizations—including trade unions, youth, women's athletic, leisure time, cultural, and other organizations—customarily described as the "transmission belts of the party"; (4) the military; (5) the security police and its adjuncts, such as the border guards, riot police, and a gray armada of informers; and, last but not least, (6) the party itself.

The structure and operational codes of these organizations are by now too well known to require elaboration here. What should be pointed out, however, are some historically unique features of the system, above all, the role of the party in welding these separate branches into a single, interlocking network that invites the designation of communist societies as "mono-organizational."[78]

The integration of these separate branches into a single unit was a key feature of the communist party state, accomplished by the presence of the party at several levels of each hierarchy. At the very top of the organization, party control was attained by the overlap between party and state functions: members of the parties' Politburos also served as key ministers of the government, trade union chiefs, generals of the army, and heads of the security

75. Kaplan 1991, vol. 2; Garlicki 1993. Both of these sources courtesy of John Connely.
76. Naimark 1995, 378.
77. Hungary 1991, 153–54.
78. Rigby 1976, 31–81.

police. At a lower level, the party wielded its power through the institution of the nomenklatura—that is, by the requirement that all executive and staff positions be filled by party members or by people carefully screened by party organs. At a third level, members of territorial organizations of the party in counties and municipalities functioned as "prefects"—that is, as arm-twisters, facilitators, arbitrators of administrative disputes, and transmitters of directives from the center to the local party cells.[79] Finally, there were the local organizations of the party, based not on neighborhood but on the workplace, a brilliant organizational design that provided the party with leverage short of coercion over the entire labor force, as well as a vantage point from which the production process could be overseen from a political point of view. Informally, this function was performed by regular consultation between management and the party secretary of the production (educational, administrative) unit; formally, by the secretary's power to confirm hiring, firing, and promotions of personnel.

A second, historically unique, aspect of the system lay in the ways in which these individual hierarchies performed their tasks. Although casually described as bureaucracies, these organizations were far from being only that.[80] Much more accurately, they could be designated as a cross between bureaucracy and revolutionary organization. As bureaucracies, they were recipients of streams of rules and regulations, transmitted through their own channels of communication. As revolutionary organizations, however, they were subject to the corrective work of party organizations, whose cadres had power to decide whether, in any particular instance, the regulations should apply or be waived in the name of the "higher" political interests of the revolutionary state. And while decisions of this kind were the prerogatives of the local party secretary, once exercised several times, other branches of organization began to act in anticipation of such interventions. In the end, the central political authority had to intervene only if the administrative or economic branch failed to act upon its own political instincts. Bit by bit, this reciprocity of expectations thus politicized and personalized what otherwise would have been a process guided by legal impersonality.

A good example is provided by the administrative allocation of living space, for which formal administrative priorities existed, usually based on the family's number of children. Yet parallel instructions also existed to ignore these priorities in cases where the applicant, or some member of his family, was deemed unreliable or had an "undesirable" social background, or, conversely, where the applicant was a party activist or politically meritorious person. An even more notorious example is provided by the classification of the rural population in the 1950s into "kulak," "middling peas-

79. Hough 1969; see also Lane 1971, 318.
80. For the operational code of communist administrative organization, see Pakulski 1986, 3–24.

ant," and "poor peasant" categories. While the administrative definition of the "kulak" category, with all its economic implications, was explicitly established in terms of the amount of land a family owned, and the definition was widely publicized in the official registers of the countries, simultaneous and confidential briefings gave local party functionaries wide discretionary powers, explicitly instructing them to take into account the class background and political reliability of proprietors. Accordingly, members of the former gentry, or of the former administrative classes, officials, gendarmes, policemen, members of proscribed former political parties, and all who were deemed to be hostile to the regimes were put on the list of kulaks, irrespective of the size of their holdings. Conversely, "revolutionary" or "anti-fascist" behavior, once again defined broadly, could result in exemptions, usually by allowing such persons to register their holdings under the names of several family members. In the end, the lists bore little resemblance to what they would have looked like under a true bureaucratic regime. Indeed, in this respect, the operational code of the communist states differed not only from those of the liberal states prior to 1931 but also from those of the fascist, or quasi-fascist, states of the prewar decade. For, compared to communism, many of those regimes had followed their perverse regulations quite punctiliously when it came to the religious mix of grandparents, spouses, dates of conversion, or military decorations earned in World War I.

Following the Stalinist model, next to the party, the security police was a major pillar of each of the East Central European party states. This is obvious from the sheer number of personnel involved, even though they exclude the auxiliary organizations of the security police, the network of informers, and the regular—that is, criminal and traffic—police. Whereas, in the estimates of Nicolas Spulber, the police forces of each of the old regimes, including their special "political" branches, consisted of 4–11,000 officials and 10–30,000 uniformed constables (including the roving rural gendarmerie that most governments maintained), the party state's uniformed and nonuniformed security forces alone were estimated at 100,000 in Poland, 70,000 in Romania, 60,000 in Czechoslovakia, 50,000 in Hungary, 40,000 in Bulgaria,[81] 25,000 in Yugoslavia,[82] and some 80,000 in the future GDR.[83] As in the Soviet Union, the functions of these communist police forces were both preemptive and punitive, and were performed both independently and in coordination with the regular police and judicial authorities.[84] In this last

81. Spulber 1957, 20–21, 388.
82. Byrnes 1957, 16.
83. Naimark 1994, 25. Of this number, though, only 13–20,000 engaged in actual investigative and interrogative functions. The same ratio was likely among the other security forces of the region. See Fricke 1984, 51.
84. On the organization and composition of the security forces, see Halecki 1957, 167; Helmreich 1957, 139–41; Dellin 1957, 155–56; also Fricke 1984, 54–59.

respect, the modus operandi of the security police was similar to that of the party. While the criminal police and the court system were supposed to follow routine procedures, these could be suspended if the security authorities deemed a case to have political implications either because of the nature of the act or the identity of the perpetrator. It was thus common practice for the regular police authorities to report to security each and every arrest they made, so that the latter could screen cases from a "broader" political point of view. Cases that were deemed to have failed that scrutiny were transferred out of the normal channels of jurisdiction to be tried in camera by special tribunals or by judges with special clearances. The condemned person would then serve his or her sentence in a labor camp under the supervision of security personnel; he or she would be forbidden to communicate with the outside world and subjected to conditions of extreme hardship. The same procedure would, of course, be followed if the person was apprehended directly by security police investigators.[85]

Although in principle the organs of the party were supreme over those of the security police, the relationship between the two organizations was both complex and poorly routinized. While there were party cells in the security organs, their secretaries had limited powers, and "official business," given its secret nature, was not discussed at party meetings.[86] Likewise, the territorial organizations of the party had only limited control over the security police agencies operating within their own jurisdiction. Thus, whether operated as a ministry (as in East Germany) or as an agency under the nominal control of the Council of Ministers, the police forces were linked to the party through the person of its first secretary, who, ignoring the functions of the various audit and control commissions of the Central Committee, was allowed to establish a personal relationship with the chief of security. This relationship, in turn, gave the first secretary his powers over party, apparatus, and Politburo.

The ascendancy of the first secretary was further enhanced by a cult of personality that was not only tolerated but encouraged by the imperial authorities as part of an informal operational code established by Stalin. This cult was sometimes as fulsome as Stalin's, sometimes more restrained. But in all the countries of East Central Europe, the special position of the first secretary was recognized by the conspicuous display of his enlarged photographs in public places. This made local leaders into "little Stalins." But little Stalins were not quite like Stalin himself. Their charisma was derivative: they were not celebrities in their own right but the "best Hungarian

85. For a revealing account of this two-track—political and criminal—justice system, see Ulc 1972, esp. 31–66.

86. Refugee interview (no. 22), June 22, 1987. For more about refugee interviews, see Introduction.

[Polish, Romanian] disciples of the great Stalin." Much like *oblast'* or re-public secretaries in the Soviet Union, they were part of an officialdom that was all-powerful in the eyes of their own constituents, yet forced to "cringe before a suspicious and omnipotent despot in the Kremlin."[87] Indeed, to make their position precarious, Stalin always kept one or two potential ri-vals in the wings and made his local satraps compete with each other for his favors, and, in the last analysis, for their own lives. These practices of the imperial government turned the local Politburos into hothouses of intrigue and bickering, so well captured in Petru Dumitriu's novel about the Ro-manian Politburo, *Meeting at the Last Judgment*.[88]

The purges and the show trials of East Central Europe must be under-stood in this context. Conceptualized, scripted, and supervised by Soviet MGB officers—Generals Boyarsky, Beshchanov, Voznesensky, Skulbashev-sky,[89] and Bielkin, a "traveling salesman of terror"[90]—the trials served two grand purposes: (1) to broadcast items of the political agenda (about class struggle, Titoism, Zionism) to the global communist movement, and (2) to keep the satellite leaders mistrustful of each other, and hence more sub-servient to their imperial masters. Certainly, the person of a first secretary was not sacrosanct. In Poland, Gomulka was removed early on, essentially for arguing with Stalin about tactical issues; the Bulgarian Dimitrov died under suspicious circumstances, perhaps related to his advocacy of a Balkan federation of communist states; the Czech Rudolf Slánský, pitted against Antonin Novotny, was tried and executed,[91] and their colleague Gottwald, while finding this form of manipulation "absolutely logical," in unguarded moments also expressed his fear and exasperation.[92] The Romanian Gheor-ghe Gheorghiu-Dej and the Hungarian Mátyás Rákosi had to engage in intrigues of epic proportions in order to prevail over their domestic ad-versaries and avoid being purged themselves. Gheorghiu-Dej played the "Zionist card" against Ana Pauker, Iosif Chişinevsky, and Vasile Luca, and Rákosi clung to the helm, despite his Jewish origins, by sacrificing other Jewish communists to satisfy the anti-Zionist hunger of Moscow.[93] The vic-tors of these top-level bouts were both brilliant backroom strategists and frightened imperial subordinates, fighting for their lives in high-stakes po-litical games.

87. Fainsod 1963, 405.
88. Dumitriu 1962.
89. Váli 1961, 62; Pelikan 1971, 102–4; Checinski 1984, 17–78; Váli 1984, 175–94.
90. Váli 1984, 184.
91. Brown 1966, 260.
92. Loebl 1976, 23, 73–74.
93. This was attained by the arrest of General Gábor Péter and other Jewish officers of the Hungarian AVH in January 1953. See Kende 1989, 134–35.

6 | The Soviet Bloc after Stalin

DIVERSITY AND DECLINE

The End of Personal Dictatorship

There are few historians of the Soviet Union today who would challenge the proposition that the Soviet system after 1930 bore the marks of Stalin's personality. He was the linchpin of the terror machine, and hence of the larger etatist design for mobilization. The monolithic features of that design could hardly have endured without his boundless energy, ruthlessness, and unusual skill in manipulating his entourage. Stalin himself shared this opinion. In a revealing diatribe shortly before his death, he berated his subordinates for their naiveté, likening them to newborn kittens, who, lacking in wisdom (and in ruthlessness), were likely to squander the patrimony he was to bequeath to them.[1]

Such forebodings, as it turned out, were exaggerated. When Stalin died on March 5, 1953, the political vacuum thereby created was quickly filled by one of the dormant institutions of the party, the Politburo. Long degraded and rarely convened by Stalin, who preferred to consult its members in twosomes and threesomes, the Politburo was nevertheless able to assume command—not least because its members, apart from their vested interest in the survival of the regime, were at the moment united by a common desire to prevent the rise of another leader who would terrorize them as Stalin had. It is well to remember that at the time of Stalin's death, the wives of Politburo members Molotov and Kalinin were under arrest,[2] while, according to the testimony of Khrushchev, the members themselves wondered at the end of each day whether they would go home or to prison camp.[3] Apparently, the only one to demur was Lavrenty Beria, the chief of Stalin's secu-

---

1. Zubok and Pleshakov 1996, 145.
2. Hingley 1974, 394; Ulam 1973, 442.
3. Khrushchev 1970, 614.

rity apparatus, who aroused suspicions as a possible claimant of Stalin's dictatorial mantle. Whether his ambitions were real or imagined, Beria's sudden emergence as the advocate of popular reforms, combined with his tight grip over the police, prompted his anxious colleagues to conspire against him. They collaborated with some high-ranking military men, who, in June 1953, arrested Beria at a weekly meeting of the Politburo, only a few days after he had led the Politburo in denouncing a cowering Hungarian delegation for the "mistakes" they committed during the Stalin years. He was then tried on the absurd charge of espionage and executed before the end of the year.

Following this coup, Beria's colleagues went on to dismantle the organizational features of personal dictatorship. They restored the authority of the Central Audit Commission to investigate charges against high functionaries, while control of the security police was removed from the chain of command of the Secretariat and placed under the supervision of a committee under the authority of the Council of Ministers. To give political substance to these formal changes in organizational charts, thousands of party members were released from concentration camps and encouraged to spread their melancholy tales of the "breaches of socialist legality" by the Stalinist police machine. This campaign reached its crescendo when Khrushchev carried the same charges before the Twentieth Party Congress in February 1956. The "secret speech," with its chilling details of torture, executions, and forced concessions turned out to be a shocker that exacted a high political price.[4] In the Soviet Union proper, it helped to delegitimate further both the routine of the purge and the "administrative measures" of the security police, but abroad it created considerable turmoil, triggering the outbreak of violence in Poland and the collapse of the communist government of Hungary in October 1956. It also sowed the seeds of the Sino-Soviet conflict and split the hitherto united international communist movement.

The Deradicalization of Ideology

These measures of "de-Stalinization," however, were embedded in a set of more profound changes in the realm of political culture and belief. These changes were not the result of ad hoc calculations of costs and benefits, but of a slow, and probably painful, process of learning by Stalin's subordinates that most likely began under the dictator's reign, although its lessons could only be articulated after his death. What we are dealing with are major differences between the way Stalin perceived the world from his isolation behind the Kremlin walls and the way his lieutenants and the lower

4. Rigby 1968.

echelons of the apparat encountered it during campaigns of collectivization, industrialization, and the war.

Unlike Stalin, as Milovan Djilas's experiences with him suggest,[5] his functionaries had to encounter some of the hard realities of Soviet life and the intractabilities of human nature and existence face-to-face. Carefully hiding their experiences behind fulsome praise of the Stalinist design, these functionaries—hardened in the trenches of economic mobilization, the war, and rural class struggle—had to cope with the inertia of the disheartened and terrorized masses and learned, without admitting it even to intimates, about the limits of human malleability and the high political costs of running a society on sheer intimidation. But after Stalin's death, these experiences became more freely articulated and, bubbling to the surface, gradually brought about what different observers of the Soviet scene subsequently described either as the "de-radicalization,"[6] or "rationalization,"[7] of the ideology of the Soviet empire, or as a transition from ideological salvationism to "incrementalism."[8] Less convincingly, at times there was also talk about the decline, or end, of ideology in Soviet-type regimes. However, the fact is that ideology, subsuming the fundamental purposes of empire and regimes, remained crucial to the legitimacy and cohesion of regimes. The justification of regime and empire was still expressed in terms of "building socialism" or "full communism." But the meaning of these terms had changed substantially in the interim. If, before, socialism was equated with paradise and the end of history, now these terms were stripped of their earlier chiliastic content and filled with a great deal of pragmatism. Communist, or Soviet-style socialist, societies were still depicted as superior forms of social organization, better than any known in human history, but the salvationist claims to total perfection and harmony were dropped.

The language of the Program of the CPSU adopted at the Twenty-Second Party Congress in 1961 is characteristic of this pragmatism. According to this program, under full communism, "co-operative wealth would flow more abundantly, and the great principle of 'from each according to his ability, to each according to his needs' will be implemented."[9] However, in the interim, "money as a medium of exchange would continue. Income differentials for specialized and skilled work would decline but persist. Some services and commodities were planned to be taken out of the price system, transport and public catering being important in this regard. . . . The posi-

5. Djilas 1962, 103.
6. Tucker 1970, 172–214.
7. Brzezinski 1967, 53–64.
8. Hough 1972, 36.
9. *The Programme of the Communist Party of the Soviet Union* (1961), 44, quoted in Lane 1971, 8.

tion of women was to be improved by the provision of collective services, but the monogamous family as a unit was to continue," although with some provisions for boarding schools.[10] There would be improvements in the educational system, health care, recreation, public transportation, and housing that would make each of them better than in any society known to humanity.[11] None of this conformed with the utopian visions of Marx, Engels, Lenin, Trotsky, and Stalin. Indeed, their earlier salvationism was now explicitly rejected. To borrow the anonymous voice recorded by yet another Soviet scholar specializing in futurology: "You rise in the morning and you begin to reflect: where shall I go today—to the factory as a chief engineer, or shall I gather and lead a fishing brigade, or perhaps fly to Moscow to conduct an urgent session of the academy? . . . thus, comrades, it will not be." [12] Or, we can listen to Khrushchev himself opining on the subject, much in the same vein: "Will there be criminals in Communist society? I personally, as a communist, cannot vouch that there will not be any. A crime is a deviation from the generally accepted standards of behavior in society, frequently caused by mental disorders. Can there be any diseases, mental disorders in a communist society? Evidently there can be." [13]

The post-Stalin regimes of the Soviet Union and East Central Europe reflect this "incrementalist" view of social engineering, which affected the images and symbolism surrounding communist leadership. By the standards of the new political culture, leaders were no longer expected to perform miracles or superhuman deeds, hence they were no longer under pressure to wrap themselves in the garb of omniscience and charismatic heroism. Indeed, rather than cultivating the imagery of miracle men and scientific geniuses, the post-Stalin leaders of the Soviet Union, as well as most of their minions in East Central Europe, were striving to gain acceptance for themselves and their parties on the basis of their skills in the more mundane arts of administration and management. Among them, Khrushchev delighted in being the "man of corn" (kukuruznik) and in dispensing advice about the milking of cows, the transport of coal, or the proper use of chemical fertilizers. Brezhnev, and later Andropov and Chernenko, were properly described as "clerks," [14] who prided themselves on their attention to petty bureaucratic detail. Some of their East Central European counterparts—Honecker, Husák, Gierek—adapted themselves to this bureaucratic model, while others, like the Hungarian Kádár, also thrived on an image of exaggerated modesty, hard work, and meticulousness. The most flamboyant of them, Roma-

10. Lane 1971, 214. See also Kelley 1980, 312–30.

11. The academician Strumilin, in Brzezinski 1967, 90.

12. Quoted in Goldhagen 1963, 623.

13. Ibid., 629.

14. See Kolakowski 1991, 139–44. For a detailed study of differences in Khrushchev's and Brezhnev's leadership styles, see Breslauer 1982, esp. 52–57, 153–68.

nia's Nicolae Ceauşescu, clearly engaged in cultivating his personality, but even he combined the sublime with the trivial and ridiculous—promoted by daily front-page press photographs showing him examining foundries, assembly lines, mine shafts, vegetable markets, and other venues that Stalin or Mao would have carefully avoided.

Such leadership styles do not in and of themselves generate legal norms or a truly bureaucratic environment. But leaders whose authority derives from the incremental, the mundane, and the paternal (as opposed to the charismatic and the salvationist) find it very difficult to exact total commitment from their subordinates or to disregard blithely their own rules and regulations in the name of revolutionary expediency. In this kind of political milieu, leaders can penalize subordinates and citizens for breaking the letter but not the spirit of the law. Rules and regulations may be broken in the name of terrestrial salvation, but hardly in the name of a higher rate of growth or of an incremental improvement in the international balance of power. Nor does the logic of incrementalist principles drive actors to either a compulsive pursuit of perfection or the accompanying pursuit of scapegoats to explain falling short of the standards of a charismatic collective. Accordingly, the norms of incrementalism discourage those very elements that had underpinned and justified the Stalinist system of terror.

The rediscovery of "socialist legality" in the post-Stalin period must be approached in this larger ideological context. At first the terminology was suspect, for in the past it had been used sometimes interchangeably with "revolutionary justice," a codeword for subjectivism and arbitrariness. But in time the term acquired new meaning and reflected a deeper commitment to more formalized, professionalized, and hence more predictable administrative and judicial systems.[15] If, under Stalin, the duty of the party functionary had been to second-guess and supersede formal regulations in the name of an ever-changing party line, now the functionary was instructed, indeed constantly exhorted, to become the guardian of the law and to supervise strict adherence to it. This, to be sure, still left it to the party to perform functions within the administrative and the judicial systems that in a full-blown legal system are performed by nonpartisan courts. Worse still, from the classical liberal point of view, while the central authorities continued to harp on the importance of observing the sanctity of legal norms, they failed to generate procedures of discovery, proof, and remedy, which are as integral to the concept of the legal state as the codification of the rules of appropriate conduct. Yet the average citizen could now be reasonably certain that he or she would not be arrested either whimsically or merely as an example to others, and functionaries could rest assured that they would not be penalized for technical difficulties and shortages beyond their control. But

15. Sharlet 1978, 320.

without the procedural component, socialist legality produced only quasi-legal states, rather than a Soviet version of the *Rechtsstaat*. Thus, although arbitrariness was mitigated by proclaimed norms, when it did occur institutional remedies were unavailable.[16]

And yet, flawed as this legalism was, it introduced a new element into the politics of communist societies and, above all, of the state machines. Under Stalin, enthusiasm, initiative, and devotion to the leader's whims took precedence over "slavish clinging" to the "dead letter" of the law; in the post-Stalin period, subordinates could do their jobs "by the book" and get away with it. Under Stalin's successors, enthusiasm, zeal, and the overfulfillment of the norms could no longer be taken for granted by a supreme leader or department head. These qualities had turned into commodities that had to be "bought" by material reward or by co-opting underlings into projects that they themselves collectively favored. This, of course, gave subordinates some latent leverage over their superiors and over the formulation of public policy, while, at the same time, inviting the subterranean bargaining, game-playing, and subtle signals of foot-dragging that T. H. Rigby, in a seminal article, has described as "crypto-politics."[17] To put it differently, while the systems did not tolerate formalized accountabilities, reciprocity between superiors and subordinates became a key element of political relationships. And even though "crypto-politicking" on the part of the common citizen was usually frustrated by the extremely broad definition of crimes such as sedition, incitement, or the revealing of state secrets, an element of this reciprocity still trickled down from the relations between leader and apparat to those between the apparat and the general population.

Still, the principal beneficiary of reciprocity was communist officialdom, whose members quickly discovered their new power and used it not only to buy immunities for themselves but also to gain a greater share of public wealth. It was at this point that Stalin's atomized officialdom turned into Djilas's "new class,"[18] capable of asserting their common interests and ensuring that their status was entrenched as well as rewarded. In Stalin's time, dismissal was tantamount to disgrace, expropriation, and death—not merely for the perpetrator, but also for his next of kin. Now, more frequently, a person dismissed from a high official position would be caught in a friendly safety net of peers who could in short order arrange for another job. That job might take the person to the provinces, and might be restricted to economic management rather than involving hard politics, but it would still be sufficiently lucrative. Moreover, dismissal, even if under less than honorable circumstances, would rarely result in the loss of personal accom-

16. For these deficiencies, see also Lipson 1963, 434–69, and Pakulski 1986, 3–24.
17. Rigby 1964, 183–94.
18. Djilas 1957.

modations, savings, cars, and other perquisites of office. In this respect, the Soviet Union and East Central Europe began to resemble their predecessors prior to communism. At this point, they also began their long slide from the Second to the Third World. For while these communist elites could still take pride in military power and in their collective international weight, by siphoning off resources from the common geopolitical project and "higher purpose" they had vowed to serve, they introduced into their societies a new source of friction and strain. However diligent they were in making their consumption inconspicuous, stories of their special stores, accounts, and accommodations began to spread, and the growing awareness of internal income inequalities now had to be added to the nagging awareness of international inequalities created by unfavorable comparisons with the material superiority of the capitalist world.

The Geopolitical Project: Continuity or Change?

The transformation of the belief system was also reflected in the international behavior of the Soviet empire. To be sure, the geopolitical ambition of creating a socialist world system was not abandoned, and at times it was even more aggressively articulated and pursued than during Stalin's days. Khrushchev, for one, boldly predicted during his first trip to the United States in 1959 that Soviet-style socialism would "bury" American-style capitalism, and then tried to lend substance to those claims by stirring up major international crises around Berlin (1961) and Cuba (1962).

Under Brezhnev (1964–81), Khrushchev's "hare-brained" schemes were abandoned in favor of a more cautious foreign policy. At the same time, as Seweryn Bialer notes, the "future expansion of the Soviet state and Communism," and the "historical vision of the victory of socialism over capitalism" [19] remained the main legitimating principles for the Soviet regime, although these objectives now rested on a revised geostrategic doctrine. From a military point of view, the new strategy accepted the doctrines of the unwinnability of nuclear wars and of mutually assured destruction, which changed the nature and principles of international class struggle and Soviet policies of anti-imperialism. In place of provoking crisis near the Western heartlands—as Stalin had done by blockading Berlin, and Khrushchev had done first by building the Berlin Wall, and then by deploying missiles a mere 90 miles off American shores—the policymakers of the Brezhnev period developed a new, two-track foreign policy. On the one hand, they accepted the necessity of strategic arms limitations, together with the principles of "peaceful competition" (and "coexistence") with the major capitalist powers; on the other hand, while maintaining a forward-looking and aggressive foreign

19. Bialer 1986, 6.

policy, they redirected its thrust from the First to the Third World by pledging to support wars of national liberation outside the European and North American continents.

Once again, the term "incrementalism" appropriately describes the changes, and it applies to both the means and the ends of this new foreign policy. As for the means (or intermediate objectives), the Soviet Union abandoned the idea of winning either by a series of insurrections in the core or by a single, bold *coup de main*. Just as significantly, but less explicitly, the classical Marxist vision of a socialist world—a global community without either national states or a single, commanding world government—gave way to a more pragmatic vision of a gradually changing balance of power between East and West. There was little doubt in Soviet minds that this gradual change would culminate in Soviet hegemony, which would be exercised for benevolent purposes,[20] much as Americans envision their global hegemony today as an instrument of expanding democratic freedoms across the world.

Intra-Bloc Relations: Reforming the Empire

Inevitably, these changes in the political culture of Soviet leadership also left their mark on the structure of the empire—that is, on the relationship between its Soviet core and East Central European periphery. In the new political milieu of restrained arbitrariness, the functionaries of the satellite parties, like Soviet functionaries, acquired a new freedom from fear and a degree of autonomy. Following the immutable laws of politics, the diminishing reliance on coercion required that these functionaries be given incentives for voluntary cooperation. In this respect, the watershed year appears to be 1955. The Polish and Hungarian crises, to be sure, raised doubts about the wisdom of tampering with the structure of the Soviet empire. But the Khrushchevite leadership, to its credit, stuck to its design, and the process of devolution continued both during and after these crises.

Some of these incentives were symbolic but psychologically significant. In Stalin's time, and even for some time after his death, as hapless Hungarian delegations were to find out in 1953 and 1954, local party chiefs were treated not merely as subordinates but as errant schoolchildren whose ways needed to be set right by their Soviet comrades.[21] Their visits to Moscow frequently remained unpublicized, and Stalin was in the habit of receiving delegations from fraternal countries one by one, in strict separation from one another. After 1956, however, these visits became well-publicized ceremonial occa-

20. See the resolutions of the Twenty-Second and Twenty-Third Congresses of the CPSU in Lane 1971, 216–17; also Kosyanenko 1974 and Kosyanenko 1976 in Kelley 1980, 315–16.
21. Váli 1960, 4–5.

sions, with honor guards, toasts, visits to the Bolshoi, and, occasionally, invitations to address the Supreme Soviet or some other Soviet conclave. Large multinational gatherings of delegations were organized to project images of the consensus and equality promised in the CPSU's resolution of October 30, 1956.[22] As part and parcel of this simulated equality and pluralism, military and economic cooperation within the Bloc became institutionalized: the former by establishing the Warsaw Treaty Organization (WTO) in 1955, the latter by revitalizing the long-dormant Council of Mutual Economic Assistance (CMEA, or Comecon) in the early 1960s. While the preponderance of Soviet influence was obvious in both organizations, regular annual or biannual meetings of delegations contributed to an atmosphere of reciprocity and good feeling.

More substantially, shortly after Stalin's death economic relations between the Soviets and their satellites were placed on a new footing. Under Stalin, the Soviet Union behaved like a classic colonial power, using very direct methods of surplus transfer from the imperial periphery to the metropole. After 1955, however, resource extraction by political means apparently came to an end, and the Soviet Union assumed another role familiar from the history of empires: it began to pay an economic price for the political structure it had built over the previous decade. One of the first and most obvious instances of this occurred in 1957, when the Soviet Union extended aid totaling 1,138 million rubles in grants and long-term credits to the embattled Kádár government in Hungary in order to stave off economic collapse in the wake of the uprising and the subsequent waves of strikes.[23] Such ad hoc grants were thereafter extended regularly to Eastern European countries experiencing economic or political trouble.

In the 1960s, then, the revitalization of Comecon brought new pricing mechanisms that, however loosely, tied barter arrangements to world market prices of comparable commodities, and thus replaced the earlier, purely arbitrary modes of pricing that had reflected disparities in political power rather than value. The consequences of this new pricing system have been the subject of considerable scholarly debate. While some economists have seen intra-Bloc trade as a source of mutual advantage (although in a system that, because of its politicized nature, was incapable of optimizing outcomes compared to other, freer, trading systems),[24] others argue that throughout the post-Stalin period, the Soviet Union's partners were consistently disadvantaged. Those who take the former position point to the composition of the commodity baskets exchanged. For, atypically in the history of empires, the exports of the imperial Soviet core region principally consisted of fuel

22. Ibid., 345.
23. Ibid., 457.
24. Desai 1987, 153–74.

and raw materials (with the share of fuel rapidly increasing after 1974), while the exports of the countries of East Central Europe consisted mainly of finished products, with the share of manufactures growing from about 60 to about 80 percent between 1950 and 1980.[25] Some economists point to the inherent disadvantages of such a trade pattern, but others speak of "implicit subsidies" granted by the Soviet Union to the countries of East Central Europe in the form of fuel deliveries below world market prices and of the world market prices the Soviet Union paid for low-quality manufactures produced in the satellite economies.

Using one, or both, of these arguments, students of these economies have come up with different numbers concerning Soviet "losses" and the overall "price of empire." At the high end, Michael Marrese and Jon Vanous suggest that in the decade of the 1970s, the Soviet Union provided a subsidy of $87.2 billion to its East European trading partners,[26] a figure later upped to $118.2 billion (in 1984 dollars) for the 1970–84 period.[27] Others, including Paul Marer and Raimund Dietz, have questioned this and come up with figures between one-half and one-third of those estimates.[28] But whatever the exact numbers, the continued disparities between the living standards of the Soviet Union and most European CMEA countries, and the consistent lagging of both Soviet and East Central European economies behind the countries of Western Europe, indicate that Comecon trade was not an engine of growth. Rather, it was an instrument for redistributing the many debilities of an imperial structure originally designed for broad political rather than narrowly conceived economic purposes.

The restructuring of economic relations was accompanied by further changes in the structure of imperial authority. In their own time, there was considerable temptation to exaggerate these, both by the Soviet Union and by Western scholars eager to treat the politics of these countries in their own terms. On the one hand, it is clear that, in the years 1956–62, the Soviet leaders withdrew personnel and largely abandoned attempts at the hands-on management of the economy and administrative affairs.[29] Some observers also speak of the greater freedom granted to satellite Politburos to make high-level appointments and to elect their own first secretaries.[30] However, the fact remains that matters of defense, intelligence, and security continued to be closely coordinated, and that the withdrawal of Soviet advisors and personnel in other domains was amply compensated for by leaving behind a good number of local "eyes and ears," including some members of the

25. See the summary analysis of Gati 1990, 118–19.
26. Marrese 1983, 48–50.
27. Gati 1990, 120.
28. Marer 1985, 155–88. For Dietz, see Gati 1990, 119–20.
29. Brzezinski 1967, 433–54.
30. Gati 1990, 33–35.

Politburos, who would regularly report to their contacts in the Soviet bureaucracy and leadership. The presumed independence of the Politburos, meanwhile, was subject to continuous Soviet attention. The circumstances surrounding the appointments of Kádár (1956), Husák (1969), or Gierek (1970) and the removal of Ulbricht (1971)—as well as the veto of the promotion of Meczar (1970)—suggest that the Soviet Union dispensed a great deal of "advice" on personnel. And over the years, even well-established leaders like Kádár were frequently forced to haggle over the membership of their own political entourages.

Still, it is fair to say that beginning in 1956 the Soviet Union moved gradually from a pattern of active to passive management of the imperial periphery, preferring to exercise a power of veto. Rather than telling their satellites what to do through "hot lines," or through the Soviet ambassador, the central authorities now established general parameters of acceptable behavior, which they tried to enforce by warnings and, if need be, by police action. These guidelines developed by trial and error over the years, and they had already been well formulated by the time their existence was acknowledged in what outsiders were quick to dub the "Brezhnev doctrine." The elements of this doctrine were first published in *Pravda* under a pseudonym on September 26, 1968, and then elaborated by Brezhnev himself in a speech to the Fifth Congress of the Polish United Workers' (Communist) Party on November 12, 1968. On the latter occasion, Brezhnev confirmed the right of "each socialist country [to] determine the concrete form of its development along the path of socialism by taking account of the specific nature of their national conditions." [31] But this permissive language was followed by stern warnings that the Soviet Union would not tolerate "deviation from [the principles of] socialism . . . and the restoration of the capitalist system." [32] "When external and internal forces hostile to socialism try to turn development of a given socialist country in the direction of a restoration of the capitalist system," Brezhnev continued, "when threat arises to the cause of socialism—a threat to the security of the commonwealth as a whole"—the Soviet Union would be ready to take "extraordinary measures," including "military assistance to a fraternal country." [33]

The key issue, then, was the definition of the term "socialism," a prerogative that the imperial party reserved for itself. Neither the document of September 26 nor the speech of November 12 explicitly confronted this task. But Soviet political practices, as they evolved between the Hungarian October and the Prague Spring, give us ample clues as to where these boundaries were supposed to lie. It is from these events—as well as from Soviet inaction in the cases of Albania and Romania—that we can infer what might

31. See the "Brezhnev Doctrine," in Stokes 1991, 133.
32. Ibid.
33. Ibid.

constitute the "restoration of capitalism." It would apparently imply (1) the restoration of a multiparty system with free elections; (2) the legalization of factions within the Communist Party itself, in violation of a tradition established at the Tenth Congress of the CPSU in 1920, on the well-founded ground that freely competing factions within the party were simply a multiparty system in disguise; and finally, (3) declaration of neutrality by a member of the Warsaw Treaty Alliance, or, more broadly, any act by its government that would change the balance of power on the European continent that had emerged after 1948. This still left some questions unanswered about the boundaries between a socialist and capitalist economy, and over the years, this last point was much debated. The Soviet Union strenuously objected to Yugoslav-type social ownership and workers' councils (see below) but finally gave in to the principles of enterprise autonomy, simulated markets, and criteria of profitability that formed the backbone of the Hungarian New Economic Model.

What the doctrine did reaffirm and permit was the choosing of "separate roads" within the common commitment to building socialism. Ill-defined, except in terms of the negative injunctions cited above, these separate roads implied some space for domestic political autonomy, and it was within this space that the post-Soviet diversity among East Central European states evolved during the last three decades of the Bloc. It is also within this space that we distinguish between "liberal" (or "soft-line") and "conservative (or "hard-line") political regimes, although it is well to remember that these terms were never used by the political actors themselves.

However, these variations in domestic politics were only one source of diversity within the Bloc. The other sources of diversity lay in interstate relations, over which the Soviet Union had lost full control even before Stalin's death. In the 1960s, these relations were becoming ever more problematic, and instead of the original, uniform imperial model, three types of relationships between the imperial center and its one-time East Central European client states emerged. In the first group, consisting of Yugoslavia and Albania, we find countries that, while retaining a communist form of government, openly proclaimed their independence from the imperial center, refused to take directions from Moscow, and did not participate in the institutions (WTO and Comecon) designed to coordinate imperial defense and trade. The three countries of the second group, Hungary, Poland, and Romania, remained part of the imperial system. On ceremonial occasions, their leaders even loudly confirmed their membership in the "socialist camp" led by the Soviet Union. But these proclamations of loyalty were not always convincing. For while they were cheering for the common cause, their leaders were increasingly distancing themselves from the Soviet geopolitical project and, pushing toward the outer limits of autonomy, were silently transforming their countries from militarized societies into socialist developmental

EXTERNAL AUTONOMY

	Independence	Simulated Conformity	Solidarity
"Soft-line" Liberalism	Yugoslavia	Poland Hungary	
"Hard-line" Conservatism	Albania	Romania	Bulgaria Czechoslovakia East Germany

FIGURE I. Variations in Communist Regimes, 1968–89.

states whose purpose was to compete in the export markets of the world. This left only East Germany, Czechoslovakia, and Bulgaria, whose leaders were most solidary with the Soviet Union in that they drew their legitimacy from the common geopolitical project of international class struggle and had domestic political arrangements closely mimicking the structure and scope of authority in the imperial center.

THE INDEPENDENTS

The "independents" were Yugoslavia and Albania, two countries that had split away from the Bloc at different times, but well before the final crisis of European communism—and without abandoning their communist identity. In neither case was the outcome of independence the result of a groundswell of popular sentiment or of a profound calculation of *raison d'état* by a local political elite. In both cases, the populations were largely unaware of the sequence of events, while the elites were less motivated by state or societal interest than by their own instinct for physical survival in a ruthless game played for the highest stakes, restrained only by the international balance of power between the Soviet Union and its major adversaries.

Yugoslavia

The story of Yugoslav independence is not without elements of irony. The leaders of the Yugoslav party had professed to be the most loyal to the

Soviet Union, were "intensely adoring"[34] of Stalin, and had expressed disappointment at not being instantly made into a Soviet republic. Tito ran a domestic regime as harsh and arbitrary as Stalin's, designed, in Tito's graphic terms, "to strike terror into the bones of those who [did] not like his kind of Yugoslavia";[35] and this rhetoric was substantiated by the massive coercion visited upon fascist collaborators, rival guerrilla groups, and members of national minority groups sympathizing with the occupying Axis countries. The Yugoslavs also faithfully copied Soviet institutions, and, not least of all, closely followed Stalinist teachings on ethnicity and nationalism. Once based on the hegemony of Serbia, Yugoslavia was turned by the communists into a federal state consisting of six republics (Serbia, Croatia, Slovenia, Montenegro, Bosnia-Herzegovina, and Macedonia) with two autonomous territories within Serbia proper (the multinational Voyvodina and the predominantly Albanian Kosovo). Initially, this federation was simply a mask for a highly centralized government, but the legitimacy of ethnic identities was recognized within the broader framework of Yugoslavism and proletarian internationalism, and over time more and more power was granted to the republics, culminating in the dispensations of the constitution in 1974.

Displays of loyalty notwithstanding, the Yugoslavs aroused Stalin's resentment by an excessive zeal that threatened to compromise a more discreet Soviet policy, by resisting efforts of Soviet advisors to micromanage local affairs, and by some of Tito's ventures in regional politics. After a few discreet warnings,[36] the Yugoslav leadership was publicly condemned, an action that Stalin believed would result in the fall of their government.[37] But personal ties forged by physical proximity in the perils of guerrilla war proved stronger than loyalty to the Soviet Union; combined with well-founded fears of being killed, these ties made the Yugoslavs strike out on their own. Viewed from a larger historical perspective, Yugoslavia was lost on account of Soviet inexperience with the process of expansion beyond the traditional boundaries of the old Russian empire.

For some time after these events, the Yugoslav communists continued their earlier style of governance, now terrorizing both the pro-Western, pro-traditionalist Right and the suspected pro-Soviet Left. But by 1950 it had become clear that both the international survival and domestic legitimacy of the Tito regime demanded more innovative political practices. The choices were limited by prevailing circumstances. On the one hand, there was as yet no great power patronage for sustaining a brand of communism more radical than that of the Soviet model; on the other, the Titoists could not contemplate a design for genuine democratization without risking their party's

34. Djilas 1962, 57.
35. Tito 1959, 355. Quotation courtesy of M. M. Drachkovitch.
36. See Stokes 1991, 57–64.
37. Khrushchev 1970, 600.

monopoly of power and their very lives. The new model thus had to be one that would put Yugoslavia somewhere between Soviet-style communism and Western democracy. For this purpose, a number of "brains" in the party turned to the classics of European Marxism, and to Marx himself, juxtaposing these teachings to the Leninist and Stalinist canons of the Soviet Union.[38] Although its true architects were Milovan Djilas and Edvard Kardelj, in deference to their leader the new ideology was informally referred to as Titoism.

The subject of a multitude of scholarly tracts,[39] this doctrine actually pivots around a few general principles. In the main, it represents an attempt to revert from Leninist voluntarism and Stalinist etatism to a classical formulation of Marxian historical determinism by rediscovering the role of autonomous social forces in history. Specifically, by returning to Marx, the architects of Titoism proclaimed that the development of socialism was driven not by the state but by the development of the means of production; and, taking a leaf from the writings of Edouard Bernstein, they argued both that the process could be gradual and that it might follow many roads, including the road of "bourgeois democracy." While to many outsiders this formula seemed needlessly arcane, its message to Marxists was clear. It implied that— contrary to Trotsky, Lenin, and Stalin—the socialist state was not the prime instrument of the international class struggle, and that, as a corollary, its internal activities, too, could be far more limited than in the Soviet model. Thus, rather than attempting to overthrow capitalism, the socialist state could pursue a course of international cooperation and coexistence, while its internal functions could be restricted to "protecting" the institutions of socialism and creating an appropriate environment for economic development. To make their differing positions more explicit, the Yugoslavs carried their Marxism one step further; they argued that the withering away of the state and the party did not have to wait until the global victory of socialism but should begin immediately after the consolidation of socialist institutions in particular national states. As a measure of these changes, Yugoslavia reverted from state autonomy to social autonomy and self-management, while the party eventually turned itself into a "league," whose functions were no longer to be those of leading but rather of "guiding" society along the path to greater prosperity and communality.

In practical terms, these principles led to three sets of reforms designed to change, and particularly to reduce, the functions of the communist state. The first of these was the dismantling of what was described as the Stalinist

38. Specifically, Marx's "Civil War in France," Friedrich Engels's *Anti-Dühring*, and several of the "revisionist" writings of Edouard Bernstein. See Rusinow 1977, 50–56.

39. Neal 1958, esp. 15–33; Hoffman and Neal 1962, 155–73; Vucinich and Zaninovich in Vucinich 1969, 235–84, 285–315. See also *Yugoslavia's Way: Program of the League of Yugoslav Communists* (1958).

model of state capitalism, and its replacement by a mixed system of private and "social" ownership. The principle of private ownership was restored in agriculture (with a ten-hectare limit on the size of individual holdings) and in the small services sector, while social ownership was retained in the other sectors of the economy. In this model, the means of production were to be owned by the producers of each particular enterprise, who would then be represented by workers' councils holding the ultimate power over management decisions. That power included the appointment of managers but excluded the power to divest and distribute assets among the presumptive owners.[40] This reform of ownership, then, went hand in hand with steps to restore the autonomy of markets by liberating enterprises from the bureaucratic planning system and subjecting them to the profit principle. In this "mixed market" or "Illyrian" model of the economy,[41] the state was still granted the power to establish priorities and to enforce them through its control over the credit system—the main source of investment and operating funds—but the managers of enterprises would be free from ministerial meddling in their choice of inputs and outputs.

Just as important as the restoration of enterprise and market autonomies were efforts to "liberalize," or "de-regiment," society and thus to restore some of the old divisions between the public and private spheres. These objectives were to be attained primarily by restoring four sets of freedoms that had been previously denied to the citizenry—those of foreign travel, of information, of artistic expression, and of personal and family decision-making. The freedom to travel abroad (for educational, recreational, or employment purposes) for the first time ended the rigorous and uniform isolation of socialist countries from the West. The freedom of information flows, including information from the capitalist West, meant both ending the practice of jamming radio broadcasts and allowing the sale of foreign newspapers. The freedom of creativity and artistic expression was promoted by limiting censorship and by taking the party (now League) "out" of the arts, sciences, and professions. Finally, and more generally, the freedom of family and personal life from external supervision and intervention included granting autonomy over decisions concerning family planning and procreation until then strictly controlled in all other communist societies.[42]

40. Of the vast literature on this subject, see the authoritative essays in Horvat, Marković, and Supek 1975, esp. Mihailo Marković, "Philosophical Foundations of the Idea of Self-Management" (1: 327–50); id., "Socialism as Self-Management" (1: 416–37); Andrija Krešić, "The Production-Relations Basis of Self-Management" (1: 445–53); Branko Horvat, "The Labor-Managed Enterprise" (2: 164–77); and Svetozar Stojanović, "Between Ideals and Reality" (1: 467–78).

41. Benjamin Ward, "The Illyrian Firm," in Horvat, Marković, and Supek 1975, 241–60.

42. For this subject, and the criteria by which to measure this "liberalization," see Korbonski 1975, 192–214, 249–85.

These reforms—the restoration of social autonomy, the "marketization" of the economy, and the deregimentation of daily life—had by the early 1960s become realities, and they would henceforth serve as a model to those aspiring to "liberalize" communism. But the success of these measures was not replicated by the elaborate reforms ostensibly designed to democratize Yugoslav society and politics. True, the term "self-management" became one of the great shibboleths of official Yugoslavia, celebrated also by a good number of enthusiasts from among the Western intellectual community. But a wide gap remained between ideals and reality, whether we examine the functioning of economic or of political democracy. First of all, the workers' councils, designed to give substance to the concept of "social ownership," could rarely perform their functions. Their often apathetic members were generally co-opted by management, were too willing to delegate authority to expertise, or remained powerless against the reality that "strong statist structures above them . . . including the military, the police and the League of Communists, still [functioned] in a hierarchical and autocratic fashion."[43] As for the structures of the state, they had been the subject of repeated tinkering in order to imbue them with a democratic appearance, but without making them truly accountable to the electorate. The character of parliamentary institutions went from an early model mimicking the Supreme Soviet to a mixture of territorial and functional representation, in which two political chambers of the Federal Assembly shared powers with chambers for dealing with issues of economics, public health, culture, and education. As stipulated by the constitution of 1963, this combination of territorial and functional chambers was replicated at the levels of the republics and autonomous territories, and, with some simplification, at the level of municipal government, mainly to lend substance to the claim that the "state" and conventional politics were withering away. However, the structure was too cumbersome to perform the tasks of routine legislation and was later abolished in favor of a more conventional bicameral National Assembly, divided between a Federal Chamber and a Chamber of Republics and Autonomous Regions. The latter—to consist of six delegations of twelve members from each of the republics and two delegations of eight members from the autonomous territories of Voyvodina and Kosovo—would eventually emerge as the hub of the parliamentary system. It would be the chamber where deals were struck and minimal consensus established among the regional representatives (encouraged by the rule that each delegation could cast one vote after polling its own members).[44] The executive, meanwhile, was turned into a collegial body, with two representatives from each republic

43. Stojanović 1975, 469–70.

44. For the most comprehensive description of these and other Yugoslav institutions, see Carter 1982. See also Rusinow 1977, 222–28, and Ramet 1984, esp. 67–86.

274 EAST CENTRAL EUROPE

and one from each of the autonomous territories. For its first six years, this body was presided over by Tito in his capacity as President for Life. After his death, it became a collective presidency with ceremonial functions rotated among its members on an annual basis.

Appearances and rhetoric notwithstanding, these institutions could hardly be regarded as genuinely representative of popular constituencies. Much celebrated as a democratic innovation, for example, was the 1963 constitution's stipulation of multiple candidacies. But these candidacies proved to have only a minimal impact on the articulation of popular interests, for all candidates were subjected to a screening procedure by the Socialist Alliance, a subsidiary of the League of Communists, with the proviso that the only candidates permitted to run would be those whose platform reflected commitment to the basic principles of socialism. Those who passed muster had to run without the benefit of organization, for such organizations were banned outright. It should also be added here that the method of electing deputies was indirect: members of local councils elected the republican organs, and these organs in turn selected delegates to the federal legislature. Thus, in the words of one observer of the Yugoslav scene, while in time these chambers were beginning to accumulate genuine political functions, their members "were not effectively representative of their ostensible constituents but of the Party and Socialist Alliance officials and organs of 'cadre policy.'" [45] Or, in the blunter language of another writer, we are dealing with "an incomprehensible [institutional] framework that made sense only as a device to prevent the organization of any rival to communist power." [46] Indeed, examination of the composition of these various legislatures reveals that throughout the 1960s and 1970s, the majority of deputies above the local level were members of the Communist League and its republican apparatus. [47]

In a like manner, reforms of the League itself, including the much vaunted rotation of personnel and the separation of state and party functions, were a far cry from democratizing the party in the sense of making its leaders accountable to the membership at large. Yet by recognizing the federal principle and by the introduction of the constitution in 1974, the League became more like a confederation of parties than a single hierarchical organization, as each of its republican and territorial branches came to exercise control over both their own assemblies and the representatives they sent to the federal institutions. The death of Tito in 1980 removed the single remaining center of power capable of overruling individual factions and territorial organizations. But even before his death, Yugoslavia had been imperceptibly

45. Rusinow 1977, 153.
46. Lampe 1996, 293.
47. Carter 1982, 125–26.

TABLE 34

Regional Income Inequalities in Yugoslavia, 1947

(per capita regional product; Yugoslavia = 100)

More Developed Regions		Less Developed Regions	
Slovenia	162	Montenegro	94
Croatia	105	Macedonia	70
Voyvodina	100	Bosnia-Herzegovina	86
Serbia proper	101	Kosovo	49

SOURCE: Ramet 1984, 183.

TABLE 35

Providers and Recipients of Development Aid, Yugoslavia

(1971–75)

Net Contributors	Population (%)	Distribution Flow
Slovenia	8.4	−22.6
Croatia	21.6	−34.5
Serbia	25.6	−29.5
Voyvodina	9.5	−13.3
Net Recipients		
Bosnia-Herzegovina	18.3	+25.6
Macedonia	8.0	+22.1
Montenegro	2.6	+12.2
Kosovo	6.1	+40.1

SOURCE: Bombelles 1991, 447.

transformed from autocracy into a political system that, while not democratic, was pluralistic in character.

No less significant than these institutional reforms and the "creeping pluralization" of Yugoslav politics were measures designed to further strengthen policies intended to eliminate economic disparities among the regions of the country (see Table 34). The previously chaotic program was streamlined in 1965 by creating an agency for the more rapid development of the underdeveloped republics and Kosovo (FADURK) as well as an official fund for financing the agency's activities.[48] The distributions from the fund (see Table 35) were supplemented by policies of preferential loan rates, forgiven loans, and a variety of tax incentives offered to individual enterprises to engage in economic activity in the underdeveloped regions.[49] While no exact figures exist for the latter, extrapolating from the total economic spending of the federation, we may estimate that the aggregate amount transferred

48. Bombelles 1991, 446–47.
49. Ibid., 445.

TABLE 36

Yugoslav Federal Budget, Percentage Share
of Investments, 1956–68

Country	Revenues contributed	Share of investments
Slovenia	21.1	6.1
Croatia	31.2	18.0
Serbia	29.2	43.5
Macedonia	4.3	10.8
Montenegro	1.3	7.9
Bosnia-Herzegovina	13.9	13.7

SOURCE: *Statisticki bilten,* FNRJ (1968), 26, 79; quoted in Djodan
1991, 105.

from the "developed" to the "underdeveloped" was in the neighborhood of
3 percent of the country's total GNP.[50]

Published in the spirit of "liberalization," information about these
amounts and distributions was likely to stir some resentment among the
populations of the contributing republics. That resentment was further aggravated by scholarly studies showing that the Serbian republic, although
politically diminished, was still favored financially by the balance of contributions and disbursements—even though much of that imbalance was due
to federal spending not in Serbia proper but in its autonomous republic of
Kosovo (see Table 36).

While nominally sustained by its unique system of social democracy, in
reality the effective functioning of the Yugoslav system depended on two
critical factors. One was the Yugoslav identity of the regional elites and their
continued adherence to the universalistic, supra-ethnic principles of the
party that kept interrepublican conflict within manageable bounds. The
other was their management of the economy, both national and regional,
which successfully garnered a modicum of support for the regime. This was
well recognized by Yugoslav officials, who, while incessantly extolling the
virtues of their system of self-management in public, in private were quick
to admit the importance of the economic factor and justify the authoritarian elements of their system in terms of developmental exigencies. To put it
somewhat differently, Yugoslavia had become the socialist version of a developmental dictatorship rather than the model of popular participation in
government.

The claims of being an effective developmental state received at least partial validation in the economic record of the country from the 1950s through
the early 1970s. During these two decades, the country's GDP was growing

50. Ibid., 449.

at an average of 6 percent per year, the output of the industrial sector at
10.1 percent, exports at 11.1 percent, imports at a more restrained 9.8 percent, and investments at 8.2 percent.[51] Altogether, GDP per capita (at 1962
prices) increased two and a half times over twenty years, infant mortality was
cut by more than half (from 118 to 55 per thousand), the struggle against
illiteracy, after a weak start in the 1950s, was beginning to show results
(down to 15.2 percent by 1970), and increases in the number of radios, au-
tos, and other consumer items indicated that some of the output growth had
been trickling down to the general population.[52] While not spectacular in
comparison to the gains of the advanced societies of the West, between 1950
and 1970, the Yugoslav economy managed to keep pace with the growth
rates of the advanced capitalist countries. Whereas, in 1937–38, Yugoslav
per capita national income (at market prices) was 13.6 percent of American and 39 percent of the Western European "six" (used elsewhere in this
study for comparative purposes), in 1970, the respective figures were 15 and
41.9 percent respectively.[53]

Yet not even in its halcyon days was everything right with the Yugoslav
economy. As in many other countries of East Central Europe, agricultural
growth was sluggish, notwithstanding—or perhaps because of—the restoration and overregulation of small peasant farms. Unemployment, hidden
and real, remained high, ameliorated only by sending almost one million
workers as "guest laborers" to the advanced industrial countries,[54] and regional income inequalities continued to increase despite the vigorous policies of income transfer (see Table 37). These disparities were most conspicuous between Slovenia and the other regions, but the gap between the
northern three—Slovenia, Croatia, and Voyvodina—and the southern five
(including Serbia proper, a region not officially classified as "less developed") was also considerable.

These economic deficiencies were magnified between 1973 and 1979, the
years of the two "oil shocks," which coincided with the end of the phase of
extensive growth.[55] The first instinct of Yugoslav technocrats was to respond to the slowdown by extensive foreign borrowing, made easy by a glut
of money in the world banking system, created as a by-product of the oil
shocks themselves. This strategy did indeed sustain a respectable rate of
growth for a period of about five years.[56] But while the economy was grow-

51. Dubey 1975, 54–60.
52. Ibid.; Lampe 1996, 289.
53. For the U.S. comparison, see Marer 1989, 72–73; for Western Europe, see Bairoch
1976, 297, 307.
54. Woodward 1995b, 200.
55. For a general discussion, see Lampe 1996, 293–324.
56. Ibid., 315.

TABLE 37

Regional Inequalities of per Capita Social Product, Yugoslavia,
1965–88

(Yugoslavia = 100)

Country	1965	1975	1986	1988
Slovenia	177	201	179	203
Croatia	120	124	117	128
Voyvodina	122	121	133	119
Serbia proper	95	92	94	101
Montenegro	71	70	80	74
Macedonia	70	69	75	63
Bosnia-Herzegovina	69	69	80	68
Kosovo	39	33	36	27

SOURCES: Ramet 1984, 183 (1965, 1975); Lydall 1989, 188; Pleština 1992, 180.

ing at a rate of 5.1 percent (in constant 1972 dollars), the rate of foreign borrowing was increasing at an annual rate of 20 percent.[57] The bubble eventually burst in 1979, and a few figures will tell the story of the 1980s. In just six years (1979–85), the country accumulated $25 billion in foreign debt (or about $1,100 per capita), and the dinar plunged from 15 to 1,370 to the U.S. dollar—as a prelude to subsequent hyperinflation.[58] The benefits of foreign trade (and tourism) were rapidly vanishing, as nearly half of income from exports went to pay interest on the debt.[59] During the same period, unemployment rose to 1.3 million, representing 17 percent of the labor force of the "socialist sector" of the economy.[60] Those still employed did not fare much better: real net personal income declined by 19.5 percent.[61] In November 1984, it was reported that two-thirds of those employed lived below the previously defined subsistence level.[62] Public consumption, investment rates, aggregate social product, and output per worker were all following downward trends,[63] and each of these items bears close correlation with the regional differentiation of the economy, spelling interrepublican political trouble (see Table 38).

Over the years, sympathetic observers have been inclined to account for this crisis in terms of particular "mistakes" made by a succession of governments: the inefficiency and overregulation of peasant farms, insistence on 51 percent Yugoslav ownership in joint ventures, or some of the excesses of workers' self-management. Yet, as time passed, the weight of scholarly opin-

57. Ibid.
58. United States, Central Intelligence Agency 1986, 59.
59. Foreign Broadcast Information Service (FBIS), October 23, 1987, 41.
60. *Radio Free Europe Research,* Yugoslavia, November 22, 1985; Lydall 1989, 82.
61. Lydall 1989, 41.
62. *Radio Free Europe Research,* Yugoslavia, November 2, 1984.
63. Lydall 1989, 41.

TABLE 38

Further Indicators of Regional Economic Disparities, Yugoslavia, 1987

	Population growth rate	Net enterprise saving[a]	Net income[b]	% of Workers abroad[c]	% Seeking employment[c]	Ratio of exports to foreign debt
Slovenia	3.4	+605	3.1	5	2	180
Croatia	2.0	−40	2.2	10	8	75
Voyvodina	0.3	−181	1.9	8	15	86
Bosnia	9.5	−845	1.7	13	24	76
Serbia	2.7	−355	1.9	9	18	90
Montenegro	9.8	−787	1.5	6	25	25
Macedonia	11.8	−413	1.4	11	27	53
Kosovo	24.5	−868	1.4	13	56	20
All	6.4	−251	2.1	10	16	83

SOURCE: Lydall 1989, 190, 192 (some figures rounded off).
[a] In US dollars per worker.
[b] In millions of dinars per worker.
[c] Percentages calculated in relation to total number of workers in the "social sector" of the economy.

ion has turned to structural factors, to contradictions built into an economic model that, even in its reformed version, could not break loose from its state socialist moorings, bureaucratic control over "entry" into and "exit" from markets, and the primacy of the political in the making of economic decisions.[64] Given this triumph of political over economic rationality, the Yugoslav economy proved no better than its counterparts in the Bloc when it came to switching from extensive to intensive, and from heavy industrial to consumer-oriented development.

There is little doubt, though, that the economic problems of Yugoslavia were aggravated by excessive political decentralization along ethnoterritorial lines.[65] More because of political exigencies than outright corruption, republican and autonomous territorial elites invested federal funds to increase their power of patronage, ignoring the logic of the division of labor. These practices resulted in functional duplication and in the notorious "bum investments" (*promašene investicije*) that, according to Yugoslav economists, swallowed up between one-third and one-half of all investments.[66] Worse still, from a political point of view, under the pressures of crisis and increasingly cutthroat competition for scarce resources, regional elites began to reach out to mass constituencies, and in so doing abandoned their former universalistic ethos. Thus, they were transformed from the en-

64. See the closing statement of a conference of 200 Yugoslav social scientists in *Radio Free Europe Research*, Yugoslavia, Mar. 8, 1985; see also Madžer 1995, i.
65. This view is shared by a wide variety of authors. See Woodward 1995, 61; Lydall 1989, 8; Vojnić 1994; Goati 1991, 51–57.
66. Žarković, in *NIN*, June 15, 1986. Mikulić, in *NIN*, June 15, 1986. Quoted in Lydall 1989, 82.

forcers of ethnic taboos into the articulators of ethnic grievances and particularism. Like all Europeans, Yugoslavs were attuned to defining economic differences as differences in *Kultur* and nursed a long list of grievances, going back to the precommunist period and the war. In their new role, Croat and Slovene party elites were thus not merely protesting unfavorable economic dispensations but quickly revived old images of Serbia as a "land of nepotism, incompetence and Levantine bakshish,"[67] qualities that made their countries the victims not just of "exploitation" but of inefficient government. Matters were not helped by the fact that Serbs and Montenegrins continued to play a disproportionate role in the League of Communists, and were represented out of proportion in the federal army and in the regional parties and police forces.[68] The Serbs in their turn complained that they were "exploited by the Slovenes, oppressed in Croatia and overrun in the Kosovo,"[69] victimized by Titoist policies of denationalization, and physically threatened by the advances of culturally alien Albanians and Moslems.[70] The southerners then responded by expressing anger at Serbian preponderance in public employment and fear of the restoration of prewar Serbian hegemony.[71]

For much of the 1980s, the Yugoslav federal state was held together, in essence, by external forces: by the latent Soviet threat to "save socialism" should Yugoslavia fall apart, and by the strong Western desire to prevent international conflict. But the centrifugal forces at work paralyzed the Yugoslav political system. Characteristically, in 1983, 18 of 25 major reform bills before the Chamber of the Republic were shelved; only 7 received the votes needed for passage.[72] This created, in the words of Josip Županov, a "situation in which the patient neither gets well nor dies, a state of prolonged malfunction in which the system still re-establishes equilibrium but does so at lower and lower levels of efficiency."[73] In this precarious situation, the "rich" republics of Slovenia and Croatia refused further contributions to the Federal Development Fund and tried to distance themselves from the rest of the federation, while the Serbian branch of the League, now a faction imbued with aggressive ethnic particularism, moved to restore its diminishing control over the Albanian majority of the Kosovo. Then came the events of

67. Originally written by Bićanić 1938, 67–68.
68. Serbs and Montenegrins together represented 38.9 percent of the total population of Yugoslavia, but made up 52.5 percent of the party membership. For the army, regional parties, and police forces, see Ramet 1984, 132; Connor 1984, 298–99; Haberl 1976, 209.
69. J. Marković 1995, vi.
70. For these charges, see the well-known document in English translation, Mihailović and Krestić 1995.
71. Allman 1993, 55–56.
72. *Radio Free Europe Research,* Yugoslavia, November 2, 1984.
73. Bekić 1985, 10.

TABLE 39
*Desertions from the League of Communists,
Membership in 1989 and 1990*

(in thousands)

Country	1989	1990
Slovenia	102	20
Croatia	298	46
Serbia	840	500
Montenegro	73	60

SOURCE: Goati 1991, 39.

1989–91, which removed the threat of Soviet intervention and, along with it, earlier Western concerns about a major international crisis.

With external constraints removed, the "rich" walked out of the federation, advancing both narrowly economic and broadly cultural arguments. Once they were on their way out, the less developed regions in turn had no economic reason to stay—and good political reasons to flee what they viewed as the likely prospect of hegemony by Serbia. Only the Serb and Montenegrin parties remained committed to the Yugoslav idea (now with a greater Serbian twist); their members rewarded them by remaining loyal to their authoritarian and nationalist leadership (see Table 39), by voting in large numbers for successor parties in the postfederal period, and, not least of all, by their willingness to fight against the forces of separatism in Slovenia, Croatia, and Bosnia-Herzegovina. While the roots of this conflict were in economic failure, the violence that attended it reflected deep-seated fears of ethnic domination and physical extinction.

Albania

The story of the separation of Albania from the Soviet Bloc is closely intertwined with other conflicts in the communist camp. It began in 1943, when the Albanian Communist (later Labor) Party was founded under Yugoslav auspices and by Yugoslav communist emissaries. After the war, with the apparent blessings of Stalin, Albania was assigned to the tutelage of Yugoslavia. While Tito did not, for reasons of his own, turn Albania into a Yugoslav republic, his advisors became de facto members of the Albanian Central Committee and proceeded to build close military and economic ties with Albania. The relationship was to be cemented by the stationing of Yugoslav troops on the Greco-Albanian border, a plan that did not materialize because of subsequent events.[74] For various reasons, some perhaps personal,

74. See Pipa 1984, 436–37.

the Yugoslavs favored one Koci Xoxe for the position of first secretary over the incumbent, Enver Hoxha, who had been first appointed as a compromise candidate among several factions upon the founding of the party.

Given such opposition and communist practices of the times, Hoxha could expect to lose not only his political office but his head as well. He was rescued by the Soviet-Yugoslav conflict, and celebrated his triumph by ordering the liquidation of Xoxe and the other favorites of the Yugoslavs. Hoxha subsequently took a major role in the anti-Tito campaign orchestrated by Moscow. But his position became precarious again in 1955 when, upon the initiative of Khrushchev, the Soviets and the Yugoslavs made up, and the aggrieved Tito demanded Hoxha's head as a token of Soviet good faith. Shortly thereafter, the Albanian's position grew still more tenuous with Khrushchev's denunciation of Stalinist methods, with which Hoxha could clearly be associated. He was saved once again by a chill in Yugoslav-Soviet relations in the aftermath of the Hungarian revolution. But when the chill was followed by yet another thaw, Hoxha took no further chances, preempting his own demise by leading his country out of the Bloc.[75] He was able to do so not only because of his country's geographic isolation and rugged terrain—which would have made military intervention a long and embarrassingly drawn-out affair—but also because military intervention would have further aggravated the then unfolding Sino-Soviet conflict and alienated a number of radical communist parties in the non-European world.

The man at the center of this vortex of events was one of the more interesting, if less well known, personalities of the communist world. A native of the Albanian Tosk south and member of a small landowner family, Hoxha was sent to France and enrolled at the University of Montpellier, but never graduated. He returned to Albania and started a tobacco business, which soon became a gathering place of politically radical elements that, in 1943, gravitated toward the communist movement. Hoxha became a member of the Politburo of the nascent party and, a few months later, as an apparent compromise candidate between the pro-Yugoslav and "nativist" factions, First Secretary of the Party. With a fine Stalinesque instinct for political maneuvering and manipulation, he would hold on to the job for forty-one years, despite numerous efforts of powerful external and internal opponents to overthrow him. But apart from that talent for intrigue and survival, he also had remarkable oratorical skills. As a writer he produced some of the best and most engaging political tracts ever written by a communist leader,[76] in which he recounts in great and credible detail his struggles with the Yugoslav, Russian, and later Chinese leaders. He was always a perfect dresser,

75. For detailed descriptions of his elaborate maneuvers and of Soviet attempts to forestall the defection, see Griffith 1963. See also Hamm 1963, 8–103.
76. See, e.g., Hoxha 1979, 1980, 1982.

with a penchant for tailor-made Italian and French suits, and most of his photographs show a smiling man with the casual elegance and good looks of a Hollywood actor.

But the easygoing, casual demeanor hid one of the most ruthless political figures produced by this century, one who swooped down mercilessly upon all whom he suspected of disloyalty or disobedience and presided over the execution of innumerable men and women from his own entourage. In 1981, he forced Mehmet Shehu, a close associate for forty years, to take his own life. Once Shehu had complied, Hoxha ordered the arrest of Shehu's wife, nephew, and son, and derided Shehu's gesture as an act of mock heroism, telling the world that instead of being given the state funeral Shehu had yearned for, "he was buried like a dog." [77] Unlike Tito, who turned "Right" after his break with the Soviet Union in 1948, Hoxha in the 1960s turned "Left" by taking advantage of the Sino-Soviet rift. But opportunism aside, Hoxha was attracted to radicalism both on grounds of temper and political exigencies. Vengeful by disposition, he thoroughly enjoyed denouncing the Soviet Union for "revisionism," while his radicalism also suited his anti-Yugoslav stand and provided justification for the terror that to the very end remained an integral part of his regime. Accordingly, he remained faithful to his revolutionary orthodoxy even after he broke with the Chinese in 1976.

Within the larger ideological framework of proletarian internationalism, the operational principles of Hoxhaism were a mixture of Stalinism and Maoism. In the 1960s, Hoxha was clearly influenced by Mao's radical hostility to tradition, bureaucracy, and the economic rationality associated with technocracy. For much of his rule, Hoxha thus preached persistent struggle against manifestations of these tendencies.[78] As part of this struggle, Hoxha imitated Mao's Cultural Revolution by making a concerted effort to destroy all vestiges of traditional institutions and forms of consciousness—above all, by banning the practice of religion outright. That policy, more severe than elsewhere in East Central Europe, produced the execution of large numbers of the clergy of both Christian and Moslem faiths and the expropriation of places of worship for secular purposes. In pursuit of these objectives, Albanian society was subjected to terror that was unmatched in scope and breadth by any other post-Stalin regime, and that succeeded in destroying the traditional fabric of human relations perhaps more completely than in any other society of communist Europe. At the same time, Hoxha found Mao's mass mobilization techniques useful and, like Stalin, put his faith in the security police and in the manipulation of state institutions. This etatism was in obvious conflict with the voluntaristic, anti-organizational strands of

77. This sentence appears in the Albanian version of Hoxha 1982, 578, but was omitted from the English translation. See Pipa 1984, 464 n. 30.
78. Kaser 1986, 4.

Hoxhaism, and the contradiction was resolved by the purges. The following list, culled from contemporary reports,[79] will illustrate the scope of these purges.

1949–51. Purge of the pro-Yugoslav communist Koci Xoxe and members of his clan (Pandi Kristo, Nesti Kerenxhi, Xhoxhi Blushi). Twenty-five percent of the party membership expelled.

1951–52. Further purges of "anti-party elements" in the army, as well as in the ministries of Communication and Industry. Among the victims, Politburo members Gjin Marku and Nexhip Vinçani.

1956. Former Politburo member Liri Gega (a pregnant woman) and her husband General Dali Ndreu executed for pro-Yugoslav tendencies.[80]

1960–61. In the wake of the Soviet-Albanian rift, pro-Soviet "revisionists" Admiral Teme Sejko, Koço Tasko, and Liri Belishova, the leading woman in the Politburo, expelled from the party and executed.

1966. Purge of all government ministries to reduce the size of the bureaucracy.

1967–68. The party expells 16,000 (of the then 50,000) members.

1969. "Anti-gossiping" campaign by the Sigurami (security police) to break up informal networks of social communication.

1970–72. Campaigns against "immature" party members.

1971. Purge of the Ministry of Finance: personnel reduced by 42 percent.

1973. Purge of the educational and cultural establishment.

1974. Purge of the Ministry of Defense; Minister of Defense General Beqir Balluku and the chiefs of the general staff and political directorate of the army executed.

1975–76. A shock wave of purges engulfs the economy: purge and execution of "specialists and pro-specialists" (among those arrested were Politburo members Abdyl Këllezi, chairman of Central Planning, and Koço Theodosi, minister of industry).

1976. Purge of the ministries of Education and Culture and of Agriculture.

1981–82. The biggest purge of all, eliminating Prime Minister Mehmet Shehu and his political clientele from the leadership in order to preempt a struggle for succession. Mehmet Shehu forced to commit sui-

79. Using periodic reports of *Radio Free Europe Research,* Albania; and monthly issues of *East Europe* 12, no. 1 (Jan. 1963) through 19, no. 12 (Dec. 1970). See also Pipa 1984, 443–51, and Kolsti 1981, 30–38.
80. For the fate of Gega, see Griffith 1963, 235. The ultimate source for this item is Khrushchev's speech at the CPSU's Twenty-Second Congress.

cide; Mrs. Fiqret Shehu (director of the Party Academy) imprisoned; Minister of Interior Feçor Shehu shot; Llambi Ziçinisti, a member of Shehu's entourage, executed; Politburo member and Sigurami officer Kadir Hasbiu sentenced to 25 years.

Although he is sometimes described as a nationalist,[81] Hoxha's Albanianism must be understood in a larger context of ideological universalism. It is true that Hoxha often invoked national symbols and heroic chapters of his country's history. But much as in the case of German National Socialism, the nation was an instrument rather than the ultimate object of communist policies. He recalled the heroic deeds of his nation in order to demonstrate that it was uniquely qualified to be in the revolutionary vanguard, liberating the oppressed of the world. Characteristically, throughout the years of his leadership, he seemed indifferent to the ethnic dimensions of Albanianism; while he quarreled incessantly over the years with the Yugoslav leadership, the fate of the oppressed Albanians of the Kosovo remained peripheral to the larger issue of Yugoslav "revisionism." Indeed, Albanians from Yugoslavia were treated with utmost suspicion, and if arriving as refugees, they were either incarcerated as spies or forcibly returned.

Affixing Hoxha's name to the doctrine and practices of Albanian communism is fully justified, and in the name of his doctrine, he did transform Albanian society—perhaps more so than Titoism transformed Yugoslavia—but like all political leaders, Hoxha could not entirely cut himself loose from the constraints of the environment within which he operated. Albanian society was divided more or less in halves along quasi-ethnic lines, between the pastoral Ghegs of the north and the feudal-agricultural Tosks of the south, with both societies further divided among clans. In principle, communism was supposed to end these differences in the name of universalistic principles. In reality, though, the communists had to develop a base of power and found southern Tosk society, chafing under the long rule of Gheg chieftains, more receptive. Whatever the original intent, the party became and remained a predominantly Tosk affair. A count of heads in the Politburo in 1983 reveals that, of its twelve members, ten were Tosks and only two were Ghegs.[82] It should also not escape attention that some of the most prominent purge victims—Liri Gega, Liri Belishova, Fadil Paçrami, Tuk Jakova, Bekir Balluku—were also Ghegs. Although the Gheg Ramiz Alia eventually succeeded Hoxha, the original members of the "Shkoder group" of Ghegs had been smashed at the time of the Yugoslav-Albanian break in 1948–50.

Like cultural divisions, the division of society into clans did not vanish with the advent of communism. Hoxha and his long-time associate Shehu

81. Lendvai 1969, 191–203.

82. Tosks: Carcani, Hasbiu, Hoxha, Isai, Kapo, Koleka, Marko, Myftiu, Shehu, Toska; Ghegs: Alia, Miska. Source: RFE *Internal Files* (Non-Circulating), June 8, 1986.

did lead a campaign against clans, doing so with particular vehemence in order to break the power of the Gheg clans of the northern highlands.[83] But once again, communism was forced to compromise, and over the decades, it used the ties of tribe and extended family to increase the solidarity of the party leadership. This was especially obvious in the ranks of the top leadership, where an inner clique of a few prominent leaders brought their wives, sons, daughters, nephews, and family retainers into the Politburo, the Central Committee, and the highest governmental posts. In the 1960s and 1970s, there were only 5 or 6 among the 36 members of the Central Committee who were not related to any other member by either blood or marriage.[84] One remarkable result of this clannish arrangement was the large number of women, not only in the party, but also in the Central Committee, the Politburo, and the Council of Ministers. While a 33 percent female party membership was not unusual, Albania, the least modern of the European communist countries, had more women in positions of responsibility than any other party. Their high positions reflect not modern predilections but rather traditional family connections. The wives of Hoxha, Shehu, and Hysni Kapo were all members of the Central Committee. Another Politburo wife, Mrs. Rita Marko, held an important position in the Ministry of Finance, and the ill-fated Fiqret Shehu, already mentioned, was the director of the Party Academy. This social pattern was also appropriately reflected in the pattern of purges. When one high-ranking communist, man or woman, fell, all of his (or her) retainers perished too. The purge did not discriminate. Women—as the cases of Liri Belishova, Fiqret Shehu, and Liri Gega illustrate—were subjected to the same treatment by the Sigurami as their male counterparts.

These peculiar mixtures of etatism and revolution, tribalism and modernity, were further reflected in the development of the Albanian economy. At first, like all East Central European countries, Albania followed the pure Stalinist model with its emphasis on investment in heavy industry. On paper at least, during these years growth rates as high as 11.4 percent were reported in the industrial sector and 13.4 percent in agriculture.[85] But in evaluating these figures, we must discount them not only for statistical sleights of hand but also for the fact that they were originally calculated from a base near zero. Albanian sources show that the share of industry in national income rose from 18.2 percent in 1960 to 43.3 percent in 1985,[86] a statistic that reflects not just the growth of industry but the chronic stagnation of agriculture. During the years of Chinese patronage, Hoxha's policies oscillated

83. Kolsti 1981, 23.
84. Interview, June 10, 1986, staff of RFE, Albanian desk, Munich, Germany.
85. Brown 1966.
86. Quoted in Biberaj 1990, 68.

between attempts at labor-intensive big leaps—the 1971–75 plan called for an annual increase of 25.8 percent in agricultural production[87]—and the most advanced "scientific techniques," including mathematical modeling, to raise the efficiency of planning and production.[88] Between these cycles, the officials in charge of the preceding economic regime would be purged. In any case, the long-term results were not impressive. After three decades of sustained, if uneven, efforts, Albanian GNP per capita was calculated at $350 (at conversion rates), half of the figure for neighboring Yugoslavia and on a par with some of the poorest African countries. Two decades later, at the close of communist rule, the Albanian figure (adjusted to purchasing power parities) was reported to have fallen further behind.[89] This dismal performance of the last two decades of Albanian communism was largely owing to the loss of Chinese patronage and foreign aid, as well as to Hoxha's decision (which may have led to the conflict with the Shehu clan) to try a model of "self-reliance." That model, with its emphasis on military production, was to turn Albania into a "socialist fortress" in order to protect one of the few authentic revolutionary regimes in the world.[90] Indeed, the figures spent on defense, according to the regime's own statistics, were substantial: the amount increased from 11.5 to 18.5 percent of the Albanian budget from 1978 to 1985, with overall "economic spending" remaining constant over the seven-year period.[91]

Hoxha's death in 1985 raised hopes of a new era of political reform and economic rationality. His successor was Ramiz Alia, former chief of Sigurami, who had later been in charge of ideology in the Politburo. Although he was one of the few Ghegs among the leadership, he had been handpicked by the Hoxha clan and was reputed to be a personal protégé of Hoxha's widow, Nexhmije. Alia did indeed take a few cautious steps toward improving relations with a few capitalist countries and, domestically, toward reining in the Sigurami. He also seemed to change course, ever so cautiously, on the issue of national identity, by taking up the cause of the Gheg Albanians of the Kosovo. But actual changes were slow in coming. The Gheg-Tosk balance in the Politburo remained more or less the same,[92] and the impulse to full-fledged irredentism was stemmed by long-standing fears that Kosovar Albanians might be "too liberal," and that their entry into the national community would upset the delicate balance between Tosk and Gheg ethnic groups. At that moment, these fears seemed to foreign observers to be exag-

87. Louis Zanga, in *Radio Free Europe Research*, Albania, July 30, 1971.
88. Kaser and Schnytzer 1977, 571.
89. United Nations 1993, 135–36.
90. Kaser 1986, 4–5.
91. Ibid., 15.
92. Three likely Ghegs (Alia, Bekteshi, Miska), one Greek, and one member of unidentifiable origins. For the list of the Politburo members, see Biberaj 1990, 57.

gerated, although they have since been justified by the resurgence of regionalism in the violence of the postcommunist years. In foreign politics, Alia reestablished relations with Albania's "capitalist" neighbors, Greece and Italy,
and some overtures were made to Austria, a long-time patron of the Albanians. In the interim, though, Alia continued to advocate "vigilance and
struggle against the aggressive plans of superpowers," [93] and thus relations
with major countries on both sides of the Cold War front lines remained
largely unchanged. The economy continued to be hamstrung by provisions
of the constitution of 1976 that banned foreign capital and borrowing. In
sum, Albania would enter the postcommunist era no better off materially,
and as devastated socially and culturally, as it had been in Hoxha's days.

DEVIANT SATELLITES: SIMULATING
SOLIDARITY AND CONFORMITY

Three other member states of the Soviet empire—Poland, Hungary,
and Romania—may be lumped together, although we must take cognizance
of significant differences in their domestic political arrangements and international behavior. As noted above, the common denominator among the
politics of these countries is that, from the 1960s onward, they were less and
less involved in common imperial endeavors. The Romanians' withdrawal
from active participation in the CMEA and the Warsaw Treaty Organization
was exceptional, but the participation of all three in the imperial trading
system declined (see Table 40), their economies opened up to world trade,
and their military budgets (despite Soviet nagging) stagnated (see Table 41).

The participation of Poland, Hungary, and Romania in Soviet geopolitical ventures, including support of movements of "national liberation" in the
non-Western world, was more symbolic than substantive and more inclined
to be humanitarian than military. As a corollary, bit by bit over the years,
the parties of these three countries reoriented their internal policies in order
to claim legitimacy in terms not of proletarian internationalism and the geopolitical designs of the imperial system but of raising the material standards
of their own populations. Even if in disguise, by the 1970s all three of these
countries became developmental states, focusing on domestic consumption
and international economic competitiveness, although each of them set out
to accomplish these purposes by different policies. In Poland, the instrument
of development was a technocracy that evolved piecemeal under accumu-
lating pressures of popular dissatisfaction; in Hungary, development was
pursued by a watered-down version of the Yugoslav model of "market socialism"; in Romania, the leadership and its economic advisors retained the

93. Louis Zanga, in *Radio Free Europe Research*, Albania, Sept. 13, 1985.

TABLE 40

Trading Patterns of East Central Europe:
Share of Intrasocialist Trade, 1970–85

	1970	1975	1980	1985
Bulgaria				
Exports	79.3	80.0	70.8	77.0
Imports	76.2	72.3	78.9	77.0
Czechoslovakia				
Exports	70.6	71.5	69.6	77.0
Imports	69.4	69.8	70.2	80.7
GDR				
Exports	73.9	73.2	69.5	65.0
Imports	69.4	66.6	63.7	67.2
Hungary				
Exports	65.6	72.2	55.1	58.6
Imports	64.5	65.7	50.6	54.4
Poland				
Exports	63.9	59.9	55.9	54.8
Imports	68.6	45.8	55.6	60.7
Romania				
Exports	58.1	46.0	44.7	42.2
Imports	53.9	43.5	37.8	50.2

SOURCE: Brabant 1989, 353.

TABLE 41

Estimated Defense Expenditures
of WTO States, 1975

(% of GNP)

Country	IISS	Alton
Bulgaria	3.0	2.7
Czechoslovakia	3.5	3.8
GDR	4.3	5.5
Hungary	2.4	2.3
Poland	2.9	3.1
Romania	1.7	1.7

SOURCES: International Institute of Strategic Studies (IISS)
1978, 88; Alton et al. 1977, 270.
NOTE: These are as yet unrevised figures that do not take into
account expenditures hidden in the civilian sector, nor of exports
used by the Soviet military establishment.

essential elements of the Stalinist economic model, based on the erroneous
assumption that this model could effectively be used to create an internationally competitive, high-consumption economy.

Poland

Seen by the Soviets as the greatest reward of the war and jewel of their
empire in 1944–45, Poland turned out to be a perennial imperial trouble

spot. Allied to the British in 1939, but liberated by the Soviets in 1944, the country's population was perhaps most actively antagonistic to the postwar arrangements. Poland was also the largest of the Soviet satellites, and the hostile attitude of its population forced even Stalin to grant it a number of concessions. In 1947, Stalin impulsively removed Wladyslaw Gomulka from the leadership of the Polish party because he advised going slow in implementing the imperial political design, in the years after his purge, but Gomulka's successors, and their Soviet patrons, showed more circumspection in their policies toward the Church, the peasantry, and the intelligentsia than was the standard in the other countries of the Bloc.

These issues of strategy split the Polish party, not only between Muscovites and nativists, but also between the "liberal" Pulawy and hard-line, but nationalist, Natolin (later Partisan) factions. These splits came into the open as early as 1954 and created an image of internal party division and political indecision among a generally hostile population. This hostility became manifest in June 1956, when violent mobs lynched security policemen in Poznan, and in October that year hundreds of thousands demonstrated on the streets of Warsaw demanding radical political change and the rehabilitation of Gomulka, by then a prominent symbol of resistance to the Stalinist regime.

Flying to Poland, Khrushchev and several members of the Soviet Politburo made the decision to compromise, mainly because the simultaneously unfolding demonstrations in Budapest had already gotten out of hand. Gomulka was restored to lead the party and, for the moment, the flaunting of national symbols and the rise of an uncensored press were tolerated to ward off massive violence. Much of this was meant only for show, but the compromise set a pattern for Polish politics that was to mark the next thirty years: an emboldened population would rise time and again to take the country to the brink of civil war, and a diffident party would each time back off at the last minute, not having the stomach for major repressive measures. Poland henceforth became the Bloc's least stable member, its history punctuated by popular protest and political crises.[94]

Although perceived as a national hero in 1956, Gomulka was just another member of the apparat who had fallen victim to the whims of the purges. This became clear in 1957, when, after effecting some cosmetic changes in the electoral system—Poles were allowed to cross out the names of candidates from the single list, which now included a handful of Catholic candidates[95]—and consenting to the dissolution of the still embryonic system of collective farms, Gomulka began to restore the lost political supremacy of the party over economy and society. He followed up the dissolution of

94. For a good summary of these crises, see Grzegorz Ekiert 1997, 299–338.
95. For more, see Olson and Simon 1982, 47–84.

TABLE 42

Comparative Economic Growth Rates: CMEA Countries
of East Central Europe, 1960–88

	1960–65	1965–70	1971–80	1981–88
Bulgaria	6.4	5.1	2.8	1.2
Czechoslovakia	2.4	3.4	2.8	1.4
East Germany	2.9	3.1	2.8	1.8
Hungary	3.9	3.0	2.6	1.0
Poland	4.5	4.0	3.6	0.8
Romania	5.4	4.9	5.3	−0.1

SOURCES: Gordon et al. 1987, 331; Kornai 1992, 200.
NOTE: Adjusted official statistics.

collective farms with a string of restrictive regulations that made the concept of property-holding purely illusory, then reined in the intelligentsia by banning its most vocal mouthpieces, the Crooked Circle Club and the newspaper *Po Prostu*. Within the party, he gradually eliminated the liberals from the leadership, but compromised with the hard-line, nationalist Partisans, now led by the politically astute General Mieczyslaw Moczar. Indeed, less by design than by default, these forces acquired increasing influence in Polish politics, and played an important role both in putting down student unrest and in purging university faculties of Jewish professors in March 1968.[96]

But the Church was hard to rein in, and the economy was ailing. As in all other countries, growth rates continued to be adequate (see Table 42), but these did not translate into private consumption and popular welfare. In 1968, Poland was the fifth-largest manufacturer of railroad cars in the world, seventh in shipbuilding and in zinc and sulphur production, ninth in heavy chemicals, and tenth in the production of steel.[97] The problem was not the rate, but the nature of growth in the industrial sector, where the Gomulka government followed essentially Stalinist priorities. The regime itself made no secret of the fact that, by 1968, "the economic situation verged on crisis,"[98] but seemed unable to change either the economy's structure or its priorities. The Stalinist model dictated austerity in times of economic stringencies, and the Gomulka regime followed this model by introducing a series of ill-timed increases in the price of consumer products, including staples, in December 1970.[99] This last attempt at austerity provoked uprisings in the major industrial centers. The party was not ready for this turn of events and, with the blessing of the Soviet Union, an emergency meeting of its Central Committee dismissed Gomulka and elected Edward Gierek, a man of technocratic credentials, to succeed him as First Secretary.

96. Gibney 1959, 56–122; Brown 1966, 50–64; Brown 1989, 160–66.
97. Ptakowski 1968, 6.
98. Ibid., 7.
99. On the movement of real wages in Poland, see Harmon 1974, 245.

Although the option of structural reform had been discussed on numerous occasions, market elements were not introduced into the Polish economy, perhaps following the advice of the Soviet leadership, who had just scrapped such reforms in Czechoslovakia and were anxiously watching developments in Hungary. Instead, Gierek experimented with a design to rationalize and decentralize the economy by transferring planning and supervisory functions from the ministries to large combinations of industrial enterprises, a model that was to show up soon thereafter in neighboring East Germany as well. But now, in the shadow of popular revolution, Gierek finally changed the priorities of the economy and embarked on a "consumer trend," hoping that such a course might also, by increasing the standard of living, increase the morale and the productivity of the labor force.[100] In this endeavor, Gierek was helped by a number of fortuitous developments. First, as a net exporter of energy and raw materials, Poland benefited from the sudden rise in world prices of these types of commodities in 1972–73. Then, as the sudden and substantial profits of the oil-producing countries found their way into the world financial system, they created a glut of money, which became available for borrowing at low interest rates. At this moment, Polish economic planners decided to hitch a ride on the "magic carpet of foreign borrowing"[101] and thereby traveled down the ultimately disastrous road of trying to stimulate both consumption and investment.[102] Ever in pursuit of his design of creating a more cooperative labor force—and in response to the popular East European motto "We'll start to work when they start to pay us"—Gierek vastly increased subsidies to agriculture and food imports, while allowing wage increases to run ahead of increases in productivity.[103] In the process, "the effort-reward equation was lost in a morass of thirteenth- and fourteenth-month bonuses."[104] While real wages increased 40 percent over a three-year period (1973–75),[105] foreign hard-currency indebtedness increased from $1.1 billion to $11.5 billion (see Table 43).

Disconcertingly for Gierek and his economists, however, this short-term borrowing did not change either labor morale or productivity. Some of the short-term loans were due, and the Polish economy had generated little capacity for repayment. The growing imbalance put Gierek under pressure to rein in the economy, but when he tried to do so by means of another series of price increases, the second best fed population of Europe (at 3,656 calories per capita per diem)[106] rioted again on a massive scale. Shots were fired

100. Gamarnikow 1972, 20–30.
101. Brown 1989, 178.
102. Tyson 1981, 122.
103. Kolankiewicz 1981, 140. See also Gitelman 1981, 147.
104. Kolankiewicz 1981, 141.
105. Gati and Triska 1981, 229.
106. Taylor and Jodice 1983, 1: 142, table 4.4.

TABLE 43

Hard-Currency Indebtedness in East Central Europe, 1971–89

(billions of US dollars)

	Bulgaria	Czecho-slovakia	GDR	Hungary	Poland	Romania	Yugoslavia
1971	0.7	0.5	1.4	1.1	1.1	1.2	—
1975	2.6	1.1	5.2	3.1	8.0	2.9	—
1976	3.2	1.9	5.9	4.1	11.5	2.0	—
1977	3.7	2.6	7.1	5.7	14.0	3.6	8.4
1978	4.3	3.2	8.9	7.5	17.8	5.2	10.7
1979	4.4	4.1	10.9	8.5	22.7	7.0	13.5
1980	3.5	4.9	14.4	9.1	25.1	9.4	17.4
1981	3.1	4.4	14.7	8.7	25.5	10.2	19.0
1982	2.8	4.0	13.1	7.7	25.2	9.8	18.5
1983	2.5	3.5	12.3	8.3	26.4	8.9	18.9
1984	2.6	4.5	—	11.0	21.1	7.8	18.8
1985	3.8	4.6	—	14.0	33.3	7.0	18.4
1986	5.9	5.6	—	16.9	36.6	7.0	19.2
1987	8.3	6.7	—	19.6	42.6	6.6	20.5
1988	8.9	7.4	—	19.6	42.1	3.0	18.9
1989	10.1	8.0	—	20.4	43.1	1.1	17.3

SOURCES: Economist Intelligence Unit 1985, 16, cited in Brown 1989, 507; World Bank 1997a; 1997b. For Yugoslavia, 1984–89: Vienna Institute 1991, 391.

but, as before, the government felt compelled to retreat. Growth rates were now plummeting from the 9.8 percent average of 1971–75 to a mere 1.2 percent per annum over the next five years. Incredibly, in retrospect, foreign bankers continued to keep the ailing economy afloat, pouring in more funds, which further raised the country's foreign indebtedness to $22.7 billion.

The day of reckoning could only be postponed, not avoided. Pressured by simple arithmetic and the inevitability of default, Gierek tried once again to clamp down on runaway spending by raising prices in August 1980. In response, the population not merely rose up against the regime but turned itself into an organized political force. Solidarity emerged and within days had a nationwide membership of eight million, clamoring for recognition as a political as well as an economic entity. As a trade union, Solidarity pressed for further wage concessions; as a political organization, it demanded more: effective power-sharing with the demoralized party and its dwindling membership.[107] These demands pushed the party state ever closer to breaking the injunctions of the Brezhnev doctrine. Pressures for intervention were building in the neighboring countries, and the Soviet Union seemed poised to make the move. It was under these circumstances that martial law was declared on December 13, 1981, by General Wojciech Jaruzelski, Poland's minister of defense.[108] He has been denounced as a traitor by his countrymen,

107. See Weydenthal 1981, 1–14.
108. Weydenthal 1982, 1–11.

but Jaruzelski's defense is that foreign intervention would have resulted in full-fledged war in Poland, and that such a war would have been a grave threat to European peace.

Jaruzelski was surprisingly successful in executing his military maneuver—Solidarity collapsed in the face of the army, and its leaders were easily rounded up by the police—but the larger political objectives of the coup remained elusive. More recalcitrant than ever, the labor force refused to cooperate in raising productivity, and, hesitant to use truly brutal measures, Jaruzelski was also hamstrung by the larger international environment in which he had to operate. East-West relations, both economic and political, now imposed considerable restraint on the Soviet Union. Jaruzelski was thus able to use enough violence to alienate his countrymen further, but not enough to project an overwhelming determination to repress. Special police forces lashed out against illegal demonstrators, and serious acts of terror were perpetrated by anonymous "thugs," or security policemen disguised as civilians. Lech Wałesa, the moving spirit of Solidarity, was now arrested, now released, and sometimes just driven around in a car to slow down his political activities.[109] Truly effective repression is incompatible with such displays of reticence, however. The Polish economy drifted on, with its restructured debt reaching $30 billion by the end of the decade. Eventually, Jaruzelski had to release the leaders of Solidarity to negotiate the regime's final surrender.

Hungary

Unlike Poland, Hungary had experienced a particularly harsh bout with Stalinism under Mátyás Rákosi, the country's Moscovite leader. The post-Stalin turmoil (1953–56) divided the party, and Khrushchev's revelations at the Twentieth Congress of his party triggered a genuine crisis, climaxing in the uprising of October–November 1956. After an initial, and somewhat restrained, intervention by local Soviet troops, Imre Nagy, leader of the reformist communists, formed a new government. He restored the multiparty system, promised free elections, and then, in an attempt to avert a second intervention, withdrew his country from the Warsaw Treaty Organization. But instead of accomplishing their objectives, Nagy's moves unleashed a full-scale attack by a large contingent of Soviet troops on November 4, 1956. The Soviet Union then set up a "revolutionary workers' and peasants'" regime headed by János Kádár, a former purge victim and apparent Nagy ally, who was either quickly persuaded or coerced to serve as Soviet advance man.[110]

109. *Radio Free Europe Research*, Poland, Feb. 21, 1985.
110. For Kádár's biography and the circumstances of his pro-Soviet conversion, see Tőkés 1996, 17–24.

As a popular and allegorical musical about the first king of Hungary (*István a király*) suggested thirty years later, Kádár may have abhorred the task, but found it historically inevitable. In any case, he presided over a particularly brutal and thorough campaign of repression, culminating in the execution of Imre Nagy in June 1958. The bloody work of repression having been accomplished, however, Kádár surprised the world and his own countrymen by changing course in 1962. He released most of the survivors of repression from jail, embraced some of the most rebellious writers, and announced a new program. Unlike Tito's, this one was not embedded in a complex doctrinal framework. It could be reduced to a few sentences that occasionally turned up unannounced in Kádár's public speeches. The most memorable of these was the declaration "He who is not against us is with us," a stunning reversal of the Stalinist principle condemning political apathy and neutrality. Yet another fragment of Kádárian wisdom, echoed and popularized by Khrushchev on one of his visits to Hungary, was that "goulash" and a full stomach were integral elements of socialism.[111] The affectionate designation of "goulash communism" then came to be used in sharp contrast to the earlier, negative connotations of "frigidaire socialism."[112] None of this was empty rhetoric. While the first principle would usher in the same "liberalization" or deregimentation that Yugoslavia was experiencing —the relaxation of censorship, the lifting of the ban on Western travel, the opening up of the country to Western tourism and cultural influence, and, overall, the ending of the party-state's interference in people's daily lives— the second maxim signaled that "consumption was not only a tactic to which one resorted out of weakness," but the fundamental purpose of Kádár's political system.[113] With a single bon mot, Kádár had elevated consumer satisfaction via economic development into the main legitimating formula of his regime.

Although real wages in Hungary were boosted in the immediate post-revolutionary period, mainly through a massive infusion of Soviet aid to hasten pacification, Kádár and his associates realized that a rigidly centralized Stalinist planned economy was an unlikely means to achieve a high-consumption society. There were thus protracted discussions from 1962 onward about the best ways of reforming the economy without incurring the hostility of the Soviet Union.[114] At various stages of these discussions, aspects of the Yugoslav model were discreetly scrutinized, but the New Economic Model (NEM) accepted by the Hungarian Central Committee in 1966 (to take effect as of January 1, 1968) turned out to be far more modest than the original design. Social ownership and workers' councils were anathema

---

111. Showcross 1974, 105. Also, "Interview with Giuseppe Boffa," in Kádár 1971, 144.
112. For the latter, see Berend 1983, 193–94.
113. Gitelman 1981, 138.
114. Berend 1983, esp. 193–218. See also Tőkés 1996, 95–96.

to both the Soviet Union and domestic conservatives, so the reformers had to be content with decentralizing economic decision-making without granting enterprises full autonomy. On the one hand, enterprises were granted a number of new powers; on the other hand, the managers continued to be appointed by the ministries and to report to them. Nor were the production units made truly responsive to the laws of supply and demand. For while profitability was to become the guiding principle of economic activities, and while production units were liberated from rigid directives by the Central Planning Office, they were hemmed in by regulations, price guidelines, and a multiplicity of exchange rates and taxes, as well as by a much touted "full employment constraint" that made the restructuring of the labor force exceedingly cumbersome.[115] To many economists, the reforms therefore did not so much restore the market as simulate it. But even these reforms were deemed to be too radical by Moscow and by domestic conservatives, both fearful of the effects of decentralization on political control and the principle of relative wage equality. Thus, after several intraparty skirmishes, in November 1972 the economy was revamped again: wage differentials among enterprises were reduced, free-wheeling entrepreneurs were reined in, and wage raises were decoupled from both profitability and productivity.[116] For the next ten years, as two unusually bold studies of the Finance Research Institute (PKK) demonstrated in 1984, the large fund established to support the competitiveness of Hungarian commodities in hard-currency markets was systematically diverted to subsidize wages in large and politically strategic, but totally unprofitable, heavy industrial enterprises.[117] The conservatives were unrepentant about this sabotage of profitability. Rudolf Tőkés quotes one of their leaders as saying in 1992: "To have a profitable enterprise with pay hikes alongside a state subsidized loss maker with no pay rise was unacceptable."[118] The real "miracle" of the Hungarian economy (often attributed to the NEM by a generally admiring Western press and academic community) was that the Hungarian population had, in spite of all the constraints, experienced fifteen years of prosperity and increases, however haphazard, in personal consumption.

That success may be explained by three factors. First, even before the inauguration of the NEM, Kádárism switched investment priorities from the military industrial complex to consumer industries. Second, the policies of reform did spawn a spirit of entrepreneurship in the services sector.[119] Third, the regime's, or at least the reformers', interest in agriculture paid off. Both

115. See Marer 1987, 278.
116. Tőkés 1996, 106.
117. Csanádi 1980, esp. 53; id. 1984, esp. 16, 157.
118. Tőkés 1996, 106.
119. By the late 1970s, 50 percent of services were provided by this sector, according to Gábor and Galasi 1981, 47–49.

collective farms and private plots flourished—often through producers' collusion with, and bribery of, local officialdom—despite efforts to divert their income.[120] Amazingly, perhaps, the collective farms made the small country the world's fifth-largest exporter of grain (mostly to the CMEA countries), while the private plots, providing 36 percent of the total agricultural product, filled grocery shelves with commodities and made Hungary the only country in the Bloc without food shortages.[121] As a result, by 1970, per capita earnings in agriculture exceeded those in industry by 7 percent, a deviation from normal patterns of income distribution and a huge change from the interwar period.[122] But, once again, a major part of the boomlet in consumption came via borrowing from gullible bankers in the glutted world financial markets. As elsewhere in East Central Europe, that borrowing began in moderation. In 1971, the country's foreign debt was a mere $1.1 billion. But by the end of the decade, the debt had risen to $9.1 billion (see Table 43), matching the Polish level in per capita terms. And just as elsewhere, the temptation was irresistible to use part of these funds as direct subsidies to consumption in order to boost political morale. Indeed, a confidential document of the Party Central Committee's Social Science Institute (TTI) in 1987 calculated that half of the hard-currency loans were spent on just such subsidies, and the other half for renewing largely antiquated technologies.[123] Kádár treated foreign borrowing largely as a technical matter for some time, but he suddenly became aware of its deep political implications in 1983.[124]

It was from this moment on that Hungary's economic crisis was officially recognized as such. Public signals were given, or permitted to be printed, in the news media,[125] and the decline in the standard of living was openly admitted in the party's own theoretical journal.[126] A public debate now began about the causes of the crisis. Some conservatives suggested that the crisis was not that of the "classical socialist" (meaning Soviet) model but of the "hybrid economy" created in the 1960s and 1970s.[127] Others lashed out against the "contradictions" between "the features of institutionalized protectionism, and the [economy's] avowed orientation toward the world economy."[128] The same writer blamed policies that "opened up the country to

120. Hare, Radice, and Swain 1981, 225–45.
121. Gábor and Galasi 1981, 48.
122. Elek 1981. Originally prepared for internal circulation only. Obtained courtesy of the Hungarian Political Science Association.
123. Huber 1987, 11. Archives of the Hungarian Political Science Association.
124. Interview with György Aczél, Sept. 20–22, 1991.
125. See Andics 1983, 1–10.
126. Szegő 1984, 66–82.
127. Szalai 1988, 50–65.
128. Salgó 1987, 7–9. Originally prepared for internal circulation only. Archives of the Hungarian Political Science Association.

foreign consumption patterns but not to foreign technology." [129] Another economist, Maria Huber, wrote angrily that the "glittering Hungarian standard of living that many [had] attributed to the copying of Western market elements was due to increased productivity only in exceptional cases. . . . If the growth rates of the 1950s were attained at the expense of agriculture, and those of the 1960s at the expense of infrastructure, the growth rates of the 1970s were essentially the products of foreign loans." [130] The debate's closure was provided by Kádár's own laconic observation: "This country has been consuming more than what it has produced over the years." [131] The crisis atmosphere of the 1980s also revived and intensified the debate about reform, which lasted until the ultimate collapse of the regime. A few new remedies were tried: some companies were given permission to trade directly with foreign customers without interference from the state monopoly of foreign trade; more private initiative was encouraged by legalizing producers' cooperatives; management positions were freed from the clutches of the nomenklatura and began to be allotted competitively; and groups of workers were allowed to form "work associations," free to contract with managers over and above customary, regulated wages. [132] None of these measures were sufficient to turn around an ailing economy, and the regime continued to the end to try to mitigate the political effects of adversity by foreign borrowing, raising Hungarian debt to $19.1 billion, the largest in per capita terms in the communist Bloc.

Romania

Although it had garnered an impressive record of terror during the Stalinist period, the Romanian Communist Party was among the weakest in East Central Europe. [133] It had little support from the population and was especially unpopular among the Romanian ethnic majority, whose members were historically suspicious of things Russian. For several years even the leadership of the party was in doubt, until Gheorghe Gheorghiu-Dej took advantage of the anti-Zionist mood in 1952 to liquidate a number of powerful Jewish communists—Iosif Chişinevsky, Vasile Luca, and Ana Pauker—then used the post-Stalin confusion in Moscow to purge Lucreţiu Pătrăşcanu, his main "nativist" rival, while he himself maneuvered back and forth between the offices of prime minister and general secretary.

Gheorghiu-Dej was an uneducated man with a rather narrow intellectual

129. Ibid.
130. Huber 1987, 16.
131. *Magyar Nemzet*, May 9, 1987, 1. Quoted also by Huber 1987, 15.
132. Comisso and Marer 1986, 273–77.
133. King 1980, 18–19; Shafir 1985, 27; Verdery 1991, 103.

horizon. This did not, however, prevent him from outwitting both domestic rivals and, later, Soviet patrons, nor did it keep him from concluding intuitively that communism with its paternalistic-communal facets might resonate better with Romanian culture (itself steeped deep in the *sabornost'* of Eastern Orthodoxy) if only it were stripped of its close association with the Soviet Union and Russia. Thus after sufficiently ingratiating himself with Moscow through loyalty demonstrated during the Hungarian revolution— he served as the jailer of the Hungarian Nagy and his associates in 1957– 58—he managed to persuade the Soviet Union to withdraw its troops from Romania. Shortly thereafter, he began to assert independence from Moscow, mainly in order to win popular legitimacy for his unpopular party. The steps he took, although minor and purely symbolic at first, were apparently understood by Romanians. He began with gestures that would seem pathetically trivial to the outside observer: he abandoned the recently slavicized spelling of the name of the country (although he changed no other analogous terms in the vocabulary), changing it from Romînia to Românâ; released from jail a number of old school, nationalist historians; and ordered his UN delegation to abstain from voting in unison with the Soviet Bloc on some thoroughly inconsequential issues. He then turned to a matter of greater substance, balking at the Soviet plan for a new division of labor within the Bloc that paid insufficient attention to Romanian industrialization.

Gheorghe Gheorghiu-Dej died a natural death in 1964, and his successor, Nicolae Ceauşescu, broadened his predecessor's policies. In domestic affairs, Ceauşescu liquidated the last vestiges of autonomy that had been granted, at Soviet insistence, to the country's Hungarian minority, and pursued a broader cultural policy that gave the party a new patriotic image and a specifically Romanian character (while carefully observing the principle of proportionality in his communist-style parliament and even in his Central Committee). In foreign affairs, he began to cultivate ties with the Chinese and to act as an intermediary between the two great powers of world communism. At the same time, he broadened relations with countries outside the Bloc. In 1967, he initiated diplomatic relations with the Federal Republic of Germany without first soliciting Soviet approval. The same year, he refused to break off diplomatic relations with Israel when all other communist nations did so in the wake of the Six-Day War. Still more consequentially, he refused to join the other members of the Warsaw Treaty Organization in the invasion of Czechoslovakia, and at home made conspicuous preparations for defending the country should the Soviet Union mount an invasion meant to discipline its refractory ally. The mass rally that he called to announce his intention to do so was unquestionably the high point both of his own political career and of the popularity of the communist regime.

The Soviet invasion did not come, and the Romanian party was now in a position to use its accumulated political capital to solve the economic problems of the country. As a legacy of the early modern period, Romanians remained obsessed with their country's economic backwardness and convinced that an aggressive policy of industrialization was the way out. Already under Gheorghiu-Dej, they had reasserted their earlier convictions by refusing the Soviet design, which had envisaged a brighter Romanian future through the modernization of agriculture and the building of extractive and agricultural processing industries. Ceauşescu and his principal planners had a more ambitious plan of combining machine building with petrochemical and extractive industries, largely aimed at exports, which they saw as the key to creating higher per capita incomes and productivity.[134] In this sense, the Ceauşescu design deviated, not only from the Stalinist objective of creating defense-oriented heavy industries, but also from the import-substitution models preferred by various neoliberal and cryptofascist governments of the interwar period. But while Ceauşescu was ready to pursue essentially export- and consumer-oriented ends, the fatal flaw in his thinking was that he wanted to accomplish these ends by retaining the key economic features of the Stalinist economy, including heavily centralized planning and a policy of generating investment capital by draining surplus from the desperately underdeveloped Romanian countryside. The ends may have been those of Adam Smith, but the means were those of Stalin and Preobrazhensky, a mismatch of monumental proportions that explains the unusually disastrous course of subsequent Romanian developments.

The consequences of this mismatch—above all, the strain that centralized management and wage egalitarianism put on the efficiency of responding to signals from external markets—were already evident in the 1960s and, together with the classical model of mobilization, reversed an incipient trend toward liberalizing. To be sure, at this early date, Ceauşescu still had the option, and enough political capital, to experiment with some version of the Yugoslav and Czechoslovak designs. But if he ever seriously considered doing so, he definitively rejected the idea in the summer of 1971, announcing instead his own version of a Maoist Cultural Revolution.[135] The main impulse for the decision is said to have come from personal experiences during a recent trip to China, although there can be little doubt that it was also shaped by his personal proclivities, which were decidedly populist in character. True, unlike the Romanian populists of earlier days, Ceauşescu exalted in the images of industrialism and technology. But, much like many non-Romanian *völkisch* thinkers, he conceived of these categories in terms of the peasant household, which remained his model for organizing economy, society, and polity throughout the rest of his life. Without being

<hr>

134. See King and Brown 1977, 201; Tsantis and Pepper 1979, 25–32, 109–31, 191–225.
135. *Scînteia*, July 7 and July 9, 1971.

fully conscious of it, in this respect Ceauşescu was more like a German National Socialist than a dyed-in-the-wool Marxist. While envisaging a landscape of cities with factories, apartment complexes, and paved streets, he believed that their denizens and workers would retain some of the wholesome characteristics of traditional rural communities. He readily acknowledged that modern industrial societies were "complex" (he did so no fewer than fourteen times at the Twelfth Congress of the Romanian Communist Party)[136] because they consisted of a number of different entities performing different tasks, but beyond this admission, there lurked the notion that, with all the differences among them, each of the entities would respond, much like the members of the peasant household, to the same central will and the same set of relatively simple rules.

This view of complexity obviated the need for subsystem autonomy and justified a system of vertical integration. The cardinal rules that guided the system were parsimony and hard work, rooted in the belief that reduction of consumption and greater expenditure of effort were the way to go about solving economic problems. Whenever a bottleneck developed in the system of production, workers were mobilized to spend longer hours at their appointed tasks, whether laying bricks or planning nuclear reactors. The task of the specialist was not to analyze but to solve problems as they arose: economists should not write essays on the nature of the international credit system but accumulate capital; veterinary scientists should not discuss why cows were dying but prevent the spread of disease among them; biologists "should not explore the 'secrets of life' but should preoccupy themselves with improving life by transforming our environment."[137]

These views were only part of a larger picture of populist neotraditionalism. If in economics the household model implied communalism and voluntarism—or, one might say, the decommodification of labor—in politics it signified a system in which the authority of the head of the household was diffuse, benevolently meddling, and supreme. Like all communist cadres of his generation, Ceauşescu had been raised politically on the images of leadership projected by Stalin. These images are obvious in the style that Ceauşescu adopted, although they were softened and modified by more direct influences of Byzantine rulership and the Orthodox ideal of the ruler as a sacrificial figure carrying on his shoulders all the burdens of the community. All of this, of course, was mixed haphazardly with impressions of twentieth-century life. The visual representations of his authority—the staples of the daily issues of *Scînteia*, the party paper, from the late 1960s until Ceauşescu's demise, and of the various collages and other "homages" given him on his

---

136. See Romania, Communist Party of, 1981.
137. Romania, Communist Party of, 1974, 75–76. See also Romania, Communist Party of, 1972, 93–116.

birthdays,[138] show a ruler surrounded by peasants presenting him with the traditional symbols of deference, a gift of salt and bread. The representations are those of a leader at work and at play. At times, they show him lost in deep thought in Stalinesque mold; at others, he is depicted inspecting mine shafts and dairy farms, accompanied by his faithful wife Elena, who, as empress, is a power unto herself, except for her subjection to the supreme ruler. The scientific element, so important in Stalin's and Mao's charisma, is not absent. But whereas Nicolae Ceauşescu was presented as a natural-born genius, the formal attributes of scientific thinking were vested in his wife, who, without genuinely earning the titles, was ritualistically referred to as "academician, doctor, engineer [inginer]"—"Adie" in the language of the disrespectful.

These homages display a surprising degree of philistinism: the nouveau riche's idea of style, a blend of Stalinist meshchanstvo and American middle-class proprieties of the 1950s. Adie is striking coy in girlish poses playing with the family dog or hovering over her children. Dad sits at his neo-baroque desk or shows off his latest hunting trophy. Their opulent-looking children are always smiling and well behaved. As a practical matter, the household model was also applied to staffing the key offices of the state. Over the years, Elena had clearly emerged as Number Two, and Nicu, a dissolute young man of loutish predispositions, had been groomed to take his father's place. But the household did not stop there. It was extended to the rest of the state apparatus through the recruitment of as many as two dozen members of the Ceauşescu and Petrescu clans into the political and administrative elite.[139]

A third, and perhaps most conspicuous, dimension of Ceauşescuism concerned the reevaluation of the concepts of ethnicity and nation-state.[140] Whereas Soviet Marxism recognized the political relevance of the concept of ethnicity, it was not seen as the final and supreme demarcator of sovereign political units. Although Romanian leaders adhered to this principle during the Stalin years, it was formally rejected after the rise of Ceauşescu to his position of national leadership. For Ceauşescu, the nation-state was an ethnically defined unit that had a historical mission to perform, the mission of building socialism. The closer the political community conformed to the ethnic one, the better the former could perform its historical task. The differences between these two views are obvious, and they emerge most

138. Perhaps the most lavish of these is the photo collage presented to him by the writers' union on his sixtieth birthday. See Omagiu preşedintelui Nicolae Ceauşescu (1978). See also King 1973b; Maier 1980.

139. For a list of those related to Ceauşescu or his wife, see "Ceauşescu Bestows More Honors on Members of His Family, Radio Free Europe Research, Romania, June 7, 1983; Shafir 1985, 76–77.

140. For a general discussion, see Fischer 1982.

clearly through comparisons of Romanian history textbooks written in the 1950s[141] and 1970s.[142] In the former, history is a struggle of antagonistic classes and the precommunist Romanian state is described as "national-ist," "bourgeois-capitalist," and even "imperialist."[143] In the latter, history is a struggle for national unification fought by Romanians against Romans, Hungarians, Ottomans, and Habsburgs. It is true that, except for the mori-bund years of the regime, these books were devoid of crude, traditional national stereotypes. But the reference to "our ancestors the Dacians"[144] hardly applied to Jews, Hungarians, or Germans. And if such were not suf-ficient hints, Ceauşescu himself made the ethnic hierarchy among the citi-zenry crystal clear. "The coinhabiting nationalities," he asserted in one of his many speeches, "did not bring with them a superior civilization . . . they found such a civilization here when they came, and assimilated it."[145] Whether or not such statements were valid or simply offensive, they provided the rationale for pursuing the goal of a homogeneous national state. As part of the plan, the Jews of Romania were discreetly let go in order to buy Ameri-can and Israeli goodwill, Germans were sold at prices constantly renegoti-ated upward, and the Hungarians of Romania, who could neither be sold nor expelled, were subject to a quiet policy of assimilation, which sought to shift the population from region to region mainly via the economy.

Some of these principles and practices rooted in the image of the house-hold did not bode well for the efficient operation of an economy designed to be export-oriented and competitive in capitalist markets. Always achieved under severe restraints on domestic consumption, the proudly announced official growth rates, 6.7 percent per annum for 1970–75,[146] or even their scaled-down Western variants (see Table 42), had no practical meaning for the average Romanian. But after 1976 (celebrated as its banner year), "the Romanian economy began to exhibit the traditional characteristics of short-age associated with excessive investment drives, including disruptions in raw material and fuel supplies, a sharp increase in the number . . . of incomplete projects and shortages in consumer markets."[147] In Marvin Jackson's cal-culations, the Romanian economy suffered a loss of $630 million in earth-quake damages in 1977, and $373 million on account of bad weather.[148] There were also losses on account of miscalculations of the country's oil re-serves. In a single year, Romania lost $1.2 billion because of price increases

141. See, for instance, Roller 1952.
142. For example, Florea and Ionescu 1971; Constantinescu 1976.
143. Roller 1952, 519.
144. Almaş and Fotescu 1971, 22.
145. "Cuvîntarea la confătuirea cadrelor din domeniul ştiinţelor sociale" (words spoken at the meeting of cadres in the social sciences), in Ceauşescu 1977, 484.
146. J. Brown 1988, 504.
147. Tyson 1984, 85–86.
148. M. Jackson 1986, 506.

for imported oil, and $200 million owing to a simultaneous fall in the prices of petrochemicals and artificial fertilizers.[149] But some of the underlying policies—including the idea of overexpanding the capacity of Romanian refineries, and investment in finished petroleum products—were the brainchildren of Ceauşescu and sycophantic economists like Manea Manescu and Emilian Dobrescu,[150] while catastrophic shortfalls in the production of oil and coal were part and parcel of the inefficiencies of institutional arrangements reflecting their populist utopianism and political rigidity.[151]

Initially restrained by populist aversions to foreign capital, after 1976, the Ceauşescu regime, too, succumbed to the temptations of borrowing easy money. As Table 43 shows, by 1981 it had accumulated $10.2 billion in foreign debt, or $423 per capita.[152] Although the latter figure compares favorably with the debt of Yugoslavia, Hungary, and Poland (with U.S.$752, $616, and $627 per head, respectively, in 1980), it was a large amount in a country where per capita income was only $1,550 in 1980, or less than half of Hungary's, and a mere 14 percent of that of the United States.[153] Indeed, servicing this debt became a critical problem in 1980. A year later, following the example of Poland, Romania defaulted and asked to reschedule its debt. The default was personally humiliating for Ceauşescu, reactivating his populist aversions, and leading to his decision to retire half of the foreign debt in five years. With many of Romania's exports already being sold below market prices, the decision was to be another major drain on domestic consumption.

The economic history of the 1980s has been described as "overorganized chaos."[154] For all practical purposes, the Romanian economy was brought to its knees. Rationing of staples was reintroduced but proved inefficient; the transportation system ceased to function in the cities (causing millions of lost man-hours); gas and electricity remained available only sporadically.[155] The country's health system collapsed: common medications became unavailable, and in many hospitals, two patients had to share one bed.[156] In a truly Orwellian scheme, workers' wages were now tied to the factory's productivity, and all social service functions, including the responsibilities for food supply, were transferred from the state to local government.

Following the Maoist model of crisis management, people were nagged, then commanded, to work on Sundays and holidays. "We must be ready to

149. Ibid., 510.
150. Ibid., 512.
151. These shortfalls alone were in the amount of $1.14 billion. Ibid., 513.
152. Ibid., 494.
153. Marer 1985, 105.
154. Verdery 1991, 100.
155. Shafir 1985, 117–18.
156. D. Ionescu 1985.

collect the harvest," Ceauşescu exhorted his people. "Let nobody come with excuses, since we will not accept any [excuse] connected with the weather. In any circumstance, working day and night, with all the force that we have, the harvest must be gathered in a minimum time."[157] To give proper weight to these exhortations, the already powerful security apparatus penetrated society as never before through a huge network of informers, whose reports and complicity in oppression served as political assets of the regime. The intrusiveness of the regime and its attempts to regulate every aspect of human life reached new heights: in a desperate attempt to raise the falling birthrate, women of childbearing age were subjected to periodic examinations to prevent abortions; a huge plan was drawn up to move villagers to the cities in order to deprive them of the last elements of personal independence; and, at the height of economic crisis, a giant project was begun—and partly accomplished—to raze the old center of Bucharest and replace it with monumental structures celebrating the victory of socialism.[158]

Having lost much of his earlier support from the West, in 1984–85, Ceauşescu attempted to move closer to the Soviet Union.[159] The experiment, however, was short-lived. In 1985, Mikhail Gorbachev arrived on the scene and began to exhort the Romanians to change their ways. Meanwhile, pressures were mounting from the West, and Ceauşescu would soon lose access to American markets and financial aid. With few gambits still available to him, he now sought to conjure up the threat of Hungarian revisionism to whip up anti-minority sentiments.

Although Ceauşescu appeared supremely confident right to the end, he nonetheless fell in 1989 and was executed by firing squad along with his wife, leaving behind him not only a broken economy but a society in a shambles, facing a long struggle merely to reestablish its system of production and common sense of identity.

SOLIDARY STATES

Three states of East Central Europe remain to be discussed: East Germany (between 1949 and 1990, the German Democratic Republic), Czechoslovakia (in the period 1969–89), and Bulgaria. Applying the designation "solidary" to these states is justified because, for long stretches of time during their nearly half century of history in the Bloc, these countries were ruled by political regimes that hewed close to the Soviet model in both their internal and external affairs, and that were capable of enforcing their will

157. "Domestic Economy," *Radio Free Europe Research*, Romania, June 10, 1980.
158. Gilberg 1990, 61–79, esp. 66–68.
159. Shafir 1985, 189.

much of the time on reluctant, although ultimately submissive, populations. Accordingly, throughout much of the post-Stalin period, they practiced politics of the "hard-line," or conservative, variety, which implied strict controls over travel, information, and creative activity, as well a rather clear line of demarcation between parties and societies at large. For these reasons, the three countries scored lower than Poland, Yugoslavia, and Hungary on the "liberalization index" constructed by the American political scientists Jan Triska and Paul Johnson to measure "subsystem autonomy," freedom of political communication, travel, censorship, and, overall, the degree of political authoritarianism—although higher than Romania and Albania.[160]

In foreign affairs, meanwhile, the three countries remained reliable supporters of the Soviet geopolitical design (except for the brief intermezzo of the "Prague Spring" in 1968). Accordingly, the political elites of these three countries not only supported the Soviet challenge to the West but made it a pivotal part of their own raisons d'être and identities. Thus, unlike the other satellite governments, those of East Germany, post-1968 Czechoslovakia, and Bulgaria were active participants in a variety of Soviet ventures outside the Bloc: the East Germans as military advisors and fighters in Angola, Ethiopia, Cuba, Mozambique, and Nicaragua; the Czechs as arms suppliers of revolutionary movements; and the Bulgarians as trainers of anti-Western terrorists, while also performing "wet jobs" for the Soviet KGB abroad—winning distinction for themselves with their famous poisoned umbrellas, as well as with their rather obvious part in the failed attempt to assassinate the pope. If only by relatively small margins, these countries were also the most loyal members of the imperial trading system of the CMEA (see Table 40), and kept their defense appropriations and spending above the East Central European average without much haggling over them (see Table 41). These acts of loyalty, and their material-logistic support to the common cause, did not go unnoticed in Moscow. When it came to the distribution of Soviet largesse in the form of indirect subsidies (Table 44), the three "solidary states" were on top of the list both in absolute and per capita terms.

There were, to be sure, some differences in political style, as well as in the actual scope and intrusiveness of public authority, among these three regimes, related mainly to differences in traditional political culture. But quite remarkably, notwithstanding significant disparities in terms of relative levels of economic development, the economic institutions of the three countries remained (except for plans hatched during the heady months of the Prague spring) quite similar over the years and closely wedded to the Soviet model. Although "reforms" were at times much touted in the public rhetoric of the

160. Triska and Johnson 1975, 255. The measurements having been taken in the late 1960s, the index for Czechoslovakia shows more "liberalism" than justified by post-1968 developments.

TABLE 44
*Net Cumulative Indirect Subsidies
from the USSR, 1971–78*

(in US dollars)

Country	Total (billions)	Per Capita
Bulgaria	$3.5	$390
GDR	4.8	290
Czechoslovakia	2.6	170
Hungary	1.0	100
Poland	2.1	60
Romania	−0.1	−0.5

SOURCE: Marer 1996, 56. Fuel and nonfood raw materials.
For higher estimates, see Marrese and Vanous 1983.

parties, they were generally designed to overhaul, rather than to abandon, central planning—seeking to make the economic process more "rational" and "scientific," and introducing individual economic incentives rather than making the system responsive to either real or simulated market signals.

East Germany

The territory of the future German Democratic Republic, Moscow's share of the defeated German Reich, was ravaged by the Soviet army and occupation authorities. Some 20–25 percent of the industrial capacity of the Soviet occupation zone was dismantled in the immediate postwar period, and an estimated 20–33 percent of its GDP was transferred to the USSR over a ten-year period (1945–55), amounting to about 3 percent of Soviet national income.[161] In the context of such policies, the building of a Soviet-style state and society was obviously off to an inauspicious start. The zone's population obviously resented these transfers and were ill disposed to forget the indignities suffered during the first years of occupation. From the very beginning, the demoralized population was acutely aware of the fact that wages were rising, and economic conditions improving, more rapidly in the Western sectors. Thus, from the very beginning, labor migration flowed from East to West, taking advantage of the open border between East and West Berlin. Moreover, this "hole in the Iron Curtain" had a psychological effect as well: those who stayed in East Germany were more insubordinate than the populations of other satellite countries, fortified by the knowledge that they were not completely at the mercy of their rulers. Further encouraged by the post-Stalin thaw, in June 1953, this insubordination exploded into open revolt, which could only be put down by Soviet tanks. But the hole remained open for another eight years, and by the time it was closed, with So-

161. Köhler 1965, 16–17; Marer 1996, 33.

viet blessings and support, in 1961, an estimated 3.7 to 4 million inhabitants of the GDR had fled to the West, half of them under the age of 25.[162]

Apart from stopping the flow of refugees and the relative indiscipline of the population, the erection of the Berlin Wall was important because it assured the leaders of the ruling Socialist Unity Party (SED) that they were now firmly implanted in the Bloc, and that their domain would not be used as a bargaining chip in international politics. At last, the building of state socialism could begin in earnest. The options were limited, however, not least because German history and nationalism provided little or nothing that the party could use to persuade the population that it was of their own flesh and blood, rather than an alien implant in German soil. The Soviet leaders were certainly wary of any attempt to link communism to the German past, and both Walter Ulbricht and Erich Honecker (together with most of their close associates) were part of a tightly knit old guard of proletarian internationalists to whom German nationalism had always been anathema.[163] The result was an awkward relationship between the party and its cultural and historical environment. As a result, the party struggled long and hard to create an East German collective identity. The first constitution of the GDR declared it to be the first socialist state on German soil, but the preamble was changed a few years later, characterizing the country as a "socialist state of workers and peasants . . . linked inseparably to the community of socialist states."[164] German history continued to be a thorny problem, at first resolved by relegating major figures like Luther, Frederick the Great, and Bismarck to subordinate clauses in a politically correct narrative about the development of the means of production, the impersonal forces of history, and the struggle among social classes.[165] It was only in the early 1980s that the regime decided to restore some dignity to German history and culture by rehabilitating previously condemned or ignored characters: Luther and Frederick the Great were now said to have hastened the demise of capitalism, while Bismarck was declared (by Politburo member Kurt Hager) to have been a "reactionary but a realist."[166] There was a tendency on the part of foreign observers to see this as a "sweeping claim to history"[167] and as a signal for the rise of a "red Prussia."[168] But the project of reclaiming the past was more an attempt to fill an absurd void in historic-cultural discourse than

162. Asmus 1981, 2. Also International Commission of Jurists 1962, 13.

163. Of 31 members of the Politburo and Secretariat featured in *Neues Deutschland* (June 27–28, 1981, 5), 23 were of worker origin, the majority prewar party members, and ten of them born before 1918. See also Bahro 1986, 73.

164. Asmus 1982, 3.

165. For a good example of this, see Bartel 1975.

166. Asmus 1983, 4; also Asmus 1980b.

167. Flaw 1984.

168. Boyse 1986, 5.

to seek a new framework of legitimation in the spirit of Romania's Ceau-şescu, or, as we shall see below, in the more muted ways of Bulgaria's Todor Zhivkov.

In principle, then, there remained the instrumentalities of raw coercion to consolidate the realm, and in the first years after the Wall was built, more people were sent to jail for political offenses in the GDR than in the rest of East Central Europe as a whole.[169] In the long run, however, this was in conflict with the imperatives of efficiency, particularly in a modern indus-trial society that was destined to be a center of high technology for the So-viet empire's military-industrial complex. Once consolidated, the Ulbricht regime therefore sought to balance coercion with economic benefits. At first, the design for doing so was distinctly Khrushchevian: SED leaders em-braced the goal of overtaking West Germany in economic development,[170] expressed in Ulbricht's ambiguous slogan of "overtaking without catching up" (*überholen ohne einzuholen*).[171] After Ulbricht's forced departure, the goal of overtaking the West was dropped, and while Honecker continued to promise rising living standards, the emphasis was increasingly on improve-ments in both quantity and quality of life—or the "integration of social and economic policy"—with quantum growth tied closely to the growth of pro-ductivity and discipline.[172]

But while consumerism—whether in the spirit of Khrushchev or of Brezh-nev—became an unmistakable aspect of East German politics, its preva-lence turned the regime into neither a technocracy nor a genuine consumer-oriented welfare regime of the Yugoslav, Polish, or Hungarian type. Unlike the Hungarian apparat and its members, who developed an identity and rai-son d'être from the belief that they would fulfill their mission by creating a consumer society, the East German apparat perceived consumerism as little more than a political bribe to keep the herd appeased. The real cohesion of the party elite came from the common geopolitical design with the Soviet Union, which SED leaders vowed to uphold and pursue with zeal.[173] As such, consumerism was a nuisance and a burden, a duty to be discharged in order that the elite could pursue its real purposes of building a high-tech economy for the imperial military-industrial machine and of fighting impe-rialism both in Europe and in the Third World. It is thus not hard to find evidence of chagrin among high functionaries about their tiresome duty to satisfy appetites—to get "politically sensitive goods" to the public on time,

169. Brown 1988, 235.
170. Gamarnikow 1966, 13–23.
171. Kopstein 1997, 65–66.
172. Baylis 1986, 212.
173. Interviews with R. B., Berlin (West), June 3, 1986; Dietrich D., Munich, June 28, 1986, and R. R., Munich, July 1–2, 1986.

to still its childish cravings for oranges and other fresh fruit during the holiday seasons,[174] so that the political class could get on with its more important task of building a new world without petty distractions from an untrustworthy populace.

There is, then, no doubt that the supply of consumer goods was a steady concern for the regime. But too much emphasis on consumerism could lead us to overlook the fact that the key aspect of the party's strategy for maintaining political stability was not to win the allegiance of the masses but to create a dedicated and militant combat elite. The term *Abgrenzung* has often been used to describe policies of ideological demarcation between East and West Germany, and it is equally applicable to the policy of demarcation between the East German masses and cadres. This was accomplished in part by a screening process that appears to have been more rigorous than in most other communist parties, and that made party membership, nomenklatura appointments, and promotions of all sorts conditional upon the performance of specific "combat tasks" (*Kampfaufgaben*). The process involved an ongoing process of testing the cadres' resolve, in order to weed out those who had "lost heart" or gotten "tired." These combat tasks included the ferreting out of unreliable colleagues, reporting on neighbors, "educating" the public by example, and harassing those who exhibited deviance from expected standards of behavior.[175] A good example of this was provided by the tale of a former waiter at one of East Germany's fancier restaurants. When interviewed in the West as a refugee, he revealed that his combat task had been to berate Westerners for lax manners and improper dress, so as to demonstrate that the East was not kowtowing to Western wealth and cosmopolitanism.[176]

An important part of this regimen of toughening up and weeding out were periodic call-ups to *Kampfgruppen* (combat groups) for two-week summer training periods. In these paramilitary groups, senior cadres and executives donned uniforms and were subjected to rigorous exercises of a military nature, in the course of which signs of slackness or lack of enthusiasm could result in dismissal or demotion upon their return to civilian ranks. Examples of these include a factory manager who was demoted for making disparaging remarks about the quality of food, and another for cursing while running uphill in full gear.[177] Functional equivalents of these *Kampfgruppen* existed, of course, in other East Central European countries. But when asked about their experiences with the Workers' Guard (*munkásör-*

174. See the exchanges between Erich Milke and Günter Schabowski in Milke and Schabowski, 1991, 144. See also Kopstein 1997, 190–91.

175. Interviews with Dr. Gernot Schneider, Hermann Raabe, Berlin (West), June 2–3, 1986, Munich, July 1–2, 1986.

176. Interview with R. R., Munich, July 1–2, 1986.

177. Ibid. Also interview with T. M., Berlin (West), June 8, 1986.

ség), Hungarian interviewees described their summer paramilitary service as a "lot of fooling around, boozing" and "an opportunity to get away from the wife and the job."[178] If "red Prussia" at the level of society existed mainly in the perfervid imagination of outside observers, the metaphor was valid at the level of an elite that cultivated the language of combat in common discourse and, collectively, was intent on projecting an image of extreme harshness. Nothing was more characteristic of this posture than the regime's open admission of, and frequent gloating over, the shooting and blowing up of people trying to escape through the Wall, or just "stupid enough" to take a wrong road or lane leading to the border of the two Germanies.[179] Apart from solidarity induced by common culpability—we may call this the "Stavrogin complex" after Dostoyevsky's hero who believed that nothing more firmly bonds six men together than their participation in the murder of a seventh—these attitudes underpinned the *Abgrenzung* of the elite from the common folk who, with good reason, were little trusted by the leadership.

In order to perform its dual tasks as provider of both guns and butter—high technology for the imperial military-industrial complex and consumer goods for a public never completely trusted—the East German elite needed a productive and sophisticated economy. Thus, in 1963, two years after the erection of the Wall, and still under Walter Ulbricht, the SED prepared the design for a New Economic System, the first one in the Soviet Bloc to envisage the decentralization of the economy.[180] But the design ran into stiff domestic opposition among leaders fearful of the political consequences of decentralizing economic production. It also touched a raw nerve in Moscow, ever fearful of political instability in this key and vulnerable member of the larger imperial family. The reform design therefore died before it was implemented, an apparent defeat for Ulbricht that may well have been one factor in his unceremonious dismissal several years later. In any case, both Ulbricht and his successor, Erich Honecker, remained steadfast within the parameters set by the Soviet leadership, and instead of a strategy of decentralization followed one of "plan improving and plan perfection." The implicit emphases here were upon scientific progress, the purchase of advanced technologies from the West, the more efficient use of machinery, the lowering of production costs, and an increasing range of product assortments, rather than any fundamental change of the economic mechanism itself.[181] To some contemporary observers, the scuttling of the reform seemed to doom

178. Interviews with Dénes Páli, Munich, June 27, 1986; and E. B., Budapest, July 8, 1986.

179. The ambassador of the GDR gave the latter explanation for the accidental shooting of an Italian truck driver at the East-West crossing point to American academics at the University of California, Berkeley, in the fall of 1978.

180. Bryson and Melzer 1991, 2.

181. Ibid., 4, 30.

hope of economic progress. But in the short run at least, the doomsayers were wrong, for the East German economy took off and, between 1962 and 1975, produced an economic miracle of sorts. By 1965, it had surged to overtake Czechoslovakia, becoming the Bloc's most productive and prosperous economy in per capita terms.[182] Indeed, albeit according to now widely suspect official figures, the GDR became the seventeenth most productive nation in the world (if we exclude a number of "new rich" oil-producing states of the Middle East from the list).[183]

While the upswing of the East German economy was directly related to the consolidation of the political system after 1961, in explaining it one cannot ignore the special relationship of its economy with the rest of Europe via West Germany. Owing to the early insistence of the German Federal Republic on the constitutional fiction of a single and undivided Germany, the GDR was a de facto associate member of the Common Market and, as such, the direct beneficiary of a common customs territory as well as indirect beneficiary of preferential treatment by West Germany.[184] Other direct benefits included a DM 800 million credit line from the federal government, loan guarantees of up to DM 1 billion (later 2.5 billion) per annum, and DM 525 million collected in tolls on the access routes to Berlin.[185] Further aid came in the form of government-inspired bank loans, ever-increasing private donations from Western relatives, and the infamous *Nasengeld*, or ransom collected in exchange for released political prisoners.[186]

And yet not all went well with the economy. Although surging ahead of its partners within the Bloc, even at its peak East Germany remained far behind the leading economies of Western Europe, of which it had at one time been a part. A few figures here may be instructive. In 1936, the part of the Reich that became the GDR in 1949—then regarded as "central" (*Mitteldeutschland*), rather than "eastern," Germany—had 28 percent of the population, 33 percent of the industrial capacity, and 30 percent of the national income of the interwar German Reich. From these figures, it has been calculated that the inhabitants of the region had per capita incomes 6.6 percent higher than the average German and 3 percent higher than those living in what would become the territory of the Federal Republic.[187] In 1936, this income structure represented about 82 percent of the average per capita income of the six most advanced industrial states of Europe,[188] and 59.6 per-

182. Shoup 1975, 10–11, tables 1–4.
183. Marer in Griffith 1989, 73.
184. For these, see Garland 1986, 173.
185. Donovan 1987, 11.
186. Asmus 1980a, 2. Asmus estimated the latter ransom fees to total DM 500 million over an 18-year period.
187. Bress 1982, 127.
188. Based on calculation by Clark 1940 for 1926–34.

cent of per capita GNP in the United States.[189] In 1980, according to some calculations, per capita GNP in the GDR was some 62–65 percent that of the six advanced industrial states of the European continent,[190] 45.9 percent that of the United States, and 64.4 percent that of the Federal Republic.[191] Per capita private consumption lagged further behind. Rationalized or not, therefore, the economy displayed some of the built-in deficiencies of centralized and militarized economies. By its very nature, it channeled too much labor and capital into the military sector, focused more on capital accumulation than on productive use of capital, and was sustained by an institutional structure that was biased against meeting the demand for both quality and quantity of a genuine consumer economy.

Economic production peaked in 1971–75. The 1976–80 plan was an outright failure.[192] Consistent with their militancy, the political leaders of the GDR responded defiantly, further raising the targets of the next five-year plan. The new targets would be achieved by acquiring costly new technologies from the West, financing the purchases through loans from Western (above all West German) banks. By the late 1970s, the GDR had already amassed $10.9 billion in foreign debt. In the first year of the new, aggressively targeted plan, foreign debt increased to $14.7 billion (see Table 43). Thereafter, foreign indebtedness leveled off, with the amounts borrowed giving the economy three relatively trouble-free years. But the improvement proved temporary, as did the restraint on foreign borrowing. After 1986, the economy was kept afloat in part by foreign funds, in part by tolerating the obsolescence of the industrial plant, along with its decreasing labor efficiency and productivity.[193] Thus, by 1987, the hard-currency debt of the GDR had reached DM 34.7 billion,[194] and by 1989, it was DM 46 billion (U.S.$27.5 billion at prevailing exchange rates).[195]

By this time, a number of East German planners, and indeed the new Soviet leadership, were counseling greater economic and political flexibility, as well as the needs for greater decentralization and for "addressing the human factor."[196] The fact of the matter was that the centralized economic model and the various attempts at perfecting it had been undertaken under Soviet auspices, and given their initial success (which the Soviet economy never duplicated), the leaders of the GDR naturally developed a reluctance

189. Marer in Griffith 1990, 72.
190. Marer 1985, 104–5.
191. Marer in Griffith 1990, 73.
192. Meher and Stahnke 1986, 131–33.
193. Janson 1991, 70–75.
194. Kopstein 1997, 65.
195. Ibid., 86–87.
196. Bryson and Melzer 1991, 2.

to change what had at one time worked well.[197] But the rate of growth was faltering, and popular frustrations with the quantity and quality of payoffs were increasing, reflected in repeated waves of emigration, or *Ausreisewellen*, in ever larger numbers of defectors via third countries, and in masses of applicants wishing to leave the country for the Federal Republic.[198] Ironically, compared with much of the world, and with the rest of East Europe, standards of living in East Germany remained high. But for the East Germans, the western half of their once-united country served as the principal, if not sole, yardstick of personal well-being.

However, through all the adversities, and through the embarrassment of human waves escaping from their imposed vision and imperial framework, the elite of East Germany held fast, showing no signs of wavering. As late as October 7, 1989, Honecker rebuffed Gorbachev's advice to soften up. A few days later, he issued an order to shoot at the demonstrating crowds— one that no doubt would have been carried out by his devoted security men. But Honecker was now betrayed by the very patrons he served. The Russian leaders' determination to abandon "international class struggle," and the challenge to the global status quo it implied, left the East German party without purpose and identity. A new group of leaders under Egon Krenz faced the regime's impending doom by bargaining to save what they could of their power, and later, of their personal wealth and freedom. The party itself remained loyal, even beyond the bitter end: 16 percent of the GDR's adult population were members, and the same percentage of votes continues to be cast in free elections for the Party of Democratic Socialism, in a gesture of unabashed nostalgia for the SED regime.[199]

Czechoslovakia

In the immediate postwar period, Czechoslovakia had a loyal Stalinist elite and a population that, if only passively, was supportive of the regime. Thus in the elections of 1946, the Czechoslovak Communist Party won 38 percent of the total vote—almost three times as much as the second party on the list—receiving 40 percent in the Czech lands and a somewhat less impressive 30 percent in Slovakia. The reasons for this surprisingly strong showing of the party were multifold: there was a deep sense of disappointment with the "West," whose major powers—England and France— had abandoned Czechoslovakia by signing the Munich accord of 1938 with

197. For this analysis of GDR anti-reformism in the Gorbachev era, see Bryson and Melzer 1991, 10–12.
198. Köhler and Runge 1984, 1280–86; Donovan 1988.
199. For the last weeks of the GDR, see Crawford 1996, 63–64; Naimark 1996, 72–96.

Hitler's Germany; there was the resentment generated by the experience of German occupation and "protectorate" during the war; and finally, there was the sense that the Soviet Union, rather than the West, was the best guarantor against German revanchism. The latter concern loomed especially large in Czech collective consciousness after the less than gentle expulsion of more than three million ethnic Germans from the Sudetenland and from the urban centers of Slovakia. In addition, the communist cause was aided by the surprising resilience of the Czechoslovak economy, which, notwithstanding "gigantomaniac" investment plans and the militarization of the industrial sector, continued to sustain a respectable standard of living, the highest in the Soviet Bloc (until overtaken by the GDR in the mid 1960s). Indeed, for some time after the war and into the immediate post-Stalin period, Czechoslovakia remained a kind of consumer paradise from which denizens of other Soviet Bloc countries would come away with shoes, shirts, raincoats, and nylon stockings generally unavailable in their own countries. Largely for these reasons, and apart from some labor unrest in Plzeň, the Czech working class remained quiescent during troubling times in adjacent Poland and Hungary in 1956.

By 1960, however, fears of German revanchism began to subside and, more or less simultaneously, the productivity of the much abused Czechoslovak economy began to decline. In 1962, a very severe winter resulted in serious food shortages, and, for the first time since the end of the war, the gross domestic product of the country declined.[200] The days of living off past assets were over.

Faced with economic adversity, the Czechoslovak party split into "liberal" and "conservative" factions, one pleading for reforms, the other staunchly defending the status quo. Despite efforts to avoid making it public, the debate spilled out into the open, and its terms were followed with considerable interest by the population, including both educated classes and industrial workers. In time, the narrowly framed technical issues concerning central planning turned into a much broader debate on the political leadership and institutions of the country. As they did so, the liberals appealed for public support in their struggle against the conservative first secretary of the party, Antonin Novotný. As it had done so often before, Moscow temporized. In October 1967, the personal intervention of Brezhnev is said to have saved Novotný from a vote of no confidence in the Czechoslovak Politburo.[201] But by December, the Czech public had become more restless, and in January 1968, with Moscow standing passively on the sidelines, the ple-

200. By some estimates as much as 11.3 percent from 1960 to 1963. See Kintner and Klaiber 1971, 273.
201. Ibid., 277.

nary session of the Central Committee of the Czechoslovak party ousted Novotný and replaced him with Alexander Dubček, a Slovak party official with
strong reformist inclinations.

The election of Dubček opened the floodgates to a public debate over
which the party could no longer exercise effective control. On March 5, trying to keep up with, or ahead of, public demands, the party's Politburo promised major changes: censorship was to be abolished; the National Assembly
was to be given new functions within new political parameters; political
prisoners were to be rehabilitated; and the long-debated New Economic
Mechanism (jointly prepared by Hungarian and Czechoslovak economists)
was to be put into effect on January 1, 1969. Moves were also made to fed-
eralize Czechoslovakia, and to turn its two parts—the Czech lands and
Slovakia—into federal republics endowed with considerable administrative
and budgetary autonomy.

While Dubček and his reformist colleagues resisted more radical demands for free elections and a multiparty system—advancing the awkward
promise that henceforth the party would not rule, but rather "continuously
earn its leading role by deeds,"[202] they were also busy preparing new party
statutes to be put before the party congress of September 1968. These draft
statutes would have done away with the Leninist principle of democratic
centralism, promised open, multicandidate elections for high party offices,
and allowed for the legalization of factions. Specifically, the Action Program
of the liberals envisaged a party in which "minorities [would] have the right
to formulate standpoints . . . to persist in their views, and to request repeated evaluations of their positions."[203]

The leaders of the Soviet Union and the other nations of the Bloc understood quite well that these provisions were not only anti-Leninist but a
design for a multiparty system in the guise of single-party rule. They also
saw Dubček rapidly losing ground to public demands, much as Nagy had
in Hungary twelve years before. There were fears, largely unfounded, of
Czechoslovakia leaving the Bloc, and of other parties' contamination by the
Czech virus of communist liberalism. Between May and August, the nations
of the Warsaw Pact met repeatedly to discuss the Czech developments and
to put pressure on Dubček and his colleagues. But these meetings, including the dramatic encounter of the Soviet and Czechoslovak Politburos at
Čierna, on the border of the two countries, failed to bring the recalcitrant
reformers to heel—in large part because, by now, they had become captives
of sweeping public expectations. It appears that shortly after the Čierna
meeting in early August, the Soviet leaders decided to intervene, inviting

202. Golan 1973, 134.
203. Ibid., 141.

their allies to join in the expedition. Except for Romania, the minor allies agreed, and on the night of August 20–21, 1968, Soviet forces invaded Czechoslovakia, joined by smaller contingents from the Hungarian, Polish, Bulgarian, and East German armies. On balance, this show of unity served Soviet public relations poorly, for it brought back memories of Germany, Hungary, and Poland dividing Czechoslovakia in 1938. In any case, the Poles and the Hungarians were unenthusiastic about the enterprise, and within a few days the satellite armies had been withdrawn to their own countries. The Soviet troops, of course, stayed on, in order to "normalize" political life in the country, essentially by returning it to the pre-1962 status quo. In this process, thousands were detained, 327,000 party members (a full one-third of the total membership) were expelled,[204] a large number of professionals were dismissed from their jobs, and an estimated 171,000 Czechoslovak citizens escaped to the West.[205] Dubček and some of his colleagues—transported in handcuffs to Moscow on August 21, and then returned—were allowed to keep their offices temporarily. This was only done, it turned out, in order to help legitimate the campaign of consolidation. But by the spring of 1969, the most difficult part of the job of pacification had been accomplished, and Dubček was replaced by Gustáv Husák, who, like the Hungarian Kádár, had been a victim of Stalin's purges. Many at the time saw significance in the parallel. But unlike Kádár, Husák remained a hard-liner who, till the end of his reign in 1988, refused to budge on matters such as censorship, repression, free travel, and the tight control of information allowed to reach the Czech public.

Although it could rely heavily on Soviet support in the short run, in the long run, the Husák regime needed to create a domestic power structure that would allow for the smoother conduct of the day-to-day business of government and economy. This was not an easy task, for in the Czech lands— the locus of communist power in the country between 1945 and 1960— both the public at large and the professional-intellectual classes were by now staunchly anti-Soviet and resentful of communism. The picture in Slovakia, however, was brighter. Whereas, in 1950, party members had made up 27.3 percent of the Czech population (as opposed to a mere 10.3 percent of Slovaks)[206] and a smaller percentage of Slovaks than Czechs had voted for the Communist Party, by now the tables had been turned. Public opinion polls show that in 1968, Slovaks were less enthusiastic about reform than about federalizing the Republic,[207] and members of the Slovak party

204. Kusin 1978, 85–86.
205. Whipple 1988, 1–7. See also Sobell 1988, 40; Ekiert 1996, 204–10.
206. Káspar 1971, 6, 11–12.
207. Leff 1988, 171–75.

were less compromised by liberal flirtations than their Czech counterparts. As a result, only 17 percent of Slovak members, as opposed to 42.5 percent of the Czechs, were purged from the party following the events of 1968.[208] This meant that Husák—or the Soviet leadership, by appointing him— could play the ethnic card, one that he was eminently qualified to draw on, given not only his ethnic origins but also his past imprisonment for being a Slovak "nationalist."

Consequently, while all the political and economic reforms of the year 1968 were removed from the table, the federalization of the country was allowed to stand. There would henceforth be separate Czech and Slovak republics within a federal structure, with the regional governments wielding considerable power over budget allocations, education, and cultural affairs. The latter were especially important, because they would allow the regional government in Bratislava to cultivate a particularistic ethnic identity and manage the affairs of troublesome national minorities. It is true that the Soviet Union did not consent to the splitting of the party itself and insisted that the Czechoslovaks follow the Soviet, rather than the Yugoslav, model. Accordingly, the Slovak party had no counterpart in the Czech lands, but remained an autonomous branch of the larger Czechoslovak party—a decision whose wisdom is hard to challenge in view of the subsequent Yugoslav experience. In any case, the Slovaks were amply compensated for this deviation from a pure model of federalism by the opening of the central party apparatus and ministries to Slovak candidates, and by the continuation of an effective policy of regional economic development. From an initial position of near complete absence with the central apparatus, within a few years the Slovaks were able to claim their 33 percent quota.[209] As for development, it was financed by a generous policy of income transfer from the Czech lands to Slovakia, representing 5 percent of Czechoslovak national income and an estimated 7.8 percent of the regional income of the Czech republic (9.1 percent in the 1970s, 5.6 percent in the 1980s).[210] These funds were channeled into the development of infrastructure, educational institutions, and industrial enterprises, mostly those with a heavy-industrial and defense-oriented production profile. Although in the long term these industries became one of Slovakia's chief economic liabilities, in the short term they were the principal device by which near parity (96:100) was achieved between regional economies that had been far apart (66:100) in 1950.[211]

While these measures were designed to cater to the sentiments of the Slovak apparat, and to certain segments of the Slovak public, the identity of the

208. Ibid., 253–54.
209. Ibid.
210. Pulpan 1992, 298.
211. Wolchik 1991, 189.

larger Czechoslovak party was cast in terms of a combative proletarian internationalism expressive of the Czech neo-Stalinists of Novotný's generation. At the very inception of the Husák regime, the fundamental purposes of the Czechoslovak party were described as "[creating] favorable conditions for building socialism in our country, and, at the same time, contributing to the common fight of the revolutionary forces against the aggressive policy of imperialism and for lasting peace, democracy and socialism in the whole world."[212] In this and in other respects, Czechoslovakia "fully acknowledge[d] her co-responsibility for the interests of international socialism."[213] These, in turn, were equated with the interests of the Soviet Union, which the reorganized and purged Czechoslovak party wished to serve as a loyal comrade-in-arms. In the words of a party spokesman in 1970:

> The military might of the Soviet Union offers a first-rate guarantee for the security of the entire socialist system [bloc]. The struggle against anti-Sovietism is therefore an objective necessity for each and every genuinely socialist movement. . . . A communist party that succumbs to anti-Soviet tendencies ceases to perform the functions of a Marxist-Leninist party, loses the ability to play the role of a leading force in its own society, dissolves internally and will gradually adopt the positions of a bourgeois ideology."[214]

It is now well-nigh impossible to establish with any degree of accuracy whether the Czech party was as tough and cohesive as was the East German SED. Relying on fragmented and anecdotal information only, this writer could find no evidence of rituals of toughening to parallel those that turned cadres of the East German party into such a ruthlessly determined and cohesive force. On the other hand, the Czechoslovak party, much like its GDR counterpart, did participate in numerous foreign ventures, was one of the main arms suppliers to terrorist and Third World revolutionary movements, and practiced many of the same policies when it came to dealing with a fundamentally unreliable public: a high degree of demarcation between party and public, along with a mixture of consumerism and coercion (leavened by a small dose of regional nationalism in Slovakia). In any case, the party's leaders remained combative to the end. As late as November 9, 1989, they ordered the police to use violence against the public. Once again, it only collapsed because the idolized Soviet party, the senior partner and leader in the anti-imperialist struggle, abandoned the common geopolitical design, leaving its junior ally with neither a raison d'être nor a sense of self-esteem.

These policies, of course, required an economy that could produce not only guns but also just enough butter to obviate reliance on full-scale terror

212. Auersperg 1970, 2.
213. Svoboda 1970.
214. Pezlar 1970.

in the Stalinist mode. The extent to which the economy was able to perform both tasks is now subject to some debate. On the one hand, the economy was able to provide a steady flow of low-quality consumer goods, while delivering the heavy industrial goods to the Soviet war machine—and it did so, alone among its neighbors, without becoming mired in foreign debt or needing to extract resources from Western states. On the other hand, like the rest of East Central Europe, the country was sliding gradually into a mode of slow growth, carefully covered up by statistical sleights of hand or simple falsification. Official data thereby came to grossly overstate rates of growth, real wages, and personal consumption. According to the calculation of economists in postcommunist Czechoslovakia, in the 1980s the country's annual GDP growth rate was overreported by 2.2 percentage points (claiming an annual growth rate of 1.5 percent where more recent studies have revealed an actual decline of −0.7 percent), the growth of consumption by 2.8 percentage points (1.3 percent instead of −1.5), investment rates by a whopping 6 points (0.9 instead of −5.1), and the growth of real wages by 1.4 points (zero instead of −1.4 percent per annum).[215]

Not surprisingly, then, although Czechoslovakia did not experience dramatic economic setbacks in the last decade of communism, the regime's ability to provide payoffs to a recalcitrant population was declining. While the Husák regime could achieve something approaching parity between the two parts of the federation, its former near-parity with Austria fell to 70 percent in 1980,[216] and to 58 percent in 1987.[217] Once again, the proximity of a major reference country was of great psychological significance. As was the case with Germans on the two sides of the intra-German boundary, Czechs and Austrians had once lived in the same political unit and were accustomed to living at approximately the same material standard. But of course it was not merely consumer goods that made the difference. By the 1980s, a courageous and vocal dissident movement had articulated widespread doubts about the capacity of a Soviet-dominated regime to govern the country efficiently and in the general interest.

Bulgaria

As noted in Chapter 4, the Communist Party of Bulgaria was well entrenched, and communist hegemony was therefore established swiftly after the country's occupation by Soviet troops in September 1944. Nonetheless, the early decades of communism were marred by considerable turmoil, much of which was caused by the Soviet Union. The very strength of the Bulgarian

215. Sujan and Sujanova 1995, 121.
216. Marer in Griffith 1989, 49.
217. World Bank 1996b, 189.

party may have led Moscow to mistrust both it and its leader, Georgi Dimi-trov, of Comintern fame. Dimitrov became especially suspect following his expressions of sympathy for the idea of a Balkan federation. After the ex-pulsion of Tito, he was invited to the Soviet Union for medical treatment and died there. The post-Dimitrov power transfer was complicated by the purge trial of Traicho Kostov, one of the heroic figures of the wartime com-munist underground. A few years later, Dimitrov's successor, Vulko Cher-venkov, like the Hungarian Rákosi, had to be dropped as part of the post-Stalin design to placate Tito, and for years the leadership of the party remained contested between Todor Zhivkov, the party's first secretary, and prime minister Anton Yugov, who held tight control over the state machine. While Zhivkov appeared to be little more than a dull apparatchik, Yugov showed considerable taste for political experiments, and was likely the mov-ing force behind Bulgaria's attempt to imitate China's Great Leap Forward. However, as in China, the leap turned into political and economic disaster, and its failure finally moved Moscow to put its client's house in order. In 1962, Khrushchev appeared in person at the Bulgarian party congress and was instrumental in confirming the dull but reliable Zhivkov, as well as re-tiring the mercurial Yugov. In 1965, Zhivkov was challenged one last time by military conspirators of ostensibly pro-Chinese proclivities. But this re-bellion was easily put down, and, with Soviet support, supreme power over the Bulgarian party thereafter remained firmly in the hands of Zhivkov un-til the very end of the communist regime.[218]

Zhivkov, his entourage, and future appointees wavered little in their loy-alty to the Soviet imperial idea. As Paul Lendvai noted in 1969, in the post-Stalin (and post-Khrushchev) years, Bulgaria was the only country where the Soviet ambassador sat upon the platform at all public occasions and ac-companied leaders on their tours of the provinces.[219] Bulgaria's press was notorious for taking its clues from the headlines of *Pravda*. Bulgaria had a leadership that made conscious efforts to construct a collective identity on the idea of a common struggle against global imperialism. The theme re-mained central to Zhivkov's public pronouncements over the decades. It was there in Zhivkov's address to the Ninth Congress of the Bulgarian Party,[220] compounded by explicit pledges of selfless "moral-political and material support to newly liberated and developing countries,"[221] and by reminders that "Bulgarians are one of the nations that bear mankind a great responsi-

218. For a more detailed description of these events, see Brown 1966, 4–19; id. 1970, 53–142. See also Bell 1986, 112–20.

219. Lendvai 1969, 206.

220. "Report to the Ninth Bulgarian Party Congress," *Radio Free Europe Research*, Bul-garia, Nov. 25, 1966.

221. "From the Draft Theses for the Twelfth Congress of the Bulgarian Communist Party," *Radio Free Europe Research*, Bulgaria, Mar. 18, 1981.

bility for [building] socialism" side by side with the Soviet Union.[222] Nor were these pledges mere rhetorical devices. Whenever the Soviet Union called upon them, the Bulgarians responded with notable enthusiasm: they provided a steady flow of logistical support to international terrorist groups, they were key players in KGB operations in the West, and they provided troops for the invasion of Czechoslovakia. They also supported the Olympic boycott of 1984 (when even the East Germans were remonstrating), despite their well-known pride in the performance of a talented national team.

This unflagging support for the Soviet imperial system went hand in hand with conscious efforts not to deviate from the Soviet institutional model. In this spirit, the Zhivkov regime relied on heavy censorship, on the active management of the press, and on strict controls of art and information flows. It effectively banned travel to the West for all but the most trusted ranks of officialdom, eschewing academic exchange agreements. But the regime was not only hard-line in the manner of its Czech and East German counterparts. It was also highly intrusive and personalized, apparently reflecting a traditional political culture with its elements of communalism and paternalism. Along with Albania and Romania, Bulgaria had a state that intruded into the most intimate aspects of private life. Examples include the aggressive promotion of pro-natalist policies—by contrast, East Germans and Czechs relied on positive rather than punitive inducements—and the virtual ban on divorce.[223]

In the same vein, and equally reminiscent of Albania and Romania, was the pervasive familialization and personalization of government. Zhivkov had his own cult of personality, only a touch more discreet than Hoxha's and Ceauşescu's, and behaved much as the patrimonial rulers of the more distant past had: treating the state as an extension of the ruler's household, recognizing no distinction between private and public funds (for which he would be tried and convicted in postcommunist days), and making his children part of the official family. He put his daughter Lyudmila in charge of the country's cultural affairs and groomed her to be his successor. She would have been the first woman to run a communist state. When she died prematurely in 1981, a similar attempt may have been made to groom Zhivkov's son Vladimir, which was frustrated only by the latter's lack of talent and willingness.

Perhaps still more strikingly, this neotraditionalism was evident in the regime's public rituals and symbolism. In 1978, the State Council issued guidelines for the "Basic Practices in Developing and Perfecting a Festive Ceremony System in the People's Republic of Bulgaria," and in 1984, "socialist

222. "T. Zhivkov's Speech on the 40th Anniversary of the Communist Regime's Founding," *Radio Free Europe Research*, Bulgaria, Sept. 24, 1984.
223. See G. S. 1984a; Nikolaev 1984. Also David and McIntyre 1981, 39.

funeral rites [were] discussed again"[224] in the highest councils of the party. These rituals were reminiscent of their religious counterparts in the Bulgarian Orthodox Church. When Lyudmila Zhivkov died in 1981, she was effectively canonized as a ruler's daughter. Thousands of little shrines were erected with candles illuminating her iconic image, in front of which schoolchildren, workers, and the communist faithful were to gather in order to gain inspiration for the next phase in the struggle for communism.

As a result of Zhivkov's loyalty to Moscow, the Bulgarian economic system remained heavily centralized, following the Soviet model. To be sure, there was frequent talk of reform, and during the regime's last decade, several official announcements were made suggesting that reforms in the system were imminent. But somehow the reforms never came to pass, perhaps because the Bulgarian economy, like the East German (at least by CMEA standards), had previously performed in an adequate manner. A loyal trading partner of the Soviet Union, Bulgaria had not objected to Soviet designs for an intra-Bloc division of labor and accepted its assigned role of agricultural and light industrial development without demur. Bulgaria was rewarded for this cooperative behavior by generous Soviet subsidies, long-term loans, and direct grants to her economy—most conspicuously by a loan of 530 million rubles, or $589 million, in 1964, much of which was subsequently forgiven.[225] It appears that the Bulgarians used these funds in a less profligate fashion than most of the other members of the Bloc, and that the emphasis on agriculture and light industry served them well in intra-Bloc trade. This was evident in rising per acre grain yields: with an average of 43 metric ctws harvested per acre (1980–82), Bulgaria surpassed all other CMEA countries in wheat yields,[226] and all but the GDR in overall productivity in this sector.[227] In the same year, at least by some calculations, Bulgaria surpassed Yugoslavia and Romania in terms of per capita GNP, becoming one of the few countries able to break out, if only briefly, from its historical position on the West-East gradient of productivity. At this point, Bulgaria was the pride of the Soviet empire, solidary and productive.

Remarkably, in spite of these encouraging economic signs, the Bulgarian government neither resorted to a massive strategy of economic payoffs nor made its economic prowess the pivot of the regime's legitimacy. Instead, the Zhivkov regime appealed to national sentiment, albeit without pursuing a policy of independence that would have been offensive to the Soviet Union. "Zhivkovism" was an ingenious amalgam of universalism and particular-

224. G. S. 1984b.
225. Brown 1966, 170.
226. Lazarcik 1985, 409.
227. Marer in Griffith 1990, 49, based on the calculations of the unpublished calculations of the Hungarian Éva Ehrlich.

ism. It invoked Bulgaria's millennial struggle against oppressive imperial regimes; made oblique references to the Bulgarian character of Macedonia (to the chagrin of the Yugoslav government); and turned historical figures, including the missionary saints Cyril and Methodius, into socialist heroes, all in the service of anti-imperialism and cooperation with the Soviet Union.[228]

However, like the rest of the Soviet Bloc countries, after its initial spurt of economic success, reformed or unreformed, Bulgaria could not avoid its long-term fate. This is to say that, after some ups and downs in the 1970s, it was sliding into progressive decline by the 1980s. True to the tested tenets of Zhivkovism, the government responded by intensifying its nationalist rhetoric and by whipping up sentiments against Bulgaria's Moslem (Pomak) and Turkish minorities. Nor did the authorities content themselves with agitation and verbal abuse: in short order the Bulgarian state was declared to have a single nationality, and a brutal campaign was undertaken to force members of minority groups to change their names and, in many cases, to seek refuge in Turkey.[229] The Soviet leadership, now under Gorbachev, was embarrassed by the spectacle and became the target of complaints by allies and friends in the Moslem world. But as Moscow was attempting to reform itself, it had already lost influence over events on the imperial periphery. For some time, the politics of whipping up hysteria was successful in blunting and diverting anti-regime sentiments produced by slipping living standards. But, as in East Germany and Czechoslovakia, the party was rapidly losing its raison d'être in the summer of 1989 as the patron party was giving up the "common struggle against imperialism." With hostile crowds gathering in the streets, the party cast about for a new formula of legitimacy. It was found in blaming Zhivkov for past mistakes and in agreeing to hold free and competitive elections.

EXPLAINING COMMUNIST DIVERSITY

The communist form of government was externally imposed on the countries of East Central Europe and thereafter sustained, directly or indirectly, by the Soviet Union. Accordingly, a great number of similarities among the individual countries must be taken for granted. Most significantly, these included the absence of formal institutions ensuring the legal and political accountability of governments; the existence of monopolistic parties serving both as instruments of mobilization and reservoirs for the recruitment of leadership; the existence of politicized, parallel bureaucracies

228. *Radio Free Europe Research*, Bulgaria, Mar. 28, 1985.
229. G. S. 1985. Mar. 28, 1985, 4; Hupchick 1985, 1–6; Brown 1988, 332–33.

of the state, party, and security organs; and the prevalence of constitutional provisions designed to simulate popular participation in government.

Still, in examining the political history of communism we have been able to observe considerable variations in the structure and scope of public authority from society to society. It was in terms of these that we could distinguish between "soft" (or liberal) and "hard" (or conservative) governments measured against the standard set by the Stalinist governments of the previous decade. The distinction between these two types was twofold: some governments were more receptive to public opinion than others, and as a corollary maintained different regimes of social discipline and regimentation by permitting or denying their citizens certain freedoms. These freedoms included (1) free access to information (including some access to information originating from outside the Bloc); (2) the freedom of artistic creativity; (3) the freedom to travel, usually with some restrictions, abroad, including travel outside the boundaries of the Soviet empire; (4) some freedom of economic distribution through a rudimentary market mechanism; and (5) a limited right to privacy, that is, some freedom from state intervention in a rather narrowly defined private sphere, usually restricted to the family. Although these freedoms do not lend themselves particularly well for exact quantification, a rather firm consensus exists that throughout most of the post-Stalin period Yugoslavia, Hungary, and Poland fell into the liberal bracket, while Albania, Bulgaria, East Germany, Romania, and Czechoslovakia (with the exception of the late 1960s), were on the conservative side of the divide.

Although they were hidden under a more convincing parliamentary façade, such variations in the exercise of political authority were not entirely unknown in the precommunist period. But then the relative power of political and economic classes, of states and civil societies, were largely circumscribed by the logic of the world market, and reflected the position of the given country on the northwest–southeast continental gradient. The further east and south a given country was, the more powerful was its state bureaucracy and the weaker were its economic classes and the overall influence of the public on the conduct of politics. This simple and elegant rule did not apply during the era of communism. Now politics no longer reflected the logic of the marketplace but the logic and interests of an imperial system together with a set of circumstances that had a bearing on relationships between the imperial core and the individual client states of its political periphery. To put it differently, the need to protect the empire and to rein in politically unreliable clients took precedence over the dictates of economic efficiency. The most obvious cases in point were Czechoslovakia and East Germany, where purely economic logic would have predicted more liberal and decentralized forms of government, but where popular recalcitrance and geographical location compelled the Soviet Union to keep in power security-conscious, hard-line elites. Likewise, in Yugoslavia, a relatively underdeveloped country of East Central Europe with great regional disparities, where a more centralized and less permissive government could well have been adopted, a fluke of imperial decision-making and the uniqueness of the country's position between East and West resulted in a model of liberal communism. In any case, Yugoslav institutions developed the way they did in part as an attempt to accommodate some Western sensitivities.

Beyond these variations in institutionalizing communist power, the political systems of East Central Europe varied with respect to their legitimacy and popularity. These aspects of the systems, of course, varied in time, from one decade to another, but there can be little argument about the fact that overall, throughout the post-Stalin period, some communist regimes were more popular than others. This proposition may be validated by examining the attitudes of both the countries' intellectual communities and their general populations. Of the two, intellectuals can play a role in politics as articulators of social discontent and as subtle critics of the prevailing political order. The common folk meanwhile can grumble and sulk, yet at times also erupt in open rebellion against an oppressive government. In East Central Europe both of these forms of protest were prevalent and deeply grounded in the political culture and its affinity for or distance from the official norms of communism. What we must remember here is that Soviet communism, while ostentatiously representing itself as a secular, modern, and universalistic ideological construct, also bore many of the marks of the cultural tradition of Russia. Because it was rooted in the communalism and paternalism of Byzantine Orthodoxy, communism resonated far more positively in the Orthodox societies of the southeast, than in the legalistic, contract societies of the northwest tier. The correlations in this respect are remarkably consistent.

Let us take first the collective response of the intellectual communities. Among them we find the bold signatories of charters and memoranda in post-1968 Czechoslovakia; the literary and religious-ethical protesters of East Germany, the well-developed literary and journalistic underground of Hungary, and the members of a genuine "second society" in Poland, starting with the Crooked Circle in the 1950s and culminating in the rise of Solidarity in the 1980s. In contrast, the countries of the southeastern tier were relatively quiescent. Open dissent was largely confined to a few lonely men and women who had the extraordinary courage to confront the power structure amid the silence of their compatriots. The dimensions of this contrast between northwest and southeast are evident from the available schol-

TABLE 45

Incidence of Dissidence and Civil Disobedience in East Central Europe, 1978–85

	1978	1979	1981	1982	1984	1985
Poland	4	12	139	128	68	55
Czechoslovakia	12	18	2	3	5	2
GDR	6	8	2	4	1	—
Romania	1[a]	—	1	—	—	—
Bulgaria	1	—	—	—	—	4[a]
Albania	—	—	—	—	—	1

SOURCE: *New York Times Index* (1978–85).
[a] Articles on protest by or harassment of ethnic minorities (Romania: Hungarians; Bulgaria: Turks).

arly literature on the subject;[230] from a survey of weekly *Research Reports* by Radio Free Europe between 1976 and 1985, which shows a 25:1 ratio of incidents reported in the two halves of East Central Europe; and finally, by the *New York Times Index* for the years 1978–85, in which a similar ratio obtains from a count of reports on oppositional activities in communist Europe (see Table 45). The same correlation is evident in culturally divided Yugoslavia as well: while a philosophical critique of the official doctrine flourished in cosmopolitan Belgrade, which was a microcosm of the larger society, embryonic parliamentarism and civil society flourished in Slovenia (where budgets were regularly voted down and regional governments were often forced to resign) and in Croatia where, in 1971, literary dissent snowballed into political dissent that was both nationist and anti-communist. In contrast, the southeastern regions of the country were largely quiescent, and their elites content to play by the official rules of the game. (There is, to be sure, some gap in the data when it comes to Hungary, for while criticism of the regime was rife in the country, it was so "normal" and frequent that it was less likely to be reported in the Western press.)[231]

As for the populations at large, the most telling evidence of these variable responses is the incidence of movements of mass protest and violent uprisings during the forty-five years of communism. The list is all too familiar, and the incidents listed occurred exclusively in countries on the western side of the continental cultural gap: East Germany (1953), Hungary (1956), Czechoslovakia (1953 and 1968), and Poland (1956, 1970, 1976, 1980–81), to which we may add the Croat "troubles" of 1971. This is not to say that on the other side of the divide communist government and subjection to the Soviet imperial system did not generate frustrations and enmities. But

230. See above all Mastny 1972; Tőkés 1979; Stokes 1991; id. 1993.
231. This point was recognized by the *Times* itself in a revealing interview with the Hungarian dissident János Kis. See the *New York Times*, October 19, 1982, 3: 1.

TABLE 46

Electoral Results of First Postcommunist/
Postindependence Elections, 1990–92

	Year	% of Vote for parliament
Albania	1991	56.2
Bulgaria	1990	47.2
Macedonia	1992	25.8
Montenegro	1990	42.6
Romania	1990	68.0
Serbia	1990	46.1
Croatia	1992	5.4
Slovenia	1992	13.6
East Germany	1990	16.4
Czechoslovakia	1991	13.5
Hungary	1990	10.9
Poland	1991	11.4

SOURCE: Dawisha and Parrott 1997a, 1: 80, 123, 174; 2: 93, 108, 161, 205, 234, 311, 377, 421.

these enmities were not sufficiently intense or widespread to burst into open resistance as long as the imperial structure was intact. Indeed, even thereafter, the rejection of communism was not as immediate and intense as in the countries of the northwestern tier. As the numbers in Table 46 demonstrate, in the critical "first elections" of the immediate postcommunist period, ex-communist parties scored in the 10 percent range in the northwest tier, but indicate, in the critical "first elections" of the postcommunist/ postindependence period, the communist successor parties, however much reformed, scored at best in the 13 to 16 percent range in the northwest tier. In the southeast, they still pulled comfortable pluralities or outright majorities, and with some cosmetic political changes, continued to govern in Albania, Bulgaria, Serbia, Montenegro, and Romania, and, with the ambiguities of a split and unstable government, in Macedonia as well.

| From Communism to Postcommunism

THE END OF EMPIRE

The Crisis of Communism

Although historical circumstances were significant contributing factors, the gradual decline and ultimate demise of the Soviet empire can hardly be understood without reexamining the nature and driving forces of the imperial system. Having reached maturity under the firm and bloody reign of the great dictator, the Soviet Union remained, even after Stalin's death, a "military society," in the sense in which Herbert Spencer once used the term. That is to say, the legitimacy of the Soviet state and the driving force behind its empire derived from an "external objective"—in its case, the perceived need to reconstruct the world by "burying" (in Khrushchev's immortal phrase) global capitalism. Given the relative underdevelopment of the Soviet economy, this objective required a system of mobilization, an authoritarian state, and an economic model geared toward political rather than social ends. Since "mobilization" often implied sacrificing a particular sector of the economy in order to accomplish short-term objectives, the expansionist impulses of the system were not only dictated by the definition of its fundamental purpose, but also reinforced by the need to replenish resources used up at the previous stage. It was by this logic that the Stalinist system had first built up its military might by destroying its agriculture and consumer economy, and then tried to recoup its losses by exploiting and dismantling some of the East Central European economies between 1945 and 1955.

Whether consciously or by pure intuition, Stalinist policies also followed what has previously been described as the "Prussian model" of expansionism. Like the policies of the rulers of resource-poor Prussia in the eighteenth and nineteenth centuries, Stalin's were guided by the maxim codified by von Clausewitz: always move toward the heartland of the opponent, in this case capitalism, and avoid any temptation to nibble around the peripheries. Stalin certainly did so in 1939–40, and then again in 1944–48, when his armies moved westward on the European continent. However, a continued thrust westward was made problematic by developments that neither von Clausewitz nor the Soviet leaders could have foreseen: the development of new weapons of mass destruction and the United States' credible commitment to use them in defense of Western Europe. Adaptation to this by the Soviet leaders was slow and grudging.[1] At first inclined to dismiss the significance of nuclear arms, Stalin may well have been considering a new thrust toward the core regions of the world economy. But by 1952, Stalin appears to have begun to grasp the implications of the nuclear age for the geopolitical design of world revolution. Although nowhere explicitly stated, this conclusion may be drawn from his 1952 essay on the "Economic Problems of the U.S.S.R.," in which he not only warned about "objective conditions" setting limits to a policy of mobilization, but also hinted at the possibility of a prolonged armistice by "predicting" that the next major war would be fought among capitalist states rather than between the socialist and capitalist world systems.[2] However, the language of this message was cast in such oblique terms that few denizens, or even functionaries, of his empire took it seriously, especially since the predictions were issued at the height of the Korean War, initiated by none other than Stalin himself. At any rate, his successors continued to grapple with the dilemma and, after some dallying with coexistence, Khrushchev returned to the earlier principles of Stalinist foreign policy. He did so by rekindling the Berlin crisis in 1958–61 and, a year thereafter, by deploying nuclear missiles in Cuba, a mere 90 miles from the shores of the United States, by now the heartland of global capitalism.

This last venture, of course, ended in something of a fiasco, and it was later branded a "hare-brained scheme" by Khrushchev's colleagues, who removed him from his post in 1964. Thereafter, the Soviet Union finally gave up on Clausewitz and the "Prussian model" and opted instead for a two-track foreign policy. Given their growing appreciation of the mutually destructive nature of nuclear war, the Soviet leaders backed away from a forward strategy on the European continent, although they did maintain large force levels, both conventional and nonconventional, in that theater as a lever against hostile engagements elsewhere in the world. Meanwhile, in order to minimize the perils of confrontation with the United States, they also began to build an edifice of treaties aimed at limiting the use and deployment of strategic nuclear arms. Yet while committed to "peaceful coexistence" in Europe, Soviet foreign policy did not abandon its external objectives, but simply switched its priorities from the global core to the non-European pe-

1. Holloway 1994, 115–29; Mastny 1996, 75–76.
2. Stalin 1972a, 469–73.

ripheries. This was not sheer rhetoric. From the 1960s onward, the Soviet Union and its sometimes reluctant allies began to pour resources into the support of revolutionaries in weak or tottering non-European states, hoping to change the global balance of power between East and West.

The way stations of this geopolitical design are well known. The strategy managed to preserve a friendly communist regime in distant Cuba even after the missiles had been removed; its steadfastness contributed greatly to the American defeat in Vietnam, Laos, and Cambodia; its more overtly interventionist components reaped political results in Angola, Ethiopia, Nicaragua, El Salvador, Mozambique, Yemen, Somalia, and, less conspicuously, in the activities of urban guerrillas and terrorists in Latin America and the Middle East. Whatever their geostrategic utility, these victories provide convincing proof of the heavily militarized, or combat, orientation of the communist movement. When future historians look back at the communist record, they will remember it not for successes in building new societies providing "to each according to his need," but for military prowess that defeated the German army in World War II, the U.S. army in Indochina, and the South African army in Angola—some of the best in history, and all of them the armies of economically more developed and technologically more sophisticated adversaries.

These policies were costly. Indeed, they required the continued mobilization of the Soviet resources, while providing no immediate economic reward. On the cost side, there were Soviet military expenditures that, growing at a rate of 4–6 percent per annum,[3] either kept abreast with or ran slightly ahead of the growth of the Soviet economy. Overall, these expenditures consumed 18–20 percent[4] of a gross national product estimated to have been between 33 and 45 percent of the GNP of the United States (or 32 to 37 percent in per capita terms).[5] The geopolitical effort claimed the best 40 percent of all machinery, 33 percent of metal products, and 20 percent of all the energy produced in the Soviet Union.[6] At those costs, the Soviet Union was able to expand its sphere of influence and transform itself from a regional hegemon into a global superpower. It did so by building a multi-ocean navy, including nuclear-powered submarines and groups of battleships, by deploying a full-fledged nuclear arsenal capable of wiping out any future military adversary, and by assembling the largest field army ever maintained by any power in peacetime, including some 170 divisions in Europe and a lesser

3. Eyal and Anthony 1988, 79; Bialer 1986, 46.
4. The calculations of these expenditures are numerous and varied, ranging from the 12.5 percent estimates of the CIA (later upped to 18 percent), to the 18 and 20 percent figures cited by Gorbachev and Ligachev respectively, and to some calculations that put the percentage figures still higher. For these, see Noren 1995, 238–76, esp. 245 and 262.
5. See Schroeder 1995, 197–234, esp. 212–16; Marer 1985, 104–5. See also Tables 60–62.
6. Schroeder 1995, 222.

force in the Soviet Far East. Last, but not least, the Soviet Union had acquired air and surface transport capabilities that enabled it to project power into virtually every corner of the world.

These expenditures in and of themselves strained the economic capacity of what was still a relatively underdeveloped country when measured against the capabilities of its principal adversaries. But the strain on the Soviet budget was further augmented by chronic pressures to subsidize some of the new allies won at such considerable expenditure of effort. Here the Soviet Union paid the price for deviating from the "Prussian model" and for ignoring the Clausewitzian injunction against nibbling at the peripheries of the enemy's heartlands. While the classical model of the mobilization system assumed that periodic conquest would allow the conqueror to replenish expended resources, the Cold War victories of the Soviet Union were all won in impoverished countries whose economies could barely sustain themselves at pre-communist levels after imposing the centralized and militarized institutions of communist rule. The failures of sugar-cane harvests in Cuba and rice harvests in Vietnam are cases in point, as is the famine that followed the imposition of a communist government in Ethiopia. The pressures to hold on to these countries were enormous and were dictated by the Soviet doctrine that socialism, once established, was irreversible. If Americans were ever fearful of the moral effects of yielding territory to Soviet expansion, the Soviet leaders were mortified at the prospect of having to surrender what had been gained, assuming that any reversal in their geopolitical fortunes would not only give their opponents momentum, but would also undermine the legitimacy of their very own political system. These Soviet fears were then taken advantage of by their newly liberated allies, who extorted large subsidies from the patron power, which in the long run contributed to the economic and administrative inefficiencies of the overseas client states. The single largest, and most consistently granted, outlay of foreign aid went to Cuba, generally estimated at an annual outlay of $6 to $9 billion. The amount of foreign aid distributed to the world peripheries is hard to calculate reliably, but it was far from trivial. In 1989, the Soviet Union was owed an uncollectible debt of 45 billion transferable rubles by non-European socialist states and another $79 billion by "friendly" Third World countries.[7]

To make matters worse, after having been exploited for ten years (1945–55), the communist countries of East Central Europe, too, became a drain on the Soviet economy. The sources of this drain were multifold. First, there were raw materials and fuel deliveries at preferential prices. Second, the smaller countries of the region profited much of the time from a structure

---

7. Marer 1997, 235–306. With author's permission, all references to this item are to the original English language version of the essay, Marer 1996. For the above, see Marer 1996, 59. One transferable ruble (TR) is more or less the equivalent of one dollar.

MAP 5. Post-Soviet Europe, 1993

of trade that favored the exporters of manufactures. Third, there was the oft-ignored foot-dragging of Soviet clients, who were continually falling short of their prescribed material contributions to the larger geopolitical effort.[8] Once again, the total cost incurred by the Soviet Union is difficult to calculate with any exactitude using one particular currency or another. But the discrepancy in respective efforts is discernible through a comparison of the economic record of the USSR with those of the East Central European members of the CMEA. Between 1945 and 1975, the Soviet economy overtook all but two of those economies—the East German and the Czechoslovak—in terms of net material product per person. But, as Table 47 indicates, in the 1980s the Soviet Union invested more yet consumed less than any of its European clients aside from Romania and, we may assume, Albania. Still more striking differences emerge from comparisons in the area of major

8. Eyal and Anthony 1988, 106–12.

TABLE 47

*Per Capita Investment and Consumption of CMEA
Countries Relative to West Germany,
France, and Great Britain*

Country	Investment	Consumption	Difference
USSR	79%	52%	27%
Czechoslovakia	98	74	24
East Germany	95	76	19
Poland	69	51	18
Bulgaria	61	46	15
Romania	50	36	14
Hungary	63	56	7

SOURCE: Winiecki 1987, 6.

consumer durables; "car density" in the USSR was, for example, a mere
fifth of Czechoslovakia's and a sixth of the GDR's in 1980.[9]

Compared to the advanced industrial countries of the capitalist orbit, per
capita personal consumption (as opposed to production) was strikingly low;
toward the end of the 1980s, levels were varyingly estimated at 22 to 28 percent of those in the United States.[10] Levels were most likely even lower in
Stalin's time; at any rate, the Soviet citizenry then clearly consumed still less.
But under Stalin, such differences carried less political weight. For one thing,
Stalin's was truly a "dictatorship over needs."[11] For another thing, Stalin's
institutionalization of the purge prevented members of the Soviet political
class from turning the state into a rent-seeking instrument—that is, from
using public office to deflect state revenue in order to raise their own standard of living to international, elite norms. All this changed after the death
of Stalin, when, on the one hand, the curtain around the Soviet Union lifted
just enough to allow the average citizen a glimpse of Western lifestyles, while,
on the other, Stalin's successors tried to compensate for the abolition of terror by promising ever-higher material standards.

Meanwhile, at the elite level, with the threat of the purges removed, members of the political class acquired the bargaining leverage of cryptopolitics,
as well as greater opportunities for self-enrichment by classical methods of
corruption. These leverages and opportunities, of course, were commensurate to rank. The upper 10,000 within Soviet officialdom were now granted
the wherewithal of a Western upper-class standard of living via privileges

9. Kornai 1992, 305.
10. I. Bauman 1989, 155; for the higher figure, see Table 47. Other estimates include the
CIA's (27.7 percent of the U.S. figure) and the UN's in 1990 (23.8 percent). For the latter, see
Schroeder 1995, 216. For Soviet economists putting consumption in the same range, see "Soviet Experts Say Their Economy Worse Than the U.S. Has Estimated," *New York Times*, re-
published in the *San Francisco Chronicle*, April 24, 1990, sec. A-6.
11. Feher, Heller, and Markus 1983.

such as hard-currency accounts, special purchasing prerogatives, and foreign travel, over and above the previously established perquisites of subsidized housing, recreation, and preferential access to elite educational institutions. At the middle level, a couple of million members of the nomenklatura class gained access to what might be described as a simulacrum of Western middle-class life, with subsidies for modest housing and for vacations, and with access to consumer goods imported from Hungary and East Germany.

It is true that Soviet elites, and particularly the members of the upper 10,000, tried to hide their privileges; indeed, they may be regarded as paragons of inconspicuous consumption, discreetly indulging behind the high walls of dachas, game preserves, and other recreational facilities reserved for themselves. But Soviet citizens were hardly ignorant of their wealth and, with consumption lagging behind production and military spending, quite justifiably saw these income differences in zero-sum terms. From the common citizens' perspective, then, the elite (or corrupt petty official) was consuming what the general population was not. These inequalities thereby served to exacerbate an already-existing sense of deprivation, especially in urban centers. Given these patterns of rent-seeking and latent dissatisfaction from the beginning of the post-Stalin period, except for its vast military power, the Soviet Union was approaching more and more the familiar model of the peripheral state described in some detail in the first part of this volume.

Conflicting demands on scarce resources were aggravated by a system of central planning and management whose weaknesses are well known to students of socialist economies. They encourage the hoarding of labor, insensitivity toward consumer demand, the worshiping of quality over quantity, and, inadvertently, the reproduction of shortage.[12] But these contradictions become even more salient where central planning is embedded in the political framework of a militarized society. The economies of such societies are inherently wasteful. They encourage "scavenging,"[13] or, to use a still stronger term, the cannibalization of the economy—that is, the use of current resources and assets for the fulfillment of politico-military goals, with scant regard for long-term damage done to the economy. In the long run, thus, the primacy of political goals, if unattained, will result in diminished labor and capital productivity. This fundamental truth was, of course, well understood by a number of economists, both foreign and domestic, and, in the 1960s, brought forth various attempts to rationalize the economies— either by Libermanist tinkering or by a modicum of decentralization, combined with simulations of the market mechanism. None of these alternatives, however, was radical enough: the problem lay not just with the bureaucratization of the economy but also with the underlying purposes of

12. G. Grossman 1962, 203–22; also Neuberger 1968; Kornai 1992, esp. 228–301.
13. For this evocative term, see Jowitt 1994, 223.

the political systems. These purposes remaining sacrosanct, the built-in deficiencies of the economic mechanism eventually brought about the economic downturn of the 1970s and 1980s (see Table 42 above).

Ironically, just as these contradictions were becoming manifest in the satellite countries, the Soviet economy was bailed out by a series of fortuitous developments in the very world market that socialism set out to abolish. Three developments are especially relevant here. First, the price of raw materials and energy shot up in the early 1970s. Although devastating for many industrial nations, including the Soviet satellites in Europe, the price rises were a blessing to the Soviet Union, with its particular export profile. By American estimates, each dollar added to the price of a barrel of crude oil on world stock markets added $1 billion in net earnings to the Soviet export economy.[14] The rise, of course, was considerable: starting from a low of $3 per barrel, at one point, the price reached $40. Second, the failure of the U.S. government to cope with its own balance of payments and budgetary problems undermined confidence in the dollar and sent the price of gold, a major Soviet export, soaring—first from its guaranteed price of $35 per ounce to $180 and then, at the end of the 1970s, to a high of $840. Altogether, these developments in commodity prices dramatically changed the terms of trade in favor of the Soviet Union over the course of the 1970s, to the extent that an equal volume of Soviet exports by decade's end bought 65 percent more foreign goods.[15] Third, and in a related development, the large amounts of petrodollars flowing in the direction of the oil-exporting states of the Middle East had been recirculated within the global financial system, creating a glut of cheap, short-term credit even in the face of the threat of inflation. The Soviet Union, like many of its Eastern European allies, took advantage of this opportunity. As a result, the mid 1970s became years of relative prosperity in the country, remembered fondly by many former members of the Soviet intellectual and political classes. For a while, the regime was able to raise both military spending and the standard of living of the masses, most directly by massive purchases of grain from the United States, Canada, and Argentina. Predictably, this prosperity did not increase the momentum toward either reform or restraint. Indeed, apparently gaining new confidence from temporary economic trends, the Soviet leaders were ready to raise the ante, seeking greater political return on their huge military investments. Thus, after the fall of Richard Nixon from the U.S. presidency, the Soviet Union attempted to tilt the balance of power in its favor through the deployment of mobile missile-launching systems. Another effort to cash in on raw military strength was made in 1979, when Soviet leaders made their ill-conceived decision to invade Afghanistan outright, in a con-

14. Schweitzer 1994, 105.
15. Ibid., 262.

scious attempt to change the hitherto accepted rules under which the Cold War had been fought in the Third World.

By this time, however, the economic fortunes of the Soviet Union were taking a downward turn.[16] Market forces were at work, although the policies of the United States also had a part in shaping them. The second oil shock had been followed by an oil glut, brought about both by the diminished consumption of the industrial countries and by the ability of the U.S. government to persuade friendly exporters to "open the oil spigot," in order to undercut Soviet exports.[17] At the same time, successful deflationary policies by the Reagan administration brought about a dramatic fall in the price of gold, from $840 per ounce to $250. As a corollary, short-term interest rates rose to double digits, making it more expensive to repay outstanding debts by new borrowing. But most significantly, the American public and federal government were recovering from their "post-Vietnam trauma," proving ready once more to increase their own military spending. The first signs of this had already appeared under the Carter administration, but the tide really turned during the Reagan presidency, with its $2 trillion rearmament program, which included appropriations for the development of the Trident missile, the B-1 and the B-2 (Stealth) bombers, the strengthening of the capabilities of U.S. land-based missiles, vast projects of research to develop new generations of defensive weapons, and a major project to modernize conventional military forces. "There would be a substantially larger navy, and greater aircraft capability. The Pentagon budget would rise by fifty percent in but a few years."[18]

Accelerated military spending may not have been, as some of its chroniclers suggest, part of a carefully crafted plan to bring the Soviet Union down.[19] But there was a clear understanding in Washington that this new cycle in the armament race would represent a severe challenge to the Soviet Union. From the very beginning of the Cold War, the Soviet Union and the United States had been competing militarily from positions of great economic disparity: with American GNP two to three times greater than that of the USSR, the United States was capable of maintaining equivalent military strength by spending just 5.5 to 7 percent of its GNP. The increases in military spending under the new Reagan program could thus be far more easily absorbed by the American than by the Soviet economy. However, America's advantages lay not only in her own economic strength but also in that of her premier allies in Western Europe and on the Pacific Rim—all of whom were laggards when it came to maintaining their own armies, yet also

16. For this turn of Soviet economic fortunes, see Aslund 1989; S. White 1991, 100–111.
17. Schweitzer 1994, 242.
18. Ibid., 62.
19. Ibid. or, more recently, d'Souza 1997, 36–40, 52–54.

sympathetic to maintaining American military strength in order to protect themselves from Soviet ambitions. At the onset of this new cycle of the armament race, researchers of the U.S. State Department estimated the gross national product of America and her allies at $7.5 trillion (1982) versus the Soviet alliance's $2.1 trillion—the latter figure broken down roughly into $1.5 trillion for the USSR, $500 billion for East Central Europe, and a pathetic $27.6 billion for the "overseas allies" of the Soviet Bloc.[20] As Gorbachev noted bitterly (and with slight exaggeration) in 1987, the United States was able to borrow two-thirds of what it would spend on arms.[21] While the figure was closer to 50 percent (much of it provided by Japanese and Germans buying U.S. treasury bonds), the ability to borrow was a major element in the program's political success, for it enabled the Reagan administration to engage in this project of military spending without asking its citizens to make any immediate sacrifices. Indeed, rather than imposing austerity via new taxes, the administration was able to accomplish its military objectives while lowering the tax burden and raising the standard of living of critical segments of the middle classes. It is at least questionable whether, without the capacity to do so, and without drawing on the liquid assets of the larger capitalist world economy, the program would have been accepted by the public as it was, almost without demur.

To assess the dilemmas of the Soviet leadership, further economic comparisons are needed. Apart from its smaller overall size, the Soviet economy was also much weaker than those of Western Europe and the United States: it operated with higher unit costs and had difficulties both in raising labor productivity and in adapting to new technologies. Moreover, in contrast to the United States, the Soviet Union was not able to draw on the accumulated wealth or trade surpluses of its allies. If America could count on Western Europe, Canada, Japan, and the newly industrialized economies of East Asia, the Soviet Union had only crisis-ridden East Central Europe, Cuba, Nicaragua, Angola, and Mozambique to look to. While the United States and its allies could raise funds without endangering the high and increasing standard of living of their citizenry, the accumulation of comparable amounts of revenue by communist governments would have destroyed the fragile "social contracts" maintained with their own citizenry.

As these developments unfolded between 1978 and 1982, the Soviet leadership faced a limited number of unpalatable alternatives; no strategy would have entailed bearable costs and bearable risks. One alternative was to take on the challenge of the new armament race. This would have required a return to Stalinist, or quasi-Stalinist, methods in order to extract the necessary

20. Block and Cline 1983, 26–27.
21. Gorbachev 1987, 115.

revenues for investment. Apart from its broader political implications, this choice was unattractive because, while it could have redirected some resources from consumption into military spending, terror would have simultaneously created an atmosphere of isolation and fear, thereby further diminishing the ability of the economic system to adapt to highly sophisticated new technologies. Another alternative was to make a bold geopolitical move before losing the existing Soviet power position in a new round of the armament race. The latter had been the strategic choice made quite explicitly by Hitler in 1938, when he explained to his generals that Germany would have to go to war with the army and industrial capacity it had, because each subsequent year would only have reduced its competitive advantage vis-à-vis its prospective enemies, then awakening from their slumber to mobilize their own industrial base.[22]

Enter Gorbachev

There was a third alternative that Soviet leaders could have considered: abandonment of the ideological underpinning and institutional framework of their militarized society, instead of merely tinkering with piecemeal reforms of its system of production and allocation. This, to be sure, would have required monumental resolve. Indeed, an explicit decision to this effect would have been tantamount to American leaders deciding to abandon their own constitutional system. Not surprisingly, the cohort of aging and ailing leaders never contemplated such a course of action. Brezhnev, Andropov, and Chernenko were too frail personally, as well as too firmly wedded to the old order, to try anything but muddling through. They would henceforth try to bear down on corruption, put down rebellions in the satellites without using Soviet troops and, in their foreign policy, maintain their strategy of national liberation, although setting new parameters for themselves by deploying Soviet troops in Afghanistan.

This strategy, however, met with little success. Domesticizing of repression in Poland pacified the country without stabilizing it, and intervening in Afghanistan without winning now only deepened the urgency of reform. Much as their predecessors had faced the dilemmas of making revolution in an underdeveloped society and of finding a strategic substitute for insurrections under Comintern auspices, this last generation of Soviet leaders faced a strategic dilemma of immense magnitude. Once again, there were no easy answers, only a deepening sense of crisis and the conviction that something unconventional would have to be done. It was in this milieu that the Politburo discussed the issue of succession after the death of K. U. Chernenko in

22. For this meeting on Aug. 22, 1938, see Berndt 1989, 214; see also Janos 1996, 42–43.

1985 and, we are told, by a narrow majority, but with a broad if vague mandate, gave the supreme command to Mikhail Gorbachev, by Soviet measures a younger, and by all appearances dynamic, man with some experience in managing both domestic and international affairs.

The breadth and opacity of the mandate to put things right gave Gorbachev considerable power, making it well nigh impossible for worried colleagues to rein him in, even when he strayed from familiar ground.[23] Nor should one forget that Gorbachev's digressions were neither immediately nor readily apparent. While, by his own subsequent accounts, the new leader's efforts were always aimed at coming to grips with the problems facing the country, his first measures were anything but bold: much in the spirit of his immediate predecessors, he first tried to improve things not by structural changes but by raising social morale—specifically, by a partial ban on the sale and consumption of vodka, which, as it turned out, created a minor economic crisis in itself. These initial forays thus remained as ineffective as Andropov's attempt to extirpate corruption largely by rhetorical means. Moreover, Gorbachev's early statements on foreign policy were full of angry bluster, denouncing the capitalist countries for trying to save themselves from their inevitable doom by accelerating the armament race.[24] As for East Central Europe, some of the region's restless leaders were "put in their place" through reminders of their obligations under the Warsaw Pact, and warnings against "undue emphasis on national attributes," as well as against the temptations of "Russophobic" appeals.[25] To the ears of anxious local satraps, these sounded more like faint echoes of the old injunctions against separate roads than the words of a bold imperial reformer.

But then, bit by bit, Gorbachev's "new thinking" began to take shape, influenced by the information that he had managed (apparently with some effort) to garner about the state of the Soviet economy and, just as significantly, by travels abroad that brought him into contact with both Western leaders and their enthusiastic constituents. His impressions of the West were favorable and apparently convinced him that his adversaries did not harbor aggressive intentions toward the Soviet Union. So impressed, by 1987 he was ready to step onto the world political stage as an "event-making man"[26] with a full-fledged design. What this design reflected was a belief that the "restructuring" of the Soviet economy required not only a freer flow of information or the transfer of skills and resources from the military to the civilian sector, but a radical change in the relations between the Soviet state and the

23. For this and other aspects of Gorbachev's evolving strategy, see Breslauer 1996, 119–39.
24. White 1991, 186.
25. On Gorbachev's first months in office, see Kusin 1986, 39–53, esp. 40–43.
26. Breslauer 1989, 317.

external world. More specifically, in a truly revolutionary turnabout, he now advocated the abandonment of the Leninist formula of relentless international class struggle in favor of a new international regime of active cooperation with the capitalist world.[27] In his own words, he was now ready to recognize "the diversity of interests in international affairs," and announced publicly his intention to join in a "search for a more secure, reliable world in which everyone would preserve their own philosophic and ideological views and their own ways of life."[28] Translated into the language of political sociology, he was ready to cross the line that separated the organizational codes of militancy and industrialism, and prepared to transform the Soviet Union from a reconstructionist to a developmental state.

Exit Communism

The premise on which the success of this transition rested was the possibility of creating a "common European home . . . sharing the cultural legacy of the enlightenment and stretching from the Urals to the Atlantic."[29] Although taken by some to be an idle propaganda slogan, and by others as the Soviet leader's visceral reaction to the adulation he received from Western crowds, the idea had deep pragmatic underpinnings and was rooted in the intellectual tradition of Bolshevism. Lenin and Trotsky had, after all, sought to foment socialist revolutions in the West in the hope that the fellow feelings of ensuing socialist governments would help backward Russia over the hump of "primitive accumulation" on the road toward a modern economy and society. Stalin may have harbored similar, although less benevolent, ideas in thinking about the rationale for a westward thrust: the economic resources of the advanced industrial countries could have been extracted by force in order to recoup the sacrifices made by the Soviet economy. Now Gorbachev was ready to discard the ideas of revolution and conquest while still looking to Europe, in the hope of solving the economic problems of his country through co-optation into the core region of the modern world economy. What he offered in exchange was acceptance of the global political status quo and removal of the ever-present Soviet military threat to the prosperous countries of the Continent.

From the point of view of the West, of course, this implicit offer would only become credible if the Soviet Union fulfilled conditions that, while not unreasonable from the perspective of one negotiating partner, eventually doomed the Soviet Bloc and the Soviet Union itself. For one thing, as a sign

27. Kubalkova and Cruikshank 1989, 3. See also Snyder 1987–88, 93–131.
28. Gorbachev 1987, 122, 125.
29. Ibid., 177, 180.

of his good faith, Gorbachev had to abandon the Brezhnev doctrine, or, to state it more rhetorically, to "pull down the wall" that divided the would-be common home. Indeed, how could the Western powers closely ally themselves with an empire whose European periphery was seething with rebellion? The Western signals were explicit, and, by 1988, Gorbachev began to respond. Rumor has it that he first expressed his willingness to abandon the doctrine of his predecessor in private conversations with the Yugoslavs, who let the word spread in both Eastern and Western Europe. In the next year, his signals got ever stronger and still less ambiguous. On July 7, 1989, Gorbachev denounced any attempt to violate the sovereignty of states, and three months later Gorbachev's spokesman, Gennady Gerassimov jokingly announced the "Frank Sinatra doctrine": Soviet clients would be allowed to go their "own way," while, it was hoped, preserving at least some elements of communist government.[30] The words, in any case, were electrifying, and their results may not have been fully anticipated. They certainly strengthened the bargaining positions of opponents of the communist regimes in Poland and Hungary: while a few months earlier the dissidents had still been willing to accept a perennially entrenched communist executive under some degree of parliamentary scrutiny, in the end such an institutional arrangement—an awkward throwback to the practices of traditional monarchies in an age of popular sovereignty—was only accepted as a temporary expedient in Poland, and not at all in Hungary. In addition, the new doctrine pithily encapsulated by Gerassimov's witticism split the parties between those who were ready to make a last stand for the imperial idea and those eager to adapt to new circumstances. Most pathetic was the lot of the solidary parties, for whom the imperial idea was also a primary source of domestic legitimacy. They found themselves still in power but devoid of a raison d'être once the Soviet Union had abandoned the idea of empire in such an apparently light-hearted manner. For these regimes, then, instead of accelerating an orderly process of devolution, the Sinatra doctrine sparked a cascade of semi-revolutions.

The last of the East Central European communists to go were the parties of Romania and Albania. Their leaders—Ceauşescu and Alia, Hoxha's successor—had previously distanced themselves from the Soviet Union, which enabled them to claim that events there had no relevance to their own countries. But the tide of change was too strong. Ceauşescu and his clan were removed by a kind of coup d'état, led by the army and disgruntled former functionaries. Alia, after holding out through the winter of 1989, preferred to negotiate a deal with a weak opposition in order to engineer the survival of his party in "free" elections. A number of contemporary observers, both

30. Crawford 1996, 74–75.

journalistic and academic, were inclined to describe the unfolding of these events as revolutions in which governments were overwhelmed by their domestic opponents. In reality, however, the locus of change was in the international sphere, where the Soviet empire had relinquished its erstwhile holdings in order to effect a deal with its global adversaries.

If one implicit condition for Western cooperation was the granting of self-determination to the countries of East Central Europe, another was reforming, or "civilizing," the institutions of the Soviet state by giving them a more representative character. No ultimatum to this effect was ever delivered, but Gorbachev knew that a "common home" would not be feasible without modifying the totalitarian constitution still in place. A series of domestic reforms thus followed, beginning with a greater freedom of expression (*glasnost'*), initially justified by technocratic arguments about the need for freer information flows in order to permit the operation of markets and to improve the efficiency of bureaucracies. Then came the creation of a deliberative body elected indirectly, under arcane rules, which produced a rather conservative assembly. None of this seemed like much by Western standards, to be sure, but it proved too much for the survival of the Soviet Union, for *glasnost'* soon revealed its potential as an instrument of separatism. In the end, like so many empires, the Soviet Union fell not because it had too many enemies but because it had too few friends. As it unraveled, the old elite ran for cover. While many at the center found refuge in the emerging new economy and in the opportunities for personal enrichment, those on the peripheries quickly converted themselves into political classes behind the flags of ethnic states and calls for national sovereignty.

There remain the unavoidable questions about the historical inevitability, and hence predictability, of these events. The answer to this question is twofold. On the one hand, the Soviet imperial system had a structure and logic that, once foiled by circumstances, produced predictable consequences typical of such entities. On the other hand, Gorbachev's rise to leadership and his role as an unwitting "executioner of the regime"[31] were far from inevitable. Even under growing pressures, the Soviet leaders could have resolved to temporize.[32] Indeed, behind the closely guarded doors of the Soviet Politburo one could have made a rational, if overly blunt, argument for more muddling through by appealing to the classical maxim about the virtues of gaining time: *habet tempus, habet vitam.* If one's fortunes are bleak, one can nonetheless hope for bad luck on the part of one's adversaries. In this instance, such a decision would have required faith in the periodic crises of

31. Schroeder 1995, 223.
32. A most convincing argument to this effect is Martin Schrenk's review of Marie Lavigne's *The Economics of Transition* (Schrenk 1995, 20–21).

capitalism or in the ill effects of social and demographic trends in the Western camp. What is most remarkable about this chapter in history is that, after seventy years of predicting the demise of capitalism, the men at the very top of the Soviet regime had so little faith in their own preachings and sacred texts.

EAST CENTRAL EUROPE: THE COMMUNIST LEGACY

Whatever the answers to this question of inevitability, the fact remains that communism in Europe did fail. The events that unfolded during the Gorbachev era turned 1989 into a landmark year. It is from this juncture that we may look back at the previous forty-five years to set the historical record straight, as well as to establish a point of departure for studying the politics of "postcommunism" and assessing the legacy left behind by the Soviet imperial regime. Humans, as Marx suggests in *The Eighteenth Brumaire*, do make their own history. But they make it out of circumstances transmitted to them by the past, reflecting designs, successes, and failures of the previous age.

The Economic Legacy

The logic of the imperial system was perhaps reflected most clearly in the economic policies of communist regimes. As we have seen from the preceding narrative, the politics of militancy and mobilization had tangibly transformed the societies of East Central Europe. As Tables 48, 49, and 50 show, under Soviet-type governments those societies had become less agricultural, more urbanized, and more industrialized, with more than 50 percent of their industrial production originating from three branches of the

TABLE 48

*Percentage of East European Labor Forces
in Agriculture, 1930–78*

Country	1930	1960	1978
GDR	—	18	10
Czechoslovakia	28	28	12
Hungary	51	38	18
Poland	65	48	33
Bulgaria	79	56	40
Yugoslavia	80	63	43
Romania	78	64	50
Albania	—	71	62
USSR	—	42	17

SOURCES: Berend and Ránki 1974, 306; World Bank 1980, 75.

TABLE 49

*Percentage of East European Population
in Urban Areas, 1960–78*

	1960	1978
GDR	72	77
Czechoslovakia	47	63
Hungary	40	54
Poland	48	57
Bulgaria	39	64
Yugoslavia	28	42
Romania	34	48
Albania	31	37
USSR	49	65

SOURCE: World Bank 1980, 77.
NOTE: Estimates are based on national definitions and are thus
more applicable for chronological than for spatial comparisons.

TABLE 50

Growth of Industry and Agriculture, 1965–82

(1975 = 100)

	INDUSTRY				
	1965	1970	1975	1980	1982
GDR	70.0	84.7	100	115.8	122.7
Czechoslovakia	67.4	82.7	100	114.1	116.1
Hungary	74.6	87.9	100	111.4	112.3
Poland	51.3	69.4	100	102.8	86.1
Bulgaria	50.2	75.7	100	117.3	123.9
Romania	37.6	64.5	100	124.0	124.9

	AGRICULTURE				
	1965	1970	1975	1980	1982
GDR	85.3	87.0	100	103.7	99.8
Czechoslovakia	75.9	89.0	100	107.4	94.8
Hungary	85.2	82.4	100	108.1	112.4
Poland	95.5	94.8	100	95.1	95.6
Bulgaria	88.2	89.9	100	84.1	92.2
Romania	81.4	77.2	100	117.2	126.8

SOURCE: Alton et al. 1983, 19.
NOTE: Comparable data on Yugoslavia and the USSR not available.

economy: machinery, metallurgy, and chemicals.[33] In the meantime, as Table
51 shows, their gross domestic product increased three- to sixfold from the
prewar year of 1937, with most of that growth coming within the 25-year
period between 1950 and 1975, or even within the still narrower time frame
between 1960 and 1973, which many economists are inclined to see as the
"golden years" of communism.[34] This record was accompanied by an im-

33. United Nations 1983, 160–61.
34. Major 1994, 328.

TABLE 51

Indices of GDP Growth for Six East Central European Countries, 1937–89

	1937	1950	1975	1989
Bulgaria	100	117.0	498.6	547.5
Czechoslovakia	100	104.2	262.5	327.3
Hungary	100	100.0	263.9	309.6
Poland	100	102.9	334.5	366.3
Romania	100	110.5	458.0	516.0
Yugoslavia	100	115.5	457.2	639.8

SOURCE: Maddison 1995, 154–55.

TABLE 52

Life Expectancy at Birth, 1960–90

	1960	1978	1990
East Germany	68	72	—
Czechoslovakia	69	70	71.8
Hungary	67	70	70.9
Poland	66	71	71.8
Bulgaria	67	72	73.4
Romania	66	70	70.8
Yugoslavia	62	69	—
Albania	62	69	72.2
USSR	68	70	69.3
West Germany	69	72	75.2
United States	70	73	75.9

SOURCES: World Bank 1980, 191; United Nations 1993, 190–91.

pressive rise in the "vital indicators" of "human development," spurred as much by the Enlightenment tradition of socialism as by the more pragmatic needs of labor management and conscript armies of the modern, militarized state. As a result of this dual impulse (the aggregate results of which appear in Tables 52, 53, and 54), infant mortality decreased from a prewar average of 150 per thousand to below 20 per thousand by the end of the communist period, while life expectancy at birth increased from 55 years to the low 70s, almost eliminating the gap between East and West in this particular respect. And although the mean number of years of education remained below Western levels, it rose considerably from before the war.

This performance earned the communist countries of East Central Europe high marks from many Western economists. In 1975, Paul Bairoch calculated that between 1950 and 1973, the communist countries of East Central Europe were doing better than 88 "underdeveloped," and 27 "nondeveloping" nations of the Third World.[35] Subsequent calculations by Bai-

35. Bairoch 1975, 193.

TABLE 53

Infant Mortality, 1960–90

(per thousand births)

	1960	1978	1990
East Germany	39	13	—
Czechoslovakia	24	19	11
Hungary	48	24	16
Poland	57	22	15
Bulgaria	45	22	17
Romania	76	31	27
Yugoslavia	88	34	21
USSR	41	—	20[a]
West Germany	34	15	12
United States	26	14	9

SOURCES: World Bank 1980, 191; World Bank 1993, 292–93.
[a] Russian Federation.

TABLE 54

School Enrollment and Mean Years of Schooling, 1960–90

	Percent of secondary school–aged enrolled		Mean years schooling
	1960	1977	1990
GDR	39	93	—
Czechoslovakia	25	38	9.0
USSR	49	73	9.0[a]
Hungary	46	68	9.6
Poland	50	67	8.0
Bulgaria	55	88	7.0
Romania	24	77	7.0
Yugoslavia	58	79	—
Albania	20	—	6.0
Fed. Rep. of Germany	—	84	11.1
United States	86	93	12.3

SOURCES: World Bank 1980, 83–84; United Nations 1993, 135–36.
[a] Russian Federation.

roch and Maurice Lévy-Leboy in 1981 suggest that while the communist countries of East Central Europe were holding on to their prewar rankings in the world economy, the countries in the Third World sample had been losing their share of global GNP.[36] In 1978, the World Bank ranked the GDR, Czechoslovakia, and Hungary as 18th, 22d, and 27th, respectively, among 125 countries.[37] Some time later, Angus Maddison, comparing the performance of the economies of the state socialist countries of the eastern Bloc (including the USSR, but excluding the GDR and Albania) with the record

36. Bairoch and Lévy-Leboy 1981, 7.
37. World Bank 1978, 79 and passim.

of the seven best-performing Latin American, eleven Asian, and ten African countries countries between 1950 and 1973, found that while the aggregate rates of GDP growth in these world regions were not dramatically different—5.2 percent for Latin America, 4.5 percent for Africa, and 5.0 percent for the Soviet Bloc—in per capita terms, the figures for Eastern Europe were substantially higher than those for the selected Latin American (2.4), Asian (3.1), and African (1.8) countries.[38] The differences were due to much higher investment and much lower birth rates under state socialism.[39]

The weak spot on this record was that while the countries of the Soviet Bloc held their own in the larger world economy, they fell short when compared with the economies of Western Europe, and it was the latter, together with the United States, that continued to be the main reference region for their populations. Exact comparison of these economies, to be sure, presents formidable challenges, which scholarship has sought to overcome by using one of three methodologies: (1) converting accounts reported in national currencies into a common denominator, usually U.S. dollars, by establishing valid exchange rates, while also compensating for the omission of the service sector from official communist statistics; (2) attempting to establish purchasing power parities (PPP) by creating consumer "baskets" of commodities, whose common value is then expressed in some international unit or familiar currency; or (3) by seeking out "physical indicators" (PI) in Western and non-Western economies, and by extrapolating the non-Western figure via comparison of the two.[40] All three methods require the intrusion of subjective elements in establishing the "true" exchange rate, or by the choice of indicators and relevant commodities. But it appears that the PPP and PI methods are likely to provide us with the smallest, and market exchange (ME) methods the largest, gaps between the Eastern and Western economies.

To compensate for these subjective elements, it may be best to choose calculations using all three methods (for the years 1975–80) and to reduce them to a single arithmetic average in comparing the economies of East Central Europe with those of the United States and the by now familiar "Western six." Three sets of calculations exist for the precommunist period, each using a different method of calculation: one set was formulated by Paul Bairoch, another by Colin Clark, and a third by the Hungarian economist Éva Ehrlich. As presented in Table 55, these can serve as a proper baseline for comparisons with the arithemetical averages yielded by the sum of different calculations on Tables 56 and 57. Since the sum of the prewar figures

38. Maddison 1995, 63.
39. Percentages for the 1970s: GDR, −0.2; Czechoslovakia, 0.7; Poland, 0.9; Hungary, 0.4; Bulgaria, 0.5; Yugoslavia, 0.9; Albania, 2.5 (World Bank 1978, 71).
40. For an extensive discussion of the relative merits of various methodologies, see Marer 1985, passim.

TABLE 55

East Central European Income per Capita, 1930s

(percentage of Western-arithmetical averages)

Researcher	Method	Year(s)	% West European Six	% US
Éva Ehrlich	PI	1937	31.0	18.3
Colin Clark	PPP	1926–34	39.9	23.2
Paul Bairoch	PPP/ME[a]	1937–38	39.3	—

SOURCES: Ehrlich 1978, 191–212 (for these figures in English text, see Marer 1989, 72); Bairoch 1976, 297; Clark 1940, 46–47, 146, 148, 151.

NOTE: East Central Europe = Czechoslovakia, Hungary, Poland, Bulgaria, Romania, and Yugoslavia.

[a] Market exchange rates in 1960 dollars, with some modifications to establish purchasing power parity.

TABLE 56

East Central European Income per Capita, 1970s, minus GDR

(% of West)

Source	Method	Year(s)	% Western Europe[a]	% US
Block (USDS)	PPP	1977–78	40.6	33.1
Marer	PPP	1980	27.8	32.2
Marer	ME	1980	22.6	26.0
Bairoch	PPP	1973	50.8	—
United Nations	PPP	1975	35.2	35.5
World Bank	ME	1978	34.0	33.5
CIA	PPP	1980	36.9	29.6
World Handbook	ME	1970s	30.5	32.1
Ehrlich	PI	1980	41.6	29.0
Arithmetical Average			35.5	31.3

SOURCES: Block 1978, 27, 33; Marer 1985, 105, cols. 8, 10; Bairoch 1976, 307, 309; United Nations 1976, 168; World Bank 1978, 69; Central Intelligence Agency 1992, 28; Taylor and Jodice 1983, 110–11; Ehrlich figures in Marer 1989, 74.

[a] "Germany" in Western Europe includes the Federal Republic only.

TABLE 57

Comparisons of East European with Western GNP per Capita (PPP), 1987–90

	1987	1988	1989	1990
% of West European	35.7	34.5	—	—
% of United States	27.9	26.9	26.4	23.9

SOURCES: For 1987, World Bank 1996, 188; for 1988, Central Intelligence Agency 1992, 28; for 1989, 1990, Havlik 1991, 37.

yield 36.7 percent, and those in Table 56 35.5 percent (more or less corroborated by the figures on Table 57), we may conclude that, notwithstanding the spurt of growth experienced by the communist economies between 1960 and 1973, the state socialist governments under Soviet auspices failed to bring about a statistically significant reduction in the East-West gap in per capita domestic product. Indeed, taken strictly, the figures suggest an increasing gap compared to the pre–World War II level. If so, much of this increase took place over the last fifteen years of the regimes' existence, when, according to Angus Maddison,[41] the economies lost ground not only in relation to the advanced capitalist countries, but also in relation to the leading countries of Asia and Latin America as well, while barely holding their ground in relation to the African economies.

The case of East Germany, not included in Tables 56 and 57, presents an instance of still greater relative decline compared to the Western economies. According to Ludwig Bress's calculations of German regional economic disparities before World War II, per capita domestic product on the territory of the future GDR was 103 percent of what it was in future West Germany (and 106 percent of the figure for the Reich as a whole).[42] Applying this multiplier to the calculations of Colin Clark for 1925–34,[43] and of Paul Bairoch for 1938,[44] we will find that per capita GDP on future East German territory was 92.2 percent of the Western index figure in the first period, and 113.8 percent in the last prewar year. The decline from these high figures is dramatic. We know, of course, that the East German economy was devastated by wartime destruction and postwar plunder. But after 1960 it made its much vaunted spurt to overtake all other socialist countries. But even so, as Table 58 shows, in the 1970s the country's per capita GDP was only 62.3 percent of the combined figures of six Western countries (including the German Federal Republic). These figures, however, may understate a more dismal reality and reflect the "creative" methods of data gathering and interpretation used by the statisticians of the GDR. More likely than not, the low figures of Marer on Table 58—hovering around the 44 percentage figure—are more realistic, in that their validity was borne out by calculations made after the fall of the GDR. These figures, reported by Havlik, compare the GDR economy with that of the United States, and report East German per capita product somewhere between 39.1 and 46.3 percent of the U.S. figure.[45]

While comparisons with Africa or Asia, whether positive or negative,

41. Maddison 1995, 62–63.
42. Bress 1982, 127. See Chapter 6, n. 187.
43. Clark 1940, 41.
44. Bairoch 1976, 297. See also Table 16 (in Chapter 4).
45. Havlik 1991, 37.

TABLE 58

German Democratic Republic, GNP per Capita Estimates, 1970s

(% of West)

Source	Method	Year(s)	% Western Europe	% US
Block (USDS)	PPP	1977–78	62.1	50.1
Marer	PPP	1980	44.8	52.0
Marer	ME	1980	—	35.0
Bairoch	PPP	1975	85.8	—
World Bank	ME	1978	60.0	58.8
World Handbook	ME	1977	55.6	58.0
Ehrlich	ME	1980	65.8	45.9
Alton	PI	1977	—	73.6
Arithmetical Average			62.3	53.3

SOURCES: Alton et al. 1983, 22–23; others as in Table 58.

had few political implications in this part of the world, the demonstration effect of the West remained a steady concern. From the 1970s onward, Western scholarship began to notice "the heightened awareness [in East Central Europe] of Western society's high levels of consumption,"[46] and the disturbing trend that consumer expectations and satisfaction were not being shaped by past experience with misery but by invidious comparisons with the West.[47] East German officialdom constantly brooded over the problem. Both Ulbricht and Honecker corresponded with their Soviet counterparts, Khrushchev and Brezhnev, about the ill effects of popular comparisons with Western standards of living,[48] and they never ceased in their efforts to prove that, all told, people lived better on their side of the border between the two Germanies. Typical of this effort was the booklet *Wo lebt man besser?* (Where does one live better?), published in 1968 by the GDR State Secretariat for West German Affairs. In it, the authors make their usual pitch about free education, subsidized housing, security of employment, and health care, while providing a list of items with comparative prices attached, but with little effort to account for obvious differences in quality, between, say, a West German Mercedes and an East German Trabant.[49] Romanian and Bulgarian officials tried to cope with the demonstration effect problem by isolating Western visitors from their own citizens, while simultaneously encouraging tourism in order to increase hard-currency earnings. In Romania, foreigners were forbidden by law from staying in the home of a citizen and, in principle, citizens were required to report all contact with noncitizens. In Hungary, one of the most "liberal" communist countries, the demonstra-

46. See Gitelman 1981, 131–34.
47. Mieczkowski 1975, 131, 244, 281.
48. Kopstein 1997, 66, 88.
49. Hell and Prien 1968.

tion effect became an important subject for the budding field of political sociology. The most remarkable product of this curiosity is the report of a symposium held in the early 1980s, published under the title of *Character, Conditions, and Tendencies of the Socialist Way of Life* in 1984.[50] Most of the contributors to the volume address the problems of deprivation and need. The lead essay, written by one of the major intellectual figures in the Hungarian party, addresses the subjectivity, flexibility, and relativity of human expectations and the paradox that the satisfaction of some needs tends to generate new ones, turning novel articles of consumption, once treated as luxuries, into necessities in the public eye.[51] Another essay agonizes over the political dilemma of whether to resist the Western model of material civilization and mass consumption society, or to succumb in the manner of the countries of the Third World.[52] Most remarkable, though, is the contribution of Kálmán Kulcsár, a renowned sociologist of law. His essay flatly states that the central problem of socialism in East Central Europe is the relative backwardness of the region, made critical by "invidious comparisons with the standards of living in adjacent capitalist societies . . . [which,] by gradually becoming the universal measure of progress . . . tend to subvert the very effort to catch up with them."[53] As for solutions, the symposium appears to suggest that leaders should accept the demonstration effect of the West as inevitable and, apart from their attempts to raise the standard of living, should try to explain to the public that the relative backwardness of the region has deep historical roots, rather than simply reflecting the relative merits of socialism and capitalism.

In view of the Soviet geopolitical design and organizational principles, it should not be surprising that the Bloc failed to overtake the capitalist West in the economic field or that communism failed to create modern mass consumption societies. It is rather more remarkable that 45 years of Soviet rule not only failed to narrow the income gap between East and West but had relatively little impact on the position of individual communist societies on the great European northwest-southeast gradient. Ironically, a trip undertaken from Vienna to Moscow or Istanbul in the 1980s would thus lead through the same way stations of progressively deteriorating material standards, agriculture, roads, accommodations, and public facilities as those encountered by a traveler 200 years before. This proposition, based on per capita GDP and GNP figures, as a first cut, is corroborated by a whole host of other indicators of "human development" in Tables 59–63 pointing to the persistence of intraregional economic inequalities.

50. Szánthó 1984.
51. Köpeczi 1984, 13–32.
52. Pataki 1984, 53–75, esp. 59.
53. Kulcsár 1984, 240–41.

TABLE 59
Ranking of Countries by per Capita GNP, 1930s

	E. Ehrlich 1937		P. Bairoch 1933–38	C. Clark 1926–34	
	% Western Europe	% US	% Western Europe	% Western Europe	% US
GDR[a]	97.1	59.6	100.8	81.8	47.5
Czechoslovakia	48.6	29.8	54.2	56.9	33.1
Hungary	38.6	23.7	43.8	44.8	25.5
Poland	34.4	21.1	36.3	35.1	20.4
Romania	23.1	14.2	33.0	29.7	17.3
Yugoslavia	22.8	14.0	32.6	40.8	23.7
Bulgaria	21.5	13.2	35.6	32.3	18.8

SOURCES: Ehrlich from Marer 1989, 73; Bairoch 1976, 297; Clark 1940, 47, 146–48, 151, and passim.
[a] GDR territory. Per capita income calculated at 6.0 percent above "German." See Bress 1982, 127.

TABLE 60
Ranking of Countries by per Capita GNP, 1977–80
(US = 100)

	PI 1977	ME 1978	PPP 1980
GDR	39%	58.0%	52%
Czechoslovakia	33	48.4	42
USSR	—	37.9	37
Hungary	24	35.6	39
Poland	23	37.3	33
Bulgaria	24	32.8	—
Romania	14	17.0	24
Yugoslavia	19	21.4	23
Albania	—	7.6	—

SOURCES: For PI, PPP, Marer 1985, 105; for ME, Taylor and Jodice 1983, 110–11.

TABLE 61
Ranking of Countries by per Capita GNP, 1987–90
(US = 100)

	1987 PPP	1988 PI	1989 PPP	1990 PI
GDR	—	45.9%	46.3%	57.4%
Czechoslovakia	44.1	42.3	37.8	52.2
USSR	—	—	44.2	52.8
Hungary	28.9	31.7	29.2	52.4
Poland	21.4	27.3	21.2	39.2
Bulgaria	23.5	29.9	27.2	49.5
Romania	22.7	21.3	16.5	35.8
Yugoslavia	—	21.9	26.1	38.1

SOURCES: For 1987, World Bank 1996, 188–89; for 1988, Ehrlich, quoted in Marer 1989, 73; for 1989, 1990, Havlik 1991, 37.

TABLE 62

Ranking of Countries by Eastern Bloc Economists, 1971–90

(per capita net material product)

	Zhelev 1971[a]	Szilágyi 1978[b]	Georgieva/Ivanov 1990[a]	
			Production	Consumption
GDR	135	124	143	174
Czechoslovakia	113	122	132	151
USSR	100	—	100	100
Hungary	82	100	—	—
Bulgaria	85	95	106	123
Poland	76	100	101	105
Romania	69	81	—	—
Yugoslavia	—	72	—	—

SOURCES: For Zhelev, Shoup 1975, 10; for Szilágyi, Marer 1985, 92; for Georgieva/ Ivanov, Havlik 1991, 13.
[a]USSR = 100.
[b]Hungary = 100.

TABLE 63

Comparison of Output per Capita, Mortality, and Occupational Structure

	Wheat yields (ktw/ha) 1976–80	Total grain output/ha 1976–80	Infant mortality (/1000) 1990	% Population in agriculture 1989–91
GDR	41.7	35.4	9	—
Czechoslovakia	40.2	36.9	11	13
Hungary	40.6	41.6	14	6
Poland	29.3	24.5	15	24
Bulgaria	37.4	35.4	17	17
Yugoslavia	31.4	—	21	—
Romania	26.8	30.1	27	31
USSR	16.4	16.0	17	—
Netherlands	54.4	—	7	5
Belgium	45.8	—	8	3
Fed. Rep. Germany	41.4	—	7	4

SOURCES: For yields: United Nations 1982, 129–30; for Yugoslavia and West Europe: Jacobs 1982, 140; for infant mortality: World Bank 1993, 292–99; for percentage of population in agriculture: United Nations 1993, 200.

A few deviations from the historical model should be noted, however. First, while the gradient is manifest, a comparison of the figures in these tables reveals that it had become somewhat less steep than before World War II. More particularly, intraregional differences between the northwestern and southeastern (Balkan) tiers of the region narrowed. This is consistent with the logic of the economic laws of Soviet-style socialism as modeled by János Kornai and demonstrated by Mária Csanádi, who empirically traced patterns of redistribution from the most to the least efficient production units.[54] It is also consistent with the hypothesis that the planning model of state socialism is less inefficient in primitive than in more complex economies. At any rate, as earlier tables have shown, over the long run the GDR turned out to be the principal loser within the larger state socialist experiment, while Bulgaria appears to have done best in relative terms. As some of the tables in this chapter indicate, there have been scholars who believed that Bulgaria overtook Poland in the 1970s or that it reached the prewar regional status of Hungary.[55] For a brief while, too, Bulgarian growth rates were matched and even surpassed by Romania (and possibly even by Albania). But by the mid 1980s, these two countries had fallen behind again, owing mainly to idiosyncratic policies that distanced them from the Bloc sufficiently to lose any possible benefit of association, yet not far enough to become true beneficiaries of large-scale assistance from the rich countries of the Western alliance. It is in this respect that the Yugoslav case is somewhat unique, for the country did profit from substantial foreign aid in the years after its "expulsion" from the Soviet Bloc. Most of these profits, however, were wasted by the country's semi-centralized economic model, in which allocations were decided at the top, but power over expenditures and investment were vested in regional units. What we saw in Yugoslavia after 1974 was, in effect, a dual economy: one in the country's northwest, oriented toward the world market and guided by principles of economic rationality; the other in the southeast, oriented toward local politics and guided by the political imperatives of building local power bases. In the medium run, the Yugoslav economy sustained high rates of growth, in which the volume of production expanded. But in the long run, the result was not the hoped-for equality among regions but an unprecedented steepening of the northwest-southeast gradient within the country itself.

Slovakia, already discussed at some length in Chapter 6, represents another special case, in that capital flows from the Czech provinces resulted in considerable narrowing of the economic gap between the western and eastern halves of the country. In this respect, the contrast between Yugoslavia and Slovakia is striking and must be accounted for in terms of differences in the overall institutional context. Whereas in Yugoslavia the expenditure of funds was the prerogative of unaccountable local elites, in Slovakia expenditures were closely monitored, not only by a single party center in Prague, but also from the imperial center in Moscow. But as with most other instances of development in East Central Europe, the success of the Slovak economy (and its near-equality with the Czech lands) was measured by the quantity of goods produced, which only had value in the context of the im-

54. Kornai 1982; Csanádi 1980, 130–31; Csanádi 1984, 163, 278.
55. See col. 4 in Marer 1985, 104, or table 10 in United States, Central Intelligence Agency 1992, 28.

perial economy and military machine. Hence Slovak success, like that of
Bulgaria or of the southern provinces of Yugoslavia, was greatly diminished
once the country exited from the Bloc and entered the world economy.

Politically, the persistence of income differentials *among* the countries of
the Bloc was of limited significance. Surely, a spurt of economic development, or expansion of consumption—whether or not it was sustained by actual growth—did buy some passive and temporary support from local populations. This was the case in Bulgaria and Slovakia and, for much shorter
spells of time, in Poland (1971–76) and Hungary (1965–73). But the absolute degree of poverty or wealth was of little consequence for the popularity and stability of communist governments, since the populations were
more attuned to their relative status vis-à-vis the West than to their ranking
within the world of state socialism. Thus the degree of latent or overt dissatisfaction had less to do with the actual standard of living than with such
factors as geopolitical and cultural proximity to the West. Indeed, in hind-
sight, we now know that economic dissatisfaction was widespread in East
Germany; although the GDR's standard of living was the highest among
state socialist societies, it was overshadowed by that of adjacent West Germany. Czechs, Hungarians, and Slovenians also had routine access to Western media, particularly to Austrian and West German television. The case
of East Germany, however, was unique in that audiences there did not have
to cope with language differences. Consequently, a sullen population had to
be kept in check by a police apparatus at least as massive as the one maintained over famished Romanians by the Ceauşescu regime. Thus, when the
imperial system began to falter, East Germans began their massive flight, ignoring all arguments about the superior virtues of state socialism. What was
most memorable about this flight was that those running across the border
from Hungary to Austria or climbing the walls of West German embassies
bore little resemblance to the ragged mass of humanity that fled westward
at the end of World War II or ran from the chaos of civil wars in Afghanistan or Rwanda. Unlike the latter, the East Germans were "well fed, clad,
educated and cosseted young professionals . . . after a wider assortment of
goods in the shops and a wider selection of holidays . . . the enticing and al-
luring spectacle of lavish consumption under capitalist auspices,"[56] motivations as disappointing to the Western Left as they were to their abandoned
communist masters.

In sum, then, continued inter- and intraregional economic inequalities
were the principal economic legacies of state socialism in East Central Europe. But this legacy was further burdened with the debts incurred by gov-

---

56. Z. Bauman 1992, 171. In Bauman's view, though, the allure was not in consumption
per se but in the availability of choice denied under state socialist discipline.

ernments eager to shore up the lagging consumer sectors of their economies in fruitless attempts to hold on to political power. The mounting sums, as we have already seen, were considerable. At the end of the state socialist era, six of the countries owed a total of $117 billion to Western creditors. The most profligate spenders of this largesse were Poland, Hungary, and East Germany; Bulgaria and Czechoslovakia were latecomers to the game. Only dirt-poor Romania and Albania remained relatively free of debt.[57] To make things worse, the five CMEA countries were themselves owed 15 billion ECUs, or $16 billion by the Soviet Union[58]—a debt that, much like the German imperial debt in 1945, had, for all practical purposes, become uncollectable upon the dissolution of the Soviet Bloc.

Structural Legacies

The state socialist governments of East Central Europe left behind a social structure that closely reflected both their policies of economic mobilization and the larger geopolitical purposes those policies served. If we were to limit ourselves to a single designation, the societies built by communism might be described as "politocracies," in which power was the prime instrument of allocating social reward, and political office was closely intertwined with social status. Not unlike the boyardom of traditional Orthodox societies, members of the party officialdom occupied a central place in both polity and society. Like the boyars of the past, this officialdom was hierarchical. Their privileges were commensurate with the position occupied in the nomenklatura, a modern version of the old tables of rank.

To be sure, not all privilege was commandeered by this political elite. Some of it they had to share with strategic groups outside the party hierarchy. These included an "elite intelligentsia" of professionals, academics, technical experts, and scientists, a cultural elite of artists and writers, and an elite of athletes, to whom the political system granted a larger share of public limelight than to the nomenklatura class itself. The privileges of the expert were a reward for performing the necessary functions of command and control over the daily tasks of running the economy; the artist was a potential "engineer of the soul" (to use Stalin's phrase); the athlete's function was to provide a focus and symbol for solidarity with the state in accordance with the spirit of a militarized society, this being one of the great common denominators, of course, between Soviet-style communism and National Socialism. At the same time, both the cultivation of the arts and competitive athletics also performed external functions for the regimes. As dual symbols

57. Vienna Institute 1991, 391.
58. Marer 1996, 59.

of state socialist prowess and refinement, they were to compensate for material deficiencies and economic inferiority. If the Soviet Union and its imperial clients could not quite equal the sophistication and productivity of the leading capitalist nations, they could match and even overtake them at the Olympic games, in the nimbleness of their dancers, or in the vocal virtuosity of their singers. Consequently, irrespective of party memberships, these categories of talent were amply rewarded, and often enjoyed greater immunities and a more inviolate private space than the members of the political class itself.

In the years 1948–65, the crafting of this social structure was a truly revolutionary enterprise and resulted in enormous social dislocations via both horizontal and vertical mobility. The first of these involved a massive shift of the population from traditional agriculture to the modern industrial and service sectors. The dimensions of these dislocations are revealed in the figures in Table 48 above.[59] Vertically, the first decade of communist rule was a time of both downward and upward mobility. On the one hand, members of the old political class were dismissed from their positions. Owners and entrepreneurs were expropriated and, together with the members of the old political class, were stigmatized and persecuted in a variety of ways, not least of which were measures barring their offspring from secondary and university education. At the same time, there was an upward flow from manual to nonmanual occupations: a change of 13.5 percent in Bulgaria, 29.0 percent in Czechoslovakia, 17.2 percent in Hungary, 16.9 percent in Poland, 20.0 percent in Romania, and 14.5 percent in Yugoslavia.[60] An estimated 2.5 percent of industrial workers and peasants were,[61] in the jargon of the day, "lifted upward" into the new political establishment.

These patterns of recruitment and social mobility began to change in the 1960s as the regimes were relaxing political criteria of admission to institutions of higher learning and to the ranks of the "elite intelligentsia." The party machines were an exception, in that they continued to draw a contingent of manual workers through special avenues of training and recruitment.[62] Simultaneously, the general rate of mobility declined rapidly. According to some studies, mobility from manual to nonmanual categories fell to levels below those prevailing in Western Europe and the United States.[63]

Most remarkably, in view of the harsh treatment meted out to them in the 1950s, substantial segments of the old prewar elites, and especially their children, began to reappear in high-status occupations. Reliable informa-

59. As to horizontal mobility, see also Connor 1988, 144.
60. Ibid.
61. Andorka 1983, 185.
62. Kolosi and Wnuk-Lipinski 1983, 4, 57.
63. Andorka 1983, 211.

tion on this subject, based on large representative samples of the general population created for census purposes, is available only for Hungary and Poland. According to these, in 1970, 16.3 percent of Hungary's and 22.3 percent of Poland's intelligentsia were members or children of prewar elite groups, indicating that no less than 40.8 percent of Hungary's and 38.4 percent of Poland's smaller prewar establishment managed to survive the intervening revolutionary experiments.[64] This "elite intelligentsia" was dispersed among all kinds of occupation but was notably underrepresented in the party machine.[65] Just as the old order once reserved positions of power for the gentry, so the communist order tried to reserve the levers of power for the members of the proletariat.

Even so, these societies created in the 1950s retained strong egalitarian elements. Indeed, their greatest achievement, at least in countries south and east of the GDR and the Czech lands, was that they pulled upward—economically, socially, and culturally—the lowest one-third of their populations, the "three [six, nine] million beggars," in the rhetoric of the populists of Right and Left, who, before World War II, had lived below subsistence levels, explaining the region's extremely low levels of life expectancy and high levels of infant mortality. Although pockets of great poverty remained in these societies, and were eagerly rediscovered by dissident sociologists in the regimes' waning years,[66] these changes brought about by communism were surely striking enough to all who possessed memories of the 1930s. Before the war, this large and predominantly rural segment of the population walked barefoot, often dressed in little more than rags, suffered chronically from tuberculosis or pellagra, and lived in hovels built with thatched roofs above dirt floors. Thirty years later, they were clad and shod, they suffered no shortage of (low-quality) staples, and they had a higher life expectancy under universal health care systems (primitive as they were by Western middle-class standards). A good part of this population lived in shoddy tenements or expropriated country mansions that for all the faulty plumbing and broken elevators were still superior to what they had before the war. The downside of such progress was that it had been partly accomplished by depressing the living standards of other strategic segments of the population, including those of the educated classes, often below prewar levels and certainly below the levels enjoyed by their occupational counterparts in the West. Comparisons of these levels hurt social morale. Some of the countries tried to deal with the problem by banning travel to capitalist lands. Others

64. Andorka 1983, 186–87; Kornai 1992, 330. See also Bálint 1983, 109.
65. Rudolf Andorka to author. At the time when the study was conducted, the publication of this particular item of information was banned in both Hungary and Poland.
66. See a report on such studies in Hungary and Poland in Lane 1983, 60–61.

did not. But those regimes that extended this most generous and gracious of all concessions—as did the Polish and Hungarian ones—sowed more seeds of bitterness, for nothing was more humiliating to members of the "elite intelligentsia" than sleeping in their cars and living off canned provisions while visiting Western Europe for vacations or scientific conferences.

At whatever the price, then, these regimes created societies with greater income equality than either the First World of advanced capitalism or the Third World of the noncommunist peripheries. They are reflected in low gini index figures (Bulgaria, 21; Poland, 25; Czechoslovakia, 21; Yugoslavia, 21)[67] that compare favorably with Brazil's score of 63 and Mexico's 50, as well as with the United States's 40, West Germany's 39, or Italy's 40.[68] We also possess data, however incomplete, that allow us to compare differences between the highest and the lowest quintiles of the income-earning populations. They show that the highest quintile in Hungary and Poland received about 3.5 times the income of the lowest, significantly different from the 8.9:1 ratio in the United States, the 8.6:1 ratio in Switzerland, or the 5.7:1 ratio for West Germany.[69] The best collection of figures divides the incomes of the top quintile by those earned by the bottom 40 percent, and using this coefficient arrives at the following rank order among six state socialist societies of East Central Europe: Czechoslovakia (1.12), GDR (1.16), Bulgaria (1.21), Hungary (1.25), and Yugoslavia (2.17)—the latter diverging on account of its regional income disparities—compared to 1.87 for Sweden and 2.70 for the United States.[70]

These figures, to be sure, tell us only part of the story of income inequality under state socialism, for they are based on earned income and therefore do not account for "perverse redistributions" via subsidies not subjected to means tests.[71] Thus, bread was subsidized for both rich and poor, and gasoline prices were subsidized by the same principle, even though the majority of the population did not own cars. And while for a manager or party chief subsidized housing often translated into a mansion, for the worker it meant an apartment in one of the tenements described above. Moreover, none of these figures take into account the fact that by the 1970s, and in step with the Soviet model, each one of these societies was governed by a political aristocracy that discreetly and inconspicuously enjoyed inordinate incomes drawn from the revenues of the state.[72]

67. Calculations by Sláma 1978 quoted in Kornai 1992, 318.
68. Ibid. See also World Bank 1996, 196–97.
69. Ibid.
70. Taylor and Jodice 1983, 135.
71. Kolosi and Boehm 1982, 94–97. See also Kornai 1992, 320.
72. This political aristocracy is estimated at 0.2 percent of the labor force. Its privileged access to goods and other perks listed are in Lane 1983, 57.

THE POSTCOMMUNIST ORDER

From Eastern Empire to Western Hegemony

The dramatic sequence of events that brought about the implosion of the Soviet Bloc posed extraordinary challenges to both participants and observers. For participants both inside and outside the region, the challenge was to create a semblance of order out of the chaos of imperial decline, regime collapse, and the dissolution of long-united political entities. For observers, not least among them political scientists, the challenge was to create intellectual order by discovering critical variables, common denominators, and appropriate analogies that would permit placing the sequence of events in a proper historical perspective.

The profession of political science rose to the occasion with commendable zeal. Indeed, it produced a plethora of paradigms long before the events had unfolded in their entirety. These paradigms may be placed along an intellectual continuum between the poles of progress and decay. On one end, we find those who rushed back either to theories of modernization and convergence[73]—perceiving an increasingly complex economic base shaking off an antiquated structure of authority—or to still larger evolutionary schemes in which the logic of rationality would prevail over irrational forces of conflict and dictatorship, culminating in a Hegelian (or Marxian) "terminal stage" of history.[74] Conversely, at the opposite end of the continuum, we find those who saw in the fall of communism an instance of political "extinction"[75] or imperial decline, with all the promises and pitfalls that political decay portends.[76] Somewhere in the middle, we find "transitologists," who, largely unburdened by theoretical assumptions, view these events as a process of transition from one type of domestic institutional order to another.[77] While these paradigms of transition have been inspired by analogies with the recent experiences of transition from authoritarian regimes in Latin America and southern Europe, there is little in these intellectual constructs that would persuade us of their general relevance, especially because they often attribute responsibility for outcomes to actors guided by virtue rather than impelled or hindered by necessity. Transforming these analogies into theory requires that we root them in empirical relationships in which outcomes are contingent.

Derived from long historical cycles of political experience, the hypotheses

73. Pye 1990, 3–19; Lewin 1988.
74. Fukuyama 1990, 75–77. In book form, Fukuyama 1992.
75. Jowitt 1992, 207–25.
76. Szporluk 1994, 21–39. Rupnik 1994, 91–114.
77. For a review of this vast literature, see Schmitter 1997, 168–74. For a major representative work, see Linz and Stepan 1996.

underlying this study point to such contingencies within the broader context of international regimes. Accordingly, especially in small states in relatively backward regions, domestic regimes—institutional designs for the structure, scope, and exercise of political authority within nation-states—are likely to rise and fall with changing hegemonic relationships, that is, in times of transition from the hegemony of one great power to that of another. We have certainly seen such transitions in the earlier history of East Central Europe, notably when the hegemony of liberal powers gave way to that of fascist states, and when the latter gave way to the regional hegemony of the Soviet Union. In each of these instances, the domestic politics of the regional small powers changed, reflecting the character, interests, and ideology of the new hegemon. These elements of hegemony provide an appropriate point of departure for our investigations, although long-term outcomes must also take account of conditions prevailing in the host societies.

In order to establish a proper baseline for comparisons, we may begin by recapitulating the principal characteristics of the Soviet-dominated "old regime." Put most succinctly, this international regime was a vertically coordinated imperial system located on the backward periphery of the modern world economy. The regime was designed to challenge the global economic and political status quo from its position of economic inferiority, an enterprise justified by an ideology of socialist internationalism. The institutions of the Soviet imperial state were defined by the logic of economic inferiority combined with the globalist ambitions of the regime: while economic inferiority called for a system of relentless mobilization, the reproduction of deprivations thereby entailed in turn demanded the strict discipline of political authoritarianism. These two elements of the system—mobilization and authoritarianism—have frequently been drawn together under the common label of "totalitarianism."

The Soviet Bloc, containing both the "inner" and the "outer" empires of Russia, was itself a product, proof, and instrument of the larger geopolitical design. This being the case, the politics of the satellites closely followed the Soviet institutional model, more as a matter of Soviet self-validation than as a matter of administrative or economic rationality. As a result, under the Stalin-Zhdanov scheme, Albania and Czechoslovakia were to be served by the very same institutions and policies, and variations from that scheme were severely limited even in later years so as not to undermine the internal legitimacy of Soviet institutions. The empire itself was a creature of armed force: it is hard to imagine any one of the "ruling" parties, including that of Yugoslavia, prevailing over their domestic opponents without the menacing regional presence of the Red Army. Force also remained the key integrative element of the Bloc once it had been consolidated. This is not to say that economic bargaining and cryptopolitics between the Soviet Union and its satellites were absent from the hegemonic relationship. But the parameters of the permissible were drawn and, in the last instance, enforced by, military power. Nothing is more illustrative of this than the fact that the Brezhnev doctrine, the grand charter of the empire, was essentially a list of negative injunctions underpinned by the threat of naked force against recalcitrant members trying to defect from the embrace of the imperial family.

The differences between the old and new international regimes are substantial. Unlike the old hegemony by the Soviet Union, the new hegemony is exercised by an alliance of some of the most prosperous societies of the world, held together by their common interest in the global economic and political status quo. Their political institutions are the products not of scarcity but of a long trajectory of material progress that, colored by shared historical traditions and memories, permitted the gradual expansion of political participation via representative government. Taken together, prosperity, participation, and representation gave rise to a political democracy that over the past few decades has operated mainly by shifting allocative functions in society back and forth between markets and state bureaucracies.

Like the Soviet Union in 1945, the more loosely coordinated Western powers in 1989 encountered a political vacuum in territories adjacent to them. But unlike the Soviet Union, they possessed no coherent geographical design and were animated neither by the desire for territorial conquest nor by prospects of an economic windfall. Indeed, while the newly opened avenues of trade with the East have consistently favored the West, these gains have been too small to matter, have been more or less offset by grants-in-aid and other forms of economic support,[78] and are unlikely to grow substantially over the next decade.[79] What motivated the future hegemon was politics, initially colored by a faint desire to live up to Western cold war rhetoric—which decried a continent torn asunder, a common culture ravaged by barbarians, and "captive nations" behind an "iron curtain"—and then by a concern about security. On the one hand, there was the more distant threat of a new Russian challenge to the continental balance of power; on the other, the more imminent prospect of chaos and disorder in lands adjacent to their own, including visions of the looming peril of waves of impoverished refugees migrating westward.

Given these differences in resources and interests, the character of the new international regime was quite different from that of its predecessor. As with any regime whose intent is the containment of conflict, force has played a role. It has been used over the years under international auspices to police Bosnia-Herzegovina, Macedonia, and, more recently, Albania. But force and

78. In 1991–95 trade with East Central Europe made up 2 percent of the total volume of EU, and 1 percent of U.S. trade. See Steven Weber 1995, 202.

79. See "Costs and Benefits of Eastern Enlargement: The Impact on EU and Central Europe," *Economic Policy*, no. 24 (Apr. 1997), cited by the *Economist*, Apr. 12, 1997, 77; Palánkai 1996, 49.

negative inducements are not the prime instruments of the new hegemony. While the charter of the Soviet Bloc spelled out an array of punishments to potential defectors, those of the new European order—incorporated in a series of documents named after cities like Rome, Maastricht, Copenhagen, and Amsterdam—are based on a major positive inducement and spell out conditions that individual countries must meet before qualifying for membership in the Council of Europe, NATO, or the European Union.[80] The major instruments of eliciting compliance with hegemonic preferences are economic inducements. Some of these take the form of traditional trade-offs: the offer of foreign aid, market shares, and investment in exchange for cooperative behavior. Others are exercised by holding out future prospects, above all the prospect of prosperity in a united Europe. To some skeptics, this may conjure up memories of Soviet calls for sacrifice holding out the prospect of full communism. However, the difference is substantial. For while no one in those days had a chance to see communism in full bloom, today the full panorama of capitalist prosperity is visible to all who can afford a visit to Vienna or Berlin. No small wonder, then, that while a large number of East Central Europeans become depressed when pondering the present, they remain relatively optimistic about their prospects for the future. If, in 1995, an average of only 17 percent (ranging from 9 percent in Hungary to 26 percent in the Czech Republic) were ready to declare that they fared better than they had 5 years earlier, 46 percent (even 37 percent of the ever-pessimistic Hungarians, along with half of the Poles) expressed the belief that they would be better off materially within the next 5 years.[81] Such future hopes are a more powerful cement holding societies together than the current economic benefits that either foreigners or their own governments can offer.

While members of the Western alliance on the two sides of the Atlantic have no formally adopted ideology, their shared interests, enmeshed with historically linked traditions and memories, have given rise to a set of common principles that, under the label of liberal universalism, provide underpinnings to the hegemonic project. At the level of economics, this universalism implies the quest for trade across national boundaries, which in the American context implies unfettered "globalization," although the latter has been restrained in Europe by strong elements of regional protectionism. Politically, the new universalism subscribes to democracy, but, in radical juxtaposition with its liberal predecessors, rejects the classical formula of the nation-state that has dominated international politics over the past three centuries. This "postnationalism," however, plays itself out differently on the two sides of the Atlantic. Whereas in the now uniting Europe, it implies

---

80. See Steven Weber 1995; Palánkai 1996, 51–52. See also Inotai 1994, esp. 15–20.
81. Rose and Haerpfer 1996, 13–14.

the gradual transfer of sovereign prerogatives from the state to supranational institutions, in the United States, it implies not so much the surrender of sovereignty as a project of replacing ethno-cultural solidarities with loyalty to institutions and collective entitlements. These are different projects. But their political fallout is the same: suspicion of ethnic-conscious majorities and a positive bias toward the ethnic solidarity of national minorities as a potential counterweight to ethno-national majoritarianism. By embracing this formula, the new universalism rejects the classical principle that the state should be the ultimate expression of cultural homogeneity and ethnic particularism. It also rejects the universalism of Soviet Marxism, which was willing to find progressive elements in the national traditions of both minorities and majorities.[82]

From a historical point of view, the rise of modern liberal universalism was closely intertwined with two major events. One of them was the civil rights movement in the United States, with its struggle for emancipation from discrimination on ethnic grounds. The other was World War II, which in and of itself looms as a giant morality tale about the potential evils of ethnic particularism and the ethnically organized state. In the United States, however, the war is not just a morality tale: it is one of the few pieces of the country's history that allows all segments of society to rally around its memory at a time when many heroes of yore are being dethroned, while others of the more recent past have yet to acquire universal acceptance and appeal. Indeed, memories of the war today provide one of the few platforms on which both Right and Left can stand. While the Right embraces it as the symbol of America in victorious ascent, the Left can celebrate it as a crusade in which an unusually odious form of radicalized particularism was decisively defeated. In Europe, meanwhile, the war is remembered as a kind of civil war among people quite similar in culture and appearance, and the morality tale it provides is a story about nations that were good or bad depending on where one stood at that particularly trying time. Ironically, in practical politics, this very division and ranking allowed Germany to reenter "Europe" after World War II, rearmed and flush with economic success, although reduced to a low moral status. This diminution in moral standing permitted Germany to participate in continental affairs but not to translate economic and military power into continental hegemony.

In this manner, and together with the American civil rights movement, World War II added a retributive and activist element to liberal universalism. Unlike the old, the new liberalism fights particularism—especially its radical manifestations in politics. Antiparticularism has become an integral part of the agenda and often outweighs such classical liberal injunctions as

---

82. For the institutionalization of the protection of minority rights, see Várady 1992, 260–82.

the advocacy of unrestrained freedoms of organization and speech. Witness the new order's injunctions against "fascism" and the seeming paradox, noticed by one Hungarian professor of law, that neo-Nazis are today to be found among the most ardent proponents of free speech.[83]

These differences between the old (Soviet) and the new (Western) hegemonies are, of course, substantial, but in contrasting these two international regimes, the observer must be careful not to overlook some elements of continuity. For one thing, we must remember that transition has not implied change from hierarchy to equality, but from one form of hierarchy to another. In East Central Europe today, there is little doubt as to who calls the shots or, in the words of the disappointed academic, as to who are the "missionaries" wielding the "bible," and who are the "local savages" awaiting conversion to the universalist canon.[84] On a first reading, this religious metaphor appears to be exaggerated. But upon reflection, it gains justification, above all because of the scope and depth of the agenda of Western emissaries. This agenda requires adaptation, not only to the exigencies of the capitalist market and to the etiquette of political democracy, but also to a wide range of cultural norms that, while they are the products of relatively recent organic changes in Western society, have under the "postmodern" label acquired an aura of global relevance. If communism set out to create a "new socialist man," the missionaries of this new universalism want to create new liberal persons endowed with the supranational sentiments of a New Age and liberated from traditional social ethics and taboos. This agenda is not only broad but in some ways more ambitious than that of Bolshevism. As a Romanian liberal suggested in personal conversation with this writer, it combines the most radical features of the conservative economic agenda of Thatcherism with those of American-style cultural liberalism.

This agenda is being pursued with considerable zeal, which brings us back once again to the metaphor of the religious mission. Such zeal has been displayed by representatives of both private and public organizations, by officials of both national and supranational governments. Illustrative here are the words of Jacques Santer, secretary-general of the European Union, excoriating an audience of Czech technocrats and political leaders. What he told them was that joining the Union required profound "emotional commitment,"[85] rather than mere legalistic compliance with documents spelling out the terms of membership. One may not wish to offend Santer by comparing him with Zhdanov, a ruthless man bent on imposing his new order

83. Sajó 1997, 46.
84. Ibid., 44.
85. Open Media Research Institute, *Daily Digest*, Apr. 5, 1996. From here on, cited as OMRI. Note that in April 1997, the name was changed to RFE\RL *Daily Newsline*, the latter distinct from the biweekly publication RFE\RL *Research Reports*, as well as from the earlier country reports published under the logo of *Radio Free Europe Research*, Munich.

on East Central Europe without a trace of regard for human cost. But there is a whiff of Zhdanovism in this statement, as well as in the doctrinaire rigidity with which the "road to liberalism" has been marked out from Prague to Tirana, with little concession to variable social, economic, and cultural conditions. This uniformity and zeal are not the products of personality or of historical accident, but of similarities that should not be overlooked when comparing the Eastern and the Western international regimes. Like the old hegemon, the new hegemons are themselves in the throes of revolutionary change, trying to cross the deep chasms from mono- to multiculturalism, from national sovereignty to supranationalism, and from the ethics of modernity to the ethics of postmodernity. These changes cry out for validation, and this search for legitimacy drives many of the Western projects in the East: the building of a multi-ethnic society in Bosnia-Herzegovina, interventions on behalf of ethnic minorities, and proposals to change the gender balance in the newly democratized parliaments by constitutional amendment.

The scope and intensity of the Western effort in East Central Europe becomes evident from the record and style of Western involvement in the affairs of these "emerging democracies," from the scrupulous monitoring of "progress" by hegemonic agencies that encourage, praise, and hector their protégés as they dispense rewards and punishments on their now regular tours of inspection. A methodical reading of daily reports of these comings and goings[86] easily yields hundreds of items, of which a few dozen will suffice to illustrate the current state of the East-West relationship with particular reference to the countries of East Central Europe.

Take the Czech lands, the model for liberal democratic progress. Here, apart from sacralizing the task of building the European Union, Jacques Santer urged an "immediate reform" of Czech law to conform with Western legal systems, "however arduous the task may be" in the short term (OMRI, 4/5/96). A U.S. congressional committee wrote to Prime Minister Václav Klaus, asking him to abrogate certain provisions of the Czech citizenship law; U.S. Senator Alphonse D'Amato and Representative C. H. Smith warned that without such reform, Czech promises to protect all minorities would sound "false and hollow" (RFE/RL, 8/25/97). The status of the Roma (Gypsy) minority was taken up again by British prime minister Tony Blair's letter to Czech political leaders (10/27/97). But legal reforms and citizenship rights were not the only concerns: some time before these warnings, the EU investigated Czech steel producers and threatened to bring anti-dumping charges against them in the European Parliament (OMRI, 07/19/95).

Like the Czech Republic, Hungary and Poland, although among the more

---

86. All dates in parentheses refer to OMRI *Daily Digest* (June 1994–April 1997) or RFE/RL *Daily Newsline*.

compliant governments, have been subject time and time again to judicious warnings about their trespasses. In Hungary, EU President Santer urged the country "to drop its 8 percent customs surcharge recently enacted by the country's legislature" (OMRI, 4/9/96). The U.S. Helsinki Committee meanwhile expressed its disappointment over Hungary hosting an "ethnic Hungarian summit" in Budapest and condemned the final communique issued by the conference (8/5/96). Other, unnamed U.S. officials in the State Department supported the rights of Hungarian minorities in neighboring countries, but condemned their aspirations for territorial autonomy (8/8/96). In Poland, officials of the OECD urged the abolition of restraints on the foreign ownership of land (7/12/96), while EU Commissioner H. van den Broek complained about vestiges of protectionism discernible in restrictions on the importation of motor vehicles (RFE/RL, 7/16/97). On the cultural-political front, the European Parliament isssued a strong reminder to the country as to what is appropriate and inappropriate in treating historical sights (OMRI, 4/26/96), while Germany has again and again raised the issue of the cultural and individual rights of the reawakened remnants of the German national minority.

Slovakia, Croatia, and, until its recent conversion, Romania, have been ruled by more recalcitrant governments that, at best, have been simulating compliance with the conditionality set up by the various agencies of the international regime. Thus they have been the objects of special attention and criticism by foreign monitoring agents. Slovakia has drawn strong and repeated warnings about its penal code (OMRI, 10/25/96; RFE/RL, 6/18/97), minority policies (OMRI, 2/17/97), and police brutality against the Roma (1/13/97). More specific issues have also been subject to critical Western review: the kidnapping of President Kováč's son (4/26/96); secret police spying on citizens (1/31/97); the publication of a right-wing book denying Slovak responsibility for the wartime deportation of Jewish citizens (RFE/RL, 6/26/97); and the building of a nuclear plant near Machovce (OMRI, 4/13/95). More recently, the Slovak government was called upon to abrogate a planned value-added tax on daily newspapers (RFE/RL, 11/3/97). The charges and the demands might well be justifiable in terms of the generalized expectations of the Western alliance, but Prime Minister Mečiar rejected them, denouncing the repeated interventions of U.S. Ambassador Ralph Johnson and EU Ambassador Georgios Zavos as "ultimatums" contrary to the classical principles of national sovereignty.[87] The net result of this recalcitrance has been the exclusion of Slovakia from the "first tier" of nations to be considered for membership in the European Union and NATO and the suspension of the membership of the country in the European Parliament for being "not yet sufficiently democratic" (11/3/97).

87. *Christian Science Monitor*, July 9, 1997, 6.

In the same vein, Croatia has been broadly and repeatedly condemned for "grave flaws" in the political and legal practices of its government, including the improprieties found by monitors of the Organization for European Security and Cooperation (OSCE) in the conduct of recent elections (RFE/RL, 6/17/97). To give this condemnation weight, U.S. Secretary of State Albright remarked that electoral irregularities "will not help Croatia's [pending] application with the World Bank" (6/17/97). Indeed, soon thereafter, the U.S. government used its veto power to stop the issuance of the loan (RFE/RL, 6/25/97). On more specific matters, there were admonitions about the publication of objectionable political tracts in Croatia, and against the promotions of thirteen officers who had served in the Croatian uniforms—whether Ustasha or regular army is debated—in World War II (OMRI, 11/5/96). More recently, the U.S. Department of State condemned Croatia for several pending parliamentary bills and for the selective application of laws. It further declared "unacceptable" the banning and "public defamation" of the Soros Educational Foundation (RFE/RL, 6/25/97). Like Slovak premier Mečiar, President Franjo Tudjman publicly rejected the "meddling of European and Transatlantic powers in Croat internal affairs" (OMRI, 11/25/96); in retaliation, the Western powers excluded Croatia from current plans of extending NATO and the EU, and gave low priority to financial aid to the country.

Monitoring Romanian behavior yields much the same results. Prior to the victory of the Liberal Democratic coalition in 1996, the country had been under steady attack for its restrictive policies toward its national minorities and for the presence of openly neofascist parties in its parliament (OMRI, 4/10/96). Western mood and expectations changed after the 1996 elections, but the new government has not been exempt from a careful review of its activities. While a recently visiting OSCE delegation under Karl Petersen expressed "cautious optimism" (RFE/RL, 10/6/97), IMF representative Paul Thompsen was "not satisfied with the progress of economic reform," was especially critical of the slow pace of privatization, and made the next installment of the IMF package conditional upon more rigorous compliance (7/30/97). On the cultural and political fronts, while more eagerly compliant than its predecessor, the government has drawn rebukes for an insufficient number of women deputies in parliament (9/27/97) and for the "delicate international implications of rehabilitating [six] members of the wartime Antonescu government" (11/10/97).

Among the countries of East Central Europe today, it is Serbia—or, more accurately, rump Yugoslavia—that has shown the greatest degree of open antagonism toward the new international regime. This pattern of behavior has persisted despite an almost daily flow of condemnations, threats, and warnings, and despite the continued, if partial, economic embargo, first declared at the onset of the war in Bosnia. Of the region's remaining countries, Bulgaria has lapsed into virtual financial receivership with the IMF. Bosnia-Herzegovina (under UNPROFOR), Macedonia (with discreet U.S. military presence, behind a UN mandate), and Albania (with the presence of an international police force since 1996) are in a state of political receivership, more reminiscent of the status of mandate territories under the Versailles treaty than of sovereign national states. Among these countries, the progress of Macedonia has received mixed reviews—of late by UN Human Rights Commissioner Elisabeth Rehn, who, while praising some of Macedonia's political accomplishments, was still concerned about "abuses of police power" and the plight of the Albanian minority (RFE/RL, 8/25/97). Albania, under the liberal democratic label, was in effect run by a Gheg tribal government between 1992 and 1996. The collapse of public authority was followed by new elections, under the watchful eyes of 450 OSCE observers (6/17/97), that, ironically, returned a group of ex-communist officials to power under a Socialist label, but to the satisfaction of both the EU and the United States. Albania has since received funds to rehabilitate its tattered economy (only two years earlier declared a spectacular success),[88] a contingent of "European" (*sic*) police officers (10/6/97), American military aid, and CIA instructors to reorganize, or dismantle, the remnants of its security police. The current, post-Berisha, Albanian government, weak and dependent on foreign policing and economic aid, tries to put up a brave front by insisting that it is running a sovereign state; in the pathetic words of the foreign minister, the Albanian leaders "are not supporting the ideas of the West because [they] are weak or in a crisis [but because they] think it is the best solution for now."[89] Others, though, less charitably, note that "they have not been heard to say 'no' to the West on anything recently."[90]

Bosnia-Herzegovina likewise remains a sore spot for Western policy. The U.S. military presence was recently extended, and NATO Secretary-General Javier Solana openly raised the possibility of a permanent military presence (RFE/RL, 11/10/97)—an echo of the Congress of Berlin's 1878 decision to give Austria-Hungary a 30-year mandate to pacify the country. Within these legal and political parameters, vertical communications between Westerners and locals tend to be unsurprisingly peremptory: the results of the Bosnian elections were not only supervised but "validated" by OSCE (9/30/97); the UN "slammed" the Moslem security police (12/12/97); EU Commissioner Jacques Klein "threatened to lock up in the National Museum leaders of the three communities" until they concluded working agreements (10/27/97); and UN Commissioner Westendorp threatened to "sack" Srpska president Krajišnik, saying: "If Krajišnik does not deliver, then I will say bye-bye to

88. Zanga 1994, 14–17.
89. Jordan 1998.
90. Ibid.

Mr. Krajišnik" (10/31/97). These are the voices of an international regime that, unlike its Soviet predecessor, does not conceal its view that national sovereignty remains little more than a "mirage," a relic of the reactionary past, soon to be superseded by the institutions of a more progressive, universalistic age.[91]

In sum, the wider collage of these items constitutes a grand strategy of co-optation, in which the richer countries of the core have sought to buy security for themselves, with the validation of their political identity as an additional bonus. Like all rational actors, their strategic efforts have involved attempts to minimize current costs while maximizing future benefits. Although no case can be made for East Central Europe being exploited in the process, there is no question that economic transfers from West to East have been far smaller than those that accompanied the grand projects of co-optation of the Cold War period, such as the efforts of the United States to save Western Europe from communism. In the latter project, the Marshall Plan alone committed 5–7 percent of the then-current GNP per annum of the United States to prospective recipients over a five-year period. This amount was in addition to $2.8 billion under the UNRRA program of 1945–47, $1.9 billion in loans under the GARIOA program to Europe, and another $7.5 billion to Greece, Turkey, and China.[92] As a percentage of American GNP, this would be the equivalent of $350–400 billion today, and that sum does not include further tangible benefits reaped by Western European countries under the Bretton Woods tariff regime. Incorporating East Germany into the Federal Republic has cost DM 1 trillion ($600 billion) thus far, and it will require the same amount over the next ten years to bring per capita income in the "new federal lands" to 90 percent of levels prevailing in western Germany.[93]

Previous enlargements of the European Union were accompanied by lesser but still substantial fiscal outlays and market concessions by the prosperous founding members. In the 1980s, Portugal received 2.53 percent of its GNP in direct benefits, Greece 1.67 percent, and Ireland 2.5 percent, amounting to some 34.6 billion ECUs.[94] Spain, with a population of 38 million, was the recipient of $29 billion of foreign direct investment (FDI) in the decade prior to its entry in the European Union and of some $80 billion between 1985 and 1991 (half in foreign direct investment, half in foreign aid).[95] The members of the "southern group" of the Union (including Spain,

91. The term mirage has been borrowed from an excellent study on how East Central Europeans confront the new age of supranationality after half a century of harangues about their loss of sovereignty to the Soviet empire. See Gombár 1996.

92. See Milward 1996, 246.

93. World Bank, world wide web: worldbank.org.htm.prdar.mayjune1997.art.htm.

94. Figures by courtesy of Yvonne Chiu.

95. Touis 1995, 95.

Portugal, Greece, and Ireland) have since 1988 been recipients of annual appropriations of 14 billion ECUs ($15.5 billion) in direct grants. In comparison, East Central Europe, with its population of about 120 million, was the recipient of $28.2 billion in foreign direct investment between 1990 and 1996, while the flow of public funds was $80 billion to Eastern European recipients (including the Baltic and Ukraine, but excluding Russia) with their combined populations of 190 million.[96] Much of the latter came in the form of loans from the IMF, the World Bank, and the European Bank of Regional Development. In any case, regardless of what the East has gained, from a Western point of view, the policy has been a success: it bought the West a fair measure of future security in return for a relatively low outlay.

The Design for Reform

Given the asymmetry of power relations between East and West, the projects of reforming the economy and politics of East Central Europe may well be seen as primarily Western projects to bring security to their part of the continent. This is not to suggest that a local impulse for reform has been completely absent, or that the peoples of the former Soviet satellites have been hostile or mere passive onlookers. Indeed, the idea of liberalizing the economy via privatization, decentralization, and the adoption of market principles of operation have been popular with both the intelligentsia and the population at large throughout the 1970s and 1980s.

As for democracy, both open dissidents and silent malcontents were fully aware that its idiom and practices were powerful weapons for delegitimizing the imperial system, and they correctly hypothesized that free elections would result either in the outright rejection of communism or in governments that would be more sensitive to local than to imperial interests. A surprising number of technocrats and academic economists were, perhaps mistakenly, inclined to link the processes of democratization and liberalization, arguing that without the first, the second project could not succeed.[97] This view found considerable support among the better-educated publics of most countries, while the "common folk" were ready to believe that democracy in and of itself was tantamount to economic prosperity. All this gave reforms a good initial momentum. But the momentum was quick to dissipate, or at least to diminish, as ideas were put to the test of political reality. Once disappointments set in, Western power began to play a crucial role, both in maintaining the momentum behind reform and in holding these emerging political systems together—whether by current inducements or by promises of a better future.

96. International Monetary Fund 1996, 107.
97. Described by McDonald 1993, 203–40. Also Michta 1997, 69.

Although there is a strong tendency in contemporary studies of East Central Europe to view postcommunist reforms as unique, and therefore as requiring their own frame of reference, historical precedents do abound and may well provide a bundle of helpful analogies. The closest and most illuminating of these arise out of the first liberal "experiment" on the peripheries in the nineteenth century. One of the centerpieces of this experiment was the "abolition of feudalism," whether domestic or foreign in origin—an act that many remember as the emancipation of the serfs in order to make them part of a modern citizenry. From an economic point of view, however, just as significant were the abolition of the corvée, which was tantamount to the commodification of labor and its adaptation to market principles, and the commodification of land via the creation of a new system of property rights—that is, the elimination of the legal fiction that all land was either royal or social property, which both landlord and peasant merely held in the form of non-negotiable tenures-in-fief. The Hungarian Count István Széchenyi's book *Hitel* (Credit), written in 1830, argued for the reform of landownership in the name, not of John Locke's natural rights but of Jeremy Bentham's utilitarianism, rejecting the old system because the fiction of royal ownership prevented the mobilization of credit by mortgaging land.[98] The logic of this argument was eventually followed throughout the European East, although in some countries (like Russia and Serbia), the road to reform was tortuous, for land was at first transferred to village communities, thereby necessitating another round of reforms. But eventually this was accomplished too, and since land represented the overwhelming share of nonliquid assets engaged in production, the process may be described as a major precursor of today's privatization programs. Much like its twentieth-century counterpart, the process was fraught with difficulties, seemingly endless litigation, and complaints about inequities and corruption. As Henry Roberts notes in his study of Romania,

> local administration . . . had ample opportunity to twist the provisions of the law to [the landlords'] advantage. Undoubtedly many injustices were committed in their application: often a landowner was able to distribute the worst land to the peasants, holding the best in his own estate; in a number of cases false measuring standards were used, an easy trick in a country lacking basic ground surveys; sometimes the landowner so divided the holdings that the peasants were unable to reach their property without paying a toll.[99]

With only a few words replaced, this text readily conjures up much of the more recent experience with privatization. While this classical example of commercializing the economy occurred, in an abstract sense, on about the

98. Széchenyi [1830] 1930. For a detailed discussion in English of Széchenyi's *Hitel*, see Barany 1968, 203–8, 211–15. And see also Chapter 3, 68–69.
99. Roberts 1951, 11.

same scale as its modern counterparts, the economy left behind by communism was undoubtedly more complex—as has been the task of adjusting it to market mechanisms. For one thing, while redistributable assets such as land and housing were on hand in each of the formerly state socialist economies, the principle of redistribution was not readily applicable to factories. Indeed, the fact that the economies were now industrialized required privatization designs of considerable subtlety. To draw up and to administer these designs, the countries of the region either vested the task in state ministries or set up privatization agencies. The latter countries passed privatization laws that recognized a number of methods of transfer, with one or another predominating. One of the dominant types, perfected in Czechoslovakia, was the method of voucher privatization, a scheme in which all adult citizens could buy voucher books containing a thousand points for the equivalent of $34 in local currency. Participants then used the points to tender bids directly or indirectly, via mutual fund managers. The plan, of course, had to anticipate excess demand and supply, and thus provided for second rounds of bidding at revised prices.[100] The Czech model was followed with some modifications in Poland and, more recently, in Romania. Both schemes provided special discounts for employees, while also holding blocks of shares in public trust either for future sales or for some useful social purpose (such as establishing social security trust funds). The major difference among these plans, however, was not in technical detail, but in the speed, determination, and efficiency with which they were executed. The Czech legislation was implemented in one major push for privatization, but in Poland the process went ahead in spurts, and in Romania, until recently it advanced at a snail's pace.

The principal alternative to voucher privatization was sale by public offerings that involved prior valuations and publicly invited bids or formal auctions, combined with the "corporatization" of enterprises and the sale of shares on stock exchanges. These methods, in their purest forms, were preferred by the Hungarian and Bulgarian privatization acts.[101] Both voucher privatization and open bidding were accompanied by what has politely been referred to as "spontaneous" privatizations—initiated by managers and politically well-connected persons even before the actual laws were passed by parliament. Indeed, some of the most notorious cases of "nomenklatura" privatization occurred before the fall of communism. Among them were the state enterprises that created subsidiaries by transferring their assets, then sold the subsidiaries to management or favored buyers, leaving the original firms as empty shells that, for lack of assets, could not subsequently be "corporatized" and sold. But even short of such shenanigans, the

---

100. Frydman, Rapaczynski, and Earle 1993, 85.
101. Ibid., 24–29, 125–40.

transfer of large amount of assets provided ample opportunity for abuse: by misrepresenting existing assets in order to diminish the purchase price; by resort to bribery and private connections in order to get favorable valuations; or by misuse of information on the part of funds set up as intermediaries between buyers and the state. In this institutional context, corruption, even if not rampant, soon reared its ugly head even in places like the Czech lands, Slovenia, and Hungary, where some reputation for probity had previously reigned. Some public organizations have attempted to assign numerical values to this phenomenon. On a 100-point scale (with Denmark and New Zealand on top, earning 97 and 94 points respectively), the World Bank gave Poland 56, the Czech Republic 54, and Hungary 49 points, as against Russia's 26 and Nigeria's 0.7. The Bank made no attempt to rank the other East Central European states.[102]

The logic of the commercialization of the economy required a second step: the establishment of a legal state capable of enforcing contracts and protecting investors, both foreign and domestic, against civil disorder and the arbitrariness of the authorities. Beyond that logic, the creation of such a legal state was also one of the conditions set by the hegemonic consortium for continued Western support and progress toward full-fledged membership in the core community of material prosperity. Thus the commercialization of the economy—its privatization and adaptation to market principles—has gone hand in hand, much as in the nineteenth century, with the drafting of new civil codes, the passage of bankruptcy and banking laws, and, of course, the reestablishment of an independent judiciary. But at the very heart of the liberal agenda lay also the restoration of representative government, the major item on the wish-list of the new hegemons and the type of reform most closely monitored in Washington, Bonn, and Brussels.

As in the nineteenth century, the institutions of representative government were inspired by foreign models. But unlike their forerunners in the "first wave" of democratization, the constitution-makers of postcommunist Europe no longer looked to Britain, the "mother of all parliaments," with an occasional nod to the written constitutions of Belgium and France. The new models were provided by Germany and the United States. The former provided a model for electoral laws whose attraction lay in its procedural compromise between the single-member, simple plurality system that the retreating communists preferred (with their organization and support spread throughout the countries) and the system of proportional representation that their opponents desired for reasons of their own. The German system also appealed to leaders because its percentual minimums for representation helped to reduce the chances of frivolity and would serve to draw a clearer line between single-issue pressure groups and political parties, al-

102. World Bank 1996a, 16–17.

though the chosen threshold varied from 3 to 8 percent (the latter for coalitions) from country to country. The American system meanwhile exerted its influence on the institutionalization of legislative-executive relationships, manifest in the popularity of presidential and quasi-presidential government—in Albania, Bulgaria, Poland, Romania, and Serbia—and provided models for constitutional courts, sometimes more powerful than the Supreme Court of the model country.[103]

Needless to say, these transplants from foreign soil do not always function along lines that run parallel to those in their original environment. Sometimes this divergence occurs because the drafters did not fully understand the operational principles involved, and sometimes it happens because in the heat of transition, the drafters were more concerned with preventing the restoration of the old order than with formulating rules that would cover a variety of contingencies. We are also dealing with circumstances and traditions grossly different from the ones prevailing in the model country. Take the case of the electoral laws. While their various thresholds have successfully cut down the number of parties to about half a dozen in the average East Central European parliament, under the given circumstances— marked by a lack of information and the inexperience of the electorate— they have failed to accomplish the second purpose of the design, that of compensating for distortions inherent in a pure single-member, simple plurality system. Indeed, differently from Germany, in East Central Europe as many as 25–30 percent of votes are "wasted" on parties that ultimately fail to win seats in parliament.[104] While such waste is inherently contrary to the principles of effective democracy, its immediate ill effect has been to distort electoral results. To give a few examples: the conservative Hungarian Democratic Forum won 42 percent of the seats in the Hungarian National Assembly in 1990 with 24 percent of the popular vote; its successor, the Hungarian Socialist Party, gained 54 percent of seats in the new parliament with 32.9 percent of the vote in 1994; the Croatian Democratic Community garnered 58 percent of seats with 44.5 percent of the vote in 1992; and the Polish Socialist-Peasant coalition took hold of 65.9 percent of parliament with a 35.8 percent share of the popular vote in 1993.[105]

Executive-legislative relations suffered as much from bad constitution-writing as from differences between political environments. Overall, as noted above, the constitutions tended to favor the prerogatives of presidents, an irony in view of the fact that the "revolutions" of 1989–90 resounded with rhetoric about the dangers of powerful executive branches in government. In a number of cases these relationships were ill defined, setting presidents

103. See Syllova, I. Jackiewicz and Z. Jackiewicz, Malová and Sivaková, Jovic, and Zajc, in Ágh and Ilonszki 1996, 322–95.
104. Crawford 1996, 186.
105. Ibid., 213, 225.

and parliaments on a collision course, frequently giving constitutional courts power over public policy. Such collisions have occurred regularly in Poland and in Hungary and, most conspicuously, in Slovakia, where the conflict between President Kováč and Prime Minister Mečiar has assumed the character of a political guerrilla war. In one of the phases of this war, Kováč engineered what may be described as a successful parliamentary coup to temporarily remove Mečiar from the office of the prime minister; Mečiar then retaliated with attempts to cut the president's staff and a campaign of vilification against Kováč,[106] which culminated in the kidnapping of the president's son by the prime minister's security detail. More recently, Mečiar has been hatching a plot to eliminate the office of the president by refusing the parliamentary quorum required for the election of a successor, taking advantage of a clause in the Slovak constitution stipulating that in case of vacancy, the powers of the presidency are to be exercised by the head of government.[107]

Still, the major source of tension experienced by these "emerging" democracies arises not from the collision of institutions but from a clash between politics and economics. To a major extent, this clash stems from the dynamics of capitalism, from processes that in Schumpeter's classical formulation involve the "creative destruction" of enterprises operating under constraints of profitability. In the case of the postcommunist transitions, these dynamics are apt to be particularly devastating, given the nature and institutions of the state socialist economy within a relatively closed imperial system. On the one hand, this economy of perennial shortage created indifferent managers, inclined to produce in bulk and inferior quality. On the other hand, a significant portion of these economies was geared to produce for a single buyer, the Soviet imperial war machine. Once the imperial economy and polity disintegrated, a considerable volume of inefficiently produced output was bereft of value, as value is calculated in the competitive marketplace. Throughout the former eastern Bloc and among the successor economies of formerly united Yugoslavia, effective demand fell off almost instantly, creating pressures for finding new markets and, in their absence, for liquidating unproductive sectors. These pressures arose in all the countries of the region, although some countries suffered more than others. The principal losers were Bulgaria, where an export-oriented agriculture and light industry were thriving during the state socialist period because its products found eager buyers in the Soviet Union and East Germany; Slovakia, where the post-1968 economic development of the region was driven by newly created armament industries serving the Soviet and other Warsaw Pact military forces, which could find no new buyers in the larger global mar-

106. See OMRI *Daily Digest,* July 13, 1995.
107. "A Mečiar Coup," *Economist,* Feb. 7, 1998, 55.

TABLE 64
Unemployment and Output Collapse

	Unemployment (%)		Output collapse[a]
	1991	1993	1994
Albania	—	—	75.0
Bulgaria	11.5	16.0	72.3
Croatia	14.1	17.2	84.0
Czech Republic	4.4	3.2	81.0
Hungary	7.4	13.0	83.4
Macedonia	24.5	28.6	53.0
Poland	11.8	15.4	91.1
Romania	3.1	9.0	73.0
Slovakia	12.7	13.5	77.9
Slovenia	10.1	14.4	94.4
Yugoslavia	21.4	25.0	—

SOURCES: For unemployment: Comander 1993, 2; for output collapse: Dobozi 1995, 19–20;
European Bank for Reconstruction and Development 1996, 185.
[a] 1989 = 100.

TABLE 65
Wage and Pension Decline
(1989 = 100)

	1990	1991	1992	1993	1994
Bulgaria	105.3	64.2	67.8	61.9	47.7
Croatia	83.8	62.9	35.5	35.2	40.1
Czech Rep.	93.3	70.4	77.4	80.1	85.3
Hungary	96.3	89.6	90.8	87.3	93.4
Poland	75.5	75.4	73.4	71.1	71.9
Romania	105.6	83.9	73.0	54.8	53.0
Slovakia	109.0	107.9	76.7	82.1	76.9
Slovenia	73.5	62.4	60.6	69.3	73.4

SOURCE: Vienna Institute 1995, 161–65. State sector employment and pensions only.

kets; the former Yugoslav republic of Macedonia, with its heavily subsidized economy; and, finally, Romania and Albania, where criteria of efficiency had been in various ways ignored by the communist government.

The dimensions of the ensuing "output collapse" are presented in Table 64 and further reflected in the rise of unemployment and in the fall of real wages and pensions shown in Table 65. These losses of output and income did not necessarily create "fifty million new poor,"[108] nor did they create conditions commensurate to those experienced by these countries during the Great Depression of 1929–34, for as we shall see later (in Tables 74 and 75), most governments of the region could shelter their populations from the worst effects of the crisis by holding the line on some of the most common

108. Milanovic 1994, 1–4.

staples. The effect, in other words, was psychological. As has been the case historically, East Central Europeans felt a sense of deprivation because the downward trend ran counter to widely held expectations that the changes in the domestic and international regimes would bring about a quick, if not instant, rise in the general standard of living.

Response to Reform: Public Opinion and the Party System

How, then, did the populations of the countries of East Central Europe respond to the costs of reforms and to the obvious hegemony of the West? The short and simple answer is that these responses have not been uniform. The validity of this statement becomes evident quickly when we examine cleavages within and among the societies of the area as they are reflected by the party system.

At first, upon the collapse of communism, public opinion was in a state of turmoil and party formation was a chaotic affair in which prospective leaders and constituents were attempting to link up with each other. On top, the main concerns of the new elite were how to find an appropriate identity, and further, how to translate this identity into concrete political programs that could be effectively articulated to the public. At the grass-roots level, the problem was uncertainty, not only about the identity and the intentions of the parties—most of whom claimed to be anti-Soviet, democratic, and reform-minded—but also about their own interests. It is not the case, of course, that people did not know that they wanted to have more prosperity, but rather that they had a limited understanding of whether particular policies would help or hurt them in their daily lives.[109] Examples of such uncertainty and ignorance abound. Thus there was at first little understanding that measures of restitution were, in the last analysis, at public expense and hence represented a zero-sum game between society as a whole and some of its individual members. There was equally little understanding among industrial workers that the rebuilding of capitalism implied the "creative destruction" of their jobs and was likely to create massive unemployment. Peasants, wherever they embraced the free market at first, as in Poland and Hungary, were unaware that the principle implies the abolition of heavy subsidies by the state. Granted, these were the "common folk," but the educated classes, and among them much of the creative intelligentsia, were not much more prescient, for they did not immediately grasp that their attacks on state paternalism would effectively destroy a generous basket of financial support for research, higher education, publishing, theater, the opera, and movie-making that sustained its practitioners in some comfort

109. For this point, see Ost 1993, 453–86, esp. 454; also Slomczynski and Shabad 1997, 167.

380 EAST CENTRAL EUROPE

and provided them with the perquisites of status. Of course, more so than the rest, this stratum and its top echelon had more recourse to mobility than the rest. Thus while some of its members opted for genteel poverty, others turned to political and economic entrepreneurship, or found mobility via emigration into the core countries of the world economy.

Although chaotic at first, things began to sort themselves out once parliaments began to make laws and people learned about their personal stakes in politics. Thus, almost immediately after the first elections, cleavages emerged between voters who saw their own stake in free markets as opposed to those who favored the distributive instruments of the state. The first group included a disproportionate number of the young (those under 45), of the highly educated, and of the residents of large urban centers, while members of the older generation, including the vast majority of old age pensioners, the rural population, and segments of the labor force with limited skills made up the second.[110] Further cleavages were soon to emerge between those who favored egalitarian redistribution as opposed to those who had a stake in redistribution to particular entities, to the Church, the family, or to those who on a variety of grounds might qualify as the victims of communism. However inchoate these divisions were, it was from them that a new political spectrum emerged, divided among liberals, socialists, and conservatives.

These divisions, to be sure, did not always coincide with political parties of the same name. One reason for this was that designations like liberal, conservative, and socialist refer to ideal types that political actors often try to synthesize to create such variants as "social liberalism" or "liberal conservatism." The other reason was that while these principles are usually articulated through political parties, these parties can only rarely boast an ideologically or programmatically homogeneous membership. Indeed, the larger the constituency of the party, the greater the likelihood that it will become what the Germans call a *Sammelpartei,* an umbrella party that collects people with divergent political interests into an alliance for electoral purposes. In trying to identify political parties by ideology, the best we can thus do is identify dominant trends within them.

Let us take the liberals first. As in earlier times, in East Central Europe today they are the principal proponents of free trade, privatization, the free flow of international capital, and the Western models of the legal state and democratic government. Some of the most conspicuous representatives of this liberalism are found in the countries of the northwestern tier: they include the Democratic Union of Poland (formerly Liberal Democratic Congress, also Union of Freedom) associated with Prime Minister Tadeusz Mazowiecki and Finance Minister Leszek Balcerowicz; the Liberal Democratic

110. See Olson 1997, 165; Georgiev 1996, 27; Demény 1993, 93; Kárpáti 1993, 337.

Party of Slovenia; and the Hungarian Free Democrats, who, in the best traditions of classical liberalism, have fought against the "reclericalization" of public life and have been aggressive protagonists of minority rights, although on economic issues they have been and are divided between "Thatcherite" free marketeers and "social liberals." For most observers, the Hungarian Young Democrats (now the Civic Democratic Party) would likewise qualify. In the Czech lands, the parties closest to the ideal type are some of the successors of the now defunct Czech Civic Forum: the Civic Alliance, the Civic Movement, and not least of all the Civic Democratic Party associated with the name of Václav Klaus, first minister of finance, then prime minister of the Republic. In the words of their party platform, "the CDP is a party of the talented, enterprising segment of society, whose members are willing to take risks, and responsibility for themselves, their family, municipality, and the governance of the country." [111] Liberalism does exist in other countries as well, although in Slovakia and the countries of the southeast it is usually well hidden under larger umbrella organizations such as the Bulgarian Democratic Union, the Romanian Democratic Convention, and the short-lived Serbian Zajedno and, more recently, DEPOS.

The conservatives of East Central Europe are sometimes competitors, sometimes allies of the liberal parties. To be sure, the label itself has been shunned by all but a few of the electorally least significant groups, such as the Polish and Hungarian Conservative parties, neither of which has been able to clear the legal threshold for representation. [112] This is mainly because when the party system reemerged after 45 years of communist rule, there seemed to be precious little for conservatives to conserve. There was, however, lingering nostalgia for some aspects of the pre-Soviet past, while traditional conservative fears of a free market continued to linger, too, together with fears that unrestrained competition might subvert traditional morality and destroy the fabric of society. These anxieties were well summarized by the Polish Cardinal Glemp, who in one of his many sermons denounced the new regime as a "mixture of liberalism and communism that replaced the formerly open persecution of the Church with a superficially chosen morality that emphasizes freedom but downplays God, religion and spirituality." [113] Indeed, most of the conservative parties of East Central Europe today wear the Christian Democratic label; some, as in the case of the Romanian Peasant Party, have added the adjective "Christian" to their earlier name.

The socialist parties of East Central Europe are either new creations or have grown out of the remnants of the ruling parties of the previous regime. The Czech and Slovak Social Democratic parties fall into the former

111. Quoted in Kárpáti 1993, 337.
112. Michta 1997, 93; Republic of Hungary, *Newsletter*, May 20, 1994.
113. OMRI, *Daily Digest*, Aug. 16, 1996.

TABLE 66

Political Parties in East Central Europe, 1990–97, by Dominant Political Orientation

	Liberal				Conservative				Socialist		
Country	Party	%Vote	Year	Country	Party	%Vote	Year	Country	Party	%Vote	Year
PROSYSTEMIC											
Czech R.	Civil Dem.	29.6	1996	Poland	Solidarity Electoral Action	33.83	1997	Czech R.	Social Democrat	28.4	1994
	Civic Alliance	6.3	1996		Independence Confederation	5.8	1993	Poland	Democratic Left Alliance	27.13	1997
Poland	Democratic Union	10.6	1993	Hungary	Democratic Forum	24.7	1990		Peasant Party	7.31	1997
Hungary	Free Democrat	19.74	1994		Christian Democrats	7.0	1994	Hungary	Socialist	33.0	1994
	Young Democrats	7.03	1994	Serbia	Smallholders	10.9	1990	Slovakia	Social Democrat	13.6	1994
	Democratic Forum	11.74	1994		Renewal (Zajedno)	13.8	1994	Croatia	Social Democrat	9.4	1995
Slovenia	Liberal Democrat	23.5	1992	Slovakia	Christian Democrats	10.0	1990	Macedonia	Social Democrat	48.3	1994
Slovakia	Democratic Union	7.3	1994	Slovenia	Christian	14.5	1992	Slovenia	Dem Ref (excom) Renewal	17.3	1990
Croatia	Social Liberal	12.0	1995					Montenegro	Democratic Socialist (DPS)	—	1997
Romania	Democratic Convention	20.01	1992								
Bulgaria	Democratic Union	34.4	1991								
Montenegro	Liberal Alliance	12.0	1992								
Macedonia	Liberal	24.1	1994								
Serbia	Democratic	7.4	1996								
ANTISYSTEMIC											
				Croatia	Dem. Comm. Rights Party	44.2	1994	Albania	Socialist[a]	56.2	1991
				Albania	Democrat	62.0	1992	Bulgaria	Socialist	47.5	1990
				Macedonia	IMRO-National Unity	30.8	1990	Romania	NSF	66.3	1991
					IMRO-Rev.	30.8	1990		DNSF-PSDR	27.7	1992
				Hungary	Justice and Life	2.6	1994		National Unity	7.7	1992
				Slovakia	National	5.4	1994		Greater Romania	3.9	1992
					MDS	35.0	1993		Soc Labor (com)	3.0	1992
				Slovenia	Nationalist	10.0	1992	Montenegro	Socialist	42.6	1992
				Czech R.	Republican	8.1	1996	Serbia	Socialist	36.7	1993
				Bulgaria	National	6.5	1994		Radical (Seselj)	22.4	1992
								Czech R.	Left Bloc	14.7	1992

SOURCES: Dawisha and Parrott 1997a, 1997b; Crawford 1996; Bihari 1993; Ágh and Ilonszki 1996.
[a] Changing over time.

category, while most of the others are successor parties that purged their ranks of compromised leaders, gave up some of their former assets, and accepted the idea of operating in multiparty systems. These include the Socialist parties of Hungary, Poland, Macedonia, Serbia, Montenegro, and Bulgaria. In Slovenia, the ex-communists, fully democratized, adopted the label Democratic Renewal; in Romania, the successor party, led by Ion Iliescu, first chose the name Front of National Salvation; somewhat later, some of its factions reappeared as the Party of Democratic Socialism. The same happened in Croatia, where the name "social democrat" signals continuity with the earlier regime. Overall, these parties, whether new or ex-communist, have been able to fill a significant niche in the political spectrum by promising to slow down market reforms, output collapse, and unemployment.

Redistribution, however, is only one issue by which we can identify political parties in East Central Europe today. By the time of the second set of post-1989 elections, publics and parties were divided by a new cleavage of great significance that opened with respect to the overall social, political, and cultural project associated with the new international hegemony. This new cleavage, as shown in Table 66, cuts across the traditional divisions between Left and Right, separating the party system into prosystemic forces willing to accept the package and trade-offs offered by the West more or less unconditionally, and antisystemic parties that either indignantly reject the package outright or merely simulate cooperation with the liberal universalist project. Remarkably, these cleavages also cut across distinctions in the spectrum of ex-communist parties. Thus the Socialist parties of Poland, Hungary, Macedonia, and Slovenia are enthusiastic participants in the Western project, even though all of them had some roots in the soil of the previous regime, while parties with a similar background in Serbia, Bulgaria, and Romania have been rejectionist in their attitude. Some of these parties, including those of Albania and Montenegro, have over the years experienced a metamorphosis in this respect by accepting the Western project after initial opposition, or else split between pro- and antisystemic factions.

While few of the liberal parties of the region—and none of the liberal parties of any consequence—can be found in the antisystemic column, conservative parties have been split as much as the socialist parties along the systemic divide. On one side of the divide, we find the array of Christian Democratic parties that, despite suspicions about the cultural agenda of liberalism, do accept the democratic capitalist agenda of the West; on the other side, we find radical Christian and populist parties that denounce the United States as the "global gendarme,"[114] human rights as "a fiction of the cowardly and the weak,"[115] and democratization as "liberty supervised by the

114. Barbu, in *România Mare*, Oct. 23, 1993, 4.
115. Quoting Radu Sorescu of the National Party of Romania. Shafir 1994, 93.

U.S.A." [116] Instead of democratization, they celebrate "the iron fist of authoritarian government," [117] or promise, as the Romanian radical Vadim Tudor has, "to govern with the Bible in one hand and with a whip in the other." [118] In the same vein, the European Union and NATO are archaic, denounced as constructs left behind from the Cold War.[119]

This "systemic" cleavage not only cuts across other ideological and programmatic commitments but is now clearly the single most important ideological divide in the region. For while much of East Central Europe today is governed by coalitions of liberals, socialists, and conservatives, there are no examples of long-term coalition agreements or alliances that cut across the pro- and antisystemic divide. Thus on the one hand the Democratic Union of Bulgaria or the Democratic Convention of Romania includes socialists, liberals, and conservatives of the democratic stripe, while on the other hand, Iliescu's Party of Social Democracy, Mečiar's Movement for Democratic Slovakia, and Milošević's Serbian Socialist Party all had national radical coalition partners, and, along with Tudjman's Democratic Community of Croatia, are umbrella parties that held together a variety of "red" and "brown" elements. Coalitions between the large, radical umbrella parties and their smaller, ideologically "pure" partners have proved particularly beneficial for antisystemic purposes, for while the large parties, especially in power, have to exercise some rhetorical restraint in a Western-dominated continental environment, their lesser partners, be they "red" or "brown," have greater freedom to "call a spade a spade," and thus keep in touch with their radical base. Thus, while Iliescu, and even Milošević, would time and again have to pay lip service to human and minority rights, Milošević's ally Vojslav Šešelj could openly demand that "Croats be dumped into trucks and deported," [120] and Iliescu's coalition partner Gheorghe Funar could demand that the Hungarians of Transylvania be expelled and that Gypsies be confined to concentration camps.[121]

Such antisystemic parties are present in all the societies of East Central Europe. But their electoral strength and political influence varies considerably from country to country with the effectiveness of the incentives provided by the West, with the proportion of winners and losers in the economic game, and, more significantly, with the proportion of those who have reason to be hopeful as opposed to those who see their future devoid of hope. These ratios, in turn, correlate roughly with the condition of the economies that communism left behind in 1989. It is not always easy, but on the

116. Barbu, *România Mare*, Oct. 23, 1993.
117. Shafir 1994, 89.
118. OMRI, *Daily Digest*, Sept. 17, 1996.
119. Shafir 1994, 93.
120. Markotić 1995, 96.
121. Shafir 1994, 89, 94.

whole it is easier, for people in Poland, Hungary, Slovenia, and the Czech Republic to be hopeful about their economic future than it is for their counterparts in Bulgaria, Romania, or Serbia, with their catastrophe economies. Antisystemic attitudes are thus less prevalent in the former than in the latter category of nations, or, to put it in more general terms, in the northwest of the region than in the southeast. The fact that the cultural divide between communal paternalism and legal impersonality closely correlates with the weakest economies may be coincidental, but it is certainly not immaterial in shaping attitudes by adding moral legitimacy to the rejection of economic and political regimes imported to these countries under Western auspices.

Democratization and Political Decay

A similar pattern emerges from the examination of the political systems that came into being after the collapse of the Soviet Bloc. Whatever the methodological limitations inherent in the enterprise, various attempts have been made to quantify differences among postcommunist polities in terms of degrees of adherence to the democratic rules of the game, freedom of association, the autonomy of civic associations, and the freedom the electronic media and the press, judged by external observers and measured on a 7-point descending scale, with 1 being the highest mark that a regime can earn. These measures appear on Table 67 and reveal considerable differences among the countries of the region with respect to the degree of de-

TABLE 67
Measures of Democracy and Freedom

	Democracy[a]	Political[b] process	Civil society[c]	Press freedom	Media independence	Rule of law
Czech Rep.	1.38	1.25	1.50	81	1.25	1.50
Hungary	1.44	1.25	1.25	66	1.50	1.75
Poland	1.44	1.50	1.25	79	1.50	1.50
Slovenia	1.88	2.00	2.00	73	1.75	1.75
Slovakia	3.81	3.75	3.25	59	4.25	4.00
Romania	3.88	3.75	3.75	51	4.25	4.25
Croatia	4.25	4.00	3.50	42	4.75	4.75
Bulgaria	3.81	3.25	4.00	—	3.75	4.25
Macedonia	3.88	3.50	3.75	—	4.00	4.25
Yugoslavia	6.00	—	6.00	23	—	—
Albania	4.50	4.25	4.25	29	4.75	4.75
Bosnia-Herzegovina	5.00	—	5.00	24	—	—

SOURCES: For columns labeled Democracy, Political process, Civil society, Media independence, and Rule of law: Shor 1997, 4; 7-point scale, 1 = best. For Press freedom: Hirschler 1996, 4–5; 100 = maximum. For Yugoslavia (Serbia-Montenegro) and Bosnia-Herzegovina, see Freedom House (1997), 579–80.
[a] Freedom of elections.
[b] Procedural correctness.
[c] Freedom of association.

ECONOMIC HEALTH

		High		Low	
POLITICAL CULTURE	Legal Impersonal	Czech Republic Hungary Poland Slovenia Slovakia	1.38 1.44 1.44 1.88 3.81	Croatia	4.25
	Communal Paternal	No Examples		Albania Bosnia-Herzegovina Bulgaria Macedonia Romania Yugoslavia (Serbia-Montenegro)	4.50 5.00 3.81 3.88 3.88 6.00

SOURCES: Shor 1997, 5; for Yugoslavia and Bosnia-Herzegovina, see Freedom House 1997.

FIGURE 2. Economic and Cultural Correlates of Democracy.

mocratization, ranging from 1.38 for the Czech Republic to 4.5 for Bosnia, and 6 for the regions of rump Yugoslavia. Upon closer examination, qualitative differences are discernible among "procedurally correct" and "troubled democracies," with two countries occupying an intermediary position as unstable, one-party dominant authoritarian systems with a record of simulating rather than practicing democratic government (see figure 2).

The first of our three categories includes four countries of the northwestern tier of the region. They are the Czech Republic, Hungary, Poland, and Slovenia. These four countries lie in the cultural sphere of legal impersonality, and, as the data in Table 68 indicate, they rate relatively high in terms of per capita GNP, liberalization, and investor confidence. As countries with favorable risk ratings, these countries have attracted the highest amounts of foreign direct investment (FDI). Politically, these four countries have earned the "procedurally correct" label by holding fair and free elections, allowing the free expression of ideas, guaranteeing the autonomy of organizations (including the cultural autonomy of ethnic minorities), and finding (after some initial wrangling) reasonable formulae for politically neutralizing the electronic media. These are also countries in which the print media have enjoyed a great deal of freedom and whose public life has been free from intimidation or open violence. Poland witnessed a number of major strikes, but on the whole these were peaceful or nonviolent. Hungary experienced a taxicab strike in 1990, in the course of which cab drivers blockaded the bridges over the Danube in Budapest. The very fact that, both

TABLE 68

Measures of Economic Liberalization, Progress, and Confidence, 1994–96

	GNP/capita (US$)	GNP world ranking	Transition progress	FDI/ capita (US$)	Credit rating	Liberalization index	Privatization (%)	Economic risk	Political risk
Czech Republic	3,200	38	3.4	586	IG[a]	9.3	70	17.48	17.83
Hungary	3,840	34	3.4	1,198	IG	9.3	60	15.46	14.95
Poland	2,410	52	3.3	121	IG	8.9	58	16.08	13.23
Slovenia	7,040	29	3.1	325	IG	8.5	38	13.59	13.75
Slovakia	2,250	55	3.2	130	IG	8.6	59	10.68	12.13
Croatia	2,560	49	3.1	122	IG	8.5	48	10.10	10.43
Bulgaria	1,250	71	2.6	166	SIG[b]	6.1	36	8.97	8.33
Macedonia	820	80	2.6	33	SIG	7.8	40	6.59	4.65
Romania	1,270	70	2.6	66	SIG	7.1	38	7.29	3.40
Yugoslavia	1,492	—	—	—	SIG	—	—	—	—
Albania	380	101	2.7	77	SIG	7.4	60	—	—

SOURCES: For GNP/capita: World Bank 1996a, 172; at market rates. For GNP world ranking: World Bank 1996a, 184–85; 133 countries ranked. For transition progress: FDI/capita. For credit rating: International Monetary Fund 1997, 94. For liberalization index: Dollar and Burns 1997, 94; rankings of 169 countries by *Euromoney*. For privatization: World Bank 1996, 14–15, with additional information from Fish 1998. For economic and political risk (optimum = 25): *Transition* 5, no. 9 (Nov.–Dec. 1994), 13–14.

[a] IG = investment guide.

[b] SIG = subinvestment guide.

in the media and in parliament, this incident has ever since been treated as a near-revolutionary event may be the best proof of the essentially peaceful standards of Hungarian politics. In all four countries of this category, the former security police force was dismantled, and politics have been more or less insulated from bureaucratic influence by the granting of broad autonomies to counties and municipalities. These latter measures seem, at least for the time being, to be the best guarantees against a return to the machine politics of precommunist days, in which the ruling parties used the centralized bureaucracies to corrupt the electoral process by turning them into political machines.

The political spectrums of these four democracies bear considerable similarities, in that the parties can be reasonably well identified by their liberal, conservative, or socialist orientation.[122] All of these parties are democratic and may well qualify for the "prosystemic" designation; they are partial to internal reform and international cooperation in the hope of eventual membership in the European Union. As noted earlier, though, in all four of these countries an "antisystemic" opposition does exist, recruited either from the ranks of unreconstructed communists or from a new Right that is attempting to rally economic discontent around the symbols of national sovereignty and unity. In Poland, accompanying a number of small extra-parliamentary parties, the representative of this trend is the Confederacy of Independent Poland, with a program that apotheosizes Pilsudski's veiled dictatorship of the interwar period and seeks to restore Poland as a great power in international affairs.[123] In Hungary, the most conspicuous antisystemic party is István Csurka's Hungarian Life and Justice Party, whose very name harkens back to the radical nationalism of the interwar period. In Slovenia, there is a Nationalist Party with anti-Serb and anti-Austrian overtones, while in the Czech Republic, radical-national conservatism is represented by the Republican Party of Miroslav Sladek. However, the overall electoral appeal and political impact of these parties has thus far been slight. Antisystemic parties have never gained the upper hand in the parliamentary process and over the years have been progressively marginalized. At their best, the Slovene Nationalists garnered 10.0 percent of the vote (1992), the Polish Independent Confederacy 7.5 percent (1991), the Czech Republicans 8.1 percent (1996), and Hungarian Life and Justice 2.6 percent in 1994 and 5.2 percent in 1998.

However, this correlation of forces does not mean that all is well in the

122. The major sources on parties and the party system in these countries have been Michta 1997, 40–66; Tőkés 1997, 67–108; and Olson 1997, 109–50; also Tálas 1993, 231–76; Kárpáti 1993, 334–55; for Slovenia, S. P. Ramet 1997, 189–225; Juhász 1993, 446–66; and Zajc 1996, 380–95.

123. Michta 1997, 94.

northwestern tier. In all of these countries, save Slovenia, procedural correctness and social peace have been purchased in part by protecting direct consumption at the expense of domestic capital formation. Even so, there remains a substantial gap between popular expectations and economic reality, and governments have so far not been able to "deliver the goods" that a large majority of the public identifies as the "good life." This clash between popular expectations and economic constraints has had tangible effects on public opinion. Democracy was generally welcome in 1989, but opinion polls soon showed a substantial loss of confidence. Although it has been suggested that these numbers reflect disappointment with political parties and particular governments,[124] the trend has also been clearly born out by answers to questions concerning the perception of democracy itself. Between 1990 and 1992, the number of those favorably inclined toward parliamentary institutions fell from 90 to 26 percent in Czechoslovakia, from 89 percent to 41 percent in Poland, and from 64 percent to 29 percent in Hungary.[125] With the exception of the Czech Republic (with no data for Slovenia), the level of this dissatisfaction continued to increase between 1992 and 1994. Since then the trend may have slowed down or even reversed. But a careful reading of the polls conducted by Richard Rose in 1996 reveals that of the people questioned in four countries of the northwestern tier, only 41 percent of the people questioned professed to be solid democrats, explicitly preferring the new regime over the old, while a somewhat larger number, 43 percent, were apathetic or cynical in that they could see no difference between the communist past and the democratic present. Finally, 16 percent remained diehards, expressing the view that the old regime was superior to the new one.[126]

This clash between economic expectations and performance is likely to create serious dilemmas for political elites. This is especially so where elites have to function in the institutional environment of democratic government, with its openness to political inputs through participation. This milieu, to quote Charles Gati, forces elites to "try to square the circle by steering a course between what should be done economically to move ahead and what can be done politically to maintain a degree of domestic stability."[127] Given this context, democracy may be relatively safe, but governments have had a great deal of difficulty holding on to power from one election to another. Unlike in the United States, in the "procedurally correct" democracies of East Central Europe, incumbency is a burden rather than a ticket to easy reelection.

124. Ibid.
125. Crawford 1996, 275.
126. R. Rose 1997, 102.
127. Gati 1996, 168–98.

TABLE 69

Disappointment with Democracy, 1991–94

(% Dissatisfied)

	1991	1994	Increase/Decrease
Albania	17	33	+16
Bulgaria	6	87	+81
Czech Republic	25	9	−16
Hungary	19	43	+24
Poland	21	40	+19
Romania	11	36	+25
Slovakia	55	62	+7

SOURCE: Eurobarometer Survey cited in Gati 1996, 168–98.

Our "troubled" category includes six Balkan countries: Albania, Bulgaria, Bosnia-Herzogovina (not included in Table 68), Macedonia, Romania, and (rump) Yugoslavia. In contrast to the four previously discussed, these countries are located within the cultural sphere of communal paternalism, and they are also the countries of the region with the weakest economies. Specifically, as Table 68 suggests, these countries possess on average one-quarter of the per capita GDP of the four countries classified as "procedurally correct." As a corollary, and direct consequence, these countries have been the slowest in making institutional adjustments in their economic systems, are seen as highly unstable, and have therefore failed to attract substantial amounts of foreign private investment. These circumstances quite obviously bear major responsibility for making their political systems "troubled," although troubled in different ways. Thus while some of these societies have simply failed to sustain themselves as functioning entities and are now democracies under direct foreign mandate, others are in virtual receivership with international lending institutions; one of them, rump Yugoslavia, is an authoritarian state with a thin parliamentary democratic façade, maintained by police terror and constant low-level violence.

The designation of "mandated" democracy is most obviously applicable to Macedonia, Bosnia-Herzegovina, and Albania. The road traveled by Bosnia-Herzegovina is the most familiar and tragic of these three. That story of war, rapine, and ethnic purification need not be retold here in detail.[128] It originated in democratic elections in which ethnic parties outpolled the partisans of a civic polity: 37.8 percent of the vote went to the political party of the Muslims, 26.5 percent to that of the Serbians, and 14.7 percent to the party of the Croatians, leaving little more than 20 percent to liberals and ex-communist proponents of a federal state.[129] An ensuing vote in fa-

128. For a concise summary of the Bosnian crisis, see Burg 1997, 123–45.
129. "Bosnia: Election Update," in *RFE/RL Research Report* 1, no. 49 (Dec. 7, 1990).

vor of secession produced a bloody civil war when the Serbs resisted loss of regional hegemony and security. The war prompted weak attempts at mediation by Western European powers, and the failure of these eventually brought about the military involvement of NATO and the United States under UN auspices. It was under these conditions that new elections were held in 1996, producing a formal political unity but little prospect for lasting peace in the absence of continued commitment on the part of the international community.[130]

Macedonia's road to receivership was less bloody, but no less illuminating. This small member republic of the larger Yugoslav federation became independent less by design than by default, but when independence came, in the spirit of the times Macedonians licensed political parties and held elections in order to gain recognition from the West. These elections produced ambiguous results. A former member of the Yugoslav Communist League, Kiro Gligorov, was elected president, while the legislature ended up split between the radical-nationalist IMRO (allied with smaller parties) and the Macedonian League of Communists.[131] The deadlock between these two forces was resolved by a temporary expedient, Gligorov's appointment of a nonparty government. Aggravated by the restlessness of a large Albanian minority, this outcome was troublesome for Western sponsors of liberal democracy. But Macedonia's real troubles were external: all four of its neighbors—Albania, Serbia, Bulgaria, and Greece—challenged, one way or another, the country's right to exist. In order to forestall domestic and international conflict, a small contingent of U.S. soldiers, once more under UN auspices, landed in the country. They brought stability and peace that set the stage for a new round of elections. This time the results were more pleasing to the West. Kiro Gligorov, who had proven to be an amicable and pragmatic leader, survived an assassination attempt and remained at the helm as president. IMRO and its radical partners conveniently disappeared from parliament, while the League of Communists transformed itself into a Democratic Socialist Union and, in alliance with a new Liberal Party, seized 86 seats in the national legislature. Owing to a modest amount of electoral engineering, nettlesome Albanian representation also declined, from 23 to a more manageable 14 seats.[132] Democracy was thus rescued and made "procedurally correct," although its durability largely depends on the external balance of power and the continued interest of the mandating states.[133]

130. For an interesting recent assessment of the record and prospects of nation-building under U.S. auspices, see Frank Viviano, "GI's Keep Uneasy Peace on Front Lines of Bosnia," *San Francisco Chronicle*, November 3, 1997, A-1, A-8, A-9.

131. Crawford 1996, 221.

132. Ibid.

133. Apart from the OMRI *Daily Digest* and RFE/RL *Daily Newslines*, see Perry 1997, 189–226, and Juhász 1993, 446–65.

The story of postcommunist Albania begins with the 1991 decision of Ramiz Alia and the Politburo of the Albanian (Communist) Party of Labor to surrender its political monopoly and to pledge its "adherence to European norms of legalism and human rights." [134] As happened elsewhere, the party's name was changed. But even when dubbed the Albanian Socialist Party, the organization still emphasized its ties with the communist past, taking credit for the accomplishments of the Hoxha period. In this vein, the party's first official program emphasized that the turn to democracy should be "in the spirit of the Albanian national character," and it continued to maintain its close identification with the Tosk clans south of the river Scumbini. [135]

Using its communist-era organizational network, the Socialist Party won the elections of 1991, garnering an overwhelming majority of seats in the new legislature. But the party would soon succumb to economic chaos and popular restiveness. In 1992, a series of menacing demonstrations demanded new and fairer elections, and these resulted in an equally sweeping victory for the Albanian Democratic party, the removal and imprisonment of Ramiz Alia, and the election of Sali Berisha to the office of president. Nominally nonpartisan, that office quickly turned into the political base from which the hold of the party was expanded, by integrating the bureaucracy and a newly created police force into a powerful political machine. As a next step, the judiciary was made subservient to the political machine, and then, one by one, the government's opponents in parliament, including the Socialist leader Fatos Nano, were arrested, tried, and sentenced to imprisonment. [136] In order to provide legal foundations for these measures, a law on Genocide and Crimes Against Humanity was passed, under which former communists as well as other opponents could be tried. In order to establish broader political support for the party and for his own personal rule, Berisha turned to Albanian nationalist themes with Gheg overtones, aggressively supporting the idea of independent states for the largely Gheg Albanians of the Kosovo and Macedonia. [137] At the same time, the economic program of the party was riddled with contradictory elements: while the Democrats committed themselves to reform and progressive privatization, their program rejected any investment scheme that could not guarantee a full return of capital within five years. [138]

After initial setbacks in the municipal elections of 1992, and even in the face of general popular disgruntlement, the Berisha machine was powerful enough to sweep the parliamentary elections of 1996. For a few months it

134. Réti 1993, 491.
135. Ibid.
136. Pano 1997, 320–22.
137. Réti 1993, 480, 484.
138. Ibid., 485.

appeared that the Democrats had indeed established their political domi-nance in the best tradition of prewar machine politics. But a barrage of for-eign criticism about all-too-obvious electoral fraud did much to undermine the ensuing effectiveness of the regime, and in January 1997, the scandalous collapse of a major pyramid scheme drove the country into a state of anar-chy. The collapse was not merely political but also cultural. It was the cri-sis of a society steeped in the values of paternalism and expecting its gov-ernment to prevent massive fraud by private enterprise. While the Tosk south was the scene of the most widespread violence, all over the country, Alba-nian turned against Albanian in an orgy of killing and plunder. Yet another international project was organized, with the Italians taking the lead. Food and funds were rushed to the country, together with a foreign police force, in order to restore a semblance of public order. Socialist prisoners, among them Nano, were released from jail, and new elections were held under in-ternational auspices. Predictably, the Socialists won and, having been re-stored to dignity under Western auspices, they pledged to transform them-selves into a social democratic party of the Western style.

Romania and Bulgaria also fall into the category of troubled democracies. In 1998, both have procedurally correct liberal governments committed to maintaining democratic institutions, but these governments have followed in the footsteps of unreformed ex-communist socialist parties whose poli-cies had brought the two countries to the verge of economic ruin, leaving them largely in the hands of international lending agencies under conditions that make governing tenuous and the prospect of democracy uncertain.

The postcommunist history of Romania began with the violent overthrow of Ceauşescu's personal dictatorship and the ascendancy of the National Sal-vation Front led by Ion Iliescu, a disgraced associate of the executed dic-tator. Originally founded as a vehicle of transition to a multiparty regime, the NSF turned into a political party under the leadership of prominent ex-communists and some newfound allies. Quick to take advantage of the old party's cadres and resources, the Front easily won the first parliamentary and presidential elections, then followed the familiar formula for creating a political machine that would assure its continued political domination: con-trol of the media; co-optation of the old regime's security police and ad-ministrative apparatus into the party; and, when challenged by mobilizing diehard-communist miners and industrial workers, repeated reigns of terror in Bucharest.[139] The Front and its machine survived a subsequent split be-tween Premier Petre Roman and Iliescu. Roman's faction kept the party's original label, but Iliescu's Democratic Front of National Salvation man-aged to keep its hands on all the important levers of power. When new elec-

139. Tismaneanu 1996, 6; Carey 1996, 16–46; Demény 1993, 277–333.

tions were held, Iliescu sailed to victory despite widespread, and rather credible, charges of electoral fraud.[140] In this respect, at least, Iliescu was heir to a political tradition going back to the Brătianus, who presided over the political machines of an earlier period in Romanian history.

Promising to be a highly pragmatic political organization, in its first days, the FNS was supposed to stand for "more food, heat, light, health, transportation."[141] But as time passed the government found it ever more difficult to deliver on these promises, as indeed on the promise of quick and efficient liberalization made to the international community.[142] With foreign capital studiously avoiding the country, and the party machine, for political reasons, continuing to subsidize both bankrupt heavy industry and unprofitable mining, the economy drifted. In order to compensate for its weaknesses, the NSF and its successors became increasingly associated with nationalist themes, presenting themselves as defenders of national sovereignty, protectors of territorial integrity from imagined revisionist invaders and, more subtly, as the heirs of policies that aimed to create a homogeneous ethnic community. By 1994, the parlous condition of the Romanian economy was conspicuously evident, with no relief in sight. In a political gamble, Iliescu made peace with the Romanian National Party and parliament turned out legislation, most prominently an Educational Law with several revisions, geared to earning the regime hard-line nationalist credentials. Elections were due in 1996, and it appeared that even in such desperate straits, the political machine would be able to eke out another victory at the polls. There may be two reasons why the attempt was not made. One was the prospect of universal condemnation by the West, the other the precarious condition of the economy, which made victory less appealing. Of course, the legal framework of democracy also allowed for leisurely retreat, without fear of harm to life and limb, and the luxury of watching the hapless Democrats cope with the economy. Iliescu could also reckon that the failure of his opponents would give his cohorts yet another chance to govern.

After a vigorous campaign, waged in the spirit of the radical Right, Iliescu lost, and, as expected, the Democratic Convention inherited a debased economy and empty treasury. Although foreign credit and investment began to trickle in, it has been too minimal to have a measurable impact on the economy. Indeed, during the first year of the new democratic government, the economy continued to deteriorate, the currency lost two-thirds of its value, and unemployment skyrocketed. These conditions severely tested

---

140. See a detailed *Report to the Committee on Human Rights of the Conference on European Security and Cooperation* (1992) by members of the Romanian opposition quoted in Owen 1993, 45–46. See also Demény 1993, 296–97, and Carey 1995, 43–66.

141. Silviu Brucan quoted in Pop-Elecheş, 1998, 6.

142. D. Ionescu 1994, 28–34; Eyal 1996, 136–37.

popular patience, as well as the staying power of a coalition that could take power only by casting its net wide, embracing even the unpopular parliamentarians of the Hungarian minority. In order to stay in power, the Democrats had to resort to political tricks. One of these was to claim, with the collusion of the West, that they had brought the country one step, or "tier," closer to paradise—that is, to NATO and the European Union. The other was to play the national card, however timidly, walking a tightrope between domestic and international politics. One instance of this was the already-noted rehabilitation of members of the wartime Antonescu government, which was followed by Western protest, a presidential apology, and an eventual compromise: a single rehabilitation. At just about the same time, the National Assembly, gratuitously deviating from its agenda, revised the already controversial Educational Law to ban instruction in Hungarian at institutions of higher learning. Parliament passed this amendment with a large majority, but the Hungarian Democratic Federation threatened to withdraw its deputies and to bring down the coalition. Once again President Constantinescu apologized and refused to sign; symbolic morsels were thrown to the Right without losing the Hungarians.[143] In any case, news of other squabbles break almost daily, and the future of democracy appears anything but bright.

The postcommunist history of Bulgaria has been troubled by a sharp divide of public opinion. Indeed, the past few years are reminiscent of the 1920s, when government followed government and no political machine emerged to stabilize either politics or economics. As in Romania and Albania, the first multiparty elections were easily won by the ex-communist Bulgarian Socialist Party (BSP). "Procedural correctness" did not suffer, but the party took obvious advantage of its organizational network to win 47 percent of the vote and 53 percent of representation in parliament.[144] As in Romania, the ex-communist party jumped on the reformist bandwagon, but the precarious condition of the economy (above all its heavy dependence on CMEA markets) limited the government's room to maneuver. As state budgets continued to subsidize producers in order to avoid massive unemployment, the country's economy deteriorated even further. Eventually the public took to the streets, demanding new elections. These resulted in a change of government under Zyelu Zhelev's presidency, and in the tenuous hold of the Democratic Union on parliament. As if anticipating the dilemmas of the Romanian Democratic Convention, the Bulgarian Democratic Union could survive only with the support of the country's ethnic minority, yet this support had to be "tacit" in view of the majority's pervasive anti-Turkish sen-

143. RFE/RL *Daily Newsline*, Nov. 26 and Dec. 10, 1997.
144. I. Szabó 1993, 134; also Troxel 1993, 413–16.

timent.[145] But privatizing the economy in the context of the loss of foreign markets caused pain that the public was not prepared to bear. So, after some experimentation with a non-party government of technocrats—an echo of the Macedonian experience—new elections were called for in December 1994. These gave the socialists 43.5 percent of the vote and exactly half of the seats in the legislature.[146] With Zhelev of the Democratic Union in the presidency, the country had a split and weak government. The new premier, Zhan Videnov, promised to pursue reform vigorously but, under pressure to raise living standards quickly, began to backtrack on the reform process and, in a move likely aimed at building a political machine, took steps to control both the media and the judiciary.[147] That he did not get very far was due primarily to the watchdog role played by the presidency.

It was at this juncture that the mismanaged and politically ravaged economy of Bulgaria collapsed. In the first months of 1996, the lev fell dramatically against the dollar, interest rates escalated, and the average wage fell to $72 a month, below the World Bank's global threshold for a substandard wage.[148] Under pressure from abroad and from below, the Videnov government resigned, and a new round of elections was held for both president and parliament. The liberal and popular Petur Stoyanov was elected president, and in parliament the Democratic Union was given another opportunity by the voters. The Union's position in 1997–98 paralleled that of the Romanian Democratic Convention: another pro-Western government kept alive by foreign material and moral support as well as by the distant hope of NATO membership.

The core of the rump Yugoslav state is Serbia, and it is from here that political authoritarianism radiates toward the Montenegrin, Kosovar, and Voyvodina peripheries. The key figure is the president of Serbia, Slobodan Milošević. While the regime can count on popular support, including the support of the radical nationalist Right and the radical ex-communist Left, the regime's parliamentary majorities have been further bolstered by electoral fraud and often blatant coercion. These methods are exercised by a military-bureaucratic-police machine—very reminiscent of similar machines of Serbia's earlier history—not only against secessionist minorities, like Croats, Hungarians, and Kosovar Albanians, but also against a weak and dispirited Serbian democratic opposition. Indeed, in this respect, no images are more enduring than the televised pictures of the police arresting a bleeding Vuk Drašković and the journalist Milovan Brkić and dragging

145. Troxel 1993, 435.

146. Crawford 1996, 200.

147. Ibid., 201. For a more extensive discussion of the Videnov government, see Bell 1997, 388–92.

148. *Transition* (World Bank) 8, no. 1 (Feb. 1997), 10.

them off for further maltreatment in captivity. In this respect, the Serbian president did not discriminate between opponents of the Left and the Right. Like Vuk Drašković of Zajedno, Vojislav Šešelj of the National Radicals was once arrested and has spent time in jail,[149] only to be embraced by the autocrat again and co-opted into his machine. When Milošević's opponents nevertheless captured key seats in local elections, the president and his government surrendered them only after months of violent clashes between demonstrators and police, but not before emptying municipal treasuries and removing files and furniture from municipal buildings.

By securing Milošević's grip on the presidency of the Serbian Republic, the political machine of the Serbian Socialist Party has assured his government a degree of political continuity that has eluded other Balkan regimes. Milošević nonetheless presides over a bankrupt and deeply divided land. Reliable statistics are generally unavailable, but by all indications the Serbian economy is the weakest in the region, having suffered from the greatest output collapse and the greatest fall in real wages.[150] The country is a reluctant host to 700,000 refugees from Bosnia and Croatia, while another 200,000, many of them urban intellectuals, appear to have emigrated.[151] The Muslim population of the Sandjak is deeply resentful, that of the Kosovo in open rebellion against Serbian rule. In 1997, secessionism reared its head even in Montenegro. It was on the issue of Serbian influence that the SPS's Montenegrin counterpart, the Democratic Socialist Party, split between Milošević ally Momir Bulatović and Milo Djukanović, who advocated independence from Belgrade. In the best tradition of the Balkans, the dispute was settled by the republic's minister of the interior, Filip Vujanović, who deployed his police in order to ensure the electoral victory of Djukanović. After months of violent wrangling and demonstrations, Djukanović did finally occupy the office of the president of Montenegro, only adding to the troubles of the federal government in Belgrade.[152]

The third group of countries consists of Slovakia and Croatia. For the years 1992–96, these countries were ranked low at 4.25 and 3.81 respectively on the seven-point democratization scale (see Figure 2 and Table 67). These lower rankings are born out by their post-independence political experience. Except for a short interlude in Slovakia between March and September 1994, both countries have been ruled by radical antisystemic coalitions that have followed a nationalist agenda pleading sovereign rights, and, in the name of these rights, have pursued bluntly discriminatory policies toward national minorities—the Serbs in Croatia and the Hungarians in Slo-

---

149. OMRI *Daily Digest*, Nov. 3 and 5, 1996.
150. Wyzan and Slay 1997, 63.
151. RFE/RL *Daily Newsline*, July 17, 1997.
152. For a summary of these unfolding events, see *Naša Borba*, Jan. 16 and 26, 1998.

vakia. Indeed, much of the Serbian diaspora in Croatia was expelled during military campaigns in eastern Slavonia and the Krajina district, while in Slovakia, Hungarians were threatened with expulsion under the guise of population exchange. In Slovakia, the Movement for Democratic Slovakia (MDS) tried to strengthen the regime by passing a law on the protection of the republic that banned many forms of anti-state, in reality anti-government, agitation in vague terms. The MDS also has tried to seize the powers of the presidency for the prime minister by manipulating loopholes in a badly written constitution, and eventually succeeded in this project in the spring of 1998. In like manner, the special powers of the presidency have been enshrined in statute. Today "Croatia is a country where one can go to jail for defaming the president." [153] To bolster the constitutional primacy of his office, President Franjo Tudjman can rely on a devoted corps of officers, much in evidence in the streets of Zagreb today, while Premier Mečiar has created political underpinnings for his regime by reestablishing a security apparatus recruited partly from the security police of the communist period.

Within the paradigm presented here, the cases of Slovakia and Croatia represent anomalies, in that both of these societies are located in the region's Western cultural sphere, while their economies, structural weaknesses notwithstanding, are closer to those of the countries of the northwest than to those of the southeast. The logic of such anomalies—of disjuncture between political outcome and its cultural and economic parameters—is the logic of instability, the validity of which is borne out by the closer examination of contemporary Slovak and Croat authoritarianism. For one thing, the often impressive parliamentary majorities of the ruling parties are in reality the products of tenuous pluralities in popular vote boosted by electoral laws and gerrymandering.[154] For another thing, the mobilization of these pluralities is much dependent on the personal qualities of leaders (one of whom, Tudjman, may be terminally ill at the time of this writing). Thus failure of leadership in the short term and economic progress in the long term may be harbingers of political change either toward greater procedural correctness or toward deadlock between pro- and antisystemic forces in the body politic.

THE RECORD OF POSTCOMMUNISM:
A STATUS REPORT, 1998

What, then, is the overall record of changes in East Central Europe within the new postcommunist continental order and under the countries'

153. OMRI *Daily Digest*, Oct. 11, 1996.
154. L. Cohen 1997, 107–9; Wolchik 1997, 212–13.

new postcommunist regimes? Just a few years ago, this question could not have been answered with any pretense of rigor, and even today, as we approach the end of the first postcommunist decade, any assessment must remain tentative, for a number of economies that at one point in time seemed to be taking off with considerable speed dipped into the negative zone once again. Economic progress has been hesitant, and the emerging social structures remain fragile. A clear pattern of social mobility is yet to emerge, so short-term indicators must be treated with extreme care. We should remember here that there is perhaps no country in this region that over the past 100 years has not experienced brief spurts of growth that seemed to defy historical trends, creating euphoria that in the long run turned out to be false.

Economics

Notwithstanding postmodern prognostications about a world in which "ideal interests" prevail over the pursuit of material gain and the romantic image cultivated by intellectual dissidents of an East Central Europe purified of greed by decades of suffering, from the point of view of the majority of the region's inhabitants the true measures of progress still lie in the material realm. Democracy itself is accepted primarily because it is perceived as a vehicle of economic development, and often as a political form to be adopted in order to curry favor with those who have the power to bring prosperity to the region from the outside world.

The economic developments of the past few years may usefully be divided into qualitative and quantitative categories. The qualitative changes are institutional, and have generally been subsumed under the label of liberalization. As we have seen above, these institutional changes include new trade regimes, reduced state subsidies, and the privatization of assets. In these respects, progress has been positive and unilinear, although varying greatly from country to country and from one geographical sector to another. On the whole, the countries of the northwestern tier of the region lead the way, while those of the southeast are followers, sometimes with a substantial lag. This pattern correlates with the countries' historical positions on the east-west gradient, although the correlation is not perfect. For example, Slovenia, although adjacent to the West, has been lagging behind in privatizing the means of production, mainly because its own liberalized communist model had been used to adapt to Western markets even before the rise of the new continental economic order. At the other end of the spectrum, Albania surged ahead for the opposite reason: its extreme backwardness provided decision makers with greater flexibility by permitting the reabsorption of unemployed industrial workers into the traditional agricultural economy.

In this manner, the Albanian clan has served as an effective substitute for the institutionalized social safety nets of the more advanced societies of the region.[155]

The quantitative side of the record takes us to the growth and decline of national product and income. As already noted, following the collapse of the Soviet Bloc and its trading system, and as part of the "creative destruction" wrought upon the economies by privatization, the countries of the region experienced a sharp output decline, then began to show a somewhat errant recovery. The turnaround from negative to positive rates occurred at various times. Poland was first in 1992. Romania and Hungary followed in 1993, and the rest of the countries, except those of the war economies of the former Yugoslavia, followed in 1994.[156] Subsequent rates of growth have varied. The most consistent leaders have been Poland and Slovakia, with annual rates of growth of 6–7 percent, although Albania had its own short-lived economic "miracle," reporting 8.2 percent growth for 1995. The next year's record was less remarkable, and in 1997, sliding into uncontrollable turmoil, Albania registered a 15 percent loss of GDP. The second echelon includes the Czech Republic and Croatia, in the 4 percent range. The rest of the countries have failed to attain these rates, with Macedonia and Hungary on the bottom rungs, reporting unimpressive growth rates of 1.0 and 1.1 percent for 1995–96.[157] Romania and Bulgaria each reported 4 percentage rates of growth in the early years of postcommunism. But in Romania this rate began to decline in 1995–96, with no signs of recovery as yet, while the Bulgarian economy went into tailspin in 1996, experiencing a 10.9 percent decline, followed by another 7 percent drop in 1997.[158]

One should be aware, however, that rates of growth do not provide a full picture of these economies. Apart from doubts about their validity, the economic effect of these rates may be marred by excessive foreign debt (a crushing percentage of GNPs and an equally high proportion of imports in Bulgaria, Hungary, Poland, and Macedonia),[159] by negative balances of trade in all but two countries (Slovenia and Slovakia) of the region,[160] or by fiscal irresponsibility. The latter most frequently takes the form of manipulating exchange rates by hiding high current account deficits or by monetary expansion financed by "flighty" short-term loans of foreign origin. These trends in some of the high-growth economies were noticed as early as 1995

155. For relative degrees of liberalization and privatization, see World Bank 1996b, 14–15 (esp. figs. 1.2 and 1.3).
156. World Bank 1996b, 26; Oesterreichische Nationalbank 1997, no pagination.
157. European Bank of Research and Development 1997, quoted in *Transition* (World Bank) 81, no. 6 (Dec. 1997), 8.
158. Ibid.
159. World Bank 1997c, 246–47.
160. Ibid., 244–45.

TABLE 70

Comparison of Communist and Postcommunist Economies, 1997

(1989 = 100)

Poland	111.8	Romania	82.4
Slovenia	99.3	Albania	79.1
Czech Republic	95.8	Croatia	73.3
Slovakia	95.6	Bulgaria	62.8
Hungary	90.4	Macedonia	55.3

SOURCE: Popov 1998, 53–84.

and served as the basis for predicting the Bulgarian fiasco two years before it occurred.[161] In terms similar to those accorded Bulgaria, the same report described Slovakia as the "worst offender" in monetary policies; Hungary and the Czech Republic were praised, while Poland was found to be "in between."[162] More recently, following the troubles of the Czech Republic in 1996–97, the prognosis was updated in still more alarmist terms, comparing the countries of East Central Europe with Mexico and Thailand in the years preceding their respective financial catastrophes. On a scale of 0 to 10 (0 indicating no risk), pre-catastrophe Mexico and Thailand received ratings of 10 and 7 respectively; meanwhile, Slovakia was rated 10, Poland 8, the Czech Republic 6, and Hungary 5. The rather tenuous fiscal policies of Croatia and the disaster-stricken economies of the Balkans were not rated by the project.[163]

Whether or not such policies have been used to boost postcommunist rates of growth in the short-term, even at their best these rates have only sufficed to overcome the effects of the output collapse experienced upon the demise of communism. As Table 70 shows, by 1997 only one country, Poland, had surpassed its level of development in the last year of communism. Four countries—Slovenia, the Czech Republic, Slovakia, and Hungary—were close to crossing the same threshold, all of them in the 90 percent range of their earlier level of development. All the others had a long way to go to reach this target, even if we assume that their rates of growth will remain in positive territory. Nor were these rates of growth sufficient to change the position of these economies in the world economy—that is, to narrow the economic gap between themselves and the more advanced countries. Indeed, with the possible exception of Slovenia, all the countries of East Central Europe lost economic ground between 1990 and 1997, whether compared with the United States (in Table 71) or with the current members of the European Union (see Table 72). A similar result emerges from a com-

161. See "The Economist Intelligence Unit Introduces Aggregate Policy Indicators," *Transition* (World Bank) 6, nos. 9–10 (Sept.–Oct. 1995): 15–17.

162. Ibid.

163. "Something Horrible Out There," *Economist,* Oct. 18, 1997, 71–72.

TABLE 71

Comparison of East Central Europe and U.S. GDP
per Capita, 1987–97

(US = 100)

	1987	1994	1997
Czech Republic	44.1%	34.4%	39.2%
Slovakia	42.3	26.6	29.1
Slovenia	33.3	24.1	39.2
Hungary	28.9	23.5	25.1
Poland	21.4	21.2	21.8
Bulgaria	23.5	16.9	13.0
Romania	22.7	15.8	15.7
Croatia	21.6[a]	—	16.8
Macedonia	—	—	8.7
Albania	3.1[a]	—	4.5

SOURCE: For 1987 and 1994, World Bank 1996b, 188–89. For 1997,
Podkaminer et al. 1998, esp. 18–23. Adjusted to Purchasing Power Parities.
[a] 1990 based on World Bank 1996b, 188–89; Podkaminer 1998.

TABLE 72

East Central Europe and the EU: GDP per
Capita Compared, 1990–97

(EU = 100)

	1990	1997
Czech Republic	62%	57%
Slovenia	60	57
Hungary	37	37
Poland	47	42
Slovakia	60	57
Bulgaria	29	19
Romania	26	23
Croatia	31	23

SOURCE: Podkaminer et al. 1998, 19.

parison of the arithmetical averages of the six countries of East Central Europe with figures from six leading Western European economies that have been used throughout this study to measure economic disparities between East and West. Of course, the six countries no longer exist within their former boundaries. To be able to compare, we have to reconstruct them and adjust the income figures for their successors to the sizes of their respective populations. This has been done in Table 73. What the comparison suggests is that, due to the coincidence of Western development and Eastern output collapse, the combined GNPs of the region have declined by almost 10 points since the end of communism, to 24.7 percent of the figure for West Europe. Accordingly, the countries of the region were more "underdeveloped" in 1997 than at any time in modern history.

TABLE 73
Comparison of per Capita GNPs (at PPP),
East and West European Six, 1995

West		East		
Belgium	$20,710	Bulgaria		$4,480
France	21,176	Czech Republic	9,770	
Germany[a]	20,070	Slovakia	3,610	
Netherlands	19,950	Czechoslovakia[b] (former)		7,716
Sweden	18,540	Hungary		6,410
Switzerland	25,860	Poland		5,400
		Romania		4,360
		Bosnia-Herzegovina	1,776	
		Croatia	3,992	
		Macedonia	2,347	
		Serbia-Montenegro	1,742	
		Slovenia	8,200	
		Yugoslavia[c] (former)		2,830
Arithmetical Average	$21,051	Arithmetical Average		$5,199
Percentage	100.0	Percentage		24.7

SOURCES: From World Bank 1997, 214–15 with missing data from United Nations 1998, 128–30, and Popov 1998 (Popov's percentages reconverted into dollar values).

[a]Germany: reunited, East and West.

[b]Czechoslovakia: Slovak and Czech figures adjusted to population (2:1 ratio).

[c]Yugoslavia: average of republics adjusted to population (Slovenia: 8.4, Croatia: 21.0, Serbia-Montenegro: 44.1, Macedonia: 8.2, Bosnia-Herzegovina: 19.30).

Social Structure and Mobility

The liberalization of the formerly communist economies and the concomitant process of "creative destruction" have brought about numerous changes in the structure of societies. In the process, new occupations have emerged and old ones have turned unprofitable or irrelevant. Some of these changes were obvious and predictable: mastery of Russian, unlike the mastery of English and German, is no longer much sought after (whether in business or in teaching); old-line engineering skills in manufacturing have become less marketable than new skills in computer programming and electronics. But even short of changing the reward structure, the market by its very nature distributes more unequally than the bureaucratized economy of the state socialist period. These inequalities became noticeable and measurable almost immediately after the demise of communism: between 1990 and 1994, gini index figures rose 11 points in Bulgaria, 8 points in the Czech Republic, 5 points in Poland, 4 in Slovenia, and 2 in Hungary.[164] In all likelihood these figures do not include the rapid accumulations of wealth that have occurred at the very top of the income scale. Reliable statistics com-

164. World Bank 1996b, 69.

paring top and bottom quintiles are not yet available, but for the time being at least, poverty has become more visible to the naked eye than it was
ten or twenty years ago.

Together with the new division of labor, the forces of the market also created new patterns of social mobility. The prevalence of these patterns varies
from country to country with the degrees of liberalization of particular
economies. Thus, in the southeast, some of the earlier patterns of mobility
seem to have survived: in Serbia and Romania at least, members both of the
old apparat and of the cultural-technical intelligentsia have been seen seeking shelter in the institutions of the state and in professional politics. Still,
compared to earlier periods, politics has lost some of its appeal, mainly because the state is no longer what it has historically been, many of its prerogatives having been transferred to supranational institutions and power
centers. This is especially true in the countries of the northwestern tier,
where the prospect of integration into supranational institutions is more
immediate, and where foreign capital and entrepreneurship, both economic
and intellectual, have a manifest interest and presence. Indeed, in these
countries a great many of the talented have chosen to act as intermediaries
between foreign business, international organizations, and academics, on
the one hand, and native "consumers" and businesses, on the other. As such
they provide nuclei for rising comprador classes: a comprador bourgeoisie
and a comprador intelligentsia. For those with marketable technical skills
in the global economy, there is yet another opportunity for upward mobility: emigration from the troubled countries of the periphery to the seats of
wealth and power in Western Europe or overseas. No exact numbers for the
latter category exist, in part because many such émigrés maintain legal ties
with their homelands. But verbal accounts in Budapest estimate the total at
100,000, and in Bucharest and Belgrade each at 200,000.

Because a new division of labor and new patterns of mobility are still
emerging, it may be premature to speak of embourgeoisement or any other
trend in class formation. Surely, in classical sociology, the concept of class
is closely related to the division of labor and to the common interests that
stem from the occupational structure. But even Marxist sociology treats
class formation as a process involving the gradual recognition of collective
identities and interests. It also involves the acquisition of social markers—
of dress, etiquette, and habits of speech—together with the evolution of social rituals that sustain collective consciousness and help to demarcate one
class from another. Such markers and rituals did exist prior to communism
and played an often grotesquely exaggerated role in social intercourse, providing rich material for social critics both in and outside the literary realm.
The markers were more or less successfully destroyed by communism, and
it was in this sense—rather than in the sense of material equality—that com-

munist societies had become "classless." The members of the nomenklatura may have had hunting lodges and Western cars, but in terms of personal habits they remained close to the working class. The same is largely true today of many private entrepreneurs and other rising stars of postcommunism. Clear differences between rich and poor already exist, but they are defined more in terms of the levels of consumption than of social style.

This particular facet of postcommunist life—the weakness, or absence, of social markers—in turn conditions social and political conflict. Those who possess are envied and often loathed. But they are loathed as individuals or as social abstractions—wily apparatchiki, mafiosi, or cheating businessmen—loathings that are not as easy to politicize as the highly visible and stylized existence of the old aristocracies or gentrified professionals and bureaucrats. As a result, politics remains remarkably devoid of class-oriented discourse. Indeed, it is closer to the pattern of mass than to that of class politics.

The most obvious downside of this state of affairs is that it focuses the free-floating chagrin of the dispossessed onto social entities marked in other terms. Communism did obliterate, or at least blur, social markers, but it did not obliterate either ethnic markers or differences in religion, physical appearance, and vernacular. Thus, while the politics of postcommunism has not as yet produced appropriate discourse of social antagonism, it has quickly given rise to various discourses of ethnic antagonism and definitions of the self in terms of the ethnic "other." This applies to all categories of ethnic minorities: those that are conspicuously successful have become symbols of inequity, those conspicuously failing have become competitors for the scarce resources of the state, and those who share a common ethnolinguistic heritage with citizens of a neighboring state have come to represent a threat to the last commonly shared social resource, the territory of the national state. The fact that the internationally hegemonic political culture has made ethnic discourse taboo, or that it has shown conspicuous solicitousness toward minorities, may make the discourse more muted, but the sentiments not necessarily less salient, for the taboos are perceived as endowments of privilege by powers located outside the political boundaries of the state.

Conclusion

As a historical study, this book has reviewed nearly two centuries of the politics of the small states of East Central Europe, divided in retrospect —and somewhat anachronistically—into three periods: those of precommunism, communism, and postcommunism. Alternatively, we may divide the period into two grand cycles: the rise and decline of liberalism, and the rise and decline of communism. The third, contemporary, period is one of a new liberalism resurrected under benevolent Western auspices. Clearly, as of writing, the future of this experiment is still uncertain. Assessing its prospects in the context of historical experience and social science will be one of the objectives of this concluding chapter.

As anticipated from the beginning, the study, while engaged in tracking the dynamics of political change, was equally engaged in calling attention to a number of historical continuities, all of them of considerable interest to both historiography and social science. Having tracked them for the better half of two centuries of history, we may now summarize their relevance for the discipline of politics.

THE POLITICS OF BACKWARDNESS

The first of these continuities, that of the problem of economic backwardness, has haunted and challenged every generation in the region since the early nineteenth century, or, more precisely, since the Industrial Revolution ran its course in Britain in the half century between 1780 and 1830. Evidence for this otherwise obvious fact has been collected by several generations of economists. While this evidence may be subjected to criticism for its margins of error, the conclusion is inescapable that generation after generation, indeed decade by decade, economic disparities between the European core and the peripheries of the world economy have not only persisted, but have steadily increased. The landmarks of this downward drift have been included in statistical tables from Chapters 3–7, usually by comparing arithmetical means of six highly advanced Western and six East Central European societies (selected on account of the availability and quality of the statistical evidence). If we take these figures, the income disparity between the two regions increased from 40 percent of Western income levels in the 1860s to 51 percent in 1910 and 60 percent in 1938. After apparently narrowing a bit during the 1950s and 1960s, the gap widened markedly once more: to 65 percent in the 1980s and 75 percent in the early years of postcommunism. Moreover, as has been pointed out again and again, these disparities persisted and increased, not only between East and West, but within the East itself, and sustained an economic gradient first observed toward the end of the eighteenth century. This gradient was steepening consistently until 1945; it flattened out somewhat under Soviet hegemony, to open up again immediately after the fall of communism. As was noted in Chapter 7, we can say that disparities between any country of the North Atlantic region and East Central Europe are today substantially higher than in 1830, 1900, or 1938.

For the political scientist, these figures raise questions of both cause and effect. Addressing these in reverse order, we can easily discern the centrality of backwardness for the formulation of public policies. It has haunted liberals, fascists, and communists in turn, as well as the new postcommunist elites. As a causal factor, international income inequalities lay behind the corruptions of the legal state and representative government, and, in the final analysis, behind the rise of fascism and communism. As a result, the political history of East Central Europe provides us with a virtual taxonomy of the politics of backwardness, including a plethora of developmental and revolutionary strategies, the first trying to close the East-West gap by institutional engineering, the second by building up the state for external conquest, or, more boldly, for reconstructing the external world by challenging (usually in the company of a great power) the existing distribution of power and wealth across the Continent or across the world.

Two hundred years of history also enables us to explore the dynamics of backwardness and to put to the test the validity of some of our general hypotheses about the conditions of progress on the periphery. Above all, we can draw some conclusions concerning the relative weight to be accorded to competing paradigms of explanation. Let us do so first by recalling again that economic disparities persisted not only between East and West but also among the peripheral countries themselves, rather closely following a continental gradient that had developed in the early modern period. The very existence of this gradient invites us to dismiss the relevance of virtue embedded in culture and national character, for the simple reason that a neat geographical distribution of these qualities is, to say the least, highly improbable. With regard to institutional explanations, the conclusion is less categorical. However, the great variety of institutional models, combined with their uniform failure to reverse the process of economic marginalization, counsels us to give these political constructs less weight than that given to "structures," or "confining conditions," imposed upon these societies by larger forces located in the external world.

The most persistent of these confining conditions has been the international demonstration effect of the material culture that grew out of the ongoing consumer revolutions of the West. This phenomenon has been observed to be worldwide and variable over time. It is more intense in the teletronic age than it was in the ages of the railroad and the mail coach. The demonstration effect has also been postulated to vary over space. It appears that it has been, and is, particularly intense in our region owing to its physical proximity to one of the great global centers of innovation and prosperity. In any case, we have seen the prevalence of this phenomenon throughout the modern age: first in the nineteenth-century gentry's yearning for Western fashions; next, in the laboring masses' desire for Western wages and working conditions in an Eastern economy; then, in the subjects of state socialism demanding cars, refrigerators, and, more generally, a style of life resembling the one fashioned by the Western middle and working classes. This steady pressure for higher consumption was effectively resisted only by the brutal, and ultimately self-defeating, methods of the Stalinist state. All others succumbed in the long run to pressures either from the masses or from the elites.

While it is difficult to strike an accurate balance among the competing explanations, it is clear that relative deprivation was not the only factor adversely affecting material progress. Markets, as noted earlier in this volume, have the capacity both to reward and to punish, often acting capriciously in ways that have less to do with virtue or institutional design than with geographical position or the availability of the right resource at the right time. Thus, while Saudi oil or, in this narrative, Scandinavian wood pulp, ore, and proximity to Britain were boons to material progress in the short and long run, East European grain, once "as good as gold," became a bain. In the 1870s, cheap land and the transportation revolutions of the time—the railroad and steam shipping—put overseas producers in command at the very moment when the countries of the region were making their first bold moves to diversify their economies through productive reinvestment of export earnings. The question of whether or not a sustained boom in cereals might have been enough to reverse the "downward drift" of Eastern economies cannot be answered with absolute certainty. But there is little doubt that six decades of sagging demand and depressed prices compounded their difficulties as they strove to break out of the vicious circle of self-reproducing scarcities. The more general lesson taught us by the world is that relative deprivation alone may not abort the take-off of development. But when it is combined with adverse market trends in historical moments of great vulnerability, it is almost certain to do so.

Although the proximity of greater wealth and market trends together may have condemned the region to a fate of progressive economic marginalization, the process of economic drift has received an additional push from political forces from outside the region's boundaries. To some observers, and mainly to the ones of the nationalist and Marxist schools, these forces were omnipresent and at work throughout the modern age. To others, like this writer, the nineteenth-century European order was less organized for intracontinental than for intercontinental exploitation. Although inferior in strength and economic worth, the countries of East Central Europe were not exploited colonies. At worst, they were the objects of economic indifference and great power neglect. Neither the concept of "foreign aid" nor the transfer of value to the "less fortunate" were part of the discourse of the age, but special relations to great powers—as was the case for Bohemia, Hungary, and Poland—were on the whole more beneficial than economically deleterious. Of course, this age of benign neglect changed drastically in the interwar period when the loose hegemonies of liberal powers were challenged in succession by great revolutionary states. With the rise of Germany and then the Soviet Union as regional hegemons and imperial states, the small powers of East Central Europe were conscripted into grand historical projects whose logic was one of political and not of economic rationality. Being part of these projects in the long run contributed further to the marginalization and peripheralization of the region in the world economy.

SMALL FISH IN BIG PONDS

Are all small powers exposed to the vagaries of history made by the great? Mostly, yes, although once again perhaps in different degrees. In the case of East Central Europe, the degree of this exposure has been unusually high. They were not only economically backward peripheries of the modern world economy but also borderlands among great powers fighting over continental hegemony. This circumstance affected not only economic but political development as well, by shaping the choice of institutions or directly imposing institutional designs and ideologies, which conventional political sociology usually attributes to "underlying" socioeconomic structures.

Such an approach is clearly inadequate in explaining the dynamics of political change in the region, for here, from the beginning of the modern age, external forces have far outweighed domestic ones as causal factors of institutional change. Insofar as changes in the means of production were relevant at all to politics, these were changes that had taken place elsewhere in the larger world. For many years, both national and Marxist historiography has shown a great predilection for explaining the rise of Hungarian, Romanian, or Bulgarian liberalism in reference to revolutions in agriculture, commerce, or industry. This may well be the right approach, except that these revolutions played themselves out, not in Hungary, Romania, or Bulgaria but in Manchester and Leeds. To use the language of Marxism, the superstructures may well have been in the East, but the base that controlled their movements was in England and in the advanced West. By the same token, fascism and communism were the products of political revolutions not in Budapest, Tirana, or Bucharest but in Berlin and Moscow.

The point here is that political change in small powers is not understandable merely as adaptation to socio-economic change within narrow political boundaries, but must be seen as adaptation to the interest and rules of hegemonic powers in international regimes. To make this point more forcefully, we may briefly re-examine the region's history of institutional change and link it not to modernization but to the changing structure of power in the larger, external context. For the modern period this re-examination must begin with the Concert of Europe, the regulator of great power relations from the Congress of Vienna to the outbreak of World War I. The main purpose of the Concert was to preserve intra-European peace in an age of massive expansion into other parts of the world, and to make the world, including the new states of East Central Europe, safe for British trade. Reflective of the key role of Britain in this system, this objective brought to our region the classical liberal design for modern government: a legal state capable of enforcing contracts, preferably embedded in a parliamentary form of government. The successor of the Concert was the Franco-British post-Versailles order, which was institutionally embodied by the League of Nations. This order brought democracy to the region when the hegemonic powers insisted that the small states of the borderlands introduce universal suffrage and grant rights to a variety of ethnic and religious minorities. When this international order collapsed in 1933–38, these democracies and codified rights also fell by the wayside. In this particular context it is especially worth remembering that the great electoral victories of the radical Right in the region were not won during the bleak depression years, but in the wake of the German ascent, which gave this particular form of political expression practical weight and meaning.

The rest of the modern history of the region leaves still less ambiguity about the external origins of internal regimes. There are few, if any, scholars left who would plead the case for the domestic origin of the ensuing communist regimes. Similarly, if today there is some debate about the origins and "base" of the post-communist regimes, it should be remembered that the "Sinatra doctrine" was enunciated in Moscow and that since then many, if not most, of the domestic policies and institutions of East Central Europe have been formulated in response to conditions set not in Budapest or Bucharest but in Brussels, Copenhagen, Maastricht, and Amsterdam. Surely the moral and material substance of these international regimes have varied considerably. But the facts of hegemony and tutelage have persisted over the decades.

But the coin of hegemony has another side as well, for the power of the great, whether "merely" hegemonic or imperial, whether "soft" or "hard" in its means, while imposing frameworks, will never be total in reach. Like the power of domestic government, that of international regimes is always subject to natural restraints. A hegemon may well dictate the form of politics and the language of discourse. But political outcomes will always deviate from the form and be subject to "corruption" by the feigned compliance of client elites laboring under the injunctions of local culture and socio-economic constraints bequeathed by a previous age. These limits on hegemonic intent, noble or base, are easily gleaned from the chapters of East Central European history and equally evident under each and every international regime. Thus the noble ideals of nineteenth-century liberalism were corrupted by political machines hiding behind the façade of splendid baroque and gothic parliaments, while the bureaucratic apparatuses and their gendarmeries effectively manufactured safe majorities. In like manner, the rising hegemony of fascist states in the 1930s produced in the region a number of one-party states. But the qualities of these states made the leaders of the hegemonic powers sneer or despair, while the grand design of communism a couple of decades later suffered the indignity of all sorts of "deviationism," ranging from Kádár's experiments with the market to Ceauşescu's radical nationalism and the Polish "social contract" with the reactionary Church. Stalin, to be sure, used the savagery of the purges to punish those suspected of simulation and to enforce uniformity across the realm. But the method was costly and inefficient. For, as developments after his death so vividly suggest, this uniformity, too, was simulated. The purge did not change minds, only appearances. It created outward conformity while strengthening the inward desire for political change.

It is at this point that we may address the role of culture in politics. Defined here as the habituated residue of traditional religious injunctions, culture has played a dual role in the East Central European experience. Culture could provide a consciously chosen rallying point against against hegemonic influence, or, subconsciously, it could shape the behavior of actors so as to corrupt the normative design of the imported political model. In the present narrative, Eastern cultures showed greater suspicion toward Western institutional imports and Western cultures to Eastern institutional imports. Subconsciously, political elites in the Eastern cultural sphere adapted more easily to Eastern institutions and political symbolism and elites in Western cultures to Western institutions and political symbolism. Nowhere is this thesis better demonstrated than in the contrast between the reactions of the societies of East Central Europe to liberalism and communism, two political models that, unlike the chaotic and ephemeral experiments with fascism, between themselves dominated the politics of the region for over a century. Recall once more the historical divide between the cultures of legalism and communalism. Whereas communism faced intellectual dissent and mass resistance by the cultures of legalism, it enjoyed at least a grudging acceptance in communal cultures, where, even at its worst, it represented something that was in some respects familiar. Contrariwise, liberalism, with its emphasis on contractual relations and the legal state, has proven to be bearable, if inadequate, in the cultures of legal impersonality but has stumbled upon considerable resistance in the cultures of communalism. This seems to be as much true in the postcommunist present as in the precommunist past.

ECONOMICS AND POLITICS: PROSPECTS OF DEMOCRACY AND DEVELOPMENT IN EAST CENTRAL EUROPE

What is historical sociology all about? In essence, it is the craft of explaining events that took place in the past, and of weaving these explanations into patterns and paradigms of generalized relationships. At their most ambitious, practitioners of the art treat these patterns as theories that have the power to predict within the confines of analogy. More cautiously put, patterns emerging from the past allow us to raise informed questions about potential sources of continuity and change based on contrast and analogy. By choosing this method to discuss the prospects of democracy in East Central Europe, we shall steer a middle course between the blind determinism of the maxim that history is destiny and the now increasingly fashionable voluntarism and "possibilism" in the social sciences that are ready to attribute institutional outcomes to sheer human will or the acumen to make the right decision at the right time. In doing so, we should once again remember Marx, who, while rightfully seen as a historical determinist, is also on record to the effect that humans make their own choices, although they are constrained by the web of circumstances handed down to them by history. To use (with some reluctance) a quasi-algebraic formula, the outcome of actions taken at Time 0 is conditioned by a mix of forces operating at Time -1, -2, and so on.

The first lesson, then, that history teaches us is that democracy cannot be created out of thin air and good will, but is conditioned by other processes —above all, the process of economic development. True, there have been instances in history when great powers were promoting and imposing democratic institutions from a position of overwhelming strength. Thus in the course of building democracies in the former Axis countries after World War II, the victorious Allies not only scripted the process but policed it in their capacity as occupiers. Something of this nature is happening in our days in a number of Balkan countries. But while foreigners can create such democratic institutions, the long-run success of such projects requires that these institutions be responsive to the aspirations of the governed, above all by being capable of generating a level of prosperity to which their constituents aspire. In this respect, it is useful to compare the "wave" of democratization initiated by the United States after World War II with that initiated by Britain and France in the interwar period. Whereas the former had firm economic underpinnings in the form of foreign aid and trade preferences, the latter lacked an economic component and came to naught upon its first encounter with economic adversity.

The real task, then, is to discuss the prospects of economic development, and more specifically the prospect of reversing the seemingly relentless historical trend toward increasing regional and continental income disparities. It is in this respect that we can take advantage of our own excursion into history, for, having done so, we can identify a number of factors that have in the past contributed to the region's increasing backwardness, and then examine whether and to what extent they are present in the contemporary international environment.

The first, and perhaps foremost, factor underlying the region's backwardness was psychological: it was an endemic sense of relative deprivation generated by images of the material progress of the countries of the advanced West. In the past, this demonstration effect weighed heavily on these societies, perhaps more heavily than on most of their counterparts on the periphery of the modern world economy, given their geographical proximity to the great centers of technological innovation and their close cultural identification with the innovators. Like the latter, they were Christian and European, circumstances that helped to convert economic differences into expectation and entitlement. The question is whether this demonstration effect is operative today as well, and how it contributes to the effectiveness of their economies and polities. By all appearances, the answer is that the effect is very much alive, and that it continues to have a negative influence on the countries' economies. Indeed, expanded opportunities for travel, free access to Western media, and growing familiarity with Western lifestyles and articles of consumption seem to have raised material expectations to new heights. True, the expectations so generated remain unfulfilled, but even in their

TABLE 74

Personal Consumption in East Central Europe, 1990–94

	Motor cars (1000s)		Meat (kg)		Sugar (kg)		Vegetables (kg)	
	1990	1994	1990	1994	1990	1994	1990	1994
Bulgaria	304	351	77.8	64.5	26.0	17.5	114	100
Czech Republic	228	261	96.5	86.5	44.0	39.5	67	70
Hungary	185	204	73.1	73.3	38.2	39.7	83	85
Poland	138	176[a]	68.6	67.5	44.1	41.3	119	122
Romania	55	76[a]	61.0	47.7	27.3	24.0	111	113
Slovakia	165	187	84.0	64.2	46.3	34.2	71	78
Slovenia	289	318	—	—	—	—	—	—

SOURCE: Vienna Institute 1995, 124–29.
[a] In 1993.

TABLE 75

Consumption and Investment as Share of GDP in East Central Europe, 1990–94

(%)

	Total consumption		Individual consumption		Collective consumption		Gross capital formation		Output collapse[a] (%)
	1990	1994	1990	1994	1990	1994	1990	1994	
Bulgaria	74.0	90.9	55.8	83.3	18.2	7.6	30.4	8.5	28
Czech Republic	70.1	79.9	50.2	57.6	19.8	22.3	28.6	20.4	19
Hungary	72.0	85.3	61.4	73.5	10.6	11.7	25.4	21.6	17
Poland	67.2	83.5	48.0	63.0	19.3	20.4	25.6	15.6	9
Romania	79.2	75.2	65.0	62.0	13.3	12.5	30.3	26.6	27
Slovakia	75.8	80.6	53.9	56.6	21.9	24.0	33.5	22[b]	22
Slovenia	66.0	74.7	48.6	54.0	17.4	20.7	16.8	20.8	6

SOURCE: Vienna Institute 1995, 124–29.
[a] Output collapse in percent.
[b] 1993 figure (21.9%).

pent-up state they have discernible consequences adverse to the cause of development. Above all, they set narrower limits on the extent to which governments can impose austerity on their publics. Thus as Tables 74 and 76 demonstrate, while in absolute terms the consumption of many articles, above all comestibles, declined substantially between 1990 and 1994, consumption relative to output has increased conspicuously, and has done so at the expense of domestic savings. Another hint of the workings of the demonstration effect is contained in figures showing the deterioration of most countries' terms of trade,[1] reminiscent of the nineteenth century, when meager savings of gold—now often illegally hoarded hard-currency reserves—and the sale of fixed assets was used to purchase higher-quality and more attractive Western articles of consumption. This kind of overspending at the expense of savings and infrastructure is just as prevalent in the public as in

1. World Bank 1997c, 245–46.

the private sector. Thus, while both the quantity and quality of state services did decline, social transfer payments still hover at 20–25 percent above what institutional lenders would find desirable given the proportion of such spending to GNP.[2]

Other challenges to the economic well-being of these societies emanate from the global market, into which they triumphantly reentered under Western auspices. Although this market, by implication at least, is often depicted as a constant (to which players can "adapt" by choosing the proper institutions), in reality it is a highly variable entity, the character of which has been changing constantly throughout the modern period. In its current shape, this market is driven by unprecedented levels of demand, generated mainly by the consumer economies of the advanced industrial societies of the West. But this very demand has stimulated the rise of a vast new industrial sector across the world, including many sectors—footware, apparel, textiles, electronics, and assembling operations—in which postcommunist economies had hoped to find their strongest comparative advantage. Likewise, Eastern agriculture, once the greatest threat to continental competitors, is now rapidly losing its competitive edge, and, as the example of the collapse of the farming sector of East Germany suggests, it may even be wiped out by more efficient, and heavily subsidized, agriculture of the West.[3]

Nor have the labor markets of the modern world become more benign. Supply is rapidly expanding, once again in the very niches initially believed to be reserved for East Central Europeans in intra-European trade. A few figures will illustrate the dimensions of the competitive challenge: 20 years ago, 66 percent of the active labor force of the world remained external to the world market, but today 90 percent, or a workforce of 4 billion, are active participants, with another 1.2 billion expected to join in the next generation. Half of this grand total, currently 2 billion workers, belong to the labor forces of countries with per capita incomes below $695—that is, below the level of the East Central European countries, with the possible exception of Albania.[4] This large, and ever-growing, labor force will be employed in the same low-value-added manufacturing sector as the workers of East Central Europe, putting pressure on wages areawide, but especially in the Balkan countries. This competitive disadvantage is mitigated somewhat by geography—that is, by the lower transportation costs of East European commodities vis-à-vis West European markets. But to overcome the pressures altogether, Jeffrey Sachs and Andrew Warner estimate, labor costs would have to fall further in the short run, to support investment levels as high as 30–40 percent.[5] Needless to say, the elasticity of wages is limited

2. Gelb 1996, 1–3.
3. Eichengreen and Kohl 1997, 21.
4. Sachs and Warner 1996, 3–4.
5. Ibid.

not only by human biology but by cultural factors as well. Today, the average worker in Hungary or the Czech Republic works for about one-fifth of the German average wage, and the ratio is as low as one-tenth in the countries of southeastern Europe. All over the region, paychecks are regarded as "starvation wages," and any further depression of these wages would result in severe social dislocation. Whatever the economic justification, at still lower wages part of the labor force would withdraw from the market and engage in self-destructive behavior and even social banditry. This already is happening in the Balkan countries, where wages range from $72 to $120 a month.[6] What we have seen in Albania and Bosnia in recent years may in part be seen as the result of such desperation, while the virulent national radicalism of some of the other countries may be viewed as attempts by political entrepreneurs to save the social fabric by taking the element of randomness out of violence and by pulling extremely scarce resources together along ethnic lines.

The capital markets of the world are equally competitive. True, the amount of money crossing international boundaries is truly staggering by the standards of the past two centuries of global capitalism. But Eastern and East Central Europe are not among the most favored destinations of this capital. Once again, the numbers tell much of the story. According to the World Bank, in a 12-month period from mid 1995 to mid 1996 foreign direct investment worldwide amounted to $325 billion. About two-thirds of this, or $228 billion, crossed boundaries among the advanced industrial states. This left $97 billion for investment in the "emerging markets" of the world. The share of Central *and* Eastern Europe (including Russia and the European republics of the former Soviet Union), with about 5.5 percent of the world's population, was $12 billion, or 3.7 percent of all foreign direct investment—a less than rousing endorsement by the world's financial community, especially in view of the fact that much of this amount went to three countries: Russia, Hungary, and the Czech Republic.[7]

Yet the balance sheet of East Central Europe has a credit side as well: an international milieu that, unlike its predecessors in modern history, is not just benign, but actively favorable to the causes of democracy and development. Unlike fascism and communism, which were openly hostile to the

6. In December 1997, average monthly wages in East Central Europe were reported as follows: Slovenia, $887; Poland, $329; Czech Republic, $302; Slovakia, $258; Serbia-Montenegro, $120; Romania, $(72)–117; Bosnia, $84; Bulgaria, $(72)–84. *Business Central Europe, Annual Supplement, 1997–98* (Dec. 1997), 22–44. Figures in parentheses from World Bank, worldbank.org.html/trans/marapril/art9.htm. In comparison, before the recent economic collapse of Southeast Asian economies, manufacturing wages in Malaysia were reported at $213, and in Thailand at $324. See United States, Department of Labor 1995, Working Papers 5211, 5219.

7. "Milestones of Transition," *Transition* (World Bank) 7, nos. 5–6 (May–June 1996): 19–24.

first and had imperial designs detrimental to the second, the new hegemony is ready to actively promote both of these projects, and unlike the liberals of the nineteenth century, who subscribed to the idea of the survival of the fittest, the new liberalism is imbued with a benevolent universalism that has internationalized some of the egalitarian impulses of the modern welfare state. It is also a hegemony of the richest and, for the time being, most powerful nations of the world, which in the past have shown impressive capabilities to co-opt and to transfer material advantage from continent to continent and from country to country—as demonstrated by the Marshall Plan, by Iberia's integration into the European Union, and by the as yet unfinished integration of the former GDR into the West German economy. So far, to be sure, the economic efforts made on behalf of East Central Europe have fallen far behind the great examples just cited.[8] Genuine integration into the European Union—a meaningful opening of markets, distributions from the European development fund, and labor mobility across the Continent—may change the picture. If so, "procedurally correct" democracies may become genuine democracies rooted in actual popular preference, and the "troubled" may advance to become procedurally more correct.

However, we must also bear in mind that world politics is not a constant, and that the balance of forces in the world and on the Continent may, as it has in the past, undergo significant change. Today's hegemons on the Continent have reasonably healthy economies, and their position has yet to be challenged politically in any major way. But economic capabilities rise and fall with booms and recessions, and the rise of new challengers to the global core is far from being outside the realm of the possible. Pliable as of this writing, Russia may once more emerge as one of these challengers, much as Germany did after defeat in World War I. Much as in the 1930s, such a challenge would likely mobilize now pent-up frustrations and disappointments and unite them as a mighty force under the red-brown flags of antisystemic movements. Such a turn of events would confront the Western alliance with strategic alternatives. It could either maximize its economic efforts to make the entire region "safe for democracy" or continue at current levels, but draw new, narrower boundaries for East Central Europe. In this case, democratization in one half of the region would accelerate, while the other half may once again turn into repressive and militant authoritarian regimes. It is with the hope that this will not come to pass that this study is concluded.

8. Projections based on current rates of growth in the West and among the "good performers" of East Central Europe are far from euphoric. The modest target of reaching 70 percent of EU per capita GNP has been estimated to require 36 years for the Czech Republic, 45 years for Hungary, and 65 years for Poland (Sachs and Warner 1996, 4).

Bibliography

Abraham, Richard. 1987. *Alexander Kerensky: The First Love of Revolution*. New York: Columbia University Press.

Abrams, Brad. 1996. "The Politics of Retribution: The Trial of Jozef Tiso." *East European Politics and Societies* 10, no. 2 (spring): 255–92.

Adelman, Jonathan R., ed. 1984. *Terror and Communist Politics: The Role of the Secret Police in Communist States*. Boulder, Colo.: Westview Press.

Ágh, Attila, and Gabriella Ilonszki, eds. 1996. *The Second Steps*. Budapest: Hungarian Centre for Democracy Studies.

Akhavian, Payam, and Robert Howse. 1994. *Yugoslavia: The Former and Future*. Washington, D.C.: Brookings Institution.

Ali, Tariq, ed. 1984. *The Stalinist Legacy: Its Impact on Twentieth-Century World Politics*. New York: Penguin Books.

Allman, T. D. 1993. "Serbia's Bloody War." In *Why Bosnia? Writings on the Balkan War,* edited by Rabia Ali and Lawrence Lifschultz. Stony Creek, Conn.: Pamphleteer's Press.

Almanahul Cuvântul, 1941 [The Almanac of the daily *Cuvânt*]. December 1940. Bucharest.

Almaş D., and E. Fotescu. 1971. *Istoria patriei: Manual pentru clasa a IV-a* [History of the fatherland: 4th grade textbook]. Bucharest: Editura Didactică.

Alton, Thad P., et al. 1977. *Research Project on National Income in East Central Europe*. New York: International Financial Research Institute, Occasional Paper No. 75.

Anderson, Charles. 1967. *Politics and Economic Change in Latin America*. Princeton, N.J.: Van Nostrand.

Andics, Jenő. 1983. "A politika és a gazdaság közötti kölcsönhatások" [Interaction between economics and politics]. *Valóság* 34, no. 7 (July): 1–10.

Andorka, Rudolf. 1983. *A társadalmi mobilitás változásai* [Changing patterns of social mobility]. Budapest: Gondolat.

Apter, David A. 1963. "System Process, and the Politics of Development." In *Industrialization and Society,* edited by Bert Hoselitz and Wilbert Moore. The Hague: Mouton.

Arendt, Hannah. 1951. *The Origins of Totalitarianism*. New York: Harcourt, Brace.

Arimia, Vasile, Ion Ardeleanu, and Stefan Lache, eds. 1991. *Antonescu-Hitler: Cor-

respondenţa si intîlnire înedite [Antonescu-Hitler: Unedited correspondence and minutes of meetings]. Bucharest: COZIA.

Aslund, Anders. 1989. *Gorbachev's Struggle for Economic Reform.* London: Pinter.

Asmus, Ronald D. 1980a. "The GDR Celebrates Martin Luther." *Radio Free Europe Research,* June 25.

———. 1980b. "The Search for Historical Roots in the GDR." *Radio Free Europe Research.* GDR, August 1.

———. 1981. "The Berlin Wall in Perspective." *Radio Free Europe Research.* GDR, August 22.

———. 1982. "Erich Honecker: The Man and His Era on His 70th Birthday." *Radio Free Europe Research.* GDR, August 30.

———. 1983. "East German Official Sets Ideological Priorities." *Radio Free Europe Research.* GDR, December 30.

Auersperg, Pavel. 1970. "The International Position of the CP of the CSSR." *Mlada Fronta* (5 May, 1970). In *Radio Free Europe Research,* Czechoslovakia, May 22.

Avakumović, Ivan. 1971. "Yugoslavia's Fascist Movements." In *Native Fascism in the Successor States, 1918–1945,* edited by Peter F. Sugar, 135–43. Santa Barbara, Calif.: Clio Press.

Avtorkhanov, Abdurakhman. 1968. *The Communist Party Apparatus.* New York: World Publishing.

Baerlein, H. 1940a. "Czechoslovakia after Munich." *Nineteenth Century,* no. 121 (March): 308–18.

———. 1940b. "Inside Slovakia Today." *Nineteenth Century,* no. 127 (March): 308–18.

Bahro, Rudolf. 1986. "The Creeping Militarization of Society." In *Leadership and Succession in the Soviet Union, East Europe and China,* edited by Martin McCauley and Stephen Carter. Armonk, N.Y.: M. E. Sharpe.

Bairoch, Paul. 1975. *The Economic Development of the Third World since 1900.* Trans. Cynthia Postan. Berkeley: University of California Press.

———. 1976. "Europe's Gross National Product, 1800–1975." *Journal of Economic History* 5, no. 2 (fall): 273–340.

———. 1977a. *Agriculture and Industrial Revolution, 1700–1914.* Fontana Economic History of Europe, 3. London: Fontana Books.

———. 1977b. *The Economic Development of the Third World since 1910.* Translated by Cynthia Postan. Berkeley and Los Angeles: University of California Press.

———. 1981. "The Main Trends in National Income Disparities since the Industrial Revolution." In *Disparities in Economic Development since the Industrial Revolution,* by Paul Bairoch and Maurice Lévy-Leboy, 3–15. London: Macmillan.

———. 1982. "International Industrialization Levels from 1750 to 1980." *Journal of Economic History* 11 (fall): 330–31.

Bairoch, Paul, and Maurice Lévy-Leboy. 1981. *Disparities in Economic Development since the Industrial Revolution.* London: Macmillan.

Baldwin, Richard E. 1994. *Towards Integrated Europe.* London: Centre for Economic Policy Research.

Bálint, József. 1983. *Társadalmi rétegeződés és jövedelmek* [Social stratification and income distribution]. Budapest: Kossuth.

Banac, Ivo. 1984. *The National Question in Yugoslavia*. Ithaca, N.Y.: Cornell University Press.

———. 1988. *With Stalin Against Tito: Cominformist Splits in Yugoslav Communism*. Ithaca, N.Y.: Cornell University Press.

———, ed. 1992. *East Europe in Revolution*. Ithaca, N.Y.: Cornell University Press.

Banks, Arthur. 1971. *Cross Polity Time Series Data*. Cambridge, Mass.: MIT Press.

Baran, Paul, and Paul Sweezy. 1971. "Notes on the Theory of Imperialism." In *Readings in U.S. Imperialism*, edited by K. T. Fann and Donald C. Hodges, 69–84. Boston, Mass.: Porter Sargent.

Barany, George. 1968. *Stephen Széchenyi and the Awakening of Hungarian Nationalism*. Princeton, N.J.: Princeton University Press.

Barany, Zoltan D. 1991. "Soviet Control of the Hungarian Military under Stalin." *Journal of Strategic Studies* 14, no. 2 (July): 148–64.

———. 1993. *Soldiers and Politics in Eastern Europe, 1945–1990*. London: Macmillan.

Barátossy-Balog, Benedek. 1930. *Japán a felkelő nap országa* [Japan, country of the rising sun]. Budapest: Author.

Bartel, Horst, ed. 1975. *Geschichte für Klasse 8* [Eighth grade history]. Berlin: Verlag Volk und Wissen.

Bauer, Otto. 1907. *Die Nationalitätenfrage und die Sozialdemokratie* [Social democracy and the problem of nationality]. Vienna: Ignaz Brand.

Bauman, Igor. 1989. *Personal Consumption in the U.S.S.R. and the U.S.A.* New York: St. Martin's Press.

Bauman, Zygmunt. 1992. *Intimations of Postmodernity*. London: Routledge.

Baxa, Jacob. 1926. *Die Geschichte der Produktivitätstheorie* [History of the theory of productivity]. Jena: Gustav Fischer.

Baylis, Thomas A. 1986. "Explaining the GDR's Economic Reform." In *Power, Purpose, and Collective Choice: Economic Strategy in Socialist States*, edited by Ellen Comisso and Laura D'Andrea Tyson, 205–44. Ithaca, N.Y.: Cornell University Press.

Beard, Charles A., and George Rodin. 1929. *The Balkan Pivot: Yugoslavia. A Study in Government and Administration*. New York: Macmillan.

Beck, Friedrich, and W. Goodman (pseud.). 1951. *Russian Purge and the Extraction of Confessions*. New York: Hurst & Blackett.

Bekić, Darko. 1985. "The Yugoslav System in Crisis: Internal Views." *Problems of Communism* 34, no. 6 (Nov.–Dec.): 70–76.

Bell, John D. 1977. *Peasants in Power: Alexander Stamboliski and the Bulgarian Agrarian National Union, 1899–1923*. Princeton, N.J.: Princeton University Press.

———. 1986. *The Bulgarian Communist Party from Blagoev to Zhivkov*. Stanford: Hoover Institution Press.

———. 1997. "Democratization and Political Participation in 'Postcommunist' Bulgaria." In *Politics, Power, and the Struggle for Democracy in South-East Europe*, edited by Karen Dawisha and Bruce Parrott, 388–92. New York: Cambridge University Press.

Bendix, Reinhard. 1967. "Tradition and Modernity Reconsidered." *Comparative Studies in Society and History* 9 (April): 296–346.

———. 1972. *Nation-Building and Citizenship*. 2d ed. Berkeley and Los Angeles: University of California Press.

———. 1977. *Max Weber*. 2d ed. Berkeley and Los Angeles: University of California Press.

Benz, Ernst. 1963. *The Eastern Orthodox Church: Its Thought and Life*. Chicago: Aldine.

Berend, Ivan T. 1982. *The European Periphery and Industrialization*. Translated by Eva Palmai. New York: Cambridge University Press.

———. 1983. *Gazdasági útkeresés, 1956–1965* [Searching for economic reforms, 1956–65]. Budapest: Magvető.

———. 1986. *The Crisis Zone of Europe*. Cambridge: Cambridge University Press.

———. 1990. *The Hungarian Economic Reforms, 1953–1988*. New York: Cambridge University Press.

———. 1996. *Central and Eastern Europe: Detour from the Periphery to the Periphery*. New York: Cambridge University Press.

Berend, Ivan T., and György Ránki. 1974. *Economic Development in East-Central Europe in the Nineteenth and Twentieth Centuries*. New York: Columbia University Press.

———. 1977. *East Central Europe in the Nineteenth and Twentieth Centuries*. Budapest: Akadémia.

———. 1982. *The European Periphery and Industrialization, 1780–1914*. Translated by E. Palmai. London: Oxford University Press; Budapest: Akadémiai Kiadó.

Berndt, Martin. 1989. *Weltmacht oder Niedergang* [World power or decline]. Darmstadt: Wissenschaftliche Buchgesellschaft.

Berry, Donald B., George Ginsburgs, and Peter B. Maggs, eds. 1978. *Soviet Law after Stalin*. 2 vols. Alphen, Neth.: Sijthoff & Noordhoff.

Bialer, Seweryn. 1986. *The Soviet Paradox: External Expansion, Internal Decline*. New York: Knopf.

Biberaj, Elez. 1990. *Albania: A Socialist Maverick*. Boulder, Colo.: Westview Press.

Bićanić, Rudolf. 1938. *Ekonomska podloga hrvatskog pitanja* [Economic foundations of the Croat question]. Split: Hrvatska Narodna Tiskara.

Bihari, Mihály, ed. 1993. *A többpártrendszerek kialakulása Kelet-Középeurópában* [The rise of multiparty systems in East Central Europe]. Budapest: Kossuth.

Black, Cyril E. 1943. *The Establishment of Constitutional Government in Bulgaria*. Princeton: Princeton University Press.

Black, Cyril E., et al. 1975. *The Modernization of Japan and Russia*. New York: Free Press.

Blobaum, Robert. 1984. *Feliks Dzierzynski and the SDKPiL: A Study of the Origins of Polish Communism*. Boulder: East European Monographs.

Bloch, Marc. 1965. *Feudal Society*. Translated by L. A. Manyon. Chicago: University of Chicago Press.

Block, Herbert. 1978. *The Planetary Product, 1977–78*. Washington, D.C.: U.S. Department of State.

Block, Herbert, and Roy S. Cline. 1983. *The Planetary Product, 1982*. Washington, D.C.: Georgetown University Center for Strategic and International Studies.

Blum, Jerome. 1961. *Lord and Peasant in Russia from the Ninth to the Nineteenth Century*. Princeton, N.J.: Princeton University Press.

Bodenheimer, Suzanne. 1971. "Dependency and Imperialism: The Roots of Latin American Underdevelopment." In *Readings in U.S. Imperialism*, edited by K. T. Fann and Donald C. Hodges, 155–82. Boston: Porter Sargent.

Body, Paul. 1972. *Joseph Eötvös and the Modernization of Hungary*. Philadelphia: Transactions of the American Philosophical Society.

Bogdan, Ivo. 1942. "Das kroatische Zeitungswesen" [Croat journalism]. In *Die Kroaten*, edited by Clemens Diederich. Zagreb and Munich: Velebit.

Böhm, Vilmos. 1922. *Két forradalom tüzében* [In the crossfire of two revolutions]. Vienna: Bécsi magyar kiadó.

Bombelles, Joseph T. 1991. "Federal Aid to the Less Developed Areas of Yugoslavia." *East European Politics and Society* 5, no. 3 (fall): 439–65.

Bonnell, Victoria E. 1991. "The Representation of Women in Early Soviet Art." *Russian Review* 50: 267–88.

Bontoux, Eugene. [1861] 1868. *Ungarn und die Ernährung Europas* [Hungary and the feeding of Europe]. 2d ed. Vienna: Waldheim.

Borcherding, Thomas F. 1977. *Budgets and Bureaucrats: The Sources of Government Growth*. Durham, N.C.: Duke University Press.

Borkenau, Franz. 1962. *World Communism: A History of the Communist International*. Ann Arbor: University of Michigan Press.

Bornstein, Morris, Zvi Gitelman, and William Zimmerman. 1981. *East–West Relations and the Future of Eastern Europe*. London: George Allen & Unwin.

Bosl, Karl, ed. 1975. *Die demokratisch-parlamentarische Struktur der Ersten Tschechoslowakischen Republik* [The parliamentary-democratic structure of the first Czechoslovak republic]. Munich: Oldenbourg Verlag.

———. 1979. *Die Erste Tschechoslowakische Republik als multinationaler Parteistaat* [The first Czechoslovak republic as a multinational party state]. Munich: Oldenbourg Verlag.

Bosnyák, Zoltan. 1937. *Magyarország elzsidósodása* [The judaization of Hungary]. Budapest: Held.

Boyse, Matthew. 1986. "The East German Experience and Soviet Economic Options." *Radio Free Europe Research*. GDR, 3 January.

Bozóki, András. 1994. *Democratic Legitimacy in Post-Communist Societies*. Budapest: T-Twins.

Brabant, Jozef M. von. 1989. *Economic Integration in Eastern Europe*. New York: Harvester Wheatsheaf.

Braudel, Fernand. 1974. *Capitalism and Material Life, 1400–1800*. New York: Harper & Row.

Breslauer, George W. 1982. *Khrushchev and Brezhnev as Leaders: Building Authority in Soviet Politics*. London: George Allen & Unwin.

———. 1989. "Evaluating Gorbachev As a Leader." *Soviet Economy* 5, no. 4: 299–340.

———. 1996. "How Gorbachev Sold His Concessionary Foreign Policy." In *Reexaming the Soviet Experience: Essays in Honor of Alexander Dallin*, ed. David Holloway and Norman Naimark. Boulder, Co.: Westview Press.

Bress, Ludwig. 1982. *Technologische Evolution im Systemwettstreit* [Technological development in the competition between two systems]. Erlangen: IGW Verlag.

Brown, James F. 1966. *The New Eastern Europe: The Khrushchev Era and After.* New York: Praeger.

———. 1970. *Bulgaria under Communist Rule.* New York: Praeger.

———. 1988. *Eastern Europe and Communist Rule.* Durham, N.C.: Duke University Press.

Brumberg, Abraham, ed. 1963. *Russia under Khrushchev.* New York: Praeger.

Bryson, Philip, and Manfred Melzer. 1991. *The End of the East German Economy.* New York: St. Martin's Press.

Brzezinski, Zbigniew K. 1961. *The Soviet Bloc.* 2d ed. New York: Praeger.

———. 1967. *Ideology and Power in Soviet Politics.* 2d ed. New York: Praeger.

Buckelow, John D. 1974. "Erich Ludendorff and the German War Effort." Ph.D. diss. University of California, San Diego.

Buday, László. 1921. *A megcsonkitott Magyarország* [Dismembered Hungary]. Budapest: Pantheon.

Buell, Raymond. 1939. "Political Conflicts in Poland." *Virginia Quarterly Review* 15, no. 2 (spring): 231–45.

Bukharin, Nikolai, and E. Preobrazhensky. [1921] 1966. *The ABC of Communism: A Popular Explanation of the Program of the Communist Party of Russia.* Ann Arbor: University of Michigan Press.

Bună Vestirea. 1937. Bucharest.

Burg, Steven L. 1997. "Bosnia-Herzegovina: A Case of Failed Democratization." In *Politics, Power, and the Struggle for Democracy in South-East Europe*, edited by Karen Dawisha and Bruce Parrott, 123–45. New York: Cambridge University Press.

Burks, Richard V. 1960. *The Dynamics of Communism in Eastern Europe.* Princeton, N.J.: Princeton University Press.

Busek, Vratislav, and Nicolas Spulber. 1957. *Czechoslovakia.* New York: Praeger.

Buzatu, Gheorghe. 1990. *Mareşalul Antonescu* [Marshal Antonescu]. Iasi: BAI.

Byrnes, Robert F., ed. 1957. *Yugoslavia under the Communists.* New York: Praeger.

Calafăteanu, Ion, ed. 1994. *Iuliu Maniu: Opinii si confruntări politice, 1940–44* [Iuliu Maniu: Political views and struggles, 1940–44]. Cluj-Napoca: Editura Dacia.

Capek, Ales, and Gerald W. Sazama. 1993. "Czech and Slovak Economic Relations." *Europe–Asia Studies* 45, no. 2: 211–35.

Carey, Henry. 1995. "Irregularities or Rigging: Romanian Parliamentary Elections." *East European Quarterly* 29, no. 3 (fall): 43–66.

———. 1996. "From Big Lie to Small Lies: State Mass Media Dominance in Post-Communist Romania." *East European Politics and Society* 10, no. 4 (winter): 16–46.

Carr, E. H. 1970. *A History of Soviet Russia.* Baltimore: Penguin Books.

Carr, Raymond. 1966. *Spain, 1808–1939.* Oxford: Clarendon Press.

Carrère d'Encausse, Hélène. 1993. *The End of the Soviet Empire: The Triumph of the Nations.* Translated by Franklin Philip. New York: Basic Books.

Carter, April. 1982. *Democratic Reform in Yugoslavia: The Changing Role of the Party.* Princeton, N.J.: Princeton University Press.

Ceauşescu, Nicolae. 1977. "Cuvîntarea la confătuirea cadrelor din domeniul ştiinţelor sociale" [Words to the meeting of cadres from the fields of the social sciences]. In *România pe drumul* [Romania on the way]. Bucharest: Editura politică.

Chalasiński, Jozef. 1947. *Przeszlość i przyszlość intelligencji Polskiej* [Present and future of the Polish intelligentsia]. Rome: Instytut Literacki.

Chapman, Janet. 1963. *Real Wages in Soviet Russia*. Cambridge, Mass.: Harvard University Press.

Chayanov, Alexander V. 1923. *Die Lehre der bäuerlichen Gesellschaft* [The theory of the peasant economy]. Berlin.

Checinski, Michael. 1984. "Polish Secret Police." In *Terror and Communist Politics: The Role of the Secret Police in Communist States*, edited by Jonathan R. Adelman, 17–78. Boulder, Colo.: Westview Press.

Childs, David. 1983. *Moscow's German Ally*. London: Allen & Unwin.

Chirot, Daniel. 1976. *Social Change in a Peripheral Society: The Creation of a Balkan Colony*. New York: Academic Press.

————, ed. 1989. *The Origins of Backwardness in Eastern Europe*. Berkeley and Los Angeles: University of California Press.

Chirot, Daniel, and Anthony Reid. 1997. *Essential Outsiders: Chinese and Jews in the Modern Transformation of Southeast Asia and Central Europe*. Seattle: University of Washington Press.

Cipolla, Carlo. 1976. *Before the Industrial Revolution*. Ithaca, N.Y.: Cornell University Press.

————. 1965. *Guns and Sails in Early European Expansion, 1400–1700*. London: Collins.

Ciurca, D. 1970. "Quelques considerations sur la noblesse féodale chez les roumaines." *Nouvelles Études Historiques* 4, no. 2: 113–37.

Clark, Colin. 1940. *The Condition of Economic Progress*. London: Macmillan.

Clausewitz, Carl von. [1832] 1943. *Vom Kriege* [On war]. In *Living Thoughts of Clausewitz*, edited and translated by Joseph I. Greene. New York: Longmans & Greene.

Clements, Barbara E. 1979. *Bolshevik Feminist: The Life of Aleksandra Kollontai*. Bloomington: Indiana University Press.

Cohen, Leonard. 1997. "Embattled Democracy: Postcommunist Croatia in Transition." In *Politics, Power, and the Struggle for Democracy in South-East Europe*, edited by Karen Dawisha and Bruce Parrott, 69–121. New York: Cambridge University Press.

Cohen, Stephen. 1975. *Bukharin and the Bolshevik Revolution*. New York: Random House.

Cohn, Norman. 1961. The Pursuit of the Millennium. 2d ed. New York: Harper & Row.

Cold War History Project. 1998. Vol. 10. Bulletins edited by David Wolff. Washington, D.C.: Woodrow Wilson Center.

Cole, G. D. H., and Raymond Postgate. 1957. *The British People, 1746–1946*. New York: Knopf.

Colson, Félix F. 1841. *De l'état présent de la Moldavie et de la Valachie* [The present condition of Moldavia and Wallachia]. Vols. 1–2. Paris: Paulin.

Comander, Simon. 1993. "Unemployment in Eastern Europe." *Transition* (World Bank) 4, no. 9 (December), 1–4.

Comisso, Ellen, and Paul Marer. 1986. "The Economic and Political Reform." In *Power, Purpose, and Collective Choice: Economic Strategy in Socialist States,* by Ellen Comisso and Laura D'Andrea Tyson, 245–78. Ithaca, N.Y.: Cornell University Press.

Comisso, Ellen, and Laura D'Andrea Tyson, eds. 1986. *Power, Purpose, and Collective Choice: Economic Strategy in Socialist States.* Ithaca, N.Y.: Cornell University Press.

Connely, John. 1996. "Foundations for Reconstructing Elites: Communist Educational Policies in the Czech Lands, East Germany and Poland, 1945–1948." *East European Society and Politics* 10, no. 3 (fall): 367–92.

Connor, Walter. 1984. *The National Question in Marxist-Leninist Theory and Strategy.* Princeton, N.J.: Princeton University Press.

———. 1988. *Socialism's Dilemmas: State and Society in the Soviet Bloc.* New York: Columbia University Press.

Constantinescu, Miron. 1976. *Istoria României. Manual pentru clasa XII-a* [Twelfth grade textbook of history]. Bucharest: Editura Didactică.

Corradini, Enrico. [1911] 1923a. "Le nazioni proletarie e il nazionalismo" [Nationalism and the proletarian nations]. In *Discorsi politici.* Florence: Vallechi.

———. 1923b. *Discorsi politici* [Discourses]. Florence: Vallechi.

"Corruption: An International Comparison." 1996. *Transition* (World Bank) 7, nos. 7–8 (July–August): 16–17.

"Costs and Benefits of Eastern Enlargement: the Impact on EU and Central Europe." 1997. *Economic Policy,* no. 24 (April).

Crampton, Richard J. 1983. *Bulgaria, 1878–1918.* Boulder, Colo. and New York: Eastern European Monographs of Columbia University Press.

———. 1987. *A Short History of Bulgaria.* New York: Cambridge University Press.

Crawford, Keith. 1996. *East Central European Politics Today.* Manchester, Eng.: Manchester University Press.

Creanga, George D. 1907. *Grundbesitzverteilung und Bauernfrage in Rumänien* [Land distribution and the peasant problem in Romania]. Leipzig: Duncker & Humblot.

Csanádi, Mária. 1980. *A differenciált erőforrás elosztás és a támogatások ujratermelődésének néhány összefüggése* [The differentiation of political resources and the reproduction of subsidies]. Budapest: PKI, Monograph no. 6.

———. 1984. *Függőség, konszenzus és szelekció: a politika es a gazdaság viszonya a gazdaság irányitásában* [Dependency, consensus, and choice-making: Interaction between politics and economics in the management of the economy]. Budapest: PKK, Monograph no. 3.

Csaplovits, Johann von. 1828. *Eine Gemälde von Ungarn* [A portrait of Hungary]. Vols. 1–2. Pest.

Ćubrilović, Vasa C. 1958. *Istoria političke misli u Srbiji XIX veka* [History of political thought in Serbia in the nineteenth century]. Belgrade: Prosveta.

Czechoslovakia, L'Office statistique de la republique tchecoslovaque. 1938. *Manuel statistique de la Republique Tchecoslovaque.*

Czempiel, Ernst-Otto. 1963. "Der Primat der auswärtigen Politik: kritische Würdigung einer Staatsmaxime." *Politische Vierteljahresschrift* 4 (September): 266–87.

Dallin, David J., and Boris N. Nikolaevsky. 1947. *Forced Labor in Soviet Russia.* New Haven, Conn.: Yale University Press.

Daniels, Robert V. 1960. *A Documentary History of Communism.* 2 vols. New York: Random House.

Danyl, R., and Z. David, eds. 1960. *Az első magyar népszámlálás, 1784–87* [The first Hungarian census]. Budapest: Allami Nyomda.

David, Henry P., and Robert F. McIntyre. 1981. *Reproductive Behavior: Central and East European Experience.* New York: Springer.

Dawisha, Karen. 1990. *Eastern Europe, Gorbachev and Reform: The Great Challenge.* 2d ed. New York: Cambridge University Press.

Dawisha, Karen, and Bruce Parrott, eds. 1997a. *The Consolidation of Democracy in East-Central Europe.* New York: Cambridge University Press.

———, eds. 1997b. *Politics, Power, and the Struggle for Democracy in South-East Europe.* New York: Cambridge University Press.

Deák, István. 1966. "Hungary." In *The European Right,* edited by Rogger and Weber, 364–407. Berkeley and Los Angeles: University of California Press.

———. 1979. *The Lawful Revolution: Louis Kossuth and the Hungarians, 1848–1849.* New York: Columbia University Press.

Dedijer, Vladimir, Ivan Božić, and Sima Ćirković. 1974. *History of Yugoslavia.* New York: McGraw-Hill.

Delbrück, Hans. 1962. *Geschichte der Kriegskunst im Rahmen der politischen Geschichte* [History of the art of war in the context of political history]. 3d ed. Berlin: deGruyter.

Dellin, L. A. D., ed. 1957. *Bulgaria.* New York: Praeger.

Demény, Lajos. 1993. "Pártosodás és pártok Romániában" [Party formation and parties in Romania]. In *A többpártrendszerek kialakulása Kelet-Középeurópában* [The Rise of multiparty systems in East Central Europe], edited by Mihály Bihari, 277–333. Budapest: Kossuth.

Desai, Padma. 1987. *The Soviet Economy: Problems and Prospects.* Oxford: Blackwell.

deSchweinitz, Karl. 1963. *Industrialization and Democracy.* Glencoe, Ill.: Free Press.

Dessewffy, Jozsef. 1831. *A "Hitel" cimü munka taglalatja* [A critical analysis of the essay "Credit"]. Kassa: Werfer.

Deutsch, Karl W. 1961. "Social Mobilization and Political Development." *American Political Science Review* 55, no. 3 (September): 493–502.

Deutscher, Isaac. 1953. *Russia, What Next?* New York: Oxford University Press.

———. 1960. *Stalin.* New York: Vintage Books.

———. 1984a. "Marxism and Primitive Magic." In *The Stalinist Legacy: Its Impact on Twentieth-Century World Politics,* edited by Tariq Ali, 106–18. New York: Penguin Books

———. 1984b. "Socialism in One Country." In *The Stalinist Legacy: Its Impact on Twentieth-Century World Politics,* edited by Tariq Ali, 95–104. New York: Penguin Books.

Deyo, Frederic C., ed. 1987. *The Political Economy of New Asian Industrialism.* Ithaca, N.Y.: Cornell University Press.

Diamant, Alfred. 1960. *Austrian Catholicism and the First Republic.* Princeton: Princeton University Press.

Diederich, Clemens, ed. 1942. *Die Kroaten.* Zagreb and Munich: Velebit.

Di Palma, Giuseppe. 1991. "Eastern Europe after Leninism: Democracy Can Work." *Current,* no. 333 (June): 34–39.

Ditz, Heinrich. 1866. *Die Landwirtschaft Ungarns* [Hungary's agricultural economy]. Leipzig: Kohler.

Djilas, Milovan. 1957. *The New Class.* New York: Harcourt, Brace & World.

———. 1962. *Conversations with Stalin.* New York: Harcourt, Brace & World.

Djodan, Šime. 1991. *Hrvatsko Pitanje, 1918–1988* [The Croatian question, 1918–1988]. Zagreb: Alfa.

Djordjević, Dimitrije. 1971. "Fascism in Yugoslavia, 1918–41." In *Native Fascism in the Successor States, 1918–1945,* edited by Peter F. Sugar, 125–34. Santa Barbara, Calif.: ABC-Clio.

Dobozi, István. 1995. "Electrical Consumption and Output Decline, 1989–94." *Transition* (World Bank) 6, nos. 9–10 (September–October): 19–20.

Dobrogeanu-Gherea, Constantin. 1910. *Neo-iobagia* [Neo-serfdom]. Bucharest: Minerva.

Dollar, David, and Craig Burns. 1997. "Good Parties Are Needed." www. worldbank.mayjune97.art3.

Don, Yehuda. 1990. "Patterns of Jewish Economic Behavior in Central Europe in the Twentieth Century." In *The Social and Economic History of Central European Jewry,* by Yehuda Don and Victor Karady, 121–54. New Brunswick, N.J.: Transaction.

Don, Yehuda, and Victor Karady, eds. 1990. *The Social and Economic History of Central European Jewry.* New Brunswick, N.J.: Transaction.

Donovan, Barbara. 1987. "Benefits to the GDR from Intra-German Economic Relations." *Radio Free Europe Research.* GDR, November 10.

———. 1988. "Emigration and Dissent in the GDR." *Radio Free Europe Research,* GDR, February 18.

Dr. Jozef Tiso, Dr. Ferdinand Durčanský a Alexander Mach pred sudom naroda [Tiso, Durcánsky, and Mach before the people's court]. 1946. Bratislava: Dovenitstvo pre informacije.

Dragaşanu, Codru. 1942. *Peregrinul Transilvan* [Transylvanian Pilgrim]. Bucharest: Ciocolescu.

Dragnich, Alex N. 1974. *Serbia, Nikola Pašić and Yugoslavia.* New Brunswick, N.J.: Rutgers University Press.

———. 1978. *The Development of Parliamentary Government in Serbia.* Boulder, Colo.: East European Monograph Series.

———. 1983. *The First Yugoslavia: Search for a Viable Political System.* Stanford: Hoover Institution Press.

d'Souza, Dinesh. 1997. "How Reagan Won the Cold War." *National Review,* November 24, 36–40, 52–54.

Dubey, Vinod. 1975. *Yugoslavia: Development with Decentralization.* Baltimore: Johns Hopkins University Press.

Duesenberry, James S. 1967. *Income, Saving and the Theory of Consumer Behavior.* 5th ed. Cambridge, Mass.: Harvard University Press.

Dumitriu, Petru. 1962. *Meeting at the Last Judgment.* Translated by Richard Howard. New York: Pantheon Books.

Dunham, Vera. 1990. *In Stalin's Time: Middle-Class Values in Soviet Fiction.* 2d enlarged ed. Durham, N.C.: Duke University Press.

Dunlop, John. 1992. *The Rise of Russia and the Fall of the Soviet Union.* Princeton, N.J.: Princeton University Press.

Dvornik, Francis. 1962. *The Slavs in European History and Civilization.* New Brunswick, N.J.: Rutgers University Press.

Dziewanowski, M. K. 1959. *The Communist Party of Poland: An Outline of History.* Cambridge, Mass.: Harvard University Press.

Eckart, Dietrich. 1925. *Der Bolschevismus von Moses bis Lenin: Zwiegespräch zwischen Adolf Hitler und mir* [Bolshevism from Moses to Lenin: My conversations with Adolf Hitler]. Munich: Hocheneichen Verlag.

Economist Intelligence Unit. 1985. *Regional Review: Eastern Europe and the USSR, 1985.* London: EIU.

Ehrenburg, Ilya. 1967. *The War, 1941–1945.* Translated by Tatyana Shebunina. Cleveland: World.

Ehrlich, Éva. 1968. "Nemzeti jövedelmek dinamikus összehasonlitása" [The dynamic comparison of GNPs with physical indicators]. *Közgazdasági Szemle* 20, no. 2: 191–212.

———. 1978. "A nemzeti jövedelmek dinamikus összehasonlitása" [Dynamic comparisons of national incomes]. *Közgazdasági Szemle* 20, no. 2: 191–212.

Eichengreen, Barry, and Richard Kohl. 1997. "The State and the External Sector in East Europe: Implications for Foreign Investment and Outward Processing Trade." Paper Presented at the Conference of the Convenor Group of the Centers for German and European Studies and of the Slavic East European Studies, the University of California, Berkeley (December 8).

Eisenstadt, Saul N. 1967. *The Protestant Ethic and Modernization.* New York: Basic Books.

Ekiert, Grzegorz. 1996. *The State Against Society: Political Crises and Their Aftermath in East Central Europe.* Princeton, N.J.: Princeton University Press.

———. 1997. Rebellious Poles: Political Crises and Popular Protest under State Socialism." *East European Politics and Societies* 11, no. 2 (spring): 299–338.

Ekonomski Institut N.R. Serbije. 1953. *Proizvodne snage N.R. Srbije* [Forces of production in the Serbian People's Republic]. Belgrade: Ekonomski Institut Srbije.

Elazar, Daniel J. 1984. "The Sunset of Bulgarian Jewry." In *The Balkan Jewish Communities: Yugoslavia, Bulgaria, Greece, and Turkey,* 1–11. Lanham, Md.: University Press of America.

Elek, Sár. 1981. *Gazdaságpolitika és paraszti jövedelmek* [Economic policy and peasant incomes]. Vol. 3 of the series *Társadalmi strukturák fejlődése* (Budapest: MSzMP-TTI [Hungarian Socialist Workers' Party, Social Sciences Institute]).

Enciclopedia Cugetarea [Encyclopedia of Thought]. 1939–40. Bucharest: Delafras.

Eötvös, József. 1846. *Die Reform in Ungarn* [Reform in Hungary]. Leipzig: Koehler.

Erdei, Ferenc. 1937. *Futóhomok* [Quicksand]. Budapest: Athenaeum.

———. 1938. *A magyar falu* [The Hungarian Village]. Budapest: Athenaeum.

Erős, Ferenc, András Kovács, and Katalin Lévai. 1985. "Hogyan jöttem rá, hogy zsidó vagyok?" [How I discovered that I was Jewish?]. *Medvetánc* 5, no. 2–3: 131–38.

Erős, János. 1981. "Hungary." In *Fascism in Europe,* edited by S. J. Woolf. London: Methuen.

European Bank for Reconstruction and Development. 1996. *Development Report.* Brussels.

———. *Transition Report, 1997.* 1997. *Transition* (World Bank) 81, no. 6 (December).

Eyal, Jonathan. 1996. "Romania." In *The New Institutional Architecture of Eastern Europe,* edited by Stephen Whitfield, 136–37. London: St. Martin.

Eyal, Jonathan, and Ian Anthony. 1988. *Warsaw Pact Military Expenditure.* Coulsden, Surrey: Jane's Information Group.

Fainsod, Merle. 1963. *Smolensk under Soviet Rule.* New York: Vintage Books.

———. 1965. *How Russia Is Ruled.* 4th ed. Cambridge, Mass.: Harvard University Press.

Fann, K. T., and Donald C. Hodges, eds. 1971. *Readings in U.S. Imperialism.* Boston: Porter Sargent.

Feher, Ferenc, Agnes Heller, and Gyorgy Markus. 1983. *Dictatorship over Needs.* Oxford: Blackwell.

Fényes, Elek. 1842–43. *Magyarország statistikája* [Statistics of Hungary]. Pest: Trattner.

Fenyo, Mario. 1972. *Hitler, Horthy and Hungary.* New Haven, Conn.: Yale University Press.

Fichte, Johann-Gottlieb. [1818] 1962. "Der geschlossene Handelsstaat" [The closed trading state]. In *Ausgewählte Werke* [Selected works], 3: 417–544. Darmstadt: Wissenschaftliche Buchgesellschaft.

Field, Mark G., ed. 1974. *Social Consequences of Modernization in Communist Societies.* Baltimore: Johns Hopkins University Press.

Filitti, Ioan C. 1929. *Domnile române sub regulamentul organic, 1834–48* [The Romanian principalities under the organic statutes, 1834–48]. Bucharest: Socec.

Fischer, Louis. 1930. *The Soviets in World Affairs.* New York and London: J. Cape and Smith.

Fischer, Mary Ellen. 1982. *Nicolae Ceauşescu and Romanian Political Leadership: Nationalism and the Personalization of Power.* Skidmore, Pa.: Skidmore College.

Fish, M. Steven. 1990. "Reform and Demilitarization in Soviet Society from Brzezhnev to Khrushchev." *Peace and Change* 15, no. 2 (April): 150–72.

———. 1998. "Democratization's Requisites: The Post-Communist Experience." *Post-Soviet Affairs* 14 (July–September): 21–48.

Fisher, Sharon. 1997. "Slovakia Heads Toward International Isolation." *Transitions* (OMRI) 3, no. 2 (February 17): 12.

Flaw, B. V. 1984. "The GDR Marks 35 Years by Sweeping Claim to German History." *Radio Free Europe Research.* GDR, 11 October.

Florea, D., and M. Ionescu. 1971. *Istoria României. Manual pentru clasa VIII-a* [Eighth grade textbook of history]. Bucharest: Editura Didactică.

Fodor, Ferenc. 1922. "A magyar képviselőválasztások térképe, 1861–1915" [Maps of elections to the Hungarian House of Representatives, 1861–1915]. In Hungarian Ministry of Foreign Affairs, *Hungarian Peace Negotiations* (Budapest), 3B, Annex vii.

Fourier, Charles M. [1829] 1892. *Le nouveau monde industriel* [The new industrial world]. Lyon.

Frank, André Gunder. 1972. "The Development of Underdevelopment" and "Economic Dependence, Class Structure, and Underdevelopment Policy." In *Dependence and Underdevelopment in Latin America*, edited by James D. Cockcroft, André Gunder Frank, and Dale J. Johnson, 231–45. Garden City, N.J.: Doubleday, Anchor Books.

Freedom House. 1997. *Freedom in the World, 1996–1997*. Philadelphia.

Fricke, Karl Wilhelm. 1984. *Die DDR-Staatsicherheit* [GDR state security]. Cologne: Wissenschaft und Politik.

Frydman, Roman, Andrzej Rapaczynski, and Jan S. Earle. 1993. *The Privatization Process in Central Europe*. New York and Budapest: Central European Press.

Fukuyama, Francis. 1990. "Are We at the End of History?" *Fortune* (January 15): 75–77.

———. 1992. *The End of History and the Last Man*. New York: Maxwell MacMillan.

Furtado, Celso. 1963. *The Economic Growth of Brazil*. Berkeley and Los Angeles: University of California Press.

Gábor, István R., and Péter Galasi. 1981. *A második gazdaság: tények és hipotézisek* [The second economy: facts and hypotheses]. Budapest: Jogi és Közgazasági Kiadó.

Gaddis, John. 1996. "Spheres of Influence: The United States and Europe, 1945–49." In *The Cold War in Europe: Era of a Divided Continent*, edited by Charles S. Maier, 211–35. Princeton: Markus Wiener.

Gaddy, Clifford. 1996. *The Price of the Past: Russia's Struggle with the Legacy of a Militarized Economy*. Washington, D.C.: Brookings Institution.

Gamarnikow, Michael. 1966. "The Reforms: A Survey." *East Europe* 15, no. 1 (January): 13–23.

———. 1972. "A New Economic Approach?" *Problems of Communism* 21, no. 5 (Sept.–Oct. 1972): 20–30.

Gannon, Robert I. 1962. *The Cardinal Spellman Story*. Garden City, N.J.: Doubleday.

Garland, John. 1986. "FDR-GDR Economic Relations." In U.S. Congress, Joint Economic Committee, *East European Economies: Slow Growth in the 1980s*, 169–76. Washington, D.C.: Government Printing Office.

Garlicki, Andrzej. 1993. *Stalinizm*. Warsaw: Wydawnyctwa Szkolne in Pedagogiczne.

Garver, Bruce M. 1978. *The Young Czech Party, 1874–1901*. New Haven, Conn.: Yale University Press.

Gati, Charles, ed. 1976. *The International Politics of Eastern Europe*. New York: Praeger.

———. 1986. *Hungary and the Soviet Bloc*. Durham, N.C.: Duke University Press.

———. 1990. *The Bloc That Failed*. Bloomington: Indiana University Press.

———. 1996. "If Not Democracy, What?" In *Post-Communism: Four Perspectives*, edited by Michael Mandelbaum, 168–98. New York: Council of Foreign Relations.

Gati, Charles, and Jan F. Triska, eds. 1981. *Blue Collar Workers in Eastern Europe*. Boston: Allen & Unwin.

Gelb, Alan. 1996. "From Plan to Market: A 28 Country Adventure." *Transition* 7, nos. 5–6 (May–June): 1–3.

Georgiev, Ivo. 1996. "Indecisive Socialist Party Stumbles into Crisis." *Transition* (OMRI) 2, no. 26 (December 27): 27.

Germany. 1929. *Statistik des Deutschen Reiches*, No. 402, Berufaufzählung [Occupational statistics]. Berlin: Reimer Habbag.

Germany, Statistisches Reichsamt. 1900, 1931, 1944, 1994. *Statistik des Deutschen Reiches* [Statistics of the German Empire].

———. 1902–14. *Vierteljahrhefte zur Statistik des deutschen Reiches* [Statistical quarterly of the German Reich].

Gerschenkron, Alexander. [1959] 1962. *Economic Backwardness in Historical Perspective*. Cambridge, Mass.: Harvard University Press.

Gibianski, Leonid. 1997. "Soviet-Yugoslav Split and the Cominform." In *The Establishment of Communist Regimes in Eastern Europe*, by Norman Naimark and Leonid Gibianski, 291–312. Boulder, Colo.: Westview Press.

Gibney, Frank. 1959. *Poland's Frozen Revolution*. New York: Farrar & Straus.

Gilberg, Trond. 1990. *Nationalism and Communism in Romania*. Boulder, Colo.: Westview Press.

Gitelman, Zvi. 1981. "The World Economy and Elite Political Strategies in Czechoslovakia, Hungary and Poland." In *East-West Relations and the Future of Eastern Europe*, by Morris Bornstein, Zvi Gitelman and William Zimmerman, 127–61. London: George Allen & Unwin.

Giurescu, Constantin, Jr. 1940. *Istoria românilor* [History of the Romanians], vols. 1–5. Bucharest: Minerva.

Giurescu, Constantin, Sr. [1918] 1943. *Despre boieri: studii de istoria socială* [About the boyars: studies in social history]. 2d ed. Bucharest: Universul.

Giurescu, Dinu. 1981. *Illustrated History of the Romanian People*. Bucharest: Editura Sport-Tourismul

Glade, William P. 1969. *The Latin American Economies: A Study of Their Institutional Evolution*. New York: American Books.

Goati, Vladimir. 1991. *Jugoslavia na prekretnici od monizma do gradjanskog rata* [Yugoslavia at the crossroads between personal dictatorship and civil war]. Belgrade: Institut za Novinarstvo.

Goebbels, Joseph. 1948. *Diaries*. London: Macmillan.

Golan, Galia. 1973. *Reform Rule in Czechoslovakia: The Dubček Era, 1968–1969*. Cambridge: Cambridge University Press.

Goldhagen, Erich. 1963. "The Glorious Future: Realities and Chimeras." In *Russia under Khrushchev*, edited by Abraham Brumberg, 616–33. New York: Praeger.

Golescu, Constantin. 1915. *Însemnare a călătoriei mele in anii 1824, 1825, si 1826* [Notes on my travels in the years 1824, 1825, and 1826]. Bucharest.

Gombár, Csaba. 1995. *Balance: The Hungarian Government, 1990–94*. Budapest: Korridor.

———, ed. 1996. A szuverénitás káprázatja [The mirage of sovereignty]. Budapest: Korridor PK Központ.

Gorbachev, Mikhail. 1987. *Perestroika: New Thinking for Our Country and for the World*. New York: Harper & Row.

Gordon, Lincoln, Brown, J. F., et al. 1987. *Eroding Empire: Western Relations with Eastern Europe*. Washington, D.C.: Brookings Institution.

Gratz, Gusztav. 1934. *A dualizmus kora* [The age of dualism], vols. 1–2. Budapest: Magyar Szemle Társasag.

Great Britain. 1934. *Census of England and Wales, 1931.* Occupation Tables. London: H. M. Stationery Office.

Grébert, Arvéd. 1975. "Dr. Joseph Tiso in the Light of Nazi Documents." *Slovakia* 25, no. 48.

Gregor, James A. 1969. *The Ideology of Fascism: The Rationale for Totalitarianism.* New York: Free Press.

———. 1979. *Italian Fascism and Developmental Dictatorship.* Princeton, N.J.: Princeton University Press.

Griffith, William. 1963. *Albania and the Sino-Soviet Rift.* Cambridge, Mass.: Harvard University Press.

———, ed. 1989. *Central and Eastern Europe: The Opening Curtain?* Boulder, Colo.: Westview Press.

Gross, Jan. 1997. "War as Revolution." In *The Establishment of Communist Regimes in Eastern Europe, 1944–1949,* edited by Norman Naimark and Leonid Gibianski, 17–40. Boulder, Colo.: Westview Press.

Grossman, Gregory. 1962. "The Structure and Organization of the Soviet Economy." *Slavic Review* 21, no. 2 (June): 203–22.

G. S. 1984a. "Draft of the New Family Code." *Radio Free Europe Research.* Bulgaria, 18 March, 1–10.

———. 1984b. "Socialist Funeral Rights Discussed Again." *Radio Free Europe Research.* Bulgaria, 23 November, 4.

———. 1985. "Officials Say There Are No Turks in Bulgaria." *Radio Free Europe Research.* Bulgaria, 28 March, 4.

Gunst, Peter. 1989. "Agrarian Systems of Central and Eastern Europe." In *The Origins of Backwardness in Eastern Europe,* edited by Daniel Chirot, 51–85. Berkeley and Los Angeles: University of California Press.

Gurr, Ted. 1970. *Why Men Rebel.* Princeton, N.J.: Princeton University Press.

Gusti, Dimitrie. 1968–77. *Opere* [Works]. Edited by Ovidiu Bădina and Octavian Neamţu. 1: 486–91. Bucharest: Editura Academiei.

Habakkuk, H. J., and M. Postan, eds. 1965. *The Industrial Revolution and After.* Vol. 6, The Cambridge Economic History of Europe. Cambridge: Cambridge University Press.

Haberl, Othmar. 1976. *Parteiorganisation und nationale Frage in Jugoslawien* [Party organization and the national question in Yugoslavia]. Berlin: Harrassowitz.

Haeffler, István, ed. 1935, 1940. *Országgyűlési Almanach* [Parliamentary almanac]. Budapest: Magyar Távirati Iroda.

Hagen, Mark von. 1996. "Rise and Fall of the Proletarian Sparta: Army, Society, and Reformism in Soviet History." In *Reexamining the Soviet Experience: Essays in Honor of Alexander Dallin,* edited by David Holloway and Norman Naimark, 51–76. Boulder, Colo.: Westview Press.

Haggard, Stephan. 1990. *Pathways from the Periphery.* Ithaca, N.Y.: Cornell University Press.

Halecki, Oscar, ed. 1957. *Poland.* New York: Praeger.

Halpern, Joel M. 1967. *Serbian Village.* 2d ed. New York: Harper.

Hamm, Harry. 1963. *Albania–China's Beachhead in Europe.* New York: Praeger.

Haraszti, Éva, ed. 1993. *Horthy, Miklós a dokumentumok tükrében* [Horthy as mirrored by documents]. Budapest: Balassi.

Harding, Neil. 1977. *Lenin's Political Thought,* vol. 1. London: Macmillan.

Hare, P. G., H. K. Radice, and N. Swain. 1981. *Hungary: A Decade of Economic Reform*. London: George Allen & Unwin.

Harmon, Chris. 1974. *Bureaucracy and Revolution in Eastern Europe*. London: Pombo Press.

Havlik, Peter. 1991. *East-West GDP Comparisons: Problems, Methods, Results*. Research Report no. 174. Vienna: WIIW.

———. *Comparison of Real Products Between East and West, 1970–1983*. Research Report no. 115. Vienna: WIIW.

Havránek, Jan. 1971. "Fascism in Czechoslovakia." In *Native Fascism in the Successor States, 1918–1945*, edited by Peter F. Sugar, 47–56. Santa Barbara, Calif.: ABC-Clio.

Hecker, Gerhard. 1983. *Walther Rathenau und sein Verhältnis zu Militär und Krieg* [Rathenau and his relationship to the military and to the war]. Boppard am Rhein: H. Boldt Verlag.

Hell, Andreas, and Hans Prien. 1968. *Wo lebt man besser? Lebensstandard in der DDR* [Where does one live better? The standard of living in the GDR]. Berlin: Staatsekretariat für Westdeutsche Fragen.

Helmreich, Ernest, ed. 1957. *Hungary*. New York: Praeger.

Herceg, Rudolf. 1923. *Die Ideologie der kroatischen Bauernbewegung* [Ideology of the Croat peasant movement]. Zagreb: Verlag Rud.

Hermann, A. H. 1975. *History of the Czechs*. London: Allen Lane.

Herr, Richard. 1958. *The Eighteenth Century Revolution in Spain*. Princeton, N.J.: Princeton University Press.

Hertz, Frederick. 1970. *The Economic Problem of the Danubian States*. New York: Fertig.

Hilberg, Raul. 1961. *The Destruction of the European Jews*. Chicago: Quadrangle Press.

Hingley, Ronald. 1974. *Stalin: The Man and His Era*. London: Hutchinson.

Hintze, Otto. 1975. *Historical Essays*. Edited and translated by Felix Gilbert. New York: Oxford University Press.

Hirschler, Richard. 1996. "Post-Socialist Media." *Transition* 7, nos. 5–6 (May–June): 4–5.

Hirschman, Albert O. 1945. *National Power and the Structure of Foreign Trade*. Berkeley: University of California Press.

———. 1962. *The Strategy of Economic Development*. New Haven: Yale University Press.

———. 1970. "Paradigms as a Hindrance to Understanding." *World Politics* 22, no. 3 (April): 329–43.

———. 1981. *Essays in Trespassing: Economics to Politics and Beyond*. New York: Cambridge University Press.

Hitchins, Keith. 1994. *Rumania, 1866–1947*. Oxford: Clarendon Press.

Hitler, Adolf. [1926] 1971. *Mein Kampf* [My struggle]. Translated by Ralph Manheim. Boston: Houghton Mifflin.

———. 1953. *Table Talk, 1941–1944*. London: Weidenfeld & Nicolson. Originally published as *Hitlers Tischgespräche im Führerhauptquartier, 1941–42*, ed. Henry Picker (Bonn: Athenäum, 1951).

Hobsbawm, Eric. 1963. *Primitive Rebels: Studies in Archaic Forms of Social Movements*. New York: Praeger.

Hoensch, Jörg. 1973. "The Slovak Republic." In *A History of the Czechoslovak Republic, 1918–1948*, edited by Victor S. Mamatey and Radomir Luža, 271–96. Princeton, N.J.: Princeton University Press.

Hoettding, Oleg. 1959. "The Soviet Union: Model for Asia: State Planning and Industrialization." *Problems of Communism* 8, no. 6 (November–December): 38–46.

Hoffman, George W., and Fred W. Neal. 1962. *Yugoslavia and the New Communism*. New York: Twentieth Century Fund.

Holloway, David. 1994. *Stalin and the Bomb: The Soviet Union and Atomic Energy*. New Haven: Yale University Press.

Holloway, David, and Norman Naimark. 1996. *Rexamining the Soviet Experience: Essays in Honor of Alexander Dallin*. Boulder, Colo.: Westview Press.

Hóman, Bálint, and Gyula Szekfű. 1936. *Magyar Történet* [Hungarian history]. Vol. 5. Budapest: Egyetemi Nyomda.

Höpken, Wolfgang. 1989. "Beamte und Verwaltung in Südosteuropa: Zu den institutionellen Voraussetzungen von Modernisierung in Bulgarien, 1879–1912" [Public officials and administration in southeastern Europe: Observations on the institutional foundations of modernization in Bulgaria, 1879–1912]. Paper presented at Conference on the Modernization of South Eastern Europe, Bad Homburg (July 5–8).

Horthy, Miklós. 1957. *Memoirs*. New York: Speller and Sons.

Horvat, Branko. 1975. "The Labor-managed Enterprise." In *Self-Governing Socialism*, vol. 2, edited by Branko Horvat, Mihailo Marković, and Rudi Supek, 164–77. New York: International Arts and Sciences Press.

Horvat, Branko, Mihailo Marković, and Rudi Supek, eds. 1975. *Self-Governing Socialism*, vols. 1–2. New York: International Arts and Sciences Press.

Horváth, Zoltán. 1961. *Magyar századforduló* [Hungarian fin de siècle]. Budapest: Kossuth Kiadó.

Hory, Ladislaus, and Martin Broszat. 1964. "Der kroatische Ustascha Staat, 1941–1945" [The Croatian Ustasha state]. *Vierteljahrhefte für Zeitgeschichte* 8.

Hoselitz, Bert, and Wilbert Moore, eds. 1963. *Industrialization and Society*. The Hague: Mouton.

Hough, Jerry F. 1969. *Soviet Prefects*. Cambridge, Mass.: Harvard University Press.

———. 1972. "The Soviet System: Petrification or Pluralism?" *Problems of Communism* 21, no. 2 (March–April): 25–45.

Hoxha, Enver. 1979. *Imperialism and the Revolution*. Tirana: The 8 Nentori Publishing House.

———. 1980. *The Khrushchevites*. Tirana: Institute of Marxist-Leninist Studies.

———. 1982. *The Titoists*. Tirana: Institute of Marxist-Leninist Studies.

Huber, Mária. 1987. *A magyar modell* [The Hungarian model]. Budapest, TTI.

Huizinga, Johan. 1954. *The Waning of the Middle Ages*. New York: Doubleday.

Hulme, Beaman Ardern. 1895. *M. Stambuloff*. London: Bliss, Sands and Foster.

Hume, David. 1970. "Of Commerce." In *Writings in Economics*, edited by Eugene Rotwine. Madison: University of Wisconsin Press.

Hungary. 1867–1944. Országgyűlés [National Assembly]. Képviselőház [House of Representatives]. *Napló* [Proceedings]. Cited as *Napló*.

———. 1878, 1890, 1927, 1938. *Magyarország tiszti cím és névtara* [Directory of Official Hungary]. Budapest: Állami Kőnyvnyomda.

———. 1892–1944. *Annuaire statistique hongrois, nouveau cours.* Budapest: Hungarian Royal Statistical Office, 1892–1944.

———. 1919. *A tanácsok országos gyűlésének naplója* [Proceedings of the National Congress of Councils]. Budapest: Athenaeum.

———. 1922. Ministry of Foreign Affairs. *Hungarian Peace Negotiations.* Budapest: Horánszky.

———. 1926–44. Országgyűlés [National Assembly]. Felsőház [Upper House]. *Napló* [Proceedings]. Cited as *Felsőház Napló.*

———. 1955–59. Magyar Munkásmozgalmi Intézet [Institute for the study of the labor movement]. *A magyar munkásmozgalom történetének válogatott dokumentumai* [Selected documents of the history of the Hungarian workers' movement]. Budapest: Kossuth.

———. 1991. Magyar Köztársaság Miniszterelnökség [Office of the prime minister]. *Törvénytelen szocializmus: A tényfeltáró bizottság jelentése* [Lawless socialism: Report of the fact-finding commission]. Budapest: Zrinyi.

Huntington, Samuel P. 1968. *Political Order in Changing Societies.* New Haven, Conn.: Yale University Press.

———. 1970. "Social and Institutional Dynamics of One Party Systems." In *Authoritarian Politics in Modern Society,* edited by Samuel Huntington and Clement H. Moore, 3–47. New York: Basic Books.

———. 1971. "The Change to Change: Modernization, Development, and Politics." *Comparative Politics* 4, no. 4 (April): 283–322.

Huntington, Samuel P., and Clement H. Moore. 1970. *Authoritarian Politics in Modern Society: The Dynamics of Established One-Party Systems.* New York: Basic Books.

Hupchick, Dennis. 1985. "Bulgaria's Moslem Troubles in the Context of Balkan History." *Radio Free Europe Research.* Bulgaria, March 29, 1–6.

Hussey, J. M. 1961. *The Byzantine World.* New York: Harper.

Inkeles, Alex. 1974. "The Modernization of Man in Socialist and Non-Socialist Countries." In *Social Consequences of Modernization in Communist Societies,* edited by Mark G. Field, 50–60. Baltimore: Johns Hopkins University Press.

Inotai, András. 1994. *The System of Criteria for Accession to the EU.* Budapest: Monograph of the Institute of World Economics.

International Commission of Jurists. 1962. *The Berlin Wall: A Defiance of Human Rights.* Geneva.

International Institute of Strategic Studies. 1978. *The Military Balance, 1973–78.* London.

International Labor Office, ed. 1945. *Wages in Germany 1800 to the Present.* Studies and Reports, no. 15. London: ILO.

International Monetary Fund. 1997. *World Economic Outlook.* Washington, D.C.

"Interrogation of Horthy." 1946. *World War II Crime Record.* National Archives, Record Group 238.

Ionescu, Andrei. 1940. "Viaţa şi moarte vitejească a lui Ion I Moţa" [Life and heroic death of Ion I. Mota]. *Almanahul Cuvântul.* Bucharest: Imprimea Cuvântul.

Ionescu, Dan. 1985. "The Limits of Health Care" and "Two to a Hospital Bed." *Radio Free Europe Research.* Romania, October 1.

———. 1994. "Romania's Privatization Program: Who is in Charge?" *RFE/RL Research Report* 3, no. 5 (February 7): 28–34.

Ionescu, Ghita. 1964. *Communism in Rumania*. London: Oxford University Press.

Isaacson, Walter, and Evan Thomas. 1986. *The Wise Men: Six Friends and the World They Made*. New York: Simon & Schuster.

Jackiewicz, Irena, and Zbigniew Jackiewicz. 1996. "The Polish Parliament in Transition: in Search of a Model." In *The Second Steps,* edited by Attila Ágh and Gabriella Ilonszki, 121–30. Budapest: Hungarian Centre for Democracy Studies.

Jackson, George D. 1966. *The Comintern and the Peasant in East Europe*. New York: Columbia University Press.

Jackson, Marvin R. 1986. "Romania's Debt Crisis: Its Causes and Consequences." In U.S. Congress, Joint Economic Committee, *East European Economies: Slow Growth in the 1980s,* 489–542. Washington, D.C.: Government Printing Office.

Jackson, Marvin R. and John R. Lampe. 1982. *Balkan Economic History, 1550– 1950: From Imperial Borderlands to Developing Nations*. Bloomington: Indiana University Press.

Jacobs, Everett, ed. 1982. *Agrarian Politics in Communist Europe*. Totawa, N.J.: Allanheld & Osmun.

James, C. L. R. 1993. *World Revolution, 1917–1936: The Rise and Fall of the Communist International*. Atlantic Highlands, N.J.: Humanities Press.

Janković, Dragoslav, and Ruzica Guzina. 1962. *Istorija države i prava Jugoslovenskih naroda* [History of government and law of the Yugoslav nation]. Belgrade: Naucna Knjiga.

Janos, Andrew C. 1970a. "The Agrarian Opposition at the National Congress of Councils." In *Revolution in Perspective: Essays on the Hungarian Soviet Republic,* edited by id. and William B. Slottman, 85–108. Berkeley and Los Angeles: University of California Press.

———. 1970b. "The One Party State and Social Mobilization: East Europe between the Wars." In *Authoritarian Politics in Modern Society,* edited by Samuel P. Huntington and Clement H. Moore, 204–36. New York: Basic Books.

———. 1974. "Gentry in the Modern World: Rumanian Boyars and Hungarian Gentry in the Politics of the Rising National States." Association International d'Études du Sud-Est Européen, IIIᵉ Congres International, Bucharest. September 4–10.

———, ed. 1976. *Authoritarian Politics in Communist Europe*. Berkeley, Calif.: Institute of International Studies Research Series, no. 28.

———. 1977. "Modernization and Decay in Historical Perspective: The Case of Romania." In *Social Change in Romania, 1860–1940,* edited by Kenneth Jowitt, 72–116. Berkeley, Calif.: Institute of International Studies.

———. 1982. *The Politics of Backwardness in Hungary, 1825–1945*. Princeton, N.J.: Princeton University Press.

———. 1989. "The Politics of Backwardness in Continental Europe, 1780–1945." *World Politics* 41, no. 3 (April): 325–58.

———. 1991. "Social Science, Communism, and the Dynamics of Political Change." *World Politics* 44, no. 3 (October): 81–112.

———. 1996a. "What Was Communism? A Retrospective in Comparative Analysis." *Communist and Post-Communist Studies* 29, no. 1, 1–24.

———. 1996b. "Modernization or Militarization? Germany and Russia as Great Powers." *German Politics and Society* 14, no. 1 (spring): 42–43.

————. 1997. "Paradigms Revisited: Productionism, Globality, and Postmodernity in Comparative Politics." *World Politics* 50, no. 1 (October): 118–49.

Janson, Carl-Heinz. 1991. *Totengräber der DDR* [Grave diggers of the GDR]. Düsseldorf: Ecolo Verlag.

Jelavich, Charles, and Barbara Jelavich, eds. 1963. *The Balkans in Transition.* Berkeley and Los Angeles: University of California Press.

Jelinek, Yeshayahu A. 1976. *The Parish Republic: Hlinka's Slovak People's Party, 1939–1945.* New York: Columbia University Press.

————. 1990. "In Search of Identity: Slovakian Jewry and Nationalism (1918–38)." In *The Social and Economic History of Central European Jewry,* edited by Yehuda Don and Victor Karady. New Brunswick, N.J.: Transaction, 1990.

Johnson, Chalmers A. 1982. *MITI and the Japanese Miracle: The Growth of Industrial Policy, 1925–75.* Stanford: Stanford University Press.

————. 1987. "Political Institutions and Economic Performance: The Government-Business Relationship in Japan, South Korea and Taiwan." In *The Political Economy of New Asian Industrialism,* edited by Frederic C. Deyo. Ithaca, N.Y.: Cornell University Press.

Johnson, Owen. 1985. *Slovakia 1918–38: Education and the Making of a Nation.* Boulder, Colo.: East European Monographs of Columbia University Press.

Jonson, Ben. [1606] 1898. *Volpone: The Fox.* London: Leonard Smithers & Co.

Jörberg, Lennart. 1975. "Structural Change and Economic Growth in Nineteenth-Century Sweden." In *Sweden's Development from Poverty to Affluence,* ed. Steven Koblik, trans. Joanna Johnson, 92–135. Minneapolis: University of Minnesota Press.

Jordan, Michael J. 1998. "Albanians Split over Kosova." *RFE/RL Daily Newsline,* 16 April.

Jovanović, Slobodan. 1933. *Ustavobranitelji i njihova vlada, 1838–1858* [The "Defenders" of the Constitution and their rule, 1838–1858]. Belgrade: Getse Kona.

Jović, Dejan. 1996. "Party System Developments from a Parliamentary Perspective." In *The Second Steps,* edited by Attila Ágh and Gabriella Ilonszki, 395–413. Budapest: Hungarian Centre for Democracy Studies.

Jowitt, Kenneth, ed. 1977. *Social Change in Romania, 1860–1940.* Berkeley, Calif.: Institute of International Studies.

————. 1987. "Moscow 'Centre.'" *East European Politics and Society* 1, no. 3 (fall): 296–348.

————. 1992. "The Leninist Legacy." In *East Europe in Revolution,* edited by Ivo Banac, 207–25. Ithaca, N.Y.: Cornell University Press.

————. 1994. "Gorbachev: Bolshevik or Menshevik." In *The New World Disorder.* Berkeley and Los Angeles: University of California Press.

Juhász, József. 1993. "A többpártrendszer kialakulása Jugoszláviában" [The rise of a multi-party system in Yugoslavia]. In *A többpártrendszerek kialakulása Kelet-Középeurópában,* edited by Mihály Bihari, 446–66. Budapest: Kossuth.

Kádár, János. 1971. *For a Socialist Hungary.* Budapest: Corvina.

Kaplan, Karel. 1987. *The Communist Party in Power.* Translated by F. Eidlin. Boulder, Colo.: Westview Press.

————. 1991. *Československo v letech 1948–1953* [Czechoslovakia in the years 1948–53]. Prague: Státni pedagogičké nakladatelstvi.

Karady, Victor. 1984. "Jewish Enrollment Patterns in Classical Secondary Education in Old Regime and Interwar Hungary." *Studies in Contemporary Jewry* 1: 225–52.

Karić, V. 1887. *Srbija: Opis zemlje, naroda i države* [Serbia: description of the land, people, and state]. Belgrade: Kraljevsko Državna Stamparia.

Kárpáti, János. 1993. "Cseh és szlovák pártstruktura" [Czech and Slovak party structures]. In *A többpártrendszerek kialakulása Kelet-Középeuropában* [The rise of multiparty systems in East Central Europe], edited by Mihály Bihari, 334–55. Budapest: Kossuth.

Karsai, Elek. 1965. *A budai vártól a gyepüig, 1941–45* [From Buda castle to the western frontier]. Budapest: Táncsics.

———, ed. 1978. *Szálasi Ferenc naplója* [Diaries of Szálasi]. Budapest: Kossuth.

Karsai, Elek, and László Karsai, eds. 1988. *A Szálasi per* [Szálasi trial]. Budapest: Reform.

Kaser, Michael. 1986. "Albania under and after Enver Hoxha." In U.S. Congress, Joint Economic Committee, *East European Economies: Slow Growth in the 1980s*, 1–23. Washington, D.C.: Government Printing Office.

Kaser, Michael, and Adi Schnytzer. 1977. "Albania: A Uniquely Socialist Economy." In U.S. Congress, Joint Economic Committee, *East European Economies: Post Helsinki*, 523–66. Washington, D.C.: Government Printing Office.

Kašpar, Jan. 1971. "Členská základna komunistické strany Československa, 1945–1948" [Basic statutes of the Communist Party of Czechoslovakia]. *Československý Časopis historický* 19: 1–26.

Kautsky, John. 1962. *Political Change in Underdeveloped Countries.* New York: Wiley.

———. 1972. *The Political Consequences of Modernization.* New York: Wiley.

Keleti, Károly. 1889. *Hazánk és népe* [Our country and people]. Budapest: Ráth Mór.

Kelley, Donald R. 1980. "Developments in Ideology." In *Soviet Politics in the Brezhnev Era*, edited by Donald R. Kelley. New York: Praeger.

Kempelen, Béla. 1911–31. *Magyar nemesi családok* [Hungarian noble families]. Budapest: Grill.

Kende, Péter. 1989. *Röpirat a zsidókérdésről* [Essay on the Jewish question]. Budapest: Magvető.

Kenez, Peter. 1985. *The Birth of the Soviet Propaganda State: Soviet Methods of Mass Mobilization, 1917–1929.* Cambridge: Cambridge University Press.

———. 1992. *Cinema and Soviet Society, 1917–1953.* Cambridge: Cambridge University Press.

Kerensky, Alexander. 1927. *The Catastrophe.* New York: Appleton.

Kernig, C. D. 1969. *Sowjetsystem und demokratische Gesellschaft*, Vols. 1–2. Freiburg: Harder.

Kessler, Joseph. 1967. "Turanism and Pan-Turanism in Hungary, 1890–1945." Ph.D. diss., University of California, Berkeley.

Khrushchev, Nikita S. 1970. *Khrushchev Remembers.* Edited and translated by Strobe Talbott. Boston: Little, Brown.

King, Robert R., ed. 1973a. *Minorities under Communism.* Cambridge, Mass.: Harvard University Press.

———. 1973b. "Nicolae Ceauşescu and the Politics of Leadership." *Radio Free Europe Research.* Rumania, 29 March.

———. 1980. *History of the Romanian Communist Party.* Stanford: Hoover Institute Press.

King, Robert R., and J. F. Brown, eds. 1977. *Eastern Europe's Uncertain Future: A Selection of Radio Free Europe Research Reports.* New York: Praeger.

Kintner, William, and Wolfgang Klaiber. 1971. *Eastern Europe and European Security.* New York: Dunellen.

Kirschbaum, Joseph. 1960. *Slovakia: Nation at the Crossroads of Europe.* New York: Speller.

Kissinger, Henry. 1994. *Diplomacy.* New York: Simon and Schuster.

Kitchen, Morton. 1976. *The Silent Dictatorship: the Politics of the German High Command under Hindenburg and Ludendorff, 1916–1918.* London: Helm.

Klein, George, and Milan J. Reban, eds. 1981. *The Politics of Ethnicity in Eastern Europe.* New York: Columbia University Press.

Klima, Arnost. 1979. "Agrarian Class Structure and Economic Development in Pre-Industrial Europe." *Past and Present,* no. 85 (October): 48–67.

Kochanowicz, Jacek. 1989. "The Polish Economy and the Development of Dependency." In *The Origins of Backwardness in Eastern Europe,* edited by Chirot, Daniel, 92–130. Berkeley and Los Angeles: University of California Press.

Köhler, Anne, and Volker Runge. 1984. "Die DDR Ausreisewelle im Frühjahr 1984" [The wave of emigration from the GDR in the spring of 1984]. *Deutschland Archiv* 17 (December): 1280–86.

Köhler, Heinz. 1965. *Economic Integration in the Soviet Bloc.* New York: Praeger.

Kolakowski, Leszek. 1991. "The Debate of the Clerks." In *From Stalinism to Pluralism: A Documentary History of Eastern Europe since 1945,* edited by Gale Stokes, 139–44. New York: Oxford University Press.

Kolankiewicz, George. 1981. "Poland 1980: The Working Class under Anomic Socialism." In *Blue Collar Workers in Eastern Europe,* edited by Jan F. Triska and Charles Gati, 136–56. Boston: Allen & Unwin.

Kollontai, Alexandra. 1970. *Autobiographie einer sexuell emanzipierten Kommunistin* [Autobiography of a sexually emancipated communist]. Munich: Rogner & Bernhard.

Kolosi, Tamás, and Antal Boehm. 1982. *Structure and Stratification in Hungary.* Budapest: Institute of Social Sciences.

Kolosi, Tamás, and Edmund Wnuk-Lipinski. 1983. *Equality and Inequality under Socialism.* Beverly Hills, Calif.: Sage Books.

Kolsti, John. 1981. "Albanianism: From the Humanists to Hoxha." In *The Politics of Ethnicity in Eastern Europe,* edited by George Klein and Milan J. Reban, 15–48. Boulder, Colo.: East European Monographs.

Kónya, Sándor. 1968. *Gömbös Gyula kisérlete a totális fasiszta diktatura megteremtéséére* [An attempt by Gömbös to create a totalitarian fascist dictatorship]. Budapest: Akadémia.

Koo, Hagen. 1987. "The Interplay of State, Social Class, and World System in East Asian Development: the Cases of South Korea and Taiwan." In *The Political Economy of the New Asian Industrialism,* edited by Frederic C. Deyo, 165–81. Ithaca, N.Y.: Cornell University Press.

Köpeczi, Béla. 1984. "A szocialista életmódkutatás elvi problémái" [Conceptual problems of researching the socialist way of life]. In *Hogyan élünk? A szocialista életmód ismérvei, feltételei és tendenciái,* edited by Szánthó Miklós, 13–32. Budapest: Közgazdasági és Jogi kiadó.

Kopstein, Jeffrey. 1997. *The Politics of Economic Decline in East Germany, 1945–1990.* Chapel Hill, N.C.: University of North Carolina Press.

Korbonski, Andrzej. 1975. "The Pattern and Method of Liberalization." In *Comparative Socialist Systems: Essays on Politics and Economics,* edited by Carmelo Mesa-Lago and Carl Beck, 192–214. Pittsburgh: Center for International Studies of the University of Pittsburgh.

Kornai, János. 1982. *Growth, Shortage and Efficiency: A Macro-Dynamic Model of the Socialist Economy.* Berkeley and Los Angeles: University of California Press.

———. 1992. *The Socialist System: The Political Economy of Socialism.* Princeton, N.J.: Princeton University Press.

Kosta, Jiři. 1975. "Die sozio-oekonomische Entwicklung der CSR: Wirtschaftliche und soziale Probleme" [Social and economic development of the CSR]. In *Die demokratisch-parlamentarische Struktur der ersten Tschechoslowakischen Republik,* edited by Karl Bosl, 7–34. Munich: Oldenbourg.

Kostrba-Skalicky, Oswald. 1975. "Bewaffnete Ohnmacht. Die tschechoslowakische Armee 1918–38" [Armed but unconscious: The Czechoslovak army; 1918–38]. In *Die Erste Tschechoslowakische Republik als multinationaler Parteistaat,* edited by Karl Bosl, 439–527. Munich: Oldenbourg Verlag.

Kosyanenko, M., ed. 1974. *Organizator stroiteltstva razvitogo sotsializma* [Organizational structure of developed socialism]. Moscow: Politizdat.

———. 1976. *Razvitoi sotsializm.* Moscow: Mysl.

Kovács, Alajos. 1923. *A zsidóság térfoglalása Magyarországon* [The ascendancy of Jewry in Hungary]. Budapest: Kellner.

Kovács, András. 1988. "Az asszimilációs dilemma" [Dilemmas of assimilation]. *Világosság* (Budapest) 29 (August–September 1988): 605–12.

Kovács, Mária, and Antal Örkény. 1991. *Káderek* [Cadres]. Budapest: ELTE.

Krešić, Andrija. 1975. "The Production-Relations Basis of Self-Management." In *Self-Governing Socialism,* vol. 1, edited by Branko Horvat, Mihailo Marković, and Rudi Supek, 445–53. New York: International Arts and Sciences Press.

Kubalkova, Vendulka, and Albert A. Cruikshank. 1989. *Thinking about Soviet New Thinking.* Berkeley, Calif.: Institute of International Studies.

Kuhn, Thomas S. 1962. *The Structure of Scientific Revolutions.* Chicago: University of Chicago Press.

Kühne, Roland. 1910. *Geschichte des Getreidehandels und Getreidepreisbildung in Ungarn* [History of grain trade and price formation in Hungary]. Ph.D. diss., Heidelberg.

Kulcsár, Kálmán. 1984. "Az életmódkutatás feladatai, távlatai és eredményei" [The tasks, perspectives and results of research about the way of life]. In *Hogyan élünk? A szocialista életmód ismérvei, feltételei és tendenciá* [How do we live? The criteria, conditions, and tendencies of the socialist way of life], edited by Szánthó Miklós, 234–46. Budapest: Közgazdasági és Jogi kiadó.

Kun, Andor, Laszló Lengyel, and Gyula Vidor, eds. 1920, 1922, 1927, 1931. *Magyar Országgyűlési Almanach* [Hungarian parliamentary almanac]. Budapest: Magyar Távirati Iroda.

Kun, Béla. 1919. *Mit akarnak a kommunisták?* [What do the Communists want?]. Budapest: Kommunisták Magyarországi Pártja.

Kurian, George T., ed. 1982. *World Press Encyclopedia.* New York: Facts on File.

Kusin, Vladimir. 1978. *From Dubcek to Charter 77.* New York: St. Martin's Press.

———. "Gorbachev and Eastern Europe." 1996. *Problems of Communism* 35, no. 1 (January–February): 39–53.

Lackó, Miklós. 1966. *Nyilasok és nemzeti szocialisták* [Arrow Cross men and national socialists]. Budapest: Kossuth.

Lacqueur, Walter, and George L. Mosse. 1966. *International Fascism.* New York: Harper & Row.

Laky, Désiré. 1932. *Statistiques des étudiants des universités en 1930* [Statistics of university students in 1930]. Budapest: Patria.

Lampe, John R. 1975. "Varieties of Unsuccessful Industrialization: The Balkan States Before 1914." *Journal of Economic History* 4, no. 1 (1975): 56–85.

———. 1996. *Yugoslavia as History: Twice There Was a Country.* New York: Cambridge University Press.

Lane, David. 1971. *Politics and Society in the USSR.* New York: Random House.

———. 1983. *The End of Social Inequality?* London: Allen & Unwin.

Laue, Theodore von. 1971. *Why Lenin, Why Stalin?* Philadelphia: Lippincott.

Lazarcik, Gregor. 1985. "Comparative Growth of Agricultural Output, Inputs and Productivity in Eastern Europe, 1962–82." In *East European Economies: Slow Growth in the 1980s,* edited by U.S. Congress, Joint Economic Committee, 1: 388–425.

League of Nations. 1943. *Agrarian Production in Continental Europe.* Geneva.

———. 1945. *Critique of Industrialization and Foreign Trade.* Geneva.

Lecca, Octav G. 1929. *Familii boereşti române* [Romanian boyar families]. Bucharest: Göbl.

———. 1937. *Dictionar istoric, arheologic si geografic al României* [Historical, archaeological, and geographic encyclopedia of Romania]. Bucharest: Universul.

Leff, Carol Skolnik. 1988. *National Conflict in Czechoslovakia: The Making and Re-making of a State.* Princeton, N.J.: Princeton University Press.

Leibenstein, Harvey. 1950. "Bandwagon, Snob and Veblen Effects in the Theory of Consumer Demand." *Quarterly Journal of Economics* 64, no. 2 (1950): 183–207.

Lendvai, Paul. 1969. *Eagles in Cobwebs: Nationalism and Communism in the Balkans.* Garden City, N.J.: Doubleday.

Lengyel, László. 1997. *Mozgástér és kényszerpálya* [Force field and room for maneuver]. Budapest: Helikon.

Lenin, Vladimir I. [1930] 1957. *Clausewitz's Werk 'vom Kriege': Auszüge und Randglossen* [Lenin's notes and excerpts from Clausewitz's work "On War"]. Berlin: Verlag Nationale Verteidigung.

———. [1898] 1964. *The Development of Capitalism in Russia.* 2nd English edition. Moscow: Progress Publishers.

———. [1902] 1970a. "The Heritage We Renounce." In *Selected Works,* vol. 1, 79–113. Moscow: Progress Publishers.

———. [1916] 1970b. *Imperialism, the Highest Stage of Capitalism.* In *Selected Works,* vol. 1, 667–763. Moscow: Progress Publishers.

————. [1917] 1970c. *The State and the Revolution: The Marxist Theory of the State and the Tasks of the Proletariat in the Revolution.* In *Selected Works,* 2: 276–376. Moscow: Progress Publishers.

————. [1905] 1970d. *Two Tactics of Social Democracy in the Democratic Revolution.* In *Selected Works,* vol. 1, 462–541. Moscow: Progress Publishers.

————. [1915] 1970e. "On the United States of Europe." In *Selected Works,* vol. 1, 662–66. Moscow: Progress Publishers.

Lerner, Daniel. 1958. *The Passing of Traditional Society.* Glencoe, Ill.: Free Press.

Lévai, Jenő. 1946. *Fekete könyv a magyar zsidóság szenvendéseiről* [Black book on the sufferings of Hungarian Jewry]. Budapest: Officina.

Lewin, Moshe. 1988. *The Gorbachev Phenomenon: A Historical Interpretation.* Berkeley and Los Angeles: University of California Press.

Lih, Lars, Oleg V. Naumov, and Oleg V. Khlevnik. 1995. *Stalin's Letters to Molotov, 1925–1936.* Translated by C. A. Fitzpatrick. New Haven: Yale University Press.

Lim, Youngil. 1981. *Government Policy and Private Enterprise: The Korean Experience in Industrialization.* Berkeley, Calif.: Institute of East Asian Studies.

Linz, Juan J., and Alfred Stepan. 1996. *Problems of Democratic Transition and Consolidation: Southern Europe, South America and Post-Communist Europe.* Baltimore: Johns Hopkins University Press.

Lipscher, Ladislaw. 1975. "Die Personalbesetztung der Verwaltungsbehörden in der Slowakei unmittelbar nach der Gründung der Tschechoslowakei" [The composition of personnel in the administration of Slovakia immediately after the founding of Czechoslovakia]. In *Die demokratisch-parlamentarische Struktur der ersten Tschechoslowakischen Republik,* edited by Karl Bosl, 149–58. Munich: Oldenbourg Verlag.

Lipson, Leon. 1963. "Socialist Legality: Road Uphill." In *Russia under Khrushchev,* edited by Abraham Brumberg, 434–70. New York: Praeger.

List, Friedrich. [1841] 1916. *Das nationale System der politischen Oekonomie.* Translated by Sampson S. Lloyd under the title *The National System of Political Economy.* London: Longmans.

Loebl, Eugen. 1969. *Sentenced and Tried: The Stalinist Purges in Czechoslovakia.* London: Elek.

————. 1976. *My Mind on Trial.* New York: Harcourt Brace Jovanovich.

Love, Joseph L. 1996. *Crafting the Third World: Theorizing Underdevelopment in Rumania and Brazil.* Stanford: Stanford University Press.

Lydall, Harold. 1989. *Yugoslavia in Crisis.* Oxford: Clarendon Press.

Macartney, C. A. 1961. *October Fifteenth: A History of Modern Hungary, 1929–44.* 2 vols. Edinburgh: Edinburgh University Press.

Maček, Vladko. 1957. *In the Struggle for Freedom.* Translated by E. and S. Gazi. New York: Speller.

Maddison, Angus. 1995. *Monitoring the World Economy, 1820–1992.* Paris and Washington, D.C.: OECD Publications and Information Center.

Madžer, Lubomir. 1995. "Ko koga eksploatiše?" [Who exploits whom?]. *Republika,* no. 123 (September 1–15): i–xv.

Maier, Anneli. 1980. "Ceauşescu Deified on His 62nd Birthday." *Radio Free Europe Research.* Romania, February 11.

Maier, Charles S. 1975. *Recasting Bourgeois Europe: Stabilization in France, Germany, and Italy in the Decade after World War I*. Princeton, N.J.: Princeton University Press.

———. 1991a. *The Cold War in Europe*. Princeton, N.J.: M. Wiener.

———. 1991b. "The Politics of Productivity." In *The Cold War in Europe*, 169–203. Princeton, N.J.: M. Wiener.

———. 1996. *The Cold War in Europe: Era of a Divided Continent*. 3d updated and expanded ed. Princeton, N.J.: M. Wiener.

———. 1997. *Dissolution: The Crisis of Communism and the End of East Germany*. Princeton: Princeton University Press.

Major, Ivan. 1994. "The Decay of Command Economies." *East European Politics and Society* 8, no. 2 (spring): 317–57.

Malaparte, Curzio. 1932. *Coup d'état: The Technique of Revolution*. Translated by Sylvia Saunders. New York: Dutton.

Malia, Martin. 1965. *Alexander Herzen and the Birth of Russian Socialism*. New York: Grosset & Dunlap.

Malová, Darina, and Danica Sivaková. 1996. "The National Council of the Slovak Republic: The Development of a National Parliament." In *The Second Steps*, edited by Attila Ágh and Gabriella Ilonszki, 342–64. Budapest: Hungarian Centre for Democracy Studies.

Mamatey, Victor S. 1973. "The Development of Czechoslovak Democracy." In *A History of the Czechoslovak Republic, 1918–48,* edited by Victor S. Mamatey and Radomir Luža, 99–166. Princeton, N.J.: Princeton University Press.

Mamatey, Victor S., and Radomir Luža, eds. 1973. *A History of the Czechoslovak Republic, 1918–48*. Princeton, N.J.: Princeton University Press, 1973.

Mandelbaum, Michael, ed. 1996. *Post-Communism: Four Perspectives*. New York: Council of Foreign Relations.

Mannheim, Karl. 1936. *Ideology and Utopia*. Translated by Louis Wirth and Edward Shils. New York: Harcourt, Brace & World.

———. 1940. *Man and Society in an Age of Reconstruction*. Translated by Edward Shils. New York: Harcourt, Brace & World.

Manoilescu, Mihail. 1922. *Ţărănismul şi democraţie* [Peasantism and democracy]. Bucharest: Minerva.

———. 1941. *Die Einzelne Partei als politische Institution der neuen Regime* [The single party as the political institution of the new regime]. Berlin: Stollberg.

———. [1930] 1986. *Forţele naţionale productive si comerţul exterior: Teoria protecţionismului si scîmbului international* [The national forces of production and foreign trade: A theory of protectionism and international exchange]. 3d ed. Bucharest: Editura Ştiinţifica.

Marczali, Henrik. 1910. *Hungary in the Eighteenth Century*. Cambridge: Cambridge University Press.

Marczewski, J. 1956. *Planification et croissance économique des démocraties populaires*. Paris: Plon.

Marer, Paul. 1976. "Has Eastern Europe Become a Liability to the Soviet Union." In *The International Politics of Eastern Europe,* edited by Charles Gati, 58–81. New York: Praeger.

———. 1985. *Dollar GNP's of the USSR and Eastern Europe*. Baltimore: Johns Hopkins University Press.

———. 1987. "The Economic System." In *Handbook on South Eastern Europe*, vol. 5, *Hungary*, edited by Klaus-Detler Grothusen, 276–301. Goettingen: Vandenhoek & Rupprecht.

———. 1989. "The Economies and Trade of Eastern Europe." In *Central and Eastern Europe: The Opening of the Curtain*, edited by William E. Griffith, 37–73. Boulder, Colo.: Westview Press.

———. 1996. "The 'Soviet Bloc' as an Integration Model: Economic, Political, and Cultural Aspects." Unpublished manuscript.

———. 1997. "A 'Szovjet Blokk' mint integrációs modell" [The Soviet bloc as an integration model]. In *Integrációs törekvések Közép és Keleteurópában* [Designs for integration in Central and East Central Europe], edited by Ignác Romsics, 235–306. Budapest: Teleki Foundation.

Marković, Jovan. 1995. "Nacija: Žrtva i osveta" [The nation: victim and vengeance]. *Republika*, no. 139 (May 1–15): i–xvi.

Marković, Mihailo. 1975a. "Philosophical Foundations of the Idea of Self-Management." In *Self-Governing Socialism*, vol. 1, edited by Branko Horvat, Mihailo Marković, and Rudi Supek, 327–50. New York: International Arts and Sciences Press.

———. 1975b. "Socialism as Self-Management." In *Self-Governing Socialism*, vol. 1, edited by Branko Horvat, Mihailo Marković, and Rudi Supek, 416–37. New York: International Arts and Sciences Press.

Marrese, Michael. 1983. *Soviet Subsidization of Trade in Eastern Europe: A Soviet Perspective*. Berkeley, Calif.: Institute of International Studies.

Marrese, Michael, and Jan Vanous. 1983. *Soviet Subsidization of Trade with Eastern Europe*. Berkeley, Calif.: University of California, Institute of International Studies, research monograph no. 52.

Marx, Karl. [1867–95] 1967. *Capital: A Critique of Political Economy*. 3 vols. New York: International Publishers.

———. [1849] 1972. "Wage Labor and Capital." In *The Marx-Engels Reader*, edited by Robert C. Tucker. New York: Norton.

Masse, Georg L. [1964] 1981. *The Crisis of German Ideology: Intellectual Origins of the Third Reich*. New York: Schocken Books.

Massell, Gregory J. 1974. *The Surrogate Proletariat: Moslem Women and Revolutionary Strategy in Soviet Central Asia, 1920–29*. Princeton, N.J.: Princeton University Press, 1974.

Mastny, Vojtech, ed. 1972. *East European Dissent*. New York: Facts on File.

———. 1979. *Russia's Road to the Cold War: Diplomacy, Warfare, and the Politics of Communism, 1941–1945*. New York: Columbia University Press.

———. 1996. *The Cold War and Soviet Insecurity: The Stalin Years*. New York: Oxford University Press.

Matlekovits, Sándor. 1900. *Das Königreich Ungarn volkswirtschaftlich und statistisch dargestellt* [An economic and statistical survey of the kingdom of Hungary]. 2 vols. Leipzig: Duncker & Humblot.

May, Arthur. 1951. *The Hapsburg Monarchy, 1867–1914*. Cambridge, Mass.: Harvard University Press.

McAdams, A. James. 1993. *Germany Divided*. Princeton, N.J.: Princeton University Press.

McCagg, William O. 1972a. *Jewish Nobles and Geniuses in Modern Hungary*. Boulder, Colo.: East European Quarterly. Distributed by Columbia University Press, New York.

———. 1972b. "Jews in Revolutions: the Hungarian Experience." *Journal of Social History* 5: 78–105.

McCauley, Martin, and Stephen Carter. 1986. *Leadership and Succession in the Soviet Union, East Europe and China*. Armonk, N.Y.: M. E. Sharpe.

McClellan, Woodford. 1965. *Svetozar Marković and the Origins of Balkan Socialism*. Princeton, N.J.: Princeton University Press.

McClelland, James. 1980. "Utopia and Revolutionary Heroism in Bolshevik Policy: The Proletarian Culture Debate." *Slavic Review* 39, no. 3 (September): 403–25.

McDonald, Jason. 1993. "Transition to Utopia: a Reinterpretation of Economics, Ideas and Politics in Hungary, 1984–90." *East European Politics and Society* 7, no. 2 (spring): 203–40.

McKendrick, Neil, John Brewer, and J. H. Plumb. 1982. *The Birth of a Consumer Society: The Commercialization of Eighteenth-Century England*. Bloomington: Indiana University Press.

McKenzie, David. 1982. "Serbian Nationalist and Military Organizations and the Piedmont Idea, 1844–1917." *East European Quarterly* 16, no. 3 (September): 323–44.

Medvedev, Roy A. 1971. *Let History Judge: The Origins and Consequences of Stalinism*. Trans. Colleen Taylor. New York: Knopf.

Meher, Manfred, and Arthur A. Stahnke. 1986. "The GDR Faces Economic Dilemmas of the 1980s." In U.S. Congress, Joint Economic Committee, *East European Economies: Slow Growth in the 1980s*, 3: 131–69. Washington, D.C.: Government Printing Office.

Meisel, James H. 1965. *Pareto and Mosca*. Englewood Cliffs, N.J.: Prentice Hall.

Mémorial Antonesco: Le IIIᵉ homme de l'Axe [In memory of Antonescu, the Third man of the Axis]. 1950. Paris: Éditions de la Couronne.

Mendelsohn, Ezra. 1983. *The Jews of East Central Europe Between the World Wars*. Bloomington: Indiana University Press.

Mesa-Lago, Carmelo, and Carl Beck, eds. 1975. *Comparative Socialist Systems: Essays on Politics and Economics*. Pittsburgh: Center for International Studies of the University of Pittsburgh.

Michta, Andrew. 1997. "Democratic Consolidation in East Central Europe: the Case of Poland." In *The Consolidation of Democracy in East-Central Europe*, edited by Karen Dawisha and Bruce Parrott, 66–109. New York: Cambridge University Press.

Mieczkowski, Bogdan. 1975. *Personal Consumption in Eastern Europe: Poland, Czechoslovakia, Hungary and East Germany*. New York: Praeger.

Mihailović, Kosta, and Vasilije Krestić. 1995. *Memorandum of the Serbian Academy of Sciences and Arts*. Belgrade: Serbian Academy.

Mikus, Joseph A. 1972. *Slovakia: A Misunderstood History*. Stoney Creek, Ontario: Battlefield Press.

Milanovic, Branko. 1994. "The Cost of Transition: Fifty Million New Poor and Growing Inequality." *Transition* (World Bank) 5, no. 8 (October): 1–4.

Milke, Erich, and Günter Schabowski. 1991. *Der Absturz* [The fall]. Berlin: Rohwolt.

Millar, James L., and Wolchik, Sharon, eds. 1994. *The Social Legacy of Communism*. New York: Cambridge University Press.

Miller, Marshall L. 1975. *Bulgaria During the Second World War*. Stanford: Stanford University Press.

Miller, William. 1908. The Balkans: Roumania, Bulgaria, Serbia and Montenegro. 2d ed. London: Unwin.

Milward, Alan S. 1996. "The Reconstruction of Western Europe." In *The Cold War in Europe: Era of a Divided Continent*, edited by Charles S. Maier, 241–70. Princeton, N.J.: Wiener, 1996.

Milward, Alan S., and S. B. Saul. 1977. *The Development of the Economies of Continental Europe, 1850–1914*. Cambridge, Mass.: Harvard University Press.

Minami, Ryoshin. 1994. *The Economic Development of Japan: A Quantitative Study*. 2d ed. New York: St. Martin's Press.

Mitchell, B. R. 1980. *European Historical Statistics*. London: Macmillan.

Mitrany, David, ed. 1930. *The Land and the Peasant in Rumania: The War and Agrarian Reform (1917–21)*. London: Humphrey Milford.

———. 1945. *Economic Development in South-East Europe*. Oxford: Political and Economic Planning Group / Oxford University Press.

———. 1951. *Marx Against the Peasant*. New York: Collier.

Moehler, Armin. 1970. *Die konservative Revolution in Deutschland* [Conservative revolution in Germany, 2nd edition]. Stuttgart.

Molnár, Erik, ed. 1971. *Magyarorszag története* [History of Hungary]. Budapest: Gondolat.

Molnár, Erik, et al. 1971. *Magyarország története* [History of Hungary]. 2 vols. Budapest: Gondolat.

Monroe, Will S. 1910. *Bohemia and the Czechs*. Boston: L. C. Page.

Montgomery, John F. 1947. *Hungary: The Unwilling Satellite*. New York: Adair.

Moore, Barrington. 1966. *Social Origins of Dictatorship and Democracy*. Boston: Beacon Press.

Moore, Clement H. 1970. "The Single Party as a Source of Legitimacy." In *Authoritarian Politics in Modern Society*, by Samuel P. Huntington and Clement H. Moore, 48–74. New York: Basic Books.

Moore, Patrick. 1994. "Croatia." *RFE/RL Research Report* 3, no. 6 (April 22): 81.

Musil, Jiří, ed. 1995. *The End of Czechoslovakia*. New York and Budapest: Central European University Press.

Mussolini, Benito. 1935. *Fascism: Doctrine and Institutions*. Rome: Ardita.

Myrdal, Gunnar. 1958. *Rich Lands and Poor*. New York: Harper.

Naimark, Norman M. 1994. "To Know Everything and to Report Everything Worth Knowing: Building the East German Police State, 1945–1949." Working Paper No. 10. Washington, D.C.: Cold War International History Project.

———. 1995. *The Russians in Germany*. Cambridge, Mass.: Harvard University Press.

———. 1996. "Ich will hier raus: Emigration and the Collapse of the German Democratic Republic." In *Eastern Europe in Revolution*, edited by Ivo Banac. Ithaca, N.Y.: Cornell University Press.

Naimark, Norman, and Leonid Gibianski. 1992. *The Establishment of Communist Regimes in Eastern Europe*. Boulder, Colo.: Westview Press.

Neal, Fred W. 1958. *Titoism in Action*. Berkeley and Los Angeles: University of California Press.

Nef, John U. 1957. *Industry and Government in France and England, 1540–1640*. Ithaca, N.Y.: Cornell University Press.

Nelson, Daniel N. 1992. *Romania after Tyranny*. Boulder, Colo.: Westview Press.

Nelson, Daniel N., and Stephen White, eds. 1982. *Communist Legislatures in Comparative Perspective*. Albany, N.Y.: State University of New York Press.

Nettl, J. P., and Ronald Robertson. 1968. *International Systems and the Modernization of Societies*. London: Faber.

Neuberger, Egon. 1968. "The Legacies of Central Planning." RM 5530-PR. Santa Monica, Calif.: RAND.

Neugebauer, Gero. 1978. *Partei und Staatsapparat in der DDR* [Party and state apparatus in the German Democratic Republic]. Opladen: Westdeutscher Verlag.

Neurath, Otto. 1919. *Durch Kriegswirtschaft zur Naturalwirtschaft*. Munich: Callway.

Nicolescu, George D., and Albert Hermely, eds. 1899. *Deputaţii noştri, 1895–99* [Our representatives]. Bucharest: Mueller.

Nicolescu, George D. 1903. *Parlamentul Român* [The Romanian parliament]. Bucharest: Socec.

Niebuhr, Reinhold. 1944. *The Children of Light and the Children of Darkness*. New York: Scribner.

Nietzsche, Friedrich. [1872, 1887] 1952. *The Birth of Tragedy and The Genealogy of Morals*. Translated by Francis Geoffrey. New York: Doubleday.

———. *The Will to Power*. [1882] 1951. Translated by Walter Kaufmann and R. J. Hollingdale. New York: Vintage Books.

Nikolaev, Rada. 1984. "Bulgaria's Stalinists." *Radio Free Europe Research*. Bulgaria, September 10, 1–10.

Nolte, Ernst. 1966. *Three Faces of Fascism*. Translated by L. Vennewitz. New York: Holt, Rinehart & Winston.

Noren, James H. 1995. "The Controversy over Western Measures of Soviet Military Expenditures." *Post-Soviet Affairs*, 11 no. 3: 238–76.

Novak, Viktor. 1948. *Magnum Crimen: Pola vijeka klerikalizma u Hrvatskoj* [Magnum Crimen: Half a century of clericalism in Croatia]. Zagreb: Tisak Nakladony Zavoda.

Nove, Alec. 1961. "The Soviet Model and Underdeveloped Countries." *International Affairs* 37, no. 1 (January): 29–38.

———. 1992. *The Economic History of the USSR, 1917–1991*. New York: Penguin Books.

Nurkse, Ragnar. 1962. *Problems of Capital Formation in Underdeveloped Countries*. New York: Oxford University Press.

Oddo, Gilbert. 1959. *Slovakia and Its People*. New York: Speller.

Oesterreichische Nationalbank. 1997. *Focus on Transition*. Vienna: OeNB.

Olson, David M. 1997. "Democratization and Political Participation in the Czech Republic." In *The Consolidation of Democracy in East-Central Europe*, edited by Karen Dawisha and Bruce Parrott, 150–96. New York: Cambridge University Press.

Olson, David M., and Maurice D. Simon. 1982. "The Institutional Development of a Minimal Parliament: the Case of the Polish Sejm." In *Communist Legislatures in Comparative Perspective*, edited by Daniel Nelson and Stephen White, 47–84. Albany, N.Y.: State University of New York Press.

Oltay, Edith. 1994. "Hungarian Socialists Prepare for a Comeback." *RFE/RL Research Reports* 3, no. 4 (March 12): 21–26.

Omagiu tovărăşului Nicolae Ceauşescu [An Homage to Comrade Nicolae Ceauşescu]. 1973. Bucharest: Editura politica.

Open Media Research Institute (OMRI), *Daily Newsline*, Open Media Research Institute, 1995–96.

Orme, Alexandra. 1950. *Comes the Comrade.* New York: Morrow.

Országgyűlési Almaanch [Almanac of the National Assembly]. See Sturm, Végváry, Kun, Haeffler.

Ort, Thomas. 1996. "The Far Right in the Czech Republic." *Uncaptive Minds* 6, no. 1 (winter–spring): 66–72.

Ortega y Gasset, José. [1930] 1957. *The Revolt of the Masses.* 3d ed. New York: W. W. Norton.

Ost, David. 1993. "The Politics of Interest in Post-Communist Europe." *Theory and Society* 22 (1993): 453–86.

Owen, Bernard. 1993. "A szavazási mód hatásai és a keleteuropai választások" [The effects of electoral laws on outcomes in East Europe]. In *A többpártrendszerek kialakulása Kelet-Középeurópában* [The rise of multiparty systems in East Central Europe], edited by Mihály Bihari, 30–64. Budapest: Kossuth.

Pakulski, Jan. 1986. "Bureaucracy and the Soviet System." *Studies in Comparative Communism* 19, no. 1 (spring): 3–24.

Palairet, Michael. 1979. "Fiscal Pressure and Peasant Impoverishment in Serbia before World War I." *Journal of Economic History* 39, no. 3 (September): 719–46.

———. 1997. *The Balkan Economies, 1800–1914: Evolution Without Development.* Cambridge: Cambridge University Press.

Palánkai, Tibor. 1996. "The Enlargement of the EU Toward the East: Monetary and Financial Aspects." *European Union Review* 1, no. 1: 41–57.

Pano, Nicholas. 1997. "The Process of Democratization in Albania." In *Politics, Power, and the Struggle for Democracy in South-East Europe*, edited by Karen Dawisha and Bruce Parrott, 320–22. New York: Cambridge University Press.

Pantazi, Ion. 1990. "Mareşalui Antonescu: după arestare, prizonier la Moscova si procesul" [Antonescu: after the arrest, imprisonment in Moscow, and the trial]. In *Mareşalui Antonescu*, edited by Gheorghe Buzatu, 343–63. Iasi: BAI.

Papadakis, Aristides. 1988. "The Historical Traditions of Church-State Relations under Orthodoxy." In *East European Christianity and Politics in the Twentieth Century*, edited by Pedro Ramet. Durham, N.C.: Duke University Press.

Parlamentul României, 1912. 1912. Bucharest: A. Grossman.

Parrish, Scott. 1997. "The Marshall Plan, Soviet-American Relations, and the Division of Europe." In *The Establishment of Communist Regimes in Eastern Europe, 1944–1949*, edited by Norman Naimark and Leonid Gibianski, 267–90. Boulder, Colo.: Westview Press.

Parsons, Talcott. 1966. *Societies: An Evolutionary and Comparative Perspective.* New York: Prentice-Hall.

Pasvolsky, Leo. 1930. *Bulgaria's Economic Position.* Washington, D.C.: Brookings Institution.

Pataki, Ferenc. 1984. "A társas alakzatok és a szocialista életmód" [Social patterns and the socialist way of life]. In *Hogyan élünk? A szocialista életmód ismérvei, feltételei és tendenciái,* edited by Miklós Szánthó, 53–75. Budapest: Közgazdasági és Jogi kiadó.

Pelikan, Jiři. 1971. *The Czechoslovak Political Trials, 1950–1954.* Stanford: Stanford University Press.

Pelin, Mihail, ed. 1993. *Mareşalul Antonescu: Epistolarul infernului* [Marshal Antonescu: correspondence from hell]. Bucharest: Editura Viitorul Românesc.

Perry, Duncan M. 1997. "The Republic of Macedonia Finding Its Way." In *Politics, Power, and the Struggle for Democracy in South-East Europe,* edited by Karen Dawisha and Bruce Parrott, 189–226. New York: Cambridge University Press.

Petrescu, Corrin. 1910. *Album corpuilor legituoare* [Almanac of the legislative body]. Bucharest: Univea.

Petrovich, Michael. 1976. *A History of Modern Serbia, 1804–1918.* New York: Harcourt, Brace, Jovanovich.

Pezlar, Ludovit. 1970. "Notes on the Function of Anti-Sovietism in the Strategy of Imperialism." *Novo Slovo* (February 12), in *Radio Free Europe Resarch.* Czechoslovakia, February 24.

Pintér, István. 1968. *Ki volt Horthy Miklós?* [Who was Miklós Horthy?]. Budapest: Zrinyi.

Pipa, Arshi. 1984. "The Political Culture of Hoxha's Albania." In *The Stalinist Legacy: Its Impact on Twentieth-Century World Politics,* edited by Tariq Ali, 435–64. New York: Penguin Books.

Platteau, Jean-Philippe. 1984. "Das Paradoxon des Staates in wirtschaftlich rückständigen Ländern" [The paradox of the state in backward countries]. *Oesterreichische Zeitschrift für Soziologie* 9, no. 4: 63–88.

Pleština, Dijana. 1992. *Regional Development in Communist Yugoslavia: Success, Failure, and Consequences.* Boulder, Colo.: Westview Press.

Podkaminer, Leon, et al. 1998. *Transition Countries: 1997 External Deficits Lower Than Feared, Stability Again a Priority.* Wiener Institut für Internationale Wirtschaftsvergleiche / Vienna Institute for Comparative Economic Studies Research Reports No. 243. Vienna: WIIW.

Polaković, Štefan. 1941. *Tisova nauka* [Tiso's teachings]. Bratislava.

Poland. 1976. *Rocznik Statystyczny* [Statistical yearbook] *1976.* Warsaw.

Polanyi, Karl. 1957. *The Great Transformation: the Political and Economic Origins of Our Time.* Boston: Beacon Press.

Politics and Political Parties in Rumania. 1936. London: International Reference Library.

Pop-Eleche§ Grigore. 1998. "The Communist Successor Parties in Romania and Hungary." M.A. thesis, University of California, Berkeley.

Popov, Vladimir. 1998. "Internationalization of the Russian Economy: What Went Wrong?" *Emergo* 5, no. 2 (spring): 53–84.

Popović, Dušan J. 1937. *O Cincarima* [About the Tsintsars]. Belgrade: Gregorović.

Postan, M. M., and John Hatcher. 1978. "Population and Class Relations in Feudal Society." *Past and Present,* no. 78 (February): 24–37.

Predescu, Lucian. 1939–40. *Enciclopedia Cugetarea* [Encyclopedia of thought]. Bucharest: Delafras.

Přihoda, Petr. 1995. "Mutual Perceptions in Czech and Slovak Relationships." In

The End of Czechoslovakia, edited by Jiři Musil, 128–39. New York and Budapest: Central European University Press.

Pritz, Pál. 1997. "Pax Germanica: Német elképzelések Európa jövőjéről a második világháborúban" [German images of the future of Europe during World War II]. In *Integrációs törekvések Közép és Keleteurópában* [Designs and movements of integration in East Central Europe], edited by Ignác Romsics, 159–235. Budapest: Teleki Alapitvány.

Pryor, Zora P. 1973. "Czechoslovak Economic Development in the Interwar Period." In *A History of the Czechoslovak Republic, 1918–1948,* edited by Victor S. Mamatey and Radomir Luža, 188–215. Princeton, N.J.: Princeton University Press.

Ptakowski, Jerzy. 1968. "Behind the Crisis in Poland." *East Europe* 17, no. 4 (April): 5–12.

Pujo, Maurice. 1933. *Les Camelots du Roi.* Paris: Plon.

Pukánszky, Béla. 1931. *Német polgárság magyar földön* [German bourgeoisie on Hungarian soil]. Budapest: Franklin.

Pulpán, Karel. 1990. *Nástin českých a československých hospodářských dějin* [An outline of Czech and Czechoslovak economic history]. Prague: Documents of Charles University.

Pulzer, Peter G. J. 1964. *The Rise of Political Anti-Semitism in Germany and Austria.* New York: John Wiley.

———. 1966. *Aspects of Political Development.* Boston: Little, Brown.

Pye, Lucian W. 1966. *Aspects of Political Development: An Analytical Study.* Boston: Little, Brown.

———. 1990. "Political Science and the Crisis of Authoritarianism." *American Political Science Review* 84, no. 1 (March): 3–19.

Radio Free Europe Research. 1963–90. Country (Target and Non-Target) Reports.

———. 1963–91. *Situation Reports.*

———. 1992–94. RFE/RL *Research Report.*

———. 1994. RFE/RL *Daily Reports.*

———. 1997–98. *Daily Newsline.*

Ramet, Pedro (later Sabrina P.), ed. 1988. *Eastern Christianity and Politics in the Twentieth Century.* Durham, N.C.: Duke University Press.

Ramet, Sabrina P. (formerly Pedro). 1984. *Nationalism and Federalism in Yugoslavia, 1963–1983.* Bloomington: University of Indiana Press. 2d ed. 1992.

———. 1997. "Democratization in Slovenia: The Second Stage." In *Politics, Power and the Struggle for Democracy in South-East Europe,* edited by Karen Dawisha and Bruce Parrott, 189–225. New York: Cambridge University Press.

Ranke, Leopold von. [1836] 1962. *Die grossen Mächte: Politisches Gespräch* [The great powers: A political dialogue]. Göttingen: Vandenhoeck & Rupprecht.

Ránki, György. 1971. "The Problem of Fascism in Hungary." In *Native Fascism in the Successor States,* edited by Peter Sugar, 65–72. Santa Barbara, Calif.: Clio Press.

Raupach, Hans. 1966. "Zur Entstehung des Begriffes Zentralverwaltungswirtschaft" [Creating the concept of a centrally administered economy]. *Jahrbuch für Sozialwissenschaft* 17: 86–101.

Réti, György. 1993. "A többpártrendszer kialakulása Albániában." In *A többpárt-*

rendszerek kialakulása Kelet-Középeurópában [The rise of multiparty systems in East Central Europe], edited by Mihály Bihari, 476–96. Budapest: Kossuth.

Rice, Condoleezza. 1984. The Soviet Union and the Czechoslovak Army, 1948–1983. Princeton, N.J.: Princeton University Press.

Rich, E. E., and C. H. Wilson. 1977. The Economic Organization of Early Modern Europe. Vol. 5, Cambridge Economic History of Europe. Cambridge: Cambridge University Press.

Rigby, Thomas H. "Crypto-Politics." 1964. Survey 50 (January): 183–94.

———, ed. 1968. The Stalin Dictatorship: Khrushchev's Speech and Other Documents. London: Methuen.

———. 1976. "Politics in the Mono-Organizational Society." In Authoritarian Politics in Communist Europe, edited by Andrew C. Janos, 31–81. Institute of International Studies Research Series, No. 28. Berkeley, Calif.: Institute of International Studies.

Riggs, Fred. 1966. Administration in Developing Countries. Boston: Houghton Mifflin.

Ring, Éva, ed. 1986. Helyünk Európában [Our place in Europe]. Budapest: Magvető.

Roberts, Henry. 1951. Rumania: Political Problems of an Agrarian State. New Haven, Conn.: Yale University Press.

Rogger, Hans, and Eugen Weber. 1966. The European Right: A Historical Profile. Berkeley and Los Angeles: University of California Press.

Roller, Mihail. 1952. Istoria RPR. Manual pentru învăţamentul mediu [History of the Romanian People's Republic. Textbook for secondary schools]. Bucharest: Editura de Stat Didactica.

Romania. 1919. Direcţiune generală a stătisticei. Anuarul statistic al României, 1915 [Statistical yearbook for 1915]. Bucharest.

———. 1931. Anuarul Parlamentar, 1931 [The Yearbook of Parliament]. Bucharest: Cantemir.

———. 1931. Recensamantul general al populaţiei româniei din 1930 [General census of the Romanian population in 1930]. Bucharest: Editura Cuvântului.

———. Presedintă Consiliului de Ministri. 1941. Pe marginea prăpastei [On the edge of the abyss]. Vols. 1–2. Bucharest.

———. 1978. Omagiu preşedintului Nicolae Ceauşescu [Homage to President N. Ceauşescu]. Bucharest: Editura politică.

Romania, Communist Party of. 1972. Documentele ale Partidului Communist Român. Rolul ştiinţei în construirea socialismului în România [Documents of the CRR: The role of science in the construction of communism]. Bucharest: Editura politică.

———. 1974. Programul Partidului Communist Român [Program of the Romanian Communist Party]. Bucharest: Editura politică.

———. 1981. Congresul al XII-lea al Partidului Communist Român [The Twelfth Congress of the Romanian Communist Party]. Bucharest: Editura politică.

"România in faţa problemilor economiei actuale." [Romania confronting concrete economic problems]. Almanahul Cuvântul, 1941 [Almanac of the daily Cuvânt, 1941].

Romsics, Ignác. 1997. Integrációs törekvések Közép és Keleteurópában [Designs of integration in East Central Europe]. Budapest: Teleki Alapitvány.

Rose, Lisle A. 1973. *After Yalta*. New York: Scribner.

Rose, Richard. 1997. "Where Are the Post-Communist Countries Going?" *Journal of Democracy* 8, no. 3 (July): 102.

Rose, Richard, and Christian Haerpfer. 1996. "Fears and Hope: New Democracy Barometer Surveys." *Transition* (World Bank) 7, nos. 5–6 (May–June): 13–14.

Rosenberg, Alfred. 1930. *Mythus des zwanzigsten Jahrhunderts* [The myth of the twentieth century]. Munich: Hocheneichen Verlag.

Rosenberg, Hans. 1966. *Bureaucracy, Aristocracy and Autocracy: The Prussian Experience*. Cambridge, Mass.: Harvard University Press.

Rosovsky, Henry. 1961. *Capital Formation in Japan, 1868–1940*. New York: Free Press.

Rostow, Walt W. 1960. *The Stages of Economic Growth*. Cambridge: Cambridge University Press.

Rotariu, Jipa. 1994. *Mareşalul Ion Antonescu: Am făcut războiul sfânt împotriva bolşevismului* [Marshal Antonescu: I waged a holy war against Bolshevism]. Oradea: Cogito.

Rothschild, Joseph. 1959. *The Communist Party of Bulgaria: Origins and Development, 1883–1936*. New York: Columbia University Press.

———. 1966. *Pilsudski's Coup d'état*. New York: Columbia University Press.

———. 1974. *East Central Europe Between the Two Wars*. Seattle: University of Washington Press.

Rothstein, Andrew. 1953. "Zionism." *Labour Monthly* (March): 124–34.

Roucek, Joseph. 1948. *Balkan Politics: International Relations in the No Man's Land*. Stanford: Stanford University Press.

Runciman, W. G. 1969. *Relative Deprivation and Social Justice*. Berkeley and Los Angeles: University of California Press.

Rupnik, Jacques. 1994. "Remapping Europe." *Daedalus* 123, no. 8 (summer): 91–114.

Rusinow, Dennison. 1977. *The Yugoslav Experiment, 1948–1974*. Berkeley and Los Angeles: University of California Press.

Sachs, Jeffrey D., and Andrew M. Warner. 1996. "How to Catch-Up with the Industrial World: Achieving Rapid Growth in Europe's Transition Economies." *Transition* (World Bank) 7, nos. 9–10 (September–October): 1–4.

Sajó, András. 1997. "Universal Rights, Missionaries, Converts and 'Local Savages.'" *East European Constitutional Review* 8, no. 1 (winter): 44–49.

Sakmyster, Thomas. 1994. *Hungary's Admiral on Horseback: Miklós Horthy, 1918–1944*. Boulder, Colo.: East European Monographs, no. 396.

Salgó, István. 1987. "Exportbővitési törekvések és a pártirányitás" [Export expansion and the party leadership]. Research Report to the Party CC. MS. Budapest: MSzMP-TTK.

Sanders, Irwin. 1958. *Collectivization of Agriculture in Eastern Europe*. Lexington: Kentucky University Press.

Scharlau, Winfried. 1964. "Parvus-Helphand als Theoretiker der deutschen Sozialdemokratie und seine Rolle in der ersten russischen Revolution" [Parvus-Helphand as theorist of German social democracy and his role in the Russian Revolution]. Ph.D. diss., Münster.

Scharlau, Winfried, and Zbynek A. Zeman. 1970. *Freibeuter der Revolution* [Free-booter of revolution]. Cologne: Verlag Wissenschaft und Politik.

Schmidt, Budomir. 1990. *Studien zur politischen Biographie Nikola Pasić* [Contributions to the political biography of Nikola Pasic]. Munich: Hieronymus.

Schmidt, Paul. 1949. *Statist an der diplomatischen Bühne.* Bonn: Athenäum, 1949.

Schmitter, Philippe. 1978. "Reflections on Mihail Manoilescu and the Political Consequences of Delayed-Dependent Development on the Periphery of Western Europe." In *Social Change in Romania, 1860–1940,* edited by Kenneth Jowitt, 117–40. Berkeley, Calif.: Institute of International Studies.

————. 1997. "Problems of Democratic Transition and Consolidation: Southern Europe, South America and Post-Communist Europe." *Journal of Democracy* 8, no. 2 (April): 168–74.

Schrenk, Martin. 1995. Review of *The Economics of Transition,* by Marie Lavigne. *Transition* (World Bank) 6, nos. 11–12 (November–December): 20–21.

Schroeder, Gertrude E. 1995. "Reflections on Economic Sovietology." *Post-Soviet Affairs* 11: 197–234.

Schumpeter, Joseph. 1947. *Capitalism, Socialism and Democracy.* New York: Harper.

Schuster, Hans. 1943. *Die Judenfrage in Rumänien* [The Jewish question in Romania]. Leipzig: Felix Meiner.

Schweitzer, Peter. 1994. *Victory: The Reagan Administration's Secret Strategy that Hastened the Collapse of the Soviet Union.* New York: Atlantic Monthly Press.

Senghaas, Dieter. 1985. *The European Experience.* Translated by K. H. Kimmig. Dover, N.H.: Berg Publishers.

Seton-Watson, Hugh. [1943] 1962. *Eastern Europe Between the Wars, 1918–1938.* Hamden, Conn.: Archon.

Seton-Watson, Robert W. 1908. *Racial Problems in Hungary.* London: Constable.

————. 1911. *Electoral Corruption and Reform in Hungary.* London: Constable.

————. 1934. *History of the Roumanians.* Cambridge: Cambridge University Press.

Shafir, Michael. 1985. *Romania: Politics, Economics and Society: Political Stagnation and Simulated Change.* London: Frances Pinter.

Sharlet, Robert. 1978. "Legal Policy under Khrushchev and Brezhnev: Continuity and Change." In *Soviet Law after Stalin,* edited by Donald B. Berry, George Ginsburgs, and Peter B. Maggs, 2: 321–92. Alphen, Neth.: Sijthoff & Noordhoff.

Shirer, William. 1941. *Berlin Diary.* New York: Knopf.

————. 1967. *The Rise and Fall of the Third Reich.* New York: Fawcett.

Shor, Boris. 1997. "Nations in Transit: 1997 Freedom House Rankings." Worldbank.org/html/trans/mayjune97, 2–4.

Shoup, Paul. 1975. "Indicators of Socio-Economic-Political Development." In *Comparative Socialist Systems: Essays on Politics and Economics,* edited by Carmelo Mesa-Lago and Carl Beck, 3–37. Pittsburgh: Center for International Studies of the University of Pittsburgh.

————. 1981. *The East European and Soviet Data Handbook.* New York: Columbia University Press.

Showcross, William. 1974. *Janos Kádár and the Politics of Hungary since the Revolution.* New York: E. P. Dutton.

Sima, Horia. 1959. *Menirea naționalismului* [The destiny of nationalism]. Salamanca: Asociación Rumano-Hispanic.

Simon, Jeffrey. 1985. *Warsaw Pact Forces: Problems of Command and Control.* Boulder, Colo.: Westview Press.

Sipos, Peter. 1970. *Imrédy Béla és a Magyar Megújulás Pártja* [Béla Imrédy and the party of Hungarian rebirth]. Budapest: Akadémia.

Slapnicka, Helmut. 1975. "Der neue Staat und die bürokratische Kontinuität: Die Entwicklung der Verwaltung, 1918–39" [The new state and bureaucratic continuity: Administrative development, 1918–39]. In *Die demokratisch-parlamentarische Struktur der Ersten Tschechoslowakischen Republik,* edited by Karl Bosl. Munich: Oldenbourg Verlag.

Slay, Ben. 1994. "The Polish Economy under the Socialists." *RFE/RL Research Report* 3, no. 33 (August 26): 66–76.

Slezkine, Yuri. 1994. "The USSR as a Communal Apartment, or How a Socialist State Promoted Ethnic Particularism." *Slavic Review* 53, no. 2 (summer): 414–53.

Slomczynski, Kazimierz, and Goldie Shabad. 1997. "Systemic Transformation and the Salience of Class Structure in East Central Europe." *East European Politics and Society* 11, no. 1, 155–90.

Smith, Adam. [1776] 1980. *The Wealth of Nations.* Edited by Andrew Skinner. New York: Penguin Books.

Snyder, Jack. 1987–88. "The Gorbachev Revolution: the Waning of Soviet Expansionism?" *International Security* 12, no. 4 (winter): 93–131.

Sobell, Vlad. 1988. "Czechoslovakia: the Legacy of Normalization." *East European Politics and Societies* 2, no. 1 (winter): 36–69.

Solzhenitsyn, Aleksandr I. 1974. *The Gulag Archipelago,* vol. 1. New York: Harper & Row.

Spencer, Herbert. [1876] 1972. *On Social Evolution.* Edited by J. D. Y. Peel. Chicago: University of Chicago Press.

Spulber, Nicolas. 1957. *The Economics of Communist Eastern Europe.* New York: Wiley & Sons.

———. 1966. *The State and Economic Development in Eastern Europe.* New York: Random House.

Stalin, Joseph. [1952] 1972a. "Economic Problems of the U.S.S.R." In *The Essential Stalin: Major Theoretical Writings, 1905–1952,* edited by Bruce Franklin, 445–81. Garden City, N.J.: Doubleday Anchor.

———. [1913] 1972b. "Marxism and the National Question." In *The Essential Stalin: Major Theoretical Writings, 1905–1952,* edited by Bruce Franklin, 54–84. Garden City, N.J.: Doubleday Anchor.

The Statesman's Yearbook. 1870, 1878, 1880, 1890, 1896, 1900. London: Macmillan.

Stavrianos, L. S. 1958. *The Balkans since 1453.* New York: Holt, Rinehart & Winston.

Stearns, Peter N. 1978. *Paths to Authority: The Middle Class and the Industrial Labor Force in France, 1820–1948.* Urbana: University of Illinois Press.

Stern, Fritz. 1961. *The Politics of Cultural Despair.* Berkeley and Los Angeles: University of California Press.

Stoianovich, Traian. 1963. "Social Foundations of Balkan Politics." In *The Balkans in Transition*, edited by Charles and Barbara Jelavich, 297–345. Berkeley and Los Angeles: University of California Press.

Stojadinović, Milan. 1939. *Jedan kralj, jedan narod, jedna država* [One king, one people, one state]. Belgrade: Sekcija za Propagandu, Jugoslovenska Radikalne Zajednice.

———. 1963. *Ni rat, ni pakt: Jugoslavija izedju dva rata* [Neither war nor concord: Yugoslavia between the two wars]. Buenos Aires: El Economista.

Stojanović, Svetozar. 1975. "Between Ideals and Reality." In *Self-Governing Socialism*, vol. 1, edited by Branko Horvat, Mihailo Marković, and Rudi Supek, 467–68. New York: International Arts and Sciences Press.

Stokes, Gale. 1975. *Legitimacy Through Liberalism: Vladimir Jovanović and the Transformation of Serbian Politics*. Seattle: University of Washington Press.

———. 1990. *Politics and Development: the Emergence of Political Parties in Nineteenth-Century Serbia*. Durham, N.C.: Duke University Press.

———, ed. 1991. *From Stalinism to Pluralism: A Documentary History of Eastern Europe since 1945*. New York: Oxford University Press.

———. 1993. *The Walls Came Tumbling Down*. New York: Oxford University Press.

Sturm, Albert, ed. 1887, 1892, 1897, 1901, 1905. *Országgyűlési Almanach* [Parliamentary almanac]. Budapest: Pester Lloyd.

Suda, Zdenek. 1980. *Zealots and Rebels: A History of the Ruling Communist Party of Czechoslovakia*. Stanford: Hoover Institution Press.

———. 1995. "Slovakia in Czech National Consciousness." In *The End of Czechoslovakia*, edited by Jiří Musil, 106–27. New York and Budapest: Central European University Press.

Sugar, Peter F., ed. 1971. *Native Fascism in the Successor States, 1918–1945*. Santa Barbara, Calif.: ABC-Clio.

Sujan, Ivan, and Milota Sujanova. 1995. "The Macro-Economic Situation in the Czech Republic." In *The Czech Republic and Economic Transition in Eastern Europe*, edited by Jan Svejnar. San Diego, Calif.: Academic Press.

Süle, Tibor. 1967. *Sozialdemokratie in Ungarn*. Cologne: Böhlen.

Sulyok, Dezső. 1954. *Magyar tragédia* [Hungarian tragedy]. Newark, N.J.: published by author.

Sündhausen, Holm. 1989. *Historische Statistik Serbiens, 1834–1914* [Serbian historical statistics]. Munich: Oldenbourg.

Suny, Ronald G., ed. 1990. *The Russian Revolution and Bolshevik Victory: Visions and Revisions*. Lexington, Mass.: D. C. Heath.

———. 1993. *The Revenge of the Past: Nationalism, Revolution and the Collapse of the Soviet Union*. Stanford: Stanford University Press.

Svejnar, Jan, ed. 1995. *The Czech Republic and Economic Transition in Eastern Europe*. San Diego, Calif.: Academic Press.

Svoboda, M. 1970. "State Sovereignty and International Socialism." *Tvorba*, August 19. In *Radio Free Europe Research*. Czechoslovakia, Sept. 4.

Syllova, Jindriska. 1996. "The Legislature of the Czech Republic." In *The Second Steps*, edited by Attila Ágh and Gabriella Ilonszki, 322–42. Budapest: Hungarian Centre for Democracy Studies.

Szabó, István. 1948. *Tanulmányok a magyar parasztság történetéből* [Studies from the history of the Hungarian peasantry]. Budapest: Athenaeum.

Szabó, Istvan. 1993. "A pártok megalakulása Bulgáriában" [Party formation in Bulgaria]. In *A többpártrendszerek kialakulása Kelet-Középeurópában* [The rise of multiparty systems in East Central Europe], edited by Mihály Bihari, 406–26. Budapest: Kossuth.

Szabó, Róbert. 1995. *A kommunista párt és a zsidóság 1945–1956* [The Communist Party and Jewry, 1945–56]. Budapest: Windsor.

Szabó, Zoltán. 1936. *A tardi helyzet* [Report from the village of Tard]. Budapest: Cserépfalvi.

Szalai, Erzsébet. 1988. "A gazdasági válság természete" [The nature of the economic crisis]. *Valóság* 31, no. 6 (June): 50–65.

Szánthó, Miklós, ed. 1984. *Hogyan élünk? A szocialista életmód ismérvei, feltételei és tendenciái* [How do we live? Criteria, conditions, and tendencies of the socialist way of life]. Budapest: Közgazdasági és Jogi kiadó.

Széchenyi, István. [1830] 1930. *Hitel* [Credit]. Fontes Edition. Budapest: Hungarian Academy of Science.

Szekfű, Gyula. 1934. *A mai Széchenyi* [Topical Széchenyi]. Budapest: Magyar Szemle.

Szegő, Szilvia. 1984. "Nominálbér, realbér, reáljövedelem" [Nominal wage, real wage, real income]. *Társadalmi Szemle* 39, no. 2 (February): 66–82.

Szporluk, Roman. 1994. "After Empire: What?" *Daedalus* 123, no. 8 (summer): 21–39.

Szűcs, Jenő. 1986. *Vázlat Európa három történeti régiójáról* [Sketch on the three historical regions of Europe]. In *Helyünk Európában* [Our place in Europe], edited by Éva Ring, 616–68. Budapest: Magvető.

Tálas, Péter. 1993. "Rendszerváltás és többpártrendszer Lengyelországban" [Transition and multi-party system in Poland]. In *A többpártrendszerek kialakulása Kelet-Középeuropában* [The rise of multiparty systems in East Central Europe], edited by Mihály Bihari, 231–76. Budapest: Kossuth.

Talmon, J. L. 1960. *The Origins of Totalitarian Democracy.* 2d ed. New York: Praeger.

Taylor, Charles Lewis, and David A. Jodice. 1983. *World Handbook of Political and Social Indicators.* 3d ed. 2 vols. New Haven, Conn.: Yale University Press.

Teleki, Éva. 1974. *Nyilas uralom Magyarországon* [Arrow Cross rule in Hungary]. Budapest: Kossuth.

Temple, Mark. 1996. "The Politicization of History: Marshal Antonescu and Romania." *East European Politics and Society* 10, no. 3 (fall): 457–503.

Tismaneanu, Vladimir. 1996. "Tenuous Pluralism in the Post-Communist Era." *Transitions* (OMRI) 2, no. 26 (December 27): 6–12.

———. 1998. *Fantasies of Salvation: Democracy, Nationalism and Myth in Post-Communist Europe.* Princeton, N.J.: Princeton University Press.

Tiso, Jozeph. 1930. *Ideologia slovenskej lúdovej strany* [Ideology of the Slovak People's Party]. Bratislava.

Tito, Josip Broz. 1959. *Govori i članci* [Speeches and articles]. Zagreb.

Todorova, Mariia Nikolaeva. 1997. *Imagining the Balkans.* New York: Oxford University Press.

Tőkés, Rudolf. 1967. *Béla Kun and the Hungarian Soviet Republic.* New York: Praeger.

————, ed. 1979. *Opposition in Eastern Europe.* Baltimore: Johns Hopkins University Press.

————. 1996. *Hungary's Negotiated Revolution.* New York: Cambridge University Press.

————. 1997. "Party Politics and Political Participation in Hungary." In *The Consolidation of Democracy in East-Central Europe,* edited by Karen Dawisha and Bruce Parrott, 67–108. New York: Cambridge University Press.

Tomasevich, Jozo. 1955. *Peasants, Politics, and Economic Change in Yugoslavia.* Stanford: Stanford University Press.

————. 1975. *The Chetniks: War and Revolution in Yugoslavia, 1941–45.* Stanford: Stanford University Press.

Tömöry, Márta. 1960. *Új vizeken járok* [On uncharted waters: A history of the Galileo Circle]. Budapest: Gondolat.

Toranska, Teresa. 1983. *"Them": Stalin's Polish Puppets.* Translated by Agnieszka Kolakowska. New York: Harper & Row.

Tovis, Alfred. 1995. "Spain in the European Community." In *Democratic Spain,* edited by R. Gillespie, 88–105. New York: Routledge.

Treitschke, Friedrich von. 1886. *Historisch-politische Aufsätze* [Historical-political essays]. Leipzig: Hirzel.

Triska, Jan F. 1968. *Constitutions of the Communist States.* Stanford: Hoover Institute Press.

Triska, Jan F., and Paul M. Johnson. 1975. "Political Development and Political Change." In *Comparative Socialist Systems: Essays on Politics and Economics,* edited by Carmelo Mesa-Lago and Carl Beck, 249–85. Pittsburgh: Center for International Studies of the University of Pittsburgh.

Troeltsch, Ernst. 1958. *Protestantism and Progress.* Boston: Beacon.

Trotsky, Leon. [1908] 1969. *Results and Prospects.* In *Permanent Revolution: Results and Prospects.* New York: Merit.

————. 1937. *The Revolution Betrayed: What Is the Soviet Union and Where Is It Going?* Translated by Max Eastman. 1st ed. Garden City, N.J.: Doubleday, Doran & Co.

Trouton, Ruth. 1952. *Peasant Renaissance in Yugoslavia, 1900–1950.* London: Routledge.

Troxel, Luan. 1993. "Socialist Persistence in the Bulgarian Elections of 1990–91." *East European Quarterly* 26, no. 4 (January): 413–16.

Tsantis, Andreas C., and Roy Pepper. 1979. *Romania: The Industrialization of an Agrarian Economy under Socialist Planning.* Washington, D.C.: World Bank.

Tucker, Robert C. 1970. *The Marxian Revolutionary Idea.* New York: Norton.

Tucker, Robert W. 1977. *The Inequality of Nations.* New York: Basic Books.

Tuka, Vojtech. 1941. *Slovenský narodny socializmus* [Slovak national socialism]. Bratislava.

Tyson, Laura D'Andrea. 1981. "Aggregate Economic Difficulties and Workers' Welfare." In *Blue Collar Workers in Eastern Europe,* edited by Jan F. Triska and Charles Gati, 108–35. London: George Allen & Unwin.

————. 1984. *Economic Adjustment in Eastern Europe.* Santa Monica, Calif.: RAND.

Újváry, Peter. 1929. *Magyar zsidó lexicon* [Hungarian Jewish Encyclopedia]. Budapest: Pallas.

Ulam, Adam. 1973. *Stalin: The Man and His Era*. New York: Viking.

Ulc, Otto. 1972. *The Judge in the Communist State: A View from Within*. Columbus: Ohio University Press.

UNESCO. 1953. *Progress of Literacy in Various Countries: A Preliminary Statistical Study of Available Census Data since 1900*. Paris: UNESCO.

United Nations. 1949. *The Relative Price of Exports and Imports of Underdeveloped Countries*. New York.

———. 1983. *Economic Survey of Europe*. New York and Geneva: Economic Commission for Europe.

———. 1993. *Human Development Report*. New York: Oxford University Press.

———. 1998. *Human Development Report*. New York: Oxford University Press.

United States. Bureau of the Census. 1975. *Historical Statistics of the United States, Colonial Times to 1970*. Washington, D.C.: Government Printing Office.

United States. Central Intelligence Agency. 1986. *Handbook of Economic Statistics*. Washington, D.C.

———. 1992. *International Economic Statistics, 1992*. Washington, D.C.: Government Printing Office.

United States. Congress. Joint Economic Committee. 1977. *East European Economies: Post-Helsinki*. Washington, D.C.: Government Printing Office.

———. 1981. *East European Economic Assessment*. Washington, D.C.: Government Printing Office.

———. 1986. *East European Economies: Slow Growth in the 1980s*. 2 vols. Washington, D.C.: Government Printing Office.

United States. Department of Labor. 1995. Bureau of Statistics Working Paper Series, Nos. 5211, 5214, 5219.

United States. Foreign Broadcast Information Service Reports. 1963–90.

Utechin, S. V. 1958. "Leninism and Bogdanovism: The Bolsheviks and Their Allies after 1917." *Soviet Studies* 10, no. 2 (October): 113–38.

———. 1963. *Russian Political Thought: A Concise History*. London: J. M. Dent.

Vago, Bela. 1981. "Communist Pragmatism toward Jewish Assimilation in Rumania and Hungary." In *Jewish Assimilation in Modern Times*, edited by Bela Vago. Boulder, Colo.: Westview Press.

Váli, Ferenc A. 1961. *Rift and Revolt in Hungary*. Cambridge, Mass.: Harvard University Press.

———. 1984. "Hungarian Secret Police: The Early Years." In *Terror and Communist Politics: The Role of the Secret Police in Communist States*, edited by Jonathan R. Adelman, 175–94. Boulder, Colo.: Westview Press.

Várady, Tibor. 1992. "Collective Minority Rights and the Problems of Their Legal Protection: the Case of Yugoslavia." *East European Politics and Societies* 6, no. 3 (fall): 260–82.

Veblen, Thorstein. [1915] 1899. *The Theory of the Leisure Class*. New York: Macmillan.

———. 1954. *Imperial Germany and the Industrial Revolution*. 3d ed. New York: Vintage Books.

Végváry, Ferenc, and Ferenc Zimmer, eds. 1910. *Országgyűlési Almanach* [Parliamentary almanac]. Budapest: Pester Lloyd.

Veliz, Claudio. 1980. *The Centralist Tradition of Latin America*. Princeton: Princeton University Press.

Verax (Radu Rosetti). 1904. *La Roumanie et les juifs* [Romania and the Jews]. Bucharest: Socec.

Verdery, Katherine. 1991. *National Ideology under Socialism*. Berkeley and Los Angeles: University of California Press.

Vida, István. 1977. "Három Chorin levél" [Three letters of Chorin]. *Századok* 111.

Vienna Institute for Comparative Economic Studies / Wiener Institut für Internationale Wirtschaftsvergleiche (WIIW). 1991. *Comecon Data, 1990*. New York: Greenwood Press.

———. 1995. *Countries in Transition*. Vienna: WIIW.

Viviano, Frank. 1997. "GIs Keep Uneasy Peace on Front Lines of Bosnia." *San Francisco Chronicle,* November 3, sec. A, 1, 8–9.

Vnuk, František. 1967. *Dr. Jozef Tiso, President of the Slovak Republic: A Commemoration*. Sydney, Australia: Association of Australian Slovaks.

Vojnić, Dragomir. 1994. "Disparity and Disintegration: the Economic Dimension of Yugoslavia's Demise." In *Yugoslavia: The Former and Future,* edited by Payam Akhavian and Robert Howse, 75–111. Washington, D.C.: Brookings Institution.

Vucinich, Wayne S. 1954. *Serbia between East and West: The Events of 1903–1908*. Stanford: Stanford University Press.

———. 1969. "Nationalism and Communism." In *Contemporary Yugoslavia: Twenty Years of Socialist Experiment,* edited by Wayne S. Vucinich. Berkeley and Los Angeles: University of California Press.

Wädekin, Karl-Eugen. 1982. "Agrarian Policies in Communist Europe: A Critical Introduction." In *Agrarian Policies in Communist Europe,* edited by Everett Jacobs. Totawa, N.J.: Allenheld & Osmun.

Wallerstein, Immanuel. 1974a. *The Modern World System, 1: Capitalist Agriculture and the Origins of the European World Economy in the Sixteenth Century*. New York: Academic Books.

———. 1974b. "The Rise and Future Demise of the Capitalist World System: Concepts for Comparative Analysis." *Comparative Studies in Society and History* 16, no. 4 (September): 382–415.

Walters, Philip. 1988. "The Russian Orthodox Church." In *Eastern Christianity and Politics in the Twentieth Century,* edited by Pedro Ramet, 61–91. Durham, N.C.: Duke University Press.

Walzer, Michael. 1967. "Puritanism and Revolutionary Ideology." In *The Protestant Ethic and Modernization,* edited by Saul N. Eisenstadt, 109–34. New York: Basic Books.

Wandycz, Piotr S. 1974. *The Lands of Partitioned Poland, 1795–1918*. Seattle: University of Washington Press.

Warriner, Doreen, ed. 1965. *Contrasts in Emerging Societies*. Bloomington: Indiana University Press.

Watts, Larry. 1993. *Romanian Cassandra*. Boulder, Colo.: East European Monographs No. 358.

Weber, Eugen. 1962. *Action Française: Royalism and Reaction in Twentieth-Century France*. Stanford: Stanford University Press.

———. 1966a. "France." In *The European Right: A Historical Profile,* edited by Hans Rogger and Eugen Weber, 71–127. Berkeley and Los Angeles: University of California Press.

————. 1966b. "The Men of the Archangel." In *International Fascism*, edited by Walter Lacqueur and George L. Mosse, 101–26. New York: Harper & Row.

————. 1966c. "Romania." In *The European Right: A Historical Profile*, edited by Hans Rogger and Eugen Weber, 501–74. Berkeley and Los Angeles: University of California Press.

Weber, Marianne. 1950. *Max Weber: Ein Lebensbild* [Max Weber: The picture of a life]. Munich: Verlag Lambert Schneider.

Weber, Max. 1892. *Die Verhältnisse der Landarbeiter im ostelbischen Deutschland* [The condition of agricultural laborers in East Elbian Germany]. Schriften des Vereins für Sozialpolitik, No. 55. Berlin: Duncker and Humblot.

————. [1904–5] 1958. *The Protestant Ethic and the Spirit of Capitalism*. Translated by Talcott Parsons. New York: Scribner.

————. 1924. *Gesammelte Aufsätze zur Sozologie und Sozialpolitik* [Collected essays on sociology and social policy]. Tübingen: J. C. B. Mohr.

————. [1925] 1947. *The Theory of Social and Economic Organization*. Translated by A. M. Henderson and Talcott Parsons. New York: Oxford University Press.

Weber, Steven. 1995. "European Union Conditionality." In *Politics and Institutions in an Integrated Europe*, edited by Barry Eichengreen, Jeffrey Frieden, and Jürgen von Hagen, 192–202. Berlin: Springer.

Weissberg, Alexander. 1951. *The Accused*. New York: Simon & Schuster.

Wereszycki, Henrik. 1971. "Fascism in Poland." In *Native Fascism in the Successor States, 1918–1945*, edited by Peter F. Sugar, 85–91. Santa Barbara, Calif.: ABC-Clio.

Weydenthal, Jan B. de. 1981. "The Political Stalemate in Poland." *Radio Free Europe Research*. Poland, October 30.

————. 1982. "State of Emergency Declared in Poland." 1982. *Radio Free Europe Research*. Poland, January 8.

Whipple, T. 1988. "Czechoslovakia in the 1980s: Redefining 'Normalcy'." *Radio Free Europe Research*. Czechoslovakia, May 11.

White, Lynn. 1963. "What Accelerated Technology in the Western Middle Ages?" In *Scientific Change*, edited by A. C. Crombie, 272–91. New York: Basic Books.

White, Steven. 1991. *Gorbachev and After*. Cambridge: Cambridge University Press.

Whitfield, Stephen, ed. 1996. *The New Institutional Architecture of Eastern Europe*. London: St. Martin.

Winiecki, Jon. 1987. *Four Kinds of Fallacies in Comparing Market-Type and Soviet-Type Economies*. Stockholm: Economic Studies Institute.

Wirth, Max. 1868. *Europa und die Bodenschätze Ungarns* [Europe and the natural resources of Hungary]. Leipzig.

Wittfogel, Karl. 1957. *Oriental Despotism: A Comparative Study of Total Power*. New Haven, Conn.: Yale University Press.

Wolchik, Sharon. 1991. *Czechoslovakia in Transition: Politics, Economy and Society*. New York: Pinter.

————. 1997. "Democratization and Political Participation in Slovakia." In *The Consolidation of Democracy in East-Central Europe*, edited by Karen Dawisha and Bruce Parrott, 230–34. New York: Cambridge University Press.

Woodward, Susan. 1995a. *Balkan Tragedy: Chaos and Dissolution after the Cold War*. Washington, D.C.: Brookings Institution.

————. 1995b. *Socialist Unemployment*. Princeton, N.J.: Princeton University Press.

Woolf, S. J., ed. 1981. *Fascism in Europe*. London: Methuen.

World Bank. 1978. *World Development Report*. Washington, D.C.: World Bank.

———. 1978, 1980. *Poverty and Human Development*. New York: Oxford University Press.

———. 1993. *World Development Report*. New York: Oxford University Press.

———. 1995. *World Development Report: Workers in an Integrated World*. New York: Oxford University Press.

———. 1996a. "Corruption: An International Comparison." *Transition* 7, nos. 7–8 (July–Aug.): 16–17.

———. 1996b. *World Development Report 1996: From Plan to Market*. New York: Oxford University Press.

———. 1997a. *Global Development: Finance 1997*. Volume 2: Country Tables / fR. Washington, D.C.: IBRD.

———. 1997b. *World Development Indicators*. CD-Rom. Washington, D.C.: IBRD.

———. 1997c. *World Development Report*. New York: Oxford University Press.

Worldmark Encyclopedia of Nations 5: Europe. 1984. New York: Worldmark Press.

Wszelaki, Jan. 1959. *Communist Economic Strategy: The Role of East Central Europe*. Washington, D.C.: National Planning Association.

Wynot, Edward D. 1971. "A Necessary Cruelty: The Emergence of Official Anti-Semitism in Poland." *American Historical Review* 76, no. 4 (October): 1035–38.

———. 1974. *Polish Politics in Transition: The Camp of National Unity and the Struggle for Power, 1935–39*. Athens: University of Georgia Press.

Wyzan, Michael, and Ben Slay. 1997. "Central, Eastern and South Eastern Europe's Year of Recovery." *Transitions* (OMRI) 3, no. 2 (February 2): 58–63.

Xenopol, Alexander D. 1882. *Studii economice* [Economic studies]. Craiova: Ralian Samitcar.

———. N.d. [1st ed. 1888–93]. *Istoria Românilor din Dacia Traiana* [History of Romania since Trajan's Dacia]. 6 vols. Bucharest: Cartea Româneasca.

———. 1911. *Istoria partidelor politice in România de la origine pâna la 1848* [History of Romanian political parties from the origins to 1848]. Vols. 1–2. Bucharest: Baer.

Xenos, Nicholas. 1987. *Scarcity and Modernity*. New York: Routledge.

Yarmolinsky, Avrahm. 1962. *Road to Revolution*. New York: Collier.

Yugoslavia. 1968. *Statistički Bilten Narodne Banka* [Statistical bulletin of the Yugoslav National Bank]. Belgrade.

Yugoslavia's Way: Program of the League of Yugoslav Communists. 1958. Translated by Stoyan Pribichevich. New York: All Nations Press.

Zacek, Joseph P. 1971. "Czechoslovak Fascisms." In *Native Fascism in the Successor States, 1918–1945*, edited by Peter F. Sugar, 56–62. Santa Barbara, Calif.: ABC-Clio.

Zagoroff, S. D., Jenő Végh, and Alexander Bilinovich. 1955. *The Agricultural Economy of Danubian Countries, 1935–45*. Stanford: Stanford University Press.

Zajc, Drago. 1996. "Legislative Developments in a New Democracy: the Case of Slovenia." In *The Second Steps*, edited by Attila Ágh and Gabriella Ilonszki, 380–95. Budapest: Hungarian Centre for Democracy Studies.

Zanga, Louis. 1994. "Albania Optimistic About Economic Growth." *RFE/RL Research Report* 3, no. 7 (February 18): 14–17.

Zaninovich, George M. 1969. "The Yugoslav Variations on Marx." In *Contemporary Yugoslavia: Twenty Years of Socialist Experiment*, edited by Wayne S. Vucinich, 285–316. Berkeley and Los Angeles: University of California Press.

Zeletin, Stefan. 1925. *Burghezia româna: origine si rolul ei istoric* [The Romanian bourgeoisie: Its origins and role in history]. Bucharest: Editura Cultura Naţionala.

———. 1927. *Neo-liberalismul: Studii asupra istoriei şi politicei burghezei române* [Neo-liberalism: studies in the history and politics of the Rumanian bourgeoisie]. Bucharest: Pagini agrare şi sociale.

Zinner, Paul. 1963. *Communist Strategy and Tactics in Czechoslovakia, 1918–48*. New York: Praeger.

"A zsidókérdés itt és most." [The Jewish question here and now]. 1989. Symposium. *Világosság* 30: 432–43.

Zubok, V. M., and Constantine Pleshakov. 1996. *Inside the Kremlin's Cold War: From Stalin to Khrushchev*. Cambridge, Mass.: Harvard University Press.

Zweig, Ferdynand. 1944. *Poland Between the Two Wars*. London: Secker & Warburg.

Zweig, Stefan, 1928. *Ben Jonson's Volpone: A Loveless Comedy of Three Acts*. New York: Viking Press.

Index

Legalism, 64, 118, 413; in Albania, 392; culture of, 44–45

Legal state, corrupted parliamentarism and, 97–99

Legal systems, reform of, 82–83, 118

Legion of the Archangel Michael, 170

Legislation, Justice and Tables of the Land of Bohemia, 43

Legislative-executive relations, 376

Lendvai, Paul, 321

Lenin, Vladimir I, 47, 152–56, 158, 160, 174, 184, 222, 260, 271, 341; book by, 153, 155; bureaucracy and, 252; death of, 219; proletarian revolution and, 154; on revolutionary justice, 159

Leninism, 159, 160, 239

Lerner, Daniel: IDE and, 21

Leszczyński, Julian, 150n

Lévy-Leboy, Maurice, 347

L'Histoire des Girondins (Lamartine), 67

Liberal capitalism, 148; crisis of, 151; principles of, 146

Liberal Constitution (1869), 122

Liberal Democratic Congress, 380

Liberal Democratic Party of Slovenia, 380–81

Liberalism, 69, 118, 148, 418; communism and, 381; corruption of, 84–97; cultural, 366; in East Central Europe, 125, 383, 413; economic, 106; ideology of, 56; intelligentsia and, 120; modern, 119; opposition to, 120; political developments and, 116; rise/decline of, 407, 411; socialism and, 172; state and, 187; Western, 67

Liberalization, 386; economic, 387 (table); in East Central Europe, 399, 403; in Hungary, 295; process of, 372, 404

Liberals, 380–81; crisis of, 148; Hungarian, 67; leftists and, 149

Life expectancy, 359; in East Central Europe, 346, 346 (table); increase in, 59

Literacy: in East Central Europe, 140, 251 (table); spread of, 139, 166, 167

Living space, allocation of, 253–54

Local government, withering of, 85

Locke, John, 373

Long sixteenth century, 54n, 57

Lord lieutenants, 86, 101

Lotz, Walter, 196

Louis, King (of Hungary), 35

Lower classes: middle class and, 67; politics and, 141; social policies for, 143

Luca, Vasile, 256, 298

Ludaks, 178, 185

Ludendorff, Erich, 223

Lueger, Karl, 187, 189

Lupu, Vasile: *Prăvila* and, 47

Luther, Martin, 308

Lysenko, Trofim D., 237

Macartney, C. A., 101, 211n

Macedonian League of Communists, 391

Mach, Alexander (Sanyo), 185; Jewish matters and, 213; New Order and, 212

Maddison, Angus, 347, 350

Madgearu, Virgil, 143

Magyars, 9, 186

Maisky, Ivan, 232

Maistre, Joseph de, 187

Malinovsky. *See* Bogdanov, Aleksandr

Malypetr, Jan, 111, 115

Manescu, Manea, 304

Maniu, Iuliu, 142, 143, 205

Mannheim, Karl: on free-floating intelligentsia, 169; fundamental democratization and, 19; reconstruction and, 23

Manoilescu, Mihai, 179n, 194; corporatist society and, 180–81; land redistribution and, 179

Manufacturing, 60, 109; in East Central Europe, 266, 416; in Poland, 291; revolution in, 55–56

Mao Zedong: charisma of, 302; Hoxha and, 283–84; personality cult of, 261

Maps, Europe: ninth-century, 30; Middle Ages, 31; nineteenth-century, 32; twentieth-century, 33, contemporary, 333

March Revolution (1848), 78

Marczali, Henrik, 51

Marczewski, Jean, 216

Marer, Paul, 266, 350

Marginalization, 166, 410; economic, 132, 139; ethnic, 171

Market principles: adaptation of, 373, 374; in Poland, 292

Markets, 409; changes in, 56

Market socialism, 288

Marko, Rita, 285n, 286

Marković, Svetozar, 119

Marku, Gjin: purge of, 284

Marrese, Michael: on subsidies, 266